BOYLE COUNTY PUBLIC LIBRARY
R 597.92 Erns 52735
Ernst, Carl Turtles of the United Stat

3 6402 2001 0185 1

LIBRARY USE ONLY

D1257742

WITHDRAWN

052735

R597.92 Ernst, Carl H
Erns
         Turtles of the
         United States

Danville - Boyle County
Public Library
Third and Broadway
Danville, Kentucky   40422

TURTLES
OF THE UNITED STATES

TURTLES
OF THE UNITED STATES

Carl H. Ernst & Roger W. Barbour

The University Press of Kentucky

ISBN: 0–8131–1272–9

Library of Congress Catalog Card Number: 72–81315

Copyright © 1972 by The University Press of Kentucky

A statewide cooperative scholarly publishing agency
serving Berea College, Centre College of Kentucky,
Eastern Kentucky University, Kentucky Historical Society,
Kentucky State University, Morehead State University,
Murray State University, University of Kentucky,
University of Louisville, and Western Kentucky University.

Editorial and Sales Offices: Lexington, Kentucky 40506

To Evelyn Chasteen Ernst
& Bernice Lewis Barbour

[COLOR PLATES FOLLOW PAGE 182]

Preface

We have long recognized the need for an up-to-date book enabling one to identify any turtle native to the United States and summarizing the information on its life history and distribution. Heretofore the most satisfactory book of this kind was Archie Carr's excellent *Handbook of Turtles*, published in 1952. Since then several new species have been described, a number of taxonomic revisions have been offered, and the knowledge of the biology of our turtles has more than doubled. Meanwhile, too, many more people—research scientists, public-health workers, naturalists, teachers, hobbyists—have become interested in turtles.

In this volume we are chiefly concerned with the ecology and ethology of these remarkable animals. We have attempted to give as complete a life history of each species as is possible in the light of present knowledge. We provide physical descriptions that should suffice for the identification of all U.S. (and Canadian) species and subspecies, and we give enough details of classification to show relationships within the group (order Testudines of the class Reptilia). Although we have ignored fossil forms, we do include a section on the origins of North American turtles. There are sections on the animal parasites and the algae harbored by U.S. turtles and on the care of turtles in captivity; and, as an aid to the understanding of scientific names, there is a glossary (with pronunciations).

In giving dimensions we have sought a compromise, dictated by the nature of this book, between scientific and popular usage, as follows: short lengths are given in millimeters, centimeters, or meters, but long distances are given in miles (not kilometers); small weights are given in grams, but large weights are given in pounds (not kilograms); large areas are given in acres or square miles (not hectares); and fluid volumes are given in gallons (not liters). Throughout, English units of all kinds, if used by other authors in works cited, have been retained for the sake of fidelity to those sources.

Readers unfamiliar with the metric units used most frequently in the text may find the following approximations helpful:

Metric	English
1 millimeter (mm) =	about 0.04 (1/25) inch
1 centimeter (cm) = 10 mm =	about 0.4 (2/5) inch
1 meter (m) = 100 cm =	about 3.3 feet = about 1.1 yards
1 gram (g) =	about 0.035 (1/28) ounce avdp.

The literature on turtles is enormous. It includes hundreds of specialized papers on such topics as morphology and physiology. Our interests, however, lie principally in natural history; so we have excluded technical matters that do not have a direct bearing on the life of the animal in the wild. In the preparation of this volume we have examined over 1,500 original papers on turtles and have combined our own observations with pertinent parts of them. With few exceptions we have listed only those articles and books that have appeared since 1949; older ones can be found in Carr's (1952) bibliography. We have included no information published since 31 December 1970.

Our experience with turtles spans more than 50 years. CHE has studied turtles and other reptiles in the eastern United States for nearly 20 years and has given special attention to the ecology and behavior of freshwater turtles. RWB has done research on aspects of the natural history of vertebrates, including turtles, since his college days; his experience as a wildlife photographer covers about 35 years. We have made several collecting trips together to various parts of the United States, seeking acquaintance with species we had not previously encountered in the field and obtaining pictures. All photographs not otherwise credited are by RWB.

We acknowledge the help of persons who have contributed in various ways: Ray E. Ashton, James F. Berry, James R. Butler, Charles C. Carpenter, J. William Cliburn, Joseph T. Collins, John E. Cooper, George W. Folkerts, Wayne Frair, Frederick R. Gehlbach, J. Whitfield Gibbons, Terry E. Graham, Helen F. Hamilton, Bobby G. Jett, Robert A. Kuehne, John M. Mehrtens, Kenneth T. Nemuras, Peter C.

H. Pritchard, M. F. Trenbeth, Harold Wahlquist, Rhoda Walgren, and George R. Zug. To others, inadvertently omitted, we express our gratitude. Faith Hershey is due special thanks for patiently typing the revisions of the manuscript, for making the line drawings, and for aiding us in countless other ways.

We also thank William H. Woodin, of the Arizona Sonora Desert Museum, and the late Charles E. Shaw, of the San Diego Zoological Gardens, for providing us with certain western turtles. The staff of the Miami Seaquarium kindly permitted us to photograph their sea turtles; all photographs of *Caretta caretta*, *Chelonia mydas*, *Eretmochelys imbricata*, and *Lepidochelys kempii* not otherwise credited were taken there. We thank the T. H. Morgan School of Biological Sciences of the University of Kentucky for help in typing. Joyce Ard, in particular, was very helpful.

Research for this volume was subsidized in part by grants from Southwest Minnesota State College (to CHE) and from the Kentucky Research Foundation (to RWB).

We would also like to express our appreciation to certain persons who have contributed indirectly. CHE is particularly indebted to his parents, George H. and Evelyn May Ernst, for the encouragement and tolerance much needed by a young herpetologist. He is also thankful to Alex Henderson and William H. Caulwell, who recognized and supported his interest in reptiles and pointed him toward graduate school; to Willard J. Trezise, who advised him during his early years of graduate study; and to Roger W. Barbour, who served as his major professor during his doctoral studies. RWB would like to express his gratitude to John W. and Laura H. Barbour, whose encouragement of his youthful interest in animals and plants went far beyond that reasonably expected of sympathetic parents.

Introduction

Everyone recognizes a turtle, of whatever size, shape, color, or origin. Would that the names applied to them were so straightforward—"turtle," "tortoise," "terrapin"—they mean one thing to one person, something else to another. Biologically all members of the order Testudines are correctly called turtles. Terrapins and tortoises are certainly turtles, regardless of whatever else they may be; *tortoise* is usually applied to terrestrial turtles, particularly the larger ones; *terrapin* is usually applied to edible, more or less aquatic hardshelled turtles.

Turtles are ancient animals that evolved a shelled form—a rare feature in the vertebrate group, to which turtles belong. They attained this feature long before mammals appeared on earth: fossils from the Triassic Period are clearly identifiable as turtles (see appendix, "Origin and Evolution of North American Turtles"). From man's viewpoint turtles are slow, harmless creatures, and in this characterization they have an important role in mythology and folklore; everyone has heard, for example, the story of the race between the hare and the tortoise. But although turtles have always been the object of much interest and speculation, surprisingly little is known of their biology; indeed, some species are known only as to their appearance.

Turtles, together with lizards, amphisbaenids, snakes, crocodilians, and the tuatara, constitute the vertebrate class Reptilia. Reptiles are ectotherms that have evolved walking limbs and—distinctively—a dry, scaly skin. They arose from the class Amphibia (limbed but moist-skinned animals) during the Pennsylvanian Period, toward the close of the Paleozoic Era, and by rapid adaptive radiation became the dominant animals on earth during the Mesozoic Era. One of the reptilian groups gave rise to the birds, another to the mammals.

Reptiles were the first vertebrates adapted to life in dry places. It is true that amphibians can spend considerable time on land, but their eggs must be laid in water or damp places. The reptiles overcame this limitation by evolving a specialized egg, which has a calcareous or parchmentlike shell that retards the loss of moisture. The egg also has embryonic membranes—amnion, chorion, and allantois—not found in amphibian eggs, as well as a yolk sac, containing nutrients. The amnion forms a fluid-filled compartment surrounding the embryo: the watery environment has been brought indoors, so to speak.

Other developments also contributed to freeing the reptiles from the water needs of amphibians. The scaly skin has few surface glands; that is, very little fluid is lost cutaneously. The well-developed lungs enable reptiles to acquire an ample oxygen supply, and modifications of the heart—incompletely four-chambered organ in most, completely four-chambered in crocodilians—have made the circulatory system more efficient, produced higher blood pressure, and led indirectly to the development of more efficient kidneys. Other, minor developments include the appearance of claws on the toes, the development of a palate separating the oral and nasal passages, and the evolution of a male copulatory organ, which allows internal fertilization.

Turtles belong to the subclass Anapsida, which is characterized by a primitive, anapsid skull—one with a solid cranium and no temporal openings. They constitute an order of shelled reptiles, Testudines, which is subdivided into the suborders Pleurodira and Cryptodira. The Pleurodira are the side-necked turtles: they withdraw their heads by bending their necks laterally. They are aquatic turtles now restricted to Australia, Africa, Madagascar, and South America; however, fossils indicate that they occurred in North America until Cretaceous times. The Cryptodira are the hidden-necked turtles: they withdraw their heads by bending their necks vertically into a sigmoidal curve. They inhabit the land, fresh water, and the seas, and they occur on all continents (although only as marine turtles in Australia). All modern turtles occurring in the United States are cryptodirans. For a more detailed anatomic comparison of the Pleurodira and Cryptodira see the appendix on the origin and evolution of turtles.

Seven of the 10 families of Cryptodira are represented in the United States and adjacent marine waters. The Chelydridae, the snapping turtles, are a New World family of three species, all of which oc-cur in the United States. The Kinosternidae, the mud and musk turtles, are a tropical American family, eight species of which range northward into the United States. The Emydidae, the semiaquatic freshwater and marsh turtles, are found on all continents except Australia; this is the most populous family in the United States, with 25 species. The Testudinidae, the terrestrial tortoises, also are found on all continents except Australia; three species occur in the southern U.S. The Cheloniidae, the sea turtles, occur in the marine waters off the coasts of North America and the Hawaiian Islands; this family is represented by five species. The family Dermochelyidae has only one living species: the leatherback, which is widely distributed in tropical and subtropical seas; it, too, occurs off the Hawaiian Islands and the continental U.S. The Trionychidae, the softshells, are found in Asia, Africa and North America; three species occur in the continental U.S., and a fourth has been introduced from Asia and established in Hawaii.

STRUCTURE: The exceptional feature of the turtle is its shell. This conservative character has remained little changed for many millions of years. The shell is divided into two parts: an upper part, the carapace, and a lower part, the plastron. The two parts are joined on each side by a bridge.

The carapace usually consists of about 50 bones. The nuchal is the most anterior bone along the midline; behind it are eight neurals, two suprapygals, and a pygal, in that order. Occasionally a preneural may be found, between the nuchal and the 1st neural. The neurals are attached to the neural arches of the dorsal vertebrae, but the other bones of the series are free from the vertebrae. On each side of the neurals are eight costal bones; in some species a precostal is also present. Outside the costals and extending along each side from the nuchal to the pygal is a series of about 11 peripherals. Each carapacial bone articulates with the adjacent bones along a suture (see Figure 1).

The forepart of the plastron is composed of a median bone: the entoplastron, which is surrounded anteriorly by two epiplastra and posteriorly by two hyoplastra. Behind these are a pair each of hypoplastra and xiphiplastra. In some primitive species a pair of mesoplastra occur between the hyoplastra and hypoplastra. Between the forelimbs and the hind limbs the hyoplastra and hypoplastra articulate with the 3rd to 7th peripherals. The forelimb emerges from the axillary notch, the hind limb from the inguinal notch. Just behind the axillary notches the axillary buttresses solidly attach the hyoplastra to the 1st costals, and in front of the inguinal notches the inguinal buttresses solidly attach the hypoplastra to the 5th costals (see Figure 1).

The bones of the shell are covered with horny scutes. The division between adjacent scutes is called the seam. A seam often leaves an impression, termed a sulcus, on the underlying bones.

Along the anterior midline of the carapace is a single cervical scute. This is followed posteriorly by a series of five vertebral scutes. Along each side and touching the vertebrals is a series of four pleurals. Outside the pleurals and extending along each side from the cervical are 12 marginal scutes. In the alligator snapping turtle (*Macroclemys*) a series of small scutes, called supramarginals, appears between the posterior pleurals and the marginals (see Figure 2).

The scutes of the plastron are divided into pairs by a median longitudinal seam. Anteriorly there is a pair of gular scutes (except that in the family Kinosternidae a single gular is usual); in some species an intergular is also present. Paired humerals, pectorals, abdominals, femorals, and anals follow, respectively, and in the Cheloniidae an interanal is present. At the posterior edge of each axillary notch there is an axillary scute, and at the front edge of each inguinal notch there is an inguinal scute (see Figure 2).

North American turtles of the genera *Sternotherus*, *Emydoidea*, and *Terrapene* have a transverse hinge located on the anterior edge of the abdominal scutes, and in *Kinosternon* there is a pair of hinges, bordering the abdominals. These hinges allow the plastron to be folded up to enclose the head and limbs.

Turtles of the genera *Dermochelys* and *Trionyx*

1. BONES OF THE TURTLE SHELL.

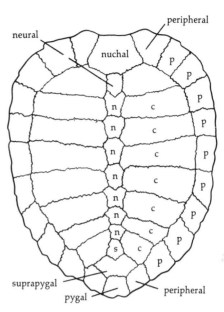

A. Carapace

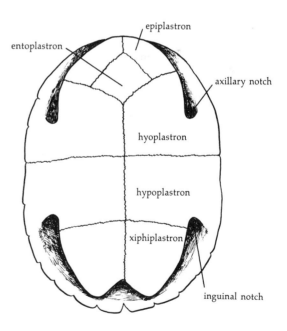

B. Plastron.
(*Drawings by Faith Hershey*)

2. SCUTES OF THE TURTLE SHELL.

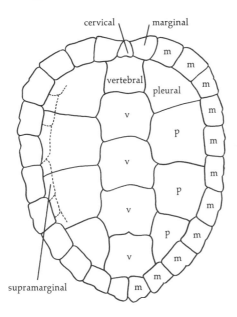

A. Carapace

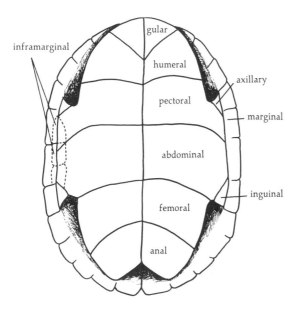

B. Plastron.
(*Drawings by Faith Hershey*)

have lost the horny covering of scutes, and the bony material in their shells is much reduced. Instead, they have a tough, leathery skin. These turtles are often referred to as leatherbacks or softshells.

Another exceptional characteristic of turtles is the migration of the limb girdles to positions inside the rib cage (which, along with the vertebral column, helps form the shell). The limbs of turtles are adapted to the medium through or on which they travel. For instance, the terrestrial tortoises of North America have evolved elephantine hind limbs, which help to support them, and shovellike forelimbs, which aid in digging. The limbs of the marine species are modified as flippers with which they quite literally fly through the seas. The semi-aquatic turtles have developed various degrees of webbing between the toes: the more webbing, the more aquatic the turtle.

Although the turtle skull is highly modified it is basically primitive; the solid cranium, with no temporal openings, has been mentioned. Posteriorly the cranium has a large otic notch on either side of an elongated supraoccipital bone. The pterygoids are solidly fused to the braincase, and the quadrate is closely attached to a lateral expansion of the otic capsule.

The jaws are toothless and are modified as sharp shearing beaks. The upper jaw is composed of two pairs of bones: the small premaxillae, in front (which are fused in soft-shelled turtles), and the maxillae, along the sides. The lower border of the maxilla may be either a sharp cutting surface or a flat crushing surface. The maxilla forms the lateral border of the nasal cavity and the lower border of the orbit. Posteriorly it articulates with the jugal. The posterior rim of the orbit is formed by the jugal ventrally and the postorbital dorsally.

The paired bones along the dorsal midline of the skull are the prefrontals, the frontals, and the parietals. The parietals form the roof and much of the lateral walls of the braincase. Laterally the parietal has a strong process projecting downward and joining the pterygoid. The lower border of the parietal also articulates with the prootic and the supraoccipital. The elongated supraoccipital extends

3. BONES OF THE TURTLE SKULL.

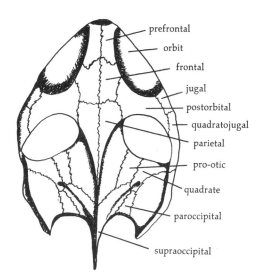

A. Dorsal view

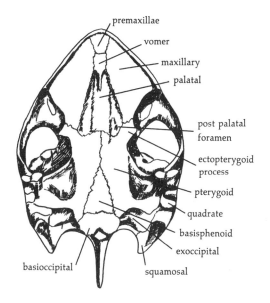

B. Ventral view.

backward and forms the upper border of the foramen magnum. Paired exoccipitals form the lateral borders, and a basioccipital forms the lower border; these three bones comprise the occipital condyle. The cheek bones are the large posterior squamosal and the smaller anterior quadratojugal. The squamosals are connected to the supraoccipital by the paroccipitals.

The palatal complex is composed, from front to rear, of the single vomer and palatine bones and the paired pterygoids. These are often covered with a secondary palate. Anteriorly the vomer touches the premaxillae. The palatines form part of the roof of the nasal passage. Between each palatine and the adjacent maxilla is an opening, the posterior palatine foramen. The pterygoids are separated posteriorly by the basisphenoid. The free lateral projections of the pterygoids are the ectopterygoid processes. The pair of quadrate bones, which lie posterior to the pterygoids, forms the lower-jaw articulation.

Each half of the lower jaw is composed of six bones. The most anterior is the dentary, which

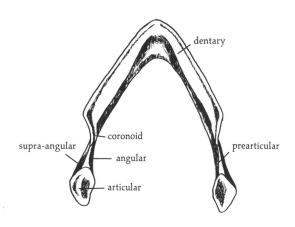

C. Lower jaw.
(*Drawings by Faith Hershey*)

5

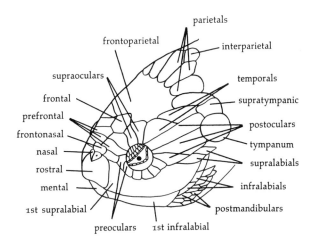

4. Scutes of the turtle head.
(*Drawings by Faith Hershey*)

forms the crushing or cutting surface; the two dentaries are firmly united at the symphysis. On the lower border of the jaw the dentary extends backward nearly to the articulation with the quadrate. On the upper side behind the crushing surface are the coronoid and supraangular bones. At the inner posterior end of the lower jaw are, ventrally, the angular bone and, dorsally, the prearticular. The articular bone forms the articulation with the quadrate (see Figure 4).

DISTRIBUTION IN THE UNITED STATES: Turtles are common in the United States. They occur in all the U.S. states except Alaska. The greatest number of species is found in Florida and the Gulf coastal states, but many species are found in the Mississippi River valley and the Atlantic coastal states. The least number of species occurs in the states west of the Rocky Mountains.

Only one turtle, *Chrysemys picta*, ranges from the Atlantic coast to the Pacific coast. It also ranges from Canada to Mexico, as do *Chelydra serpentina* and *Sternotherus odoratus*. Other species with extensive ranges in the United States are *Kinosternon subrubrum*, *Chrysemys scripta*, and *Terrapene carolina*. In contrast to these are *Chelydra osceola*, *Kinosternon baurii*, and *Chrysemys nelsoni*, which

are restricted to Florida; *Chrysemys alabamensis*, which occurs rarely in scattered localities along the Gulf coast; and the sawbacks, of the genus *Graptemys*, each of which is restricted to a single river system. *Clemmys muhlenbergii* has an interesting disjunct distribution: it occurs only in relict populations over a once rather large range. Several populations of *Chrysemys scripta* apparently originated from released or escaped captives.

HABITAT: Although a turtle species may be widespread it shows a preference for a particular habitat. Many North American species are aquatic to a considerable extent; these are found in lakes, ponds, cypress swamps, marshes, bogs, rivers, streams, and other freshwater habitats. Some prefer deep water, but most occur only in relatively shallow water, and nearly all avoid swift currents. Other aquatic species live in the brackish water of estuaries and coastal salt marshes. The sea turtles inhabit the warmer oceans and seas but occasionally enter bays and river mouths.

Several North American turtles have evolved a terrestrial way of life. The box turtles (*Terrapene*) vary in habitat preferences from deciduous hardwood forests in the eastern United States to the semiarid grasslands of the southwest. The tortoises (*Gopherus*) are found in the sandy pine woods of Florida, in the open dry woodlands of Texas, and in the deserts of the southwest. They somewhat overcome the rigors of their environment by burrowing.

ACTIVITY: In the United States most turtles are active from April through October. Feeding and other activities begin when the water or air temperature warms to 15–20 C. Typically, mating occurs in the spring, the eggs are laid in June and July, and hatching begins in late August and lasts through September. Many turtles are forced to aestivate during dry, hot periods. In winter they hibernate in the soft bottom of some waterway or under the soil and vegetable debris of the woodland or prairie. In some southern states, notably Florida, turtles may remain active all year.

The daily round normally includes sleeping, basking in the sun, and foraging for food. Most tur-

6

tles are diurnal, but mud turtles, musk turtles, and snappers are decidedly nocturnal.

REPRODUCTION: In North America spermatogenesis begins in the testes of the mature male in the spring and is completed in the early fall. The sperm pass from the testes and are stored over the winter in the epididymides. Ovulation in the female typically occurs in May and June, and new ova start to mature soon after.

A courtship precedes the actual mating. Courtship varies with the species: it may include a "tickling" of the female's head with the forefoot claws, as in *Chrysemys* and *Graptemys*; chasing, ramming, or biting, as in the *Gopherus*; or some combination of these. Sperm may be stored by the female and remain viable for a long time; for example, diamondback terrapin females have laid fertile eggs after four years in isolation.

The digging of the nest, the arranging of the eggs in the nest, and the covering of the nest are completed with the hind feet only. All of this is done instinctively; the female never turns to look into the nest. After filling the nest she walks away, never to return; that is, the eggs are left to hatch or not, as environmental conditions dictate. After hatching, the young receive no parental care and are strictly on their own. Several clutches of eggs may be laid each season.

GROWTH: Growth of the epidermal scutes in those turtles that do not periodically shed is stimulated presumably by growth of the bony shell. The scutes adjust to the growth of the bones beneath them by eccentric growth around the granular infantile scute. A layer of germinal epithelium lies beneath the scute, and, as the bones of the shell grow, this layer increases correspondingly. The scute is enlarged by new material applied over the entire undersurface. When growth ceases, at the beginning of hibernation or aestivation, the thin edges of the scutes are slightly depressed where they meet the seams. When growth is resumed the germinal layer of the epidermis, rather than continuing to add to the edge of the existing scute, forms an entirely new layer. It is thin and indistinct under the central part of the

scute but becomes more distinct toward its periphery. Near the edge of the scute the new layer becomes greatly thickened, and it bulges upward where it passes under the edge; this recurves the free edge of the scute above, forming a major growth-ring, or annulus. The newly formed epidermis, projecting from under the edges of the scute, is paler and softer than the older parts; from this one is able to determine readily whether a turtle is growing. The epidermal scutes are like low pyramids only in appearance; their apparent thickness is enhanced by the contours of the bony shell, which correspond to the contours of the scutes.

In *Graptemys*, *Chrysemys*, and *Deirochelys*, a fracture zone develops between the old and new layers of the scute as the new layer of epidermis is formed, and the older layer is shed, annually and in one piece.

Growth is rapid in young turtles but slows considerably after maturity is reached. As long as environmental conditions are favorable some growth occurs; probably the ability to grow is never lost.

The relative lengths of the abdominal scutes and the plastron remain approximately the same throughout the turtle's life. The original abdominal scutes of hatchlings do not increase in size; rather, they remain constant as new growth in initiated around them. Thus, an approximation of the growth rate can be obtained by measuring the plastron length, the abdominal-scute length, and the lengths of the various annuli of the abdominal scutes and then applying the equation $L_1/L_2 = C_1/C_2$, where C_1 represents the length of the annulus, C_2 the length of the abdominal scute, L_2 the plastron length, and L_1 the unknown length of the plastron at the time the annulus was formed.

Some turtles grow to very large size. The leatherback may become more than 7 feet long and weigh close to a ton. Green turtles and loggerheads occasionally weigh close to 1,000 lb. The giant tortoises of the Galápagos Islands may weigh more than 500 lb. The alligator snapping turtle reaches a weight of more than 200 lb: it is the largest freshwater turtle in the United States.

Turtles may attain an age greater than any other

living vertebrate; the great longevity of some species is well documented. Box turtles (*Terrapene carolina*) have lived for more than a century, and several giant tortoises (*Geochelone*) are thought to have lived for 120–150 years.

FOOD AND FEEDING: Although some species have rather exclusive diets, most of our turtles are omnivorous. Animal food taken includes many kinds of invertebrates and vertebrates. Various algae and the fruits, stems, and leaves of terrestrial and aquatic plants are eaten. The green turtle (*Chelonia mydas*) and the tortoises (*Gopherus*) are strict herbivores. Some map turtles (*Graptemys*) feed almost exclusively on mollusks. Many species are carnivorous when young but become herbivorous with advancing age.

Turtles usually stalk their prey or actively seek it out, but some may lie in ambush. After the food is seized it is torn apart by the sharp, horny beak and the forefoot claws; then it is swallowed in portions. If the morsel is small it may be ingested whole.

ECONOMIC IMPORTANCE: Turtles may be of considerable importance to man in several respects. They serve as a ready source of meat and are eaten locally; the green turtle, the diamondback terrapin, and the snapping turtle are marketed commercially for their flesh. The hawksbill turtle is the source of the tortoiseshell used in jewelry and toilet articles. Probably more than a million dollars is spent on turtles annually in the pet trade. On the negative side, several common species are known to transmit some of the *Salmonella* diseases to man.

CONSERVATION: Turtle populations have been decreasing at an alarming rate in the United States in recent years. The exact causes of the decline are unknown, but a number of circumstances are suspected.

Overcollecting is certainly a factor. The volume of the pet trade has resulted in the removal of many adults from the populations, and the gathering of eggs and juveniles reduces the rate of replacement of those adults left to die of natural causes. With their slow rate of maturation our turtles cannot withstand heavy cropping and still maintain their populations.

Although there is no direct proof of their harmful effects on turtles, insecticides and herbicides probably contribute to the decrease in the numbers of turtles. Large quantities of chlorinated hydrocarbons (ingredients in many pesticides) surely are stored in the body fat in late summer and fall and could well cause the death of many turtles as they use this fat during hibernation.

The automobile has a detrimental effect: thousands of turtles are killed crossing highways each year. Many drivers even go out of their way to run over them, just to hear them "pop."

The general deterioration of the natural environment has eliminated large populations in certain regions. Swamps and marshes have been drained for additional farmland or for the construction of highways, housing developments, shopping centers, drive-in movies, and the like. The U.S. Army Corps of Engineers dams rivers and floods low-lying woodlands and marshy ground, thus eliminating shallow water and terrestrial habitats. And man has polluted many bodies of water so badly that turtles can no longer live in them.

If turtles are to remain a conspicuous part of our fauna we must initiate conservation measures. Although we do not yet know enough about turtle biology to formulate an adequate conservation plan, certain needs are obvious. The waterways and lands harboring important populations should be protected from undue human disturbance and pollution. The trend away from the use of the dangerous residual pesticides must be continued. States must pass and enforce legislation controlling the capture of these creatures in the wild.

Equally important: more people must become acquainted with the many fascinating aspects of turtle biology. Such awareness should make people more interested in the protection of these shy creatures. The creation of such an attitude—not only toward turtles but also toward our dwindling wildlife resources generally—is a major purpose of this book.

The Identification of Turtles

The accompanying key to the turtles of the United States is designed to enable one to identify the animal in hand. The characters most often used are those of the shell, limbs, and head—usually the least variable characters within a species. Occasionally it is necessary to refer to some character of the skull for positive identification. (Figures 1–4.)

Within a population of turtles any character will show individual variation; the larger the sample the greater the extremes. In most cases, however, a specimen will have the character as described in the key or at least can be placed within the middle range of measurements. Still, one occasionally encounters a turtle in which the character is quite different or in which the measurements fall outside the given range. For this and other reasons no key is infallible; so, after one has arrived at a name by use of the key, the animal should be compared with the photographs and the description in the species account.

Difficulties in keying are most frequent when the turtle is immature (or, sometimes, a preserved specimen). Then one should follow each alternative down to species and in each case examine that possibility by reference to the photographs and text.

If the reader still cannot identify his specimen, it is likely to be a foreign turtle—somebody's pet, escaped or released. In this case we suggest the reader consult the works of Wermuth and Mertens (1961) or Pritchard (1967a) (see bibliography).

3a. & 4a.

3b.

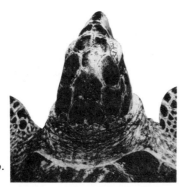

4b.

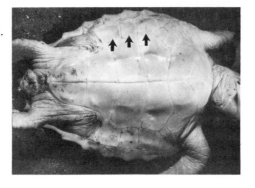

5a.

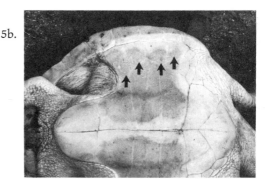

5b.

KEY TO THE TURTLES OF THE UNITED STATES

(Identification characters apply to living *adults*. Before attempting to key immature or preserved specimens see the introductory remarks.)

1a. Shell covered with horny plates   2

  b. Shell covered with leathery skin   46

2a. Limbs paddlelike; strictly marine (Family Cheloniidae)   3

  b. Limbs not paddlelike; not strictly marine   7

3a. Four pairs of pleurals; cervical not in contact with the first pleurals   4

  b. Five or more pairs of pleurals; cervical in contact with the first pleurals   5

4a. One pair of prefrontal scales; lower jaw strongly serrated: *Chelonia mydas*, page 207

  b. Two pairs of prefrontal scales; lower jaw only weakly serrated: *Eretmochelys imbricata*, page 222

5a. Bridge with three inframarginals: *Caretta caretta*, page 231

  b. Bridge with four inframarginals   6

6a. Usually only five pairs of pleurals; color gray. *Lepidochelys kempii*, page 239

b. Usually more than five pairs of pleurals; color olive: *Lepidochelys olivacea*, page 244

7a. Hind feet elephantine and not webbed; forefeet shovellike and modified for digging; strictly terrestrial (Family Testudinidae) 8

b. Hind feet not elephantine and more or less webbed; forefeet not shovellike; aquatic or semiaquatic 10

8a. Distance from base of first claw to base of 4th claw on forefoot approximately equal to the same measurement on hind foot 9

b. Distance from base of 1st claw to base of 3rd claw on forefoot approximately equal to the distance from base of 1st claw to base of 4th claw on hind foot; restricted to the southeastern United States: *Gopherus polyphemus*, page 200

9a. Paired axillary scutes; restricted to southern Texas: *Gopherus berlandieri*, page 191

b. Single axillary scute; restricted to the southwestern United States: *Gopherus agassizii*, page 184

10a. Plastron small and cross-shaped; tail more than half the carapace length (Family Chelydridae) 11

b. Plastron not small or cross-shaped; tail less than half the carapace length 13

11a. A row of supramarginal scutes above the marginals on each side; upper jaw strongly hooked; carapace with three prominent keels extending the entire length: *Macroclemys temminckii*, page 29

b. No supramarginals; upper jaw not strongly hooked; carapacial keels not extending the entire length 12

7a.

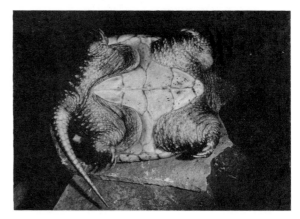

10a.

11a.

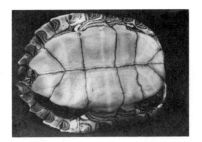

13a.

13b.

14a.

15a.

16a.

16b.

12a. Width of 3rd vertebral the same or greater than height of 2nd pleural: *Chelydra osceola*, page 26

b. Width of 3rd vertebral much less than height of 2nd pleural: *Chelydra serpentina*, page 19

13a. Plastron composed of 12 horny scutes; pectoral scute in contact with the marginals (Family Emydidae)   14

b. Plastron composed of 10 or 11 horny scutes; pectoral scute not in contact with the marginals (Family Kinosternidae)   39

14a. Plastron with a well-developed hinge   15

b. Plastron without a well-developed hinge   17

15a. Upper jaw notched; chin and throat bright yellow: *Emydoidea blandingii*, page 179

b. Upper jaw not notched; chin and throat not yellow   16

16a. Carapace keeled; pattern variable: *Terrapene carolina*, page 87

b. Carapace not keeled; pattern of radiating lines on pleurals and plastron constant: *Terrapene ornata*, page 96

17a. Neck extremely long (distance from snout to shoulder approximately equal to the plastron length): *Deirochelys reticularia,* page 174

b. Neck not long (distance from snout to shoulder approximately equal to half the plastron length) 18

18a.

18a. Upper jaw with a prominent notch bordered on each side by toothlike cusps 19

b. Upper jaw without a prominent notch bordered by cusps 23

19a. Carapace not serrated posteriorly: *Chrysemys picta,* page 138

b. Carapace serrated posteriorly 20

19b.

20a. Prefrontal arrow absent; restricted to Texas and New Mexico: *Chrysemys concinna texana,* page 156

b. Prefrontal arrow present 21

21a. Paramedial stripes end in back of the eyes: *Chrysemys nelsoni,* page 169

b. Paramedial stripes continue forward between the eyes and onto the snout 22

20b.

22a. Carapace elevated medially; restricted to Gulf coastal plain: *Chrysemys alabamensis,* page 172

b. Carapace flattened medially; restricted to Atlantic coastal plain: *Chrysemys rubriventris,* page 165

21a.

13

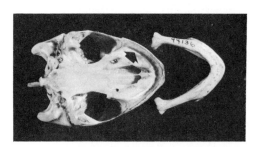

23a. & 24a.

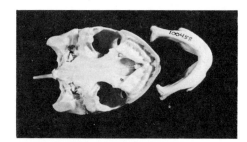

23a. & 24b.

24a.

24b.

25a.

23a. Crushing surface of the upper jaw with a ridge or tuberculate row extending parallel to its margin   24

b. Crushing surface of the upper jaw smooth or undulating but not ridged   26

24a. Crushing surface of upper jaw not serrated; underside of chin rounded: *Chrysemys scripta*, page 147

b. Crushing surface of upper jaw serrated; underside of chin flat   25

25a. C-shaped mark present on 2nd pleural; plastral figure present: *Chrysemys concinna*, page 155

b. C-shaped mark absent on 2nd pleural; no plastral figure: *Chrysemys floridana*, page 161

26a. Crushing surface of the upper jaw narrow   27

b. Crushing surface of the upper jaw broad   30

27a. Carapace with some indication of a keel   28

b. Carapace smooth, without a keel   29

26a.

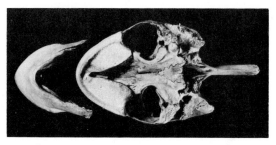

26b.

30a.

31a.

28a. Temporal region of head with a conspicuous orange blotch; carapace weakly keeled: *Clemmys muhlenbergii*, page 76

   b. Temporal region of head without an orange blotch; carapace strongly keeled: *Clemmys insculpta*, page 80

29a. Carapace blue-black and marked with rounded yellow spots; found east of the Mississippi River: *Clemmys guttata*, page 71

   b. Carapace mottled but without rounded yellow spots; found west of the Rocky Mountains: *Clemmys marmorata*, page 84

30a. Scutes of the carapace rough, with concentric ridges or striations; head and neck without longitudinal stripes: *Malaclemys terrapin*, page 103

   b. Scutes of the carapace smooth, without concentric ridges or striations; head and neck striped   31

31b. & 33b.

31a. Vertebral keel low, without prominent spines or knobs   32

   b. Vertebral keel well developed, with prominent spines or knobs   33

32a. Horizontal or J-shaped reddish to orange mark behind the eye; scutes of carapace distinctly convex; small size: *Graptemys versa*, page 127

   b. Yellowish spot behind the eye; scutes of carapace not convex; medium to large size: *Graptemys geographica*, page 109

32a.

32b.

33a.

34a.

35a.

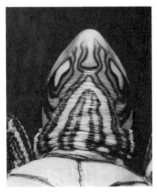

37a.

37b.

33a. Vertebral keel with blunt, rounded black knobs: *Graptemys nigrinoda*, page 135

b. Vertebral keel with sharp, narrow spines 34

34a. A large solid orange or yellow spot on each pleural: *Graptemys flavimaculata*, page 132

b. Solid orange or yellow spot absent from pleurals 35

35a. A light ring or oval mark on each pleural: *Graptemys oculifera*, page 129

b. No ring or oval mark on each pleural 36

36a. Large, solid light mark behind the eye 37

b. Narrow light lines behind the eye 38

37a. A longitudinal light bar under the chin; broad light bars on the marginals: *Graptemys pulchra*, page 116

b. A curved or transverse bar under the chin; narrow, light bars on the marginals: *Graptemys barbouri*, page 113

38a. Yellow crescent behind the eye prevents neck stripes from reaching the eye: *Graptemys kohnii*, page 119

b. Yellow spot behind the eye does not prevent neck stripes from reaching the eye: *Graptemys pseudogeographica*, page 122

38a.

38b.

39a. Pectoral scutes squarish; a single, indistinct transverse hinge between the pectoral and abdominal scutes   40

  b. Pectoral scutes triangular; two prominent transverse hinges bordering the abdominal scutes   42

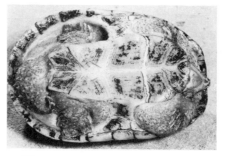

39a.

40a. Two light stripes on the side of the head; barbels on the chin and throat; nonoverlapping carapacial scutes: *Sternotherus odoratus*, page 33

  b. Light stripes absent from side of head; barbels on chin only; overlapping carapacial scutes 41

39b.

41a. Gular scute absent; very prominent vertebral keel: *Sternotherus carinatus*, page 42

  b. Gular scute present; vertebral keel not strongly developed (but two lateral keels may be present on young individuals): *Sternotherus minor*, page 46

42a. Carapace with three longitudinal light stripes: *Kinosternon baurii*, page 56

  b. Carapace plain, not striped   43

40a.

43a. Ninth marginal much higher than the 8th: *Kinosternon flavescens*, page 60

  b. Ninth marginal as high as or only slightly higher than the 8th   44

41b.

42a.

43a.

17

44a.

45a.

46b.

47a.

47b.

48a.

44a. First vertebral widely separated from the 2nd marginal: *Kinosternon subrubrum*, page 50

b. First vertebral in contact with the 2nd marginal 45

45a. Carapace keeled, arched as viewed directly from front; shell less than twice as broad as deep: *Kinosternon hirtipes*, page 66

b. Carapace depressed, flattened when viewed directly from front; shell twice as broad as deep: *Kinosternon sonoriense*, page 64

46a. Limbs paddlelike; snout not tubular; entirely marine (Family Dermochelyidae): *Dermochelys coriacea*, page 249

b. Limbs not paddlelike; snout tubular; entirely freshwater (Family Trionychidae) 47

47a. Nostrils round with no ridge projecting from the septum; anterior edge of carapace without tubercles: *Trionyx muticus*, page 256

b. Nostrils crescentic, with a ridge projecting from the septum; anterior edge of carapace with tubercles 48

48a. Marginal ridge present 49

b. Marginal ridge absent: *Trionyx spiniferus*, page 261

49a. Head plain or with a yellow band from the posterior corner of the eye to the base of the lower jaw; restricted to the extreme southeastern United States: *Trionyx ferox*, page 266

b. Head plain or with fine black lines radiating from the eyes; no yellow band on side of head present; restricted to the Hawaiian Islands: *Trionyx sinensis*, page 270

CHELYDRIDAE: Snapping Turtles

This New World family contains two genera, *Chelydra* and *Macroclemys*. The three species range from Canada to Ecuador.

These are among the largest of the freshwater turtles. All have big heads, powerful jaws, and vile tempers. The well-developed, rough carapace is strongly serrated posteriorly, has 11 marginals on each side, and is connected to the cross-shaped plastron by a narrow bridge. The tail is long and saw-toothed above.

The temporal region of the skull is little emarginate, and the frontals do not enter the orbit. The maxilla is not connected to the quadratojugal, and only rarely is its crushing surface ridged. The quadrate encloses the stapes. There is no secondary palate. The 10th dorsal vertebra lacks ribs, and there is only one biconvex vertebra in the neck. The nuchal bone has rib-shaped lateral processes, which extend below the marginals. The costals are reduced laterally, and there are 11 peripherals. A T-shaped entoplastron is present.

CHELYDRA SERPENTINA (Linnaeus)

Snapping Turtle   I

RECOGNITION: A large (20–47 cm) turtle having the temporal region and the back of the head covered with flat juxtaposed plates, the dorsal surface of the neck with rounded, wartlike tubercles, and the width of the 3rd vertebral much less than the height of the 2nd pleural and less than one-third the length of the five vertebrals. The carapace is massive, is strongly serrated posteriorly, and has three low keels, which are composed of knobs located well behind the centers of the scutes; with increasing age the keels become less conspicuous, and old individuals are often smooth. The carapace varies from tan, brown, or olive to black, and there may be a pattern of radiating lines on each scute. The bridge is small and the hingeless plastron is reduced, giving a cross-shaped appearance; the bridge width is usually one-10th the plastron length or less. The plastron is yellowish to tan and usually without a pattern. The skin is gray to blackish, with some yel-

5. Adult *Chelydra serpentina serpentina*.

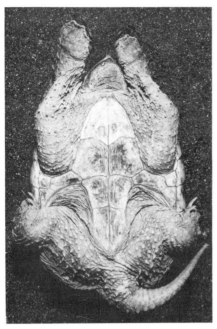

6. Plastron of adult *Chelydra serpentina serpentina.*

7. *Chelydra serpentina serpentina.* Note blunt tubercles on neck.

low or white flecks. The tail is as long as or longer than the carapace; the lateral rows of tubercles are much less conspicuous than the median row, so that there appears to be only one saw-toothed row; and the lower surface of the tail is covered with large, flat scales. The head is large. The eyes are dorsolateral: the orbits can readily be seen from above. The large and powerful jaws may be barred, and the upper jaw is somewhat hooked. The snout is short, and there are only two barbels on the chin. Adults may weigh more than 75 lb.

Males grow larger and have longer preanal tail-lengths (86% of the length of the posterior plastral lobe) than females (less than 86%). In males the anal opening is posterior to the carapacial margin.

GEOGRAPHIC VARIATION: Four subspecies of *C. serpentina* have been described. We consider one to be a distinct species, *C. osceola* (page 26), and two do not occur in the United States. The nominate subspecies, *C. s. serpentina* (Linnaeus), is the only subspecies considered here.

CONFUSING SPECIES: *C. osceola* has the temporal region and the back of the head covered with granular scales and scattered tubercles, the dorsal surface of the neck with long pointed tubercles, and the width of the 3rd vertebral the same as or greater than the height of the 2nd pleural. *Macroclemys temminckii* has a row of supramarginals between the marginals and the pleurals, a strongly hooked beak, lateral eyes, and three high keels on the carapace at all ages. *Kinosternon* and *Sternotherus* have short tails and hinged plastrons.

DISTRIBUTION: *C. serpentina* ranges from Nova Scotia, New Brunswick, southern Quebec, and southeastern Alberta southward east of the Rocky Mountains to northern Florida and the Texas coast, in the United States, and south through Mexico and Central America to Ecuador. In the U.S. it occurs to elevations of at least 6,700 ft.

HABITAT: The common snapping turtle has been taken in almost every freshwater habitat within its range, and it also enters brackish tide pools. It prefers water with a soft mud bottom and abundant aquatic vegetation or an abundance of submerged brush and tree trunks. This species associates with nearly all the freshwater turtles sharing its range.

BEHAVIOR: The snapping turtle is one of the more aquatic species. It spends most of its time lying on the bottom of some deep pool or buried in the mud in shallow water with only its eyes and nostrils exposed. The depth of the water above the mud is usually comparable to the length of the neck, for the nostrils must be periodically raised to the surface. This turtle also hides beneath stumps, roots, brush, and other objects in the water and in muskrat lodges and burrows.

Although sluggish by day, the common snapping turtle apparently is quite active at night. It usually moves about by creeping slowly over the bottom; however, when disturbed it can swim rapidly. By day it often floats lazily just beneath the surface with only its eyes and nostrils protruding. It may bask in this fashion. Legler (1956a) described a social relationship in which *Chrysemys picta* basked on the back of floating *Chelydra serpentina*. Snappers sometimes leave the water to bask on shore or to climb tree trunks, rocks, or stumps at the edge of the water; however, they do not bask out of water as often as other freshwater species.

Hutchison *et al.* (1966) found the mean critical thermal maximum of eight *C. serpentina* to be 39.46 C (37.4–40.6); this was one of the lowest maxima among several species they examined. Ernst (1968b) found that *C. serpentina* had a water-loss gradient of 0.64g/hr, which was the greatest gradient among the five species examined. Thus, basking in *C. serpentina* probably is restricted by intolerance of high temperatures and by rapid loss of moisture.

Snapping turtles are most active during the warmer months, but they have been observed crawling along under the ice in midwinter. Most enter hibernation by late October: they burrow into the mud bottom, settle beneath logs or vegetable debris, or retreat into muskrat burrows or lodges.

Distribution of *Chelydra serpentina* in the United States.

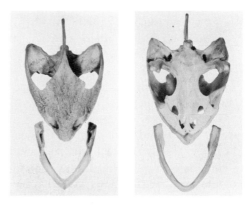

Skull of *Chelydra serpentina*

Large congregations sometimes hibernate together, and other species of turtles may join them. Pell (in Brattstrom, 1965) found the temperature of the mud and water as well as the body temperature of a submerged hibernating *C. serpentina* to be 5 C. Snappers emerge in March, April, or May, depending on latitude and temperature. In summer, if their habitat dries, some snappers aestivate in the mud and others emigrate to more suitable habitats nearby.

The snapping turtle has a vicious temper and should be handled carefully. It strikes with amazing speed and its jaws are capable of tearing flesh severely. The strike often carries the forepart of the body off the ground. The safest way to carry a snapping turtle is to grasp it by the hind limbs while keeping its head down and the plastron toward you and well away from your legs. Do not carry large specimens by the tail: they can be severely injured by having their caudal vertebrae separated or the sacral region stretched. When handled, snappers emit a musk as potent as that of musk turtles. Snapping turtles normally are docile when submerged, but even then they can and sometimes do bite viciously.

Brode (1958) found that juvenile *C. serpentina* would grasp a stick with their tails and could hang by it—sometimes for a few seconds, sometimes for several minutes. He suggested that snappers may maintain their position in swift water by hooking their prehensile tails over fixed objects.

REPRODUCTION: Both sexes of *C. serpentina* become sexually mature when the carapace is about 20 cm long.

Mating occurs from April to November. Each encounter may be preceded by courtship. Legler (1955) showed that precoital behavior varies. In his laboratory a male often directly approached a female on the bottom of the tank and mounted her at once. Several times a male followed a female for a few minutes and then mounted her at or near the surface; together they sank slowly to the bottom. Legler once observed a pair facing each other on the bottom with necks extended and noses about 1 inch apart. Each was positioned so that the anterior edge of the plastron touched the bottom and the hindquarters were elevated to a maximum by the hind legs. The turtles made sudden, simultaneous sideward sweeps of their heads and necks, but in opposite directions; subsequently they slowly brought their necks back to the straight-forward position. This sequence was repeated about 10 times at intervals of approximately 10 sec. Taylor (1933) found two *C. serpentina* with their heads close together in shallow water; they appeared to be gulping water and violently forcing it out their nostrils, causing an upheaval of the surface above their heads.

In coital position the male is astride the carapace of the female, gripping its edges firmly with all four feet. When in place he curls his tail under her body, and at the same time extends his chin over her snout so that she cannot extend her neck. He then begins a series of violent, coordinated muscular contractions of the legs, neck, and tail. The neck is thrust forward and downward. He may bite the female about the head and neck or grasp a fold of loose skin. Flexure of his tail elevates her tail and improves cloacal contact. Muscular spasms occur before, during, and after intromission; perhaps they facilitate penetration. The female is passive, except that at times she may struggle violently and attempt to retaliate as the male bites her. According to Smith (1956), sperm may remain viable in the female for several years.

Nesting occurs from late May through September; June is the peak month. An open site, which may be several hundred meters from the water, is selected and the nest is dug with the hind feet, in sand, loam, or vegetable debris. Muskrat lodges often are used as nesting sites. The nest usually is flask-shaped: a narrow opening descends at an angle to a large egg-chamber below. The depth of the nest ranges from 4 to 7 inches, and its dimensions vary with the size of the female. The eggs are laid at intervals of approximately 1 minute and are put in place by alternate movements of the hind feet. When the clutch is complete the nest is filled and concealed by alternate scraping with the hind feet.

If the female is visited by an intruder while she is nesting, she may go steadily on with the job or else wait quietly until she is left alone.

Hammer (1969) found that nesting activity was influenced by air temperature and by precipitation. Rising air temperatures above a minimum of 50–60 F resulted in greater nesting activity. Light rain coincident with or slightly preceding rising night temperatures also increased the activity. Most nesting was between 5 and 9 AM and between 5 and 9 PM. Larger females apparently nested earlier in the season than did smaller ones. The smallest nesting female weighed 9 lb. and had a carapace length of 10 inches; the largest weighed 23.5 lb. and had a 14.6-inch carapace.

Mammals destroyed 48% of 102 nests at the first predatory visit; 11% were visited more than once before all eggs were destroyed. Nests in which some of the eggs remained intact comprised 12% of the total. Twenty-five percent of the nests escaped destruction by predators or by the actions of men repairing dikes. Considerably more nests were destroyed by predators in 1966 (63%) than in 1967 (46%): abnormally high rainfall in 1967 apparently helped conceal the nests. Skunks destroyed 25% of the nests, raccoons 22%, and minks 9%. A high correlation existed between nest concentration and predation levels: dikes having the highest number of nests per mile also had the highest percentages of nests destroyed (Hammer, 1969).

The number of eggs in a clutch is 11–83 but is usually 20–30. The larger females lay the most eggs. More than one clutch probably is laid each season. The white, tough, spherical eggs are 23–33 mm in diameter and weigh 7–15 g. In a fresh egg one pole is white and the other pinkish, and an air chamber occupies nearly half the space within the shell.

Incubation periods are 55–125 days, depending on environmental conditions. Emergence from the nest normally occurs from late August to early October but may be delayed until the following spring.

Hatchlings have nearly round, dark-gray to brown, wrinkly carapaces with three distinct keels.

8. Hatchling *Chelydra serpentina serpentina.*

There is often a pattern, consisting of a light spot on the underside of each marginal, and the plastron is black with some light mottling. The skin is dark gray, and the head and jaws may be somewhat mottled. A buttonlike yolk sac 7–10 mm in diameter is attached to the center of the plastron; it usually is absorbed within the first 3 days. The caruncle or egg-tooth usually is shed within the first 3 weeks. Hatchlings are about 26–31 mm in carapace length and 24–29 mm in carapace width. They weigh about 5.7 g.

GROWTH: Gibbons (1968e) calculated the age/size classes of six *C. serpentina* taken from the polluted Kalamazoo River near Otsego, Michigan: 1 year, 54–66 mm; 2 years, 83–108 mm; 3 years, 124–145 mm; 4 years, 146–184 mm; 5 years, 177–211 mm; and 6 years, 204–238 mm. The mean carapace length of five specimens increased 32mm/year from the 1st through the 6th year, but the rate of growth declined each year; for example, the average increase in length in a 15-year-old, 257-mm turtle was about 18.5 mm/year through the 14th year but less than 10 mm/year for the last 2 years. Gibbons found no evidence that the growth rate slows more rapidly once maturity is reached. Hammer (1969) found that annual growth increments were large in young snappers but small in older ones—an indication that growth follows a sigmoidal curve. Lagler and Applegate (1943) gave the length/weight relationships of Michigan *C. serpentina* as 197 mm/1,873 g, 248 mm/3,357 g, 298 mm/6,033 g, 349 mm/9,979 g, and 375 mm/13,608 g.

As *C. serpentina* grows, the carapacial keels become less conspicuous, the carapace becomes smoother, the length increases faster than the width, and the tail becomes relatively shorter. Examples of this species have lived for at least 20 years in captivity.

FOOD AND FEEDING: *C. serpentina* is omnivorous. It consumes insects, crayfish, fiddler crabs, shrimp, water mites, clams, snails, earthworms, leeches, tubificid worms, freshwater sponges, fish (adults, fry, and eggs), frogs and toads (adults, tadpoles, and eggs), salamanders, snakes, small turtles, birds, and small mammals. Among the plants it eats are various algae, *Elodea*, *Potamogeton*, *Polygonum*, *Nymphaea*, *Lemna*, *Typha*, *Vallisneria*, *Nuphar*, *Wolffia*, and *Najas*.

Lagler (1943) observed that fish, invertebrates, and plant material occurred most frequently in snapping turtle diets. Alexander (1943) found that plant material composed 36.5% by volume (60.0% frequency) and animals 54.1% by volume (64.7% frequency) of the contents of 470 stomachs. Crayfish occurred in 31% of 569 stomachs examined by Penn (1950). Carrion is sometimes consumed; when baits in turtle traps begin to decay, *C. serpentina* is more likely to be attracted.

Young snappers actively forage for food, but older individuals often lie in ambush to seize their prey. Small prey is seized and swallowed intact; larger prey is held in the mouth and torn to pieces with the aid of the long foreclaws. Larger animals are sometimes dragged beneath the surface and held until they drown. Feeding usually takes place underwater.

Burghardt and Hess (1966) fed three groups of hatchlings either meat, fish, or worms. When tested after a period of 12 daily feedings, each group preferred the diet to which it had become accustomed. Thereafter, for 12 days, each group was given an uncustomary food, and at the end of this period each still preferred its initial diet. Burghardt and Hess concluded that food-imprinting may influence the feeding behavior of this turtle.

PREDATORS: Crows, mink, skunks, foxes, and raccoons raid snapping turtle nests and eat the eggs. Hatchlings and juveniles are the prey of herons, bitterns, crows, hawks, bullfrogs, large fish, and snakes. Man is the chief predator of the adults, but alligators probably take a few.

MOVEMENTS: *C. serpentina* sometimes travels considerable distances, both overland and in water. Barbour (1950) found a juvenile snapper on top of a wooded mountain 1.5 miles from the nearest stream large enough to support fish and more than

5 miles from the nearest pond. Klimstra (1951) reported that a pair of snapping turtles moved overland 610 yards from a drying pond to a stream. He calculated their overland speed at 0.125 mph, but this included two brief stops. In Pennsylvania nine adults, recaptured a total of 16 times, moved an average of 74.5 m between recaptures and had estimated home ranges averaging 4.55 acres (Ernst, 1968c).

Hammer (1969) found that the average distance traveled by 107 turtles was 0.69 mile (0–3.75). The mean distance moved in one year was 0.57 mile. One female moved 2.11 miles in 10 days, but most traveled considerably less and many were recaught in the same location 4 to 6 days later. Most of the movements occurred within the same marsh. Fifty-three percent of the recaptures were on the dike where nesting females were originally marked, and 74% had not left the pool where they had been marked; that is, there was little movement between pools.

Hatchlings are attracted to large areas of intense illumination and thus find their way from the nests to the water. Their escape from the nest is aided by a marked negative geotropism in the dark. They also are attracted toward areas of high humidity; but the presence of a light source in a drier area will counteract any tendency to move into a wet area (Noble and Breslau, 1938). Gibbons and Smith (1968) presented evidence that adult *Chelydra* use the sun as their directional guide while traveling overland. Ernst and Hamilton (1969) found that two *C. serpentina* chose blue 69% of the time and red 25% in trials with a choice of red-, yellow-, green-, or blue-lighted compartments; the significance of this was not determined.

POPULATIONS: Cagle (1942) found *C. serpentina* comprised 1–11% of five southern Illinois turtle populations, and Cagle and Chaney (1950) found they made up from 2.4–17.2% of six Louisiana populations. At White Oak, Pennsylvania, *C. serpentina* comprised only 3.6% of 1,218 turtles, and at Lake Reba, Madison County, Kentucky, they comprised 32.6% of 43 turtles collected. Because

C. serpentina is secretive and may not be attracted to baits in traps as readily as are other species, these figures probably do not truly reflect the relative abundance of snapping turtles. We feel they are the most abundant aquatic turtles in Kentucky, and they are common throughout their range.

Hammer (1969) estimated the snapping turtle population of Lacreek Refuge, South Dakota, at about 860 sexually mature females in the areas sampled. An estimate of the mature population was obtained by doubling that number, for the sex ratio was approximately 1:1; thus 1,720 mature turtles were believed to exist in the portions of the refuge sampled. Extrapolation to include areas not adequately sampled gave an estimate of 2,415 sexually mature snapping turtles on Lacreek Refuge: approximately one turtle for every 2 acres of marsh.

The sex ratio of hatchlings is about 1:1, and this ratio is maintained into adulthood (Mosimann and Bider, 1960). Deviations from this ratio in a series of large individuals is due to the fact that males attain larger size.

REMARKS: In a study of the penial morphology of cryptodiran turtles Zug (1966) found that the glans penis is nearly identical in *Chelydra* and *Macroclemys*, except for an additional fold in the latter. This suggests close relationship between these genera.

The snapping turtle sometimes comes into disrepute because it takes game fish and ducklings. Coulter (1957) reported that predation by snapping turtles resulted in losses of 10–13% of the estimated duckling populations in two study areas in Maine.

The flesh of the snapping turtle is delicious and is eaten throughout the range; an excellent soup can be made from it. The fresh eggs are edible if fried (they will not hard-boil). A detailed account of the economic value of this species was given by Clark and Southall (1920).

Danville-Boyle County
Public Library
Third and Broadway
Danville, Kentucky 40422

C52735

9. Adult *Chelydra osceola.*

CHELYDRA OSCEOLA Stejneger

Florida Snapping Turtle   I

RECOGNITION: A large (20–47 cm) turtle having the temporal region and the back of the head covered with granular scales and a scattering of low tubercles and having the dorsal surface of the neck covered with long, pointed tubercles. The large carapace is strongly serrated posteriorly and has three low keels: a central keel on the vertebrals and two lateral keels on the pleurals; with increasing age the keels become less conspicuous, and old individuals are often smooth. Knobs on the keels are located near the centers of the large scutes. The width of the 3rd vertebral is about one-third the total length of the five vertebrals and as much as or more than the height of the 2nd pleural. The carapace is olive-brown to dark brown and may have a pattern of pale radiating lines on each scute. The bridge is narrow and the hingeless plastron is reduced, giving a cross-shaped appearance. The plastron is yellowish to tan and, usually, immaculate. The skin is gray to black, with small whitish flecks. The tail is as long as or longer than the carapace and has the lateral rows of tubercles about the same size as the central row, so that there appear to be three saw-toothed rows; the lower surface of the tail is covered with large scales. The head is large. The eyes are dorsolateral; they can readily be seen from above. The jaws are large and powerful and may have a barred pattern; the upper jaw is somewhat hooked. There are paired barbels on the chin. Adults may weigh more than 50 lb.

Males have the anal opening posterior to the carapacial margin, but in females it is under or anterior to the margin.

GEOGRAPHIC VARIATION: No subspecies have been described.

CONFUSING SPECIES: *C. serpentina* has the temporal region and the back of the head with flat juxtaposed plates, the dorsal surface of the neck with rounded wartlike tubercles, and the width of the 3rd vertebral much less than the height of the 2nd pleural.

(Richmond [1958] discusses additional characters that separate *C. osceola* from *C. serpentina*.) *Macroclemys temminckii* has a strongly hooked beak, lateral eyes, three high persistent keels, and a row of supramarginals interposed between the marginals and the pleurals.

DISTRIBUTION: *C. osceola* is restricted to peninsular Florida.

HABITAT: The Florida snapping turtle occurs in freshwater having an abundance of aquatic plants and a soft bottom. It is often encountered in canals, sloughs, and pools and is one of the few tetrapods regularly found in the acidic, muck-bottomed hammock streams. Juveniles often take refuge in clumps of water hyacinth. *C. osceola* has been observed in association with all freshwater turtle species within its range.

BEHAVIOR: Little is known of the habits of this turtle. It appears to be largely nocturnal. Individuals either migrate or burrow into the mud when their habitats dry, and Carr (1952) thought they could remain buried for weeks without suffering damage. Extensive droughts, however (as recently in the Everglades) kill many individuals.

REPRODUCTION: This species probably matures at a carapace length of about 20 cm; a 15.5-cm female examined by Duellman and Schwartz (1958) was immature.

Nesting occurs during June, but the procedure has not been described. Carr (1952) speculated, from the appearance of the ground around several nests and the pile of sand usually found on the backs of recently ovipositing females, that they must at least occasionally dig a preliminary cavity, as some sea turtles do.

Hatchlings are rich chestnut-brown, with black at the seams: they are much brighter than adults. The ridges, keels, and tubercles on the carapace are very prominent. The plastron is black. The skin is gray and mottled, with the mottling tending to form lines on the head and neck. The barbels on the

Distribution of *Chelydra osceola*.

10. Plastron of adult *Chelydra osceola*.

11. *Chelydra osceola*; note elongate tubercles on neck.

chin are whitish. The caruncle is sharp and has the tip inclined slightly downward. A newly hatched *C. osceola* measured 31 mm in carapace length, 26.5 mm in carapace width, 18 mm in shell depth, and 11.5 mm in head width; 30 mm of tail extended beyond the shell (Carr, 1952). The smallest juvenile examined by Duellman and Schwartz (1958) had a carapace length of 28 mm, a carapace width of 29 mm, and a shell depth of 17 mm.

FOOD AND FEEDING: *C. osceola* is omnivorous. Stomachs examined in southern Florida by Frank J. Ligas contained numerous opercula of *Pomacea* snails, crayfish, a water snake (*Natrix*), an adult red-winged blackbird, sawgrass seeds, duckweed (*Lemna minor*), and arrowhead (*Sagittaria*). Fish are also occasionally taken. Carr (1952) reported that the few stomachs he examined all contained some plant remains.

POPULATIONS: *C. osceola* is quite common over its range but probably is most abundant in the canals of the Everglades.

REMARKS: Some authorities consider *C. osceola* to be conspecific with *C. serpentina* (page 19) and classify it as a subspecies of the latter. The problem has not been resolved, but we have elected to separate *C. osceola* in accordance with the findings of Richmond (1958).

Although the Florida snapping turtle is little favored as food, its flesh is palatable.

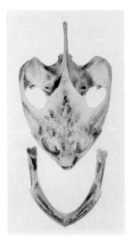
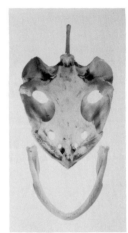

Skull of *Chelydra osceola*

MACROCLEMYS TEMMINCKII (Troost)

Alligator Snapping Turtle   II

RECOGNITION: A large (38–66+ cm) turtle with a hooked jaw, lateral eyes, three keels on the carapace, and a row of supramarginal scutes along the sides. The large, rough, dark carapace is strongly serrated posteriorly and has three rather high persistent keels: a central keel on the vertebrals and two lateral keels on the pleurals; knobs on the keels are elevated and somewhat curved posteriorly. A row of three to eight supramarginal scutes is located between the marginals and the first three pleurals on each side. The bridge is small and the hingeless plastron is reduced, giving a cross-shaped appearance. The plastron is grayish; in juveniles it may be somewhat mottled with small whitish blotches. The skin is dark brown to gray above and lighter below; there may be darker blotches on the head. The tail is about as long as the carapace and has three rows of low tubercles above and numerous small scales below. The huge, pointed head has the eyes placed so much to the side that the orbits cannot be seen from above. There are numerous dermal projections on the side of the head, on the chin, and on the neck. The jaws are large and powerful, and the upper jaw is strongly hooked. There is a wormlike process on the tongue; it is attached, approximately at its center, to a rounded muscular base, and both ends are freely movable. In the young, each end of this elongate process may bear a small branch, but in larger specimens the ends are entire. Adults are known to attain a weight of at least 219 lb.

Males have longer preanal tail-lengths than females and have the anal opening posterior to the carapacial margin.

GEOGRAPHIC VARIATION: No subspecies have been described.

CONFUSING SPECIES: *Chelydra serpentina* and *C. osceola* lack supramarginal scutes, have low keels on the carapace or none at all, and have the eyes situated so high that the orbits can be seen from above.

12. Adult *Macroclemys temminckii*; note the supramarginal scutes.

13. Plastron of *Macroclemys temminckii*.

14. *Macroclemys temminckii.* Note the sharply hooked jaws, the radiating tubercles about the eye, and the "worm" on the floor of the mouth.

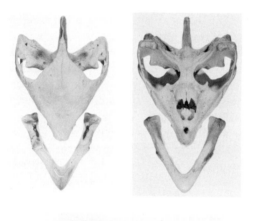

Skull of *Macroclemys temminckii*

DISTRIBUTION: *Macroclemys* ranges south in the Mississippi valley from Kansas, Iowa, and Illinois to the Gulf and on the coastal plain from southeastern Georgia and northern Florida to eastern Texas.

HABITAT: The alligator snapper occurs most frequently in the deep water of rivers, canals, lakes, and oxbows. It has also been found in swamps, bayous, and ponds that are situated near deeper, running water, and it sometimes enters brackish coastal waters. Mud bottoms and abundant aquatic vegetation usually are present. *Macroclemys* has been taken in association with most of the freshwater turtles in its range.

BEHAVIOR: Little is known of the habits of this deepwater turtle. It does not bask, and it seems to be quite sedentary. It seldom swims for any distance; rather, it creeps along the bottom. It seems to be nocturnal. Apparently only nesting females come out on land.

Juveniles will grasp a stick with their tails and can hang from it for periods ranging from a few seconds to several minutes. Possibly they maintain their position in swift water by hooking their prehensile tails around fixed objects (Brode, 1958).

These animals cannot remain submerged as long as many other species of turtles. After 15–20 min in warm water, if prevented from reaching the surface they will stretch their necks upward as far as possible; and if unable to reach air they begin to open and close the mouth rapidly and vigorously, gulping water in evident distress. At water temperatures of 70–75 F they show signs of distress when submerged for 40–50 min. While submerged they slowly open and close the mouth and pulsate the throat, perhaps for pharyngeal respiration. Dye added to the water reveals the presence of a current swirling about the mouth (Allen and Neill, 1950).

Hutchison *et al.* (1966) found the mean critical thermal maximum temperature of two *Macroclemys* to be 39.35 C (38.5–40.7). Allen and Neill (1950) reported that captives refused to eat when the air temperature fell below 65 F.

Captives soon become tame. Wild ones, if aroused, can be formidable: like *Chelydra*, they can strike with amazing speed and with a force great enough to raise their bodies off the ground and carry them forward in the direction of the strike. Cahn (1937) reported that a 103-lb specimen was able to cut through a broom handle with one snap of the jaws; the wood appeared to have been cut by a sharp axe. However, Allen and Neill (1950) reported that 35–40-lb specimens were scarcely capable of biting an ordinary pencil in two, although they deeply scored the wood, and specimens weighing 90–100 lb merely dented a broom handle. They also reported that on one occasion a large individual they were capturing bit a chunk of spruce wood out of a canoe gunwale. Human flesh is hardly as tough as wood, so extreme care should be taken when handling these turtles. Futhermore, they scratch vigorously with their long claws and often void the bladder. They also emit a musky odor, which is neither as strong nor as unpleasant as that of *Chelydra*.

REPRODUCTION: Mating occurs in February, March, and April in Florida but probably occurs later in the Mississippi valley. The male pursues the female and persistently tries to mount her. When successful he moves his body slightly to one side and pushes his tail beneath her tail as she pulls it upward and to one side. Mating lasts 5–25 min. A pair of large captives copulated on 28 February and the female laid 44 eggs on 21 April (Allen and Neill, 1950).

In Florida nesting occurs from April through June; in the Mississippi valley it probably takes place later, perhaps in June or July. Our only information on mating and nesting in this species consists of the observations of Allen and Neill (1950) on captives. The nests were dug entirely with the hind feet and, apparently, always during the daylight hours. A nest illustrated by Allen and Neill was dug in the bottom of a 14-cm pit similar to the preliminary cavity dug by some sea turtles. The nest cavity was flask-shaped, with a 7-by-12-cm neck and a 16-by-24-cm egg chamber. The greatest depth below the surface was 35.5 cm.

The eggs are nearly spherical and have a hard white shell, which is unglazed and smooth. Their diameter is 30–44 mm. Clutch size is 15–50, apparently in relation to the size of the female. Allen and Neill (1950) reported that 29 eggs laid on 3 June started to hatch on 11 September and continued to hatch through 19 September—an incubation period of 100–108 days.

The hatchling is brown, with a roughened carapace and a long, slender tail. The head is covered with elaborate papillae, and the eye is ringed with conical tubercles. The dark skin may show some lighter mottling. The jaws are long, relatively narrow, and pointed at the tip. The inside of the mouth is light gray-brown with black mottling. Allen and Neill (1950) have given the following dimensions of a typical hatchling: carapace length 44 mm, plastron length 32 mm, distance from the anterior margin of the carapace to the tail tip 104 mm, and weight 23.2 g. The specimen figured by Agassiz (1857) is of hatchling size (though the egg-tooth is lacking) and has the following dimensions: carapace length 43.5, carapace width 41 mm, carapace depth 21 mm, and plastron length 28 mm.

GROWTH: Two *Macroclemys* kept by Allen and Neill (1950) were 84 mm and 90 mm in carapace length when 5 years old. A September 1942 hatchling with a carapace length of 44 mm grew to 85 mm by January 1949. Hunt (in anon., 1967) found that a *Macroclemys* grew from a carapace length of 3.50 inches in June 1958 to 10.75 inches (weight 12 lb) in April 1967.

Conant and Hudson (1949) reported longevity records of 58 years 8 months and of 47 years 7 months for two *Macroclemys* in the Philadelphia Zoological Garden; the older specimen was still alive at the time the article was published.

FOOD AND FEEDING: *Macroclemys* probably feeds on any animal it can capture, subdue, and swallow. In captivity it is known to eat fish, beef, pork, frogs, snakes, turtles, snails, worms, mussels, crayfish, and various aquatic plants. Allen and Neill (1950) reported that captives stalked, caught, and ate turtles of the genera *Deirochelys*, *Chrysemys*, *Kinosternon*, and *Sternotherus*. These authors also reported that a large *Macroclemys* killed but did not eat a smaller example of its own kind. A juvenile we kept killed and partly ate individuals of several species of *Graptemys* and *Chrysemys*. Excrement from newly caught captives often contains numerous fragments of snail and mussel shells.

Carr (1952) suggested that *Macroclemys* forages actively by night and reserves the use of the "worm" to provide an occasional fish during the more passive daytime period. The "worm"—gray at rest but suffused with red when active—is the double-ended movable process on the tongue. Captives have been seen to open the jaws, wriggle the process, and lure fish into the mouth.

PREDATORS: Man is the chief predator of this species, but alligators and large gars probably eat smaller individuals, and skunks and raccoons raid the nests.

MOVEMENTS: In three years a *Macroclemys* inhabiting an Oklahoma river moved upstream at an average rate of 6 miles a year (Wickham, 1922). Smith (1956) thought this migration might be correlated with the fact that fish in a given locality soon learn not to bite at the tongue lure; therefore *Macroclemys* may constantly seek new waters in which the lure may succeed.

Allen and Neill (1950) observed aggression that may represent territorial defense; this occurred when a 65-lb *Macroclemys* was introduced into a tank that for several years had been the home of a 93-lb individual. The latter had been living in peace with several small *Macroclemys* and a number of other turtles of several species. The 93-lb turtle attacked the 65-lb one, bit it, and overturned it on the tank bottom.

POPULATIONS: Cagle and Chaney (1950) found *Macroclemys* relatively rare in Louisiana: 12.5% of 24 turtles trapped during 496 trap-hours at Lake Iatt, 4.2% of 46 turtles during 1,413 trap-hours at Caddo Lake, 12.1% of 99 turtles during 390 trap-

hours at Tensas Bayou, and only 4% of 25 turtles trapped in Lake Arthur. They thought *Macroclemys* might have been more abundant than their results indicated: the trap throat was such that it was difficult for a large turtle to enter, and the trap was so short that a large individual could rest in the throat and reach the bait.

REMARKS: The alligator snapping turtle was called "*Macrochelys*" for many years (Schmidt, 1953), until Smith (1955) pointed out that the name *Macroclemys* has priority.

Economically, *Macroclemys* is of little importance. It is eaten locally in the south and occasionally has been sold in the markets of the larger cities, but the flesh is not as tasty as that of *Chelydra*. The eggs are sometimes eaten.

Cahn (1937) reported that a 103-lb individual was capable of walking about with a 165-lb man standing on its back.

The fact that these turtles eat fish and probably destroy some waterfowl makes them unpopular in some places.

Distribution of *Macroclemys temminckii*.

KINOSTERNIDAE:
Musk & Mud Turtles

The Kinosternidae are a New World family of small to medium-sized freshwater turtles ranging from Canada to South America. The four genera —*Sternotherus*, *Kinosternon*, *Staurotypus*, and *Claudius*—contain 23 species; most of them are Central American, but the 3 species of *Sternotherus* and 5 of the 16 species of *Kinosternon* occur in the United States.

There are only 10 or 11 scutes on the single- or double-hinged plastron. Musk glands, associated with the bridge, exude malodorous secretions when the turtle is disturbed. The carapace has a nuchal bone with riblike lateral processes extending below the marginals; 10 peripheral bones; and 23 marginal scutes. The 10th dorsal vertebra lacks ribs, and there is only one biconvex vertebra in the neck. The temporal region of the skull is moderately emarginated. The frontal bones are reduced and do not enter the orbit. The maxilla contacts the quadratojugal, and its crushing surface lacks a ridge. The quadrate does not enclose the stapes. A secondary palate is present. The entoplastron may be absent.

Electrophoretic variation in the serum albumins and other blood proteins of *Kinosternon baurii*, *K. scorpioides*, *Sternotherus minor*, and *S. odoratus* were studied by Crenshaw (1962). The presence of albumin fractions in the Kinosternidae indicates a distinction between this family and the related Chelydridae, which appear to lack significant plasma albumin components.

STERNOTHERUS ODORATUS (Latreille)
Stinkpot   III

RECOGNITION: A small (8.3–13.6 cm) turtle with two prominent light lines on the side of the head, a small plastron with 11 scutes, and an inconspicuous single hinge. There is a single, well-developed gular scute. The deep carapace is highly arched, elongated, and narrow. In younger individuals there may be a prominent vertebral keel, but this is lost in adults. The carapacial margin is unserrated, and the carapacial scutes usually do not overlap. The carapace is gray-brown to black; in adults it is un-

15. Adult *Sternotherus odoratus*; note striped face.

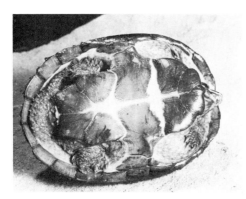

16. Plastron of male *Sternotherus odoratus*; note roughly rectangular pectoral scute.

17. *Sternotherus odoratus*.

marked, but juveniles often have a pattern of scattered spots or radiating dark streaks. The plastron ranges in color from yellowish to brown. The skin is gray to blackish, and the sides of the head and neck usually have a pair of conspicuous yellow or white lines, which begin on the snout and extend backward, passing above and below the eye; these lines may be faded or broken, and in some Florida specimens they may be lacking. Barbels are present on both the chin and the throat.

Males have longer, thicker tails, which end in a blunt terminal nail, and more exposed skin around the median plastral seams than females; they also have two small patches of tilted scales on the inner surface of each hind leg.

GEOGRAPHIC VARIATION: *S. odoratus* is a monotypic species.

CONFUSING SPECIES: All other species of *Sternotherus* lack the two light lines on the side of the head, have barbels on the chin only, and have each large scute of the carapace slightly overlapping the scute behind it. The mud turtles (*Kinosternon*) have large plastrons with two prominent hinges.

DISTRIBUTION: *S. odoratus* ranges from New England and southern Ontario south to Florida and west to Wisconsin and central Texas. There are scattered records from south-central Kansas, western Texas, and Chihuahua, Mexico.

HABITAT: The stinkpot occurs in almost any waterway with a slow current and soft bottom: rivers, streams, lakes, ponds, sloughs, canals, swamps, bayous, and oxbows. It may, however, occasionally occur in almost any sort of stream; for example, we have taken a specimen in a gravel-bottomed stream in northwestern Arkansas. Tinkle (1959a) showed that the fall line usually limits the distribution of stinkpots; they are found above it only in the rivers draining into the Gulf of Mexico.

Although this species usually prefers shallow water, McCauley (1945) and Carr (1940, 1952) found it in water 10–30 ft deep. *S. odoratus* apparently is not tolerant of brackish water: Conant and Baily (1936) reported that it disappeared when a habitat in New Jersey became brackish due to the opening of a canal.

This turtle associates with practically all other aquatic turtles found within its range.

BEHAVIOR: During the daylight hours *S. odoratus* is generally inactive, remaining buried in the mud or resting on the bottom; however, an occasional individual may be found crawling along the bottom at any time. Mahmoud (1969) reported that the 24-hr cycle of the stinkpot in Oklahoma showed morning and evening activity from May to August. The activity was from 4 to 10:20 AM and from 5:40 to 9 PM. From September to April most of the activity occurred between 10 AM and 4 PM. Lagler (1943) and Carr (1952) noted nocturnal activity in stinkpots. Root (1949) showed that submerged *S. odoratus* require only one-eighth the oxygen they normally use in air and so can remain submerged for long periods. He concluded that buccopharyngeal respiration contributed little to the ability of *S. odoratus* to remain submerged and suggested that the throat movements that are prominent while the turtle is underwater are primarily concerned with olfaction.

The basking habit is poorly developed: stinkpots are seldom found out of the water. Most basking occurs while the turtle rests in shallow water with just the top of the carapace exposed to the sunlight or when floating at the surface among aquatic vegetation. They do, however, occasionally climb onto the bank or onto fallen trees to bask. McCauley (1945) and Conant (1958) both remarked on the climbing tendencies of this species. It sometimes climbs 6 ft or higher above the surface of the water on small tree trunks. Older individuals drop into the water when disturbed, but the younger ones hold on with such a grip that it is difficult to remove them.

Temperature relationships of Oklahoma *S. odoratus* have been studied by Mahmoud (1969). He found a mean difference between the cloacal and environmental temperature, throughout the year, of $\pm$ 0.58 to $-$ 0.05 C. The thermal activity range was 10–34 C and the field-preferred body temperature was 24.14 C. The minimum and maximum body temperatures at which *S. odoratus* would accept food in the laboratory were 13 and 35 C. In captivity the stinkpot showed greater activity at water temperatures of 21–26 C. Mahmoud's specimens had a mean critical thermal maximum of 40.25 C (39.5–41.9) and lost their righting ability at an average temperature of 38.7 C (38.4–39.0). Brattstrom (1965) reported that the 19 stinkpots he examined were active at body temperatures of 16.2–28.8 C, with a mean of 21.2 C. Hutchison *et al.* (1966) found that the critical thermal maximum of 19 *S. odoratus* was 40.1–41.7 C. Under field conditions Edgren and Edgren (1955) found that temperatures of stinkpots were higher than the water temperatures when the water temperatures were low (17–19 C) and lower when the water temperatures were high (28–30 C); but in the laboratory the turtles' cloacal temperatures and the water temperatures were about the same, which suggests that thermoregulation resulting from behavioral mechanisms was precluded by laboratory conditions. At lower water temperatures in the laboratory the stinkpots were slightly but significantly warmer than the water, which suggests the possibility of a slight endogenous thermoregulation.

When fully grown stinkpots are kept out of water for a period of time with like-sized specimens of other species, such as *Chrysemys picta*, *Clemmys guttata*, and *Kinosternon subrubrum*, they usually are the first to show signs of distress. Ernst (1968b) compared evaporative loss of water in *S. odoratus*, *Chelydra serpentina*, *Clemmys guttata*, *C. insculpta*, and *Terrapene carolina*; he found that *S. odoratus* suffered the greatest total weight loss (20%) and had a weight-loss gradient of 0.24 g/hr. Two young died during the study after losing 33.4% and 33.1% of their weight, respectively.

Mahmoud (1969) found that Oklahoma *S. odoratus* were active most of the year. There was some inactivity during December, January, and February, when the water temperature was below their thermoactivity range. He estimated the annual activity

35

period to be 330 days. Conant (1951a) collected Ohio *S. odoratus* in every month from March to October; the earliest record was 3 March (1933), the latest 20 October (1929). Evermann and Clark (1916) collected or observed active *S. odoratus* at Lake Maxinkuckee, Indiana, from 18 March to 31 December; the last record was of one walking beneath the ice.

Stinkpots hibernate buried 12 inches or so in the mud bottom under water; beneath rocks, logs, or trash in or near the water; in recesses beneath banks; or in muskrat dens or lodges. They begin to burrow when the water temperature falls below 10 C—sometimes congregating in numbers at suitable hibernacula. Thomas and Trautman (1937) found an estimated 450 stinkpots in an area approximately 45 ft by 6 ft in the mud bed of a drained canal at Buckeye Lake, Ohio.

The temperament of individuals varies. Some are shy, pulling into their shells when handled, but most bite and scratch viciously. In addition to the biting and scratching they void the contents of their musk glands readily, and the resulting odor is vile enough to have earned them their common name, stinkpot. The odor arises from a yellowish, volatile fluid secreted by two glands located on each side beneath the border of the carapace: one gland is located at the posterior end of the bridge, the other about midway between the bridge and anterior edge of the carapace. Similar glands are found in all kinosternids.

REPRODUCTION: Studies of Michigan *S. odoratus* by Risley (1933) indicated that males mature in their 3rd or 4th year and that females mature in their 9th to 11th year. Tinkle (1961) reported, however, that males mature in 3 years, at a length of 60–70 mm, and females mature in 2 to 7 years, at a length of 80–95 mm. Oklahoma males mature in 4 to 7 years, females in 5 to 8 years; sexual maturity is reached at a carapace length of 65–85 mm (Mahmoud, 1967).

Southern stinkpots mature faster than those in the north. Tinkle (1961) found that the minimum size at maturity of southern males was 54 mm

(mean 65 mm), of southern females 61 mm (mean 82 mm). Comparable figures for northern males and females were 63 mm (mean 73 mm) and 80 mm (mean 96 mm). No mature northern female had fewer than three growth annuli, and most had four or more; the oldest immature female examined had seven. The youngest mature northern male had three annuli, but several with this number were immature. Northern males 4 years old or older were mature. The youngest mature southern female had three annuli; no specimens were available with more than three annuli, but all of the southern females with three were mature. The youngest mature southern male had three annuli, and none with more than three was immature. A southern male with a single annulus was mature, but all others with one or two annuli were immature.

Risley (1934, 1938) studied the sexual cycle of male *S. odoratus* from Michigan. Spermatogenesis began with the multiplication of spermatogonia in early May, before the completion of the periodic involution of the testes. Primary spermatocytes and maturation divisions appeared near the middle of June, continued through July, and occurred sporadically until late August. Spermiogenesis began in the latter part of July, was in full progress in August, and was practically completed by the end of September or early October. A pronounced decrease in the size of the testes and a corresponding increase in the size of the epididymides occurred at the end of the cycle. Restoration of germinal epithelium occurred primarily in March, April, and May, with some recovery occurring over the winter.

Edgren (1960a) reported that ovulation in Wisconsin females occurs in late April or early May. He calculated that the life of the egg in the oviduct is between 5 and 8 weeks. According to Pope (1939), ovulation takes place in southern Michigan between 15 and 20 May, and the eggs are retained in the oviducts for 20–35 days, while the albumen and shell are being formed. At Lake Maxinkuckee, Indiana, Evermann and Clark (1916) noted quite well-developed eggs in a female they found crushed on the road on 20 September 1907.

Courtship and mating occur sporadically

throughout the year, with peaks in the spring and fall. Most mating occurs in April and May, before the nesting period. A second period of mating occurs in September and October but may extend into December. There is evidence that sperm from the late matings may be retained through the winter in viable condition in the oviducts. Mating occurs underwater, in shallows, at night or in the early morning.

Mahmoud (1967) studied the sexual activities of *S. odoratus*, *S. carinatus*, *Kinosternon subrubrum*, and *K. flavescens*; he has given a most detailed composite account of their courtship and mating. There were three phases: tactile; mounting and intromission; and biting and rubbing. During the tactile phase a male with head extended approached another turtle from behind and felt or smelled its tail, apparently to determine sex. Courtship usually proceeded no further if the approached turtle was a male; if a female, the male, with head still extending forward, moved to her side and nudged the region of her bridge with his nose. This movement apparently was directed at the musk glands there. If the female was not receptive she moved away. The male responded either by giving chase or by going elsewhere. If chasing occurred, the male, with head fully extended, persistently attempted to nudge or bite the female about the head as he followed. The chase was either by walking or swimming and was sometimes followed by mounting, a few seconds later. If initially receptive, the female remained immobile while the male, with head fully extended, gently nudged her just behind the eye and a few seconds later assumed the mounting position. This tactile phase varied in length from a few seconds to 3 min.

The mounting phase usually followed the tactile phase. Males approached females either from behind or from the side. The male positioned himself with his plastron directly over the female's carapace by grasping the margins of her carapace with the toes and claws of all four feet. By flexing one knee the male held the female's tail between the two scaly patches on the opposing posterior surfaces of the upper and lower leg throughout coitus.

Distribution of *Sternotherus odoratus* in the United States.

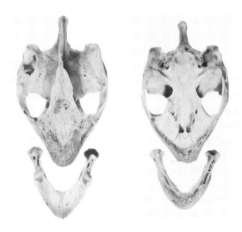

Skull of *Sternotherus odoratus*

The male's tail was looped so that the terminal nail was in touch with the skin at one side of the female's cloaca; this brought the vents together, and insertion of the penis followed. The male's head extended forward to gently touch the top of the female's head and neck. These actions occurred simultaneously. When the coital position was attained the rubbing-and-biting phase began. The time between mounting and penial insertion was 5–10 sec.

Finneran (1948) discovered a pair of Connecticut *S. odoratus* copulating plastron-to-plastron, with the male holding the female with all four feet. This is the only record of this mating position in this species, and it must be considered exceptional.

The nesting season of *S. odoratus* varies with latitude: in the south the egg-laying lasts from March through July, in the north from May through August. Nesting takes place from early morning into the night. Nests have been dug as far as 150 ft from the water.

Some females lay their eggs on the open ground; others dig well-formed nests as deep as 4 inches. Most nests, however, are shallow and are formed by scraping away debris such as decaying vegetable matter, leaf mold, or rotting wood. Many eggs are laid under stumps and fallen logs and in the walls of muskrat houses. When a nest is excavated it usually is dug with the hind feet only; however, Newman (1906) saw a female dig with all four feet and her snout. Female stinkpots are noted for sharing nesting sites: often several lay their eggs at the same place. Cagle (1937) found 16 nests under one log 3 ft long; these nests were so close together that many of them were intermingled. Edgren (1942) found 130 eggs buried in the debris of an abandoned duck blind.

S. odoratus eggs are elliptical, with a thick, white, brittle shell that appears slightly glazed when dry. Cahn (1937) reported that the average size of 112 eggs was 27.6 mm in length and 14.8 mm in width. The average size of 75 eggs taken by Risley (1933) was 27.1 mm in length (24–31) and 15.5 mm in width (14.2–17.0). Two deposited eggs weighed by Conant and Downs (1940) were 3.5 and 3.6 g, and

10 viable eggs removed from three females by Edgren (1960a) averaged 4.02 g. Edgren (1956) reported that *S. odoratus* eggs do not increase in size during incubation. Tinkle (1959c) showed that eggs released from one ovary may reach the opposite oviduct by transcoelomic migration.

The number of eggs per clutch varies from one to nine; the normal number is two to five. The average number of eggs laid by southern stinkpots is 2.2 (1–4), by northern stinkpots 4.6 (2–9); and there is an average prereproductive potential of 10.8 in the north and only 4.2 in the south. Clutch size increases with a decrease in the isotherm zone: at an isotherm zone of 70–75 F the mean clutch size is 1.8, at 50–55 F it is 3.5, and at 45–50 F it is 5.5 (Tinkle, 1961). There is a correlation between clutch size and the body size of the female: the largest females lay the most eggs per clutch. Gibbons (1970b) suggested that at least two clutches are laid each year in Florida.

Hatchlings emerge in August and September in Florida and in September and October in the north. Risley (1933) reported that the incubation period of eggs kept in the laboratory was 60–75 days. Carr (1952) gave the following account of the hatching of a stinkpot egg:

At 6 PM noticed a small crescentic piece of shell, about 2.5 mm long and 1 mm wide that was loose but remained in place. By 11 PM this hole enlarged to 3.5 mm in diameter and another hole, on the opposite side of the same end, has appeared, giving the egg two separate openings. From the larger (the first-made) of these the toenails of the hatchling protrude. August 13, 11 AM: no change except holes slightly larger, now irregularly so, and with jagged outlines; the inner membrane is not broken under the newer hole. Nine PM: the two holes are now continuous, the band of shell separating them having been fractured. August 14, 9 AM: several cracks now radiating from the single large hole in the end, 12 noon, hatchling out; it did not emerge by forcing its way through the initial hole but by breaking out the entire end of the egg in one large and two small pieces.

Gibbons (1970a) believed hatchlings overwinter in the nest in South Carolina.

The hatchling carapace is rough and has a prominent vertebral keel and two smaller lateral keels. It is black, with a light spot on each marginal. The plastron lacks hinges and is rough in texture; it is dark with lighter mottlings. The skin is black and the two light stripes on the head are prominent. Risley (1933) measured 200 recently hatched southern Michigan *S. odoratus* and found the carapace to average 23 mm (19–25). Carr (1952) reported that three newly hatched young had carapaces 21.0–22.2 mm long, 15.5–16.0 mm wide, and 11.5–12.8 mm high. Dodge (1956a) gave the length and width of the carapace of four hatchlings as, respectively, in millimeters, 24, 19; 23, 18; 22, 19; and 22, 17.

GROWTH: As *S. odoratus* grows it becomes more elongated and flattened. Risley (1933) reported that stinkpots with carapaces over 80 mm in length are at least 10 years old. He showed that stinkpots averaged approximately 32.5 mm, 42.5 mm, 52 mm, 61 mm, 67 mm, 71 mm, 74.5 mm, 77.6 mm, and 80 mm in length, respectively, for each of their first 9 years. Mahmoud (1969) found that Oklahoma males having a carapace length of 41–60 mm increased an average of 12.1 mm (21%) per growing season; those 61–80 mm increased 1.6 mm (2.3%); and those over 81 mm increased only 0.78 mm (0.96%). Females having a carapace length of 41–60 mm increased 26.6 mm (52%); those 61–80 mm increased 0.88 mm (1.3%); and those over 81 mm increased only 0.23 mm (0.25%). Three *S. odoratus* over 10 years old did not grow during the 2 years they were kept in captivity.

In one month the hatchlings of a clutch increased in length from 18.3 mm to 19.9 mm and in width from 14 mm to 18.2 mm, and those of another clutch increased from 22 mm to 23.7 mm in length and from 16.3 mm to 20.9 mm in width (Adler, 1960).

Mahmoud (1969) found that the growth period of *S. odoratus* in Oklahoma was limited to the warm months and was approximately 190 days long.

A stinkpot lived for more than 53 years 3 months in the Philadelphia Zoological Garden (Conant and Hudson, 1949).

18. Hatchling *Sternotherus odoratus* on a twenty-five cent piece. Even this baby has become encrusted with algae.

19. Juvenile *Sternotherus odoratus*.

FOOD AND FEEDING: *S. odoratus* is omnivorous. Stinkpots under 5 cm in carapace length feed predominantly on small aquatic insects, algae, and carrion, whereas those above 5 cm feed on any kind of food. They are bottom feeders, often walking about, with head extended, in search of food. They probe soft mud, sand, and decaying vegetation with their heads, apparently looking for food. They prefer slow-moving prey. A piece of food too large to be swallowed whole is held between the jaws while the claws tear the main mass away from the part in the mouth.

The stinkpot is known to eat earthworms, leeches, clams, snails, crabs, crayfish, aquatic insects, fish eggs, minnows, tadpoles, algae, and parts of higher plants. These usually are eaten underwater, but Newman (1906) observed stinkpots, at dusk, crawling about on land and seizing and eating slugs. He also reported that they are scavengers, feeding on all sorts of material, from dead mollusks to kitchen refuse. Lagler (1943) reported that insects and snails were the foods most often found in the stomachs (34.2% and 28.3% of occurrence, respectively). Mahmoud (1968b) found the following percentages of frequency and volume, respectively, of food items in Oklahoma *S. odoratus*: Insecta 98.3, 46.4; Crustacea 61.1, 5.0; Mollusca 96.2, 23.7; Amphibia 5.2, 1.1; carrion 37.4, 3.4; and aquatic vegetation 97.4, 20.4.

PREDATORS: Stinkpot eggs are eaten by skunks, raccoons, herons, and crows and, probably, by other animals on occasion. The remains of juveniles have been found in largemouth bass, bullfrogs, and cottonmouths. There is some evidence that muskrats sometimes feed on adults. Man occasionally takes one on a hook and line and usually destroys the turtle for its efforts.

MOVEMENTS: Maximum and minimum distances between successive points of capture of Oklahoma *S. odoratus* were 1,724 and 6 ft. The average first-last capture distances for periods of more than 100 days were 166 ft for females and 227 ft for males; for less than 100 days, 126 ft for females and 217 ft for males. The average distance traveled by 39 males was 222 ft, by 37 females 146 ft. Average home range of Oklahoma stinkpots was 0.06 acre for males and 0.12 acre for females (Mahmoud, 1969).

Among 23 Pennsylvania *S. odoratus* recaptured by one of us (CHE), the average distance between recaptures was 152 m (166 m for 15 males, 113 m for 6 females, and 185 m for 2 juveniles).

Stinkpots occasionally move overland, but the home range is probably confined to one body of water. Overland movements are likely seasonal or forced.

Newly hatched stinkpots find their way from the nest to the water primarily because of the attraction of large areas of intense illumination. Escape from the nest is facilitated by their marked negative geotropism in the dark. They are attracted toward areas of high humidity, but the presence of a light source in a drier area will counteract any tendency to move toward a wet area (Noble and Breslau, 1938).

The retina of *S. odoratus* contains both rods and cones; that is, the species can see color (Ernst *et al.*, 1970). Ernst and Hamilton (1969) reported that *S. odoratus* chose red or yellow compartments over green or blue in 64% of trials; this color-selection, they thought, may be of aid in orientation.

POPULATIONS: Mahmoud (1969) estimated that there were 60.7 stinkpots per acre in an Oklahoma study area in 1958. Cagle (1942) found *S. odoratus* made up 5–48% of six turtle populations in southern Illinois, and Wade and Gifford (1965) found that it made up 34% of the turtle population of a northern Indiana lake. However, stinkpots comprised only 4.5% of 1,218 turtles caught at the White Oak Bird Sanctuary, in Pennsylvania (Ernst, 1969).

Risley (1933) reported that of 255 adults taken in the field, 77 were males and 178 were females—a sex ratio of 1:2.3. Cagle (1942) found that males comprised 41% of his samples. The sex ratio of all *S. odoratus* examined by Tinkle (1961) in which sex could be determined was slightly skewed in favor of females: among 51 hatchlings there were 36 females and 15 males, and of 647 stinkpots over 50 mm in carapace length 339 (52%) were females and 308 (48%) were males.

REMARKS: Zug (1966) found that in *Sternotherus* the structure of the glans penis is of two general types: a *minor–odoratus* type and a *carinatus* type. He gave a thorough description of each.

A sexual difference in the total serum lipoprotein concentration during the spring and summer months was found by Smith (1968): males exhibited significantly lower values than females. Apparently the female sex hormone mobilized the lipoproteins and maintained a higher serum level. Sexual and seasonal variations in the total hemoglobin content also occurred. Males exhibited a significant decrease in the hemoglobin count from spring to summer. A significant increase in total hemoglobin was noted in both sexes from summer to fall; this increase was believed to result from increased food intake.

S. odoratus is of little value commercially, because the flesh has a musky flavor. At times this species is a nuisance to hook-and-line fishermen: it is an accomplished bait-stealer.

20. Subadult *Sternotherus odoratus* showing characteristic juvenile carapacial pattern.

STERNOTHERUS CARINATUS (Gray)

Razor-backed Musk Turtle   III

RECOGNITION: A small (10–15 cm) turtle having a prominent vertebral keel and a small plastron with 10 scutes and an indistinct hinge. The deep, steeply sloping carapace is slightly serrated posteriorly, and each vertebral scute usually overlaps the one behind it; the marginals are slightly flared. The carapacial scutes are light brown to orange, with dark spots or radiating streaks and dark posterior borders on each; this pattern may be lost with age. The immaculate yellow plastron lacks a gular scute; that is, it has only 10 instead of the 11 scutes found in other kinosternids. An indistinct hinge is located between the pectoral and the abdominal scutes. The skin is gray to brown or pinkish, with small dark spots, and the jaws are tan with dark streaks. The snout is somewhat tubular, and there are two barbels on the chin. All four feet are webbed.

Males have thick, long tails, with the anal opening located posterior to the carapacial margin.

GEOGRAPHIC VARIATION: No subspecies are recognized.

CONFUSING SPECIES: Other *Sternotherus* lack a pronounced vertebral keel and have a gular scute. Mud turtles (*Kinosternon*) have two well-developed plastral hinges and triangular pectoral scutes.

DISTRIBUTION: *S. carinatus* ranges from southeastern Oklahoma, central Arkansas, and Mississippi south to the Gulf of Mexico; that is, the range is almost completely within the Gulf coastal plain.

HABITAT: This species occurs in rivers, slow streams, and swamps. Little current, soft bottoms, abundant aquatic vegetation, and some basking sites are the preferred conditions. It is found with most of the other freshwater turtles in its range.

BEHAVIOR: Oklahoma *S. carinatus* have an annual active period of about 310 days, from March through November. They hibernate in cavities be-

21. Adult male *Sternotherus carinatus*.

neath overhanging banks as well as beneath rocks on river bottoms. In summer they apparently do not aestivate; instead, they retire to deep water. From June to September they are most active from 3 to 10 AM and from 4:40 to 11 PM (Mahmoud, 1969).

S. carinatus basks much more than other *Sternotherus.*

Oklahoma *S. carinatus* showed differences between the cloacal and the environmental temperature, throughout the year, of $+1.0$ C to -0.11 C. The temperature range for active individuals was 14–34 C, and the field-preferred body temperature was 33.29 C. Captives accepted food at body temperatures of 16–34 C. The mean critical thermal maximum was 40.25 C (39.5–41.9), and the righting ability was lost at a mean of 38.7 C (38.4–39.0) (Mahmoud, 1969).

Razor-backed musk turtles are more shy than other *Sternotherus.* When handled they seldom bite or expel musk.

REPRODUCTION: Females mature at a carapace length of about 100 mm, which is reached in 4 or 5 years; males, at 100–120 mm, in 5 or 6 years.

The courtship of this turtle is divisible into three phases: tactile; mounting and intromission; and biting and rubbing. These phases are identical with those of *S. odoratus* (which see for details).

The only data on nesting are those of Tinkle (1958a), who found a clutch of two eggs halfway up a steep bank on the Pearl River. By dissection he estimated that a female lays an average of 7.3 eggs a season, in two clutches. Females with oviducal eggs were found in early April and early June.

The carapace of the hatchling is 23–31 mm in length and is nearly as wide as long. Hatchlings are similar to adults, differing only in their greater tendency toward overlapping of the vertebral scutes, more accentuated markings of the head and upper shell, and a paler plastron. Many have three carapacial keels.

GROWTH: The growth period in Oklahoma is 180 days and is limited to the warm months. The growth

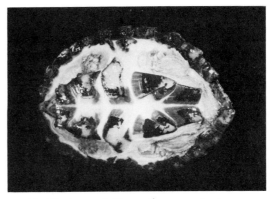

22. Plastron of *Sternotherus carinatus.*

23. *Sternotherus carinatus.*

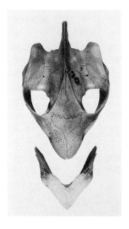
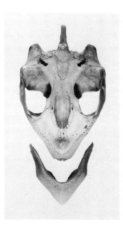

Skull of *Sternotherus carinatus*

24. Juvenile *Sternotherus carinatus*.

rates of two groups of Oklahoma *S. carinatus* were determined by Mahmoud (1969). In the first group, females having an initial carapace length of 21–40 mm increased an average of 12.7 mm (42.3%) per growing season; those 41–60 mm increased 26.6 mm (52%); those 61–80 mm increased 0.88 mm (1.3%); and those over 81 mm increased only 0.23 mm (0.25%). Males of this group having an initial carapace length of 41–60 mm increased 12.1 mm (21%); those 61–80 mm increased 1.6 mm (2.3%); and those over 81 mm increased only 0.78 mm (0.96%) per growing season. In the second group, females having an initial carapacial length of 21–40 mm had the same growth rates as those of the first group; those 41–60 mm increased 13 mm (37.3%); and those 61–80 mm increased 15.3 mm (21%) per growing season. Males of the second group were 61–80 mm in carapace length initially and increased only 0.2 mm (0.18%). Mahmoud also found that the growth rate continued at approximately the same rate beyond the first 6 years. Three *S. carinatus* ranging from 11.3 to 14.2 cm in carapace length showed no apparent growth over 1 to 3 years. Two individuals more than 10 years old showed no growth during the 2 years they were captive.

FOOD AND FEEDING: *S. carinatus* is omnivorous. Mahmoud (1968b) found the following percentages of frequency and volume of food items, respectively, in *S. carinatus*: Insecta 91.6, 42.9; Crustacea 38.7, 2.8; Mollusca 96.7, 24.3; Amphibia 3.1, 2.5; carrion 61.2, 10.6; and aquatic vegetation 88.9, 16.6. Turtles under 5 cm in carapace length fed predominantly on small aquatic insects, algae, and carrion, whereas larger ones fed on any kind of food, regardless of its size, but preferred mollusks. Tinkle (1958a) reported that *S. carinatus* fed predominantly on insects, snails, and clams; some took decapods and plants. Captives feed readily on any kind of meat or fish offered them.

Razor-backed musk turtles are bottom feeders. They frequently walk along the bottom, with neck fully extended, searching for food. They also probe with their heads in soft mud, sand, and decaying vegetation, apparently for food. Occasionally they feed at the surface.

PREDATORS: Nests of this turtle are robbed by many species of mammals. Fish, water snakes, and other turtles prey on the hatchlings. Man destroys the adults; for example, Mahmoud (1969) reported that two fishermen caught and killed 51 adults in 2 hr on the Blue River near Milburn, Oklahoma.

MOVEMENTS: The maximum and minimum distances between successive captures of Oklahoma *S. carinatus* were 308 and 15 ft. The average distance between first and last captures during more than 100 days of activity was 57 ft for females and 127 ft for males (Mahmoud, 1969).

POPULATIONS: Mahmoud (1969) estimated 92.6 *S. carinatus* per acre of suitable habitat in Oklahoma. He found an adult sex ratio of 36 females to 22 males. Tinkle (1958a) found a ratio of 73 females to 50 males.

REMARKS: Skull structure and external morphology show *S. carinatus* to be more closely related to *S. minor peltifer* and *S. m. minor* than to *S. m. depressus*.

Distribution of *Sternotherus carinatus*.

25. Adult *Sternotherus minor minor.*

STERNOTHERUS MINOR (Agassiz)

Loggerhead Musk Turtle   III

RECOGNITION: A small (7.5–11.5 cm) turtle with overlapping vertebral scutes, a small plastron with a single indistinct hinge and 11 scutes, and no prominent facial stripes. The deep carapace is slightly serrated behind and has a vertebral keel and two lateral keels; the latter often disappear with age. It is dark brown to orange with dark-bordered seams; juveniles often have a pattern of scattered spots or radiating dark streaks. The plastron is pink to yellowish and, usually, immaculate; it has a single gular scute, and the hinge is located between the pectorals and the abdominals. The skin is gray-brown to pinkish, with dark dots on the head, neck, and limbs; some have orange skin with dark stripes on the neck. The jaws are tan with dark streaks. The snout is somewhat tubular, and there are two barbels on the chin. All four feet are webbed.

Males have thick, long, spine-tipped tails, and the anal opening is posterior to the carapacial margin.

GEOGRAPHIC VARIATION: Three subspecies have been described. *S. m. minor* (Agassiz), the loggerhead musk turtle, ranges from central Georgia and southeastern Alabama to central Florida. This subspecies usually lacks stripes on the head and neck; has three carapacial keels in the juvenile (these may disappear with age); has the sides of the carapace forming an angle of less than 100°; and shows a mean angle/height ratio of about 5:1 for those with a vertebral keel. *S. m. peltifer* Smith and Glass, the striped-necked musk turtle, ranges from eastern Tennessee and Alabama to the Pearl River, in south-central Mississippi. This subspecies has distinct wide stripes on the neck, a vertebral keel (which disappears with age), the sides of the carapace forming an angle of less than 100°, and a mean angle/height ratio of about 5:1 in those with a vertebral keel. *S. m. depressus* Tinkle and Webb, the flattened musk turtle, is restricted to the Black Warrior River system, in northwestern Alabama. It has few, if any, narrow stripes on the neck; a blunt middorsal keel; a wide, flattened carapace

26. Adult *Sternotherus minor depressus.* (*Photo by Isabelle Hunt Conant*)

27. Front view of *Sternotherus minor depressus.* (*Photo by Isabelle Hunt Conant*)

with an angle always greater than 100°; and a mean angle/height ratio of about 9.5:1 in juveniles.

DISTRIBUTION: *S. minor* ranges from eastern Tennessee and central Georgia south to central Florida and west to the Pearl River system, in south-central Mississippi.

HABITAT: This species inhabits rivers, creeks, spring runs, oxbows, and swamps. It occurs most commonly around snags and fallen trees, and it prefers a soft bottom. It associates with most of the aquatic turtles in its range.

BEHAVIOR: *S. minor* is active both day and night. It can be found prowling along the bottom, probing for food, or else resting on submerged objects. This turtle is an adept climber, often reaching high and difficult perches for basking. However, the basking habit is not well developed: *S. minor* cannot long withstand the direct rays of the sun. Hutchison *et al.* (1966) found the mean critical thermal maximum was 40.4 C (39.7–41.4) and that the loss of righting response occurred at a mean of 38.3 C (37.8–38.7).

S. minor often remains submerged for long periods of time. Belkin (1968a) showed that it can obtain oxygen from the water via the buccopharyngeal lining.

This turtle is pugnacious, often biting viciously and expelling a strong musk when handled. Neill (1948b) reported that the young are capable of emitting musk even before they hatch.

REPRODUCTION: Both sexes of *S. m. minor* mature at a carapace length of about 80 mm. Females ma-

28. Plastron of *Sternotherus minor minor.*

29. *Sternotherus minor minor.*

47

30. Juvenile *Sternotherus minor minor*. The dorsal keel is obvious, but the lateral keel is less conspicuous.

31. Juvenile *Sternotherus minor peltifer*. The heavily striped neck is characteristic of this subspecies.

Distribution of *Sternotherus minor*.

ture in 5 or 6 years, males in 4 to 7. *S. m. depressus* matures in about 4 years: females at a carapace length of 90–100 mm, males at about 75 mm (Tinkle, 1958a).

Neither courtship, mating, nor nesting of this turtle has been described. Carr (1952) observed several females walking in the woods in Florida, and in mid-April he scratched out numerous eggs—singly or as many as three together—that had been shallowly buried at the bases of trees or beside logs.

Tinkle (1958a) dissected females and found the mean number of potentially ovulatory follicles in *S. m. minor* to be 2.7, in *S. m. peltifer* 7.0, and in *S. m. depressus* 5.5. Inasmuch as a female *S. m. minor* captured in early June had five corpora lutea and several follicles of ovulatory size, there may well be two clutches a season.

The hatchlings of *S. m. minor* and *S. m. peltifer* have a medial keel and two lateral keels. The carapace is only slightly longer than wide and has a pattern of streaks, blotches, or spots. The plastron of *S. m. minor* is pinkish-white; that of *S. m. peltifer* is yellow-orange. Hatchlings of *S. m. peltifer* have strongly striped necks. The hatchlings of *S. m. depressus* have not been described.

GROWTH: The rate of growth declines after age 3 or 4 years. The carapace in all subspecies becomes progressively flatter with increasing size (Tinkle, 1958a).

FOOD AND FEEDING: Tinkle (1958a) found insects, arachnids, isopods, crayfish, and clams in *S. m. depressus*. In *S. m. minor* he found insects, millipedes, snails, clams, fish, and aquatic plants. Folkerts (1968) found snails and insects to be the leading food of Alabama *S. m. peltifer*; he also found that they consumed filamentous algae, vascular plants, clams, crayfish, spiders, fish, bits of rock, and detritus. A captive juvenile *S. m. minor* killed and partially ate two juvenile *Chrysemys scripta*, a hatchling *S. m. minor*, and a juvenile *S. m. peltifer* over a 2-year period. It is likely that older individuals are somewhat cannibalistic and that they prey on small turtles of other species as well.

In *S. m. minor* increasing size brings a shift from an insectivorous to a molluscivorous diet. This subspecies develops heavy lower-jaw musculature and an expanded crushing surface on both jaws—apparently adaptations to eating mollusks. This parallels the crushing-apparatus development in *Graptemys barbouri* and *G. pulchra.*

Folkerts (1968) saw *S. m. peltifer* feeding on algal mats or mats of riverweed (*Podostemum*). On several occasions individuals bit down on clumps of algae, drew the head back, and pulled the algae between the jaws. These clumps were covered with tiny snails, and many were scraped off by this action.

Trapping evidence indicates that *S. m. minor* feeds at twilight and in the forepart of the night but not during the morning; *S. m. peltifer* feeds mostly during the morning but not at night; and *S. m. depressus* feeds late at night and during the early morning.

POPULATIONS: Marchand (1942) reported that 500 or more razor-backed musk turtles could be seen during a day of water-goggling in Rainbow Springs River, Marion County, Florida. Samples collected by Tinkle (1958a) had sex ratios of 169 (49%) males to 178 (51%) females in *S. m. minor*, 32 (52%) males to 30 (48%) females in *S. m. peltifer*, and 10 (24%) males to 32 (76%) females in *S. m. depressus.*

REMARKS: *S. m. depressus* was described by Tinkle and Webb (1955) as a species, *S. depressus.* We have relegated it to the status of a subspecies of *S. minor* on the basis of information supplied by Dr. George W. Folkerts, whose student, Ronald Estridge, found that this turtle intergrades with *S. m. peltifer* in the Black Warrior River above Tuscaloosa, Alabama. Intergradation between *S. m. minor* and *S. m. peltifer* occurs from the eastern rim of Mobile Bay to the Choctawhatchee River. Intergrade juveniles differ from *S. m. minor* in lacking lateral keels and from *S. m. peltifer* in lacking head stripes.

Tinkle (1958a) discussed the relationships be-

tween the species and subspecies of *Sternotherus* and speculated about their immediate origins.

Hybridization between a captive male *S. odoratus* and a captive female *S. m. minor* was reported, with a description of the progeny, by Folkerts (1967).

Three juvenile *S. minor* (two *S. m. minor*, one *S. m. peltifer*) chose a red-lighted compartment in 46% of the trials over yellow (25%), blue (25%), and green (4%) (Ernst and Hamilton, 1969).

There is a surprising paucity of information on the natural history of this rather abundant turtle. A serious study of almost any facet of its biology would be rewarding.

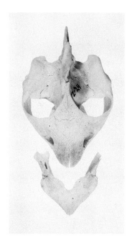 

Skull of *Sternotherus minor*

32. Adult *Kinosternon subrubrum subrubrum.*

33. Adult *Kinosternon subrubrum hippocrepis.* The facial stripes are characteristic of this race.

KINOSTERNON SUBRUBRUM (Lacépède)

Mud Turtle   IV

RECOGNITION: A small (7.5–12.4 cm) turtle with 11 scutes on the double-hinged plastron, a keelless carapace lacking stripes, and the 9th marginal not enlarged. The carapace is oval, smooth, and often depressed; the sides are straight, and the carapace drops abruptly behind. The 1st vertebral scute is widely separated from the 2nd marginal. The carapace varies from yellowish to olive or black and is patternless. The immaculate yellow-to-brown plastron has a single gular scute and two well-marked transverse hinges (which tend to ossify in old individuals). The skin is brown to olive and may exhibit some markings. The head is medium-sized and usually dark brown with some yellow mottling; sometimes there are two light lines on each side of the head and neck. All four feet are webbed.

Compared with females, males have larger heads; longer, thicker, nail-tipped tails; deeper posterior plastral notches; longer and more curved foreclaws; and two small tilted patches of scales on the inner side of each hind leg.

GEOGRAPHIC VARIATION: Three subspecies are recognized. *K. s. subrubrum* (Lacépède), the eastern mud turtle, ranges from southwestern Connecticut and Long Island to the Gulf coast and northwest through Kentucky to southern Indiana and Illinois. This subspecies has a wide bridge, a spotted or mottled head, and the anterior lobe of the plastron shorter than the posterior lobe. *K. s. hippocrepis* Gray, the Mississippi mud turtle, ranges in the Mississippi Valley from Louisiana and eastern Texas northward to Missouri and western Kentucky. It has a wide bridge, two distinct light lines on each side of the head, and the anterior lobe of the plastron shorter than the posterior lobe. *K. s. steindachneri* (Siebenrock), the Florida mud turtle, is restricted to peninsular Florida. It has a narrow bridge, a plain or mottled head, and the anterior lobe of the plastron often longer than the posterior lobe.

CONFUSING SPECIES: *K. flavescens* has an enlarged 9th marginal scute. *K. baurii* has a striped carapace. The musk turtles, *Sternotherus*, have small plastrons with a single hinge.

DISTRIBUTION: *K. subrubrum* ranges from Connecticut and Long Island south to the Gulf coast, west to east-central Texas, and north to Missouri, southern Illinois, and southern Indiana. Isolated colonies exist in northwestern Indiana and in west-central Missouri.

HABITAT: The mud turtle prefers slow-moving bodies of shallow water with soft bottoms and abundant aquatic vegetation. Frequently it inhabits the lodges of muskrats. It has been taken from ditches, sloughs, wet meadows, ponds, marshes, bayous, lagoons, and cypress swamps. *K. subrubrum* shows a marked tolerance for brackish water: it is often abundant in salt marshes. It associates with most of the aquatic turtles within its range.

BEHAVIOR: The 24-hr cycle of Oklahoma *K. s. hippocrepis* showed two activity periods during June through August: between 4 and 9 AM, with a peak between 5:20 and 8 AM, and between 4:40 and 10 PM, with a peak between 7 and 8 PM (Mahmoud, 1969). In Florida *K. s. steindachneri* shows similar summer-activity periods.

The mud turtle spends much of its time crawling on the bottom but occasionally floats on the surface. It is quite terrestrial and prowls about on land, usually in the early morning or early evening.

Carr (1952) found *K. s. steindachneri* in holes in clay canal-banks. He watched a large male dig such a hole just below the waterline, using all four feet to remove the soil. When finished the turtle emerged, turned around, and backed into the burrow.

The annual activity period of *K. s. hippocrepis* in Oklahoma was 265 days. Most of the turtles disappeared during late October and remained secluded until early April, but a few were observed during the winter (Mahmoud, 1969). The earliest and latest dates on which Nichols (1947) found

34. Plastron of *Kinosternon subrubrum subrubrum*. Note the triangular pectoral scutes.

35. Plastron of *Kinosternon subrubrum steindachneri*. The posterior lobe is narrowest in this subspecies.

36. Front view of *Kinosternon subrubrum subrubrum*.

active mud turtles on Long Island were 11 April and 11 November.

K. subrubrum can be seen basking at times on submerged brush or on the shore, but it does not bask often. Mahmoud (1969) found a mean difference between cloacal and environmental temperatures throughout the seasons of ± 0.46 to — 0.8 C. The thermoactivity range was 16–36 C, the field-preferred temperature was 23.65 C. *K. subrubrum* took food, in the laboratory, at body temperatures of 13–38 C. It had a mean critical thermal maximum of 40.95 C (39.0–42.5) and lost the righting ability at 38.8 C (38.1–39.4).

Two *K. s. steindachneri* lost moisture at hourly rates of 0.46% and 0.61% of their initial weights. The larger lost 23.6% of its initial weight in 51 hr in a drying-chamber at 38 C and 37% relative humidity (Bogert and Cowles, 1947).

When the habitat dries, mud turtles burrow into the mud and aestivate; they are often plowed up at the edges of ponds and swamps. A large population of mud turtles inhabited a pin oak flatwoods in southern Illinois that was covered with water during the early spring; the woods dried by late April, and the turtles dug burrows and aestivated. The 1963 population was estimated to be active only about 6 weeks (Skorepa and Ozment, 1968).

With the onset of cold weather in the north (usually in late October) *K. subrubrum* enters hibernation. It digs into the soft bottom of a waterway or digs a burrow some distance from the water or retreats under logs or piles of vegetable debris. However, in southern portions of the range mud turtles may remain active all year.

The disposition of mud turtles is variable: some are very timid but others bite savagely. The specimens of *K. s. steindachneri* we have handled were particularly fiery-tempered. The musk secreted by this species is weak compared with that of *Sternotherus* or *Chelydra*.

REPRODUCTION: Oklahoma *K. subrubrum* mature at a carapace length of 8–12 cm: males when 4–7 years of age, females when 5–8 years of age (Mahmoud, 1967).

Mating occurs from mid-March through May; copulations are earliest in the south. Courtship and mating are as in *S. odoratus* (which see). Mating usually takes place underwater but sometimes occurs on land.

Most nesting occurs during June but has been observed from February through September in various parts of the range. The nesting site usually is open ground not far from water. Sandy, loamy soils are preferred, but piles of vegetable debris also are used. In some localities mud turtles often nest in muskrat tunnels. Eggs have been found on the surface of the ground and under piles of boards.

A female may try several places before finding a suitable site. When satisfied she starts digging with her forefeet, thrusting the dirt out laterally until she is almost concealed; then she turns around and completes the nest with her hind feet. At this time and while she is laying, only the head of the turtle is visible. After the eggs are deposited she crawls out and may proceed directly to the water; or she may make a slight effort to conceal the nest cavity by leveling the site and scratching around it. Of the 14 completed nests examined by Richmond (1945) only 3 showed indications that the turtles had tried unsuccessfully to conceal them, for the scratchings were conspicuous.

The completed nest usually is a semicircular cavity 3–5 inches deep and entering the ground at about a 30° angle. The cavity is dug slightly higher and wider than the space to be occupied by the clutch; and, after the eggs are laid, soil is packed firmly around and above them. In loose sandy soil the nest cavity is soon obliterated by rains.

The normal complement of eggs is two to five; clutches of three and five are the most common. However, there are abundant records of a single-egg clutch. Tinkle (1959b) found six eggs beneath a pile of boards, and McCauley (1945) found one clutch of eight eggs and another of nine. These latter clutches could represent the contributions of more than one female.

The eggs are elliptical, pinkish-white or bluish-white, and brittle-shelled. The shell surface is covered with a fine, irregular network of impressed lines, which cause the surface to appear finely granular or pebbled, although not evenly so. The eggs are 22.0–29.2 mm long and 13–18 mm wide. They do not take up water during incubation as do most turtle eggs.

Hatching occurs in late August and September, but the hatchlings may overwinter in the nest and emerge the following spring. Sabath (1960) incubated a single egg laid on 21 June; it hatched 110 days later.

The hatchling carapace is shaped like that of the adult but has a vertebral keel and two weak lateral keels, is rough, and is not depressed anteriorly or sharply turned down posteriorly. It is dark brown or black, with light spots along the marginals. The plastron is irregularly mottled with orange or red, and the hinges are poorly developed. The skin is brown or black, and in the subspecies *K. s. hippocrepis* there may be two faint yellow lines on each side of the head and neck. The carapace length is 20–27 mm, the width 10–20 mm, and the depth 11–14.5 mm.

GROWTH: Mahmoud (1969) found the growth period of *K. subrubrum* in Oklahoma to be 170 days, limited to the warm months. Females having an initial carapace length of 21–40 mm increased an average of 16.6 mm (44%) per growing season; females 41–60 mm increased 13.7 mm (27.5%); females 61–80 mm increased 2.6 mm (3.5%); and females over 81 mm increased only 0.38 mm (0.39%). Males 61–80 mm in initial carapace length increased 3.0 mm (1.24%) and those over 81 mm increased only 0.83 mm (0.98%) per growing season. There was an increase in length in both sexes during the first 6 years, after which the growth rate steadily declined. Sixteen were kept 2 years in captivity without any apparent growth; annual rings indicated that they were more than 10 years of age.

Skorepa and Ozment (1968) reported that five captive hatchlings increased 4–8 mm in carapace length, 4.0–6.5 mm in carapace width, and from 1–2 mm in height between 4 May 1962 and 4 April 1963. At the end of this period they had carapace lengths of 26–30 mm.

37. Front view of *Kinosternon subrubrum steindachneri*. The V-shaped dark mark on top of the head is characteristic.

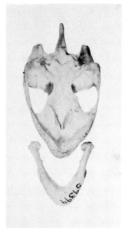
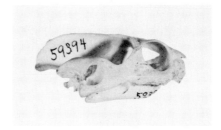

Skull of *Kinosternon subrubrum*

A female *K. subrubrum*, which was an adult when it was received, lived for 38 years in captivity (Pope, 1939).

FOOD AND FEEDING: *K. subrubrum* is an omnivorous feeder. Mahmoud (1968b) reported the following percentages of frequency and volume respectively of food items: Insecta 98.3, 30.4; Crustacea 15.0, 1.4; Mollusca 93.1, 31.8; Amphibia 30.0, 2.2; carrion 68.6, 11.9; and aquatic vegetation 89.6, 22.3. Mud turtles under 5 cm in carapace length feed predominantly on small aquatic insects, algae, and carrion; those above 5 cm feed on any kind of food. Captives feed readily on canned and fresh fish, canned beef, hamburger, dog food, snails, insects, tomatoes, and watermelon.

K. subrubrum occasionally feeds at the surface but is predominantly a bottom feeder. It frequently walks along the bottom, probing into soft mud, sand, and decaying vegetation with its head.

PREDATORS: The eggs are eaten by king snakes, opossums, weasels, skunks, and raccoons. Juveniles are known to be attacked by blue crabs, gars, water snakes, hognose snakes, cottonmouths, and crows. The shells of adults are sometimes gnawed by rodents. Many mud turtles are killed by automobiles.

MOVEMENTS: Mahmoud (1969) reported that the maximum and minimum distances between successive points of capture for Oklahoma mud turtles were 1,340 ft and 2 ft. The average first-last capture distances for periods of more than 100 days were 267 ft for females and 188 ft for males; for less than 100 days, 140 ft for females and 154 ft for males. Eleven were recaptured at their original capture point. During July 1957 he released 15 *K. subrubrum* into Lake Texoma at one place and during August 1959 recovered 7 within an estimated radius of 150 ft from the release point. This restricted movement suggests a limited home range, which Mahmoud estimated to average 0.12 acre for males and 0.13 acre for females.

In South Carolina, radioactively tagged *K. subrubrum* spent 3–142 days on land and traveled 1–600 m from the capture sites. They generally moved short distances (less than 2 m/day), burrowed below litter or sand to depths of 2–11 cm for up to 2 weeks in one location, and then moved longer distances (10 m/day). The time spent in the first burrow was 7 days (2–16). The cycle—short movements, burrowing, then longer moves—was repeated until December, when the mud turtles ceased to move. The mean rate of travel was 3.6 m/day (Bennett *et al.*, 1970).

Strecker (1926) observed a migration of *K. s. hippocrepis* near Waco, Texas. A marsh was rapidly drying, and as he walked along the levee Strecker counted 45 mud turtles traveling overland in the same direction. At first he thought they were moving to a ditch along a railroad track about 200 yards away, but he found that there was very little water in the ditch and that the mud turtles were scattered over a damp meadow on the other side. He followed the line of march and discovered that the turtles were headed for a large tank more than half a mile away.

Ernst and Hamilton (1969) found that *K. subrubrum* selected a blue-lighted compartment in 60% of the trials and a red-lighted compartment in 22%; it entered yellow and green compartments in only 9%, each, of the trials. This color selection may have some significance in orientation.

POPULATION: Mahmoud (1969) estimated 64.5 *K. subrubrum* per acre of suitable habitat in Oklahoma in 1956 and 104.6 in 1957. Skorepa and Ozment (1968) reported that it was often possible to find 10 adults within an estimated 7-m² area in the southern Illinois population they studied. Gibbons (1970a) estimated 170 mud turtles in the approximately 10-hectare basin of Ellenton Bay, South Carolina.

Sex ratios of mature Oklahoma *K. subrubrum* were 47 males to 71 females in Cowan Creek, 16 males to 24 females at the Tishomingo Fish Hatchery, and 16 males to 28 females in Lake Texoma (Mahmoud, 1969).

REMARKS: Intergradation between *K. s. subrubrum* and *K. s. steindachneri* occurs in the region from Tallahassee to Lake Placid, Florida, and between *K. s. subrubrum* and *K. s. hippocrepis* in Covington and Jackson counties, Mississippi.

Zug (1966) observed no differences in the structure of the glans penis of the four species of *Kinosternon* occurring in the United States.

The small size and the musky flavor of the flesh of this turtle render it unsuitable as food for man. It occasionally steals the bait from a fisherman's hook.

Distribution of *Kinosternon subrubrum*.

38. Adult *Kinosternon baurii palmarum*.

39. Front view of *Kinosternon baurii*. The three carapacial stripes are sometimes more, but often less, conspicuous than in this individual.

KINOSTERNON BAURII (Garman)

Striped Mud Turtle   IV

RECOGNITION: A small (7.5–12.0 cm) turtle with 11 plastral scutes and three variable light stripes on the tan-to-black carapace. The broad, smooth carapace is keelless and unserrated and usually has its widest and highest points behind the middle. The vertebrals may be depressed, forming a broad, shallow middorsal groove. The broad plastron has two well-developed transverse hinges bordering the abdominal scutes; it is olive to yellow and either plain or with dark seam-borders. The skin is tan to black, and the neck and head may show dark mottling. The small, conical head has two light lines extending posteriorly from the orbit—one above and one below the tympanum. All four feet are webbed.

Females are larger than males and have short, stubby tails. Males have long, thick, spine-tipped tails and two patches of tilted scales on the inner surface of each hind leg.

GEOGRAPHIC VARIATION: Two subspecies are recognized. *K. b. baurii* (Garman), the Key mud turtle, occurs on the lower Florida Keys, from Big Pine Key to Key West. This race has opaque carapacial scutes, and the sutures between the bony plates beneath do not show through. The shell stripes are sometimes obliterated, and the lower jaw is weakly streaked if at all. *K. b. palmarum* Stejneger, the striped mud turtle, ranges from southern Georgia to the upper Florida Keys. The scutes of the carapace are thin and transparent, and the sutures of the underlying bones show through. The lower jaw is heavily streaked with dark pigment.

CONFUSING SPECIES: No other North American *Kinosternon* has a striped carapace. *Sternotherus* have rectangular pectoral scutes and a single, indistinct plastral hinge.

DISTRIBUTION: *K. baurii* ranges from southern Georgia south through the Florida Keys.

HABITAT: The striped mud turtle is most often found in quiet water with a soft bottom—swamps, sloughs, and ponds. It also frequents wet meadows, and it enters brackish water. Occasionally it inhabits the lodges of the round-tailed muskrat (*Neofiber alleni*). It occurs with all the other aquatic turtles in its range.

BEHAVIOR: *K. baurii* seldom basks. It is most often seen when it is moving overland across highways and dikes; these journeys occur at any hour of the day but seem to be most frequent at dusk and at daybreak. During cold spells *K. baurii* sometimes seeks temporary shelter in piles of moist decaying vegetation.

Hutchison *et al.* (1966) found the mean critical thermal maximum was 40.6 C (39.9–41.2). The mean loss of righting response occurred at 39.1 C (38.2–40.4).

The striped mud turtle is a gentle creature, seldom biting unless severely provoked.

REPRODUCTION: Both sexes of *K. baurii* mature at a carapace length of about 7.5 cm.

A possibly sex-related act of aggression of one male toward another and a presumed courtship act of the same male with a female were described by Carr (1940). On 2 May he saw two males fighting on the bank of a little stream. A female was about 2 ft away, and Carr assumed the males were fighting over her. After a struggle lasting about 5 min one of the males lost his footing and fell into the water. The victorious male immediately turned to the female, thrust his snout beneath her plastron, and crawled under her, leaving her balanced upon his carapace. They remained motionless in this position 30 min before Carr collected them.

Nesting occurs from April to June. The nests are dug in sand or in piles of decaying vegetation.

A clutch varies from one to four eggs, and possibly as many as three clutches may be laid each season. The eggs are elliptical, whitish, and brittle-shelled. Einem (1956) found that 20 oviducal eggs were 25.0–31.8 mm long and 15.8–17.2 mm wide.

40. The two plastral hinges are obvious in this view of *Kinosternon baurii*.

41. The facial striping in *Kinosternon baurii* is variable; many show more distinct stripes than this individual, some even strongly reminiscent of *Sternotherus odoratus*.

Skull of *Kinosternon baurii*

The eggs do not vary in size during incubation and apparently do not absorb water. Evidently the shell not only resists water-absorption but also resists desiccation, for eggs left completely dry for some time will develop normally.

The incubation period at room temperature is 96–129 days. Einem (1956) found that after 2 or 3 months of incubation a single longitudinal crack formed in each eggshell. The crack extended to and around the ends of the egg as incubation proceeded. Later the crack exuded small amounts of albumen and expanded slightly. At hatching the eggshell ruptured a second time: close to one end and opposite each of the hatchling's eyes, two jagged holes about 3 mm in diameter formed, first in the shell and then in the shell membrane. The turtle's forefeet seemed to accomplish this. Cracks radiated from these holes in various directions; some intersected the prehatching split. The turtle usually emerged through this end of the eggshell, most often without completely halving the egg longitudinally. Complete liberation from the shell required 2–65 hr.

Hatchlings are black with yellow spots on each marginal. The rough carapace has three weak keels, one beneath each stripe. The yellow plastron has a dark central blotch and dark-bordered seams. The plastral hinges are not functional until about the 3rd month after hatching. The yellow stripes on the head are pronounced. Six hatchlings measured by Einem (1956) were 20.5–25.0 mm in carapace length, 18.1–20.9 mm in plastron length, 14.0–17.2 mm in carapace width, and 14.5–18.2 mm in depth. They had yolk sacs 5–7 mm in length, and each possessed a caruncle.

GROWTH: Einem (1956) reported that hatchling *K. baurii* increased their dimensions in three months as follows: carapace length, 1.0–5.2 mm; plastron length, 1.8–3.7 mm; carapace width, 3.9–8.8 mm; and depth, 0.4–1.4 mm. Two of these hatchlings decreased 1.2 and 1.5 mm, respectively, in shell depth.

K. baurii does well in captivity. One specimen has lived more than 25 years.

FOOD AND FEEDING: *K. baurii* is omnivorous. Natural foods include seeds of the cabbage palm (*Sabal palmetto*), juniper leaves, various algae, small snails, insects, and dead fish. This turtle is easily caught on a hook and line baited with liver, grasshoppers, worms, or dough. Duellman and Schwartz (1958) reported *K. baurii* were attracted to traps baited with small-mammal carcasses: they must have some scavenging tendencies. While on land they often forage in cow dung, perhaps seeking insects.

PREDATORS: Various mammals feed on the eggs. Many vertebrates take juveniles. Alligators and man are probably the most destructive animals to adults. Frank J. Ligas once observed a South Florida king snake (*Lampropeltis getulus brooksi*) scrape up and eat three eggs.

POPULATIONS: *K. baurii* is extremely common in southern Florida.

REMARKS: Uzzell and Schwartz (1955) in redefining the subspecies of *K. baurii*, showed that *K. b. baurii* is restricted to the lower Florida Keys and *K. b. palmarum* to the mainland and the upper Keys; the reverse had previously been thought to be the case.

An apparent case of DDT poisoning in *K. baurii* was reported by Herald (1949). A female was discovered a day after an application of DDT had killed many fish. She seemed anesthetized—unable to retract the head or legs or to make any attempt to escape. Four days later she laid two eggs; on the 12th day she died. After incubation the eggs did not hatch, so it is likely that they had been aborted. (Poisoning with DDT often causes viviparous fish to abort.)

Distribution of *Kinosternon baurii*.

59

KINOSTERNON FLAVESCENS (Agassiz)
Yellow Mud Turtle   v

RECOGNITION: A small (7.5–12.8 cm), yellowish turtle with 11 scutes on the plastron and with both the 9th and the 10th marginals elevated. The broad, smooth carapace is not serrated, lacks a vertebral keel, and may be depressed medially. The 1st vertebral touches the 2nd marginal. The carapace is yellow to brown and the scutes are dark-bordered. The bridge and underside of the marginals are yellow with dark pigment along the seams. The plastron has two well-developed transverse hinges bordering the abdominal scutes; it is yellowish to brown, with dark pigment along the seams. The skin is immaculate yellow to gray. The head is flattened. The jaws are hooked and, usually, whitish to yellow; they may be spotted. All four feet are webbed.

Males have short, concave plastrons; long, thick, spine-tipped tails; and two patches of tilted scales on the inner surface of each hind leg.

GEOGRAPHIC VARIATION: Three subspecies are recognized. *K. f. flavescens* (Agassiz), the yellow mud turtle, ranges, in the United States, from southern Nebraska south to Texas, New Mexico, and southeastern Arizona. It has a yellow chin, throat, and carapace. The gular scute is approximately 41% as long as the anterior lobe of the plastron. *K. f. stejnegeri* Hartweg, the Mexican yellow mud turtle, occurs mainly in northern Mexico but has been reported by Smith and Hensley (1957) from southern Arizona. It has a yellow chin and throat and an olive carapace. The gular scute is approximately 63% as long as the anterior lobe of the plastron. *K. f. spooneri* Smith, the Illinois mud turtle, is restricted to northwestern Illinois and adjacent Iowa and Missouri. The soft parts are dark gray to black, with yellow pigment restricted to the barbels and the anterior half of the lower jaw. The carapace is dark brown. The gular scute is approximately 51% as long as the anterior lobe of the plastron.

CONFUSING SPECIES: No other *Kinosternon* in the United States has an elevated 9th marginal. *Sterno-*

42. Adult *Kinosternon flavescens flavescens.*

43. Plastron of male *Kinosternon flavescens flavescens.*

therus odoratus and *S. carinatus* have rectangular pectoral scutes and a single, indistinct plastral hinge.

DISTRIBUTION: The yellow mud turtle occurs in northwestern Illinois and adjacent Iowa and Missouri and from southern Nebraska south through Texas, New Mexico, and southern Arizona to Sonora, Durango, and Tamaulipas, Mexico. It has been found at elevations as great as 5,000 ft.

HABITAT: *K. flavescens* inhabits almost any quiet water within its range: swamps, sloughs, sinkholes, rivers, creeks, ponds, lakes, reservoirs, cisterns, and cattle tanks in semiarid grasslands or open woodlands. A mud or sand bottom is preferred, and aquatic vegetation is often present. This species has been taken with *K. subrubrum*, *K. sonoriense*, *Chelydra serpentina*, *Sternotherus odoratus*, *S. carinatus*, *Trionyx spiniferus*, *T. muticus*, *Chrysemys picta*, and *C. scripta*.

BEHAVIOR: In Oklahoma, *K. flavescens* is most active between 9 AM and 8 PM during April and May. During June and July the 24-hr cycle has two periods of activity: between midnight and 7:40 AM and between 4 and 7 PM. The annual activity period is 140 days (Mahmoud, 1969).

K. flavescens spends much time basking, or foraging on land. It occasionally migrates overland between bodies of water.

Mahmoud (1969) found a mean difference between cloacal and environmental temperatures throughout the year of ±0.3 C to −20 C. The thermoactivity range was 18–32 C and the field-preferred body temperature was 25.06 C. His captives accepted food at body temperatures of 16–38 C. The mean critical thermal maximum was 43.25 C (39.2–43.7), and the righting ability was lost at a mean of 39.7 C (38.1–40.1).

With the onset of cold weather these turtles burrow into natural depressions, such as old stumpholes, and beneath shrubs, brushpiles, logs, or leaf litter. Some dig burrows in loose sandy soil; others hibernate in muskrat dens or in the mud at the bot-

44. The head of *Kinosternon flavescens flavescens* is quite plain.

45. *Kinosternon flavescens spooneri*, as shown in these Cass County, Illinois, specimens, is a much darker race than *Kinosternon flavescens flavescens*.
(*Photos courtesy of the Illinois Natural History Survey*)

61

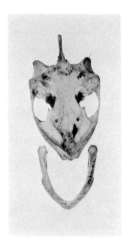
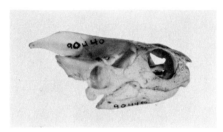

Skull of *Kinosternon flavescens*

tom of pools. Carpenter (1957) found them hibernating in close association with *Terrapene ornata* and *T. carolina*. During the hottest parts of summer they seek out sheltered spots, where they aestivate.

In disposition they are shy and retiring. They seldom attempt to bite or to expel their musk.

REPRODUCTION: Sexual maturity is reached at a carapace length of 8–12 cm. Males are mature at 4–7 years of age, females at 5–8.

The courtship pattern of *K. flavescens* is divisible into three phases: tactile; mounting and intromission; and biting and rubbing. The phases are identical to those of *Sternotherus odoratus* (which see for details). *K. flavescens* may stay in coitus for 10 min to 3 hr. Courtship usually takes place in water varying in depth from 1 inch to several feet, but a mating pair has been seen on the bank of a pond (Mahmoud, 1967).

The nest and the nesting activities have not been described, but observations on captives suggest that the nesting season includes July and August. Clutches range from two to four eggs, which are elliptical, hard, and white. The eggs are 24.0–28.5 mm in length and 13.5–16.5 mm in width. The duration of incubation is unknown.

The hatchling carapace is 21–30 mm long, and the width nearly equals the length. It is slightly keeled and has the 9th and 10th marginals the same height as or slightly lower than the 8th. Cahn (1937) reported that elevation of the marginals first appears at a shell length of about 67 mm. Young *K. f. flavescens* and *K. f. stejnegeri* are similar to adults. Young *K. f. spooneri* are distinctly different: they have a dark shell, dark soft-parts, and a pattern of small, irregular light markings on the chin.

GROWTH: The growth period in Oklahoma is only 90 days. Turtles having an initial carapace length of 21–40 mm increased 7.7 mm (22%) per growing season; those 41–60 increased 7.9 mm (16.5%); those 61–80 mm increased 3.1 mm (4.5%); and those over 81 mm increased only 2.7 mm (0.3%).

Ten *K. flavescens* over 10 years old did not grow during the 2 years they were kept in captivity (Mahmoud, 1969).

FOOD AND FEEDING: *K. flavescens* is omnivorous. Mahmoud (1968b) found the following percentages of frequency and volume, respectively, of food items in *K. flavescens*: Insecta 94.7, 27.8; Crustacea 99.2, 27.7; Mollusca 93.7, 23.5; Amphibia 91.2, 9.2; carrion 13.2, 3.2; and aquatic vegetation 37.2, 8.5. Turtles under 5 cm in carapace length fed predominantly on small aquatic insects, algae, and carrion, whereas those over 5 cm ate a greater variety of items.

Yellow mud turtles are essentially bottom feeders but sometimes feed at the surface or on land. Their acute sense of smell or taste under water aids them in locating food.

PREDATORS: Many species of mammals rob the nests. Fish, water snakes, and other turtles commonly prey on the hatchlings. Man seems to be the only important enemy of the adults.

MOVEMENTS: The maximum and minimum distances between successive points of capture of Oklahoma yellow mud turtles were 1,428 ft and 11 ft. The average distance between first and last capture during more than 100 days of activity was 845 ft for females and 444 ft for males; for periods of less than 100 days, 556 ft for females and 801 ft for males. The areas traversed were 3,680–28,000 sq ft and averaged 0.26 acre for males and 0.31 acre for females (Mahmoud, 1969).

POPULATIONS: Mahmoud (1969) estimated 11.3 *K. flavescens* per acre of suitable habitat in Oklahoma. The male/female ratios of mature individuals at three Oklahoma localities were 23:35, 64:88, and 20:13.

REMARKS: Many aspects of the life history of this turtle are poorly known.

Distribution of *Kinosternon flavescens* in the United States.

KINOSTERNON SONORIENSE Le Conte

Sonora Mud Turtle   v

46. Adult female *Kinosternon sonoriense*.

47. *Kinosternon sonoriense* plastron.

RECOGNITION: A medium-sized (10.0–16.5 cm), dark turtle with 11 scutes on the plastron, an elongated carapace, and a mottled pattern on the head, neck, and limbs. The smooth carapace usually is depressed, but one or three low keels may be present. The 1st vertebral touches the 2nd marginal. The posterior marginals are flared, and the 10th on each side is higher than the 9th or the 11th. The carapace is olive-brown to dark brown, and the seams are patterned with darker pigment. The underside of the marginals and the bridge are yellowish to brown with a dark mottled pattern. The plastron has two well-marked transverse hinges bordering the abdominal scutes and is yellow to brownish, with dark bordered seams. The skin is gray, and the head, neck, and limbs have mottled dark markings. The head is flattened. The jaws are hooked; they are cream-colored and may show dark flecks. All four feet are webbed.

Males have concave plastrons; long, thick, spine-tipped tails; and two patches of tilted scales on the inner surface of each hind leg.

GEOGRAPHIC VARIATION: No subspecies have been described.

CONFUSING SPECIES: *K. flavescens* has the 9th marginal higher than the 8th. *K. hirtipes* has a strongly keeled carapace, which is arched as viewed from the front. *Sternotherus odoratus* has rectangular pectoral scutes and a single, poorly developed hinge.

DISTRIBUTION: *K. sonoriense* ranges from southwestern New Mexico, central and southeastern Arizona, and southwestern Arizona and adjacent California south to Sonora, Chihuahua, and Durango, Mexico.

HABITAT: This turtle occurs at elevations up to 6,700 ft. It inhabits rivers, creeks, ditches, ponds, springs, and waterholes, usually in woodlands.

REMARKS: Little is known of the biology of this turtle. It sometimes leaves the water to bask. Occasional rains stimulate it to sporadic emigration, and it congregates in waterholes during dry periods. It is carnivorous and is sometimes taken on hooks baited with meat. Captives readily eat fresh and canned fish and various kinds of meat. One lived 21 years 9 months in the Philadelphia Zoological Garden (Conant and Hudson, 1949).

Hatchlings are only a little longer than wide. One figured by Agassiz (1857) was 28.5 mm in carapace length, 24.0 mm in carapace width, 14.0 mm in depth, 23.5 mm in plastron length, and 14.5 mm in plastron width. The hatchling carapace usually has a low, broad central keel and two elongated lateral ridges. The upper posterior edge of each marginal often has a black smudge, and the 10th marginal is not noticeably elevated. The plastral seams are dark-bordered.

48. *Kinosternon sonoriense* is a shy animal, and rarely exhibits more face than shown here when disturbed.

Distribution of *Kinosternon sonoriense* in the United States.

Skull of *Kinosternon sonoriense*

65

49. Adult male *Kinosternon hirtipes murrayi.*

50. Adult female *Kinosternon hirtipes murrayi.*

KINOSTERNON HIRTIPES (Wagler)

Rough-footed Mud Turtle v

RECOGNITION: A small (10.0–14.6 cm) turtle with 11 scutes on the plastron, an elevated and keeled carapace, and a finely reticulated head-pattern. The oval carapace is smooth and is less than twice as broad as deep. The well-developed keel appears somewhat arched when viewed from the front, and it slopes gently anteriorly but rather abruptly posteriorly, forming a hump over the sacral region. The 1st vertebral is in contact with the 2nd marginal. The marginals are narrow except for the 10th, which is elevated, and those posterior to the bridge are somewhat flared. The carapace is olive to brown, and the seams are distinctly black-bordered. The plastron is short and narrow, with the hind lobe not broader than the front lobe. There are two well-developed hinges, one on each side of the abdominal scutes. The plastron ranges from brown to tan, and the seams are bordered with darker brown. The bridge is of medium length. The limbs are gray to tan. The head and neck are tan to black, with light reticulations if black and with dark reticulations or spotting if tan. The jaws are tan to gray and may be finely streaked with dark brown or black. All four feet are webbed.

Males have long, thick, spine-tipped tails; concave plastrons; and the posterior marginals more flared than those of females.

GEOGRAPHIC VARIATION: Two subspecies are recognized. *K. h. hirtipes* (Wagler), the rough-footed mud turtle, is nearly confined to Mexico but has been reported from southern Arizona by Smith and Taylor (1950). In this subspecies the lengths of the interpectoral and interfemoral seams do not exceed 76% of the length of the interhumeral seam. *K. h. murrayi* Glass and Hartweg, the Big Bend mud turtle, occurs in the lower Big Bend region of western Texas and in adjacent northeastern Chihuahua. It has the lengths of the interpectoral and interfemoral seams exceeding 80% of the length of the interhumeral seam.

Wermuth and Mertens (1961) used the character

51. Plastron of *Kinosternon hirtipes murrayi.*

52. *Kinosternon hirtipes murrayi* has a mottled head pattern. (*Photo by Frederick R. Gehlbach*)

53. The dorsal keel of *Kinosternon hirtipes murrayi* is most obvious posteriorly.

of a large gular scute—twice as long as the interhumeral seam and more than half as long as the anterior lobe of the plastron—as their key character for *K. h. murrayi.* This character is illustrated in a figure of one of the paratypes (Glass and Hartweg, 1951) but may not be present in all of the type series.

CONFUSING SPECIES: *K. flavescens* has the 9th marginal elevated above the 8th. *K. sonoriense* has a shell that is more than twice as broad as deep. *Sternotherus odoratus* has a small plastron with a single, poorly developed hinge and rectangular pectoral scutes.

DISTRIBUTION: *K. hirtipes* ranges from the Big Bend region of western Texas and, possibly, extreme southern Arizona, southward on the Mexican Plateau to Mexico City.

HABITAT: The rough-footed mud turtle inhabits bodies of water in mesquite-grasslands. It usually is found in lakes, ponds, or rivers flowing into lakes but also enters temporary pools, stock ponds, and marshy ground. In Michoacán it ranges between the altitudes of 1,500 and 2,200 m (Duellman, 1965). Smith *et al.* (1963) collected this species in the Rio Conchos of Chihuahua and found little difference between its abundance in lowlands and in mountains. It is often associated with *K. integrum, K. flavescens, Chrysemys scripta gaigeae,* and *Trionyx spiniferus emoryi.*

Distribution of *Kinosternon hirtipes* in the United States.

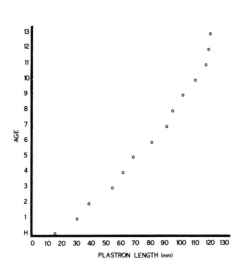

54. Growth rate of a 13-year-old male
Kinosternon hirtipes murrayi.
(*Figure prepared by Faith Hershey*)

Skull of *Kinosternon hirtipes*

BEHAVIOR: Little is known of the natural history of this turtle. It is chiefly nocturnal but sometimes active by day. Frederick R. Gehlbach found rough-footed mud turtles to be most active between 9 PM and midnight in Texas.

Beltz (1954b) reported that a captive adult female kept in southern California escaped and overwintered under a pile of leaves and debris without any ill effects. He thought this same individual, when placed out of water in the sun, became uneasy and appeared to search for water. If the carapace is not kept moist, parts of the scutes dry and peel off, leaving permanent patches of discoloration.

REPRODUCTION: Four to seven elliptical white eggs, averaging 28 by 17 mm, are laid in June.

GROWTH: The growth rate of a 13-year-old, 120.7-mm male *K. h. murrayi* is illustrated in Figure 54.

FOOD AND FEEDING: Captives readily eat canned and fresh fish. Legler (1960b) reported that *K. hirtipes* were attracted to nets baited with canned sardines in soybean oil.

POPULATION: Frederick R. Gehlbach collected six adults (two females 109–122 mm in plastron length, four males 116–125 mm) and two juveniles (51–70 mm), and observed three other individuals in a 6,250-sq-ft, 13-ft-deep, *Chara*-choked stockpond in Texas.

In the Rio Grande at Lajitos, Brewster County, Texas, *Trionyx s. emoryi* was the most abundant turtle, *Chrysemys s. gaigeae* was uncommon, and *K. hirtipes* was rare, and about the same situation prevailed in the Río Conchos, one mile northwest of Ojinaga, Chihuahua. However, at the junction of the Río San Pedro and the Río Conchos, in Chihuahua, *K. hirtipes* was the dominant turtle (Legler, 1960b). Williams *et al.* (1960) found a similar situation in the Río Florida, 1 mile east of La Cruz, Chihuahua, where they collected 17 *K. hirtipes* and only 2 each of *T. s. emoryi* and *C. s. gaigeae*.

REMARKS: Studies are needed on the natural history and the intra- and interspecific systematic relationships of this species.

EMYDIDAE:
Semiaquatic Pond & Marsh Turtles

This, the largest family of living turtles, contains 25 genera and more than 80 species (the exact number is debatable). The family is represented in the Americas, Europe, Asia, and northern Africa. The United States has 25 species in seven genera. Most U.S. species are medium-sized, with a low-arched carapace. The bridge and plastron are well developed, and hinges may be present between the plastral scutes. The feet are somewhat elongated and have varying amounts of webbing between the toes.

Turtles of this family have the temporal region of the skull widely emarginated posteriorly and the frontal bones often entering the orbit. The maxilla rarely touches the quadratojugal, and its crushing surface is often ridged. The quadrate does not inclose the stapes. The nuchal lacks lateral rib-like processes, and there are 11 peripherals on each side. The neck usually has two biconvex vertebrae, and the dorsal vertebrae have well-developed rib-heads. An entoplastron is present.

The Emydidae of the United States form three distinct species-complexes, as follows:

1. The *Clemmys–Terrapene* complex. These turtles have the crushing surfaces of the jaws narrow and ridgeless. The upper crushing surface lacks portions of the palatine or the pterygoid bone, and the lower surface is without a distinct lingual border on the dentary, so that it slopes gradually into the medial face of the dentary. The nasopalatine foramen is small, and the interorbital region is broader than the nasal chamber. The lower parietal process is well separated from the palatine by the pterygoid bone. The neck vertebrae are not elongated, and the 2nd to 8th vertebrae are shortest. The dorsal rib-heads are normal.

Four species of *Clemmys* and two of *Terrapene* occur in the United States. This complex also contains two Mexican species of *Terrapene* and the European *Emys orbicularis*. McDowell (1964) showed that on the basis of skull morphology the Old World turtles formerly placed in *Clemmys* are sufficiently different from the North American species to warrant placing them in a separate genus, *Mauremys*; thus the name *Clemmys* is reserved for those occurring in North America. Milstead (1969) suggested that *Terrapene* and *Emys* have a common ancestry in *Clemmys*, either in Asia or in North America. According to Milstead, *Terrapene* later formed two species-groups in North America: (i) the *carolina* group, including *T. c. carolina, T. c. bauri, T. c. major, T. c. triunguis, T. c. mexicana, T. c. yucatana, T. c. putnami* (extinct), and *T. coahuila*; and (ii) the *ornata* group, including *T. o. ornata, T. o. luteola, T. o. longinsulae* (extinct), *T. n. nelsoni,* and *T. n. klauberi.*

2. The *Chrysemys* complex. These turtles have the crushing surfaces of the jaws broad, with or without ridges and with the upper surface containing portions of the palatine or the pterygoid bone. The lower surface has a sharp angulation setting off the horizontal crushing surface from the vertical medial surface of the dentary. The nasopalatine foramen is much larger than the posterior palatine foramen, and the interorbital region is broader than the nasal chamber. The lower parietal process touches the palatine (except in some *Chrysemys picta*). The neck vertebrae are not elongated, and the 2nd to 8th vertebrae are shortest. The dorsal rib-heads are normal. This complex includes the genera *Chrysemys, Malaclemys,* and *Graptemys.*

Chrysemys is composed of 15 species from Canada to Brazil and in the West Indies. All of the species have the crushing surface of the upper jaw with a well-developed middle ridge. *C. picta, C. scripta, C. concinna, C. floridana, C. rubriventris, C. nelsoni,* and *C. alabamensis* occur in the United States. All but *C. picta* formerly were placed in "*Pseudemys.*" After a study of cranial characteristics, McDowell (1964) revised *Chrysemys* to include *Pseudemys.* An osteologic study by Weaver and Rose (1967) and a study of penial morphology by Zug (1966) support this inclusion.

Malaclemys and *Graptemys* occur only in North America. These turtles have the crushing surfaces nearly flat, with only a low indication of a middle ridge. *Malaclemys* is monotypic, but there are at least nine species of *Graptemys.* McDowell (1964), on the basis of skull features, combined *Graptemys*

(map turtles) and *Malaclemys* (the diamondback terrapin) under the latter name (by priority). However, because he examined only six specimens of *Malaclemys* and only nine specimens of four of the nine species of *Graptemys,* we believe this combination needs more study.

3. The *Deirochelys-Emydoidea* complex. The crushing surfaces are narrow and ridgeless, with the upper surface lacking portions of the palatine or the pterygoid bone and the lower surface not sharply defined medially. The rhamphotheca-bearing part of the dentary slopes into the vertical medial surface of the dentary. The nasopalatine foramen is small but the posterior palatine foramen is large. The interorbital is less wide than the nasal chamber, and the lower portion of the parietal touches the palatine bone. The neck is extremely long, and the 2nd to 7th vertebrae are much longer than the 8th. The dorsal rib-heads are extremely long, slender, and bowed outward ventrally.

Only two species are included: *Deirochelys reticularia* and *Emydoidea blandingii.* Both occur in the United States. *Deirochelys* probably is derived from a *Chrysemys scripta*-like ancestor but has been much modified, particularly in the narrowing of the crushing surfaces and the elongation of the neck. For many years *Emydoidea* was placed in *Emys,* but Loveridge and Williams (1957) showed it is more closely related to *Deirochelys* than to the European *Emys orbicularis,* and they reassigned it to *Emydoidea.* McDowell (1964) was unable to find significant cranial differences between *Emydoidea* and *Deirochelys,* and Zug (1966) found only minor differences between these two genera in the structure of the glans penis. *Emydoidea* probably is derived from *Deirochelys.*

CLEMMYS GUTTATA (Schneider)

Spotted Turtle

RECOGNITION: A small (8.0–12.5 cm), blue-black turtle with round yellow spots on its broad, smooth, keelless, unserrated carapace. The spots are transparent areas in the scutes, overlying patches of yellow pigment; they may fade with age, and some old individuals are spotless. The ventral surface of the marginals is yellowish and may have a pattern of black blotches at the outer edge in the young; the bridge is marked with an elongated black blotch. The hingeless, yellow or orangish plastron has large black blotches on the outer portions; sometimes in older individuals these cover the entire plastron. The skin is gray to black; there are occasional yellow spots on the head, neck, and limbs. The head has a broken yellow band near the tympanum and, in some individuals, another extending backward from the orbit.

The spotting varies with age—young individuals have fewer spots—and may also vary geographically. Richmond and Goin (1938) found smaller and less conspicuous spots in adults from Virginia than in those from farther north. Conant (1951) counted 14–114 spots in Ohio specimens. The 124 individuals from southeastern Pennsylvania examined by one of us (CHE) had 21–101 spots (males 27–101, mean 46.9; females 21–78, mean 42.6). However, Yerkes (1905) claimed that females usually have more spots than males. He also reported a greater number of spots on the left side of the carapace in both sexes; in this regard he postulated a correlation with right-handedness and right-eyedness.

Males have tan chins; brown eyes; long, thick tails, with the anal opening near the tip; and slightly concave plastrons. Females have yellow chins, orange eyes, and flat or convex plastrons, which are slightly longer than those of the males and extend closer to the carapacial margin.

GEOGRAPHIC VARIATION: Although some geographic variation has been recorded, no subspecies have been described.

55. The bright spots on *Clemmys guttata* are quite evident.

56. The plastral pattern of this *Clemmys guttata* is typical of the species.

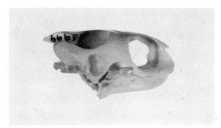

Skull of *Clemmys guttata*

57. *Clemmys guttata.*

CONFUSING SPECIES: *Emydoidea blandingii* has an elongated, blue-black carapace with tan to yellowish spots or radiating lines like *C. guttata*, but has a bright-yellow neck and a hinged plastron. Old, spotless *C. guttata* may be confused with *C. muhlenbergii*, but the latter has a slightly keeled carapace and a large orange blotch on each side of the head.

DISTRIBUTION: *C. guttata* is restricted to eastern North America. It ranges from southern Ontario and Maine southward along the Atlantic coastal plain to southern Georgia and westward through Ontario, New York, Pennsylvania, central Ohio, northern Indiana, and Michigan to northeastern Illinois. There are scattered records from northern Florida.

HABITAT: *C. guttata* is equally at home on land or in water. Although most frequently found in bogs and marshy pastures, it also occurs in small woodland streams. It requires a soft substrate and prefers some aquatic vegetation. It has been seen or taken in association with *C. insculpta*, *C. muhlenbergii*, *Chelydra serpentina*, *Sternotherus odoratus*, *Kinosternon subrubrum*, *Terrapene carolina*, *Emydoidea blandingii*, and *Chrysemys picta*.

In a marshy pasture in Lancaster County, Pennsylvania, where all three eastern species of *Clemmys* occur, *C. guttata* was the most aquatic, followed by *C. muhlenbergii* and *C. insculpta* in that order.

BEHAVIOR: In the water this turtle is shy and attempts to burrow into the mud when disturbed. Fond of basking, it is often seen lying in the sun on logs or in clumps of grass. Spotted turtles often congregate on a suitable log; if disturbed there, they dive directly to the bottom and bury themselves in the mud. This habit makes them rather easy to collect by feeling about in the mud under their basking sites. Individuals have favorite basking sites to which they return regularly throughout the season.

One commonly finds individuals of either sex walking about on land adjacent to their aquatic retreats. They are usually solitary while wandering on land; if disturbed, at that time they quickly withdraw into their shells, to remain so until all is quiet.

Of 416 Pennsylvania captures 18% were taken in March, 22% in April, 29% in May, and 26% in June. Conant (1951) found Ohio specimens in every month from February to November, but most were obtained in the spring: 12% in March, 28% in April, and 49% in May.

Spotted turtles prefer cool temperatures. Ernst (1967c) found them mating at cloacal temperatures of 8–10 C; that is, at or below the minimum voluntary temperatures of other aquatic turtles. During the warm summer days they are not easily found: apparently they aestivate in the mud bottom of some waterway or in a muskrat burrow or lodge. This is surprising, because Hutchison *et al.* (1966) found they had a mean critical thermal maximum of 41.98 C (41.2–42.5), which is higher than that of many other turtles. However, Ernst (1968b) found that they have an evaporative-water-loss gradient higher than that of *Terrapene carolina*, which is a more terrestrial species.

In the colder part of winter *C. guttata* hibernates in the mud bottom of some waterway.

REPRODUCTION: The smallest courting or mating male *C. guttata* observed in Pennsylvania was 83.4 mm in plastron length, the smallest female 80.8 mm. The smallest nesting female had an 80.9-mm plastron. Both sexes probably become mature at about 80 mm in plastron length.

Courtship was observed on 24 March and on 5 and 28 April; it occurred both morning and afternoon at water temperatures of 8.8–18.9 C and air temperatures of 10.0–22.3 C. Courtship included frantic chases of the female by one or several males. The chases covered 30–50 m, lasted 15–30 min, and took place in shallow water and on the adjacent land. The female's hind legs and tail were sometimes bitten during the chase. Often she turned to look at her pursuers. On 28 April two males were seen chasing a female around a shallow pool. The males repeatedly bit each other and the female.

Finally they stopped chasing her to fight, and during the savage struggle the smaller male was driven from the pool.

When the female is finally caught the male mounts her from behind and, while tightly grasping her carapace, places his tail beneath hers. At times the male slides off and comes to lie on his side; such copulating pairs form an L-shaped figure. Copulating *C. guttata* were found on 19 March and on 1 and 15 April. During the 19 March observation four copulating pairs and another pair, clasping but not copulating, were found in one small pool; the water temperature was 8.5 C, the air temperature 12.0 C, and cloacal temperatures 8.0–10.1 C. The matings observed on 1 and 15 April occurred at water temperatures of 15.5 C and 18.0 C and air temperatures of 16.3 C and 20.1 C, respectively. All the matings occurred underwater and lasted 15–30 min (Ernst, 1967c, 1970b). However, copulation may also occur on land (Carr, 1952).

Twelve nests were examined; all were in well-drained loamy soil in a marshy pasture exposed to full sunlight. They were flask-shaped, with plugs of hard earth, and had the following average dimensions: depth 50.3 mm (45.0–58.7), greatest diameter of cavity 50.1 mm (45.2–53.8), and diameter of the neck 31.1 mm (29.3–32.5).

Eight complete and three partial nestings were observed from 2 to 29 June. Ten occurred between 6:30 and 9 PM and one occurred at 9:30 AM. Completion of the nesting required 45–120 min; those dug in hard dry soil took longest to complete.

When the female emerges from the water she pauses on the bank and looks around, possibly for orientation. Then she crawls until she finds a suitable place to dig. Several trial cavities may be dug and abandoned. When a suitable site is found the female braces her front legs and begins to dig, using the hind feet alternately. As one foot digs, the other three are used for support. The body pivots in a semicircle as the hind feet are changed. Often more digging is done with one foot than the other; this results in a larger pile of dirt on one side. The toes are cupped while dirt is lifted out of the cavity. Digging lasts 29–75 min and ceases when the cavity is as

58. Hatchling *Clemmys guttata* are sometimes nearly immaculate.

Distribution of *Clemmys guttata* in the United States.

deep as the hind feet can extend; thus it is the largest females that dig the deepest nests.

After the cavity is completed the female rests for a few minutes before ovipositing. The neck is extended in a straining attitude before each egg descends and is retracted as the egg is expelled. The eggs are arranged in the nest by alternate movements of the hind feet. After all the eggs are laid another rest period, of about 5 min, occurs before the covering of the nest begins. The hind feet are used alternately to scrape soil and grass back into the nest cavity. When the cavity is filled the female rubs her plastron from side to side over the nest; then she returns to the water. No bladder contents were voided during any of the nestings that we observed.

Twelve Pennsylvania clutches contained an average of 3.58 (3–5) eggs. Adler (1961) reported a clutch of eight eggs laid by an Indiana *C. guttata.* Average dimensions of 37 eggs were as follows: length 32.9 mm (31.0–33.7), width 16.7 mm (15.9–17.2). They were elliptical and white and had flexible shells. Many had indentations after laying, but these disappeared as incubation progressed.

Eighteen of 43 Pennsylvania eggs failed to hatch: 6 because they were destroyed by predators or drought and 12 because they were either infertile or decayed.

Estimated incubation periods are 70–83 days (mean 76). The longest incubation periods occur when the soil is hard and dry. Earliest hatchings take place in late August. Perhaps hatchlings from late nestings overwinter in the egg or in the nest: springtime observations and measurements of the young by Conant (1951) and Nemuras (1967a) indicated that overwintering occurs in Ohio and Maryland.

Hatchlings are blue-black and usually have one yellow spot on each carapacial scute except the cervical, which has none; some hatchlings lack spots. The yellow plastron has a black central figure. The head is spotted and in some the neck is spotted as well. Average dimensions are as follows: carapace length 29.8 mm (28.0–31.2), carapace width 31.3 mm (28.5–33.1); plastron length 26.4 mm (25.2–

26.9), and plastron width 16.0 mm (15.8–16.3). The head and the tail are larger in proportion to shell length than those of adults. A caruncle is present at hatching but drops off by the end of the 1st week. The external yolk sac averages 16.5 mm (12.1–18.9) in diameter.

GROWTH: Graham (1970) studied the growth of Rhode Island *C. guttata* and found the following relationships of age to plastron length: hatchlings, mean 24.73 mm (22.9–26.7); 1 year, 35.36 mm (30.5–46.2); 2 years, 42.57 mm (35.6–52.8); 3 years, 48.8 mm (39.6–58.9); 4 years, 54.89 mm (44.6–64.8); 5 years, 59.82 mm (48.5–70.1); 6 years 67.47 mm, 53.1–78.2); and 7 years, 72.92 mm (57.0–83.8). The percentage increase in plastron length ranged from 42.98% the 1st year to 8.08% the 7th year. Babcock (1919) reported that at hatching a *C. guttata* had a carapace length of 26 mm and in 5 months grew to 32 mm.

Pope (1939) reported a longevity of 42 years for a captive, and Graham (1970) found a wild individual in its 26th growing season.

FOOD AND FEEDING: *C. guttata* is omnivorus. Surface (1908) found animal food in all 27 stomachs he examined and vegetation in 3. The animals eaten included worms, slugs, snails, small crustaceans, crayfish, millipedes, spiders, and insects of the orders Ephemerida, Plecoptera, Odonata, Hemiptera, Neuroptera, Lepidoptera, Coleoptera, Diptera, and Hymenoptera. Many of the insects were not aquatic species; perhaps these were captured on land. Conant (1951) observed *C. guttata* eating frogs, earthworms, grubs, and the grass growing in a flooded meadow. Two stomachs of Pennsylvania specimens examined by us included only filamentous green algae. Our captive specimens feed well on fresh and canned fish, cantaloupe, and watermelon.

PREDATORS: Grant (1936a) found spotted turtles in northern Indiana whose shells had been gnawed by rodents and others that had been mutilated or killed by unidentified predators, which ate the legs or head. A mutilated Pennsylvania specimen was surrounded by raccoon tracks. The eggs are sometimes eaten by skunks and raccoons.

MOVEMENTS: Netting (1936) reported an apparent spring migration of *C. guttata* from an upland hibernaculum to a small swamp. Adult spotted turtles in a Pennsylvania marsh had home ranges of approximately 1.3 acres. They returned to their home ranges after being displaced 0.5 mile; probably visual clues were used in their homeward orientation (Ernst 1968a, 1970a).

POPULATIONS: *C. guttata* numbered 124 (10.2%) of the 1,218 turtles captured at the White Oak Bird Sanctuary, Lancaster County, Pennsylvania. The spotted turtles included 13 (10.5%) juveniles, 51 (41.1%) adult males and 60 (48.4%) adult females.

REMARKS: The spotted turtle is of little economic value, except that it may be a factor in the control of obnoxious insects.

59. Adult female *Clemmys muhlenbergii.*

60. Plastron of *Clemmys muhlenbergii.*

CLEMMYS MUHLENBERGII (Schoepff)

Bog Turtle   VI

RECOGNITION: A small (8.0–11.5 cm), brownish turtle with a large, bright blotch on each side of the head. The elongated, rough carapace is moderately domed and has an inconspicuous keel. The sides of the carapace are nearly parallel or slightly divergent behind, and the posterior margin is smooth or only slightly serrated. Color varies from light brown through mahogany to black; each scute usually has a light center. The lower sides of the marginals and the bridge are the same color as the rest of the carapace. The hingeless plastron is dark brown to black, with a few irregularly dispersed light marks. The skin is brown and may be mottled with red above and orange or red below. The head is brown with a large, usually orange but sometimes yellow or red, blotch above and behind the tympanum.

Males have long, thick tails, with the anal opening posterior to the carapacial margin; concave plastrons; and thick foreclaws. Females have high wide carapaces and flat plastrons; the plastron has a wide notch at its posterior margin.

GEOGRAPHIC VARIATION: No subspecies are recognized.

CONFUSING SPECIES: *C. insculpta* is larger, has a sculptured shell, a strongly serrated posterior carapacial margin, and a strong vertebral keel, and lacks the large bright blotch on each side of the head. An old *C. guttata* may have lost its spots, but it has a more rounded, flatter carapace and lacks the large bright head-blotches. An old *Terrapene carolina* may resemble the bog turtle in color, but it always has a hinged plastron.

DISTRIBUTION: *C. muhlenbergii* has a discontinuous range in the eastern United States. The main range is from western Connecticut and eastern New York southward through eastern Pennsylvania and New Jersey to northern Delaware and Maryland. It is also found in northwestern New

York, in northwestern Pennsylvania, and in southern Virginia and adjacent western North Carolina. There is a doubtful record from Rhode Island. The bog turtle is rare throughout its range.

HABITAT: Sphagnum bogs, swamps, and marshy meadows having clear, slow-moving streams with soft bottoms are the preferred habitat. *C. muhlenbergii* occurs from sea level to elevations of more than 4,000 ft (in the Appalachians of North Carolina). It is most often found with *C. guttata* but also occurs with *C. insculpta, Chrysemys picta, Terrapene carolina, Sternotherus odoratus, Kinosternon subrubrum,* and *Chelydra serpentina.*

BEHAVIOR: Little is known of the biology of this small turtle. In Pennsylvania it is active only during the warmer parts of the day; we have never taken it earlier than 11 AM or later than 4 PM. After emerging from its nocturnal shelter it basks for a time before foraging. Our observations indicate that the bog turtle requires more heat to initiate and support activity than does *C. guttata, Chrysemys picta,* or *Terrapene carolina;* on many days sufficiently warm and sunny to arouse these turtles, *C. muhlenbergii* remains in seclusion.

A muskrat burrow is often used as a hibernaculum. Bog turtles emerge from hibernation in April and return in midautumn. They are most active in April, May, June, and September, and they may aestivate during the dry months (July and August). An aestivating individual was found embedded in hard clay under a board on 8 August.

The burrowing habit is well developed: when alarmed the bog turtle rapidly digs into the mucky substrate with which it usually is associated. When handled it retires into its shell, and it rarely makes any attempt to bite or scratch.

REPRODUCTION: May through early June is the mating period. Females remain secluded in the mating season: the males must search them out. The only data on courtship we have are the observations of Cramer, as reported by Barton and Price (1955). A captive pair was provided with a piece of ground and a pool whose depth was more than twice the height of the turtles. Several days after capture the male mounted the female underwater, hooking the claws of all four feet under her marginals. He then thumped his plastron against her carapace several times, making a noise like two turtles shaken together in a bag. She withdrew her head and he moved forward without losing his footholds; then, putting his head down in front of her, he blew bubbles through his nostrils. This procedure was repeated two or three times, and all the while the male continued thumping lightly against the female's carapace. Next he moved back as far as possible without losing his footholds and attempted to copulate. The entire performance was repeated several times at later dates, and each time both participants were entirely submerged.

The nesting of the bog turtle has not been adequately described. However, Alexanderson (in Eglis, 1967) observed that the female does not burrow under moss to lay her eggs, as had been supposed; rather, she digs and covers a nest in the ground as other turtles do. The nesting season extends through June into July, but Nemuras (1967b) reported a 21 August nesting by a captive.

The normal complement of eggs is three to five. Only 10% of the nests examined by Alexanderson contained three eggs; 30% had four and 60% had five. In 1964 her turtles laid six clutches between 12 June and 3 July; of these, four clutches consisted of five eggs each, and the other two consisted of four each. The eggs are elliptical and have white shells. Six shelled oviducal eggs were 28.3–31.1 mm in length and 14.1–15.8 mm in width.

The duration of incubation in nature is not known, but some indication of it has been given by Nemuras (1969) and Alexanderson (in Eglis, 1967). Nemuras took four eggs, laid on 9 June, and placed them in a jar containing damp moss; on 30 July one egg was pipped and on 1 August hatchlings emerged from two eggs—an incubation period of approximately 55 days. Alexanderson artificially incubated 28 eggs, laid between 12 June and 3 July, at 75 F nights and 90 F days; she had 18 hatchlings emerge between 3 and 21 August. Barton and Price

61. A bright orange blotch behind the eye is characteristic of *Clemmys muhlenbergii.*

Skull of Clemmys muhlenbergii

(1955) reported the emergence of a hatchling from a nest on 7 September in Lancaster County, Pennsylvania, and Wright (1918) found one on 18 July in New York.

Hatchlings are 23–34 mm in carapace length; the width is about 80% of this. They have dark-brown, immaculate carapaces and yellow plastrons with a large, dark central figure. The bright head-blotches are well developed. The tail is relatively long.

GROWTH: Barton and Price (1955) kept a young male bog turtle at room temperature from 2 September 1951 to 28 December 1953. It grew as follows: from 53.2 to 84.0 mm in carapace length (58% increase), from 46.8 to 69.0 mm in carapace width (47% increase), from 45.2 to 71 mm in plastron length (57% increase), and from 36.5 to 51.0 mm in plastron width (40% increase). A free-living adult male we measured in Lancaster County, Pennsylvania, grew 0.7 mm in plastron length between 25 April and 20 June 1967. A yearling, also from Lancaster County, had the following measurements: carapace length 37.9 mm, carapace width 34.1 mm, plastron length 31.7 mm; posterior plastron width 20.5 mm, and tail length 21.4 mm.

FOOD AND FEEDING: *C. muhlenbergii* is omnivorous, and it feeds both on land and underwater. Surface (1908) found that the stomach of one individual contained 80% insects and 20% berries. Barton and Price (1955) reported the stomach contents of two adults consisted primarily of insects, with one lepidopterous larva comprising nearly half the total amount in each stomach. Beetles were the next most common food item, followed by the fleshy seeds of pondweed (*Potamogeton*). Large numbers of sedge (*Carex*) seeds had been consumed by these turtles and by nine others subsequently examined. Also represented were caddisfly larval cases and the cocoons of a parasitic hymenopteran or dipteran. The upper intestine of one turtle contained the shells of several young snails (*Succinea ovalis*); that of the other had pieces of a millipede and a cranefly wing. The most common item found in the feces of six turtles caught in mid-August was the exoskeleton of the Japanese beetle (*Popillia japonica*). Campbell (1960) observed bog turtles feeding on a dead pickerel frog (*Rana palustris*) and the larvae of the butterfly *Euphydrys phaeton*. Captives eat earthworms and canned or fresh fish.

PREDATORS: The nests are destroyed by skunks and raccoons, and the young are eaten by several kinds of birds and mammals. Adults are the prey of raccoons, skunks, dogs, and foxes.

MOVEMENTS: A Pennsylvania male recaptured three times within 1 month had moved an average of 12 m between recaptures. The same turtle, when released approximately 0.25 mile away, returned to the capture area in 1 day.

Barton (in Eglis, 1967) attached thread dispensers to bog turtles and observed a migratory pattern. Apparently they left the hibernation sites in April or May and moved upstream to feeding and nesting places where the water was less deep. The return trip was made in late August. One walked 56 ft a day in free movement and did most of its moving from 9 AM to 1 PM. It took this turtle less than 2 weeks to travel across a 600–700-ft meadow. Barton observed that the migration urge apparently was not triggered by a drying or draining of the habitat; instead, the turtles dug deeper into the mud.

POPULATIONS: *C. muhlenbergii* represented only 0.8% of the turtles (10 of 1,218) captured at the White Oak Bird Sanctuary, Lancaster County, Pennsylvania, over a 3-year span. These were one yearling, six adult males, and three adult females. Barton (in Eglis, 1967) censused representative plots of his study area and found that a 10-acre habitat may harbor up to 500 individuals; yet in other areas commercial collectors obtained only two bog turtles per acre after digging up and sifting the mud of entire bogs.

This is the rarest of our turtles and has been considered so for more than 50 years (Babcock, 1919). The population is dwindling.

REMARKS: Draining of the habitat has virtually eliminated *C. muhlenbergii* over most of its original range. Because of its scarcity and restricted distribution it has been placed on the list of rare and endangered species by the Bureau of Sport Fisheries and Wildlife of the United States Department of the Interior. As mankind increases in numbers while altering the face of the land, this shy little creature seems surely doomed to extinction.

The bog turtle is too small to have any commercial food value. It may have a role in the destruction of injurious and obnoxious insects.

Distribution of *Clemmys muhlenbergii*.

62. Adult female *Clemmys insculpta.* The strongly sculptured carapace is characteristic of this species.

63. Plastral scutes of *Clemmys insculpta* usually bear dark blotches at their outer ends.

CLEMMYS INSCULPTA (Le Conte)

Wood Turtle   VII

RECOGNITION: A medium-sized (12.5–23.0 cm) turtle with a keeled, sculptured carapace. The broad, low carapace is rough: each large scute supports an irregular pyramid formed by a series of concentric growth-ridges and grooves. The posterior marginals are strongly flared and serrated. The carapace is slightly widened posteriorly and in some individuals is slightly indented in the region of the bridge. It is gray to brown, often with black and yellow lines radiating from the upper posterior corners of the pleurals. The bottom of the marginals and the bridge often have dark blotches along the seams. The hingeless, yellow plastron has a pattern of oblong dark blotches on each scute. The skin is dark brown to black, often with some orange or red pigment on the forelegs and neck. The tail is rather long.

The male has a long, thick tail, with the anal opening posterior to the carapacial margin; a concave plastron with a deeply notched posterior margin; and prominent scales on the anterior surface of the forelimbs.

GEOGRAPHIC VARIATION: No subspecies have been described.

CONFUSING SPECIES: *C. muhlenbergii* is small and has a feeble keel, a bright blotch on each side of the head, and a relatively smooth shell. *Emydoidea blandingii* and *Terrapene carolina* have hinged plastrons.

DISTRIBUTION: The wood turtle ranges from Nova Scotia south to northern Virginia and west through southern Ontario and New York to northeastern Ohio, Michigan, Wisconsin, eastern Minnesota, and northeastern Iowa.

HABITAT: Next to the box turtles (*Terrapene*) and the tortoises (*Gopherus*) this is our most terrestrial turtle. It can be found in most habitats within its range. We have observed it in deciduous woods, woodland bogs, and marshy fields (in Pennsylvania,

Maryland, and New York). It occurs with *C. guttata,* *C. muhlenbergii, Chrysemys picta, Terrapene carolina, Sternotherus odoratus,* and *Chelydra serpentina.*

BEHAVIOR: The wood turtle is diurnal and often wanders about on land during the midday hours. It is fond of basking in the morning—for example, on a log in the middle of a large creek. In the dry summer months it often soaks in mud puddles.

C. insculpta is active from late March to mid-October. The winter months are spent in hibernation in the mud bottom of some waterway or in a hole in the bank.

Hutchison *et al.* (1966) reported that the mean critical thermal maximum for four *C. insculpta* was 41.3 C (39.6–42.5) and that the mean loss of the righting response occurred at 39.8 C (39.0–40.5). Ernst (1968b) found that cutaneous evaporative water-loss by *C. insculpta* was similar to that of *C. guttata.* These two semiaquatic species fell between the terrestrial *Terrapene carolina* and the aquatic *Chelydra serpentina* and *Sternotherus odoratus* in this environmental relationship.

REPRODUCTION: Powell (1967) showed that, in Nova Scotia, female *C. insculpta* do not have a typical emydid ovarian cycle; it differs conspicuously in the relative uniformity of follicular growth and ovulation. Two specimens collected on 5 June contained oviducal eggs, and on 21 June in the same locality nesting activity was observed. From these data Powell estimated that *C. insculpta* retain their eggs for a minimum of 3 weeks. Only one clutch is laid per season, and virtually all large follicles are ovulated in this single clutch; Powell's single September specimen had a distinct group of 10 large follicles, representing one clutch.

Brenner (1970) found a positive correlation between the ovarian fat content and the maturation of ova. The amount of fat increased significantly with the increase in ovarian weight. There was an inverse relationship between body fat and gonadal weight and a direct correlation between the rate of fat depletion and that of ovarian development. Both

64. The dark head of *Clemmys insculpta* is quite flat.

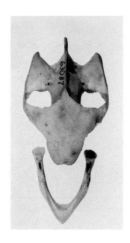
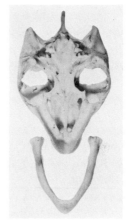
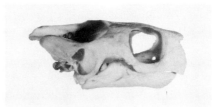

Skull of *Clemmys insculpta*

81

the photoperiod and the temperature influence the amount and use of fat and thus affect the reproductive cycle of the species.

Courtship and mating have been observed in the wild on 26 March, 14 May, and 1 October, and in captives during December. The procedure includes a sort of dance, in which the male and the female approach each other slowly with necks extended and heads held high; when the turtles are within about 8 inches of touching each other they suddenly lower their heads and swing them from side to side—a movement that may continue for as long as 2 hr without stopping (Carr, 1952). Wright (1918) reported that wood turtles emit a courting whistle, not unlike that of a teakettle.

Copulation occurs in the water. According to Carr (1952) the male holds the shell of the female with all four feet: his forefeet are close together around the front edge of her carapace and the claws of his hind feet are clamped under the rear edge. In courtship the male usually is the more aggressive, but the female sometimes takes the initiative: Fisher (1945) twice saw a female turn, tip up a male, and crawl under him.

Nesting occurs in late May and June. An account by Pallas (1960) of nesting by a captive is the most complete on record. On 12 June a female was discovered digging at 8:50 AM, during a fine drizzle. At that time she had already dug a hole perhaps half the depth her hind legs could reach. Digging continued until 10:24 AM; it was done entirely with the hind feet, which alternated without once missing a turn. After digging the hole she formed an egg chamber at the bottom by scraping the right side with her left foot, and vice versa. Her head was stretched far out during the digging and the front feet were stationary. She dug slowly and did not pause to rest.

At 10:25 AM the first egg was laid. Seven more followed—the last at 10:34 AM. During laying, her head was partly withdrawn, and one hind leg rested on the ground, the other at the edge of the hole or just inside it. As each egg appeared she raised her posterior high and lifted her tail. After each egg was dropped she inserted one foot inside the hole—the feet alternated in this—but pulled it out as the next egg appeared.

She rested for 2 min, and then began to fill the nest with earth. Filling and tamping continued until about 11:20 AM; during this period the turtle retained her original position while pivoting farther and farther to the sides. Then, for another 20 min., filling and tamping continued, but she moved her front feet from their stations and swung in an irregular circle that finally brought her some inches from the nesting site.

The filling action consisted of scratching with her claws at the sides of the hole, scraping with her toes and the sides of her feet to bring dirt from the surface into the hole, packing with the soles of her feet held flat and the feet rapidly alternating, and tamping with the sides of the feet, the back of the feet, and occasionally with the whole side of the lower leg. She also pounded the dirt with the rear of her plastron, until the nesting site was indistinguishable from the surrounding ground. Her head was extended during this stage, and she rested several times, for as long as 2–4 min. At 11:48 AM she left the site.

The elliptical eggs are whitish, have smooth, thin shells, and are about 40 mm long and 26 mm wide. Clutch size is from 4 to 12; 7 or 8 is usual.

Pope (1939) reported that four of eight eggs deposited on 26 May hatched about 1 October. Allen (1955) recorded an incubation period of 77 days. Hatchlings normally emerge in August, September, or October, but Wright (1918) found one in New York on 20 April.

Hatchlings are gray-brown and lack any orange or red pigment on the neck or legs. The tail is long: about equal to the carapace length. The keelless shell is low and about as broad as long. A newly hatched individual had a carapace 32 mm in length and, although not fully expanded, was 27.5 mm in width at the bridge (McCauley, 1945). Pope (1939) gave the carapace lengths and widths, respectively, of three hatchlings as 32.0 mm and 30.0 mm, 33.0 mm and 35.0 mm, and 31.5 mm and 34.5 mm. Swanson (1952) reported that the combined weight of six hatchlings was 1 3/8 oz.

FOOD AND FEEDING: The wood turtle is omnivorous. Plants eaten include filamentous algae, moss, grass, willow leaves, strawberries, blackberries, and sorrel. Animal foods include a wide variety of insects and mollusks as well as earthworms and tadpoles. Surface (1908) found plant remains in 76% and animal remains in 80% of the 26 specimens he examined. He also found bird remains, indicating scavenging tendencies. Captives readily eat apples and canned dog food, and they relish hard-boiled eggs.

PREDATORS: Thoreau (in Babcock, 1919) observed a hawk or crow attack a wood turtle and saw a skunk rob a nest. Surface (1908) took a young wood turtle from the stomach of a largemouth bass. Nests surely are robbed by a variety of mammals, and carnivorous vertebrates of several kinds devour the young.

MOVEMENTS: A male we recaptured three times had moved an average of 90 m between recaptures, but a female we recaptured once had moved only 15 m. Woods (1945) reported a land speed of 0.2 mile/hr for a wood turtle. This turtle is an accomplished climber: we have seen one ascend a chain-link fence.

POPULATIONS: *C. insculpta* comprised 2.3% of the turtles (28 of 1,218) caught over a 3-year period at the White Oak Bird Sanctuary, Lancaster County, Pennsylvania. All were adults; 16 were males and 12 were females.

REMARKS: Tinklepaugh (1932) ran *C. insculpta* through a maze and reported that it had learning ability about equal to that of a rat.

Tests of hearing ability by Wever and Vernon (1956a, 1956b) indicated sensitivity of 500 cps—comparable with that of a cat.

The wood turtle is edible but is seldom marketed.

Oliver (1955) recorded a longevity of 58 years in captivity.

Distribution of *Clemmys insculpta* in the United States.

65. The western pond turtle, *Clemmys marmorata*.

66. Plastral view of *Clemmys marmorata*.

CLEMMYS MARMORATA (Baird and Girard)

Western Pond Turtle   VII

RECOGNITION: A small to medium-sized (9–18 cm) turtle with a low carapace and, usually, a pattern of spots or lines that radiate from the centers of the scutes. The short, broad carapace is smooth, widest behind the bridge, and keelless. It is olive, dark brown, or black, and the pattern may be absent in some individuals. The 1st vertebral is in contact with four marginals and the cervical. The bottom of the marginals and the bridge are marked with irregular dark blotches or lines along the seams. The hingeless, pale-yellow plastron sometimes carries a pattern of dark blotches along the posterior margins of the scutes. The skin is gray, with some pale yellow on the neck, chin, forelimbs, and tail. The head is plain or reticulated.

In males the plastron is concave; in females it is flat. In males the anal opening is posterior to the carapace margin; in females it is ventral to the margin.

GEOGRAPHIC VARIATION: Two subspecies are recognized. *C. m. marmorata* (Baird and Girard), the northwestern pond turtle, ranges from British Columbia south to San Francisco Bay and also occurs in western Nevada. It has a pair of well-developed, triangular inguinal scutes on the bridge, and the neck and head are well marked with dark dashes. The throat is pale in contrast with the sides of the head. *C. m. pallida* Seeliger, the southwestern pond turtle, occurs from San Francisco Bay south into Baja California. It can be distinguished by its poorly developed inguinal scutes (absent in 60% of individuals) and by the uniform color of the throat and neck.

CONFUSING SPECIES: The only other freshwater turtle within its range in the United States is *Chrysemys picta*, which has a large, dark blotch spreading along the seams of the plastron, a notched upper jaw, a reticulate pattern of light lines on the carapace, red pigment on the marginals, and yellow stripes on the neck and limbs.

DISTRIBUTION: *C. marmorata* ranges chiefly west of the Cascade–Sierra crest from extreme southwestern British Columbia to northwestern Baja California. Isolated colonies exist in the Truckee and Carson rivers in Nevada. There is a questionable record from Jerome County, Idaho.

HABITAT: This is the most aquatic species of *Clemmys*. It inhabits ponds, marshes, slow-moving streams, and irrigation canals with rocky or muddy bottoms and abundant aquatic vegetation. It also occurs in clear, swift streams to an elevation of 6,000 ft, and it has been reported from brackish coastal waters.

BEHAVIOR: *C. marmorata* often can be seen sunning itself on rocks, logs, mudbanks, or mats of vegetation. Shy and wary, it dives into the water at the least disturbance. According to Pope (1939), during the middle of the day those not basking rest on the bottom of pools, but in the early morning and evening they move upstream or downstream, from one pool to another.

Evenden (1948) reported that the earliest date of occurrence in the central Willamette valley, in Oregon, was 28 February, the latest date 19 November. In California, *C. marmorata* usually disappears toward the end of September and reappears in late March or early April (Storer, 1930). Hibernation is spent in the mud bottoms of streams or ponds.

Brattstrom (1965) found afternoon body temperatures of three *C. marmorata* to be 21.8 C, 25.5 C, and 27.0 C. One collected at 9:30 AM in water of 8.3 C had a body temperature of 9.0 C.

REPRODUCTION: Courtship and mating in this turtle have not been described. Nesting occurs from late April through August; the peak period is June to mid-July. Most nests are dug in the morning. Usually they are located along stream or pond margins; however, they have been found in fields 300 ft. above and hundreds of yards from the water. Full sunlight seems to be required.

Clutch size ranges from 3 to 11. The hard, white eggs are elliptical-oval, measuring 32.8–42.6 mm in

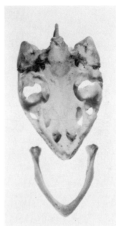

Skull of *Clemmys marmorata*

67. Although often reticulated, the head of *Clemmys marmorata* is sometimes plain.

length and 19.7–22.6 mm in width. The incubation period is unknown.

Hatchlings are about 25 mm in carapace length. The rounded and keeled carapace is brown or olive, with yellow markings at the edge of the marginals. The carapacial scutes have numerous small tubercles, which give them a grainy appearance. The plastron is yellow and has a large, irregular, dark central blotch. The head, limbs, and tail are marked with pale yellow. The tail is nearly as long as the carapace.

GROWTH: Storer (1930) found that at the beginning of their 2nd season *C. marmorata* were 27.8–33.8 mm in carapace length. A 48.7 mm juvenile was in its 2nd season of growth; one 58.0 mm long was in its 3rd season; two, 58.5 and 64.0 mm long, were at the beginning of their 3rd growing season; and one 66.0 mm long was well into its 3rd growth period. Those in their 4th growing season were 71.5–79.5 mm long, and one in its 5th year was 95.0 mm long. These rates indicate that *C. marmorata* may be expected to attain a carapace length of about 140 mm in 10 years.

Seeliger (1945) found that the granular condition of the hatchling carapace disappears with age. She gave the following average lengths of carapace in relation to the progressive changes: granular condition at 30.1 mm; granular portion together with radiating and concentric ridges in each scute at 67.9 mm; concentric ridges only at 125.7 mm; and smooth shell at 145.9 mm.

FOOD AND FEEDING: *C. marmorata* is omnivorous but shows a strong preference for animal food. It feeds on the pods of the yellow lily (*Nuphar polysepalum*), adult and larval insects, fish, worms, and crustaceans. It also takes carrion. Bogert (in Carr, 1952) saw a captive pick up a large sow bug on land and carry it to water before attempting to swallow it. Captives feed well on canned and fresh fish, liver, raw beef, and canned dog food.

REMARKS: Seeliger (1945) found intergrades between the two subspecies in Alameda, Contra

Costa, Santa Clara, Mariposa, Madera, Fresno, Tulare, and Kern counties, California.

This turtle is edible and previously was sold in the markets of San Francisco. Storer (1930) cited prices of $3–$6/doz during the 1920s.

Distribution of *Clemmys marmorata* in the United States.

TERRAPENE CAROLINA (Linnaeus)

Box Turtle

RECOGNITION: A small (10–20 cm) terrestrial turtle with a hinged plastron and a keeled, high-domed, elongated carapace having its highest point posterior to the plastral hinge. The carapace is rounded dorsally and is not serrated posteriorly; a prominent vertebral keel is usually present on the 2nd to 4th vertebral scutes. The 1st vertebral is elevated at a steep angle (50° or more), and the 1st marginal is usually rectangular in shape. The carapace is brownish, usually with an extremely variable yellow or orangish pattern of radiating lines, spots, bars, or irregular blotches on each scute. The plastron lacks a bridge and has a strong hinge between the pectoral and abdominal scutes; this forms two movable lobes. The hinge usually arises at the 5th marginal. The plastron is often as long as or longer than the carapace, and its lateral margin may be indented at the femoroanal seam. Frequently an axillary scute is present, at the 4th marginal. In color the plastron is tan to dark brown; it may be patternless, show dark blotches or smudges, or have a dark central area with branches along the seams. The skin is black to reddish-brown, with yellow or orange spots and streaks; on the head the markings are variable. The upper jaw is hooked terminally and is usually without a notch.

In most adult males the iris is red; in females it is yellowish-brown. The posterior lobe of the plastron is concave in males, flat or slightly convex in females. The claws of the hind foot are, in males, short, stocky, and considerably curved; those of females are longer, more slender, and straighter. Males have longer and thicker tails than the females do.

GEOGRAPHIC VARIATION: Of the six extant subspecies, four occur in the United States. *T. c. carolina* (Linnaeus), the eastern box turtle, ranges from southern Maine south to Georgia and west to Michigan, Illinois, and Tennessee. It has a short, broad, brightly marked carapace with the marginals nearly vertical or only slightly flared. *T. c. major*

68. Adult *Terrapene carolina carolina.*

69. The carapacial pattern of *Terrapene carolina carolina* is quite variable.

70. *Terrapene carolina carolina.*

71. The single plastral hinge of *Terrapene carolina* allows almost complete closure of the shell.

(Agassiz), the Gulf Coast box turtle, ranges along the Gulf coastal plain from the Florida panhandle to eastern Texas. This, the largest of the box turtles, sometimes exceeds 20 cm in carapace length. It has an elongated carapace on which the markings often are absent or are obscured by black or tan color; the rear margin flares strongly outward. *T. c. triunguis* (Agassiz), the three-toed box turtle, ranges from Missouri south to Alabama and Texas. It usually has only three toes on the hind foot. The carapace typically is tan or olive with an obscure pattern. Orange or yellow spots usually are conspicuous on both the head and the forelimbs, but in males the head often is solid red. *T. c. bauri* Taylor, the Florida box turtle, is restricted to peninsular Florida and the Keys. It, too, usually has only three toes on the hind foot, but the carapace has a bright pattern of light radiating lines, and there are two characteristic stripes on each side of the head.

CONFUSING SPECIES: *T. ornata* lacks a prominent vertebral keel and has the 1st marginal irregularly oval or triangular in shape, the plastral hinge usually arising at the seam between the 5th and 6th marginals or at the 6th marginal, and usually a plastral pattern of radiating yellow lines on each scute. *Emydoidea blandingii* has a notched upper jaw, a bright-yellow neck and chin, and a keelless carapace. Tortoises (*Gopherus*) and *Clemmys insculpta* lack plastral hinges.

DISTRIBUTION: *T. carolina* ranges from southern Maine south to the Florida Keys and west to Michigan, Illinois, eastern Kansas, Oklahoma, and Texas. It has been reported from isolated localities in New York and western Kansas. In Mexico it occurs in the states of Campeche, Quintana Roo, San Luis Potosi, Tamaulipas, Veracruz, and Yucatan.

HABITAT: *T. carolina* is predominantly a species of open woodlands, although in the northeast it also occurs in pastures and marshy meadows. It occasionally shares its habitat with *T. ornata, Emydoidea blandingii, Clemmys insculpta, C. guttata, C. muhlenbergii,* and *Gopherus polyphemus.*

BEHAVIOR: In the summer, activity of *T. carolina* is largely restricted to mornings or after rains. Often these turtles avoid the heat of the day by sheltering under rotting logs or masses of decaying leaves, in mammal burrows, or in mud; in the hottest weather they frequently enter shaded shallow pools and puddles and remain there for periods varying from a few hours to a few days. In other words, thermoregulation is accomplished by changing the microenvironment; by this means the body temperature is kept within the range of 29 to 38 C. Hutchison *et al.* (1966) reported that loss of the righting response in *T. carolina* occurred at 39.0–42.2 C and that the critical thermal maximum was 41.5–43.9 C; they found no significant variation in the critical thermal maximum in *T. carolina* from five widely separated U. S. states.

In the cooler temperatures of spring and fall box turtles can be found foraging at any daylight hour. This species is decidedly diurnal, and it scoops out a form in which to spend the night.

McCauley (1945) noted that a large box turtle repeatedly returned to swim in a lily pond. Latham (1916) found that box turtles sometimes enter salt water.

Under natural conditions of temperature (10–29 C) and humidity (45–95%), unfed *T. c. carolina* we studied lost 3.6% of their total weight; this was a weight-loss gradient of 0.14 g/hr for 5 days. During the same period, the semiaquatic *Clemmys guttata* and *C. insculpta* lost 10.0% and the aquatic *Chelydra serpentina* and *Sternotherus odoratus* lost 17.8%. Obviously, there is a significant difference in the water-holding ability of turtles from different habitats: greatest in terrestrial species, least in aquatic species. Bogert and Cowles (1947) found *T. c. bauri* lost 17.3% of its weight (gradient of 0.38 g/hr) in 45 hours at 38 C and 37% relative humidity in a drying chamber.

In the northern part of its range *T. carolina* enters hibernation in late October or November. In the deep south it may remain semiactive throughout the winter. In Louisiana, Penn and Pottharst (1940) found that *T. c. major* hibernated when the temperature fell below 65 F.

72. The four subspecies of *Terrapene carolina*. From the left, *Terrapene carolina bauri*, *Terrapene carolina carolina*, *Terrapene carolina triunguis*, and *Terrapene carolina major*.

73. *Terrapene carolina triunguis* and *Terrapene carolina bauri* usually have only three toes on each hind foot; the other two races normally have four.

74. In hot dry weather, *Terrapene carolina carolina* often seeks the cooling shelter of a mud puddle. (*Photo by John MacGregor*)

89

When entering hibernation these turtles burrow into loose soil, sand, vegetable debris, the mud of ponds or stream bottoms, or old stump holes; or they may enter mammal burrows. The same hibernaculum may be used in successive winters. They go deeper as the soil temperature drops: as much as 2 ft deep before winter is over. The depth to which the soil freezes seems to be the factor limiting the northern distribution. We have observed that the hibernacula often are shared by as many as four *T. carolina*. Carpenter (1957) found Oklahoma *T. carolina* hibernating in close association with *T. ornata* and/or *Kinosternon flavescens* and *Chelydra serpentina*.

Box turtles usually emerge from hibernation in April. Carpenter (1957) reported that the longest period an Oklahoma individual remained in the same hibernaculum in one season was 154 days: from 11 November to 8 April. He found that many box turtles changed hibernacula during the winter. The average length of time that 73 turtles remained in one place was 63.4 days.

During warm spells in winter or early spring many emerge and soon thereafter are killed by rapid declines of temperature. Neill (1948a) thought that more box turtles were killed by cold than by all other factors together, and he suggested that the wholesale destruction may actually be of advantage to the species by eliminating weaker individuals. Mortality during hibernation must surely be high.

Oliver (in Brattstrom, 1965) thought that box turtles (mostly *T. carolina*) that do not hibernate or otherwise lower their body temperatures during the winter usually die the following summer. However, we have kept both *T. carolina* and *T. ornata* in captivity at room temperature for several years, and mortality was low.

Cahn (1937) compared the hibernation of several individuals of *T. carolina* and *T. ornata* under the same environmental conditions in Illinois. *T. ornata* burrowed into the ground in October—2 weeks before *T. carolina*—and continued to burrow, to a maximum of 22.5 inches. Some individuals of *T. carolina* spent the entire winter in the mud bottom of a puddle and became active on warm winter

days; others burrowed nearly as deep as *T. ornata* did. *T. ornata* emerged from hibernation 1 or 2 weeks later in the spring than did *T. carolina*.

REPRODUCTION: Spermatogonia divide from May to July. Primary spermatocytes appear in June, peak in July, and decrease in number until fall. Maturation divisions and spermiogenesis occur in July, and both increase greatly in early August. Spermatogenesis is past its peak by mid-September, after which the seminal epithelium is greatly reduced in size. Following hibernation the testis is composed chiefly of Sertoli cells, lipoidal debris, and spermatogonia; the epididymis is filled with spermatozoa throughout the year. Interstitial cells are large and heavily laden with lipoids during May, but in July and August they are small. In the fall they increase in size, but there is little increase in lipoidal material.

The oogenetic cycle begins in July and August, when the oogonia divide and grow in the germinal ridges located at sites scattered about the periphery of the ovary. New follicles are formed at this time, and usually two to eight of them accumulate yolk during the fall. Ovarian weight is greatest in May. In June, after ovulation, the collapsed follicles are transformed into corpora lutea, which atrophy by mid-August (Atland, 1951).

Courtship and mating usually occur in the spring but may extend through the summer into autumn. Data collected by Evans (1953) from 72 matings of *T. c. carolina* show that courtship is divided into three phases: a circling, biting, and shoving phase; a preliminary mounting phase; and a copulatory phase.

In phase 1 the male approaches the female but stops when about 4 inches away, with his legs straightened, his head held high, and often with one leg raised above the ground. The female retracts her head but watches him. He then walks around the female, nipping her shell as he goes, or pushes her shell a few degrees upon its axis, bites it, and then pushes it farther around and bites it again. Up to 1 hr may elapse during this phase, depending on the readiness of the female to open her plastron. He eventually mounts and almost instantly hooks his toes into the posterior plastral opening, where she holds them tightly. Apparently titillation of the claws upon the posterolateral edges of the female's carapace is the final stimulus inducing her to open the rear part of the plastron.

In phase 2 the male's hind feet follow the edge of the plastron forward and, when near the hinge, the claws hook on and the rear plastron closes upon them.

The stimuli that bring about phase 3 are the contact of plastron and carapace; the downward projection of the male's head in front of the female's head as he bites the forward edge of her shell; the touch of his forefeet upon her shell; and the slight motion of his pinioned claws on the plastral edge. For copulation, the male slips backward until his carapace rests on the ground, while the rear ankles of the female press downward and medially upon his feet, which have shifted farther in under her carapace. After several seconds he leans still farther back and then returns to the vertical position, in which intromission occurs.

This, the courtship pattern of *T. c. carolina*, is perhaps the ancestral type. In *T. c. triunguis* the male stops a few inches from the female and, with head held high, pulsates his orange-colored throat. She comes alongside; he mounts, scratches her scutes with all four feet, is pinioned, and then for several minutes exposes his pulsing throat to her. In *T. c. bauri* the male climbs upon the female's carapace with all four feet. After a moment of rubbing and scratching her he pulsates his yellow throat above her head. When pinioned in the usual manner he nibbles gently at her neck. The mating of *T. c. major* sometimes takes place in shallow water, but in other respects it resembles that of *T. c. carolina*.

Males sometimes die as a result of falling on their backs after copulation in a place where they cannot gain sufficient leverage to right themselves (Allard, 1939).

Female *T. carolina* may lay viable eggs for up to 4 years after mating (Ewing, 1943).

Nesting occurs from May through July. Most nests are started at twilight and finished after dark;

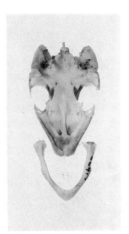

Skull of *Terrapene carolina*

Distribution of *Terrapene carolina* in the United States.

however, Smith and List (1955) found a Mississippi female laying at 7 AM.

The nest site usually is in an open, elevated patch of sandy or loamy soil. The 3–4-inch flask-shaped cavity is dug entirely with the hind feet and its size is correlated with the length of the hind leg. At the beginning of excavation the forefeet are braced and subsequently not moved; the hind feet dig alternately. The eggs are extruded at intervals of 1–6 min and are arranged in the nest by the hind feet; the entire nesting process may take as long as 5 hr to complete. The bladder contents may be voided into the cavity during the nesting. When the clutch is complete the nest cavity is filled by broad lateral sweeps of one hind foot or by scooping soil forward with both hind feet in unison. Filling also involves much tamping and treading with the toes, feet, knees, and plastron.

The eggs are elliptical and have thin, white flexible shells. They are 29–40 mm in length, 19–23 mm in width, and 6–11 g in weight. Clutch size ranges from three to eight; four or five is the usual number. Ewing (1933) reported a fertility rate of 78.6%.

The incubation period depends on soil temperature, which in turn depends on such factors as mean air temperature, shading, soil characteristics, rainfall, and exposure. About 3 months' time normally is required before hatching, which takes place from early September into October. Sometimes hatchlings overwinter in the nest. The shortest incubation period recorded was 69 days, the longest 136 days (Allard, 1948).

Hatchlings have a flat, brownish-gray carapace with a yellow spot on each large scute, and there is a vertebral keel. The plastron is yellow to cream-colored, with a brownish central blotch; the hinge is nonfunctional. The tail is long in comparison with that of the adult. Allard (1948) gave the following dimensions for 17 newly hatched *T. carolina*: plastron length 28.1 mm (26–30), plastron width 24.3 mm (21–27), shell height 15.5 mm (15–18), carapace length 31.0 mm (30–33), carapace width 29.5 mm (28–33), and weight 6.5 g (5.7–7.7). At hatching a caruncle is present between the nos-

75. Hatchling *Terrapene carolina carolina*. The caruncle (egg tooth) is still attached to the beak.

76. Plastron of a hatchling *Terrapene carolina carolina*; the yolk sac is still attached.

trils; it is lost, and the yolk sac is retracted, within 1 week. Neill (1948c) commented that during the earlier stages young *T. carolina* emit a strong odor when molested, but this is lost as further development occurs.

GROWTH: Allard (1948) followed for several years the growth of 22 turtles hatched in 1934. Their average weight on 11 July 1935 was 11.5 g; on 15 September 1935, 20.6 g; and on 17 October 1936, 39.6 g. They were again weighed on 14 May 1937 and found to have an average weight of 38.6 g, which meant an average loss of 1 g after almost 7 months; during this period they had hibernated and subsequently had probably been without food: on 14 May they had barely begun feeding. On 28 October 1937, at the end of their 3rd year after hatching, their average weight was 53.9 g.

Ditmars (in Pope, 1939) reported a Connecticut *T. carolina* attained a carapace length of about 5 inches in slightly more than 5 years. Rosenberger (in Pope, 1939) reported a male grew to 4.75 inches in plastron length and a female to 4.00 inches in 4 years. Carr (1952) stated that during the first 4 or 5 years of life box turtles may grow at a rate of 0.5–0.75 inch a year. Nichols (1939a) found the maximum growth rate to be 3/8 inch/year. Sexual maturity is reached in about 4 or 5 years. Nichols believed that full growth is attained in about 20 years, but we have seen 20-year-old individuals with new growth rings.

The box turtle's shell has great regenerative powers: Smith (1958) reported a case of total regeneration of the carapace of a badly burned *T. carolina.*

Oliver (1955) reported that a *T. carolina* lived 138 years in the wild. Graham and Hutchison (1969) have given evidence for centenarian box turtles in New England.

FOOD AND FEEDING: *T. carolina* is omnivorous. When young it is chiefly carnivorous, but it becomes more herbivorous with age. Babcock (1939) kept a young *T. carolina* for 6 years after hatching before it took any plant material. Stomachs of 40 individuals of various sizes examined by Surface (1908) had animal material in 80% and plant material in 62% of those containing food. Klimstra and Newsome (1960) found plant remains in 89% and animal remains in 98% of stomachs containing food. Barbour (1950) noted snails 60%, crayfish 15%, and plant material 12.5%, by volume. Bush (1959) found snails and slugs 52.5%, mushrooms 10%, caterpillars 10%, carabid beetles 4%, and centipedes 3.5%, by volume. Roots, stems, leaves, fruits, and some seeds are eaten. Among the plants are mushrooms, blackberries, blueberries, mulberries, plums, strawberries, sweet cicely, wintergreen, ground cherry, mosses, *Rubus*, *Polygonum*, *Ambrosia*, *Galium*, *Vitis*, and the grasses *Bromus*, *Paspalum*, and *Hordeum*. Box turtles occasionally damage tomato, lettuce, cucumber, cantaloupe, and strawberry crops. Invertebrates eaten include snails, slugs, earthworms, spiders, crayfish, millipedes, grasshoppers, flies, beetles, ants, termites, cicadas, caterpillars, insect grubs, and maggots. Vertebrate food includes fish, frogs, toads, salamanders, lizards, and various snakes (*Carphophis amoenus*, *Coluber constrictor*, *Storeria dekayi*, *Thamnophis sirtalis*). Box turtles also consume carrion: they have been seen feeding on dead birds, amphibians, mice, shrews, and even a dead cow. Conant (1951a) saw captives feeding on a broken duck egg, and one of us (CHE) saw a female eating several of her own eggs.

Myers (1956) reported an unusual feeding habit in *T. carolina.* When confronted with several mealworms a captive subadult picked up each in turn and with a few bites killed or disabled it. Only when all were incapable of escape did the turtle start to feed. This behavior was observed on several occasions when more than one mealworm was offered.

Our captives feed well on canned dog food, tomatoes, lettuce, bananas, apples, hard-boiled eggs, watermelon, cantaloupe, and bread. Cahn (1937) reported that if his young captives were not permitted to hibernate they ceased to eat, no matter what food was offered, and died before the end of winter. We have found this not to be the case as long as they are kept at 75–80 F.

93

PREDATORS: Large numbers of nests are destroyed by skunks, foxes, raccoons, and crows. Crows, copperheads (Murphy, 1964), and cottonmouths (Klimstra, 1959b) are known predators of juveniles, but surely many other species take the young. The numerous limb mutilations seen on adults are probably caused by such carnivores as raccoons, skunks, coyotes, dogs, and foxes. Few species are able to prey effectively on adults; however, Culbertson (1907) observed hogs crushing and eating them.

Man is the leading killer of box turtles: thousands die annually on the highways. Adler (1970) has suggested that the Indians (primarily the Iroquois) were responsible for the elimination of *T. carolina* in western New York and possibly in southern Ontario by using them for food, medical, ceremonial, burial, and hunting purposes.

MOVEMENTS: The home ranges of Long Island *T. c. carolina* had a diameter of 250 yards or less, and were moved somewhat with the passage of years. One exceptional turtle wandered more than 0.5 mile (Nichols, 1939b). Dolbeer (1969) estimated the home range of Tennessee *T. c. carolina* to be only 250 ft; but Stickel (1950) reported that in Maryland the average diameter of the ranges of adult males was 330 ft, of females 370 ft. Ranges of box turtles of all ages and both sexes overlap; the turtles frequently occur together and show no antagonism. Movements within the home range vary from random meanderings to fairly direct traverses. In many cases certain routes are used repeatedly. Some box turtles use only one portion of the home range at a time and may take several days or weeks to use the entire range. Some have a divided home range and travel between the divisions at infrequent intervals. Occasional trips outside the range are made by some individuals; these trips include searches for nesting sites (Stickel, 1950).

Nichols (1939b) found most adults (89.5%) showed some homing tendency. All adults displaced 0.50–0.75 mile moved back 1,000–1,400 yards. Only three of seven young showed any tendency to home; the greatest distance returned was 700 yards. Two adults, displaced 4 and 20 miles

respectively, remained near the places where they were liberated. Gould (1957) reported that 22 of 43 *T. carolina* moved in a homeward direction when released in open fields up to 5 miles from their original points of capture. They oriented themselves by the sun: homeward headings were inaccurate or lacking on overcast days, and light reflected from a mirror caused them to alter course. Later studies by Gould (1959) revealed that box turtles released in unfamiliar localities sometimes headed in a direction other than that of home. Lemkau (1970) released 14 *T. carolina* in unfamiliar territory and found that each individual tended to move in a single direction; however, for the group as a whole no particular direction was discernible. These data suggest that the box turtle is able to move in a predetermined direction over periods of several days and for considerable distances; this would facilitate the maintenance of a direct course when orientation cues are temporarily obscured. Ernst and Hamilton (1969) found that *T. carolina* made no significant color choice, so colors are probably not used in orientation.

POPULATIONS: Dolbeer (1969) collected 270 box turtles in a 22-acre woodland near Knoxville, Tennessee, and by recapture estimated the population to be 7–9/acre. Stickel (1950) collected 245 adults on 29 acres at Laurel, Maryland, and estimated the population to be 4–5/acre. Her recapture records showed that some of these adults had ranges entirely within the study plot and that others ranged beyond it. Still others were transients; so the number of box turtles collected was somewhat greater than the permanent population. The transient population was estimated to be about 6.7% of the total at any one time. Juveniles constituted less than 10% of the total population, or about 0.1–0.5/acre.

In spite of the abundance of *T. carolina* in some regions, hatchlings and juveniles are rarely found. The young that hatched in a pen immediately entered a puddle of water and hid in the vegetation or beneath the bottom debris, and when brought into a laboratory they immediately burrowed under sphagnum and remained there for weeks at a time

(Cahn, 1937). This secretiveness may be a clue to the seeming scarcity of juveniles. Legler (1960a) found that *T. ornata* juveniles were more plentiful than they appeared to be and that they were also rather secretive. Stickel (1950) thought the problem of estimating numbers of juveniles was complicated by the fact that small turtles are not numerous, are not readily seen, and are more mobile than adults.

REMARKS: Hybridization between *T. carolina* and *T. ornata* occasionally occurs where the ranges overlap. Intergradation between the subspecies of *T. carolina* has been discussed by Milstead (1969).

Carpenter (1956) reported carapace-pitting in Oklahoma *T. c. triunguis.* This involved both the scutes and the bone and was associated with the anterior borders of the 3rd pleural scutes. The condition was more common in females, and it was positively correlated, in both sexes, with increasing carapace length. Neither the cause nor the significance of the pitting is known.

Whole-body x-ray exposures of *T. carolina* revealed an LD50 (median lethal dose) of 850 r (roentgens). The course of the acute radiation syndrome was prolonged, with delayed and prolonged hemopoietic depression; assessment of radiation lethality took 120 days (Cosgrove, 1965).

Stickel (1951) found no significant difference in either population size or growth rate of *T. carolina* in an area treated with DDT annually for 5 years. However, Ferguson (1963) reported a *T. carolina* death possibly from heptachlor poisoning. Perhaps the mortality from pesticides and herbicides is higher than we know.

Although many injurious insects are included in their diet, box turtles are probably of little economic importance. They may disseminate chiggers, and there is a possibility that they sometimes destroy the eggs of ground-nesting birds. They are sometimes eaten, but this is risky: Babcock (1919) reported that Pennsylvania miners ate box turtles (during a strike) and became ill. It is likely that the turtles had fed on a poisonous fungus, which did not affect them but made their flesh temporarily poisonous. Carr (1952) retold an anecdote of his father's: box turtles that were accidentally roasted in burning brushpiles in Mississippi were eaten by several boys, all of whom subsequently became ill. Goldfield and Sussman (in Nolan *et al.*, 1965) isolated the virus of western equine encephalitis from the blood of *T. carolina*, which may serve as a reservoir for this disease.

77. *Terrapene ornata ornata.*

TERRAPENE ORNATA (Agassiz)

Ornate Box Turtle IX

RECOGNITION: A small (10–14 cm) terrestrial turtle with a hinged plastron, a keelless carapace (almost always), and a conspicuous pattern of radiating light lines. The carapace generally is round or oval and is high-domed; the highest point is directly above or anterior to the plastral hinge. The carapace is without posterior serrations and is flattened dorsally; rarely a weakly developed middorsal keel occurs on, usually, the posterior half of the 3rd and anterior half of the 4th vertebral scutes. The 1st vertebral is elevated at a low angle (45° or less), and the 1st marginal usually is irregularly oval or triangular. The carapace is dark brown to reddish-brown, often with a yellow middorsal stripe; each scute shows radiating yellowish lines. The plastron has a strong hinge between the pectoral and abdominal scutes; this divides the plastron into two movable lobes. The hinge usually arises at the seam between the 5th and 6th marginals or at the 6th marginal. The plastron is often as long as or longer than the carapace, and its lateral margin is usually entire (not indented). It lacks a bridge. There is usually no axillary scute; if present it is at the 5th marginal. The plastron has a pattern of radiating lines on each scute. The skin is dark brown with yellow spotting, especially on the dorsal surface of the head and limbs; the chin and the unnotched upper jaw are yellow. In some individuals the head is greenish. The tail may have a yellow dorsal stripe. There usually are four toes on the hind foot; rarely there are but three.

In adult males the iris is red; in females it is yellowish-brown. In males but not in females the first toe on the hind foot is thickened, widened, and turned in. The hind lobe of the plastron is slightly concave in males, flat or convex in females. Females grow larger than males.

GEOGRAPHIC VARIATION: Two subspecies are recognized. *T. o. ornata* (Agassiz), the ornate box turtle, ranges from Indiana and eastern Wyoming south to Louisiana and New Mexico. It is distinguished by the five to eight radiating lines on the 2nd pleural and by its generally dark appearance. *T. o. luteola* Smith and Ramsey, the salt basin box turtle, ranges from the Trans-Pecos region of Texas and southeastern Arizona south into Sonora and Chihuahua, Mexico. This turtle has 11 to 14 radiating lines on the 2nd pleural and is generally yellowish. The shells of old individuals often lose their pattern and become uniformly pale greenish or straw-colored; this pigment loss does not occur in *T. o. ornata*.

CONFUSING SPECIES: *T. carolina* has a prominent middorsal keel (usually) on the 2nd to 4th vertebral scutes; has the 1st marginal nearly rectangular; has the plastral hinge usually at the 5th marginal; often has only three toes on the hind foot; and, except in the Florida subspecies, lacks a plastral pattern of radiating yellow lines on each scute. *Emydoidea blandingii* has a notched upper jaw and a bright-yellow neck and chin. The tortoises (*Gopherus*) do not have hinged plastrons.

DISTRIBUTION: *T. ornata* ranges from Illinois, Iowa, South Dakota, and eastern Wyoming south to southwestern Louisiana, Texas, New Mexico, southeastern Arizona, and Sonora and Chihuahua, Mexico. It also occurs locally in northwestern Indiana, and there is a record from Wisconsin.

HABITAT: This is a "prairie" turtle, inhabiting treeless plains and gently rolling country with grass and scattered low brush as the dominant vegetation. It shares its habitat with *T. carolina*, *Gopherus berlandieri*, and *G. agassizii*, and it also occurs near waterways that harbor many species of aquatic turtles.

BEHAVIOR: The daily cycle of activity of *T. ornata* consists of periods of basking, foraging, and rest that vary in length in keeping with environmental conditions. These turtles emerge from their nighttime burrows, forms, and other places of concealment soon after dawn and ordinarily bask for at least a few minutes before beginning to forage. Although foraging sometimes continues in shady

78. The pattern of radiating lines on the carapace of *Terrapene ornata* also occurs on the plastron.

79. *Terrapene ornata luteola* is a lighter race with more radiating lines than *Terrapene ornata ornata*.

97

spots throughout the day, it usually ceases between midmorning and noon, when the turtles seek shelter. They remain under cover until midafternoon or late afternoon, when they again become active. Activity of all except nesting females ceases at dusk.

As temperatures rise in summer the period of midday quiescence is lengthened and the turtles sometimes spend the warmest hours in pools of water. At least in the southwestern portion of its range *T. ornata* seems to be largely controlled by rainfall: it becomes specially active during and after thunderstorms.

T. ornata is active from March to November. Anderson (1965) reported that in Missouri this species emerges from hibernation in mid-April and tends to remain in woodlands for several weeks, feeding little and spending much of the time partly embedded in the soil. In May they become more active, and by June ornate box turtles are often seen sunning themselves or crossing highways.

Ornate box turtles begin to enter hibernation in October; by the end of November most or all of them are underground. In Kansas autumn activity is characterized by movement into ravines and other low places and into wooded strips along fields or small streams (Legler, 1960a)—places good for basking and burrowing as well as for protection from the wind. The turtles often use animal burrows along the banks of a ravine for temporary shelter, and the overhanging sod at the edge of the ravine provides cover beneath which the turtles can easily dig.

Low air-temperature is probably the primary stimulus for hibernation. A decrease in general activity usually follows the autumn rains. Rain probably facilitates burrowing by softening the ground; more often than not, ornate box turtles excavate their own hibernacula. These are deepened gradually during the winter; depth seems to be governed by the temperature of the soil. Hibernacula in woods and other sheltered places ordinarily are shallower than those in open grassland.

Ornate box turtles usually hibernate singly. In the rare instances in which more than one turtle is found in a hibernaculum, the association has no social significance; it is simply a reflection of the availability and suitability of the hibernaculum.

Legler (1960a) reported that body temperatures of hibernating *T. ornata* approximated that of the surrounding soil. In November and December body temperatures tended to be slightly higher than soil temperatures; in February and March slightly lower. The lowest body temperature of any turtle that survived the winter was 2.7 C; body temperatures 1–3° higher than this were common in the coldest part of winter.

Emergence from hibernation usually occurs in April, but in some years a few emerge as early as the 1st week of March. Emergence is delayed until the ground has been sufficiently moistened and air temperatures have reached 26 C (Fitch, 1956). In early March, turtles face upward in their hibernacula, and as the temperature rises they move slowly upward, usually following the route by which they entered. They remain just below the surface of the ground for a week or two before actually emerging; emergence is probably hastened by the ground-softening spring rains.

Cahn (1937) compared the hibernation of *T. ornata* and *T. carolina* in an outdoor pen. *T. ornata* entered hibernation before *T. carolina*; every individual disappeared fully 2 weeks before the first *T. carolina* made any effort to hibernate. Once *T. ornata* had dug into the ground, they did not emerge until spring. Like *T. carolina*, they were only a few inches under the surface of the ground in October but dug deeper as the temperature dropped. *T. carolina* ceased its descent at 19 inches, but *T. ornata* went to a depth of 22.5 inches. *T. ornata* did not emerge until a week or two after *T. carolina* had become active. Altogether, then *T. ornata* remained in hibernation nearly a month longer than did *T. carolina*. The greater depth of the hibernaculum perhaps suffices to account for the longer period of inactivity.

Peters (1959) noted the existence of an air dome above hibernating *T. ornata*. This space was about half the size of the turtle and was filled with loose dirt, which provided a little air space.

In a study of the effects of hibernation on the

physiology of *T. ornata*, Peters (1959) found an increase of 19% in the number of red blood cells, an increase of 30% in the number of white blood cells, an increase of 57% in the amount of blood sugar, no significant change in the amount of serum protein, a 50% decrease in liver fat, and a total weight loss of 1.2–10.4 g.

Legler (1960a) took about 500 body temperatures under natural conditions and found 30 C to be the optimum temperature for activity. Emergence usually occurs when the body temperature is 24 C or higher and almost never occurs when it is below 15 C. Body temperature is raised to optimum by basking; if this is impossible, activity begins at suboptimal temperatures. Shelter in dens, burrows, or forms is sought when the body temperature rises above 30 C. A temperature of 40 C for a prolonged period is lethal; prolonged exposure at 0 C or below is also fatal. Brattstrom (1965) found the mean body temperature of 57 active *T. ornata* to be 28 C (13.0–35.9).

T. ornata with the scutes experimentally removed lost about 26% of their initial weight after 6 days of desiccation; controls lost only 3%. When exposed to direct sunlight they warmed more slowly than did the controls and lost heat faster in cooling. This suggests that the scutes retard water loss and thereby aid in temperature regulation (Rose, 1969).

REPRODUCTION: Sexual maturity seems more closely correlated with size than with age. There is evidence that males mature when smaller and younger than females: 76% of the males studied by Legler (1960a) were mature at 100–109 mm in plastron length and at age 8–9 years, and 66% of the females were mature at 110–119 mm in plastron length and at age 10–11 years.

The spermatogenic cycle begins in May and reaches its peak in September, when large numbers of sperm and spermatids are present in the testes. The cycle is completed in October, when sperm pass into the epididymides, where it is stored over the winter; thus females are inseminated with sperm produced in the preceding year.

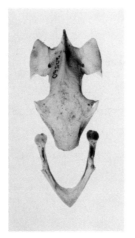
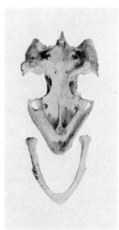
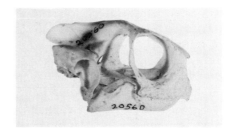

Skull of *Terrapene ornata*

80. *Terrapene ornata luteola.*

The ovarian cycle begins in midsummer, soon after ovulation, and continues until the next ovulation. Follicular growth is rapid during the period from spring emergence to ovulation. Large follicles remaining after ovulation represent, in many instances, eggs that will be laid later in the same season.

Courtship and mating occur most commonly in spring, soon after emergence from hibernation but sometimes they occur in summer. Brumwell (1940) described mating in *T. o. ornata*. A male pursued a female for nearly 30 min, first nudging the margins of her shell and later approaching rapidly from the rear and hurling himself on her back while emitting a stream of liquid from each nostril. Presumably the liquid was water: both turtles had imbibed in a pond just before courtship began. (Brumwell suggested that pressure on the plastron of the male had forced the water out his nostrils.) After the male had achieved intromission the pair remained in coitus for 30 min; however, the act may last as long as 2 hr. In another instance Brumwell saw four males pursuing a single female; they exhibited the same nudging and lunging behavior. Males that attempted to mount other males were repelled by defensive snapping. The female, too, snapped at some of the males that tried to mount her. One male was finally successful and thereafter was unmolested by the other males. In the several matings that Legler (1960a) observed, the male, after mounting the female, gripped her just beneath her legs or on the skin of the gluteal region with the first claws of his hind feet and used the remaining three claws to grip the posterior edges of her plastron. In most instances she secured his legs by hooking her own around them. This coital position differs from that of *T. carolina*, at least in the position of the male's legs.

Nesting extends from early May to mid-July and is most frequent in June. However, Bissett (1968) observed a nesting on 15 April by a captive. Some females that nest early in the season lay a second clutch in July.

Nesting sites that are open, well-drained, and have a soft substrate are preferred. The site is selected after a period of wandering during which the female tests the substrate at a number of places;

the search may continue for more than a week. Nest-digging begins in the evening and usually is completed after dark. The female uses her hind feet only. She prepares a preliminary cavity, in which she lies while digging the main cavity. Often the bladder is voided on the surface and inside the cavity, softening the soil. The typical nest is flask-shaped: roughly 55 mm deep, 80 mm wide at the bottom, and 60 mm wide at the opening.

Clutch size ranges from two to eight; four to six eggs are usual. The ellipsoidal eggs have finely granulated but somewhat brittle white shells. Data from 42 eggs in nine clutches were as follows: length 36.06 mm (31.3–40.9), width 21.72 mm (20.0–26.3), and weight 10.09 g (8.0–14.3). The smaller clutches tended to have the larger eggs: the largest and heaviest were in a clutch of two eggs, the smallest in a clutch of eight (Legler, 1960a).

Incubation periods for 49 eggs kept in a laboratory were 56–127 days, depending on the air temperature. Eggs kept at a daily average temperature of 91 F had a mean incubation period of 59 days (56–64); at 82 F, 70 days (67–73); and at 75 F, 125 days (124–127) (Legler, 1960a). The incubation periods averaging 59 and 70 days more nearly reflect natural conditions than does the excessively long period of 125 days.

During incubation the eggs expand by absorption of water. A temporary lack of moisture usually will not kill embryos, but prolonged dryness is lethal. Of 60 eggs studied in the laboratory by Legler (1960a), 45 (75%) were fertile, and 36 (80%) of the fertile eggs hatched.

The almost round hatchlings are approximately 30 mm in carapace length and weigh about 7 g. The carapace is dark brown to black, with yellow spots on the scutes and a yellow dorsal stripe along the vertebral ridge. The plastron is yellow to cream-colored, with a large, dark central blotch; the hinge is not yet developed. The caruncle remains on the beak for a variable period of time.

GROWTH: Scute growth in *T. ornata* begins with the spring formation of a new layer of epidermis beneath the existing scute. The peripheral projection of the new layer is distinct in texture and color and is separated from the older part of the scute by a major growth-ring. Minor growth-rings form when growth slows or temporarily stops during periods of quiescence; no new layer of epidermis is formed. The scutes are not shed. Early hatching and early emergence from the nest are factors contributing to maximum growth in the first season. Hatchlings that overwinter in the nest do not grow there, but they emerge early. Growth is rapid at first but slows gradually until maturity is reached, and it stops 2 or 3 years later; the total growing period is probably not more than 15–20 years out of *T. ornata*'s lifespan of approximately 50 years. Legler (1960a) recorded mean increments in plastral length of 68%, 29%, and 18% for the first 3 years.

The average number of growing days for *T. ornata* in Kansas is approximately 160 days/year; the amount of growth depends on climatic influences on food supply and foraging conditions. Growth rate is directly correlated with precipitation, being highest when large populations of grasshoppers and long periods of favorable weather occur in the same year (Legler, 1960a).

A number of changes in structure and appearance occur in the period from hatching to maturity. Fontanelles of the bony shell close at or before maturity, and the hinge of the plastron becomes functional the 4th year. The markings on the carapace and plastron change with age to distinct, straight-sided radiating lines.

FOOD AND FEEDING: Under natural conditions *T. ornata* is chiefly carnivorous; captives, however, eat a variety of vegetable matter as well as meat. Insects (chiefly beetles, caterpillars, and grasshoppers) comprise approximately 90% of the food. Dung beetles constitute the most important staple element of the diet: the disturbance of piles of dung by turtles in the course of their foragings is a characteristic sign of *T. ornata*. Insects form the bulk of the diet most of the year, but certain other foods (for example, mulberries) are eaten in quantity when especially abundant—sometimes to the exclusion of other foods. *T. ornata* also eats carrion.

Metcalf and Metcalf (1970) observed *T. ornata* eating grasshoppers, caterpillars, scavenger beetles, fish, a dead woodrat (*Neotoma floridana*), mulberries, cantaloupes, tomatoes, strawberries, blackberries, a pod of the green bean, a groundcherry (*Physalis*) fruit, and a dandelion during their study of these turtles in Kansas. They also found an individual stuck in a can that contained a small amount of honey. Another specimen, which had been confined in an automobile trunk in which honey had been transported, was found with some honey around its mouth. Whether these turtles were eating honey or were seeking bees attracted to it is not known.

Captive ornate box turtles displayed surprising agility in capturing and eating tadpoles of the spadefoot toad (*Scaphiopus*); this suggests that *T. ornata* may be an important predator upon *Scaphiopus* larvae (Norris and Zweifel, 1950).

Legler (1960a) found stones up to 7 mm in diameter in the stomachs of ornate box turtles. He presumed that these were swallowed accidentally with food; however, Skorepa (1966) observed captives deliberately eating bits of stone 3–5 mm in diameter.

PREDATORS: Dogs, badgers, coyotes, crows, white-necked ravens, copperheads, and bullfrogs feed on *T. ornata*. Raccoons, striped skunks, domestic cats, opossums, bullsnakes, red-tailed hawks, and marsh hawks likely take them as opportunity arises. Adult *T. ornata* sometimes eat juveniles. A bullsnake was seen to swallow an entire clutch of newly laid eggs before the female turtle could cover the nest (Legler, 1960a). Western hognose snakes also eat the eggs. Adult *T. ornata* have few enemies other than man; probably more adults are killed by automobiles than by all the predators combined.

MOVEMENTS: Fitch (1958), who recovered 14 marked *T. ornata* a total of 30 times in 7 years, found the average radius of the home range to be 274 ft, indicating an area of approximately 5.4 acres; a female, possibly gravid, moved 1,830 ft in 53 days. Legler (1960a) found that the ranges of males and of females did not differ significantly. The radius of the home range of 44 adults (146 captures) averaged 278 ft (71–913); the average area of the home range was 5.6 acres. Home ranges of turtles of all ages and sexes overlapped broadly, and there was no indication of territoriality or social hierarchy.

Of two ornate box turtles removed more than 0.25 mi from their home range by Legler (1960a), one homed and one did not. A female studied by Metcalf and Metcalf (1970) homed from 1.03 mi to the approximate site of capture, between 23 August 1965 and 21 July 1966. Another displaced female (studied with a trailing device) traveled 1,450 ft in 9.67 hr. She traveled 910 ft between 8 AM, the time she was released, and 10:45 AM; then she rested in a form until 3 PM. She traveled 70 ft the next hour and 470 ft between 4 and 5:40 PM.

POPULATIONS: Population density in certain areas of favorable habitat in Kansas was 2.6–6.3/acre. The total number of individuals on the study area was estimated to be 286. A marked population consisted of 53% adult or subadult females, 31% adult males, and 16% juveniles. Only six individuals had plastrons shorter than 60 mm. Small box turtles are surely not as rare as these samples indicate; they are just more difficult to find. More females than males were found in all months of the season of activity except April and August, when more males were found; the preponderance of females was greatest in the nesting season (Legler, 1960a).

For 29 years Anderson (1965) kept road counts in Missouri on the number of live ornate box turtles encountered during late May and early June. He gave particular attention to one test stretch of 100 miles in a region where they were common. One-way drives over the test road in 1940 yielded counts of 90–156 turtles. Counts made in 1959 when conditions of weather, time, and temperature were approximately the same showed counts of only 5–35 turtles. Anderson attributed this decline to the enormous highway-traffic toll, which seemed to have reduced the populations adjacent to the highway.

REMARKS: Legler (1960a) reported that ornate box turtles occasionally eat the eggs and young of

ground-nesting birds and slightly damage vegetables, but in no instance do these feeding habits significantly affect the economy of man. *T. ornata* probably benefits man by destroying large numbers of crop-damaging insects. In doing so they surely must accumulate considerable quantities of insecticides, and this may well be a factor contributing to their decline.

Distribution of *Terrapene ornata* in the United States.

MALACLEMYS TERRAPIN (Schoepff)

Diamondback Terrapin

81. Note the sculptured shell and spotted head of this *Malaclemys terrapin terrapin.*

82. Plastron of *Malaclemys terrapin terrapin.*

RECOGNITION: A small to medium-sized (10–23 cm) salt-marsh turtle with markings and concentric grooves and ridges on each large scute and having the limbs and head flecked or spotted. The oblong carapace is widest behind the bridge, highest at the bridge, and slightly serrated posteriorly, and it has a vertebral keel that varies from low and inconspicuous to prominent and knobby. The posterior marginals may be curled upward. The carapace is gray, light brown, or black; if it is light brown, the scutes are ringed concentrically with darker color. The undersides of the marginals and the bridge are often marked with dark flecks. The oblong, hingeless plastron usually is yellow to greenish in ground color and marked with dark blotches or flecks. The skin varies from grayish to black, with light flecks. The head is small, flat, and of uniform color dorsally. Although the head and neck are without stripes, they may show flecks or curved markings. The black eyes are large and prominent. The jaws are light in color, and the chin may be blackish. The crushing surface of the upper jaw is wide and smooth. The hind feet are large and strongly webbed.

Adult males are smaller than females in carapace length: males 10–14 cm, females 15–23 cm. The females have broader, blunter heads, deeper shells, and shorter tails than do males, and the anal opening is closer to the body and in front of the posterior carapacial margin.

GEOGRAPHIC VARIATION: Seven subspecies are recognized. *M. t. terrapin* (Schoepff), the northern diamondback terrapin, ranges along the Atlantic coast from Cape Cod to Cape Hatteras. The vertebral keels are not expanded distally and the sides of the carapace diverge posteriorly. *M. t. centrata* (Latreille), the Carolina diamondback terrapin, ranges from Cape Hatteras south along the coast to northern Florida. It also has the keels of its vertebrals unexpanded distally, but the sides of the carapace are nearly parallel and the plastron curves inward posteriorly. *M. t. tequesta* Schwartz, the Florida east coast terrapin, occurs along the Atlantic coast of Florida. The carapace is dark and lacks a pattern of concentric ridges, and the centers of the large scutes are only a little lighter than the areas around them. *M. t. rhizophorarum* Fowler, the mangrove terrapin, is restricted to the Florida Keys. This subspecies has a carapacial keel with terminal expansions and carapacial scutes without light centers. The ventral seams of the marginals and those of the plastron are often bordered with black. The spots on the neck are fused to form a streaked pattern, and the hind legs are vertically striped. *M. t. macrospilota* Hay, the ornate diamondback terrapin, ranges along the Gulf coast from Florida Bay to Alabama. The keel has terminal expansions, and the centers of the carapacial scutes are orange or yellow. *M. t. pileata* (Wied), the Mississippi diamondback terrapin, ranges from the Florida panhandle to western Louisiana on the Gulf coast. The oval carapace has a keel with terminal expansions, and the carapacial scutes lack light centers. The top of the head, the upper lip, and the neck and limbs are black or dark brown. *M. t. littoralis* Hay, the Texas diamondback terrapin, ranges along the Gulf coast from western Louisiana to western Texas. This subspecies has a carapacial keel with terminal expansions and carapacial scutes without light centers. The carapace is deep, with its highest point toward the rear; the plastron is nearly white. The upper lip and the top of the head are white, and the greenish-grey neck and legs are heavily spotted with black.

CONFUSING SPECIES: Our only other turtles inhabiting brackish water are the sliders, of the genus *Chrysemys*, which have obviously striped necks and heads, *Chelydra serpentina* and *Macroclemys temminckii*, which have long, saw-toothed tails, and the mud turtles (*Kinosternon*), which have hinged plastrons.

DISTRIBUTION: *Malaclemys* occurs along the Atlantic and Gulf coasts from Cape Cod to Texas; it also occurs on the Florida Keys.

83. *Malaclemys terrapin terrapin* often has a handsome "mustache."

84. *Malaclemys terrapin macrospilota* has very pale skin and large yellow blotches on the carapace.

HABITAT: A resident of brackish water, *Malaclemys* lives in coastal marshes, tidal flats, coves, estuaries, and the lagoons behind barrier beaches. *Chelydra serpentina*, *Kinosternon subrubrum*, *Chrysemys picta*, *C. alabamensis*, and *C. concinna* also enter these brackish habitats and may come in contact with *Malaclemys*.

BEHAVIOR: The diamondback terrapin spends the daylight hours basking on mud flats or debris, prowling through the tidal marshes, or buried in depressions in the mud. It apparently spends the night buried in mud.

The basking habit is well developed: *Malaclemys* is quite tolerant of high temperatures. Hutchison *et al.* (1966) reported the critical thermal maximum to be about 42 C.

Malaclemys hibernates in the mud of streams or ponds, but hibernation is not continuous: the terrapins sometimes emerge during warm spells. Hatchlings enter hibernation shortly after hatching in autumn and may remain buried until well into the next spring. In Georgia and North Carolina *M. t. centrata* bury themselves rather deeply in the mud of tidal flats in late October or early November and remain there until March, except that they may emerge on warm days in winter. After emergence in March they do not begin feeding immediately; instead, they spend some time shallowly buried in mud banks.

Movements of this turtle on land are poorly known. Females come on land to nest, and both sexes crawl on exposed mud flats for basking. During June 1961 we found a large female crossing a road on Cape May, New Jersey, in midafternoon. She was approximately 500 yards from the ocean and was moving toward the shore; her dryness suggested that she had been wandering overland for some time.

Living in brackish water, *Malaclemys* is subject to varying salt concentrations, which complicate the osmotic regulation of body fluids. Bentley *et al.* (1967) found that the diamondback terrapin slowly loses water and gains sodium ions while in a hypertonic environment but when returned to freshwater

gains water and excretes accumulated excess sodium salts. Thorson (1968) found a relatively large volume of circulating fluid and a low total water content; this suggests that seawater is not a normal environment for *Malaclemys*. However, Bentley *et al.* (1967) believed that the species could survive for extended periods, though not indefinitely, in the absence of freshwater. *Malaclemys* has a pair of orbital salt glands, which excrete excess sodium ions. Schmidt-Nielsen and Fange (1958) demonstrated this salt excretion when they gave 10% sodium chloride, in the amount of 10 ml/kg of body weight, to *Malaclemys*: the salt reappeared as "tears" in the eye. The sodium-ion concentration of the secretion was 616–784 milliequivalents of sodium ions per liter; this is well above that of seawater (about 500). Cowan (1967, 1969) reported that the salt glands of *Malaclemys* varied with the salinity of the environment. Dunson (1970) caught wild *Malaclemys* at salinities of 11.3–31.8%. Acclimation of these turtles to seawater resulted in a 2.4-fold increase in the sodium-ion concentration of orbital fluid and a small rise in plasma sodium-ion concentration. Maximum rates of salt-gland excretion by *Malaclemys* acclimated to seawater varied from 16.8 to 26.6 micromoles of sodium ions per 100 gram hours. In those acclimated to freshwater, secretion was less than 1 micromole of sodium ions per 100 gram hours. Diamondback terrapins have a salt gland that is intermediate in excretory capacity between those of terrestrial and marine reptiles.

REPRODUCTION: Female *M. t. centrata* become sexually mature when they reach a plastron length of about 137 mm, but one became mature at 121 mm. Males develop secondary sexual characters at a plastron length of 80–90 mm (Hildebrand, 1932). Intergrade male *M. t. pileata* × *M. t. littoralis* mature during their 3rd season, but females do not mature until after the 6th year (Cagle, 1952c).

Hay (1904) reported that soon after hibernation ends *Malaclemys* seeks out others of its kind and mates. Copulation usually takes place at night or in the early morning—always in water. The smaller male is carried on the back of the female.

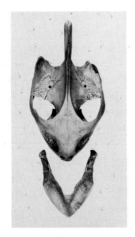

Skull of *Malaclemys terrapin*

85. Hatchling *Malaclemys terrapin terrapin.*

The nesting season extends from April through July, depending on the latitude. *M. t. terrapin* nests in May or June, *M. t. centrata* from May through July, and *M. t. macrospilota* from April through July. The nests are located above high tide mark along the sandy edges of salt marshes and rivers, in the dunes of sea beaches, and on offshore islands. They are flask-shaped to triangular, and are 4–8 inches deep, depending on the size of the nesting female. A triangular nest described by Reid (1955) was 5 inches deep; one side was 4 inches long and the other two were each 3 inches long. A parapet approximately 1.5 inches high had been thrown up along the two shorter sides. The nests are dug entirely with the hind feet, and many females empty the bladder into the cavity, probably to facilitate digging. When a suitable nesting place cannot be found the eggs are dropped at random.

Clutch size ranges from 4 to 12 eggs, and more than one clutch may be laid each season. Captives have laid as often as five times a year. Egg production in captives has occurred as early as the 4th year. In females that are fed through one or two winters, egg production generally begins in the 5th or 6th year; in those hibernating it rarely occurs before the 7th year. Egg production is low immediately after penning but increases to normal in about the 3rd year of captivity. For at least the first 6 years of sexual maturity, and probably for much longer, it is greater among the fed terrapins of a brood than among those of the same brood that are allowed to hibernate. Maximum egg production occurs when a terrapin is approximately 25 years of age. An average annual egg production of 35 eggs per female has been recorded, with a maximum hatch per female of 31.2 young (Barney, 1922).

The oblong to elliptical eggs are pinkish-white when fresh and have thin, easily dented shells; the surface is coated with minute, scattered calcareous bumps. Twelve eggs measured by McCauley (1945) averaged 31.1 mm in length (28.5–35.0) and 21.2 mm in width (20.0–22.5).

Four fresh eggs desiccated to constant weight by Cunningham and Hurwitz (1936) contained about 68% water and 32% solids. This proportion of water is less than that of the chicken egg (72–77%). The original dry weight of eight other terrapin eggs, calculated on the basis of 68% water, was found to average 3.31 g. After incubating for 54 days these eggs were desiccated for 48 hr and the average dry weight was found to be 2.83 g. During incubation these eggs averaged an increase in volume of 3.1 cc and an average total weight increase of 4.8 g; the increase surely represented absorbed water.

Females have produced fertilized eggs after 4 years of isolation, although with a marked decrease in fertility after the 2nd year (Hildebrand, 1929). A normal 90% hatch can be obtained among mature terrapins in a ratio of one male to three females. The percentage of hatch is not increased by the presence of a larger proportion of males. The eggs are rather delicate: even the most careful handling has the effect of reducing the hatching percentage by as much as 75% (Barney, 1922).

The average incubation period is about 90 days; it varies considerably with temperature. The young may overwinter in the nest.

Hatchlings are patterned much like adults but usually are brighter. The shells are round, and the head and tail are large in comparison with those of adults. Four hatchlings of *M. t. terrapin* examined by Reid (1955) on the 4th day after hatching had the following measurements: carapace length 27.0–28.5 mm, carapace width 27.0–28.5 mm, plastron length 26.0–28.0 mm, and plastron width 23.0–24.0 mm.

GROWTH: The scutes are not periodically shed; rather, the layers of new growth push up the older layers so as to give a pyramidal appearance to each scute—hence the name diamondback. As the terrapin grows, each scute extends peripherally; that is, each period of growth adds a ring of new tissue, which is separated from the preceding ring by a depressed line. Although these rings are spoken of as concentric, growth is not equal in all directions. Scutes other than those of the anterior margins of the carapace and plastron grow faster anteriorly; on most of the scutes the center of each ring is anterior to that of the preceding ring.

Young *M. t. terrapin* increase in length about 1 inch/year for the first 2 years, slightly less in the 3rd year, and about 0.5 inch/year in the 4th and 5th years (Babcock, 1919). Few 6-inch terrapins are less than 7 years of age.

Cagle (1952c) calculated the plastron length of 12 *M. t. pileata* × *M. t. littoralis* intergrades as 18.0–35.7 mm at hatching, as 30.3–61.1 mm at the end of the 1st growing season, 24.4–86.7 mm at the end of the 2nd season, and 75.4–107.3 mm at the end of the 3rd growing season. Only 10 of these turtles had rings representing the 4th season of growth; these turtles were 91.1–115.5 mm in plastron length. Six with 5th-season growth rings were 102.5–117.5 mm, and two representing the 6th season were 109.9 and 115.0 mm. Growth rate slows at sexual maturity. The mean annual growth for the first 6 years of five captive broods of *M. t. terrapin* in North Carolina was similar for the first 2 seasons but much slower thereafter (Hildebrand, 1929, 1932).

Allen and Littleford (1955) studied the growth rates of captive juveniles through 2 years of age and found the following average length and weight increments: initial plastron length 30.65 mm (27.1–32.8), initial weight 6.5 g (4.4–7.8); end of 1st year, length 61.93 mm (59.5–65.6), weight 81.8 g (75.2–95.8); end of 2nd year, length 89.63 mm (68.5–95.7), weight 143.08 g (134.6–153.7). Much information on the growth rates of captive *Malaclemys* reared commercially is available in papers by Coker (1906), Barney (1922), and Hildebrand (1929, 1932). Generally, about a year's growth can be gained during the 1st winter by keeping captive hatchlings in a brooder house at a temperature of 80 F or higher. Barney (1922) reported that mortality among yearling terrapins fed in a warmed nursery house during the winter was 7–29%; mortality among adult terrapins was about 0.5%.

Hildebrand (1932) estimated the longevity of *Malaclemys* to be well over 40 years.

FOOD AND FEEDING: Diamondback terrapins probably are scavengers, but they also take live food. Coker (1906) examined 14 *M. t. centrata* and found remains of the snail *Littorina irrorata* in the stomachs of 12; he also found the snail *Melampus lineatus*, fiddler and other crabs, marine annelids (*Nereis*), and some fragments of marsh plants. Cagle (1952c) found only remains of small clams and snails in the stomachs of the *M. t. pileata* × *M. t. littoralis* intergrades he examined. In 14 *M. t. macrospilota* Carr (1952) found the stomach contents consisted almost wholly of rather finely crushed fragments of shells, about 90% of which was shells of the Venus clam *Anomalocardia cuneimeris*. Captives feed readily on chopped fish, crabs, snails, oysters, clams, insects, marine annelids, and beef.

PREDATORS: The adults have few predators other than man, but the eggs and hatchlings are destroyed by crows, hogs, Norway rats, muskrats, raccoons, skunks, and mink.

POPULATIONS: Of 70 adult Louisiana *M. t. pileata* × *M. t. littoralis* intergrades caught offshore in nets, 13 were females and 57 were males. All of the males and only two of the females were sexually mature. This ratio—4.4 males to one female—is unusual: the common ratio in Reptilia is two or more females per male. Probably the ratio was abnormal—a reflection of the tendency of females to move inshore during the nesting season (Cagle, 1952c). Hildebrand (1932) stated that of 1,442 terrapins raised in captivity and sexed by external characters, 209 were males and 1,233 were females—a ratio of one male to 5.9 females. However, many of those called females probably were juvenile males that had not yet developed secondary sex characters. One brood consisted of 148 females and no males; another had 54 males and 93 females, or one male to 1.7 females. Hildebrand found 86 males and 53 females (1.66 males to one female) in three broods obtained by cross-breeding Carolina and Texas terrapins.

REMARKS: The flesh of the diamondback terrapin is renowned for its flavor. At one time the population was severely decimated by hunters, but since the popularity of terrapin meat has declined the species has made a strong comeback in many localities. McCauley (1945) reported that more than 89,000 lb were taken in Maryland in 1891 and sold for 25¢/lb. By 1920 the price had risen to $1.22/lb, but the Maryland terrapin population had so declined that the total catch in that year was only 823 lb. A 1929 revision of the laws favored the turtle, and by 1935 the population increase was such that 5,800 lb were taken. In its heyday the diamondback was so popular that the U.S. Bureau of Fisheries established a program of artificial propagation, at Beaufort, North Carolina. The papers of Hay, Coker, Barney, and Hildebrand document the results of this project and other research on *Malaclemys* conducted there.

Except for its value as food for man, *Malaclemys* apparently is of little economic importance. It probably aids in the control of salt marsh mosquitoes. Goldfield and Sussman (in Nolan *et al.*, 1965) found the virus of western equine encephalitis in the blood of New Jersey specimens. It is possible that *Malaclemys* serve as a reservoir for this mosquito-borne disease.

Distribution of *Malaclemys terrapin.*

RECOGNITION: A medium-sized to large (10–27 cm) turtle with an olive to brown carapace having a distinct but low vertebral keel, a strongly serrated hind margin, and a reticulate pattern of fine yellow lines. The lower edge of the marginals is yellow with circular markings. The bridge is marked with light bars. The hingeless plastron is immaculate yellow to cream-colored in adults, but in juveniles it carries a pattern of dark lines bordering the seams. The skin is olive to brown, with yellow stripes. The post-orbital mark is somewhat triangular and variable in size. Frequently the anterior end of one neck-stripe turns upward across the tympanum, and a few always reach the orbit. The lower jaw is marked with longitudinal yellow lines, of which the central line is the widest.

Adult males have long, thick tails, with the anal opening behind the carapacial margin. Females have broad heads, males somewhat narrower heads. In males the carapace is oval, tapering posteriorly; in females it is rounded. Males are 10–16 cm in carapace length, females 17.5–27 cm.

GEOGRAPHIC VARIATION: No subspecies are recognized.

CONFUSING SPECIES: *G. kohnii* has a crescentic post-orbital mark that separates the neck stripes from the orbit and a vertebral keel with well-developed tubercles. *G. pseudogeographica* has a tuberculate vertebral keel. *Chrysemys picta* has no vertebral keel, and the posterior margin of the carapace is not serrated.

DISTRIBUTION: *G. geographica* ranges from southern Quebec and northwestern Vermont west to southern Wisconsin and, west of the Appalachians, south to Arkansas and Georgia. It also occurs in the Susquehanna River drainage of Pennsylvania and Maryland.

HABITAT: *G. geographica* most often frequents large

86. A female *Graptemys geographica*.

87. Plastron of *Graptemys geographica* showing the seam-following pattern.

bodies of water, such as rivers or lakes. Mill ponds, oxbows, and the overflow ponds of rivers often contain many individuals. Abundant basking sites, much aquatic vegetation, and a soft bottom are required. Rapid currents are avoided. This species has been collected or observed with *G. pseudogeographica, Chelydra serpentina, Kinosternon subrubrum, Sternotherus odoratus, S. minor, Chrysemys scripta, C. floridana, C. picta,* and *Trionyx spiniferus.*

BEHAVIOR: Evermann and Clark (1916) found that at Lake Maxinkuckee, Indiana, map turtles crawled out of the water at about 8–9 AM—earlier if the day was bright and warm—and basked for most of the day. They are quite gregarious, often piling up several deep while basking. From the amount of time the turtles were inactive during the day, Evermann and Clark thought they were primarily nocturnal feeders. Individuals in Elkhorn Creek, in Kentucky, were quite active at twilight.

Map turtles are extremely wary while basking: they dive into the water at the slightest disturbance. Their gregariousness makes them difficult to approach, for when one becomes alarmed and slides into the water all promptly follow.

This turtle ordinarily comes ashore only to bask or nest, but it will move overland during droughts.

Map turtles are most active from April until September. They go through periods of inactivity during the winter but may not hibernate. They are often seen moving sluggishly about under ice. Smith (1956) and Anderson (1965) stated that the map turtle uses its skin and the lining of the pharynx and the cloaca for aquatic respiration in winter; this may be correct, but it has not yet been adequately demonstrated.

REPRODUCTION: Courtship and mating apparently occur in both spring and autumn. Evermann and Clark (1916) reported that on 4 October and later, pairs of map turtles—or a small one following a larger one—frequently were seen walking about on the bottom of Lake Maxinkuckee. On 27 April smaller ones were again seen following larger ones

88. Head pattern of *Graptemys geographica.*

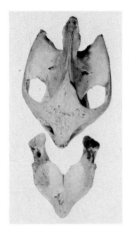
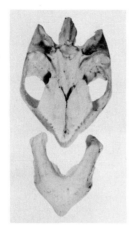
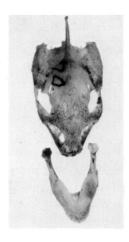

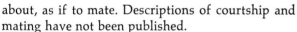

Skull of Female
Graptemys geographica

Skull of Male
Graptemys geographica

about, as if to mate. Descriptions of courtship and mating have not been published.

Nesting occurs from late May through mid-July, with a peak during the 2nd and 3rd weeks of June. Females leave the water and may wander some distance before selecting a suitable site. Soft, plowed soil or clean, dry sand away from beaches seem to be preferred, although clay is sometimes used. Often several trial cavities are dug before the proper soil conditions are found. Most nests are dug in places receiving full sunlight. Most nesting occurs early in the day—usually before 8 AM.

The nest is flask-shaped and somewhat smaller than those of other species. It is dug entirely with the hind feet, and its total depth depends on the length of the hind limbs.

If disturbed while digging, the female pulls into her shell but usually does not abandon the nest. When convinced the danger is past, she resumes digging.

The eggs are placed in a double layer, often with a thin layer of dirt between. The last few eggs may lie in the neck of the nest, quite close to the surface. When laying is completed loose dirt is scraped into and over the hole and the surface is smoothed by dragging the plastron over it; this effectively camouflages the nest. As soon as she is finished the female returns to the water.

Newman (1906) reported that none of the females he found nesting was under 19 cm in carapace length or less than 14 years old.

The dull white, ellipsoidal eggs are soft and easily indented when fresh but become firmer as water is absorbed. A clutch varies from 10 to 16, with 12 to 14 being usual; however, Thompson (in Babcock, 1919) reported nests containing as many as 20 eggs. The number apparently depends on the size and age of the female. Thompson dissected a female that contained 14 eggs in the oviducts and about the same number of well-developed eggs in the ovaries. This may indicate that second clutches are laid during a season. The eggs are 32–35 mm in length and 21–22 mm in width.

Eggs laid early in the season hatch from mid-

111

August through September. Those laid in July over-winter in the nest, and the young emerge during May and June.

Hatchlings are nearly round, and the dorsal keel is prominent. The reticulate pattern of the carapace is bright, and the plastral pattern is well developed.

FOOD AND FEEDING: *G. geographica* feeds primarily on freshwater snails and clams; but insects (especially the immature stages), crayfish, and water mites are also taken. Fish are occasionally eaten, usually as carrion; and some plant material is consumed. Penn (1950) found crayfish made up 24% of the food.

Newman (1906) observed that two methods of feeding prevail. The favorite one is to bite off the extended soft parts of mollusks and leave the shell behind. When this fails the broad, flat surfaces of the jaws crush the shell, and the broken pieces are picked out of the mouth with the foreclaws. While hunting, a map turtle prowls about on the bottom and probes the aquatic vegetation. Food is always swallowed underwater.

PREDATORS: The eggs and young are as subject to attack and destruction by predatory animals as are those of other species, but no one has identified the chief predators. Man probably does not destroy many map turtles directly, but his constant destruction and pollution of the habitat undoubtedly kills many each year.

POPULATIONS: Tinkle (1959a) reported that *G. geographica* represented only 2% of the total number of turtles collected from the Tombigbee River in Alabama over a 4-year period; above the fall line the representation was only 1%. In many parts of its range this turtle formerly was abundant, but pollution and other habitat-damaging effects have thinned its population. In places where map turtles are still common they may seem to be rare, because of the difficulty of capturing them.

REMARKS: The relationship of *G. geographica* to the other map turtles is not well understood: this is the most divergent species. It probably is most closely related to the broad-headed group, which comprises *G. kohnii*, *G. pulchra*, and *G. barbouri*.

The flesh of map turtles is palatable, but the difficulty of capturing them in numbers precludes commercial use. Map turtles are of some economic importance because of their food habits. They consume large numbers of the snails that serve as intermediate hosts of parasitic trematodes of man and domestic animals.

Distribution of *Graptemys geographica* in the United States.

89. A male *Graptemys barbouri.*

90. Plastron of a reluctant *Graptemys barbouri.*

RECOGNITION: A small to medium-sized (9–26 cm), broad-headed turtle with a black-tipped, tuberculate vertebral keel. The 2nd and 3rd vertebrals bear slightly concave tubercles; the 1st and 4th bear a low spine or ridge. The posterior margin of the carapace is strongly serrated. The carapace is olive to dark brown, and the pleurals and marginals have a pattern of pale-yellow to white oval markings, which are open posteriorly; these are often lost in large individuals. The bottoms of the marginals are marked along the posterior seam with a dark, semicircular blotch. The hingeless, deep plastron is greenish-yellow to cream-colored, with a narrow black border along the posterior margin of each scute except the anals; the border tends to fade with age. There are well-developed spinelike projections on the pectoral and abdominal scutes. The skin is dark brown to black, with cream-colored stripes. Head markings consist of three broad light areas, which are interconnected: one on the snout and two behind the eyes. The 12 to 14 stripes on the nape of the neck are connected with the postocular blotches. The chin exhibits a curved light bar, which often parallels the curve of the jaw.

Adult males are 9–13 cm in carapace length, adult females 17–26 cm. Males have long, thick tails, with the anal opening posterior to the carapacial margin. In males the head is small and narrow; in females it is large and short-snouted.

GEOGRAPHIC VARIATION: No subspecies are recognized.

CONFUSING SPECIES: *G. pulchra* has a longitudinal light bar under its chin, a well-developed spine on the 4th vertebral, broad light bars on the marginals, and it lacks spines at the bridge on the pectoral and abdominal scutes. *G. nigrinoda* has rounded vertebral knobs.

DISTRIBUTION: *G. barbouri* occurs in the Gulf coastal streams of the Florida panhandle and adjacent

91. *Graptemys barbouri* has a striking head pattern.

Distribution of *Graptemys barbouri.*

Georgia and Alabama from the Appalachicola River system to the Escambia River. It apparently occurs only below the fall line.

HABITAT: The habitat of *G. barbouri* is a clear, limestone-bottomed stream with an abundance of snags and fallen trees. Associated turtle species include *Chrysemys floridana, C. concinna, C. scripta, Sternotherus minor, Macroclemys temminckii,* and *Trionyx* sp.

BEHAVIOR: This is a confirmed basker, spending much of its time on logs and snags. Shy and difficult to approach, it dives at the first sign of disturbance. It often spends the night resting just under the surface, on submerged tree limbs and snags. It seldom travels overland.

G. barbouri becomes inactive when the water temperature is low. Marchand (in Carr, 1952) found it lethargic but open-eyed, on the bottom in limestone depressions, while *Chrysemys concinna* was active.

REPRODUCTION: Twenty-five females (plastron 20.4–25.0 cm) contained 105 oviducal eggs. The presence of excess corpora lutea and corpora albicantia showed some had previously nested. One (24.0 cm) had three oviducal eggs and eight corpora lutea; another (24.2 cm) had nine oviducal eggs and 18 corpora lutea. Third clutches would probably have been deposited: some of those containing oviducal eggs also had 4 to 33 ovocytes larger than 1 cm in diameter. Each female may deposit up to 51 eggs a season. Shelled oviducal eggs averaged 3.71 cm (3.10–4.04) in length and 2.59 cm (2.22–2.93) in width. The largest eggs (length 3.69–4.04 cm, width 2.65–2.93 cm) were removed from a female containing 11 eggs; the smallest (length 3.10–3.68 cm, width 2.36–2.55 cm) were from a female containing 6 (Cagle, 1952b).

The smallest sexually mature female examined by Cagle (1952b) had a plastron length of 17.6 cm, and the smallest sexually mature male was 6.9 cm long and in its 4th growing season; however, Wahlquist (1970) saw two 2nd-year males, 5.3 and

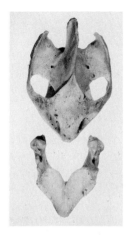

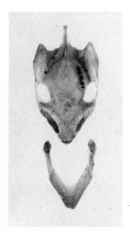
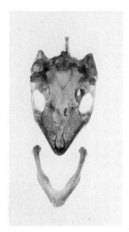

Skull of Female
Graptemys barbouri

Skull of Male
Graptemys barbouri

5.6 cm in plastron length, court other captive *Graptemys*.

During courtship the male approaches the female with his neck extended. He swims around her until they are face to face, and after nose contact he strokes her head with the inner side of his forelegs (Wahlquist, 1970).

GROWTH: Plastron length of hatchlings is 1.76–3.60 cm. Cagle (1952b) calculated average lengths for subsequent years as follows: 1st year, 4.36 cm (3.09–5.10); 2nd year, 5.89 cm (4.94–6.50); 3rd year, 7.86 cm (6.78–9.09); and 4th year, 9.93 cm (9.63–10.22). Juveniles of both sexes apparently have comparable growth rates. Growth slows considerably after maturity.

FOOD AND FEEDING: Crenshaw (in Carr, 1952), examining the intestinal tracts of two adult females from Georgia, found shell fragments of two gastropod species and one pelecypod species, together with four minute plant fragments. Wahlquist (1970) reported that the females eat mussels and snails and that males eat smaller snails, insects, crayfish (probably), and an occasional fish. Our captive male will eat any fish, fowl, or red meat given it, and it readily consumes lettuce. Carr (1952) believed that an exhaustive study of the food habits of *G. barbouri* probably would show sexual differences in diet, because the jaws of males and juveniles are more lightly constructed than those of females and obviously are less well suited to crushing mollusk shells.

POPULATIONS: Marchand (in Carr, 1952) found *G. barbouri* at a ratio of 2–3 to 1 *Chrysemys concinna* in the Chipola River of Florida. Chaney and Smith (1950) caught 382 adult *G. barbouri* there in 13 hours of nighttime collecting. A field crew from Tulane University, collecting in the same locality, found this turtle scarce in 1953. Probably the population in this portion of the Chipola River was decimated by overzealous collectors.

REMARKS: *G. barbouri* is in danger of extinction; it urgently needs to be protected. It should be added to the federal list of rare and endangered species.

GRAPTEMYS PULCHRA Baur

Alabama Map Turtle   XI

RECOGNITION: A small to medium-sized (8.7–21.0 cm), broad-headed turtle with laterally compressed, black spinelike vertebral projections arranged along a black middorsal line. The posterior margin of the olive carapace is slightly serrated. Each pleural has a pattern of yellow-to-orange, black-bordered lines in a semicircular or reticulate arrangement, and the marginals have wide, semicircular light markings. The cervical is nearly square. The hingeless, shallow, yellow plastron has a narrow, black border on the posterior edge of each scute. Often both the carapacial and the plastral pattern fade with age, especially in large females. The skin is dark brown to black, with yellow stripes, and the head pattern is distinct: the interorbital area is covered with a large yellow blotch extending backward on each side, and a longitudinal light bar extends backward from the point of the chin.

Females are larger and have broader heads than males. Adult males are 8.7–12.5 cm in carapace length, adult females 17–21 cm. In males the tail is long and thick, with the anal opening behind the carapace margin.

GEOGRAPHIC VARIATION: No subspecies are recognized.

CONFUSING SPECIES: The range of this species overlaps that of five other map turtles. *G. barbouri* has a curved or transverse bar under the chin, narrow light bars on the marginals, a low ridge on the 4th vertebral, and spines on the pectoral and abdominal scutes at the bridge. *G. nigrinoda* has a narrow head, narrow light semicircles or circles on the marginals, and blunt vertebral knobs. *G. flavimaculata* has a narrow head and solid light markings on the pleurals. *G. oculifera* has a narrow head and broad light circles on the pleurals. *G. kohnii* has a narrow, crescentic postorbital mark.

DISTRIBUTION. This turtle lives in Gulf coastal streams, ranging from the Escambia River system

92. Male *Graptemys pulchra*.

93. Large female *Graptemys pulchra*.

in Alabama and the Florida panhandle west to the Pearl River system of eastern Louisiana.

HABITAT: Deep water with a slow current and a sand or gravel bottom is preferred, and basking sites such as logs or debris are necessary. *G. pulchra* is found with *G. oculifera*, *G. nigrinoda*, *G. flavimaculata*, *Chrysemys scripta*, *C. floridana*, *C. concinna*, *Sternotherus carinatus*, *S. minor*, *S. odoratus*, *Chelydra serpentina*, and *Trionyx spiniferus*.

BEHAVIOR: Little is known of the behavior of this common turtle. Long periods of the day are spent in basking. Like other map turtles *G. pulchra* is extremely wary and dives into the water at the slightest disturbance; therefore, by day it can be adequately observed only through binoculars or a telescope. At night these turtles usually sleep near their basking sites, clinging a few inches below the water surface to submerged objects—often the branches of uprooted or flooded trees. If extreme caution is used they may be approached at this time and collected by hand.

REPRODUCTION: The smallest mature male caught by Cagle (1952b) had a plastron length of 7.12 cm and was in its 4th growing season; the smallest mature female was 17 cm long. He collected a female with a plastron length of 17 cm from the Pearl River on 8 June; she contained three eggs, which were 42.7–47.3 mm in length and 25.0–27.0 mm in width. The ovaries contained six large (8–22 mm) ovocytes. The oviducal eggs apparently would have constituted the first clutch of the season, and a second clutch probably would have been laid. Another female, 20.7 cm in plastron length, was collected 15 July from the Escambia River; she contained six eggs, five of which were 38.0–40.0 mm in length and 24.2–25.0 mm in width. The right ovary had eight ovulation points and the left had six; no enlarged ovocytes were found on either ovary. This female had produced 14 eggs that season: 8 in the first clutch (or clutches) and 6 ready to be laid (Cagle, 1952b). Exposed sandbars are the favored nesting sites.

94. The yellow plastral scutes of *Graptemys pulchra* are often stained with dark deposits.

95. Head pattern of *Graptemys pulchra*.

Distribution of *Graptemys pulchra*.

Skull of Female
Graptemys pulchra

Skull of Male
Graptemys pulchra

GROWTH: Hatchlings average 3.02 cm (2.15–3.53) in plastron length, and the average lengths for subsequent years are as follows: 1st year, 4.37 cm (3.53–5.41); 2nd year, 5.11 cm (4.56–5.93); 3rd year, 6.09 cm (5.60–6.57); and 4th year, 6.74 cm (6.32–6.90). Juveniles of both sexes have similar growth rates. Growth slows considerably after maturity is reached (Cagle, 1952b).

FOOD AND FEEDING: Insects, snails, and clams comprise the diet of *G. pulchra*. The females, with their heavy jaws, can crush mollusks; the males, which have weaker jaws, probably rely mainly on insects.

MOVEMENTS: Hatchling *G. pulchra* react negatively to bright sunlight: those placed on sand within 2 ft of water turn and move to the nearest shade. Hatchlings usually leave the nest within 3 hr after sunset. Tests suggest that light reflected from water

is not an attractant, but there is a negative reaction to dark objects; thus the dark shadow of the forest background might direct orientation to the water (Anderson, 1958).

POPULATIONS: *G. pulchra* probably is the most populous turtle in the Pearl, Tombigbee, and Escambia rivers.

REMARKS: *G. pulchra*, *G. barbouri*, and *G. kohnii* form the broad-headed group of map turtles. However, the skull of *G. pulchra* is unique among *Graptemys* in having the jugal bone excluded from the orbit.

GRAPTEMYS KOHNII (Baur)

Mississippi Map Turtle

RECOGNITION: A medium-sized (9–25 cm), broad-headed map turtle having a dark-brown vertebral keel with the tubercles on the 2nd and 3rd vertebrals pronounced and convex anteriorly. The carapace is strongly serrated posteriorly. It is olive to brown; each pleural has a reticulate pattern of one or more circular markings interconnected by bars, and each marginal has a light figure, which often is open posteriorly. The bridge is marked with light bars. The hingeless plastron is greenish-yellow, with a pattern of double dark lines extending along the seams; this pattern fades with age. The skin is olive to brown, with yellow stripes. A crescent-shaped postorbital mark extends below the eye on each side and prevents the neck stripes from reaching the eye. A straight yellow line extends from the tip of the snout to each crescentic mark. The lower jaw bears a round spot at the symphysis.

Adult males have elongated foreclaws and long, thick tails, with the anal opening posterior to the carapacial margin. Females are larger and have proportionately larger heads. Adult females are 15–25 cm in carapace length, adult males 9–13 cm.

GEOGRAPHIC VARIATION: No subspecies are recognized.

CONFUSING SPECIES: Four other map turtles occur within the range of *G. kohnii. G. geographica* lacks a pronounced vertebral keel and plastral pattern, and some of the neck stripes reach the eye. *G. pseudogeographica* has the neck stripes reaching the eye. *G. versa* has the neck stripes reaching the eye and the light postorbital stripes extending backward. *G. pulchra* has a wide, light interorbital mark.

DISTRIBUTION: *G. kohnii* occurs in the Mississippi River valley from central Illinois and eastern Nebraska south to the Gulf. It ranges chiefly west of the Mississippi River, but there is a record from as far east as Mobile, Alabama.

96. Male *Graptemys kohnii*. The postorbital stripe effectively separates the neck stripes from the eye.

97. Adult *Graptemys kohnii* may retain the intricate plastral pattern of the young.

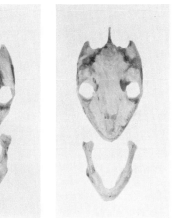

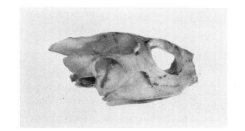

Skull of Female
Graptemys kohnii

Skull of Male
Graptemys kohnii

Distribution of *Graptemys kohnii*.

98. *Graptemys kohnii*.

HABITAT: The quieter parts of silt-bearing rivers, lakes, sloughs, and bayous, always with abundant aquatic vegetation, are the home of this turtle. It occurs in association with *G. pseudogeographica, Chrysemys scripta, C. floridana, C. concinna, C. picta, Kinosternon subrubrum, Sternotherus odoratus, S. carinatus,* and *Chelydra serpentina.*

BEHAVIOR: Little is known of the habits of *G. kohnii.* It is fond of basking and is shy and difficult to approach. Apparently it seldom travels overland.

REPRODUCTION: During courtship the male strokes the female's face with his foreclaws. The only observation of nesting was at Natchez, Mississippi, on 1 June.

FOOD AND FEEDING: Apparently *G. kohnii* is omnivorous. Stomach contents have included the aquatic plants *Ceratophyllum, Cabomba,* and *Potamogeton* and various species of the duckweed family (Lemnaceae), as well as dragonfly and damselfly nymphs, clams, snails, and a blue-tailed skink (*Eumeces fasciatus*) (Carr, 1952). Captives will eat fish, liver, kidney, and lettuce.

POPULATIONS: *G. kohnii* is numerous in the Ouachita and Sabine rivers of Louisiana. Tinkle (1958a) found it and *Chrysemys concinna* to be the dominant species in the Tensas River.

REMARKS: Juvenile *G. kohnii* closely resemble juvenile *G. oculifera* in skull characteristics: these species may be closely allied. *G. kohnii* is also close to *G. pseudogeographica,* with which it was considered conspecific for many years.

Baby Mississippi map turtles often appear in the pet trade, where they are called graybacks. Although attractive animals, they do poorly in captivity and soon die.

G. kohnii is palatable and is eaten locally in the lower Mississippi valley.

99. A hatchling *Graptemys kohnii* is a handsome little animal.

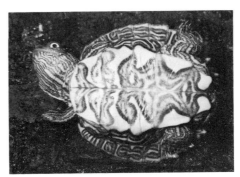

100. The plastral pattern of hatchling *Graptemys kohnii* is more conspicuous than that of the adult.

101. Male *Graptemys pseudogeographica ouachitensis.*

GRAPTEMYS PSEUDOGEOGRAPHICA (Gray)
False Map Turtle XII

RECOGNITION: A medium-sized to large (9–27 cm) turtle with a concave anterior profile and a distinct vertebral keel bearing conspicuous low spines. The carapace is olive or brown, and each pleural has yellowish oval markings and dark blotches. Both the upper and the lower edges of the marginals have a yellow ocellus at each seam. The posterior carapacial margin is strongly serrated. The bridge is marked with light bars. The hingeless plastron is cream-colored to yellow; it is immaculate in adults but has a pattern of dark lines bordering the seams in the young. The skin is olive to brown, with numerous narrow yellow stripes on the legs, tail, chin, and neck. The postorbital mark is variable but usually consists of a downward extension of a neck stripe behind the orbit of the eye; always, some of the neck stripes reach the orbit. The head is only moderately broad.

Adult males have long, thick tails, with the anal opening posterior to the carapacial margin, and elongated foreclaws (especially the third). Adult males are 9–15 cm in carapace length, females 12–27 cm.

GEOGRAPHIC VARIATION: Three subspecies are recognized. *G. p. pseudogeographica* (Gray), the false map turtle, is the largest and most northern of the races, ranging along the upper Mississippi River and in the Missouri River valley in North Dakota, South Dakota, Nebraska, and Iowa. It has a narrow postorbital mark, has four to seven neck stripes reaching the orbit, lacks large spots on the jaws, and has fewer leg stripes. *G. p. ouachitensis* Cagle, the Ouachita map turtle, ranges from the Ouachita River system of northern Louisiana northward to Indiana, Ohio, and northern West Virginia in the east and to Nebraska in the west. In this subspecies the postorbital mark is square to rectangular; one to three neck stripes reach the orbit; and there are two large, light spots on each side of the face: one just under the eye and another on the lower jaw. A broad belt of intergradation exists where the ranges of the false and Ouachita map turtles meet. *G. p. sabinensis* Cagle, the Sabine map turtle, is restricted to the Sabine River system of Texas and Louisiana. It has an elongate or oval postorbital mark, five to nine neck stripes reaching the orbit, and transverse bars under the chin.

CONFUSING SPECIES: In *G. kohnii* a crescentic postorbital mark separates the neck stripes from the eye, and the head is broad. *G. geographica* has a low, spineless vertebral keel and a rather broad head. Although not occurring in the range, two other turtles may also be confused with *G. pseudogeographica*; they are *G. versa*, which has a low keel and, usually, a J-shaped postorbital mark extending backward from the eye, and *Chrysemys scripta gaigeae*, which lacks a keel and has a large, black-bordered postorbital mark.

DISTRIBUTION: *G. pseudogeographica* ranges from the Sabine River system of western Louisiana and eastern Texas northward to the Dakotas, Minnesota, Wisconsin, Illinois, Indiana, central Ohio, and northwestern West Virginia.

HABITAT: The false map turtle occurs in lakes, ponds, sloughs, large rivers and their backwaters, and drowned forests in large reservoirs. It prefers water with abundant aquatic vegetation. Apparently it is more common in slow currents, but it occurs in the swiftly flowing main channel of the Missouri River. The false map turtle is found with *G. geographica*, *G. kohnii*, *Macroclemys temminckii*, *Chelydra serpentina*, *Kinosternon subrubrum*, *Sternotherus odoratus*, *S. carinatus*, *Trionyx spiniferus*, *Chrysemys scripta*, and *C. floridana*.

BEHAVIOR: This species spends many of the daylight hours basking. For this it prefers sites remote from shore. Basking *G. pseudogeographica* often pile up several deep. Extremely wary, they slip into the water at the least disturbance and remain hidden in aquatic vegetation for a long period before resurfacing.

Except while nesting, false map turtles seldom

102. The plastron of adult *Graptemys pseudogeographica*, although immaculate, is often randomly stained.

103. The postorbital stripe of *Graptemys pseudogeographica* does not separate the neck stripes from the eye.

123

venture overland. When encountered on land they seem extremely shy and withdraw into their shells, where they remain for an extended period after the disturbance is over.

In the northern part of the range false map turtles enter hibernation in October and remain inactive until after the ice has melted. They burrow to a depth of 4–12+ inches in the soft bottom; often they select the underwater entrance of a muskrat lodge as a hibernaculum. In the south they may not hibernate but remain sluggishly active throughout the winter.

Hutchison *et al.* (1966) reported that the mean critical thermal maximum was 41.0 C (40.4–42.0), and that the mean loss of the righting response occurred at 38.9 C (38.5–39.4).

REPRODUCTION: The smallest mature male *G. p. sabinensis* measured by Cagle (1953a) was 6.4 cm in plastron length. The only two mature males that still had recognizable growth-rings were in their 3rd season of growth; one was just becoming mature and the other was apparently in its 2nd season of maturity. The smallest mature male *G. p. ouachitensis* found in Lake Texoma, Oklahoma, by Webb (1961) was 7.3 cm in plastron length and was in its 2nd year. Timkin (1968) reported his smallest mature male *G. p. pseudogeographica* from the Missouri River was 10.3 cm in plastron length.

The smallest adult female *G. p. sabinensis* measured by Cagle (1953a) had a plastron length of 12.55 cm. Webb (1961) reported the smallest adult female *G. p. ouachitensis* from Lake Texoma was 15.4 cm in plastron length; he calculated that females of this subspecies do not become mature until their 6th or 7th year. Timkin (1968) found that some but not all female *G. p. pseudogeographica* were sexually mature at plastron lengths of 18–19 cm.

During courtship the male swims over the female, makes an abrupt turn to face her, extends his head, and strokes her head and neck with his elongated foreclaws. When she settles to the bottom he swims behind and settles over her.

Nesting occurs in late June and July. In Illinois,

females contain only shell-less eggs until about 6 July, when nesting begins (Cahn, 1937). Nests usually are situated in full sunlight, and they are dug entirely with the hind feet. Anderson (1965) found a captive digging a nest at 10 AM on 29 June in Missouri; egg-laying began at 10:12 AM and continued until 10:42 AM.

A typical nest descends at an angle of about 60°, is about 5.5 inches deep, has a 2-inch opening, and terminates in a rounded chamber about 3 inches across.

The egg complement ranges from 6 to 13, with 9 or 10 being usual. The elliptical white eggs have soft, leathery shells of fine texture. Webb (1961) reported that oviducal eggs obtained on 6 July averaged 34.7 mm (32.8–35.9) in length and 23.2 mm (22.2–23.8) in width. Six taken on 21 June averaged 38.5 mm (36.5–40.3) in length and 20.4 (18.7–22.0) in width.

On the basis of numbers of oviducal eggs and follicle counts in three Oklahoma females, Webb (1961) estimated the annual reproductive capacity to be at least 21 eggs, in three clutches or fewer, and the realized annual reproductive capacity to be 19.5 eggs.

The duration of incubation is unknown.

The hatchlings are nearly round. The black keel is well developed on the first three vertebrals, and the posterior margin of the carapace is more serrated than that of the adult. The carapace is bright olive, with yellow markings, and the plastron shows a well-developed pattern. Webb (1961) gave the average plastral length of seven male hatchling *G. p. ouachitensis* as 3.0 cm (2.6–3.2) and of 19 females as 2.9 cm (2.2–3.4). Cagle (1953a) recorded the measurements of six hatchling *G. p. sabinensis*: carapace length 3.3–3.5 cm, carapace width 3.07–3.35 cm, plastron length 2.81–3.16 cm, and depth 0.77–0.84 cm.

GROWTH: Webb (1961) reported that at the end of their 1st year six free-living Oklahoma males were 4.8–5.3 cm in plastral length and had increased 1.6–2.6 cm, and 17 females were 3.6–6.0 and had increased 0.7–3.5 cm. At the end of the 2nd year

Skull of Female
Graptemys pseudogeographica

Skull of Male
Graptemys pseudogeographica

two males were 6.3–7.3 cm and had increased 1.1–2.4 cm, and eight females were 6.0–8.1 cm and had increased 1.4–2.6 cm. One female in her 3rd year was 9.5 cm and had increased 2.3 cm. A subadult female *G. p. sabinensis* studied by Cagle (1953a) was 1.72 cm in plastron length at hatching, 3.63 cm at the end of the 1st season of growth, 5.13 cm at the end of the 2nd, 5.96 cm at the end of the 3rd, and 7.45 cm at the end of the 5th. Growth slows as sexual maturity is reached.

A *G. pseudogeographica* lived for 21 years 6 months in the Philadelphia Zoological Garden (Conant and Hudson, 1949).

FOOD AND FEEDING: False map turtles are predominantly carnivorous. Insects, crayfish, mollusks, worms, bryozoa, fish carrion, algae, and parts of various aquatic higher plants are eaten. The narrow crushing surface of the jaws indicates that this species probably does not feed preponderantly on mollusks.

PREDATORS: Many kinds of animals feed on the eggs and young, but man is the leading predator on adults. Many false map turtles find their way into the pet trade, and overzealous collectors have decimated populations.

POPULATIONS: Of 180 *G. p. pseudogeographica* collected from the Missouri River by Timken (1968), 144 were females. Of the females, 36 were mature and 108 were immature. All 36 males were mature. The overall sex ratio was 4:1, with a 1:1 ratio in mature adults. Of 26 *G. p. ouachitensis* hatchlings sexed by Webb (1961), 19 were females and 7 were males—a 3:1 sex ratio at hatching.

Webb (1961) reported that *G. pseudogeographica* made up 15% of the 156 turtles trapped in Lake Texoma. Cagle and Chaney (1950) found it comprised 2.1% of the turtles trapped in Caddo Lake, Louisiana, and 3.4% of those trapped in the Caddo Lake spillway. These turtles are difficult to trap, because they do not readily react to bait.

Chaney and Smith (1950) collected 175 specimens of *G. pseudogeographica* and *G. kohnii* from the Ouachita River near Harrisonburg, Louisiana, and 325 *G. pseudogeographica* and *G. kohnii* from the Sabine River near Negreet, Louisiana. The num-

125

bers show how abundant these turtles have been in certain localities.

REMARKS: *G. pseudogeographica* is most closely related to *G. kohnii* and *G. versa.* Hybridization between *G. pseudogeographica* and *G. kohnii* has been reported.

Commercial fishermen told Anderson (1965) that this turtle was abundant 25 or more years earlier in the Missouri and Mississippi rivers but had become uncommon. They attributed the decline to stream pollution and asserted that an increasing discharge of pollutants in recent years had virtually eradicated turtles for many miles below Kansas City and St. Louis.

The false map turtle is palatable and is sometimes eaten by man; females are especially selected because of their larger size.

Distribution of *Graptemys pseudogeographica.*

104. Male *Graptemys versa*.

105. Plastral pattern of *Graptemys versa*.

106. A J-shaped postorbital mark is characteristic of *Graptemys versa*.

GRAPTEMYS VERSA Stejneger

Texas Map Turtle　　　　　XII

RECOGNITION: A small (6.5–12 cm), narrow-headed map turtle having a vertebral keel with low knobs. The knobs often are dark-tipped, and there is a yellow area anterior to each. The carapacial scutes are distinctly convex, and the posterior margin of the carapace is strongly serrated. The carapace is olive, with reticulating yellow lines on the scutes. The marginals are patterned dorsally with reticulating yellow lines and ventrally with fine dark lines surrounding irregular yellow blotches. The bridge is patterned with fine, dark longitudinal bars; the hingeless plastron is yellow and has a pattern of dark lines along the seams. The skin is olive, with many dark lines surrounding yellowish areas. The orange or yellow postorbital marks (one on each side) are horizontal or J-shaped and extend backward at their lower (outer) edge; these marks may be broken. Fine yellow lines extend up the neck from the tympanum and enter the orbit. The chin often has a pattern of orange or yellow blotches with dark borders.

Adult males are 6.5–8.2 cm in carapace length, adult females 9–12 cm: this is the smallest of the map turtles. Males have long, thick tails, with the anal opening posterior to the carapace margin.

GEOGRAPHIC VARIATION: No subspecies are recognized.

CONFUSING SPECIES: *Chrysemys scripta elegans* lacks a vertebral keel and has black smudges on the plastron. *C. concinna texana* also lacks a vertebral keel and has broad stripes, spots, or vertical bars on the head. *Graptemys kohnii* has a crescent-shaped postorbital mark that prevents any neck stripes from reaching the eye. *G. pseudogeographica* is larger and lacks the horizontal or J-shaped postorbital mark.

DISTRIBUTION: This species is restricted to the Edwards Plateau of central Texas.

127

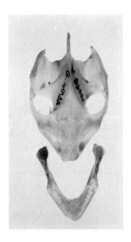

Skull of Female
Graptemys versa

Skull of Male
Graptemys versa

REMARKS: Little is known of the habitat preferences and biology of *G. versa*. A captive male ate fresh and canned fish, chicken, beef, hamburger, dog food, insects, and occasionally lettuce. This same turtle was observed on several occasions to bob its head, at a rate of approximately five bobs per second, at a male *G. barbouri* kept in the same aquarium. Perhaps this represented a part of the courtship behavior of *G. versa*.

G. versa is apparently most closely related to *G. pseudogeographica*, with which it was formerly considered conspecific.

There appears to be an undescribed form of *Graptemys* in the Colorado River system of Texas —a system having tributaries from the Edwards Plateau. The affinities of this form with *G. versa* are unknown.

Distribution of *Graptemys versa*.

GRAPTEMYS OCULIFERA (Baur)

Ringed Sawback

RECOGNITION: A small (7.5–22 cm), narrow-headed map turtle with laterally compressed, black, spine-like vertebral projections and a slightly serrated posterior carapacial margin. The carapace is dark olive-green; each pleural has a broad yellow or orange circular mark, and each marginal is marked with a wide yellow bar or semicircle. The hingeless plastron is yellow or orange, with an olive-brown pattern extending along the seams; this pattern fades with age. The skin is black with yellow stripes, and the ventral surface of the neck bears three wide longitudinal lines. The variable postorbital marks (one on each side) are ovoid, rectangular, or rounded and usually are not connected with the narrow dorsal longitudinal line. Two broad yellow lines enter the orbit of the eye. The intraorbital line is wide and is equal to or greater than the width of the broadest neck lines. The lower jaw is marked with longitudinal yellow lines as wide as the black interspaces.

Adult males have long, thick tails, with the anal opening posterior to the carapace margin and close to the tail-tip. Males also have elongated foreclaws. Adult females are 12–22 cm in carapace length, adult males 7.5–11.0 cm.

GEOGRAPHIC VARIATION: No subspecies are recognized.

CONFUSING SPECIES: *G. flavimaculata* has olive-green skin, a light cream-colored plastron, the postorbital mark connected to the longitudinal dorsal neck-line, and a large yellow blotch on each pleural. *G. nigrinoda* has broad, rounded, knoblike projections on the vertebrals, postorbital marks connected dorsally to form a Y-shaped mark, and four yellow neck-lines entering the orbit. *G. pulchra* has a wide head, a longitudinal light bar on the chin, and broad light bars on the marginals.

DISTRIBUTION: *G. oculifera* is restricted to the Pearl River system of Mississippi and Louisiana.

107. Male *Graptemys oculifera.*

108. Plastron of *Graptemys oculifera.*

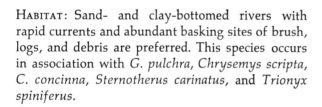

Skull of Female
Graptemys oculifera

Skull of Male
Graptemys oculifera

HABITAT: Sand- and clay-bottomed rivers with rapid currents and abundant basking sites of brush, logs, and debris are preferred. This species occurs in association with *G. pulchra, Chrysemys scripta, C. concinna, Sternotherus carinatus,* and *Trionyx spiniferus.*

BEHAVIOR: The habits of *G. oculifera* are poorly known. It spends much of the day basking and is difficult to approach. It seldom ventures on land.

REPRODUCTION: The eggs are deposited in early June, on sandbars. Cagle (1953b) described an incomplete nest as a hole 3 cm in diameter and 3 cm deep leading to a cavity 9 cm in depth. The temperature was 28.8 C in the nest and 29.2 C at the surface. The smallest mature female collected by Cagle (1953b) had a plastron 12.8 cm long. This female, captured on 4 June, had three eggs in the left oviduct and none in the right. Two of the oviducal eggs measured 4.03 by 2.06 cm and 4.00 by 2.10 cm, respectively. The ovaries contained four ovo-

cytes, which were 1.6 cm, 1.6 cm, 2.1 cm, and 2.3 cm in diameter. When found, this turtle was depositing her first clutch of the season, and she probably would have deposited a second clutch, of four eggs. A female collected in April had four ovocytes, 0.7–1.5 cm in diameter, in each ovary.

Males become sexually mature at about 6.5 cm in plastron length. A male of this size collected by Cagle (1953b) had motile sperm in the testes, but the foreclaws and preanal area were not conspicuously elongated. It was apparently in its 1st season of maturity and was in its 5th season of growth.

GROWTH: Hatchlings are 2.23–3.27 cm in plastron length. Juveniles are 3.57–5.37 cm long in the early part of their 1st growing season and 3.90–5.80 cm long in their 2nd growing season. Juvenile females apparently grow more rapidly than juvenile males: a female 6.8 cm in length was in the 2nd growing season and one 7.12 cm long was in the 5th growing season. The growth rate slows as maturity is reached (Cagle, 1953b).

FOOD AND FEEDING: Insects and mollusks are the primary food items of this turtle, whose scissors-like jaws are well adapted for dismembering such animals.

MOVEMENTS: Hatchling *G. oculifera* showed negative reactions to bright sunlight. Those placed on the sand within 2 ft of water turned and moved to the nearest shade. Tests suggested that light reflected from the water is not a factor, but that the dark mass of shadow formed by the forest background might affect orientation. There is possibly a negative orientation to dark objects at night. Hatchlings leave the nest within 3 hrs after sunset (Anderson, 1958).

POPULATIONS: A sample of 51 *G. oculifera* included 6 mature males, 3 mature females, and 42 juveniles, of which 35 were hatchlings and 7 were in their 2nd growing season (Cagle, 1953b).

REMARKS: *G. oculifera* is most closely related to the other narrow-headed sawbacks, *G. flavimaculata* and *G. nigrinoda*, and in skull features it also closely approaches juvenile *G. kohnii*.

Distribution of *Graptemys oculifera*.

109. Head and forelegs of *Graptemys oculifera* are brilliantly striped. The circular pattern on the pleurals is characteristic of the species.

GRAPTEMYS FLAVIMACULATA Cagle

Yellow-blotched Sawback　　　　XIII

RECOGNITION: A small (7.5–16 cm), narrow-headed turtle with laterally compressed, black, spinelike vertebral projections and a slightly serrated posterior carapacial margin. The carapace is olive to brown; each pleural has a broad ring or yellow blotch covering most of its surface, and each marginal has a wide yellow bar or semicircle. The hingeless plastron is light cream-colored, with a black pattern extending along the seams; this pattern fades with age. The skin is olive with yellow stripes. There are about 19 longitudinal yellow lines on the neck; those on the ventral surface are twice as wide as those of the dorsal surface. The postorbital mark usually is rectangular, and it joins a longitudinal dorsal neck-line that is at least twice as wide as the next widest neck-line. Two to four neck-lines reach the orbit. The interorbital line is narrower than the neck lines. The lower jaw is marked with longitudinal yellow lines, which are wider than the olive-green interstices; thus the yellow is predominant.

Adult males have long, thick tails, with the anal opening posterior to the carapacial margin; they also have elongated foreclaws. Adult females have broader heads and are larger than males. Adult females are 10–16 cm in carapace length, adult males 7.5–11.0 cm.

110. Large yellow spots on the spiny carapace are characteristic of *Graptemys flavimaculata.*

111. Plastral pattern of *Graptemys flavimaculata.*

112. *Graptemys flavimaculata.*

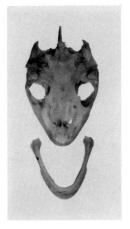
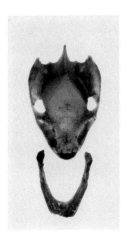

Skull of Female
Graptemys flavimaculata

Skull of Male
Graptemys flavimaculata

GEOGRAPHIC VARIATION: No subspecies are recognized.

CONFUSING SPECIES: *G. oculifera* usually has the postorbital mark separated from the longitudinal dorsal lines; black skin; a broad yellow or orange circle on each pleural; and a yellow or orange plastron. *G. nigrinoda* has broad, rounded, knoblike vertebral projections; postorbital marks connected dorsally to form a Y-shaped mark; black skin; a narrow yellow or orange semicircle or circle on each pleural; and a yellow plastron. *G. pulchra* has a wide head, a longitudinal light bar on the chin, and broad light bars on the marginals.

DISTRIBUTION: *G. flavimaculata* is restricted to the Pascagoula River system of Mississippi and Alabama.

HABITAT: Sand- and clay-bottomed streams with

moderate to rapid currents form the habitat of *G. flavimaculata*. Piles of brush and debris serve as basking sites, and the tangled roots are used as shelters. This species shares its habitat with *G. pulchra, Chrysemys concinna, C. scripta,* and *Sternotherus carinatus*.

BEHAVIOR: Almost nothing is known of the behavior of the yellow-blotched sawback. Like other map turtles it is a confirmed basker and is extremely difficult to approach. It seldom ventures overland.

REPRODUCTION: Little is known of the reproductive habits of *G. flavimaculata*. Cagle (1954a) reported females were mature at a plastron length of 13.3 cm, males at 6.7 cm.

During courtship the male approaches the female with his neck extended. She faces him and extends her neck. He then stretches out his forelimbs and strokes the sides of her head with his claws; she simultaneously attempts to stroke him (Wahlquist, 1970). This behavior is quite similar to that of *Chrysemys picta*.

GROWTH: Growth is rapid: males may mature during their 2nd growing season. In their 3rd and 4th seasons they are 7.4–8.0 cm in plastron length.

FOOD AND FEEDING: The diet consists largely of snails and insects.

POPULATIONS: *G. flavimaculata* is apparently the dominant turtle species in the Pascagoula River system.

Distribution of *Graptemys flavimaculata*.

GRAPTEMYS NIGRINODA Cagle
Black-knobbed Sawback

RECOGNITION: A small (7.5–15 cm), narrow-headed turtle with broad, rounded, black, knoblike vertebral projections and a strongly serrated posterior carapacial margin. The carapace is dark olive; each pleural and marginal has a narrow, yellow or orange, semicircular or circular mark. The hingeless yellow plastron is often tinted with red and has a black, branching pattern. The skin is black, with yellow stripes on the head, neck, limbs, and tail. The postorbital mark is a vertical crescent connecting dorsally with that of the opposite side to form a Y-shaped mark. Usually two to four neckstripes enter the orbit, and the interorbital line is narrower than the neck lines. The lower jaw has longitudinal yellow lines as wide as the black interstices.

Adult males have long thick tails, with the anal opening posterior to the carapacial margin; they also have elongated foreclaws. Adult females are 10–15 cm in carapace length, adult males 7.5–10.0 cm.

GEOGRAPHIC VARIATION: Two subspecies are recognized. *G. n. nigrinoda* Cagle, the black-knobbed sawback, is restricted to the upper portions of the Tombigbee and Alabama river systems of Alabama and Mississippi. It has a poorly developed plastral figure, which never occupies more than 30% of the plastron. The postocular mark is, typically, crescentic and strongly recurved. The light lines that reach the eye are seldom interrupted, and the soft parts are predominantly yellow. *G. n. delticola* Folkerts and Mount, the delta black-knobbed sawback, occurs in the interconnecting streams and lakes of the delta of the Mobile Bay drainage, in Baldwin and Mobile counties, Alabama. It differs from the nominate race in having a plastral figure that occupies more than 60% of the plastron. The postocular mark is neither crescentic nor strongly recurved laterally. In many individuals the light lines that reach the eye are interrupted, and the soft parts are predominantly black.

113. The carapacial keel of *Graptemys nigrinoda* bears blunt, rounded spines.

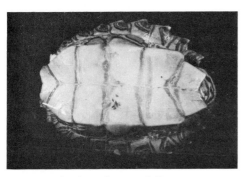

114. The broad seam-following plastral pattern of *Graptemys nigrinoda.*

CONFUSING SPECIES: *G. oculifera* usually has the postorbital mark separate from the broad longitudinal dorsal line; the carapace margin only slightly serrated; and laterally compressed, spinelike vertebral projections. *G. flavimaculata* has olive skin; the carapace margin slightly serrated; laterally compressed, spinelike vertebral projections; a large yellow blotch on each pleural; and a cream-colored plastron. *G. pulchra* has a large head, a longitudinal light bar on the chin, and broad light bars on the marginals.

DISTRIBUTION: *G. nigrinoda* occurs below the fall line in the Alabama, Tombigbee, and Black Warrior river systems of Alabama and Mississippi.

HABITAT: Sand- and clay-bottomed streams with moderate currents and abundant basking sites of brush, logs, and debris are the favorite habitats. *G. nigrinoda* is found in deeper waters than either *G. oculifera* or *G. flavimaculata*. It occurs in association with *G. pulchra*, *Chrysemys concinna*, *C. scripta*, *Sternotherus carinatus*, and *Trionyx* sp.

BEHAVIOR: Little is known of the behavior of *G. nigrinoda*. It spends much of the day basking and is difficult to approach. It spends the night sleeping on brush piles and logs. It seldom ventures overland.

REPRODUCTION: The reproductive biology is poorly known. Males are sexually mature at 6.8 cm in plastron length in their 3rd season of growth (Cagle, 1954a). Two sexually mature females had plastron lengths of 13.5 cm and 14.2 cm (Shoop, 1967).

FOOD AND FEEDING: Snails and insects are the preferred foods. Wahlquist (1970) observed black-knobbed sawbacks swimming after beetles and dragonflies that had fallen into the river. If an insect fell within 3 ft of a turtle that was at or near the surface, the turtle quickly swam to the insect and consumed it bit by bit. The greatest concentration of this species observed by Wahlquist was in the 1st mile of a river below a domestic

115. *Graptemys nigrinoda*.

Distribution of *Graptemys nigrinoda*.

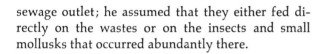

Skull of Female
Graptemys nigrinoda

Skull of Male
Graptemys nigrinoda

sewage outlet; he assumed that they either fed directly on the wastes or on the insects and small mollusks that occurred abundantly there.

POPULATIONS: *G. nigrinoda* is abundant in the waterways of its restricted range.

REMARKS: Cagle (1954a) and Tinkle (1958a) discussed speciation in *G. oculifera, G. flavimaculata,* and *G. nigrinoda*—the narrow-headed, saw backed map turtles. Although quite distinct, they form an obvious species-group. *G. oculifera* and *G. flavimaculata* occupy two of the geologically youngest rivers on the Gulf coastal plain; both Cagle and Tinkle concluded that they had differentiated in situ, so they must have evolved rapidly. *G. nigrinoda* shows the greatest divergence and is perhaps the oldest. Tinkle (1958a) believed that all three species may have had a common origin in the Tennessee River system or the Tombigbee River system during early Pleistocene. Stream piracy in the adjacent headwaters of the Pearl, Pascagoula, and Tombigbee

rivers may eventually cause a mingling of the gene pools of these species.

Tinkle (1962) demonstrated a similarity between the narrow-headed *Graptemys* and *Chrysemys picta* in the marginal contacts of the 3rd carapacial seam. McDowell (1964) found resemblances in the skull structure of *Graptemys* (=*Malaclemys, sensu lato,* of McDowell) and some members of the genus *Chrysemys* and thought the latter to be ancestral to the map turtles.

116. The subspecies *Chrysemys picta picta* has the pleural and vertebral seams aligned, which distinguishes it from all other North American turtles.

117. *Chrysemys picta dorsalis* has a prominent red or yellow middorsal stripe.

CHRYSEMYS PICTA (Schneider)

Painted Turtle　　　　　　　　　XIV, XV

RECOGNITION: A small (10–25 cm) turtle with red markings on the marginals and a notched upper jaw. The carapace is smooth, oval, flattened, and keelless; the highest and widest points are at the center; and the posterior margin is without serrations. It is olive to black, with yellow or red borders along the seams and red bars or crescents on the marginals. Some individuals have a well-developed longitudinal middorsal stripe, which is red or yellow. The bridge is plain, and the hingeless plastron is yellowish, often with a black or reddish-brown blotch of varying size and shape. The skin is black to olive; the neck, legs, and tail are striped with red and yellow. The head is striped with yellow. A yellow line extends rearward from below the eye and may meet a similar line from the lower jaw. There is a large, yellow dorsolateral spot and a yellow streak on each side of the head behind the eye. The chin is marked with two wide yellow lines, which meet at the tip of the jaw and enclose a narrow yellow stripe.

Males have elongated foreclaws and long, thick tails, with the anal opening posterior to the carapacial margin. Females are larger in all shell dimensions.

GEOGRAPHIC VARIATION: Four subspecies are recognized. *C. p. picta* (Schneider), the eastern painted turtle, ranges from southeastern Canada through New England and the Atlantic coastal states to Georgia and thence west into eastern Alabama. This subspecies has the vertebral and pleural carapacial seams aligned; light borders along the carapacial seams; and a plain yellow plastron. The middorsal stripe is narrow; it may be poorly developed or absent. *C. p. marginata* Agassiz, the midland painted turtle, ranges from southern Quebec and Ontario south in the central United States to Tennessee and northern Alabama. Its range is east of the Mississippi River, and extends eastward into New England, Pennsylvania, West Virginia, and Maryland. It has alternating vertebral and pleural seams, dark borders along the carapacial seams, and a variable dark figure on the plastron. This figure is usually no more than half the width of the plastron, and it does not extend out along the seams. The middorsal stripe is normally absent or poorly developed. *C. p. dorsalis* Agassiz, the southern painted turtle, is found from southern Illinois and Missouri southward along both sides of the Mississippi River to the Gulf coast of Louisiana and eastward through the northern part of Mississippi into Alabama; there is a relict population in southeastern Oklahoma. It has a conspicuous red or yellow middorsal stripe, alternating vertebral and pleural seams, and a plain plastron. *C. p. bellii* (Gray), the western painted turtle, ranges from western Ontario across southern Canada to British Columbia and south to Missouri, northern Oklahoma, eastern Colorado, Wyoming, Idaho, and northern Oregon; it is also found in many scattered localities in the southwestern U.S. and in one locality in Chihuahua. This, the largest of the painted turtles, has alternating vertebral and pleural seams; a reticulate pattern of lines on the carapace; and a large, dark plastral figure, which branches out along the seams and occupies most of the plastral surface. The middorsal stripe is absent or poorly developed.

CONFUSING SPECIES: The other members of the genus *Chrysemys*—the sliders, cooters, and red-bellied turtles—all have the rear margin of the carapace serrated and usually are larger as adults. *Deirochelys reticularia* has an extremely long neck, a wide foreleg-stripe, and the hind legs vertically striped.

DISTRIBUTION: This is the only North American turtle that ranges across the continent. It occurs across southern Canada, from Nova Scotia to British Columbia, and south to Georgia, Alabama, Mississippi, Louisiana, Oklahoma, Colorado, Wyoming, Idaho, and Oregon. It is also found in scattered localities in Texas, New Mexico, Arizona, Utah, and Chihuahua, Mexico.

HABITAT: *C. picta* prefers slow-moving shallow water, as in ponds, marshes, lakes, and creeks. A

118. *Chrysemys picta marginata* lacks a carapacial pattern, and has the pleural and vertebral seams disaligned.

119. *Chrysemys picta bellii* has a reticulate carapacial pattern.

120. Both *Chrysemys picta picta* (shown) and *Chrysemys picta dorsalis* usually have an immaculate plastron.

121. *Chrysemys picta marginata* has a central plastral figure. The animal shown also exhibits considerable staining of the plastral scutes.

122. *Chrysemys picta bellii* has an intricate, branching, plastral pattern.

soft bottom, basking sites, and aquatic vegetation are required. Along the Atlantic coast it sometimes enters brackish waters. Painted turtles have been observed or taken in association with almost every other species of freshwater turtle occurring within its range.

BEHAVIOR: *C. picta* is diurnal; it spends the night sleeping at the bottom or on a partially submerged object. It becomes active about sunrise and basks for several hours before beginning to forage, in the late morning. Another period of basking follows, and foraging is resumed in the late afternoon, to continue into the early evening.

The basking habit is well developed: as many as 50 painted turtles can be seen on a log at a time. Hatchlings also bask—an indication, perhaps, that the practice is instinctive. A period of basking usually lasts about 2 hr, and the periods occur most commonly in the early morning, at midday, and in early afternoon; however, some of these turtles can be found basking at any daylight hour. Basking is most frequent from April through September, and some individuals bask during warm spells in winter. Painted turtles commonly share basking sites with other species of turtles. Cloacal temperatures of eight basking painted turtles in Pennsylvania averaged 25.2 C (22.5–29.0).

Cloacal temperatures of active *C. picta* in Pennsylvania ranged from 8 C to 29 C, with a mean of 22 C. Fifty percent fell between 17 C and 23 C, which may be the optimum temperature range. The critical thermal maximum of an adult female was 41 C (Ernst, 1971j). Brattstrom (1965) found the mean critical thermal maximum to be 42.3 C; it was lower in smaller individuals. Hutchison *et al.* (1966) discovered a correlation between the critical thermal maximum and the habitat and geographic distribution of painted turtles. Differences in the critical thermal maxima were found in different parts of the range; the lowest (40.9 C) was recorded in *C. p. picta* from Rhode Island and *C. p. bellii* from Minnesota, the highest in *C. p. marginata* from Michigan (42.2 C) and *C. p. dorsalis* from Louisiana (41.6 C). Hutchison and Kosh (1965) discovered that *C. picta* exposed to longer photoperiods had higher critical thermal maxima than those exposed to shorter photoperiods at the same acclimation temperatures. This probably results in seasonal variations in resistance to temperature extremes. Kosh and Hutchison (1968) found indications of a circadian rhythm in temperature tolerance. The critical thermal minimum is approximately —2 C.

C. picta is most active from March through October. Although individuals may be active throughout the year, most become dormant during the colder months. Active feeding does not occur until water temperatures approach 20 C, but painted turtles may feed lethargically at temperatures of 15 C or below.

Sexton (1959a) divided the annual cycle of activity and movements of Michigan *C. picta* into the following separate seasons: "prevernal," beginning with the final melting of the ice and lasting until 25 March, or when mass movements out of hibernation ponds first occurred; "vernal," from 26 March to 31 May, or when submerged aquatic plants important to *C. picta* grow to the surface; "aestival," from 1 June until 31 August, or when the turtles return to winter quarters; "autumnal," extending from 1 September until 1 December, or when the permanent cover of ice forms; and "hiemal," lasting while water is permanently covered with ice. There is little activity during the prevernal season. During the vernal season the turtles emigrate from the hibernating ponds to outlying bodies of water. In the aestival season they gradually filter back into the hibernating ponds and congregate in the aquatic vegetation. They tend to move into deeper water during the autumnal season, and dormancy occurs during the hiemal period.

Hibernation is not prolonged in these turtles, and they become active during warm periods. The water of the hibernation site may be as much as 3 ft deep, and the turtles bury themselves as much as 18 inches in the soft bottom. Cloacal temperatures of 22 hibernating Pennsylvania *C. picta* averaged 6.2 C; in 20 of them the temperature was higher than that of the water, and in 15 it was higher than that of the bottom.

123. The bright yellow spots behind the eye of *Chrysemys picta picta* often enables one to identify it from a distance.

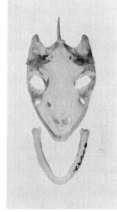

Skull of *Chrysemys picta*

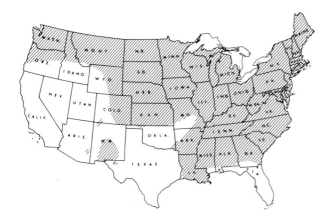

Distribution of *Chrysemys picta*
in the United States.

124. Reticulate melanism commonly
occurs in some populations of
Chrysemys picta bellii.

REPRODUCTION: Male painted turtles mature in Pennsylvania at a plastron length of 80–90 mm, apparently in their 4th year, but do not mate until the spring of the 5th year. Evidence from other populations indicates that maturity is a correlate of size rather than of age. Cagle (1954b) reported that southern male *C. p. dorsalis* may become mature during their 1st growing season but that northern males require at least 2 and possibly 3 seasons to attain maturity.

Spermatogenesis begins in March and reaches its peak in July and August. The cycle is completed in September, when the sperm pass into the epididymides.

Females are mature when the ovaries contain follicles with diameters greater than 15 mm or when there are oviducal eggs. This usually occurs in Pennsylvania at a plastron length of 100 mm, in the 5th year; but mating probably does not take place until the spring of the 6th year. The attainment of maturity varies with latitude and the length of the growing season.

The ovarian cycle begins in July or August and is completed by the end of October. Ovulation occurs the following May. Ovarian activity alternates: in any one season, one ovary produces more eggs than the other.

Courtship and mating usually occur from March to mid-June but sometimes extend into summer and fall. Courtship observed in Pennsylvania always took place in water less than 2 ft deep and at temperatures of 10.0–27.8 C.

Courtship begins with a slow pursuit of the female; when at last she is overtaken the male passes and turns to face her. He then strokes her head and neck with the backs of his elongated foreclaws. Receptive females respond by stroking his outstretched forelimbs with the bottoms of her foreclaws. Between the periods of stroking, the male swims away, seemingly trying to entice the female to follow. After this behavior has been repeated several times the female sinks to the bottom, the male swims behind and mounts her, and copulation begins.

Nesting occurs from late May until mid-July,

with peak activity in June and early July. Most nests are dug in the early evening, but morning nestings have also been reported. The flask-shaped nests are dug with the hind feet in loamy or sandy soil, in the open. Average dimensions of 14 Pennsylvania nests were as follows: greatest diameter of cavity, 72 mm (65–72); diameter of the neck, 45 mm (41–51); and depth, 104 mm (99–111).

The number of eggs per clutch varies from 2 to 20 and differs with the subspecies. The largest race, *C. p. bellii*, lays the most eggs per clutch: 4–20. The medium-sized subspecies *C. p. picta* and *C. p. marginata* lay 2–11 and 3–10 eggs, respectively. Fifteen clutches of intergrade *C. p. picta* × *C. p. marginata* from Pennsylvania averaged 4.73 eggs (4–6). The smallest subspecies, *C. p. dorsalis*, lays only 2–7 eggs per clutch, but this southern turtle may nest several times a season.

The eggs normally are elliptical, are white to cream in color, and have smooth, slightly pitted surfaces; they are flexible when first laid but become firmer as water is absorbed. Eggs in Pennsylvania averaged 32.1 mm (28.8–35.1) in length, 19.2 mm (17.6–22.2) in width, and 7.2 g (6.1–9.1) in weight.

Artificially incubated eggs in Pennsylvania took 65–80 days (mean 76) to hatch; those naturally incubated in the nest took 72–80 days (mean 76). The earliest natural hatching took place on 14 August, the latest on 29 August.

Hatchlings from eggs laid late in the season (July or August) often are not ready to emerge from the nest before the onset of cold weather; in that case they apparently overwinter in the nest. Conceivably, some of these late eggs do not hatch until the following spring. Overwintering in the nest is well known and has been reported from many localities in the northern part of the range; it seems to be a well-established protective mechanism in painted turtles.

The hatchling *C. picta* is essentially round and has a keeled carapace. The head, eyes, and tail are proportionally larger than in the adult. A deep crease exists across the abdominal plate. The pigmentation and patterns of the shell and skin are brighter and more pronounced than in adults. The

125. Hatchling *Chrysemys picta picta*.

hatchling has an external yolk sac 10–25 mm in diameter, and a caruncle that usually drops off by the 5th day.

GROWTH: The growth period is limited by water temperature, amount of rainfall, and availability of food. In southeastern Pennsylvania the growth period is from 1 June until 31 August—92 days. Cagle (1954b) thought the growing season of *C. picta* in Louisiana was from the end of February to the end of December—approximately 307 days—and in southern Illinois from the end of May to the end of October—approximately 153 days.

Growth during the 1st season depends on the date of hatching: hatchlings that overwinter and emerge the following spring grow more than those that hatch and emerge in late summer. Growth is initiated as soon as the shell unfolds—usually 7–10 days after hatching—and the youngsters start to feed. It is rapid the 1st season: some hatchlings double their size. After the 1st season, growth is variable: the smaller individuals usually grow faster than the larger ones. Pennsylvania *C. picta* in their 1st year were as much as 45 mm in plastron length; in the 2nd year, 60 mm; in the 3rd year, 75 mm; and in the 4th year, 90 mm. Once maturity is reached, growth slows or essentially ceases; some painted turtles show no growth whatever from one year to the next.

The longevity in nature is unknown. Sexton (1959b, 1965) referred to *C. p. marginata* that were in their 13th growing season, and Schwartz (1961) believed the longevity was about 20 years. Conant and Hudson (1949) gave a longevity record of a *C. p. bellii* in the Philadelphia Zoological Garden as 11 years 3 months 10 days.

FOOD AND FEEDING: Painted turtles obtain food by foraging along the bottom and among clumps of algae and other aquatic vegetation. Most animal food is sought out, but occasionally they lie in ambush to seize prey. Sexton (1959a) described the hunting technique: the turtle makes exploratory strikes with the head into vegetation to disturb potential prey sufficiently to make it move, then actively pursues it. Large prey is held in the jaws while the forefeet tear it apart.

Belkin and Gans (1968) described a surface-skimming feeding method they termed neustophagia. The head is projected out of the water at an angle of about 45°. The mandible is dropped so that its cutting edge is parallel to the surface; at the same time the hyoid is protracted, to increase the capacity of the pharynx. The head and neck are then slowly retracted until the surface film is broken and water flows into the throat. After several seconds, when the throat has been partially filled, the turtle closes its mouth; this traps the fine particulate matter (neuston) found on the water surface.

Painted turtles are omnivorous: most species of plants and animals, living or dead, found in their habitat may be eaten as opportunity arises. Fifty-six Pennsylvania adults contained animal food in 64% of the stomachs (61.2% by volume) and plant remains in 100% (38.8% by volume): see Table 1. Young painted turtles are carnivorous but become more herbivorous as they mature.

PREDATORS: Thirteen-lined ground squirrels, gray squirrels, skunks, foxes, badgers, raccoons, garter snakes (*Thamnophis radix*), and men take the eggs. Mink, muskrats, crows, black racers (*Coluber constrictor*), larger turtles, bullfrogs, and larger fish feed on the young turtles. In the south alligators eat adults. Man, with his automobiles and pesticides, is the worst foe of adult *C. picta*.

MOVEMENTS: The size of the home range in *C. picta* has not been reported, but it may include several bodies of water. Homing ability is well developed. Cagle (1944b) reported the return of many Illinois painted turtles that were released some distance from where they were collected; a few of these returns required overland journeys, and one turtle removed five times returned four. Williams (1952) released 98 *C. picta* at varying distances from their collection points; of 57 that were recovered 41 had returned.

Ernst (1970e) found that *C. picta* returned from 1 mile with the current and from 2 miles against the current. Those returning upstream had to leave the water and climb a 20% grade beside a dam.

Forty-five turtles studied by Emlen (1969) displayed a marked tendency to orient homeward when displaced 100 m; however, none returned from 1 mile. He thought that painted turtles do not orient by simple positive geotaxis, although downhill movements could partly explain his results. Homeward orientation did not correlate with wind direction at the time of release; therefore olfactory cues emanating from the home pond probably were not guiding stimuli. Turtles released under completely overcast skies displayed accurate homeward orientation. This argues against the use of celestial cues; however, Gould (1959) observed *C. picta* apparently were using the sun to get their directional bearings. Emlen found a deterioration in both homeward orientation and the straightness of the paths traversed by blindfolded *C. picta*. He thought that visual recognition of landmarks is important in enabling *C. picta* to home. The possession of such a simple, short-distance homing ability would seem well adapted to the needs of a relatively sedentary species like the painted turtle.

Ortleb and Sexton (1964) found positive responses to water temperatures and to light and negative responses to water current, aromatic water, and variously colored water. Heidt and Burbidge (1966) reported that painted turtles at hatching prefer red light over green or blue, and Ernst and Hamilton (1969) recorded similar results for adults. The research of Noble and Breslau (1938) showed hatchling *C. picta* were attracted toward the maximum area illuminated by the open sky.

POPULATIONS: *C. picta* was the most abundant turtle at the White Oak Bird Sanctuary, Lancaster County, Pennsylvania, during a 3-year study: seven species were present, and *C. picta* made up 76% of the individuals caught. In all, 929 *C. picta* were marked, and the Lincoln index estimate was 1,913 individuals —a mean density of 239/acre of water (Ernst, 1971g). Sexton (1959a) estimated the density of a Michigan population to be 166/acre during a dry period and 40/acre during high water. Gibbons

TABLE 1

STOMACH CONTENTS OF 56 ADULT *CHRYSEMYS PICTA* FROM PENNSYLVANIA

Food item	No. of stomachs	% occur-rence	Total found (all stomachs)	% by volume
ANIMALS	36	64.3	—	61.2
Planaria				
(*Dugesia*)	1	1.8	12	4.1
Rotifers	3	5.0	10	0.3
Slugs	3	5.0	4	4.5
Snails	16	28.6	—	12.1
Physa	14	25.0	37	8.1
Unidentified				
snail remains	10	18.0	—	4.0
Amphipods	4	7.1	12	3.0
Crayfish				
(*Cambarus*)	4	7.1	4	7.5
Insects	18	32.1	—	11.5
Diptera	16	28.6	100	6.2
Odonata	10	18.0	53	3.0
Coleoptera	10	18.0	27	1.6
Colembola	2	3.6	4	0.5
Unidentified				
insect remains	7	12.5	—	0.2
Fish (*Lepomis*)	3	5.0	—	13.0
Unidentified				
animal remains	5	8.9	—	5.2
PLANTS	56	100.0	—	38.8
Algae	56	100.0	—	14.7
Cladophora	51	91.1	—	7.6
Spirogyra	48	85.7	—	7.1
Vascular plants	22	39.3	—	24.1
Typha seeds	14	25.0	32	10.2
Typha stems	12	21.4	—	12.8
Lemna	3	5.0	—	0.3
Unidentified				
plant remains	23	50.0	—	0.8

TABLE 2

A COMPARISON OF *CHRYSEMYS PICTA* POPULATIONS REPORTED IN THE LITERATURE

Place	Juveniles	Males	Females	Total	Reference
Cora, Illinois	25 (44%)	18 (32%)	14 (25%)	57	Cagle, 1954b
Elkville, Illinois	42 (70%)	18 (30%)	0	60	Cagle, 1954b
Herrin, Illinois	46 (52%)	39 (44%)	3 (3%)	88	Cagle, 1954b
Jacob, Illinois	42 (34%)	39 (31%)	44 (35%)	125	Cagle, 1942
Marion, Illinois	11 (28%)	14 (36%)	14 (36%)	39	Cagle, 1954b
Nigger Creek, Michigan	141 (58%)	51 (21%)	51 (21%)	243	Cagle, 1954b
Sheriff's Marsh, Michigan	521 (53%)	265 (27%)	215 (22%)	1001	Gibbons, 1968b
University Bay, Wisconsin	69 (9%)	416 (52%)	306 (39%)	791	Ream & Ream, 1966
White Oak, Pennsylvania	180 (19%)	374 (40%)	375 (40%)	929	Ernst, 1969

(1968b) estimated 233/acre in a study of another Michigan population.

The 929 marked turtles at White Oak consisted of 40.3% adult males, 40.3% adult females, and 19.4% juveniles; that is, a sex ratio of 1:1 and a 1:4 ratio of juveniles to adults. Small turtles probably were not as scarce as the ratio indicates; they were just difficult to find and catch. There was an estimated 51% annual turnover in the population, with most of the mortality in the young. Table 2 compares several *C. picta* populations reported in the literature.

In an investigation of the influence of sampling methods on the estimation of population structure in *C. picta*, Ream and Ream (1966) found that each method yielded a different size-class distribution and sex ratio.

Gibbons (1968b) found that only about 2% of the eggs develop into juveniles that become part of the population. He thought that most of these juveniles reach maturity, for he found no evidence that mortality increases with age in immature *C. picta*.

REMARKS: Bleakney (1958) offered an explanation for the present distribution of the subspecies of *C. picta*. He suggested that at the time of the latest retreat of the glaciers the painted turtles were divided into three separate populations, which may

well have been separate species: *C. picta* in the southeastern Atlantic coastal region, *C. dorsalis* in the lower Mississippi River region, and *C. bellii* in the southwest. However, the populations did not develop complete reproductive isolation. The retreat of the glaciers was accompanied by northward extensions of the three populations. According to Bleakney, *C. dorsalis* spread up the Mississippi River and met *C. bellii* near the mouth of the Missouri River; hybridization of these two forms produced *C. marginata*, which spread up the Ohio River valley into the eastern Great Lakes Region. Meanwhile *C. picta* spread northward along the Atlantic coastal plain and westward along the Gulf coastal plain, eventually meeting *C. marginata* in the north and *C. dorsalis* in the west. Wherever these forms met, they eventually interbred, indicating that the whole complex consists of a single species with four subspecies. Intergradation between the subspecies has been well studied in several regions; the findings have been summarized by Ernst (1967a, 1970d) and by Ernst and Ernst (1971).

C. picta is palatable but is not often eaten. It is a common laboratory animal, and it sometimes appears in the pet trade.

126. Female *Chrysemys scripta scripta* showing the conspicuous light vertical blotch behind the eye.

127. *Chrysemys scripta elegans* (shown) has a carapacial pattern very similar to *Chrysemys scripta troostii*.

CHRYSEMYS SCRIPTA (Schoepff)

Pond Slider   XV, XVI

RECOGNITION: A medium-sized (12–28 cm) turtle with a prominent patch (or patches) of red or yellow on each side of the head and a rounded lower jaw. Because the species consists of several well-defined subspecies, the following description is highly generalized; see under "Geographic Variation" for particulars of color and pattern.

The carapace is oval, is weakly keeled, and has a slightly serrated posterior margin. It is olive to brown with yellow markings varying geographically from stripes and bars to reticulations and ocelli. The markings on the marginal scutes also are variable but usually take the form of a dark blotch partly surrounded by a light band. Old males often have become black. The bridge markings vary from dark blotches to bars. The hingeless plastron is yellow and exhibits a pattern that varies geographically from a single blotch on each scute (or, rarely, no pattern) to an extensive pattern covering most of the plastron. The skin is green to olive brown, with yellow stripes. The supratemporal and orbito-mandibular headstripes are conspicuous; a postorbital stripe of red or yellow is present (in our subspecies); and a prefrontal arrow is formed as the supratemporal stripes pass forward from the eyes to meet a sagittal stripe on top of the snout. The neck is marked with numerous stripes and a central chin stripe runs backward and divides to form a Y-shaped mark. The limbs have numerous narrow stripes.

Males usually are smaller than females. Adult males have elongated, curved claws and long, thick tails, with the anal opening posterior to the carapacial margin.

GEOGRAPHIC VARIATION: Four subspecies occur in the United States. *C. s. scripta* (Schoepff), the yellow-bellied turtle, ranges from southeastern Virginia to northern Florida. It has a wide yellow stripe on each pleural scute; a conspicuous yellow postorbital blotch, which may join a neck stripe; and a yellow plastron, which usually has ocelli or smudges

147

128. *Chrysemys scripta gaigeae* has a reticulate carapacial pattern and a large orangish blotch behind the eye.

129. The nearly immaculate plastral pattern of *Chrysemys scripta scripta.*

on each anterior scute. *C. s. elegans* (Wied), the red-eared turtle, occupies the Mississippi valley from Illinois to the Gulf. It has a wide red postorbital stripe, narrow chin stripes, a transverse yellow stripe on each pleural, and a plastral pattern of one large dark blotch or ocellus on each scute. *C. s. troostii* (Holbrook), the Cumberland turtle, occurs in the upper portions of the Cumberland and Tennessee rivers, from southeastern Kentucky to northeastern Alabama. It has a narrow yellow postorbital stripe, broad chin stripes, a transverse yellow stripe on each pleural scute, and a plastral pattern of ocelli or small black smudges. *C. s. gaigeae* (Hartweg), the Big Bend turtle, is found in the Big Bend region of Texas and adjacent Mexico. It has a reticulate carapacial pattern, often with small ocelli; an oval, black-bordered red-to-orange spot behind the eye and well separated from it; the chin medially striped, with the lateral stripes shortened to ovals that are almost ocelli; and a plastral pattern that varies from a large blotch on each scute to a large, dark central figure spreading out along the transverse seams.

CONFUSING SPECIES: *C. rubriventris, C. nelsoni,* and *C. alabamensis* are deep-shelled and have a prominently notched upper jaw with a cusp on each side of the notch. *C. floridana* and *C. concinna* have deep shells and lack the prefrontal arrow. *C. picta* has a notched upper jaw, with cusps, and an unserrated carapace. *Deirochelys reticularia* has an extremely long neck and a broad foreleg-stripe.

130. *Chrysemys scripta troostii* has a plastral pattern of paired hollow blotches.

DISTRIBUTION: *C. scripta* ranges, in the United States, from southeastern Virginia south to northern Florida and west to Kansas, Oklahoma, and New Mexico; thence it ranges through Mexico and Central America to Brazil.

HABITAT: Although most freshwater habitats are occupied by *C. scripta*, it prefers quiet waters with soft bottoms, an abundance of aquatic vegetation, and suitable basking sites. It shares its habitat with most other freshwater turtles within its range.

BEHAVIOR: Feeding may occur at any time but usually is restricted to early morning and late afternoon; trapping records suggest that the greatest feeding activity is in early morning. Basking frequently occurs in late afternoon and on dark days, but it is at its height from midmorning to mid-afternoon on sunny days. At night the pond slider sleeps while lying on the bottom, floating at the surface, or resting near the surface on brush piles or the limbs of overturned trees.

The basking habit is well developed: these turtles sometimes pile up in several tiers on a convenient log. They also bask while floating at the surface. *C. scripta* often bask in company with other species of *Chrysemys* as well as *Graptemys* spp. and *Deirochelys*. A warm rain apparently does not affect them, but a cold rain will drive them into the water.

During basking, water is lost through cutaneous evaporation. Boyer (1965) found that at normal summer temperatures and humidities his largest *C. s. elegans* lost 0.43 g/hr and his smallest lost 0.23 g/hr. He thought that heat loss from evaporation was negligible.

Submersion of *C. s. elegans* reduces heat production by as much as 80%. This reduction depends on the oxygen concentration available prior to the onset of diving. Uptake of oxygen from water was found to be only 6% of that from air. A profound reduction in the metabolic rate follows diving, but not until the oxygen stores are depleted. Only a very low metabolism can be supported by oxygen extracted from water, and the metabolism of submerged turtles is primarily anaerobic (Jackson and Schmidt-Nielsen, 1966; Jackson, 1968).

The combined function of the cloacal bursae and the urinary bladder in *C. scripta* is analogous to that of ballast tanks in a submarine. The cloacal bursae are used for water storage and for active, short-term adjustments of water volume. A larger volume of fluid usually occupies the urinary bladder, which acts as a relatively static depot involved in large or long-term buoyancy adjustments (Jackson, 1969).

Cagle (1950) reported that Illinois *C. scripta* were active through a temperature range of 10 C to 37 C. Brattstrom (1965) found that the mean body temperature of two pond sliders was 25.5 and that their critical maximum was 41.2 C. Hutchison *et al.* (1966) reported a similar critical thermal maximum: 40.2–42.8 C.

Pond sliders become inactive when water temperatures drop below 10 C; hence, feeding usually stops after October. Many hibernate underwater,

131. *Chrysemys scripta elegans* has a plastral pattern of paired, solid dark blotches.

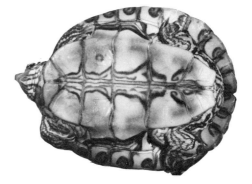

132. *Chrysemys scripta gaigeae* has an intricate central plastral pattern.

149

133. *Chrysemys scripta scripta.*

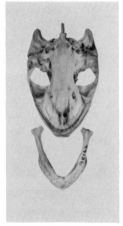

Skull of *Chrysemys scripta*

and others seek protected places near the waterline; muskrat burrows and hollow stumps are often used. Pond sliders usually do not congregate to hibernate unless forced to do so by low water. They often become active during the winter's warm periods; we have often seen them basking at such times in Kentucky.

REPRODUCTION: Cagle (1948a) reported that male *C. s. elegans* become sexually mature when they reach a plastron length of 9–10 cm, at 2–5 years old. Webb (1961) stated that of 47 Oklahoma males 7.7–18.4 cm in plastral length, 42 (89%) were mature. Eleven mature male *C. s. gaigeae* examined by Legler (1960b) had an average carapace length of 13.8 cm (11.5–16.6). Burger (1937) found that the male sexual cycle is dependent on the length of the daily photoperiod.

Female *C. s. elegans* become mature when they reach a plastron length of 15–19.5 cm; in this respect no difference was apparent when populations from Illinois, Tennessee, and Louisiana were compared (Cagle, 1950). Cahn (1937) found that the females first nest when they are 17.8–19.0 cm in carapace length (equivalent to plastron lengths of 14–16 cm). Known mature female *C. s. gaigeae* were 16.9–20.8 cm in carapace length (Legler, 1960b).

We observed courtship in Kentucky from March to early June, but Cagle (1950), reported it also occurred from late September into November. In the breeding season sexually active males seem to search constantly for females during the daylight hours. Several may simultaneously attempt to court a single female. Taking a position in the water directly in front of the female, the male places his forefeet close together, soles outward, and vibrates the backs of his long foreclaws against her head and neck. As she swims forward he swims backward. After a time she sinks to the bottom, where she retreats slowly with the male following. Eventually he assumes a position directly over her—clasping her carapace with the claws of all four feet, bending his head down to touch hers, and curling his tail in an attempt to place the cloacas in contact. After intromission the male withdraws his head and forelimbs and swings backward to assume an almost vertical position, which he maintains during the 15-min copulation.

Such a *Liebespiel* has often been observed in our tanks. The courtship act is quite similar to that of *C. picta*; but despite ample opportunity we have never seen a male of the one species courting a female of the other.

C. scripta normally nests in June and July; eggs may be laid in late April or May in the south, however, and an occasional female may nest as late as August. Captives may deposit eggs at irregular periods; this probably results from the ability of the female to retain the eggs within the oviducts for many weeks when no favorable nesting site is available (Cagle and Tihen, 1948).

In late afternoon or early evening the female seeks an open site where the soil is damp and friable. The nest often is located on the nearest land providing such a site, but a female sometimes moves a considerable distance from the water to dig her nest. In Kansas, Taylor (1935) observed females digging nests on the summit of a hill 400 yards from the nearest pond and about 175 ft above the water level. It is questionable whether hatchlings could reach the water from such a distance.

Often several trial holes are dug before a satisfactory place is located; such shallow holes are especially abundant where the soil is rocky. Examination of these holes usually shows the presence of exceptionally hard soil or a barrier of some sort.

The female digs the nest cavity with her hind feet; if the earth is hard she voids her bladders and softens it. Once a hole is dug to a depth of 1–4 inches, the hind feet are used alternately to enlarge the cavity and form the nest. The excavation of 18 different nests took 26–187 min; the longer periods may have been required by females disturbed by repeated visits (Cagle, 1950).

Nests are exceedingly variable; apparently they reflect the condition of soil. In soft moist earth the nest cavity is ovoid, slanting back 1–4 inches from the entrance and enlarged at the bottom; the entrance is about three-fourths the diameter of the egg chamber. In hard soil the entrance usually is shorter

and the egg chamber almost spherical. Taylor (1935) found a nest that was 11.4 cm deep and about 5.6 cm in greatest diameter and had an entrance about 4 cm in diameter.

Cahn (1937) reported that the eggs are laid at about 40-sec intervals. After the eggs are deposited the female pushes the loose soil and associated debris into the nest entrance and presses it in place with the hind limbs and the rear part of the plastron. It is freely moistened with fluid from the cloacal bursae. Ordinarily the filling is not forced into the egg chamber and therefore does not touch the eggs; occasionally, however, it is sufficiently fluid to come in contact with some of the eggs, and those eggs that are completely enclosed often fail to hatch. When finished, the plug of wet soil and debris closing the nest has the appearance of a mud ball thrown forcibly against the ground.

The ovoid eggs have flexible white shells with many regularly distributed calcareous grains. During incubation the eggs increase in size and become more rigid as water is absorbed. A sample of 221 oviducal eggs from Illinois averaged 36.2 mm (30.9–43.0) in length, 21.6 mm (19.4–24.8) in width, and 9.71 g (6.1–15.4) in weight. A sample of 406 eggs from Louisiana averaged 37.7 mm (23.5–44.2) in length, 22.6 mm (18.4–24.6) in width, and 11.1 g (9.0–14.0) in weight. There was no significant correlation between the size of the eggs and the size of the female (Cagle, 1944c).

Clutch size varies slightly over the range of the species. Cagle (1950) found the number of eggs in 129 nests in southern Louisiana averaged 7 (2–19); in 102 nests in Illinois, 9.3 (4–18); and in 47 nests in Tennessee, 10.5 (5–22). Cahn (1937) reported that in Illinois 15–18 eggs usually are laid, but one nest contained 23. There is a correlation between clutch size and the size of the female: larger females lay more eggs. Of 67 Illinois females the smallest (15.8 cm) contained 5 eggs, and the largest (26.0 cm) contained 20 eggs; of 59 Louisiana females the smallest (15.9 cm) contained 4 eggs and the largest (22.0 cm) contained 11 (Cagle, 1950). Legler (1960b) found that four female *C. s. gaigeae* with carapace lengths of 20.2 cm, 18.6 cm, 19.4 cm, and

134. *Chrysemys scripta elegans* has a red bar behind the eye. It is the commonest turtle in the pet trade. *Chrysemys scripta troostii* is similar but has a yellow or orange bar behind the eye.

Distribution of *Chrysemys scripta* in the United States.

16.9 cm contained 11, 9, 7, and 6 oviducal eggs, respectively. However, Webb (1961) found no correlation between the number of eggs and the plastron lengths of 53 Oklahoma *C. s. elegans*.

In some regions, at least, females deposit more than one clutch per season. Webb (1961) found in Oklahoma that females could deposit three 12-egg clutches per season, but the actual number laid was estimated at 26.4 (mean 8.8 eggs per clutch).

Eggs hatch from early July to late September. Of 200 eggs shipped from Reelfoot Lake, Tennessee, on 8 September, 100 hatched before they arrived in Southern Illinois, on 12 September; the remainder hatched before the end of September. Eggs in 34 Louisiana nests hatched as follows: 1–15 July, 1; 16–31 July, 16; 1–15 August, 9; 16–31 August, 6; and 1–4 September, 2. Five of 12 Illinois nests that were opened in late September contained young turtles; the remainder contained eggs near hatching. The young may emerge in late fall or overwinter in the nest. Eggs dissected from females and incubated in the laboratory at 30 C hatched in 68–70 days (Cagle, 1950).

Hatchlings are round and are more brightly colored than adults. The carapace is green with yellow markings, and there are smudges or ocelli on the underside of the marginals, the bridge, and the plastron. The tail is proportionately longer than in adults. The yolk mass is 1–3 cm in diameter and is absorbed just before or immediately after hatching. Cagle (1950) found the average weight of the yolk sacs of 62 hatchlings was 0.8 g (0.2–1.9).

GROWTH: Cagle (1950) reported that, ordinarily, individuals 2.0–3.5 cm in length are hatchlings; those 3.5–5.5 cm usually are in their 1st season of growth; and those 5.5–6.5 cm usually are in their 2nd season. Under excellent growing conditions an individual may attain a size greater than 5.5 cm in one growing season. Using annuli of the femoral scute, Webb (1961) calculated that the average plastron length of 26 individuals at hatching was 3.1 cm (2.3–3.9), and he found no appreciable difference in size between the sexes. At the end of the 1st growing season 7 males were 5.4 cm (4.1–6.3) in plastral length and 18 females were 6.2 cm (4.2–7.8). At the end of the 2nd season of growth 6 males were 7.1 cm (6.0–8.3) and 12 females were 9.1 cm (6.2–11.3). After the 3rd season 4 males were 8.9 cm (7.4–10.9) and 7 females were 11.4 cm (8.0–14.0). Three females in their 4th growing season were 14.5 cm (12.9–17.6).

Gibbons (1969a, 1970c) found that *C. s. scripta* in an artificially heated reservoir at the Savannah River Atomic Energy Plant reached exceedingly large body sizes and exhibited extraordinary growth rates. This was thought to be due to the increased availability of food plants, not directly to the warmth of the water.

For additional data on growth in this species the reader is referred to the excellent papers by Cagle (1946, 1948b).

Cagle (1950) thought the natural longevity of *C. scripta* is 50–75 years; we think that few, if any, individuals ever reach such extreme age.

FOOD AND FEEDING: The food preferences of *C. scripta* change with age: juveniles are highly carnivorous, but as they become older they eat progressively larger quantities of vegetable matter. Adults are omnivorous and exhibit no obvious preference for animal or plant food. They will take almost any food item available.

Foods recorded from *C. scripta* include algae, duckweed, and assorted emergent herbaceous plants. Animals include tadpoles, small fish, insects (adults and larvae), crayfish, shrimp, amphipods, and various mollusks, mostly snails. Captives readily consume fresh and canned fish, raw beef and hamburger, canned dog food, lettuce, bananas, watermelon, and cantaloupe.

Webb (1961) thought its omnivorous habits allowed the pond slider to thrive in places subject to an alternating availability of different foods because of fluctuating water levels. Mahmoud and Lavenda (1969) found that hatchling *C. s. elegans* established preferences for the initial diet fed them, but that these preferences are transitory.

PREDATORS: Man is the greatest destroyer of *C. scripta*. Every year untold numbers of adults are wantonly shot while basking, beheaded after being hooked by fishermen, crushed as they wander across highways, or sacrificed for research and teaching. Thousands of juveniles and eggs are collected annually for the pet trade; few of these survive the improper care to which they are subjected. Alligators, gars, crows, mink, raccoons, otters, and perhaps muskrats prey on adults. Juveniles are eaten by fish, frogs, snakes, carnivorous turtles, wading birds, and various mammals. Nests are frequently robbed by skunks and raccoons. Ants, maggots, and molds attack the eggs. It is a marvel that the species survives.

MOVEMENTS: *C. scripta* tends to remain in one place, near good basking and feeding sites, where they sometimes aggregate in large numbers. Each individual has a home range that may include two or more bodies of water, between which it makes frequent overland journeys.

Cagle (1944b) marked and released 1,006 pond sliders in a drainage ditch in Illinois. Most remained within 0.5 mile of the release point, but some moved greater distances. In 27 days one moved approximately 2 miles up the ditch, then 0.25 mile overland to a pond. A male recaptured by Webb (1961) had moved approximately 1.5 miles between 23 July 1953 and 21 June 1954. Another male, which had moved about 0.66 mile between 23 July 1953 and 18 June 1954, was recaptured on 20 June and found to have moved about the same distance in this 2-day period. A female moved about 0.33 mile between July 1953 and 22 June 1954.

Cagle (1944b) released *C. scripta* at distances away from the point of capture to test homing ability. Of 51 displaced *C. scripta* recovered once, 16 returned to the area of original capture. Records of turtles recovered more than once also demonstrated homing behavior. However, seasonal movements away from the home range occur during early spring and late fall, in response to reproductive urges or the need to find quarters for hibernation.

Turtles inhabiting shallow waters may be forced to move when the water level is lowered in summer, but they are reluctant to leave established home waters. They can survive without food for several months and will tolerate severe crowding; thus they tend to remain until forced to move by the drying of the bottom. When conditions become intolerable they finally move to more favorable habitats. This ability to move successfully from an untenable place to a better one is doubtless a significant factor in the successful maintenance of large populations of this species.

POPULATIONS: Over the eastern portions of its range *C. scripta* is one of the most abundant turtles. Cagle (1950) reported that in southern Illinois and Louisiana pond sliders constituted 71–87% of the turtle population and were most abundant in the larger bodies of water. In Kentucky they comprised 75% of the turtles we trapped. Gibbons (1970a) estimated the population in Ellenton Bay, South Carolina, as 880 turtles in approximately 10 hectares. The composition of five southern Illinois populations is presented in table 3.

REMARKS: With age, males and some females become increasingly dark, losing all color pattern. Good historical accounts of the resulting taxonomic confusion were given by Viosca (1933) and Carr (1952). The age at which melanism first appears is geographically variable. McCoy (1968) has documented the development and progression of melanism in Oklahoma *C. s. elegans*.

The flesh of the pond slider is palatable: it is eaten locally in the South. Clark and Southall (1920) reported that this turtle was common in the fish markets of Chicago and was sometimes shipped as far as Philadelphia and Washington, D.C. In recent years its popularity has declined, and it now appears less frequently in the markets.

Juvenile *C. s. elegans* appear in great numbers in the baby turtle trade; indeed, this is the most popular pet turtle in the United States. Lately a number of *Salmonella* infections in human beings have been traced to pet turtles, most of which were *C. scripta*. Kennedy (1968) isolated nine serotypes of *Salmonella* and samples of *Arizona*, *Citrobacter*, and *Proteus* from pet *Chrysemys*; he thought they should

be considered potential vectors of salmonellosis when more obvious sources prove negative. Care should be taken to prevent the contamination of food with water in which a pet turtle lives; this is especially important in the case of children, who should be taught to wash their hands after touching the water or the turtle.

TABLE 3

COMPOSITION OF FIVE SOUTHERN ILLINOIS POPULATIONS OF *CHRYSEMYS SCRIPTA*
(after Cagle, 1942)

Locality	Juveniles	Males	Females	Total
Marion	10 (77%)	2 (15%)	1 (8%)	13
Elkville Pond	12 (43%)	6 (21%)	10 (36%)	28
Elkville Lake	29 (55%)	9 (17%)	15 (28%)	53
Grimsby Lake	37 (27%)	58 (43%)	40 (30%)	135
Jacob	175 (15%)	396 (35%)	576 (50%)	1,147

CHRYSEMYS CONCINNA (Le Conte)
River Cooter

RECOGNITION: A large (22–32 cm) freshwater turtle with a C-shaped light mark on the 2nd pleural and a patterned plastron. The elongated, narrow, flattened carapace is highest at the middle, occasionally restricted in the region of the 6th marginals, and slightly serrated posteriorly. It is brown with yellow to cream-colored markings. Dorsally each marginal has a dark area, usually in the form of two concentric circles, and some individuals have a light bar on each marginal. Ventrally each marginal has a dark light-centered spot bordering the seams. The bridge has one or two dark bars. The hingeless, yellow plastron has a dark pattern that follows the seams, may be present only on the anterior half of the plastron, and usually fades with age. The skin is olive to brown, with yellow or cream stripes. On the head the supratemporal and paramedial stripes lie parallel, and the sagittal stripe passes anteriorly between the eyes but does not meet the supratemporals. There are wide yellow stripes on the underside of the neck, and a central chin-stripe extends posteriorly and divides to form a Y-shaped mark.

Adult males have long, straight foreclaws and long, thick tails, with the anal opening behind the carapacial margin.

GEOGRAPHIC VARIATION: Five subspecies are recognized. *C. c. concinna* (Le Conte), the river cooter, ranges from Virginia to eastern Alabama in the streams of the Piedmont and the Atlantic coastal plain. Its markings are essentially as described above. *C. c. suwanniensis* (Carr), the Suwanee cooter, lacks stripes on the outer surface of the hind foot. The head stripes are light yellow, and the plastron is yellow to orange, with a well-defined pattern. *C. c. mobilensis* (Holbrook), the Mobile cooter, occurs in the Gulf coast streams from the Florida panhandle to extreme southeastern Texas. It is similar to the Suwanee cooter but is paler, smaller, and has orange to red head-stripes. *C. c. hieroglyphica* (Holbrook), the slider, is the upper

135. *Chrysemys concinna concinna.*
(*Photo by Kenneth T. Nemuras*)

136. *Chrysemys concinna suwanniensis.*

137. Male *Chrysemys concinna mobilensis.*

138. Male *Chrysemys concinna hieroglyphica.* Note the C-shaped mark on the second pleural. Elongated foreclaws are characteristic of males.

139. A faint X-shaped mark usually occurs on the anterior plastron of *Chrysemys concinna.*

Mississippi valley representative of this species, ranging from southern Illinois and adjacent Missouri south to Tennessee and Alabama and west to Kansas, Oklahoma, and Texas. The C-shaped mark and the plastral pattern are well developed, and the shell usually is indented at the bridge. *C. c. texana* (Baur), the Texas slider, is the most divergent of the subspecies: the head pattern is highly variable but always contains broad yellow stripes, spots, or vertical bars; the C-shaped mark is also variable and may be absent altogether; and the upper jaw is notched, with a cusp on each side. This subspecies ranges from central Texas and New Mexico south to Chihuahua, Coahuila, Nuevo Leon, and Tamaulipas, Mexico.

CONFUSING SPECIES: No other species has a C-shaped mark on the 2nd pleural. *C. floridana* lacks a plastral pattern. *C. picta* lacks serrations on the carapace and has a notched upper jaw. *C. nelsoni, C. alabamensis,* and *C. rubriventris* have a notched upper jaw and there is a prefrontal arrow, formed by the junction of the saggital and supratemporal head stripes. *C. scripta* has a prefrontal arrow.

DISTRIBUTION: *C. concinna* ranges along the Piedmont and the Atlantic and Gulf coastal plains from Virginia into Mexico; inland in the Mississippi valley to southern Illinois, southern Missouri, southeastern Kansas, and Oklahoma; and west across Texas to New Mexico.

HABITAT: *C. concinna* is predominantly a turtle of rivers, preferring those with moderate current, abundant aquatic vegetation, and rocky bottoms. It also inhabits lakes, ponds, oxbows, swamps, large ditches, and cattle tanks. It has been taken in lagoons, brackish tidal marshes, and the Gulf of Mexico. It occurs with most of the other freshwater and salt-marsh turtles within its range.

BEHAVIOR: The river cooter is shy and leaves the water only to bask or nest. The basking habit is well developed: large aggregations often are seen on logs or other favored sites. It often shares basking sites with other species of *Chrysemys* and with *Deirochelys reticularia*. While basking it is very wary: it will dive into the water at the slightest alarm.

C. concinna seems less resistant to solar radiation than are some of the thicker-shelled *Chrysemys*; however, Hutchison *et al.* (1966) found the critical thermal maximum to be 41.8 C (40.4–42.8), which is rather high.

Much time is spent submerged, either resting on the bottom or walking slowly about in quest of food; but the river cooter must periodically go to the surface to breathe. Belkin (1964) reported that not even the tip of the snout protrudes above the surface when a river cooter breathes. The lining of the nares is hydrophobic, so that once the turtle is at the surface the nares open at the bottom of a small depression in the surface film. The turtle is able to maintain this position with respect to the surface, despite the bobbing of the body caused by breathing; thus it can breathe without any part of the body projecting above the surface film.

Belkin (1964) studied the diving physiology and behavior of *C. concinna*. Each of his turtles spent most of the time lying quietly on the bottom of the aquarium with eyes closed; during this time it only stirred, periodically, to open its eyes, raise its head and the forepart of its body, breathe, and again submerge. Periods of submergence ranged from a few minutes to more than 2 hr; the average was about 1 hr. In some the submerged periods were of equal length; in others they varied greatly. Breathing periods ranged from 30 sec to about 4 min. On average, the duration of submergence was more than 50 times that of the breathing periods. Belkin found that, except in instances of unusually prolonged submergence, the time spent breathing after a dive was not influenced by the duration of the dive. Typically, *C. concinna* began to breathe as soon as its nares were emptied of water and continued to breathe for 5 to 20 cycles, each cycle consisting of an exhalation followed by an inhalation and lasting about 3 sec. This was followed by a period of apnea and then another period of breathing; the last inspiration was followed almost immediately by submergence. Belkin also found that the oxygen-storage capacity was sufficient to allow a 2–3-hr dive at 22 C.

River cooters apparently venture away from water only to nest. When on land they are slow and awkward, and their orientation seems poor. Cahn (1937) remarked that fishermen often throw them ashore into a maze of cypress knees and that many perish before they can find their way back to the water. When picked up these turtles withdraw into their shells and remain there for a considerable time.

Neill (1948a) could not find river cooters during the winter months in Richmond County, Georgia, when other species were still active. Perhaps this indicates a tendency toward deep hibernation in the more northerly portions of the range.

REPRODUCTION: The smallest mature female recorded by Jackson (1970) was 140 mm in carapace length, the smallest male 146 mm.

On 21 January, Marchand (1944) observed several Florida female *C. concinna* swimming slowly, usually 3–4 ft below the surface, with a (smaller) male following each. A male would swim up and over a female until they were about even anteriorly. They continued slowly forward—she with head and neck extended, he with head thrust forward and downward until it was only 0.5 inch above hers. His forefeet were held close together, almost touching her neck. The pairs swam in this manner for variable distances up to 25 yards. The turtles seemed oblivious of their surroundings and paid no attention to Marchand as he made his underwater observations. The male's tail was extended straight down and curved forward at its end. Males swimming alone, presumably in search of females, also had this characteristic downward extension and hook of the tail. Frequently, after a pair had swum about for awhile in this fashion, the male slipped backward on the female and curved his tail under the rear of her carapace; in this position they usually settled slowly to the bottom. Marchand did not actually observe copulation, nor did he note a male stroking a female with the foreclaws. In

140. Male *Chrysemys concinna hieroglyphica.*

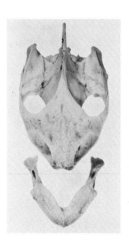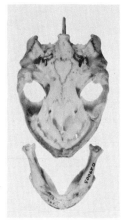

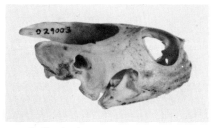

Skull of *Chrysemys concinna*

our experience a male always approaches a female from above and behind and attempts to maintain a position just above her, from which he can vibrate his foreclaws against her head. This kind of courtship behavior probably is similar to that of *C. floridana,* since these species hybridize in nature.

The nesting of this turtle has never been described. The nests are located in sandy soil usually not more than 100 ft from water. Late May through July is probably the nesting season in the South.

The eggs are ellipsoidal and have a fine granular texture and a faint, pinkish-white, dull coloration. The shell is quite flexible and parchment-like. Nine eggs from a large *C. c. hieroglyphica* female averaged 37.6 mm (35–42) in length and 26.1 mm (22–28) in width (Cahn, 1937). Jackson and Jackson (1968) reported that 72 *C. c. suwanniensis* eggs were 32.9–43.3 mm in length and 24.4–30.5 mm in width; 17 of these eggs averaged 19.9 g (16.4–22.4) in weight. The Jacksons obtained three intact clutches of 17 to 19 eggs.

Three groups of eggs incubated in the laboratory by Jackson and Jackson (1968) hatched after 84–92 days; hatching percentages in the three groups varied from 47.0% to 91.3%. In nature, hatching occurs in August and September. Some hatchlings may overwinter in the nest, especially in the north.

Hatchling *C. c. suwanniensis* examined by Jackson and Jackson (1968) retained yolk sacs that were 6.2–12.8 mm in width. Within a week the sacs had been retracted through the umbilical area of the plastron. Loss of the caruncle occurred in 8–17 days (average 11 days). Measurements of 30 hatchlings were as follows: carapace length 35.0 mm (32.7–36.5) carapace width 29.8 mm (26.3–35.4), plastron length 31.7 mm (29.2–33.8), and weight 12.4 g (10.4–13.8). The carapace was yellow-green with numerous brownish-green blotches. The plastron was citron-colored and had a seam-following gray-brown pattern. A dark longitudinal bar of variable width occurred on the bridge. The head-and-neck striping was similar to that of adults.

Anderson (1965) described a hatchling *C. c. heiroglyphica* from Missouri as having a round-arched, dull-olive carapace with a median keel. The pattern was quite intense. This hatchling was 33 mm in carapace length and 31 mm in width and weighed 10.2 g. The orange-yellow plastron had an extensive dark pattern.

GROWTH: About two weeks after hatching, the typical juvenile pattern develops, the hatchling becomes brighter green, and the C-shaped mark on the second pleural becomes discernible.

Marchand (1942) calculated that in 1 year a young female *C. c. suwanniensis* increased 23% in shell length, a young male 17%. The average growth rate for all recaptured turtles was 5–10% per year; the smaller individuals showed the more rapid rates. Jackson (1966, 1968, 1970) found the season of active growth in this subspecies to be from March to November. He found a progressive decline in the growth rate with increasing size; the rate of increase of carapace length was greater in females than in males.

Conant and Hudson (1949) reported that a *C. c. mobilensis* lived 12 years 6 months in the Philadelphia Zoological Garden.

FOOD AND FEEDING: *C. concinna* adults are predominantly herbivorous. Allen (1938) noted a slight tendency of *C. c. suwanniensis* to scavenge but no predaceous tendencies; rather, he observed a marked preference for both aquatic and terrestrial plant food. Marchand (1942) examined the stomachs of 10 adult *C. c. suwanniensis* and found the following percentages, by volume, of plants present: *Naias* 82.3%, *Lemna* 7.2%, *Ceratophyllum* 5.5%, *Sagittaria* 2.5%, and filamentous algae 2.5%. In saltwater habitats this subspecies feeds largely on turtle grass. Parker (1939) found that the stomach of a large *C. c. hieroglyphica* contained *Phaeophycea*, *Oscillatoria*, and Lemnaceae, and he remarked that small captives will eat bits of meat and insects, as well as plants. Cahn (1937) thought *C. c. hieroglyphica* is largely carnivorous, feeding upon almost any animal matter that is available. The stomachs he examined contained crayfish, tadpoles, small fish, snails, many kinds of insects, aquatic sedges, algae, and numerous shallow-water

141. Juvenile *Chrysemys concinna mobilensis*.

142. On the plastron of young *Chrysemys concinna* the X-shaped mark is often pronounced.

plant species. He stated that the scavenging habit is well developed. Our captives, both adults and juveniles, feed exclusively on plants.

Strecker (1927b) found only mollusks (*Sphaerium, Planorbis, Lymnaea*) in the digestive tracts of *C. c. texana*.

PREDATORS: Skunks, raccoons, opossums, and hogs are egg predators. Fish, turtles, snakes, wading birds, and mammals eat hatchlings and juveniles. Alligators occasionally prey on adult river cooters. Man is the greatest persecutor of this turtle: adults are eaten, are crushed on highways, and are driven from their habitats by pollution, drainage, or other forces of "progress," and the young appear in the pet trade.

MOVEMENTS: Some *C. c. suwanniensis* marked by Marchand (1942) wandered 700 yards or more between recaptures; one was recaptured 3.5 miles below the release site. He thought some of this movement could be attributed to abnormal population pressures created by releasing many individuals at one site.

POPULATIONS: Among the 1,022 turtles collected from Rainbow Springs Run, Marion County, Florida, Marchand (1942) found 37.3% *C. c. suwanniensis* and 33.3% *C. floridana peninsularis*.

REMARKS: Pritchard (1967a) synonomized *C. concinna* and *C. floridana*. He pointed out that although some authorities place the races having a plastral pattern in the *C. concinna* group and those without a plastral pattern in the *C. floridana* group, this convenient system is not accurate: the two forms intergrade completely. However, this probably is not intergradation but hybridization: although *C. concinna* and *C. floridana* are quite closely related, cranial and other osteologic characters show them to be separate species (McDowell, 1964; Weaver and Rose, 1967), as does an analysis of their serum proteins (Zweig and Crenshaw, 1957).

Allen (1950) reported that he often heard *C. c.*

suwanniensis utter a short, deep-throated grunt. The calling turtle always was afloat on the surface with head held high, and the call was given with the mouth closed; the neck pulsated with each grunt. He thought it likely that this utterance played a part in courtship. No other observations of this behavior have been reported.

The flesh of *C. concinna* is palatable and is often eaten locally in the South. It is said that *C. c. suwanniensis*—known locally as "Suwannee chicken"—is the most tasty of the subspecies.

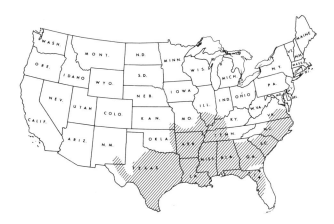

Distribution of *Chrysemys concinna* in the United States.

CHRYSEMYS FLORIDANA (Le Conte)

Cooter XVII

RECOGNITION: A large (22–40 cm) freshwater turtle with a wide transverse stripe on the 2nd pleural and an immaculate, yellow, hingeless plastron. The elongated and highly arched carapace has the highest point at the center and the widest point behind the center, and the posterior margin is slightly serrated. The carapace is brownish with yellow markings; the wide stripe on the 2nd pleural may be forked at the upper or the lower end or at both. Each marginal has a central yellow bar on the dorsal surface and, on the ventral surface in some individuals, a dark, light-centered spot, which usually covers the posterior seam. The skin is brown to black, with yellow stripes. The supratemporal and paramedial stripes usually are joined behind the eyes. The underside of the neck is marked with wide yellow stripes, and a central chin-stripe extends back and divides to form a Y-shaped mark.

Males have elongated foreclaws and long, thick tails, with the anal opening behind the carapacial margin. Males are slightly smaller and flatter than females which sometimes show an indentation in the carapace just anterior to the bridge.

143. Subadult *Chrysemys floridana peninsularis.*

GEOGRAPHIC VARIATION: There are three subspecies. *C. f. floridana* (LeConte), the Florida cooter, occurs on the Atlantic coastal plain from Virginia to northern Florida and west on the Gulf coastal plain to Alabama. This race has numerous head-stripes, but they do not form hairpin markings. *C. f. peninsularis* (Carr), the peninsula cooter, is restricted to peninsular Florida. It has a pair of light lines resembling hairpins on the top of its head; these may be broken or incomplete. *C. f. hoyi* (Agassiz), the Missouri slider, inhabits the lower Mississippi valley and extends west along the Texas coast. It has numerous broken and twisted head-stripes and is the smallest of the three races.

144. The plastron of all *Chrysemys floridana* is immaculate.

CONFUSING SPECIES: In *C. scripta, C. rubiventris, C. nelsoni,* and *C. alabamenis* there is a prefrontal arrow, and in the latter three the upper jaw is notched.

161

C. concinna has a C-shaped mark on the 2nd pleural and has a patterned plastron. *C. picta* is much smaller and has a notched upper jaw and an unserrated carapace. *Deirochelys reticularia* has a netlike pattern of light lines on the carapace, an extremely long neck, and a very wide foreleg-stripe.

DISTRIBUTION: *C. floridana* ranges along the Atlantic coastal plain from Chesapeake Bay to about the Tamiami Trail in southern Florida; west across the Gulf coastal plain to eastern Texas; and north in the Mississippi valley to eastern Oklahoma, southeastern Kansas, southern Missouri, and southern Illinois.

HABITAT: The cooter inhabits almost any aquatic habitat having a slow current, soft bottom, basking sites, and abundant aquatic vegetation. It can be found in association with almost any freshwater turtle occurring within its range.

BEHAVIOR: *C. floridana* is quite fond of basking and spends many of the daylight hours so occupied. Cooters are gregarious: often as many as 20 or 30 may bask on the same log. Such a group is difficult to approach, but individuals do not seem especially wary. In Florida they often bask with *C. nelsoni* and *C. concinna*; however, they apparently cannot tolerate direct sun for as long as *C. nelsoni* (Pritchard and Greenhood, 1968). This is surprising, because Hutchison *et al.* (1966) found that *C. floridana* has a critical thermal maximum of 40.85 C (40.4–41.3) which is slightly above that of *C. nelsoni*. Bogert and Cowles (1947) kept a large specimen for 40 hr in a chamber in which the temperature was maintained at 38 C and the relative humidity at 37%. During this period the turtle maintained a body temperature of 35.0–36.9 C and lost 14.4% of its original weight. When replaced in water it regained its original weight plus 115 g.

The cooter is predominantly diurnal, and it is most active early and late in the day. Carr (1952), however, observed on several nights that two or three were feeding when most were asleep or, at least, inactive. Marchand (1942) found that cooters

spent midday in hiding along the edges of a stream, with concentrations in such places as caves, sunken trees, and patches of water lilies (*Nymphaea*). At night they slept on the bottom or among the water lily stems.

In the deep South *C. floridana* does not truly hibernate, but it does become less active, and during cold spells it sometimes burrows into the mud. Cooters are more frequently terrestrial than most other *Chrysemys*. Carr (1952) found that during unseasonably warm days in winter they often wander about on land; although sometimes this may be attributed to a migratory urge set up by low water-levels in their home ponds, at other times no satisfactory explanation is evident. Both sexes wander; therefore a nesting urge cannot be the driving force in all cases. Many of the wandering cooters are killed by predators or automobiles, and others perish when they become overheated.

REPRODUCTION: The courtship of *C. floridana* has not been described but probably is similar to that of *C. concinna*, with which it hybridizes.

The length of the nesting period varies geographically. *C. f. peninsularis* usually nests from November to June, but there are indications that it may do so sporadically throughout the year. South Georgia *C. f. floridana* nest during May and June, and Kansas *C. f. hoyi* nest in June (Carr, 1952; Smith, 1956).

The nest is roughly flask-shaped and is dug with the hind feet in friable soil in open places. Sometimes there are one or more additional cavities, located 2–5 inches from the principal nest and ordinarily containing a single egg. Carr (1952) observed that peninsula cooters kick out trenches on either side of the nest and rest their hind feet in these during oviposition.

Nesting usually begins in the afternoon and sometimes continues until late at night. Cooters nest at least twice a year, and the number of eggs per clutch depends on the number of times the turtle has previously nested during the season. A clutch is usually 20 but ranges from 12 to 29. Goff and Goff (1932) found that an average of 46 sec (25–105) elapsed between the laying of each of 13 eggs, but Allen (1938) reported an interval of 20–29 sec for another turtle.

The elliptical eggs have white, well-calcified shells with a coarse granular surface; they are soft when laid but rapidly harden. Variable in size, they average 34 mm (29–40.5) in length and 25 mm (22–27) in width. Goff and Goff (1932) reported that 19 eggs weighed from 11.5–12.5 g.

Incubation lasts 80–150 days, depending on soil temperature. In the northern portions of the range hatchlings may overwinter in the nest.

Hatchlings are brighter than adults. The carapace is about as wide as long, has a well-developed keel, and is more highly arched and flared than that of adults. The immaculate yellow plastron bears a yolk sac at hatching; this soon disappears, leaving a yolk scar. The caruncle persists for more than a week. Sixteen hatchlings were 27.0–33.0 mm in length, 25.0–31.2 mm in width, and 16.1–18.2 mm in depth (Carr, 1952). Goff and Goff (1932) found that hatchlings averaged 9.1 g.

GROWTH: The hatchling shell remains comparatively broad for some time; at maturity it has lost about 10% of its relative width. The depth of the shell relative to its length appears to remain fairly constant with growth. Carr (1952) measured a series of 30 *C. f. floridana* from North and South Carolina and found that in growing from a length of 46 mm to 240 mm the shell became 24% narrower and 9% lower and the head became 11.2% narrower, compared with the total shell-length. The greatest growth shown by any *C. f. peninsularis* retaken by Marchand (1942) was that of a male, which increased its initial 160-mm shell-length about 12% per year; the next greatest was that of a 240-mm female, which gained 8%. The greater gains were made by the smaller adults. (Juveniles were not studied.)

FOOD AND FEEDING: Adult *C. floridana* are largely herbivorous; they eat a wide variety of aquatic plants, including *Sagittaria, Ceratophyllum, Myriophyllum, Naias,* and *Lemna,* and they probably also

145. Head pattern of *Chrysemys floridana peninsularis.*

146. Old male *Chrysemys floridana hoyi.*

147. Head pattern of *Chrysemys floridana hoyi.*

163

eat algae. In captivity they accept lettuce, spinach, cabbage, watermelon, cantaloupe, and bananas. The young take animal food but become less carnivorous as they grow older.

PREDATORS: Many eggs are destroyed by skunks, raccoons, opossums, bears, and hogs. The young are eaten by large wading birds, large fish, snakes, carnivorous turtles, and various mammals. Adults are eaten by alligators.

MOVEMENTS: Marchand (1945) reported that of 33 marked cooters retaken once, 16 were at the release point; 6 of these were recaptured within 1 month, and the greatest elapsed time was 7 months. Of the 17 cooters that had moved, 8 wandered 100 yards or less, and the greatest distance was 300 yards (three cases; 7 months, 1.5 months, and 7 days, respectively). Of eight retaken twice, the greatest distance traveled was 265 yards, in a month's time. Two showed no movement, and two had returned to the site of initial capture. Of three that were retaken three times, two showed attachments for certain places, but the third wandered extensively, covering 400 yards in 19 days, although the total distance from the initial capture point was only 225 yards. One recaptured four times had not moved on one occasion, and the maximum distance covered in any of its movements was 175 yards in 18 days. Marchand (1945) also studied the movements of *C. floridana* and *C. concinna* at another site. Here 20 returns were obtained; they were

equally divided between the two species, and 14 of the turtles had wandered 700 yards or more.

Gibbons and Smith (1968) discovered that *C. floridana* uses the sun to find a particular direction when moving overland.

POPULATIONS: The total turtle population of Rainbow Springs Run, Marion County, Florida included 33.3% *C. floridana* and 37.3% *C. concinna* (Marchand, 1942).

REMARKS: Both the flesh and the eggs of the cooter are palatable and are eaten locally in the South, but this turtle is seldom marketed. Young cooters occasionally appear in the pet trade.

Pope (1939) reported a local decrease in cooters after pollution of waters by sewage and industrial wastes in Raleigh, North Carolina.

Despite the local abundance of this species, little is known of its biology.

 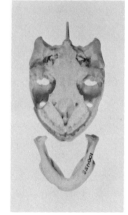

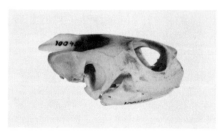

Skull of *Chrysemys floridana*

164   Distribution of *Chrysemys floridana*.

148. Subadult *Chrysemys rubriventris rubriventris.*

CHRYSEMYS RUBRIVENTRIS (Le Conte)

Red-bellied Turtle

RECOGNITION: A large (25–40 cm) freshwater turtle having a reddish plastron and a prominent notch at the tip of the upper jaw, with a toothlike cusp on each side. The elongated carapace usually has the highest point at the middle and widest point behind the middle, usually is flattened dorsally, and is slightly serrated posteriorly. It is brown to black, with red or yellow markings on the pleurals and marginals. The 2nd pleural has a wide, light, central transverse band, which is forked at the upper or the lower end or at both ends. Each marginal has a red bar on the upper surface and a dark blotch with a light central spot on the lower surface. Melanism is common in old individuals. The bridge and the plastron are deep. The hingeless plastron is reddish-orange and in the young has a dark mark that spreads along the seams; this fades with age and is absent in old individuals. The bridge has a wide dark bar. The skin is dark olive with yellow stripes. On the head, the sagittal stripe passes anteriorly between the eyes and meets the joined supratemporal stripes on the snout, forming the prefrontal arrow that is characteristic of the red-bellied group. Five to eight stripes occur between the supratemporals behind the eyes. The paramedial stripes pass forward from the neck across the occipital region and terminate between the orbits. A supratemporal stripe bends upward from the neck on each side and enters the orbit.

Males have long, straight foreclaws; large, thick tails, with the anal opening behind the carapacial margin; and lower, slightly narrower shells than females. Females are slightly larger than males.

GEOGRAPHIC VARIATION: Two subspecies are recognized. *C. r. rubriventris* (Le Conte), the red-bellied turtle, ranges on the Atlantic coastal plain from central New Jersey south to northeastern North Carolina and west up the Potomac River to eastern West Virginia. *C. r. bangsi* (Babcock), the Plymouth turtle, is restricted to relict populations in Plymouth County and Naushon Island, Massachusetts.

149. Plastral pattern of subadult *Chrysemys rubriventris rubriventris*. This pattern fades with age and may be absent in old individuals.

150. Head pattern of *Chrysemys rubriventris rubriventris*.

C. r. bangsi is recognized on the basis of a higher carapace than that of the nominate race. In *C. r. bangsi* the greatest length of the carapace is 2.4 times its greatest height; in *C. r. rubriventris*, 2.6 times. Studies by Conant (1951b) on Pennsylvania individuals and by Graham (1969) on those of Naushon Island indicated a variation encompassing the supposedly diagnostic extremes; this character may well be insufficient to distinguish the populations.

CONFUSING SPECIES: *C. floridana* and *C. concinna* usually lack a notch at the tip of the upper jaw and a prefrontal arrow; also, *C. concinna* has a C-shaped figure on the 2nd pleural. *C. picta* lacks serrations on the carapace and has two large yellow marks on each side of the head.

DISTRIBUTION: *C. rubriventris* occurs along the Atlantic coastal plain from central New Jersey south to northeastern North Carolina and west up the Potomac River to eastern West Virginia. It also has relict populations in Plymouth County and Naushon Island, Massachusetts.

HABITAT: Relatively large, deep bodies of water with basking sites are the preferred habitat. The red-bellied turtle has been found in creeks, rivers, marshes, ponds, and lakes and has also been taken from brackish water. The New England form is restricted to ponds. *C. rubriventris* has been found with *Chrysemys picta*, *C. floridana*, *Chelydra serpentina*, *Sternotherus odoratus*, and *Kinosternon subrubrum*.

BEHAVIOR: The red-bellied turtle spends much of the day lying in the sun, on logs and rocks. It is shy and difficult to approach, and the basking sites usually are adjacent to deep water, into which it dives at the slightest alarm. Apparently it ventures on land only to lay eggs.

New England red-bellied turtles are active from May until mid-October, except for a short period of aestivation, in August (Babcock, 1916). The colder months are spent in hibernation, buried in or resting on some deep mud bottom.

166

REPRODUCTION: Courtship and mating in *C. rubriventris* have not been described.

Nesting takes place in June and July. The nest is dug with the hind feet, most frequently in sandy clay or loam. The site usually is in full sunlight in a cultivated tract adjacent to the water and may be more than 100 ft from the water's edge. The nest is flask-shaped and averages about 4 inches deep and 4 inches wide at the bottom, with a 3-inch opening. When laying is completed the female scrapes dirt into and over the hole, using her hind feet to do so. She packs the dirt firmly by rising as high as possible on all four legs and dropping heavily onto the nest site. Nesting may occur more than once a season; Conant and Bailey (1936) reported that a New Jersey female, caught on 26 June, laid 6 eggs on 21 July and 12 more on 10 August.

The eggs are elliptical and white-shelled. They are 25–37 mm in length, and about 19 mm in width, and they vary with the size of the female. The usual complement numbers 10 to 12, but Smith (1904) remarked that the largest females lay as many as 35 eggs and possibly more.

The young probably hatch in late summer, but the actual incubation period is unknown. They may overwinter in the nest and emerge the following spring.

Hatchlings are brightly colored and have rounded, keeled carapaces. The reddish plastron has a large dark figure that spreads somewhat along the seams. This pattern is similar to that of *C. concinna*.

GROWTH: Graham (1969) reported that specimens 12.94 cm and 23.02 cm in carapace length were in their 4th and 9th growing seasons, respectively.

FOOD AND FEEDING: The red-bellied turtle apparently is omnivorous. Known food items include snails, fish, tadpoles, crayfish, and aquatic vegetation. The fact that it is not often lured into traps baited with fish seems to indicate that fish are not a normal part of the diet. The median ridges on the crushing surfaces of the jaws are tuberculate, like those of *C. floridana* and *C. concinna*; this probably is an adaptation to a herbivorous diet, so it is likely that

151. Juvenile *Chrysemys rubriventris rubriventris*.
(*Photo by Kenneth T. Nemuras*)

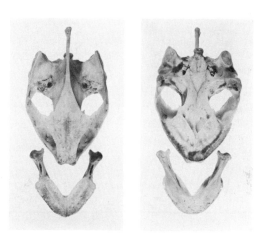

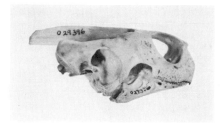

Skull of *Chrysemys rubriventris*

C. rubriventris depends to a substantial degree on aquatic vegetation for nourishment.

PREDATORS: Crows, skunks and raccoons rob nests and prey on hatchlings. Man is the chief destroyer of adults.

POPULATIONS: Graham (1969) reported that the Plymouth populations contained substantial numbers of juveniles. This implies the reproductive success necessary to maintain the relict group.

REMARKS: *C. rubriventris*, *C. nelsoni* and *C. alabamensis*, form the red-bellied, or *rubriventris*, group of the genus *Chrysemys*. They share external characters—notched upper jaw, prefrontal arrow, and reddish plastron—and have the skull with the vomer contributing to the triturating surface and with the middle ridge of the lower triturating surface set well to the side of the lingual margin of the surface. The red-bellied group is closely related to the *C. floridana* complex; in fact, *C. rubriventris* and *C. floridana* sometimes hybridize. Crenshaw (1965) discovered a hybrid swarm of *Chrysemys* in North Carolina that included 62 *C. floridana* showing apparent introgression from *C. rubriventris* and 2 *C. rubriventris* having some *C. floridana* characteristics.

In the northern part of its range the future of this species is bleak. The continued existence of suitable habitat along the Delaware River is doubtful in view of industrial expansion, the demand for property, the drainage of wetlands, and the application of insecticides to control mosquitoes. Collection of young for the pet trade from the Massachusetts localities will certainly deplete and probably eliminate the species there.

The red-bellied turtle is tasty and has been sold in the markets as a substitute for the diamondback terrapin. McCauley (1945) found them at 75¢ each and up, according to size, in the markets of Washington, D.C. The eggs are sometimes eaten by people who live near the breeding grounds.

Distribution of *Chrysemys rubriventris*.

CHRYSEMYS NELSONI (Carr)

Florida Red-bellied Turtle XVIII

RECOGNITION: A large (20–34 cm) freshwater turtle having a reddish plastron and a prominent notch at the tip of the upper jaw, with a toothlike cusp on each side. The high-arched, elongated carapace has the highest point usually anterior to the middle and the widest point at the middle, and the posterior margin is slightly serrated. The carapace is variable in color but usually is blackish, with red or yellow markings on the pleurals and marginals. The 2nd pleural has a light central band, which passes dorsoventrally and, just below the dorsal edge, usually bends sharply toward the rear and passes to the upper rear edge of the pleural; often this band is branched, to form a Y-shaped figure. Each marginal has a red bar located centrally on its dorsal surface; the ventral surface exhibits a dark smudge-like blotch. Melanism may occur in older individuals of both sexes. The bridge is deep; although usually immaculate, it sometimes has several dark blotches. The hingeless plastron is reddish-orange and may be plain or carry a medial pattern; this usually fades with age. The skin is black with yellow stripes. The head shows a prefrontal arrow, formed by the junction of the sagittal and supratemporal stripes on the snout. One to three stripes occur between the supratemporals behind the eyes, and the paramedial head-stripes usually are reduced and always end behind the eyes.

Males have elongated, slightly curved foreclaws and long, thick tails, with the anal opening posterior to the carapacial margin. Females are slightly larger than males.

GEOGRAPHIC VARIATION: No subspecies are recognized.

CONFUSING SPECIES: *C. floridana* and *C. concinna* usually lack the notch and cusps on the upper jaw and always lack the prefrontal arrow; also, *C. concinna* has a C-shaped figure on the 2nd pleural. In *C. alabamensis* the prominent paramedial head-

152. Large adult female *Chrysemys nelsoni.*

153. Subadult *Chrysemys nelsoni.*

154. Plastral pattern of subadult *Chrysemys nelsoni*. This pattern fades with age and may be absent in old individuals.

155. Young *Chrysemys nelsoni*.

stripes are rarely reduced, and they continue forward between the eyes.

DISTRIBUTION: *C. nelsoni* is restricted to Florida south of a line from Apalachicola eastward to the Atlantic Ocean.

HABITAT: This turtle has been taken from ponds, lakes, ditches, sloughs, marshes, and mangrove-bordered creeks. Water containing abundant aquatic vegetation is preferred. It shares its habitat with *C. floridana*, *C. concinna*, *Deirochelys reticularia*, *Chelydra osceola*, *Sternotherus minor*, *S. odoratus*, *Kinosternon baurii*, *K. subrubrum*, and *Trionyx ferox*.

BEHAVIOR: This species, a confirmed basker, spends much of the day lying in the sun on logs or floating mats of vegetation; it often shares these sites with *C. concinna* and *C. floridana*. Pritchard and Greenhood (1968) studied the basking habits of *C. nelsoni* and stated that this turtle seemed to bask for longer periods than either *C. concinna* or *C. floridana*. Possibly *C. nelsoni* can tolerate longer basking periods because its thicker shell retards the conduction of

heat to the viscera. However, it shows no marked tolerance for high body-temperatures. Hutchison *et al.* (1966) reported a mean critical thermal maximum of 40.42 C (39.7–41.0), and Pritchard and Greenhood (1968) reported a lethal temperature range of 43–44 C. The critical thermal maximum is slightly lower than those of *C. concinna* and *C. floridana* and corresponds closely to that of *C. scripta*.

C. nelsoni apparently does not hibernate. It is active all year.

REPRODUCTION: Little is known of the reproductive habits of the Florida red-bellied turtle. Although nesting may occur throughout the year, the peak comes in late spring and early summer. Females hunting for nesting sites are often found with nesting *C. floridana*.

The elliptical, white eggs measure approximately 47 mm by 19 mm. Duellman and Schwartz (1958) removed 12 eggs from a hybrid *C. nelsoni* × *C. floridana peninsularis* in late June; they hatched on 10 September.

The hatchlings are brighter than adults, and the carapace is rounded and slightly keeled. The plastron is orange or reddish, and the dark plastral

Skull of *Chrysemys nelsoni*

Distribution of *Chrysemys nelsoni*.

markings are solid semicircles with the flat sides along the seams.

FOOD AND FEEDING: Adult *C. nelsoni* are highly herbivorous; the young, like those of other species of *Chrysemys*, probably are more carnivorous. The adults prefer *Sagittaria, Lemna,* and *Naias.* Jim Butler, naturalist at the Corkscrew Swamp Sanctuary, has observed them eating lesser duckweed (*Lemna minor*), broad-leaved arrowhead (*Sagittaria latifolia*), climbing hempweed (*Mikania*), and water-hemlock (*Cicuta*). Adults show some scavenging tendencies and will feed on carrion, such as dead fish. Captive adults eat fish and various meats.

PREDATORS: Many nests are destroyed by skunks, raccoons, opossums, and hogs. Newly hatched turtles are eaten by fish, turtles, mammals, and wading birds, but adults are relatively free of predators. Besides man, the only major predator on adults is the alligator.

POPULATIONS: Marchand (in Carr, 1952) found *C. nelsoni* to comprise 2.1% of a turtle population that included six other species, the most numerous of which were *C. concinna* and *C. floridana.* There is little difference in the habitat preference of *C. nelsoni* and *C. floridana,* but the latter is the more abundant species nearly everywhere they occur together. *C. nelsoni, C. floridana,* and *C. concinna,* which have similar basking habits and practically identical diets, coexist in the Rainbow River in apparent defiance of Gause's rule, which states that species having the same ecologic requirements cannot concurrently occupy the same niche. The rule applies only to populations in equilibrium: either this population is not in equilibrium or else there are subtle, unknown differences in the requirements of the three species.

REMARKS: *C. nelsoni* is closely related to *C. alabamensis* and is likely ancestral to it. Hybridization with *C. floridana* and *C. concinna* apparently occurs (Duellman and Schwartz, 1958; Pritchard and Greenhood, 1968). Zug (1966) reported that *C. nelsoni, C. scripta, C. floridana,* and *C. concinna* form a homogeneous group in respect to the morphology of the penis.

C. nelsoni is palatable. It is eaten locally but is seldom marketed.

171

156. *Chrysemys alabamenis.*

157. Plastron of male *Chrysemys alabamensis.*

CHRYSEMYS ALABAMENSIS (Baur)

Alabama Red-bellied Turtle   XVIII

RECOGNITION: A large (20–25 cm) salt-marsh turtle with a reddish plastron and a prominent notch at the tip of the upper jaws, bordered on either side by a toothlike cusp. The elongated carapace is highly arched and is elevated along the vertebrals; its highest point is often anterior to the middle and its widest point is at the middle. The posterior margin is slightly serrated. The carapace is olive to black, with red to yellow bars on the pleurals and marginals. The second pleural has a wide, light, centrally located transverse bar, which may be Y-shaped. The bridge and the plastron are deep. The hingeless plastron is reddish-yellow and may show a dark, mottled pattern, which may also occur on the carapace and bridge. The skin is olive to black, with yellow stripes. The supratemporal and paramedial head-stripes are prominent and parallel, and

Skull of *Chrysemys alabamensis*

172

they do not join posterior to the orbit. The supratemporals pass forward from the orbit, joining well above and posterior to the nostrils. A sagittal stripe passes anteriorly between the orbits and joins the supratemporal stripes at their juncture to form the prefrontal arrow characteristic of the red-bellied turtle group.

Males have long, straight foreclaws and long, thick tails, with the anal opening behind the carapacial margin.

GEOGRAPHIC VARIATION: No subspecies are recognized.

CONFUSING SPECIES: Variants of *C. floridana* and *C. concinna* occasionally possess the deep notch and toothlike cusps at the tip of the upper jaw, but neither has the prefrontal arrow. Also, *C. concinna* has a light, C-shaped mark on the 2nd pleural, and in *C. floridana* the supratemporal and paramedial head-stripes are joined behind the eyes. In *C. nelsoni* the paramedial stripes are reduced or absent.

DISTRIBUTION: *C. alabamensis* is restricted to the Gulf coast, from Apalachee Bay, Florida, to Mobile Bay, Alabama. There is a questionable record from eastern Texas.

HABITAT: Salt marshes and coastal swamps are the primary habitats of *C. alabamensis*, but it sometimes enters rivers and streams. It shares its habitat with *C. concinna* and *Malaclemys terrapin*.

FOOD AND FEEDING: This species seems to be primarily herbivorous, consuming many species of plants. Captives readily eat lettuce but also take fish.

REMARKS: Because of its confused taxonomic status, *C. alabamensis* has been largely ignored. Carr and Crenshaw (1957) gave a resumé of the problem.

Probably some natural-history data have been reported, but because of the confusion of names these data cannot be isolated.

C. alabamensis is most closely related to *C. nelsoni*, from which it probably arose; in fact, these two may represent populations of a single, variable species. However, Carr and Crenshaw (1957) reported that their small sample suggested that the two forms overlap geographically in the Apalachicola area and behave as perfectly valid species. A more detailed study of their relationship is needed.

The flesh is palatable and is eaten locally, but because of the scarcity and limited distribution of *C. alabamensis* it is of little economic importance.

158. Note the rugose carapace and the notched upper jaw of *Chrysemys alabamensis*.

Distribution of *Chrysemys alabamensis*.

173

159. Male *Deirochelys reticularia reticularia.*

160. Male *Deirochelys reticularia chrysea.*

DEIROCHELYS RETICULARIA (Latreille)

Chicken Turtle   XIX

RECOGNITION: A small to medium-sized (10–25 cm) turtle with an extremely long neck and a reticulate pattern of yellow lines on the tan to olive carapace. The long, narrow, and somewhat depressed carapace is widest behind the middle, and in adults is neither keeled nor posteriorly serrated. The surface is somewhat rough, because the scutes are sculptured with small longitudinal ridges. The 1st vertebral is in contact with four marginals and the cervical, and the undersides of the marginals are yellow and may have a dark blotch at the seam. One or two black blotches may also occur on the bridge. The hingeless plastron is yellow and in the western race may have a dark pattern bordering the seams. The skin is olive to brown, with yellow or white stripes. There is a characteristic pattern of vertical light stripes on the rump, and the foreleg stripe is very wide. The length of the head and neck, measured from snout to shoulder, is approximately equal to the plastron length, and about 75–80% of the carapace length.

Adult males have long, thick tails, with the anal opening posterior to the carapacial margin. Females are larger than males.

GEOGRAPHIC VARIATION: Three subspecies are recognized. *D. r. reticularia* (Latreille), the eastern chicken turtle, occurs along the Atlantic and Gulf coastal plains from southeastern Virginia to the Mississippi River. This subspecies has narrow, net-like lines on the olive to brown carapace, a narrow yellow carapacial rim, and often a spot at the juncture of the femoral and anal scutes. Black spots are present on the ventral surface of the marginals at the level of the bridge in about 72% of individuals (Schwartz, 1956a). *D. r. chrysea* Schwartz, the Florida chicken turtle, is restricted to peninsular Florida. This race has a network of broad, bright, orange or yellow lines on the carapace and a wide, orange carapacial rim. Black spots are present on the ventral surface of the marginals at the level of the bridge in about 43% of individuals (Schwartz,

1956a). *D. r. miaria* Schwartz, the western chicken turtle, occurs west of the Mississippi River from southeastern Missouri and central Oklahoma south to the Gulf, and there is a record from western Mississippi. This subspecies is flattened, has a network of broad, faint lines on the carapace, and has a plastral pattern of dark markings along the seams. Adults have unstreaked chins and throats.

CONFUSING SPECIES: The species of *Chrysemys* and *Graptemys* lack the long neck and have the 1st vertebral in contact with only two marginals and the cervical.

DISTRIBUTION: *Deirochelys* occurs from southeastern Virginia south along the Atlantic coastal plain to southern Florida, west along the Gulf coastal plain to Texas, and northward west of the Mississippi River to southeastern Oklahoma and southeastern Missouri. There is a record from northeastern Mississippi. There are fewer than a half-dozen records of this species from above the fall line.

HABITAT: The chicken turtle is fairly common in still-water habitats, such as ponds, lakes, ditches, and cypress swamps; sometimes large aggregations can be found in temporary pools. Apparently it does not occur in moving-water habitats. It can be found with nearly all of the freshwater turtles occurring within its range.

BEHAVIOR: Surprisingly little has been reported about the behavior of the chicken turtle. Like other aquatic emydids, it spends much of its time basking; while basking it is wary and easily alarmed. Chicken turtles are well adjusted to high temperatures. Hutchison *et al.* (1966) found that three *Deirochelys* lost the righting ability at 39.1 C (38.5–39.5) and that their mean critical thermal maximum was 41.3 C (40.8–42.2).

This turtle often wanders overland, and large numbers are crushed on the roads or otherwise destroyed at such times. Neill (1948a) suggested that an abundance of shells found in a woods in Richmond County, Georgia, might be explained by their

161. Black spots are present on the undersides of the marginals and on the bridge of *Deirochelys reticularia reticularia.*

162. Black spots on the undersides of the marginals and on the bridge are much reduced, or absent in *Deirochelys reticularia chrysea.*

165. There is apparently no literature record of ecdysis in *Deirochelys*. It does occur, however, and effectively rids the animal of algae and ectoparasites.

163. Female *Deirochelys reticularia reticularia* showing the wide foreleg stripe and rugose carapace found in this species.

164. The "striped pants" of *Deirochelys reticularia*.

having been caught by sudden cold weather. The chicken turtle has three phases of terrestrial activity: a period of gravid-female activity in early spring, a period in April when both sexes are active, and a period in late spring when adult males predominate (Gibbons, 1969b).

At least in the northern part of its range, *Deirochelys* hibernates in mud and aquatic vegetation along lake margins and becomes active on the first warm days of spring. In the deep south it does not hibernate but remains active except on cold days.

The disposition varies: some bite and scratch viciously; others are shy and retiring.

REPRODUCTION: Males reach maturity at 75–85 mm in plastron length, presumably during their 2nd or 3rd growing season. Females greater than 160 mm in plastron length are mature, those 145–160 mm are just attaining maturity, and females greater than 180 mm are apparently sterile or have biennial or triennial reproductive cycles (Gibbons, 1969b). Courtship and mating have not been recorded.

In Florida the chicken turtle apparently nests throughout the year: eggs have been found from mid-November through January. Females have been observed wandering among nesting *Chrysemys* in June, although no nests have been observed in that month. Gibbons (1969b) found that egg-laying in South Carolina began as early as the middle of March. Seven females captured between 11 and

166. Hatchling *Deirochelys reticu-laria reticularia.*

22 March contained eggs. Of 17 captured between 30 March and 13 June only three contained eggs. Anderson (1965) reported that a captive *D. r. miaria* laid a total of 10 eggs, on the soil surface, at irregular intervals between 13 and 19 July.

Shelled eggs have been found in the oviducts at widely spaced intervals throughout the year. However, Cagle and Tihen (1948) have shown that this does not necessarily indicate the nesting season. They found that eggs may be retained in the oviducts for months if suitable nesting conditions are lacking. In some cases the eggs are retained so long that they cause erosive destruction of the oviducal wall and escape into the abdominal cavity.

The nest is cylindrical, approximately 4 inches deep, and 3 inches in diameter at the mouth.

The elliptical, white eggs are 32–40 mm in length and 20.0–23.3 mm in width. Clutch size varies from 5 to 15. Anderson (1965) found a female that had laid 12 eggs contained three size-groups of developing follicles. One group, of 11, averaged 18 mm by 20 mm; a second group, of 10, averaged 10 mm by 13 mm; and a third group, composed of numerous small follicles, ranged down to 1 mm in diameter. These data indicate that *Deirochelys* may nest several times a year. In South Carolina some hatchlings overwinter in the nest (Gibbons, 1969b).

Hatchlings are nearly round; Carr (1952) found a Louisiana hatchling, still possessing a caruncle, that had a carapace length of 28 mm, a carapace

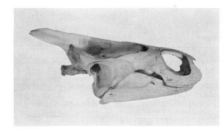

Skull of *Deirochelys reticularia*

177

width of 25.5 mm, a depth of 14 mm, a plastron length of 26 mm, a tail length behind the carapacial margin of 7 mm, a neck-and-head length in front of the anterior carapacial margin of 21 mm, and a head width of 8 mm. The carapace usually has a slight keel and rugose scutes. The shell and skin markings are similar to the adult's but brighter, and there may be more head-and-neck stripes. Hatchling *D. r. miaria* have dark pigment along the plastral seams.

GROWTH: Growth rates of South Carolina individuals were 25–30 mm/year up to a plastron length of 90–100 mm for males and 130–150 mm for females (Gibbons, 1969b). When maturity is reached the growth rate apparently slows dramatically.

FOOD AND FEEDING: *Deirochelys* probably is omnivorous. Carr (1952) observed free-living chicken turtles eating tadpoles, crayfish, and what appeared to be a bud of the water plant *Nuphar*. Cagle (1950) reported that chicken turtles react best to bait in advanced decay, whereas other turtles refuse to enter a trap containing rotten bait. Our captive adults readily consume lettuce and fresh or canned fish; the juveniles refuse vegetable matter. This species probably becomes more herbivorous with increasing age.

PREDATORS: Little has been published about predation on the chicken turtle. Raccoons, skunks, and other mammals surely dig up and eat the eggs. Juveniles are the prey of large fish, snakes, alligators, otters, raccoons, and large wading birds. Man is no doubt the worst enemy of adults, but alligators capture and eat them on occasion.

MOVEMENTS: A marked chicken turtle moved 670 yards in slightly more than 8 months (Marchand, 1945).

POPULATIONS: Cagle and Chaney (1950) reported that *Deirochelys* comprised only 4.4% of the total turtle population of the Lacassine Refuge, in southwestern Louisiana; traps operated for 456 trap hours yielded only four *Deirochelys*.

Gibbons (1970a), using the Lincoln index, estimated there were approximately 401 *Deirochelys* in the 10-hectare Ellenton Bay, in South Carolina. The sex ratio was 1.85 males per female. He thought this probably was biased, due to the differing behavior of the sexes. Such bias was particularly evident when two methods of trapping were compared: swim-in traps caught 31 males and 4 females, but terrestrial traps caught 11 males and 20 females.

REMARKS: *Deirochelys* is not a river turtle; thus it is not surprising that the Mississippi River has proven such an effective barrier between the subspecies *D. r. reticularia* and *D. r. miaria*. The great river appears to be uninhabited by chicken turtles, and with few exceptions it effectively prevents gene-flow between the populations on the eastern and western banks.

It seems preferable to regard *D. r. reticularia* as ancestral to both *D. r. chrysea* and *D. r. miaria*.

The chicken turtle apparently was named for its palatable flesh. It was once common in the markets of southern cities but is not often sold today. It is still eaten locally in the South.

Distribution of *Deirochelys reticularia*.

EMYDOIDEA BLANDINGII (Holbrook)

Blanding's Turtle   XIX

RECOGNITION: A medium-sized to large (12.5–26 cm) turtle with a yellow chin and throat and a well-developed hinge between the pectoral and abdominal scutes. The elongated, smooth, blue-black carapace is neither keeled nor serrated. The 1st vertebral is in contact with four marginals and the cervical; each pleural and vertebral has tan to yellowish spots or slightly radiating lines; and the marginals are heavily spotted. The hinged, yellow plastron has large, dark, symmetrically arranged blotches, which may be so large as to hide most of the yellow color. The skin is blue-gray with some yellow scales on the tail and legs. The large head is flat; the eyes protrude; and the upper jaw is notched terminally and may be marked with dark bars. The neck is extremely long for a North American turtle. The hind feet are weakly webbed.

Sexual dimorphism is not pronounced. In males the anal opening is behind the carapacial margin and the plastron is slightly concave.

GEOGRAPHIC VARIATION: No subspecies are recognized.

CONFUSING SPECIES: The box turtles, *Terrapene carolina* and *T. ornata*, also have a well-developed plastral hinge, but neither has a yellow throat and chin or a notched upper jaw; also, *T. carolina* has a keeled carapace. *Clemmys guttata* has a blue-black carapace with yellow spots, but it lacks a plastral hinge.

DISTRIBUTION: Blanding's turtle ranges from southern Ontario south through the Great Lakes region and west to eastern Nebraska. It also occurs in scattered localities in eastern New York, Massachusetts, southern New Hampshire, and Nova Scotia.

HABITAT: *Emydoidea* prefers shallow water with a soft bottom and abundant aquatic vegetation; it is found in lakes, ponds, marshes, creeks, and sloughs. It occurs with *Chelydra serpentina*, *Sternotherus*

167. *Emydoidea blandingii.*

168. *Emydoidea blandingii* has a long neck and can extend the head a surprisingly long distance.

169. Hinged plastron of *Emydoidea blandingii.*

170. A bright yellow chin and neck are characteristic of *Emydoidea blandingii.*

odoratus, Trionyx spiniferus, Chrysemys picta, C. scripta, Graptemys geographica, Clemmys guttata, and *C. insculpta.*

BEHAVIOR: Little is known of the behavior of this turtle. It is fond of basking and has been observed sunning itself on muskrat houses, steep banks of dikes and ditches, stumps, logs, and driftwood. When disturbed it immediately dives and either burrows into the bottom, hides under debris, or swims rapidly away. It is often found prowling along the bottom in shallow water.

When handled these turtles withdraw into their shells and close the movable lobes of the plastron as tightly as possible. They are timid and usually make no attempt to bite.

Ohio *Emydoidea* may be active in all months of the year. Evermann and Clark (1916) found them active from 29 March to 4 November in northern Indiana. Individuals have been seen swimming slowly beneath the winter ice.

Hibernation is apparently spent in mud at the bottom of some body of water. Blanding's turtles have been found in the underwater entrances of muskrat houses and in the mud of spring-fed ditches. At the Toledo Zoo two spent the winter under wet leaves several feet from water, but most hibernated successfully beneath masses of soggy leaves in their pool (Conant, 1951a).

Hutchison *et al.* (1966) found the mean critical thermal maximum of 12 *Emydoidea* to be 39.5 C (38.2–40.6 C). This is one of the lowest maxima among the 25 species they examined and probably is a reason for *Emydoidea's* restriction to northern latitudes.

REPRODUCTION: There is no information on the size at which maturity is attained. Gibbons (1968d) dissected a female that was 101 mm in plastron length and found her to be immature.

Richmond (1970) observed a male swim around a female and nudge and bump her several times before forcing her to the bottom by mounting and firmly hooking the claws of all four feet over the edges of her carapace. The entire mating took place in water and lasted 17 min. Conant (1951a) observed males actively pursuing females on a number of occasions. Copulation has been recorded in every month from March to November but is most common in March, April, and May. The mating on 17 November reported by Smith (1961) was surely a belated one, because these turtles are less active at that time of the year.

Nesting has been observed only in Canada, where late June and July seem to be the peak period (Logier, 1925; Brown, 1927; Bleakney, 1963). However, Evermann and Clark (1916) captured females on 17 and 18 May at Lake Maxinkuckee, in northern Indiana; the turtles were walking about on dry land as if hunting for nesting sites. Nesting probably occurs earlier in the United States.

Early evening is the normal time of nesting, and places with sandy soil are preferred. The nest is flask-shaped and about 7 inches deep; the opening is 3–4 inches in diameter, and the terminal chamber is about 7 inches wide. The nest is dug entirely with the hind feet. A nesting observed by Snyder (1921) took 45 min to complete.

The number of eggs in a clutch varies from 6 to 11; the mean is 8, but two clutches may be laid each season. The ellipsoidal, dull-white eggs average 36 mm (36–38) in length and 24 mm (22–26) in width.

Hatching and emergence in September has been reported by several observers. Smith (1961) found a number of hatchlings dead and desiccated on 26 August in Illinois; apparently they had been killed by the hot sun before they could make their way to water.

The rounded, keeled carapace of the hatchling is dark brown to black, sometimes with spots, and is 29–35 mm in length. The plastron has a large, black central blotch, and the future hinge is suggested by a crease. The tail is proportionately much longer than in adults.

Food and Feeding: Lagler (1943) examined 51 *Emydoidea* and found that crustaceans made up more than half and insect remains almost a quarter of the food volume; fish and other vertebrates, snails, leeches, and plants made up the remainder.

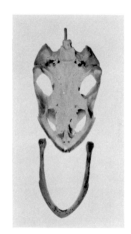

Skull of *Emydoidea blandingii*

These turtles apparently had fed entirely on aquatic materials. Penn (1950) found that crayfish constituted 78% in frequency and 58% in volume of the food of 92 *Emydoidea* he examined.

Cahn (1937) reported that this species eats leaves, grasses, berries, and other succulent vegetation, slugs, grubs, insect larvae, and earthworms on land, and insect larvae, tadpoles, frogs, crayfish, and minnows in water. Although there is some question about the ability to feed out of water, individuals we kept readily and easily ate dog food from a dry dish.

Distribution of *Emydoidea blandingii* in the United States.

PREDATORS: The eggs and young of *Emydoidea* are eaten by a number of species of fishes, reptiles, birds, and mammals. Grant (1936a) found several shells in northern Indiana that had been severely gnawed by a rodent. Man, by draining swamps and marshes, has destroyed much of the suitable habitat and thus has unwittingly eliminated large numbers of this innocuous animal.

MOVEMENTS: Although *Emydoidea* frequently ventures on land, it apparently does not travel extensively. Four recaptured by Gibbons (1968d) were found less than 100 m from the site of original capture. This suggests a rather small home range. The time between initial and subsequent captures ranged from 4 days to more than 14 months. All instances of travel overland were in April, June, or September.

REMARKS: Blanding's turtle is palatable but is too rare to be profitably marketed. Lagler (1943) reported the presence of 111 fish eggs in the stomach of a Michigan individual, but as far as fish are concerned this species probably is of greater importance as a food competitor than as a predator.

Conant and Hudson (1949) reported that a Blanding's turtle lived 11 years 7 months in the Philadelphia Zoological Garden. Surely they are able to live considerably longer than that.

Common Snapping Turtle
Chelydra serpentina serpentina

Florida Snapping Turtle,
Chelydra osceola

Alligator Snapping Turtle,
Macroclemys temminckii

"Worm" of Alligator Snapping Turtle

Stinkpot,
Sternotherus odoratus

Razor-backed Musk Turtle,
Sternotherus carinatus

Loggerhead Musk Turtle,
Sternotherus minor minor

Eastern Mud Turtle,
Kinosternon subrubrum subrubrum

Striped Mud Turtle,
Kinosternon baurii palmarum

V

Yellow Mud Turtle,
Kinosternon flavescens flavescens

Sonora Mud Turtle,
Kinosternon sonoriense

Big Bend Mud Turtle,
Kinosternon hirtipes murrayi

Spotted Turtle,
Clemmys guttata

Bog Turtle,
Clemmys muhlenbergii

Wood Turtle,
Clemmys insculpta

Western Pond Turtle,
Clemmys marmorata

Eastern Box Turtle,
Terrapene carolina carolina

Three-toed Box Turtle,
Terrapene carolina triunguis

Gulf Coast Box Turtle,
Terrapene carolina major

Florida Box Turtle,
Terrapene carolina bauri

Ornate Box Turtle,
Terrapene ornata ornata

Northern Diamond-backed Terrapin,
Malaclemys terrapin terrapin

Map Turtle,
Graptemys geographica

Barbour's Map Turtle,
Graptemys barbouri

Alabama Map Turtle,
Graptemys pulchra, male

Alabama Map Turtle,
Graptemys pulchra, female

Mississippi Map Turtle,
Graptemys kohnii

Ouachita Map Turtle,
*Graptemys pseudogeographica
ouachitensis*

Texas Map Turtle,
Graptemys versa

Ringed Sawback
Graptemys oculifera

Yellow-blotched Sawback,
Graptemys flavimaculata, male

Yellow-blotched Sawback,
Graptemys flavimaculata, female

Black-knobbed Sawback
Graptemys nigrinoda nigrinoda

Eastern Painted Turtle,
Chrysemys picta picta

Southern Painted Turtle,
Chrysemys picta dorsalis

Midland Painted Turtle,
Chrysemys picta marginata

Western Painted Turtle,
Chrysemys picta bellii

Yellow-bellied Turtle,
Chrysemys scripta scripta

Red-eared Turtle,
Chrysemys scripta elegans

Cumberland Turtle,
Chrysemys scripta troostii

Big Bend Turtle,
Chrysemys scripta gaigeae

Slider,
Chrysemys concinna hieroglyphica

Peninsula Cooter,
Chrysemys floridana peninsularis

Red-bellied Turtle,
Chrysemys rubriventris rubriventris

Florida Red-bellied Turtle,
Chrysemys nelsoni

Alabama Red-bellied Turtle,
Chrysemys alabamensis

Eastern Chicken Turtle,
Deirochelys reticularia reticularia

Blanding's Turtle,
Emydoidea blandingii

Desert Tortoise,
Gopherus agassizii

Texas Tortoise,
Gopherus berlandieri

Gopher Tortoise,
Gopherus polyphemus

Green Turtle,
Chelonia mydas

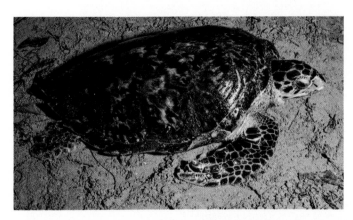

Hawksbill,
Eretmochelys imbricata

Loggerhead,
Caretta caretta

Atlantic Ridley,
Lepidochelys kempii

Pacific Ridley
Lepidochelys olivacea
(*photo by Charles M. Bogert*)

Leatherback,
Dermochelys coriacea
(*photo by Peter C. H. Pritchard*)

Midland Smooth Softshell,
Trionyx muticus muticus

Eastern Spiny Softshell,
Trionyx spiniferus spiniferus

Florida Softshell,
Trionyx ferox

Chinese Softshell,
Trionyx sinensis sinensis

TESTUDINIDAE:
Tortoises

The family consists of 10 genera and 39 living species of tortoises; they occur in the Americas, Europe, Africa, and Asia and on certain oceanic islands. The giant *Geochelone elephantopus* of the Galápagos Islands, and *G. gigantea* of the Seychelles Islands, are the largest living land turtles. Three species of the genus *Gopherus* occur in the United States.

These are medium-sized to large, strictly terrestrial turtles with columnar, elephantine hind limbs. The forelimbs are covered anteriorly with thick, hard scales. The feet are short and broad, with heavy-clawed, webless toes having no more than two bones in any digit. The high-arched carapace is firmly sutured to the bridge; the plastron is well developed and contains an entoplastron. The nuchal bone is without lateral costiform processes and there are 11 peripherals. There are two biconvex neck vertebrae and the dorsal rib-heads are often vestigial. The temporal region of the skull is widely emarginated posteriorly, and the frontal bones enter the orbit. The quadrate bone always encloses the stapes. The maxilla rarely touches the quadratojugal, and its crushing surface is rigid.

Auffenberg (1966a) pointed out that, on the basis of differences in carpus structure as well as a number of other anatomic features, two species-groups of *Gopherus* may be recognized: a *polyphemus* group, consisting of *G. polyphemus* and the Mexican *G. flavomarginatus*, and an *agassizii* group, comprising *G. agassizii* and *G. berlandieri*. Further evidence of the close relationship of *G. agassizii* and *G. berlandieri* is given by Woodbury (1952), who described hybrids produced by a mating of these two species. The proposal of Wermuth and Mertens (1961) that all four forms of *Gopherus* are only subspecifically distinct seems incorrect in view of present evidence. Grant's (1960b) contention that *G. flavomarginatus* is synonymous with *G. agassizii* or at most is a subspecies thereof is strongly contradicted by their carpal structure and other differences in gross anatomy.

171. An adult female *Gopherus agassizii.*

GOPHERUS AGASSIZII (Cooper)

Desert Tortoise   XX

RECOGNITION: A large (15–37 cm) terrestrial turtle of the southwestern United States that has large, elephantine hind feet, shovellike forefeet, and a gular projection on the plastron. The rough, ridged, but keelless carapace is oblong and is highest behind the middle; the rear margin is serrated, and the marginals above the hind limbs are flared. The carapace is black to tan, and often the centers of the scutes are yellowish or orange. The bridge is well developed and has a single axillary scute. The plastron is large and hingeless; the elongated gular scutes project anteriorly and may bend upward. The plastral scutes are black to tan; some of them may have yellowish centers. The skin of the limbs is brown and that of the limb sockets and neck yellowish; the head usually is tan but may be reddish. The head is somewhat rounded, and the crushing ridges of the upper jaws form less than a $65°$ angle with each other. There are well-developed integumentary glands beneath the chin. The iris usually is greenish-yellow. The forefeet and hind feet are about the same size; the distance from the base of the 1st claw to the base of the 4th on the forefoot approximately equals the same measurement on the hind foot. The toes are not webbed, and there is a single, large femoral spur.

Males are larger than females and have longer, thicker tails, longer gular projections, concave plastrons, and more massive claws.

GEOGRAPHIC VARIATION: No subspecies have been described.

CONFUSING SPECIES: Within its range only *Terrapene ornata, Kinosternon sonoriense,* and *K. flavescens* could be confused with the desert tortoise; each of these has a hinged plastron and lacks a gular projection.

DISTRIBUTION: In the United States *Gopherus agassizii* ranges through southern Nevada, extreme southwestern Utah, southwestern California, and western Arizona. In Mexico it occurs in northern Baja California, western Sonora (including Tiburon Island, in the Gulf of California), and northwestern Sinaloa.

HABITAT: This tortoise inhabits desert oases, washes, canyon bottoms, and rocky hillsides in drylands having sandy or gravelly soil; it occurs to an altitude of at least 3,500 ft. Thorn scrub, creosote bushes, and cacti often are present in the habitat. Although *Terrapene ornata* occurs with *G. agassizii* in some localities, no other North American turtle shares the more severe of the habitats occupied by this species.

BEHAVIOR: *G. agassizii* constructs a burrow, which is its home. The turtle digs by scraping alternately with the forelimbs; when the hole becomes deep enough the turtle turns around and pushes the dirt out with its shoulders. The burrows are dug in dry, gravelly soil and are located under a bush either in an arroyo bank or at the base of a cliff. In cross-section they are somewhat oval; may be straight, curved, or forked; and many have enlarged chambers. Although sometimes just long enough to admit the tortoise, they are occasionally over 30 ft in length. Woodbury and Hardy (1948) reported that two kinds of burrows—dens and summer holes—are used in southwestern Utah. Dens are horizontal tunnels dug in banks of washes, usually for distances of 8–15 ft but occasionally for 20–30 ft. Summer holes are scattered over the flats and benches and are dug downward at angles of about 20–40° for a distance of 3–4 ft. In Sonora, Mexico, Auffenberg (1969) found that the summer retreat was most commonly a shallow hollow dug into the base of an arroyo wall; several tortoises may use the same shelter during a single season. In Utah, woodrats (*Neotoma* spp.) often share the winter burrows with desert tortoises.

Once in their burrows, desert tortoises resist almost all attempts to remove them. They brace their forefeet against the walls or else firmly plant them on the floor of the burrow, lean forward, and raise their backs against the roof. This is quite effective, and they are difficult to extract. A captive female

172. Growth annuli are evident on the plastron of this *Gopherus agassizii.*

173. The forelegs of all *Gopherus* are broad and flattened as in this *Gopherus agassizii.* Note also the gular extension of the plastron beneath the chin.

that shares the house of one of us (CHE) often successfully uses these tactics to resist removal from beneath furniture.

In the warm season the daily activity of *G. agassizii* is governed largely by temperature. It forages for a short period after sunrise and again in the late afternoon. Between the active periods the tortoise rests in its burrow, which is a special microhabitat: the humidity is higher and the temperature is lower and more constant in the burrow than outside it. By retreating into the burrow the tortoise relieves the problems of evaporative water-loss and high body temperature. In extremely hot weather the tortoise may keep to its burrow all day. On the other hand, it is specially active during rains: the cooler temperature and higher humidity make conditions outside the burrow more tolerable. In the wild this turtle seldom basks except on cool days, but captives in more temperate climates often spend considerable time lying in the sun.

Generally speaking, *G. agassizii* is active from March through September and enters hibernation in October or November. Woodbury and Hardy (1940) found that in southwestern Utah desert tortoises congregate in large communal dens during the winter. These were dug as deep as 33 ft into gravel banks, and some had multiple openings. As many as 23 tortoises were found in one burrow, and some returned to the same burrow annually. Auffenberg (1969) reported that in Pima County, Arizona, individuals often returned year after year to particular hibernacula. These winter burrows were always located well above the floor of arroyos and usually were enlarged ground-squirrel burrows. The typical burrow extended just far enough so that the rear portion of the tortoise's shell was even with the arroyo wall. This depth apparently was sufficient to shelter the tortoise from the cold night winds but allowed the exposure of a part of the shell to the rays of the afternoon sun: the burrows were always located in a south-facing slope, and four or five tortoises sometimes occupied adjacent burrows. Nichols (1953) saw several captives combine their efforts to dig a communal hibernaculum. Nichols (1957) reported that several young captive tortoises

hatched in California did not hibernate during their 1st winter, but all hibernated the 2nd winter.

Woodbury and Hardy (1948) reported that some desert tortoises first became active at temperatures as low as 15 C; activity gradually increased with rising temperature, until at about 26.7–29.4 C all were active. Brattstrom (1965) found that the temperatures of more than 10 active *G. agassizii* were 15.0–37.8 C (mean 30.6) and that the critical thermal maximum was 39.5 C. On the other hand, Hutchison *et al.* (1966) found that a *G. agassizii* lost its righting ability at 39.0 C and that the critical thermal maximum was 43.1 C. The latter figure seems more reasonable. An individual kept on its back in direct sunlight will die in a short time, but these tortoises can right themselves by using their head, neck, and forelimbs.

Woodbury and Hardy (1948) and Auffenberg (1969) have shown that the desert tortoise occupies a rather small home range wherein water may not be available. In the driest parts of its range the desert tortoise has opportunities for drinking only after rains, which are infrequent—sometimes years apart. Intake of water by drinking is reduced to a minimum; however, when water is available the tortoise will drink. Miller (1932) reported that individuals increased their weights as much as 43% by drinking. The basic water supply of a desert tortoise must come from food: the plants eaten are not entirely dry, and additional water is produced metabolically from them. Tortoises accumulate fat for hibernation, and this is also a source of metabolic water.

Desert tortoises lose water by evaporation and urination. Some water is always lost by evaporation from the lungs; however, the skin permits the passage of less water than that of turtles in damper climates (Schmidt-Nielsen and Bentley, 1966). Dantzler and Schmidt-Nielsen (1966) showed that the urinary bladder of the desert tortoise is more permeable to water than that of freshwater turtles and that the tortoise excretes nitrogenous wastes in the semisolid form of urates. When water is available it excretes liquid urine, but it is able to go for months without discharging water from the bladder.

G. agassizii has rather unusual social relationships. When two tortoises meet, each nods its head rapidly, and sometimes they touch noses before they pass. When two males meet, a fight is likely to ensue. After the preliminary nodding they separate a little distance, then with heads down partway into their shells rush toward one another. They meet head-on, and the gular projections are butted violently together. The fights do no damage, but one of the tortoises may be turned over; the vanquished struggles for some time, with one foreleg vibrating vigorously in the air and the other pawing for a foothold on the ground, before he rights himself.

A captive female *G. agassizii*, when first introduced to a male *G. polyphemus* of about the same size, rammed him several times, causing him to withdraw into his shell. She then walked away. She has never again shown such aggressiveness toward him during the several years they have been kept together; indeed, they often seek out the other's company, especially when about to retire for the night. When a small male *G. berlandieri* was introduced to the female she circled and sniffed him for about 1 min and then ignored him.

Nichols (1957) reported that after one of her adults drank water it occasionally urinated in its house. Until the house had been thoroughly hosed and aired, other tortoises—one male especially—would not sleep inside unless forced to do so.

174. *Gopherus agassizii.*

REPRODUCTION: Woodbury and Hardy (1948) calculated that sexual maturity is reached in 15–20 years, when females are 230–265 mm in carapace length and males are 250–316 mm. Miller (1955) reported that male secondary sexual characteristics begin to appear at 16 years, are definite at 17 years, and are complete at 20 years. A female 165 mm in carapace length (10–11 years old) stimulated courting activity in a large male.

Courtship and mating occur in the spring and possibly continue into the summer months. During courtship the male extends his head and bobs it up and down; he may also bite the female's nose, forelegs, and shell and ram her with the gular extension. Males may also utter grunts at this time. Accord-

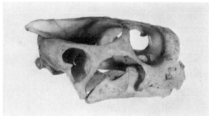

Skull of *Gopherus agassizii*

ing to Weaver (1970), most reports of vocalizing during breeding activities suggest that the sounds are a by-product of the copulatory effort; nothing indicates that they serve as an auditory signal. Campbell and Evans (1967) found two types of sounds: a short grunt and a drawn-out moan. The fundamental frequency varied by at least an octave—from 0.5 kc to 1.0 kc—and in most cases the signal contained two or three harmonics. These sounds were not recorded in courtship or in combat, and their biologic significance is not known. Nichols (1953) reported that each spring a captive male chose a mate for the season—usually a different female from that of the previous year. Nichols (1957) reported a female initiating courtship.

During copulation the male mounts the female from the rear and assumes a nearly erect position, with his forelimbs resting on her carapace. He then performs vertical pumping movements, accompanied by puffing and grunting noises.

The nesting season extends from mid-May through July. Early morning and late afternoon seem to be the favorite nesting times. Captives have been known to lay eggs as late as September and October and to nest two or three times in one season (Stuart, 1954; Miller, 1955). The eggs normally are deposited in cavities dug in sandy soil but are occasionally laid in the mouths of burrows or are deposited singly at random.

The hind feet are used to dig the nest, to arrange the eggs in the nest, and to scratch and drag soil back into the cavity after the eggs are laid. The female may urinate into the nest cavity before filling it or on it after filling it. Excavation of the nest may take from 1 hr to several hours, and egg laying from 15 to 30 min. Booth (1958) reported that a nesting female scooped out a depression with her front legs; then, from the bottom of it, she dug the egg cavity with her hind feet.

The nest is funnel-shaped; that is, wider at the entrance than in the egg chamber. The depth is 3–10 inches. Nichols (1953) gave the measurements of a typical nest as approximately 6 inches deep, 9 inches in diameter at the top, and 7 inches across at the bottom.

In the days just prior to nesting the female often becomes extremely restless and spends considerable time scratching the soil with her forefeet. She may refuse to eat during this period.

Clutches consist of 2 to 14 eggs; about 5 is the usual number. The eggs vary from elliptical to nearly spherical in shape; four elliptical ones were 41.6–48.7 mm in length, 36.7–39.6 mm in maximum transverse diameter, and 34.9–38.2 mm in minimum transverse diameter (Miller, 1932). Fresh eggs are moist, translucent, and extremely hard, with a coarse, rough texture and without gloss, chalky layer, or pigment. The translucence, which permits observation of a small gas bubble within the egg, disappears upon drying. The gas bubble remains for several months without change in volume—an indication that the shell is moisture-proof.

Hatching occurs from mid-August to October, with the peak in September and early October. Natural incubation periods usually are more than 100 days, but artificially incubated eggs have hatched in 82–92 days. Grant (1936b) reported a case of overwintering in the egg, with hatching the following spring.

Hatchlings are nearly as wide as long and are 36–48 mm in carapace length, 35–43 mm in carapace width, and 20–24 mm in depth. The carapace varies from dull yellow to brownish, with darker-brown areas on each of the scutes. It is pliable, and there are wrinkles on the sides and a deep crease across the plastron that had allowed curling of the fetus in the egg. In the center of the plastron is a yolk sac about one-third the size of the young turtle; the sac greatly impedes its movements. This is rapidly resorbed over a 2-day period, leaving only a soft umbilical scar by the 3rd day; it remains visible for several weeks and does not completely heal for several months. The caruncle disappears gradually. The cervical and the 12th marginals are incomplete at hatching and are deeply notched and crenulated on the margin. Color and shape of the hatchling are such as to render it practically invisible among stones and dry grasses.

Both Grant (1936b) and Booth (1958) have commented that hatchlings differ radically from adults in their disposition. Hatchlings are very pugnacious —advancing, hissing, and biting when touched; adults are quite docile.

GROWTH: A captive juvenile increased in carapace length from 44.7 mm to 72.3 mm in 3 years, and a hatchling grew from 46.9 mm to 70.4 mm in 1 year. Ten tortoises increased 2.1–50% per year (Miller, 1932). Bogert (1937) reported that a wild female grew 22 mm in 680 days and a smaller female grew 70 mm in 818 days. Woodbury and Hardy (1948) found that young *G. agassizii* grew to a carapace length of about 100 mm in 5 years. The most rapid growth recorded by them was a tortoise that grew from 206 to 302 mm in a little more than 52 months.

Miller (1955) presented carapace-length growth curves of three desert tortoises captured as hatchlings and kept for 18–20 years. Carapace growth showed remarkably uniform gradients. A male kept for 20 years increased from 44.7 mm to 232 mm. At 5 years of age the plastron was still slightly soft at the center; at 11 years it was entirely rigid; at 16 years the concavity in the pelvic region was beginning to develop; and at 20 years the gular projection was fully extended and curved upward. Two probable females kept for 17 years did not develop secondary sex characteristics in that time, and two small tortoises picked up at the probable ages of 6 and 7 years showed no secondary sex characteristics by the age of 25 years.

Nichols (1953, 1957) reported that a male *G. agassizii* captured in 1929, when 4 or 5 years old, was still alive when 32 or 33 years old.

FOOD AND FEEDING: The serrated jaws of *G. agassizii* are well adapted to the shredding of vegetation. The species is mostly herbivorous, subsisting on various grasses, cacti, and the blossoms of *Encelia canescens* and other desert Compositae. Captives eat radishes, dandelions, watermelon, cantaloupe, lettuce, cabbage, spinach, bananas, figs, peaches, clover, grasses, grapes, apples, bread, cheese, snails, insects, and bird eggshells. Nichols (1953) reported that captives will consume the eggs of their own species.

PREDATORS: Coyotes, bobcats, and ravens are known to feed on desert tortoises, and badgers, skunks, foxes, ring-tailed cats, and hawks are suspected predators. Man sometimes uses the desert tortoise as food; more important is his destruction of many of them on the highways.

MOVEMENTS: *G. agassizii* is a slow and deliberate animal. Woodbury and Hardy (1948) measured rates of travel as being 720–1,584 ft/hr; at such steady rates it would take 3.3–7.3 hr to travel 1 mile. The velocity in feet per second ranged from 0.25 at 25.8 C to 0.44 at 33.0 C.

Utah desert tortoises perform yearly migrations between the winter hibernacula and the summer feeding grounds, where they occupy home ranges that usually cover 10–100 acres and overlap the ranges of other desert tortoises. There is no evidence that they defend territories (Woodbury and Hardy, 1948). A female was recaptured 200 yards from the place of liberation after 58 days; when recaptured again, 619 days later, she had traversed a minimum distance of 150 yards. After 4 years an adult male was recaptured approximately 300 yards from the original capture site (Bogert, 1937).

POPULATIONS: Woodbury and Hardy (1948) found approximately 300 *G. agassizii* in about 1,200 acres. Of the 281 tortoises they studied, 101 were males, 151 were females, 10 were of indeterminate sex but were thought to be equally divided between males and females, and the sex of the remainder was unrecorded. They estimated that young tortoises made up less than 5% of the population and that the average annual mortality was 1–5%.

REMARKS: The desert tortoise is a surprisingly good climber and often digs its winter den at the top of a steep bank. Woodbury and Hardy (1948) reported that to enter one such den a tortoise had to climb 51 ft at an angle of about 45°, ascend a vertical gravel ledge 12 inches high at its lowest point, and then climb an additional 4 ft at an angle of about 40°. At another den the tortoise had to climb 16 inches; the first 4 inches led to a narrow ledge, just wide enough to accommodate the hind feet. Above this a vertical 10 inches led to a 2-inch slope, which in turn led to the entrance to the den.

Our captive female spends much time attempting to climb walls and pieces of furniture. On several occasions she has climbed vertically 6–8 inches up a living room sofa. In accomplishing this she reached up with her forefeet, hooked them under the sofa cushions, and then did a pull-up, raising her hind limbs clear of the floor.

Desert tortoises are sometimes eaten by man, but this probably is not common now. Indians may use the shells for containers and have also used them as ornaments and rattles in their dances. It has been suggested that the liquid stored in the bladder could be a source of water for persons lost in the desert. The above uses are of little economic importance; but the sale of *G. agassizii* in the pet trade is a source of considerable revenue, and for that reason the species is still being relentlessly hunted. This is especially pathetic because the desert tortoise makes a poor pet outside its natural range; it requires particular care, and very few survive in captivity. Continuation of the trade in desert tortoises probably would result in their extinction. Fortunately, both California and Arizona have passed legislation to protect *G. agassizii*.

Distribution of *Gopherus agassizii* in the United States.

175. Adult male *Gopherus berlandieri.*

GOPHERUS BERLANDIERI (Agassiz)

Texas Tortoise   XX

RECOGNITION: A small to medium-sized (10.5–22 cm) terrestrial turtle having elephantine hind feet, shovellike forefeet, and a gular projection on the plastron. The short, oblong, keelless carapace has its highest point back of the middle and drops off sharply to a serrated rear margin. It has a somewhat rough, ridged appearance, caused by the usually well-marked growth-rings. The carapace is brown, and the scutes may have yellow centers. The marginals above the hind limbs are flared. The bridge is well developed and usually has two axillary scutes. The hingeless, yellowish plastron is large, and the gular scutes are elongated and project anteriorly, sometimes bending upward. The limbs, neck, and head are yellowish. The head is wedge-shaped, and the snout is somewhat pointed. The angle between the upper crushing ridges is usually more than 65° but less than 70°. There are well-developed glands beneath the rami of the lower jaw. The iris often is greenish-yellow. The forefeet are large and shovellike and have thick, blunt claws; the hind feet are large and flat. The distance from the base of the 1st claw to the base of the 4th claw on the forefoot approximately equals the same measurement on the hindfoot. The toes are not webbed.

The males have slightly longer and narrower carapaces than females, a longer and more deeply forked gular projection, and a concave plastron.

GEOGRAPHIC VARIATION: No subspecies have been described.

CONFUSING SPECIES: Within the Texas tortoise's range *Terrapene ornata* is the only other turtle that habitually lives on land; it has a hinged plastron and lacks a gular projection.

DISTRIBUTION: *G. berlandieri* occurs from southern Texas through eastern Coahuila and Nuevo León to southern Tamaulipas, Mexico.

191

HABITAT: This species is found in habitats ranging from near-desert in Mexico to scrub forests in humid and subtropical parts of southern Texas. Sandy, well-drained soils are preferred, and open scrub woods seem to be specially favored. In southern Texas the species occurs from sea level to a few hundred feet; in Tamaulipas it extends up to 2,900 ft.

BEHAVIOR: Unlike the other two species of *Gopherus* in the United States, *G. berlandieri* usually does not dig an extensive burrow. Instead, it uses its gular projection, forelimbs, and the lateral edges of the shell to push away the surface debris and soil to create a resting-place, to which it often returns. This so-called pallet usually is located under a bush or the edge of a clump of cactus and is simply a ramp sloping just steeply enough to accommodate the anterior edge of the shell below the surface. There are usually several pallets within a tortoise's home range. Continued use of a pallet, together with the clearing away of accumulated soil and debris, tends to deepen it; the deepest one found by Auffenberg and Weaver (1969) was 4 inches deep at its anterior end and 13 inches long. They also found that the use of pallets is seasonal. Pallets in thick brush near Brownsville, Texas, are used throughout the year, but in summer proportionately more tortoises are found in pallets in such places. In winter a greater proportion of tortoises are found in pallets in open brush or in grassland.

Texas tortoises sometimes occupy empty mammal burrows of suitable size. On occasion they excavate burrows as much as 4 ft long and 1 ft deep. Conant (1958) pointed out that where digging is difficult *G. berlandieri* excavate barely enough to hide themselves or else take shelter beneath rocks, stumps, or debris.

Auffenberg and Weaver (1969) thought that the factors governing the kind and use of shelters by all three species of *Gopherus* were the extent of seasonal surface-temperature extremes and the composition of the substrate.

Texas tortoises have two principal activity periods: one in the morning and another in the after-noon. In April the greatest activity occurs at midday, but as the season progresses the two periods become better defined. By July most tortoises are active in the late afternoon (after 3 or 4 PM), but by November midday movements again become more common at the expense of morning and late-afternoon excursions. There are no apparent differences in the activity period with respect to size or sex (Auffenberg and Weaver, 1969).

Carr (1952) reported that in Tamaulipas in December, Texas tortoises go into a state of semihibernation during periods of chilly weather. Because the soils there are too heavy for effective burrowing, they passively await warmer temperatures, often with no more than half the shell under cover. Of six individuals he observed, one was actively moving about in the middle of a bright, warm day. Strecker (1927a) reported that in December a captive lapsed into a semitorpid condition.

G. berlandieri does not often bask. In its natural habitat, prolonged exposure to the direct rays of the sun is fatal. Grant (1960a) reported that a healthy male exposed to direct sunlight died in 20 min while several other tortoises, kept in the shade at 103 F (39.4 C), were not affected. Hutchison *et al.* (1966) reported that the mean loss of righting response of four specimens occurred at 40.4 C (39.8–40.7) and that the mean critical thermal maximum was 42.85 C (42.5–43.2).

In semiarid country *G. berlandieri* may not have access to free water for long periods. Like other species of *Gopherus* it has adapted to this lack by reabsorbing water through the bladder and excreting nitrogenous wastes as semisolids. Baze and Horne (1970) found that in freshly collected *G. berlandieri* ammonia was most concentrated in the blood and uric acid was highest in the urine. The rise in osmotic concentration associated with high levels of urea in dehydrated *Gopherus* may be important in reducing evaporative water-loss during hibernation or other times of stress; this is especially important to turtles living in arid or semiarid habitats. The integument of *Gopherus* is relatively impermeable to water by comparison with that of other turtles; this, too, is important in water conservation. In many localities the most important, and sometimes the only, water available to *G. berlandieri* is the water it extracts metabolically from its food.

Males often engage in combat before the breeding season, but the frequency of fighting declines sharply before the breeding season ends. Weaver (1970) saw combat between captive males (in an outdoor pen in Gainesville, Florida) as early as 12 March and in the field as late as July. In confrontations where neither male is subordinate, both engage in ramming and biting and each attempts to overturn the other with his gular projections. Dominance is apparently established when one overturns the other or when one flees the combat ground after a ramming and pushing contest. Evidence of the combat often remains on the ground in the form of a circle within which the soil has been tamped down by the feet and plastrons of the combatants. At the end of combat the victorious male holds his head higher than that of the defeated male. If combat ends with one tortoise fleeing, the loser retreats with his head extended directly forward and the winner pursues with his head inclined upward about 30°.

Another kind of combat occurs between males when only one of the two is aggressive. The aggressive tortoise rams and bites the other on the front feet, head, and shell in a series of movements similar to those of courtship. The unaggressive male tries to avoid him by pivoting about. The combat ends when the unaggressive male escapes to a pallet or withdraws his head and limbs and remains still (Weaver, 1970).

REPRODUCTION: Auffenberg and Weaver (1969) found that secondary sex characters are clearly evident only in individuals larger than 105 mm in carapace length. Sexual maturity is attained at a carapace length of 105–128 mm; that is, at 3–5 years of age.

Chromatographic analyses of chin-gland secretions of adult male *G. berlandieri* by Rose (1970) revealed the presence of nine fatty acids, and behavioral analyses he conducted indicated that these

176. Plastron of a male *Gopherus berlandieri*.

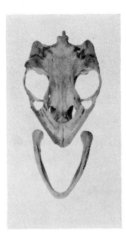

Skull of *Gopherus berlandieri*

served as an olfactory cue during courtship or combat.

Courtship and mating occur in Texas from June to September. Weaver (1970), who studied reproductive activities in the wild and in captivity, has divided the precopulatory behavior of *G. berlandieri* into four stages. The following are his descriptions of the stages:

STAGE ONE: Stage one is a relatively passive phase during which the female shows little active response to the male's presence, but during which she modulates his behavior . . . Courtship behavior begins by the male trailing a female . . . Initially he walks 3 to 10 feet behind her, and his behavior is modulated by hers as two major characteristics of the trailing stage show: (1) he stops whenever she stops, and (2) he often bobs his head in her direction. During the early portion of the trailing stage the male usually walks with his neck only partly extended. During this initial stage of courtship the female's behavioral role is largely one of indifference and she does not bob her head at any time. She normally grazes and noses at various items on the ground, displaying the same movements and activity as lone, unattended females do. Occasionally she makes one or more stops in the shade, during which the male appears to lose interest and may even graze. When she resumes walking, the male continues his trailing. These shade stops may be temperature regulating behavior.

Late in the trailing stage, which may last from a few minutes to nearly an hour, the male shortens the distance between himself and the female. When he is about 3 feet directly behind her he increases the frequency and vigor of head bobbing and when not bobbing holds his head parallel to the ground in a high, arched position, his neck inclined between 25° and 35°. At this point the female increases her walking speed, and ceases all grazing. This shift in the female's behavior marks the end of stage one.

STAGE TWO: The second stage of courtship . . . is more intense than the first, and begins when the male tries to overtake the female and confront her face to face. On overtaking her he stops her by biting her head, front feet, and the top front edge of her carapace, and ramming her forcibly with his massive, elongate gular projection . . . The female at first avoids him by turning away from him so that both tortoises move in a circular path of constantly diminishing diameter. As the male increases the intensity of his biting and ramming, the female finally withdraws her head and front legs but continues to pivot her anterior end away from his by driving with her rear feet. With his increased biting tempo, the male's head bobbing stops or loses any recognizable pattern, and he increasingly confines his biting to the female's nuchal and anterior peripheral bones. The bites now become quite forceful, the male often grasping the female's shell in his mouth and alternately pushing and pulling her, and she soon withdraws her head and front feet, leaving her rear feet extended so she is in an incline with the rear of her shell highest. She no longer pivots, and the male attempts to mount her. The stimulus or releaser for mounting behavior in the male seems to be the female's inclined position. Observations Walter Auffenberg made near Laredo, Texas suggest that the female selects the place where stage two and the subsequent stages occur, usually one relatively free of underbrush.

STAGE THREE: The male may try to mount from any place on the female's shell. If the initial attempts occur at other than the rear of the female's shell, he works his way to the rear with his front feet on the dorsal surface of her carapace and his rear feet on the ground . . .

STAGE FOUR: None of the unions I observed lasted 10 minutes and were terminated when the female walked out from under the male. Housholder (1950) reported that a female *G. berlandieri* (which he thought was a female *G. agassizi*) everted part of her cloaca, apparently to facilitate intromission by the male. This occurs in female *polyphemus* . . . but I did not witness it in *berlandieri* courtships.

Each thrust by the male during copulation pushes the female forward. To compensate for her change of position the male performs a series of hopping steps with his rear feet. Occasionally his rear legs become tangled in grass, which impedes his hop-stepping and interrupts copulation. Thus the female's selection of a relatively clear area helps ensure successful coition.

The length of the nesting season has not been determined. All observed nestings have been in June or July. Auffenberg and Weaver (1969) found small holes that appeared to be trial nest sites, in late April and in August. They also found shelled eggs in a female accidentally killed in November; and freshly caught females sacrificed in the laboratory contained shelled eggs as late as 16 September and ovarian eggs larger than 10 mm in diameter as late as November. They reported that shelled eggs

have been found in the oviducts as early as April and eggs 10 mm or larger as early as March. Ovarian eggs were present in sacrificed females in March and April and again in September, October, and November. Two mature females sacrificed in June and July had no ovarian eggs. These data, which are supported by field observations, suggest two periods of egg-laying in Texas: one in late June and July, the other in late August and September.

Auffenberg and Weaver (1969) thought that soil texture, soil moisture, and orientation with respect to the sun were influences on the choice of nest site. Field data permit some generalizations as to nest sites. The nest normally is dug in soil relatively free of vegetation—usually under or near the drip zone of bushes. No correlation is evident between the chosen site and the shade pattern of the bushes. A positive correlation exists between density of nest sites and density of tortoises. Females use no special nesting grounds. Nests usually are found in small clusters, and there is considerable distance between clusters regardless of tortoise density. Nests are often found near, and even in, the same spot under a particular bush in successive years.

Auffenberg and Weaver (1969) observed the nesting of a captive. At 7:45 AM she scraped the bare floor of the pallet occupied the previous night, using her gular projection as a scoop. Starting at the pallet's shallow end, she pushed a small amount of dirt before her to the deep end. At that end of the pallet, and with her plastron still in contact with the ground, she twisted her shell from side to side so as to shift the loose dirt laterally. She then used her front feet alternately to push the dirt either outside the pallet or onto her carapace. She then backed up to her original starting position, at the shallow end of the pallet, and repeated the sequence. In 30 min she deepened the pallet's far end about 0.5 inch. She then turned in the pallet to face in the opposite direction and, with the rear portion of her shell in the deep end, started to dig the nest with her hind limbs. Alternately she placed each hind leg medially under the plastron; as she drew the leg back to its normal position the

195

outer edge of the plantar surface picked up a small amount of dirt and deposited it forward and to the side. After repeating the scraping movement two or four times she shifted the rear of her shell in the direction of the leg last used, thus bringing the opposite leg over the nest. By 9 AM she was removing less dirt with each stroke: the hole was now so deep that she had to draw each foot vertically to the surface, which meant that she could bring up less soil; furthermore, the soil became increasingly hard with depth. The hardness she partly overcame by urinating into the cavity. Bladder release seemed to be correlated with digging activity, for she dug more rapidly immediately after urinating, and at the increased tempo she removed considerably more earth. And, because the soil had been moistened, it stuck better to the edge of her foot. As the soil again became dry the digging tempo decreased. Observations by Brown (1964) and on another female by Auffenberg and Weaver (1969) differ little from the above account.

There is some evidence that the eggs may be laid on the ground surface if a substrate suitable for nesting cannot be found.

The nest is somewhat flask-shaped, in that the opening is not as wide as the chamber below. Auffenberg and Weaver (1969) gave the measurements of two nests: greatest depth, 2.50 inches and 2.00 inches; greatest width, 2.50 inches and 2.75 inches; and diameter of the opening, 1.50 inches and 1.75 inches, respectively. Sabbath (1960) reported a nest 1.75 inches in diameter and 3.00 inches in depth.

The number of eggs per clutch ranges from one to three. Of 60 nests examined by Auffenberg and Weaver (1969), 38 contained one egg each, 19 contained two eggs each, and 3 had three eggs each.

Grant (1960a) reported that a captive female laid three eggs in a nest on 8 June and deposited single eggs on the surface on 19 June and on 9 and 13 July. Auffenberg and Weaver (1969) felt that under normal conditions this female probably would have made at least two nests. Probably, multiple nestings occur during a single nesting season.

The elongate, white, hardened eggs are 40.0–53.7 mm in length, and 29.0–34.0 mm in width. The average width/length ratio of nine eggs measured by Auffenberg and Weaver was 0.71 (0.61–0.80) to 1, and the same ratio of six eggs measured by Grant (1960a) was 0.73 (0.66–0.82) to 1.

Grant (1960a) and Paxson (1962) have presented evidence that the eggs of *G. berlandieri* must be flexible to be laid. Measurements of eggs and of the maximum space between the posterior carapacial and plastral margins showed that a firm (hardened) egg could not possibly be expelled from the body.

The incubation period is unknown.

Hatchlings are nearly round: about 40–50 mm in both length and width. The umbilical scar disappears at about 50 mm. Pigmented areas of the hatchling shell are brown, unpigmented areas creamy-white. The unpigmented areas are restricted to the posterior edge of the anterior marginals, to the free edges of the lateral and posterior marginals, and to the center of each pleural and vertebral scute. On the plastron, pigment is restricted to the seam areas except on the femoral scutes, where pigment covers all but the free lateral edges. The head has a yellowish stripe extending from below the anterior corner of the eye to the angle of the jaw. The tympanic region is unpigmented. There is a faint, yellowish temporal patch and a small unpigmented spot around the egg tooth and both nostrils. The throat and chin are creamy-white, with a dark spot at the mandibular symphysis. The horny mandibles are dark; the remainder of the head is brown. The scales at the base of the forefeet and the hind feet are black, and the dark scales on the hind feet continue around the side of the heel and up the leg for a short distance; the remainder of the hind leg is creamy-white except for yellowish thigh-scales. The dorsal tail-surface is grayish. The outer brachial scales are black, those of the middle anterior portion of the forelimb have light yellowish centers, and those of the inner edge are creamy-white. The scales of the posterior brachial surface are dark dorsally and lighter below, the sharp differentiation occurring just above the elbow. The gular scute is greatly projected. Laminal spurs and marginal denticulations are absent (Auffenberg and Weaver, 1969).

GROWTH: Auffenberg and Weaver (1969) found that at 1 year of age *G. berlandieri* is 70–81 mm in length; the mean increase in length during the 1st year is 50.3%. When 3–5 years old they are 105–128 mm in length, and they are about 130 mm long in their 6th year. After the 6th year the growth rate slows markedly and remains more or less constant, at approximately 5% per year. The maximum number of major growth-rings counted by Auffenberg and Weaver in any specimen was 18 (at 201 mm), but the number could not be counted accurately in most specimens that were more than 180 mm long. They found that the average absolute growth of males was 7.9 mm/year and 12.5 mm for 2 years, of female specimens 11.1 mm/year and 18.9 mm for 2 years; this suggests that females grow faster than males.

FOOD AND FEEDING: In the wild, *G. berlandieri* seems to prefer the stems, fruits, and flowers of cacti (*Opuntia*); grasses, violets, asters, and other plants also are eaten. In addition to plant remains, a crayfish claw, land-snail shells, and a few fragments of beetles have been recovered from feces. Auffenberg and Weaver (1969) observed Texas tortoises feeding on the feces of other tortoises and of rabbits, and they also saw them biting the bleached bones of cows and rabbits. Captive specimens eat lettuce, tomatoes, grass, clover, and bananas; Pope (1939) reported they eat raw meat.

Several studies (Grant, 1960a; Auffenberg, 1969; Auffenberg and Weaver, 1969) have shown that Texas tortoises prefer red and green foods over blue. They prefer green in spring and shift to red in August and September. This matches the natural color changes, as the red fruits of *Opuntia* mature at that time.

PREDATORS: Skunks, raccoons, and possibly the woodrat *Neotoma micropus* prey on the eggs of the Texas tortoise. The young are eaten by almost any predator that encounters them: foxes, coyotes, skunks, bobcats, raccoons, and snakes. Coyotes and bobcats may prey on adults, but predation pressure on adults is surely low.

177. *Gopherus berlandieri.*

197

Man is by far the chief destroyer of *G. berlandieri*. Texas tortoises formerly were collected and sold in the pet trade, where most died because of inadequate care and diet; fortunately, a Texas law now protects them. Many are crushed by automobiles, and some ranchers kill them because of a mistaken belief that they eat quail eggs.

MOVEMENTS: Auffenberg and Weaver (1969) found that the cumulative average yearly movement for males more than 150 mm in length was 98.6 m for 1 year, 153 m for 2 years, and 130 m for 3 years. Males under 150 mm had average movements of 30 m, 149.1 m, and 178 m for 1, 2, and 3 years, respectively. The cumulative average for females over 150 mm in length was 94.1 m for 1 year, 92.4 m for 2 years, and 164.1 m for 3 years; those under 150 mm had movements of 93.7 m, 162 m, and 302 m for the same time periods. The average maximum distance traveled per day was 20.6 m (5.2–52.5). The tracks made by four *G. berlandieri* in a single day across wind-blown silt measured 46 m, 161 m, 142 m, and 480 m. The mean distance of daily movement for 3 years was 267 m. Daily movements indicated that the tortoises, although nomadic, maintained restricted home ranges for short periods of time.

Hamilton (1944) reported an apparent migration of *G. berlandieri* in the vicinity of Corpus Christi Lake, Texas. Sixteen solitary tortoises were counted on a road in about 3 miles, and at least as many more were observed beside the road, just after the cessation of torrential rains. Most of the tortoises were headed generally east, away from the lake, but the directions varied from NNE to SSE. They were moving as individuals, not as any sort of group. Grant (1936b) also reported a migration of these tortoises in southern Texas but did not give details.

Auffenberg and Weaver (1969) released *G. berlandieri* at various distances from the pallets in which they found them and traced their movements for 36 hr in a test of homing ability. One individual removed 77.6 m to the east returned to its pallet and another removed 42.5 m to the east was 20.7 m from its pallet at the end of the test. The distance and direction removed and the final distance from the pallet of three other specimens were as follows: 31 m S, 31.0 m; 49.6 m WSW, 27.9 m; and 100.1 m SSE, 37.2 m. Of 11 tortoises released on flats at distances of 49.6 to 108.5 m from their homes on bushy lomas (broad-topped hills) only four returned.

Auffenberg and Weaver (1969) presumed that visual or olfactory cues were used in homing. That local features may aid the turtle in remaining on the home range is suggested by the movements of the tortoises released on the featureless flats: they showed no consistent ability to reach the loma from release points 50 and 125 m distant from the loma edge. Tortoises apparently avoid wandering onto the flats; there is no evidence that tortoises regularly cross them from one loma to another, or that they even make short forays onto the flats from a home loma.

POPULATIONS: Auffenberg and Weaver (1969) reported the following parameters for three populations in southeast Texas: Loma Tío Alejos, 27.7% adult males, 57.6% adult females, and 14.7% subadults; Port Isabel Loma, 46.6% adult males and 53.4% adult females; and Mesa del Gavilon, 20% adult males, 40% adult females and 40% subadults. On Loma Tío Alejos the minimum overall density was one tortoise per 430 m², but densities in the major plant associations differed widely, as follows: in brush, one tortoise per 82 m²; in the *Baccharis* zone, 1/300 m²; in grass and cactus, 1/1,231 m²; and in the clay zone, 1/1,575 m². In the open, drier brush of Falcon Dam State Park, Starr County, Texas, the density was about 1/42,000 m².

REMARKS: Although most human activities are harmful to *G. berlandieri*, Auffenberg and Weaver (1969) have pointed out that several human activities, notably managed grazing, favor them. The most dramatic and long-range effects can be seen where brush control is practiced. This practice initially kills many tortoises but in the long run increases grass production; under current practices, the scattered brush-cover the tortoises need reappears very quickly. If the area is grazed by cattle, it is maintained in a dynamic equilibrium in which tortoises can maintain their minimum densities over long periods of time. Slight overgrazing under these conditions encourages the growth of prickly pear (*Opuntia* sp.), one of the staple foods of *G. berlandieri* when grasses become dry in the summer.

G. berlandieri is of little or no economic importance to man.

Distribution of *Gopherus berlandieri* in the United States.

178. Adult male *Gopherus polyphemus.* Elephantine hind feet are characteristic of all the *Gopherus.*

179. A large, old male *Gopherus polyphemus.* With increasing age the older growth annuli are worn away, resulting in a much smoother shell.

GOPHERUS POLYPHEMUS (Daudin)

Gopher Tortoise   XX

RECOGNITION: A large (15–37 cm) terrestrial turtle of the southeastern United States with elephantine hind feet, shovellike forefeet, and a gular projection on the plastron. The keelless, oblong carapace is widest in front of the bridge and, usually, highest in the sacral region; and it may be somewhat constricted behind the bridge. It drops off abruptly to the rear, and the posterior marginals are only slightly serrated. The growth rings usually are well marked and give the dark-brown to grayish-black carapace a somewhat rough, ridged appearance; the scutes often have light centers. The bridge is well developed and usually has a single axillary scute. The gular scutes of the large, hingeless, yellowish plastron are elongated and project anteriorly; they may curve upward. The skin of the head and limbs is grayish-black, that of the limb sockets yellowish. The head is large and rounded, with an angle between the upper crushing ridges of 73° or more. There are well developed integumentary glands beneath the chin. The iris is dark brown. The hind feet are relatively small; the distance from the base of the 1st claw to the base of the 3rd claw on the forefoot approximately equals the distance from the base of the 1st claw to the base of the 4th claw on the hind foot. The toes are not webbed.

Males have more concave plastrons and larger integumentary glands under the chin than females have.

GEOGRAPHIC VARIATION: No subspecies are recognized.

CONFUSING SPECIES: This species can be separated from all the other turtles in its range by its elongate gular projection, small elephantine hind limbs, and shovellike forelimbs.

DISTRIBUTION: *G. polyphemus* ranges from South Carolina south along the Atlantic coastal plain through Florida and west along the Gulf coastal plain to extreme eastern Louisiana.

HABITAT: The gopher tortoise usually lives on well-drained, sandy soils in transitional areas (ecotones) where two different ecologic communities, such as forest and grassland, come together. Only *Terrapene carolina* shares its terrestrial habitat, but adjacent aquatic habitats may contain *Macroclemys* and species of *Chelydra, Kinosternon, Sternotherus, Chrysemys, Deirochelys,* and *Trionyx.*

BEHAVIOR: Like other members of the genus, *G. polyphemus* is a burrower; however, its forelimbs and feet are more specialized for digging than are those of its two U.S. congeners. In *G. agassizii* and *G. berlandieri* the wrist is movable to a limited degree, but in *G. polyphemus* it is kept virtually immovable by strong, sheetlike ligaments that bind the bones into a relatively solid unit (Auffenberg, 1966a). Thus the forelimbs of the gopher tortoise are notably effective soil-moving devices—a pair of built-in shovels.

G. polyphemus digs a long burrow, which it usually inhabits throughout its life, although it may have some alternate burrows. The burrow, dug in sandy soil, is mostly dry but at the deepest point is usually somewhat moist. Within the burrow the temperature and humidity remain relatively constant throughout the year; that is, the burrow is a microhabitat in which the gopher turtle is unaffected by climatic changes on the surface.

The burrows usually are straight and unbranched; sometimes they curve around obstructions. Hansen (1963) recorded the dimensions of 13 burrows as follows: length 106–242 inches, depth 55–110 inches, angle of decline 17–39°, entrance width 7.3–12.5 inches, entrance depth 2.5–6.5 inches, width at 2 ft, 5.3–9.0 inches, and depth at 2 ft, 2.5–5.5 inches. He also reported one burrow 47.5 ft long. In 54 burrows the height/width ratio of the burrow entrance was 0.51 to 1, and at 2 ft down it became 0.54 to 1. There usually is an enlarged chamber at the end of the burrow; there the tortoise sleeps and can turn around. The tortoise often defecates in its burrow, and fecal matter frequently accumulates in the terminal chamber. Brode (1959) saw gopher tortoises in late summer backing out of their holes, dragging and scraping dung and trash and depositing it several feet beyond the entrance.

Many animals find the burrow of a gopher tortoise a suitable permanent home or a temporary shelter. Among vertebrates found in the burrows are skunks, red foxes, raccoons, opossums, rats, rabbits, quail, burrowing owls, diamondback rattlesnakes, black racers, indigo snakes, six-lined racerunners, gopher frogs, leopard frogs, and toads (Carr, 1952; Brode, 1959). Many arthropods also occur as commensals or obligates in these burrows: Young and Goff (1939) listed 32 species of spiders, ticks, and insects.

In Florida the gopher tortoise often is active during the warmest hours of the day. From about 10 AM to 2 PM they wander about, browsing as they go; other times usually are spent in the burrow. On cool days they bask at the entrance before starting on their journeys, but warm rain does not seem to upset the daily routine. Fluctuations of light and temperature entrain their internal clock, which under constant light and temperature (26 C) shows a mean period length of 22:33.4 hr (Gourley, 1969).

Gopherus polyphemus characteristically basks with its head in an elevated position—in marked contrast to *G. berlandieri* and *G. agassizii.* Often it extends its forefeet to the sides and its hind feet to the rear.

In Florida the gopher tortoise is, essentially, active all year: it remains in the burrow during cold spells but emerges on warm days. Farther north it may truly hibernate briefly, during severe weather.

It can withstand high body temperatures. Bogert and Cowles (1947) found 34–35 C to be normal for active individuals. Hutchison *et al.* (1966) recorded a critical thermal maximum of 43.9 C—the highest they found in any turtle.

Bogert and Cowles (1947) found that a *G. polyphemus* kept in a desiccation chamber at 38 C and 37% relative humidity lost moisture at a mean rate of 0.42% of the initial weight per hour for more than 79 hr. A total loss of 30.4% of the original weight (43% water loss) was recorded; the tortoise died. Auffenberg and Weaver (1969) reported that of all *Gopherus* species *G. polyphemus* desiccates most rapidly in captivity if deprived of a burrow. This may explain why this species is so consistently associated with burrows over most of its range; the only places where they do not dig burrows are both warm and moist.

Carr (1952) observed fights between male and female *G. polyphemus*. Weaver (1970) saw ramming between a captive male and female, but it was not clear whether this was courtship or combat. He also saw one moderate-sized, malformed male *G. polyphemus* repeatedly ram a subadult *Geochelone elephantopus* and an adult *Geochelone pardalis*, each of which was at least 20 lbs heavier than its assailant. A 19.7-cm male we have, when introduced to a 35.6-cm male first sniffed and bobbed its head and then repeatedly rammed the larger male and drove it into a shelter.

Weaver (1970) gained some data on combat in *G. polyphemus* by watching confrontations between males in the laboratory. When a newcomer is placed in their pen, males either remain still, immediately proceed toward the intruder, or (in a few cases) retreat into a corner. When approaching an intruder, a highly motivated tortoise walks rapidly with his neck fully extended; under normal circumstances the pace is slower and the neck is only partly extended. When the tortoises are about 2.5 ft apart, head-bobbing begins. The fact that he head is always pointed in the direction of another tortoise when bobbing occurs suggests that a visual cue is involved, but a highly motivated tortoise will walk toward another tortoise in the absence of reciprocal bobbing or locomotion. At contact the vertical bobs of both males become more lateral and finally lose any recognizable pattern. Each sniffs the head and feet of the other. The vertical bobs associated with these sniffing movements often are interrupted by a lateral wiping motion across the surface of one of its forelegs. After 1 or 2 min of mutual sniffing, one of the tortoises becomes more active than the other, and they clearly demonstrate dominance relationships by their postures. The dominant tortoise supports its weight on all four of its extended legs. He may walk around

the submissive one, stopping often to smell his rear legs. The submissive tortoise holds his head low, with his neck only partly extended. If the dominant tortoise continues to investigate, the submissive one positions himself at an angle of approximately 45° to the dominant one and maneuvers to keep one side or the other presented to the front of the dominant individual. He does this with his hind legs by pivoting on the anterior portion of the plastron, keeping the front legs withdrawn. After 1 or 2 min of this behavior the dominant individual turns away, apparently having lost interest in the other tortoise. Perhaps in meetings between two males, or a male and a female *G. polyphemus* in the nonbreeding season, noncombative recognition of dominance results in the subordinate tortoise leaving the dominant individual's presence. Weaver's experiments failed to show that a given *G. polyphemus* always dominates an intruder introduced into its home pen; instead, certain individuals tended markedly to be dominant both in their own pen and in those of others.

When surprised away from its burrow *G. polyphemus* may retreat into its shell or merely try to walk away. It never bites but may scratch if picked up. Captives quickly become tame and seldom retreat into their shells when handled.

REPRODUCTION: Mating occurs in the spring. Courtship apparently consists of several basic sequential activities. The first of these Auffenberg (1966b) termed the "male orientation circle": the male walks in a circle and periodically stops and bobs his head, perhaps to attract the attention of a sexually responsive female. When a female approaches he bobs his head violently, then bites her on the forelegs, head, anterior edge of the carapace, and, especially, the gular projection. (This is probably the method of sex identification; females do not bite one another or males.) The female then backs in a semicircle, stops, and stretches her hind legs. Later she pivots 180°, so that the posterior part of her shell is nearest the male's head; this may be a primitive form of presentation. The attempts to mount—usually unsuccessful—are followed by more biting, which in turn is followed by a successful mounting and coition.

Auffenberg (1969) found that in some instances, just before the male's behavior changed from head-bobbing to biting, the female rubbed the side of her face and chin across her outstretched front legs. Adults of all four species of *Gopherus* have a pair of glands on the chin; although they are small most of the year, these glands usually become swollen in the breeding season. Both sexes have an enlarged scale, more prominent than the rest, on each front leg near the elbow. Scent probably is transferred by the female from her chin to her front legs by means of this scale. Her chin-rubbing seems to be a response to the male's head-bobbing, and Auffenberg speculated that this action causes the male to change his behavior from bobbing to biting. His bobbing may provide the female with more than just a visual cue: he has glands beneath the lower jawbone, and the bobbing may also serve to spread a scent that is a signal to the female.

Nesting occurs from late April to mid-July. Most nests are located at a considerable distance from the burrow, but some are dug in the burrow entrances. Arata (1958) found two nests in the conspicuous mound of sand at the entrance to gopher tortoise burrows. In each of these nests the eggs were in one plane, about 6 inches beneath the surface. The sand above the eggs was exposed to the full rays of the sun.

Perhaps the only description of the nesting process has been given by Kenefick (1954). On 27 June, at 10:50 AM, a captive female started digging a nest. (She had been found mating on 23 April.) She first swung her body in a circle while scraping a shallow, bowl-shaped depression with her front feet; it was about 2.5 ft in diameter. Then, using her hind feet only, she dug a cylindrical cavity, slightly flared at the bottom; it was about 5 inches in diameter and 5 inches deep—apparently as far as she could reach. At 11 AM, while straddling the cavity with her rear feet, she laid her first egg. This action was accompanied by long sighs as the neck was moved in and out of the shell. As each egg was laid in the cavity it was pushed to the front by a hind foot. The last

180. Plastral view of *Gopherus polyphemus.*

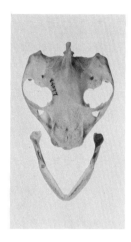
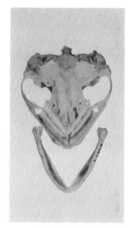

Skull of *Gopherus polyphemus*

Distribution of *Gopherus polyphemus*.

181. Face of *Gopherus polyphemus*.

of seven eggs was laid at 11:30 AM. After this she scraped dirt from the sides of the hole with her hind feet and lightly covered the eggs; then she used her front feet to complete the covering—a 20-min job, in all. After the nest was filled she walked back and forth over it, brushing it lightly with her foreclaws. The entire procedure, from first digging to final brushing took 1 hr.

Clutch size ranges from four to seven eggs; five or six are usual. The white, brittle eggs usually are almost spherical, but Arata (1958) reported the eggs of one clutch to be somewhat elliptical. The diameter is 38–46 mm, with the greater diameter usually about 43 mm and the least about 41 mm. Often there is less than a 1-mm difference between the greatest and least diameters. Eleven eggs weighed approximately 33.5–47.0 g.

Brode (1959) studied 40 nests in Mississippi and found that most of the five or six eggs in each hatched but only about half the young dug their way out. He attributed this mortality to the fact that the overburden was hard-packed.

Hatching and emergence occur in August and September. At hatching the yolk sac is large, averaging 10 by 10 by 5 mm, but it is completely resorbed within 18–24 hr. The deep transverse flexure across the yellow plastron essentially disappears within 3 days. The granular carapace is almost round, being only slightly longer than wide. The dorsal scutes have yellow centers; their edges and the marginals range from a deep grayish-brown to brown. There are two tiny points on the anterior edge of each gular, a similar one at the tip of each anal scute, and an even more minute one on the lateral margin of each femoral scute. A hard, sharp laminal spur is present on the posterolateral margin of each humeral scute; it disappears after a time. Young at hatching averaged 42.9 mm in carapace length and 43.4 mm in width; within 6 hr the proportions changed to 43.4 mm in length and 42.1 mm in width as a result of the straightening of the body axis (Arata, 1958).

GROWTH: Goin and Goff (1941) recovered 33 of 131 marked Florida individuals. The greatest growth was that of a female, which increased in length from 148 mm to 190 mm between June 1937 and March 1938; during this period her weight increased from 545 g to 800 g. The average gain in length for all 33 tortoises was 10.5 mm for an average period of a little less than a year. The average gain in weight was 137.3 g, the greatest 535 g.

The longevity of the gopher tortoise is unknown, but growth annuli show some specimens to be more than 25 years old.

FOOD AND FEEDING: The digestive tracts of wild gopher tortoises examined by Carr (1952) contained large amounts of grass and leaves, with occasional bits of hard fruits, bones, charcoal, and, on one occasion, insect chitin. Brode (1959) observed them eating mushrooms. Captives are known to eat lettuce, grasses, dandelions, various fruits, canned salmon, hamburger, and dog food.

PREDATORS: Auffenberg and Weaver (1969) reported that, in Florida, nests destroyed before hatching usually are lost within the 1st week. Scents associated with nest-building and egg-laying probably are more important in leading predators to a nest than is the scent of the eggs themselves. These associated scents probably disappear or become masked after a few days. Skunks and raccoons are the leading nest predators. Adult indigo snakes (*Drymarchon corais*) are known to feed on hatchlings, but man is the leading killer of adults: many are crushed on the highways, and they are also slaughtered for food. Many juveniles and adults are captured and sold in the pet trade, where they do poorly and usually die soon after removal from their natural habitat. Rattlesnake hunts in parts of the range are decimating many populations, because the gasses introduced into the burrows to kill the snakes also kill the tortoises. Many populations are being destroyed by the steady press of housing developments, shopping centers, and agriculture.

MOVEMENTS: The gopher tortoise has a well-defined home range. As a tortoise becomes older and larger it increases the size of its home range, which for some old individuals may be extensive. The largest recorded home range is 31,400 m² for a 20.3-cm specimen (Gourley, 1969). Several alternate burrows may be made within the home range, and well-marked pathways often connect them. Burrows seldom are located more than 50 m from places where the tortoise grazes, and well-defined trails usually connect the burrows with these places.

Layne (in Goin and Goin, 1962) trapped a gopher tortoise in its burrow and released it at 10:20 AM in a fire lane about 140 m from the mouth of the burrow. A few minutes later it had moved to within 45 m of the burrow. It progressed at a leisurely but steady pace, pausing momentarily now and then to nip at some vegetation. When near the burrow site the tortoise turned and headed directly for the burrow, which was about 18 m from the fire lane and screened by brush; it arrived back at the burrow at 10:32 AM. Layne then took the tortoise about 180 m west of the burrow into thick brush and released it at about 10:40 AM. He then removed the trap from the burrow entrance, smoothed the soil, and departed. At 2:30 PM he discovered tracks leading into the burrow—probably those of the tortoise handled in the morning.

Some form of orientation is used by *G. polyphemus* to return to a particular burrow. Gibbons and Smith (1968) recorded the compass bearings of tortoises crossing roads in Florida. Each of the tortoises was then put into a closed cardboard box, taken 1 mile farther down the road, released in the middle of the road, and pointed in a randomly chosen direction. The sun was visible at the time of release in all instances. Most captures and releases were made between 9 AM and 11 AM and between 4 AM and 6 PM. Of 18 released, 9 went in the direction of their original movement, 6 moved in the opposite direction, and 3 at right angles to the original direction. Gibbons and Smith thought the simplest explanation was that the tortoises were using the sun to find a particular compass direction.

Gourley (1969) conducted orientation tests in an open field and in an arena. In the field, 56.5% of individuals showed statistically significant direction preferences. The chosen directions had no relation to the homeward direction and were widely divergent for tortoises from the same population. In the arena, 51.4% showed significant direction preferences. A comparison of the preferred directions in the field and the arena indicated that landmarks may have had a disruptive effect on orientation. Gourley also subjected the tortoises to an advanced phase shift of 6 hr. This resulted in a change in the expected (counterclockwise) direction, and the mean shift was not significantly different from the expected shift of 90°. These data indicate that the gopher tortoise is probably capable of sun-compass orientation.

Yerkes (in Pope, 1939) showed that *G. polyphemus* has judgment about walking off elevated surfaces: at heights of about 1 ft there was hesitation at the edge, whereas at 6 ft great fear was exhibited.

The gopher tortoise will swim of its own accord in both fresh and brackish water. Brode (1959) observed one at the Gulf Coast Research Laboratory in Mississippi swim the boat slip—a dredged channel about 60 ft wide—in order to get to a woods. It was a slow swimmer and maintained a fairly regular course.

REMARKS: National Audubon Society biologist Frank J. Ligas showed us photographs of a 16-inch (40.6-cm), 29-lb male that was collected on the Brighton Indian Reservation, Florida. Unfortunately, this specimen was not available for examination.

These tortoises are surprisingly strong for their size. Knight (in Carr, 1952) reported that one carried a full-grown man on its back with apparent ease. A large specimen kept at home by one of us (CHE) often moved the furniture around, causing much consternation.

Auffenberg (1969) found that in at least one locality on the west coast of Florida some tortoises do not dig burrows. Individuals in this recently discovered population do construct the feeding trailways characteristic of the species. However, they live on land that is close to sea level which has soil only a few inches thick over limestone bed-rock; that is, the ground conditions make burrowing impossible. Suitable temperature and humidity the year around permit tortoises to survive there without burrows.

G. polyphemus is of little economic importance. It is eaten in some parts of the south, and in the past its shell was used as a sun helmet. Some revenue is gained from its sale in the pet trade. The ancient Indians had a monetary system in which gopher tortoises played a part like that of wampum, and the shells were used as baskets and pots. Gopher tortoises may cause slight damage to crops or gardens, and livestock sometimes trip in the burrows. Gopher tortoise burrows undoubtedly are a factor in the survival of many species, which shelter in them during times of stress.

CHELONIIDAE: Marine Turtles

Four living genera and six species of Cheloniidae occur in the warmer marine waters. Five species inhabit the coastal waters of the United States.

These large sea turtles have a heart-shaped carapace, which is covered with horny scutes. The fore limbs are paddlelike, with elongated digits. The neck is short, and the ability to retract the head has been lost. The carapace retains the embryonic spaces between the ribs; thus the neurals and pleurals are greatly reduced in size. The nuchal is attached ventrally to the neural arch of the 8th vertebra. The 4th vertebra is biconvex. The carapace and plastron are connected by ligaments; the plastron is somewhat reduced and has a small entoplastron. The deltopectoral crest of the humerus is far down the shaft, the trochanteric fossa of the femur is greatly restricted, and the trochanters are united. The temporal region of the skull is completely roofed. The premaxillae are not fused, meet the vomer, and separate the internal nares and palatines. A secondary palate is present, but palatine fenestra are lacking. The pterygoids separate the basisphenoid from the palatines but do not touch the maxilla. The maxilla does not contact the quadratojugal. The dentary is confined to the anterior half of the lower jaw.

CHELONIA MYDAS (Linnaeus)

Green Turtle   XXI

RECOGNITION: A medium-sized to large (76–153 cm) sea turtle having paddlelike forelimbs, a single pair of prefrontal scales on the head, and a serrated cutting edge on the lower jaw. The broad, low, heart-shaped carapace lacks a vertebral keel and is serrated posteriorly. There are four pairs of pleurals, and the 1st pleural is not in contact with the cervical. The carapacial scutes are olive to brown and may contain a mottled, radiating or wavy pattern. The bridge has four inframarginal scutes, which lack pores. The hingeless plastron is immaculate white or yellowish. The skin is brown or, sometimes, gray to black, and many of the head scales may have yellow margins. The horny inner surface of the upper jaw

182. Female *Chelonia mydas*. This turtle is hunted for food wherever it occurs.

has well-developed vertical ridges, and the cutting edge of the lower jaw is strongly serrated.

In males the carapace is more tapering posteriorly and the hind lobe of the plastron is narrower than in females. In males the tail is strongly prehensile in a vertical plane, is tipped with a heavy, flattened nail, and extends far beyond the posterior carapacial margin; in females the tail barely reaches the margin. The forelimb in males has a single claw that is large and curved.

The common name of this turtle is derived from the greenish color of its body fat.

183. Plastral view of *Chelonia mydas*.

GEOGRAPHIC VARIATION: Two subspecies are recognized. *C. m. mydas* (Linnaeus), the Atlantic green turtle, ranges in the Atlantic Ocean from New England and the British Isles to Argentina and extreme South Africa. It is often abundant about Ascension Island, in the Cape Verde Islands and the Cayman Islands, and off Bermuda. This subspecies is predominantly brown and has an elongated, shallow carapace that is not markedly indented above the hind limbs. *C. m. agassizii* Bocourt, the Pacific green turtle, ranges from Ethiopia around the Cape of Good Hope to western Africa, and east through the Indian and Pacific oceans to the western coast of the New World, from the United States to Chile. This turtle is greenish or olive-brown and has a broad, deep shell that is often markedly indented above the hind limbs. Some individuals of this subspecies are melanistic, becoming slate-gray to black in overall color. Caldwell (1962c) described a *C. m. carrinegra* from the Gulf of California on the basis of this dark pigment; however, since such black turtles occur also in Guatemala and the Galápagos Islands and paler individuals can be found in the Gulf of California, there seems to be no geographic distinction between the two color-forms and all eastern Pacific green turtles should be considered *C. m. agassizii*.

CONFUSING SPECIES: *Eretmochelys imbricata* has two pairs of prefrontal scales, and the large scutes of the carapace overlap. *Caretta caretta* and the two species of *Lepidochelys*, L. kempii and L. olivacea, have five or more pairs of pleurals, with the first pair touching the cervical.

DISTRIBUTION: *Chelonia mydas* ranges through the Atlantic, Pacific, and Indian oceans, chiefly in the tropics.

HABITAT: The green turtle migrates across the open seas but feeds in shallow water supporting an abundance of submerged vegetation. It shares its nesting beaches with all species of sea turtles (including the Australian flatback, *C. depressa*).

BEHAVIOR: *Chelonia mydas* spends most of the daylight hours browsing on the vast underwater beds of turtle grass. It occasionally climbs out onto beaches and rocky ledges to bask; in fact, it is the only marine turtle that habitually does so. At night it sleeps on the bottom or on a ledge above the water level.

Walker (1959) reported that when *Chelonia mydas* is resting underwater it closes its nostrils. Closure occurs within each nostril, not at the tip; and it is effected by the meeting of three bulges from the wall of each nasal passage. When *Chelonia* is prowling underwater it keeps its nostrils open and slowly moves the floor of the mouth up and down, apparently for olfaction.

Berkson (1966, 1967) studied the physiologic adjustments to prolonged and deep diving in *Chelonia mydas*. He found that in prolonged dives the green turtle can survive up to 5 hr with no measurable oxygen in the trachea or in the blood of the carotid artery and that as long as 9 min may elapse between heartbeats; intervals of 4–5 min were common.

The cloacal temperatures of seven females were recorded just after they had crawled out of the ocean to nest. The average temperature taken 3-20 min after they had left the water but before laying was 29.9 C; that taken 1-2 hr after emerging—by which time laying had been completed—was 30.0 C. The temperature of shallow water offshore was 27.5–28.5 C during the period (Hirth, 1962).

McGinnis (1968) reported that *C. mydas* does not consistently seek out either warm or cool layers

of water. Captives were more active at cooler water temperatures (18–22 C) and became torpid at higher water temperatures (26–30 C).

The green turtle has large salt-secreting glands located in the orbits. These glands consist of closely packed and branched tubules that radiate from central ducts; that is, they are similar to salt glands in birds. The glands remove excess salts from the blood and help maintain osmotic balance.

In temperament green turtles usually are inoffensive, but they can bite viciously.

REPRODUCTION: Sexual maturity in *C. m. mydas* is reached sometime between 5 and 13 years. Of 1,146 nesting female *C. m. mydas* at Tortuguero, Costa Rica, the smallest was 69.2 cm in carapace length, the largest 117.5 cm; average length was 100 cm (Carr and Ogren, 1960). Mature females at Ascension Island (Carr and Hirth, 1962) averaged 108 cm (83.8–141.0). Pritchard (1969a) found that mature female *C. m. mydas* at Shell Beach, Guyana, measured 96.5–116.8 cm and those at Bigi Santi, Surinam, 100.3–121.9 cm. The average mature female *C. m. agassizii* of the China Sea population is about 97.8 cm in carapace length (Hendrickson, 1958). Hendrickson thought that maturity in *C. m. agassizii* is attained in 4–6 years. Hirth and Carr (1970) reported that nesting female *C. m. agassizii* in the Gulf of Aden were 78.7–114.3 cm long and averaged 96.0 cm. Grazing males in the Gulf of Aden have a mean carapace length of 90.4 cm (71–104). Caldwell (1962c) thought it possible that individuals from the Gulf of California mature at a smaller size. He reported that males as small as 63.5 cm in carapace length had well-developed tails, many at 71 cm had tails that seemed fully developed, and all had fully developed tails at a carapace length of 76.2 cm.

Mating occurs during the laying season and in the water off the nesting beaches. Although mated pairs have been seen more than 1 mile from shore, the greatest concentration is close to shore. Copulation occurs at any hour, but whether it takes place before or after the first nesting emergence is unknown. Several males may simultaneously court and attempt to mate with a single female. Loveridge and Williams (1957) reported that in Aldabra Island lagoon the males fight desperately with each other during the breeding season.

Copulating pairs float at the surface, with the male atop the female. The enlarged claws on the front flippers and the strong nail at the tip of the prehensile tail provide a firm three-point attachment; moreover, the male's claws cut into the female's carapace at the third intermarginal seam and leave deep, bleeding wounds.

C. m. mydas is known to nest on the beaches of Costa Rica, Guyana, Surinam, Vera Cruz (Mexico), Ascension Island, Mona Island, Aves Island, the Cape Verde Islands, Trinidad, the Dry Tortugas, and Mujeres Island. It also may occasionally nest on the coasts of Florida, Bermuda, Alta Vela, and the Cayman Islands. On the beaches of the Caribbean, the Gulf of Mexico, and the Cape Verde Islands the nesting season extends from March to October, with the greatest activity in May and June. On Ascension Island the season extends from December to July, with the period from February to April being most important.

C. m. agassizii is known to nest on the western coast of Africa and on the beaches of Ethiopia, Madagascar, the Seychelles Islands, Mauritius, the Maldive Islands, Yemen, Ceylon, Pakistan, Burma, Malaya, Thailand, Borneo, the islands of the Strait of Malacca, Talang Islands, northern Australia, the Caroline Islands, the Marshall Islands, the Hawaiian Islands and other central-Pacific islands, the Galápagos Islands, and the Pacific coasts of Central America and Mexico. Carr (1952) reported that the nesting season in Australia extends from late October to mid-February; in the Gulf of Siam the year around, with a July-to-November peak; on Ceylon from July to November; in the Malacca Straits from December through January; in the Seychelles Islands the year around with a March-to-May peak; and in Borneo from May to September. Loveridge and Williams (1957) reported that on the western coast of Africa the laying season is from September to January.

Hendrickson (1958) found that the nesting beaches on islands usually were on the leeward side, and in Sarawak (Borneo) the principal ones had fringing coral reefs below mean low tide. Hirth and Carr (1970) compared the characteristics of the nesting beaches at South Yemen, Aldabra Island, Ascension Island, Aves Island, and Tortuguero, Costa Rica. They found that the sand varied from fine to coarse in texture and from olive-gray to white in color. The pH ranged from 6.9 to 8.0 and the carbonate content was high in all beaches except at Tortuguero. Organic content was 0.30-1.18%.

Nesting occurs at night. The following account of the nesting of *C. m. mydas* is quoted from the observation by Carr and Giovannoli (1957) on a female found at 9:15 PM on 25 August 1955 as she was emerging from the breakers at Tortuguero, Costa Rica:

After a few stops to "smell" the sand . . . the turtle dragged herself out of the water and started up the beach. The trip took her a distance of about 55 paces, and, with many pauses and periods of apparent appraisal of the outlook, consumed 20 minutes. When the turtle reached the edge of the beach vegetation (largely sea grapes at this point), she crawled uncertainly back and forth a few times, then settled herself and at 9:35 P.M. began making tentative "swipes" at the sand with her front flippers. These strokes led gradually into purposeful digging. The first operation was the thrashing out of the nesting pit (a broad depression, in this case about 4 feet wide) dug by violent throwing of sand by all four feet, the body meantime rotating slowly. As the depression deepened, the body of the turtle, or its back three-quarters, was lowered into it.

At 10:00 P.M. the turtle was well planted in her pit, the pivoting had stopped, and the deepening and enlarging of the hole continued largely by means of alternate kicking by the hind feet. At 10:16 P.M. the kicking stopped. The turtle pushed the distal edge of a hind flipper against the bottom of the pit, curled it, and scooped out the first sand from what was to become the egg cavity.

From then on the digging of the egg chamber continued for nearly half an hour, the two hind fins being thrust alternately into the deepening hole to "palm" out perhaps a teacupful of sand each time. Then a curious maneuver was observed—one not mentioned in the sketchy accounts in the literature of nesting by the

Pacific form and not noticed by us during careful observance of nesting by the loggerhead turtle and by the Pacific ridley. As the working flipper was thrust into the hole for its load of sand, the other flipper was spread firmly on the sand beside the mouth of the hole. The excavating fin raised its burden of sand out of the hole, slowly moved it to the side, and dropped it. Immediately the off flipper shot out laterally and upward and struck the under margin of the shell a hard back-hand blow. There was great force in this movement, and the thumping sound it made could be heard above a moderate surf when the observer moved away to a distance of 40 paces. This mannerism is typical and is continuously executed throughout this stage of the digging. We have twice located nesting turtles in the dark by tracing the sound. The aim of the movement seems to be to rid the site of any loose sand that might fall into the cavity. The action is too fast to follow with the eye, but when such a stroke has been completed the lip and environs of the hole on the side where the flipper rested are clean and firm. As the flippers alternate in digging, the process is repeated in reverse, and the whole operation of excavating the urn-shaped egg cavity is a series of such bilateral reciprocal actions.

At 10:45 P.M. the turtle stopped digging, dropped her tail low in the cavity, and began to lay. The complement was dropped singly and by two's, the intervals between extrusions of eggs varying between one and 10 seconds except for a few periods of rest of as long as 30 to 60 seconds towards the end of the operation. Throughout the time that the eggs were being dropped, the two hind flippers were spread and held horizontally close together over the opening of the cavity, covering it completely . . . . This seems to be a typical, though not invariable, maneuver, for it was noticed in every case except one that was watched at this stage of the process (at least several dozen). It is a marked departure from the behavior of *Caretta* and *Lepidochelys* which press the vertically oriented back fins against the upper part of the wall of the cavity as if to keep sand from falling in.

At 11:08 P.M. laying was completed, and the filling of the egg hole was begun. . . . The turtle reached laterally with alternately working hind flippers, raked in sand, and kneaded it into the hole. When the hole was full the raking and packing continued, so that the mound grew beneath the after edge of the shell. From time to time the turtle bunched and squeezed this mound between her flippers, and as it continued to grow the back end of her body was pushed up until it was nearly horizontal, in-

184. Swimming *Chelonia mydas*. The limbs of all sea turtles, as shown here, are highly modified for an aquatic existence.

stead of being inclined on the slope of the nest pit as it had been throughout the laying process.

At 11:15 P.M. work with the hind flippers stopped and the fore fins began to thrash and to sling sand. After a few strokes, the hind flippers joined in this work. As the turtle threw sand, she shifted the orientation of her body, and the indiscriminately flung sand gradually filled the nesting pit and sprinkled the surroundings through a radius of 6 to 8 feet. As the pit filled, the shifting stopped, but the scooping and throwing of sand with the fore fins continued, and eventually produced two good-sized basins (one for each flipper) at some distance from the former rim of the now indistinguishable nest excavation. Gradually the scattering of sand was discontinued, and the turtle began shuffling and scuffing about, over and near the site (but doing nothing like the pounding mentioned in the literature on other species). When all work was done the two depressions scooped out during the filling process by the fore flippers remained as the most conspicuous features of the local topography and may reasonably be regarded as diversionary in function.

At 11:32 P.M. all concern with the nest seemed to leave the turtle suddenly, and she made for the sea, moving towards it at an angle of roughly 20 degrees and disappearing in the surf at 11:43 P.M.

Carr and Hirth (1962) reported that the high threshold of alarm of the emerging Ascension Island turtle is the most striking behavioral difference between it and a member of the Tortuguero population: when the latter strands and starts up the beach she can be turned back into the surf by the slightest show of artificial light or by the movement of something silhouetted against the starlit sky. In the Ascension population the pattern of behavior, which in most turtles begins with the digging process and thereafter keeps the animal oblivious to outside interference, appears to take over at the time of stranding. The turtles could thus be watched at close quarters—which permitted the observation that sand-smelling (whatever its function may be) is standard procedure with the Ascension turtles. Hendrickson (1958) found that the nesting process of *C. m. agassizii* in Sarawak was very similar to that described above.

Bustard and Greenham (1969) found that several aspects of the behavior of Heron Island, Australia, *C. m. agassizii* differed from that of Costa Rica females. Protracted smelling of the beach at the water's edge was not performed by the Australia turtles. During oviposition the rear flippers were either spread together over the nest or else one or both flippers projected posteriorly into and were pressed against the rear of the egg chamber. Both positions occurred with equal frequency. The striking of the shell with the off flipper and the consequent clearing of the nesting hole of loose sand was not seen to occur in the Heron Island green turtles.

Hirth and Carr (1970) reported that, on the average, *C. m. agassizii* on the beaches of South Yemen took about 2 hr to complete the nesting sequence. A typical schedule was as follows: clearing of nest site and excavating a body pit, 35 min; digging the nest cavity, 35 min; oviposition, 10 min; filling and packing the nest cavity, 10 min; and filling the body pit and concealing the site, 40 min. If one were to include the time it took the turtle to emerge from the sea, select a nest site, and crawl back to the sea after nesting, the total time on land would be increased by 0.5–1.5 hr. Some noteworthy variations in the nesting behavior of Yemen green turtles were (1) the relatively deep body-pits—sometimes more than twice the depth of the shell; (2) the audible sound made by the backstroke of the hind foot during the digging of the egg chamber; and (3) a peculiar shuffle in the early part of the same stage. The depth of the body pits no doubt is accounted for by the extremely loose character of the sand at most of the rookery beaches. In this respect the body pits in South Yemen suggest those made by Ascension Island green turtles (Carr and Hirth, 1962). In approximately 60% of the nest-hole excavations observed by Hirth and Carr the extreme forward swing of the hind limb that flips sand forward during egg-chamber excavation brought the foot sharply against the shell with a thudding sound. Caldwell, Carr, and Ogren (1959) and Carr and Ogren (1960) reported that when digging the egg chamber several species of sea turtles regularly pivot the body on the anterior part of the plastron to swing the working flipper into position over the hole. In most of the South Yemen nestings there was a distinct two-step movement at this stage. After the left hind flipper was jerked forward, to kick away the loose sand on that side and make the sound just described, the body was pivoted slightly to the right, stopped, then shifted again to the right, and finally stopped with the flipper in position to dig. This shuffle was most pronounced during the initial stages of the nest-digging sequence; as the hole became deeper the shuffle sometimes was continued on only one side, and as the hole neared completion all pivoting usually ceased.

Carr and Carr (1970) calculated, from 447 returns of the turtles tagged during 15 years at the nesting beach at Tortuguero, Costa Rica, that some females nest every 2 years and others every 3 years; the latter is the more frequent cycle. Returns after absences of 4 years were so frequent that they thought it probable that a regular cycle of this duration also exists. A growing list of two-time and three-time returns showed that, although an individual usually maintains a constant cycle, modulation may occur and that the change may be either from 3 to 2 years or vice versa. They suggested that the modulation reflects ecologic conditions on the feeding ground. Hendrickson (1958) reported results indicating that Sarawak females probably follow a 3-year nesting cycle.

Female *Chelonia mydas* usually nest several times in a given season. Pritchard (1967a) reported that they may nest as many as eight times in a season. Carr and Ogren (1960) found a maximum of six nestings, at a mean interval of 12.5 days (12–14), on Tortuguero, Costa Rica. Hendrickson (1958) found the mean interval between nestings on the Talang Islands, off Sarawak, was 10.5 days. Carr and Hirth (1962) reported 14.5 days as the interval at Ascension Island. Pritchard (1969a) reported an interval of 13 days in Guyana and of 13–14 days in Surinam.

Carr and Hirth (1962) reported that the average number of *C. m. mydas* eggs per clutch at Tortuguero was 110 (18–193), at Ascension Island 115.5 (53–181). Pritchard (1969a) reported that the average number of eggs in 20 nests of this race at Bigi

Santi, Surinam, was 142.8 (87–174) and that the average for 248 nests at Eilanti, Surinam, was 141.9. The largest number of eggs in one nest at Eilanti was 226—which is the largest clutch of eggs known to have been laid by any green turtle. Hendrickson (1958) reported that the mean number of eggs from 8,147 clutches of *C. m. agassizii* in Malaysia was 104.7 (3–184). Banks (1937) reported an average of 108 eggs per clutch for 16,690 clutches in Borneo in 1934 and 107 eggs for 10,726 clutches there in 1932.

The nearly spherical, soft, white eggs are 35–58 mm in diameter and weigh 44–65 g. Under normal conditions dehydration sets in after deposition, and within 48 hr the shell is somewhat shriveled and brittle.

Hirth and Carr (1970) reported that nondeveloping eggs comprised about 40% of each clutch in South Yemen. Moorhouse (1933) reported that in 11 undisturbed clutches in Australia the hatching percentages were 41–86%.

The incubation period is 30–72 days but usually is 45–60 days.

Carr and Hirth (1961) stated that "turtles in a nest are not independent individuals but a group that meets the shared predicament of its interment with group action. The first young that hatch do not start digging at once but lie still until some nestmates are free of the egg. Each new hatching adds to the working space, because the spherical eggs and the spaces between them make a volume greater than that of the young and the crumpled shells. The vertical displacement that will carry the turtles to the surface is the upward migration of this chamber, brought about by a witless collaboration that is really a loose sort of division of labor. Although the movements involved are only a generalized thrashing, similar to those that free the hatchling from the egg, they accomplish four different (and perhaps indispensable) things, depending on the position of the turtle in the mass. Turtles of the top layer scratch down the ceiling. Those around the sides undercut the walls. Those on the bottom have two roles, one mechanical and the other psychological: they trample and compact the sand that filters down from above, and they serve as a receptor–motor device for the hatchling super-organism, stirring it out of recurrent spells of lassitude. Lying passively for a time under the weight of its fellows, one of them will suddenly burst into a spasm of squirming that triggers a new pandemic of work in the mass. Thus, by fits and starts, the ceiling falls, the floor rises, and the roomful of collaborating hatchlings is carried toward the surface."

Tests conducted at Ascension Island by Carr and Hirth (1962) indicated that metabolic heating raises the temperature in nests of developing eggs and suggested that this may constitute thermal cooperation affecting the fitness of the sets of eggs and young as evolutionary units. Hendrickson (1958) recorded nest-temperature gains at the China Sea rookeries of 5.9 C over the outside average at the same depths during a 2-week period. At Ascension Island the average gain was 2.3 C in nests.

Hatchlings emerge from the nest after dark. Nocturnal emergence has marked survival value, because a high temperature of the surface sand would kill them and because the danger of predation is much greater by day. Bustard (1967b) found nests in which a few hatchlings were visible at the sand surface during the heat of the day; in most cases only the head protruded, but occasionally part of the anterior region of the carapace also was exposed. They gave no sign of life, remaining completely immobile for many hours; detailed observation, however, showed that in this position they were able to remain alive under conditions in which total exposure would have been fatal. After dark they became active, emerged from the nest with the rest of the brood, and made for the water. Bustard (1967b) never saw day-emergent hatchlings bury themselves, but this has been described by Moorhouse (1933). Any account of the mechanism preventing daytime emergence must include an explanation of how inactivity, caused by bright light or high temperature, is transmitted to the hatchlings deeper down which are unable to experience these conditions directly. Bustard (1967b) suggested that the comatose condition of the few turtles that reach the surface has a damping effect on the activity of

those below. Furthermore, those at the surface act like corks in a bottle, occupying the opening of the nest shaft and making exit difficult if not impossible for those below. Experimental removal of individuals whose heads are protruding from the sand, together with the removal of others then immediately visible, has led to activity within the nest and emergence of the turtle brood within minutes, during the day. Mrosovsky (1968) found that diurnal activity is inhibited at temperatures above 28.5 C and that the heat of the sand on the nesting beaches usually is high enough to confine the hatchlings to the nest until after dark. Once the temperature falls to 28.5 C at night, they become active. He pointed out that in the morning the temperature just beneath the surface frequently is below 28.5 C. This is most often the case on rainy days; and in fact hatchlings often emerge after a rain, sometimes even by day.

In hatchlings the carapace is keeled and is dark green to brown; it may have a mottled pattern and a light border. The plastron is white or yellow and has two longitudinal ridges. The skin is blackish, and the flippers have white borders. The upper beak is light in color, and the caruncle is merely its sharply pointed but smoothly continuous upper-anterior projection. Hatchlings are 44–54 mm in carapace length and 31–43 mm in width, and they weigh about 25 g.

The color pattern of hatchling green turtles is an example of countershading. Bustard (1970) thought that the black dorsal coloration is disadvantageous: the hatchlings are conspicuous to predators when crossing pale-colored sand to the sea. He suggested that the dark carapace plays an important role in elevating the body temperature when the hatchling is floating at the surface. The increased body temperature would result in faster growth, due to heightened metabolism, and more rapid growth-rate during this extremely vulnerable stage of the life history has decided survival value.

GROWTH: Ingle and Smith (1949) reported that *C. m. mydas* has an early growth rate of about 7 lb in body weight and 7 inches in carapace length per year. Schmidt (1916) found that in the Danish West

Indies (= Virgin Islands) there was a monthly increase in weight of 138–442 g. According to him a *C. m. mydas* of 5 lb was 1.0–1.5 years old; one of 12 lb, 2.0–2.5 years; and one of 20 lb, 3.0–3.5 years. Caldwell (1962b) recorded the growth rates of four captive hatchlings as 100 mm the 1st year and 115 mm in each of the following 2 years. The mean weight increase was about 135 g the 1st year, 2,725 g the 2nd year, and 5,000 g the 3rd year. Ingle and Smith (1949) reported that this subspecies does not greatly exceed 150 lb or a carapace length of 30 inches and in heavily fished waters probably does not exceed 120 lb. They also reported West Indies records of green turtles weighing 850 lb and having carapaces more than 5 ft long. Carr and Caldwell (1956) found that the relationship between carapace length and body weight in 208 *C. m. mydas* (mostly young turtles) from the Florida fishing grounds could best be expressed by the following equation: $\log W = \text{minus } 2.195 + 2.87 \log L$, where L is length and W is weight. Australian *C. m. agassizii* reach a carapace length of 203 mm in their 1st year (Moorhouse, 1933). Carr (1952) reported that yearlings of this subspecies are usually 203–254 mm in carapace length, mature females about 890 mm, and 10-year-olds as much as 1,110 mm. Hendrickson (1958) plotted the growth and calculated the following age-size relationships: 1 year, 275 mm; 2 years, 460 mm; 3 years, 630 mm; and 4 years, 810 mm.

Caldwell (1962d) found Gulf of California males to be smaller (maximum 35.5 inches) than females (maximum 38.5 inches). The tendency for males to weigh less than females begins at a carapace length of about 30 inches, when sexual dimorphism first becomes evident. The female becomes somewhat deeper-bodied, the posterior portion of the male's carapace becomes proportionately more pointed, and the length of the male's tail increases greatly by comparison with the female's. Caldwell found the relationship between carapace length (L) and body weight (W) in these specimens could best be expressed by the following equation: $\log W = \text{minus } 2.14 + 2.60 \log L$.

In Ascension Island *C. m. mydas*, as well as those in Costa Rica, adult body size is influenced more by

185. Hatchling *Chelonia mydas*. (*Photo by Wayne Frair*)

maturation size and by factors having to do with migration than by growth after maturity. The Ascension turtles are selectively large because they have to travel farther without feeding (Carr and Goodman 1970).

A *C. m. agassizii* lived 15 years in the New York Aquarium. Eleven *C. m. mydas* were kept for more than 20 years at Marineland, in Florida.

FOOD AND FEEDING: *Chelonia mydas* is omnivorous, but the adult prefers plant food; in other words, the juvenile is more carnivorous than the adult. Plants consumed include green, brown, and red algae, mangrove (roots and leaves), and *Zostera, Cymodocea, Thallasia, Halophila, Posidonia, Halodule,* and *Portulacca*. Roots seem to be the preferred part of the plants. Animal food includes small mollusks, crustaceans, sponges, and jellyfish. Deraniyagala (1939) reported that green turtles scavenged near a house, feeding on the kitchen refuse thrown into the water. Captives feed readily on liver, kidney, beef, and fish.

The serrated lower jaw of *Chelonia* probably is an adaptation to grazing. Green turtles are the only marine turtles subsisting mainly on plants—a diet poor in vitamin D. They are also the only marine turtles that come to the shore to bask—perhaps a means of producing the needed vitamin D, through the action of the sunlight on skin sterols.

Smith (1961) proposed that the papilla-like rakers in the choanae (the internal openings of the nasal passage in the roof of the mouth) of *Chelonia* are correlated with a distinctive behavior whereby the choanae are used specifically as strainers. Since *Chelonia* is more herbivorous than other sea turtles, he felt that a reasonable possibility exists that the so-called choanal rakers and a unique (among sea turtles) compressive role of the tongue evolved as an adaptation to a primarily vegetarian diet. Development of the rakers seems correlated closely with the shift from a carnivorous to an herbivorous diet.

PREDATORS: Hendrickson (1958) reported that ghost crabs (*Ocypode*), monitor lizards (*Varanus*), long-tailed macaque monkeys (*Macacus irus*), and man

are the chief egg predators in the Malayan region. DeSilva (1969a) observed a Brahminy kite (*Haliastur indus intermedius*) and white-bellied sea eagles (*Haliaeetus leucogaster*) preying on hatchlings in Sabah (northeastern Borneo). On the American nesting beaches, raccoons, foxes, dogs, jaguars, pigs, and man are the leading nest predators. Hatchlings on the beaches are preyed upon by rats, cats, dogs, lizards, snakes, gulls, frigatebirds, herons, and other birds. Once they enter the sea the hatchlings fall victim to a great host of carnivorous fishes. Man is the major predator on adults, but dogs, tigers, and jaguars attack nesting females, and various sharks feed on adults at sea.

MOVEMENTS: *Chelonia* is a powerful swimmer. Oliver (1955) recorded 23 observations on a 3.5-ft individual as it cruised leisurely in a large saltwater stockade. At no time did it make any noticeable effort toward haste, yet it maintained a speed of 0.88–1.4 mph.

During their lifetimes green turtles migrate over long distances. Their principal nesting beaches and feeding grounds may be as far as 1,400 miles apart: Carr (1965) reported that nine females tagged on the nesting beaches of Ascension Island were recovered 1,400 miles or more away, along the coast of Brazil. Table 4 gives some other distances known to have been traveled by *C. m. mydas*.

Returns from the 15-year tagging program on nesting females at Tortuguero, Costa Rica, furnish data for generalizations on migration. No correlation has been evident between the post-tagging interval and the distance of site of recovery from Tortuguero; this may be taken to mean that green turtles are not wanderers but are scheduled migrants between the nesting beach and a special feeding-place. No turtle marked at Tortuguero has ever been recovered in Costa Rica after the end of the nesting season; this suggests that the resident population is small. None marked at Tortuguero has ever been found nesting elsewhere; this implies that Tortuguero is the exclusive and ancestral nesting ground for the populations sampled there. The recovery sites are spread throughout the western Caribbean

TABLE 4

SOME LONG MIGRATIONS OF TAGGED FEMALE
CHELONIA MYDAS MYDAS

Tagged at	Recovered at	Elapsed time	Miles	Reference
Tortuguero, Costa Rica	Mujeres Island, Mexico	725 days	775	Carr and Ogren, 1960
Tortuguero, Costa Rica	Morant Cays, Jamaica	277 days	684	Carr and Ogren, 1960
Tortuguero, Costa Rica	British Honduras	139 days	705	Carr and Ogren, 1960
Tortuguero, Costa Rica	southern coast of Cuba	220 days	793	Carr and Ogren, 1960
Tortuguero, Costa Rica	near Cartagena, Colombia	33 days	535	Carr and Ogren, 1960
Tortuguero, Costa Rica	near Cartagena, Colombia	67 days	535	Carr and Ogren, 1960
Tortuguero, Costa Rica	near Cartagena, Colombia	118 days	535	Carr and Ogren, 1960
Tortuguero, Costa Rica	Gulf of Morrosquillo, Colombia	168 days	540	Carr and Hirth, 1962
Tortuguero, Costa Rica	Riohacha, Colombia	373 days	713	Carr and Hirth, 1962
Tortuguero, Costa Rica	Doce Leguas Cays, Cuba	982+ days	795	Carr and Hirth, 1962
Tortuguero, Costa Rica	Cortés, Cuba	364 days	800	Carr and Hirth, 1962
Tortuguero, Costa Rica	near Campeche, Mexico	275 days	1,219	Carr and Hirth, 1962
Bigi Santi, Surinam	São Luiz, Brazil	72 days	1,000+	Pritchard, 1969a

and throughout the Gulf of Mexico, as far away as the Florida Keys; the eastern Caribbean is barely represented (Venezuela). Each season the nesting assemblage at Tortuguero is composite, with contingents arriving from various feeding localities. Although a given female nests on a 2–4-year cycle, the nesting schedule is not synchronous for a given resident population, because each feeding locality may be represented yearly at the nesting beach (Carr and Ogren, 1960; Carr and Hirth, 1962; Carr, 1965).

Long-distance migrations also are made by *C. m. agassizii*. Carr (1952) offered some evidence that the feeding population of the Mozambique Channel moves to the Aldabra Islands for the nesting season. Hirth and Carr (1970), reviewing the recoveries off the coast of Somalia of females tagged on the Yemen nesting beaches, noted that some had traveled more than 400 miles, and one had traveled at least 420 miles in 39 days. They calculated that the average minimum rate of two of the turtles tagged the same night and recovered 85 days later was 14 miles/day, assuming they traveled close to shore around the Gulf of Aden.

Where the hatchlings go once they leave the nesting beaches is unknown. Carr and Caldwell (1956)

examined a feeding population of immature green turtles, averaging 24.9 inches in carapace length and weighing 3–30+lb, in the vicinity of Cedar Key and Crystal River, on the western coast of Florida. The turtles are regular residents from April to November. Nobody knows whence they come or where they go. Apparently they first appear from the south and usually are in small but definite groups. Carr and Caldwell found that these juveniles could home from a distance of about 30 miles.

Carr (1967a) theorized that hatchling Atlantic green turtles become associated with clumps of *Sargassum* and drift passively with the weed into the Sargasso Sea. Here they could feed on the invertebrates associated with the weed or on the *Sargassum* itself until they grew to sufficient size to journey to the Florida feeding grounds.

Ninety-eight hatchling green turtles were transported from Tortuguero to Florida, raised for 1 year in concrete tanks, and tagged and released in the Indian River on 10 November 1964. Witham and Carr (1968) reported that only two had been recovered. The first was caught on 15 January 1965 in the Indian River about 7 miles north of the release point. The second was recovered off Sandy Cay,

217

186. Swimming juvenile *Chelonia mydas*.

Grand Bahama Island, on 13 May 1967. It had traveled 65 nautical miles and had crossed the Gulf Stream. In another experiment a similarly treated individual released 17 October 1967 at Bahía Honda State Park, in the Florida Keys, was recovered more than 800 miles away on 15 November 1968 off Cape Hatteras Light in Pamlico Sound, North Carolina (Carr and Sweat, 1969).

Caldwell (1969) reported that fishermen have taken hatchling and barely posthatchling Pacific green turtles at the surface around Clarión and Socorro islands, in the Revilla Gigedo group, 420 miles off the coast of central Mexico, and that turtles of this age have been similarly taken about 50 miles southeast of Manzanillo, which is on the Pacific coast. The young turtles were attracted to floodlights hanging over the sides of the vessels at night and were easily netted. Caldwell felt that these turtles were from either the rookeries on the coast of Michoacán (south of Manzanillo) or the rookeries on the Revilla Gigedo islands.

A number of studies have been made to discover how green turtles find their way. Some of them have concerned vision. Studies by Ehrenfeld and Koch (1967) on visual accommodation in *Chelonia mydas* indicate that the species is extremely myopic in air but approximately emmetropic in seawater. Mrosovsky and Carr (1967) found that hatchlings preferred the shorter wavelengths (green and blue) over the longer wavelengths (yellow and red).

Mrosovsky and Shettleworth (1968) found that in blue–red and yellow–red preference tests the attractiveness of red could be boosted by increasing its intensity relative to the blue or yellow alternative. Although there was a preference for blue over red of equal intensity, this preference could be reversed if the intensity of the red was made sufficiently high—an indication that brightness was an important factor. They also reported that if there is a blue preference, the part it plays in sea-finding can only be secondary compared with brightness. Simultaneous comparison of differential brightness from a wide field of view enables the turtle to head for the center of an open horizon. The underlying mechanism involves a balancing of brightness inputs in both eyes, and the hatchling orients itself to maintain such a balance. For the green sea turtle on the nesting beach the most open horizon is nearly always seaward and is nearly always brighter than the landward direction. Because it has a brightness preference and a tropotactic reaction to light, the bright illumination from the open horizon is the turtle's principal cue in sea-finding.

Experiments by Ehrenfeld (1968) in which spectacles holding a variety of color filters were placed over the eyes of *Chelonia mydas* confirmed that light-intensity discrimination rather than color discrimination is the basis for seafinding.

Studies by Ehrenfeld and Carr (1967) on seafinding showed that there was no evidence of an innate compass-direction preference based on celestial information, that a direct view of the sea or surf was not necessary for seaward orientation, and that light polarized by reflection from the surface of the sea was not used as a primary cue when the water was not in sight.

How green turtles orient themselves in the open sea is unknown, but the studies by Ehrenfeld and Koch (1967) on visual accommodation have effectively eliminated navigation by the stars: the turtles cannot see them. The location of nesting grounds on mainland beaches and feeding grounds near the mainland makes it difficult to prove that at least some do not locate these places by following shorelines. However, a number of major nesting beaches are located on isolated islands, and apparently the turtles have no difficulty in finding them. Perhaps the most outstanding island-finding feat is the travel from the feeding grounds along the Brazilian coast to the nesting beaches on Ascension Island, over 1,000 miles away in the South Atlantic.

The Brazil-to-Ascension migration has been discussed at length by Carr (1967b). Ascension Island, only 5 miles across, lies in the westward flow of the Equatorial Current, directly upstream from the bulge of Brazil. Before this current strikes the mainland, it splits—some of its waters flowing to the West Indies and the Caribbean and becoming the Gulf Stream, the rest turning southward along the coast as the Brazil Current. The Ascension nesting

colony consists of turtles that come from both north and south of the point on the bulge opposite which the current splits. Two advantages are at once apparent in the Brazil–Ascension migration. One is the current that comes directly from the island toward the feeding grounds. The other is the position of Ascension: it is on the same parallel of latitude as the nearest point on the mainland. These special features may have favored development of the Ascension-seeking pattern, but they increase our difficulty in reasoning out the mechanics of the guidance process: they favor no one navigation process over another. Celestial, inertial, magnetic-field, and Coriolis-force guidance would all be simplified to some extent by the geography of the situation. In addition the relationship between the direction of the current and the direction of the nearest course between the island and the mainland makes it impossible to rule out a fifth possibility, namely landmark-piloting by an olfactory emanation from the island, possibly detectable from far out at sea. Koch *et al.* (1969) evaluated the possibility of orientation based in part on the detection of some chemical substance originating at Ascension Island. Calculations based on the turbulences and structure of the oceanic currents in the South Atlantic showed that the concentration of any substance emanating from the island would be only 100– to 1,000-fold lower in the Brazilian coastal region than in the upstream waters in the immediate vicinity of the island. To follow this chemical trail to the island the turtle would have to be able to follow the gradient of increasing concentration to the center of the stream and then travel against the current in an easterly direction. In doing so the turtle would have to solve four problems: (1) It must be able to selectively detect emanation from the target. (2) It must be able to detect the direction of the current or else must be provided with a time-compensated suncompass sense and a knowledge of the approximate direction of the goal. (3) It must be able to detect a difference in concentration at one time compared with another time—hours apart. (4) It must be capable of going far enough in a fixed direction with a crosscurrent component to sense a meaningful

TABLE 5

ESTIMATED RATES OF LOSS IN *CHELONIA MYDAS* TO VARIOUS FACTORS DURING
THE EARLY STAGE OF THE LIFE CYCLE
(after Hendrickson, 1958)

Decimating factor	Percentage loss	Remnant of the Hypothetical 1,800 units after loss	Percentage Remnant
Nondeveloping eggs	40	1,080 developing eggs	60.0
Nest destruction by turtles	50	540 developing eggs	30.0
Predators on nests	25	405 developing eggs	23.0
Beach predators on hatchlings	40	243 hatchlings	14.0
Shallow-water predators on hatchlings (during 1st hr or so in water)	50	122 hatchlings	7.0
Deep-water predators on hatchlings (during 1st week at sea)	75 (?)	31 juveniles	1.7

change in concentration and alter course according-ly. (If chemical orientation actually does occur, then obviously the imprinting of the hatchlings with the taste or odor of the waters near their nesting beach would be a tremendous advantage.)

We still do not know how turtles find their way in the open sea. Many explanations have been proposed and many have been rejected; the research continues. The use of radio transmitters attached to free-swimming oceanic turtles, with the signals reflected from a satellite to onshore receivers, is providing valuable clues.

POPULATIONS: Carr and Caldwell (1956) estimated that approximately 5,600 turtles were present in the feeding population of immature *Chelonia mydas* along the western coast of Florida. However, this was based on recaptures of tagged turtles by commercial fishermen, who were selective: they took only turtles weighing more than 20 lb, and many smaller turtles probably were not accounted for. Also, the tagged turtles were not released on the fishing grounds; that is, not all of them are likely to have entered waters where recapture was possible.

Sex ratios of two groups of *C. m. mydas* caught on Miskito Bank by commercial fishermen were, respectively, 27 males to 66 females and 105 males to 271 females (Carr and Giovannoli, 1957). Hirth and Carr (1970) reported a sex ratio of 56% females and 44% males among 4,376 *C. m. agassizii* caught on the feeding grounds between Aden and Ras al Ara.

The mortality rate in hatchlings and nesting females is high. In some cases none of the hatchlings from a given nest survive the trip to the sea. Hendrickson (1958) estimated the rates of loss to various factors during the early stages of the life cycle of *C. m. agassizii* in Malaysia (Table 5). Bustard and Tognetti (1969) found that nest destruction is dependent on population density and is a means of regulating population size.

REMARKS: The exploitation of the green turtle on both the nesting beaches and the feeding grounds makes the future of this species bleak. It has already disappeared from many beaches where it formerly was numerous. The collection of eggs on the nesting beaches is particularly injurious to the species. If

Chelonia mydas is to survive, conservation methods must be applied wherever the turtles breed or feed. In particular the nesting beaches must be rigorously protected by governmental regulation and must be adequately patrolled during the breeding season.

Economically, *Chelonia mydas* is the most important reptile in the world. Its flesh and its eggs serve as an important source of protein in many impoverished parts of the world where protein is scarce. In more affluent societies this turtle has long been in demand for the delicious soup which can be prepared from it. The demand for turtle soup has supported commercial fisheries since the 17th century. Green turtles formerly provided fresh meat to the crews of naval, whaling, and pirate ships. Also, a thin oil is obtained from the turtle and the eggs. Parsons (1962) gave a detailed account of the commercial exploitation of this animal.

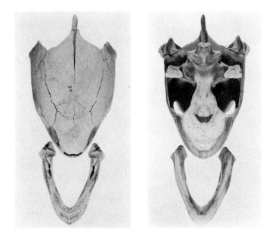

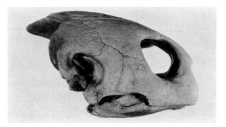

Skull of *Chelonia mydas*

ERETMOCHELYS IMBRICATA (Linnaeus)

Hawksbill XXI

RECOGNITION: A small to medium-sized (43–91 cm) sea turtle having dark paddlelike flippers, four pairs of pleurals with the first not touching the cervical, and two pairs of prefrontal scales. The carapace is shield-shaped (heart-shaped in the young and more elongated and straight-sided in the adult), has a keel on at least the last four vertebrals, and is serrated posteriorly. In the young the carapacial scutes strongly overlap the next posterior ones, but as the turtle matures the overlapping becomes progressively less, until finally the scutes lie side by side. The carapace is dark greenish-brown; in the young it shows a tortoiseshell pattern. There are four poreless inframarginal scutes on the yellow bridge. The plastron is hingeless and yellow; in juveniles it may have two longitudinal ridges and a few dark blotches, especially on the anterior scutes. The head scales are black to chestnut-brown at the center and lighter at their margins; the jaws are yellow with some brown streaks or bars. The chin and throat are yellow, and the neck is dark above. The cutting edge of the lower jaw is smooth or only slightly serrated; that of the upper jaw is without strongly elevated vertical ridges on the inner surface. The snout is elongated and narrow—rather like a hawk's beak—and is not notched at the tip. The floor of the mouth is deeply excavated at the mandibular symphysis.

Males have somewhat concave plastrons; long, thick tails, which extend beyond the posterior carapacial margin; and long, heavy claws.

GEOGRAPHIC VARIATION: Two subspecies are recognized. *E. i. imbricata* (Linnaeus), the Atlantic hawksbill, ranges through the warmer parts of the western Atlantic Ocean, from Massachusetts through the Gulf of Mexico to southern Brazil. It also has been recorded from Scotland and Morocco. This subspecies has a nearly straight-sided carapace that tapers posteriorly; a keel that is continuous on the last four vertebrals only; ridges that converge posteriorly on the last two vertebrals only; and the upper surfaces of the head and flip-

187. Young female hawksbill, *Eretmochelys imbricata*. Commercial "tortoise-shell" is prepared from the carapacial scutes of this species.

pers with less black. *E. i. bissa* (Rüppell), the Pacific hawksbill, ranges through the tropical portions of the Indian and Pacific oceans, from Madagascar to the Red Sea on the east coast of Africa and east to Australia and Japan in the western Pacific, to the Hawaiian Islands in the central Pacific, and from Peru to Baja California in the eastern Pacific. Stragglers occasionally reach California. It has a more heart-shaped carapace, a fully continuous vertebral keel, all vertebrals with ridges that converge posteriorly, and the head and flippers almost solid black.

CONFUSING SPECIES: *Chelonia mydas* has only one pair of prefrontals and a strongly serrated lower jaw. *Caretta caretta, Lepidochelys kempii,* and *L. olivacea* have five or more pairs of pleurals with the first touching the cervical.

DISTRIBUTION: The hawksbill ranges in the Atlantic, Pacific, and Indian oceans from California, Japan, the Red Sea, the British Isles, and Massachusetts south to Peru, Australia, Madagascar, northwestern Africa, and southern Brazil.

HABITAT: This marine turtle is characteristically an inhabitant of rocky places and coral reefs. It also occurs in shallow coastal waters, such as mangrove-bordered bays, estuaries, and lagoons with mud bottoms and little or no vegetation, and in small, narrow creeks and passes. It is occasionally found in deep waters and has been taken from floating patches of *Sargassum* weed. *Eretmochelys* shares its water habitat and its nesting beaches with all other species of marine turtles.

BEHAVIOR: Little is known of the behavior of the hawksbill. Apparently it is diurnal except during the nesting season. In temperament, newly caught individuals are very aggressive, biting and snapping at anything within their reach. When it seizes an object the turtle does not release it readily, and the strong, sharp jaws inflict a painful bite. Loveridge and Williams (1957) remarked that the hawksbill bites so freely that Malagasy fishermen carry in their boats a piece of wood that they hold out to a harpooned turtle. Once the reptile has seized the proffered wood it does not soon let go. It is said that if this procedure is not followed the turtle is likely to bite their frail boats when being hauled aboard and may cause considerable damage. Furthermore, the sharp edges of the overlapping scutes can cause deep wounds if a struggling specimen is carelessly handled.

Hawksbills are at times aggressive toward their own kind, and they have been known to attack *Chelonia mydas* in captivity. On one occasion Parrish (1958) observed two captive females fighting, possibly over food. He stated it was not uncommon for one turtle to bite another when regaining a resting-place. The bitten turtle was never observed to fight back; it always left the resting-place immediately.

Hirth (1962) took the cloacal temperatures of two *Eretmochelys* just after they had finished nesting; one had a temperature of 28.5 C, the other 29.0 C. Shallow water offshore varied only 1.0 C during the period of the study, averaging 27.9 C (27.5–28.5).

REPRODUCTION: Carr (1952) reported that *Eretmochelys* matures sexually at 3 years of age and on attaining a weight of about 30 lb. Carr *et al.* (1966) found that at Tortuguero, Costa Rica, mature females had a mean carapace length of 32.72 inches (29.5–36.0), mature males 31.56 inches (31.25–32.0). At Shell Beach, Guyana, Pritchard (1969a) found that the mean carapace length of nesting females was 33.1 inches (31.5–35.0).

Mating occurs in the shallow water off the nesting beaches. According to Hornell (1927), copulation begins soon after the spent females return to the sea, but males have been observed to follow a female onto the beach. Whether mating takes place at any other time or place is not known.

The Atlantic hawksbill nests on beaches in Florida, Jamaica (Pedro and Morant cays), the Cayman Islands, Aves Island, the Virgin Islands, Grenada, Tobago, Trinidad, Guyana, Surinam, French Guiana, Panama, Costa Rica, Mexico, and the islands and keys off the Central American coast. Nesting lasts from April through November and is at its peak in June and July.

The Pacific hawksbill nests on beaches on the eastern coast of Africa (December to February); the Seychelles Islands (throughout the year, with a peak from September to November); Ceylon (November to February); and in Honduras, Nicaragua, and El Salvador (August to November).

Paul Kawamoto, aquatic biologist for the state of Hawaii, has sent us a copy of a recent report from the files of the Hawaii Division of Fish and Game (Turtle 321.08). The report follows:

On Tuesday, October 14, 1969, Mr. Michael Tancayo, Jr., of Kaunakakai, Molokai, came down to the Kaunakakai Wharf with his son to release two (2) young turtles (about 2-inch carapace length). Mr. Tancayo offered these turtles to Warden Ronald Kama who was on Molokai on assignment to dive for starfish, *Acanthaster planci*. The two turtles were accepted by Kama and thus this discovery and story was related to H. Sakuda and K. Ego.

Mr. Tancayo and his family visited Halawa Beach on Sunday, October 12, 1969 about 7:00 a.m. and found and collected 26 baby turtles on the beach. Upon digging in the nearby sand they were able to uncover a nest with about a dozen eggs. At home, Mr. Tancayo found that he could not keep and feed the two turtles as well as he would like to have, so he came down to the harbor to release the young turtles.

On Friday morning, K. Ego and Fish and Game personnel inspected the beach at Halawa and during our discussion, Warden Leroy Mollena of Molokai who as a young boy lived and grew up in Halawa Valley, mentioned that many years ago many young turtles were occasionally seen in the shore and beach at Halawa.

The two young turtles were brought back to Oahu and identified as Hawksbill turtles, *Eretmochelys imbricata* . . .

This is apparently the first report of the Pacific hawksbill nesting on Hawaii.

The females come onto the beach at night, and nesting takes about 1 hr. Carr *et al.* (1966) recorded nesting returns to Tortuguero, Costa Rica, of 3 years and 6 years, respectively, for two tagged females—which suggests that the hawksbill nests

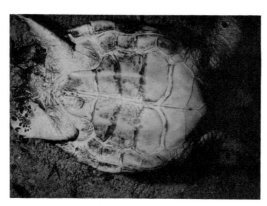

188. Plastron of *Eretmochelys imbricata*.

in 3-year cycles, as does *Chelonia mydas.* Hornell (1927) reported that in the Seychelles Islands females marked while nesting came back to nest again after 13–15 days. Carr *et al.* (1966) recorded three cases of renesting at Tortuguero after 17, 18, and 30 days, respectively. They thought that the 30-day interval could have represented a return after two previous nestings at 2-week intervals, with one of these not observed.

Carr *et al.* (1966) gave a lucid account of the nesting of *Eretmochelys,* as follows:

The first contact that an observer has with an emerging turtle comes when she is stranded by the wave wash. At this point, as during the whole trip up the beach, the hawksbill is exceptionally wary. If a light is played on her, she usually turns and goes rapidly back to the sea. On moonlight nights, or even in strong starlight, if the shell of the turtle is not heavily fouled with algae and barnacles it glints with reflections and even without artificial light sometimes attracts the attention of a watcher. If it does, one may sometimes crawl close to the emerging turtle and watch as she appraises the stranding site. The process is essentially the 'sand-smelling' described by Carr and Ogren (1960) for *Chelonia.* The muzzle is pressed against the sand and held there a second or more, then the head is lifted, and the turtle peers about the foreground and back and forth into the gloom of the upper beach. This process is kept up both while she rests in the wave wash and after her emergence onto dry beach. Whether it is actually an olfactory assessment or merely a tactile one is not known. In any case the habit is much more strongly developed in the hawksbill than in the green turtle and is usually continued all the way up to the site the turtle finally chooses for nesting. Besides this nuzzling of the sand, the turtle cranes her neck and peers about warily, presumably assessing the topography and security of the situation. At this stage, when a dog or man moves near a turtle she still is likely to return to the sea.

TRAVEL FROM SURF TO HIGH BEACH. The gait of the hawksbill involves little of the breast stroke of *Chelonia* —the labored dragging forward of the body by simultaneous movements of all the legs. *Eretmochelys* uses a more reptilian style of walking, with diagonal limbs working together. When the turtle is tired, a few breast strokes may be made, but the alternating style is usually quickly resumed. This marked difference in gait, com-

bined with the active peering and neck craning and more frequent sand smelling of the hawksbill, makes her journey up the beach strikingly different from the machine-like locomotion of *Chelonia* . . .

SELECTION OF NEST SITE. As the turtle approaches the dry, tumbled sand above the tidal zone she starts making trial sweeps with the fore fins, and lowers her snout against the ground more frequently. She may move directly inland on a more or less zigzag course, but sometimes for no evident reason will crawl long distances up or down the upper beach before finally stopping, crossing broad expanses of territory that, to the observer, appears suitable nesting ground. The prenesting prospecting of the hawksbill seems on the average to be more protracted than that of *Chelonia.* One hawksbill trail that we paced off was 450 paces long, with the nest situated about 400 paces along the trail from the point of emergence. To the observer, the process of selection of the nest site seems to be a direct visual assessment of the terrain, augmented by tactile and possibly olfactory corrections. Even on the darkest nights obstacles appear to be avoided visually. Nests are rarely made in wave-washed, hard-surfaced, or turf-grown ground. The discrimination by which these are avoided seems to involve trial scraping with the flippers, supplemented by more of the sand-smelling maneuver. When a satisfactory site is finally reached, the turtle makes a few sweeps with the fore flippers, used singly; then the back feet are brought into play and the actual digging begins.

CLEARING THE SITE AND EXCAVATING THE BODY PIT. The whole site-clearing, pit-thrashing, nest-digging operation is a sequence of intergrading stereotyped movements. The hawksbill makes no such deep basin as that in which the green turtle and trunkback rest while nesting. The process of site clearing, in which sand is thrown back by first the front and then the back fins, is sometimes continued until a shallow excavation is formed, but in other cases only a few scratches that do little more than clear the vines or debris away from the site may be made. The fore fins start to work first, then hesitantly the hind feet begin, working alternately, and alternating also with front fins. During this action the body may inch forward slightly and may shift back and forth, to right or to left. After several minutes the action of the fore flippers stops, and that of the back foot changes gradually from a kick to a scraping stroke applied to the sand just beneath the tail, and then becomes the scooping action used in digging the nest.

EXCAVATION OF THE EGG CAVITY. The egg cavity is a

189. Underwater view of a juvenile
Eretmochelys imbricata.

flask-shaped hole. It is dug by the hind feet only, working alternately. The foot is brought in beneath the hind edge of the shell, and its edge is pressed against the ground and curled to pick up a small amount of sand. The cupped foot is then lifted and swung laterally, and the sand is dropped several inches out from the rear margin of the shell. As the sand falls, the other hind foot, which until then has rested on the sand beside the beginning of the egg cavity, snaps sharply forward, throwing sand from beside the hole to the front and side. This whole operation is then repeated in reverse. The entire nest-digging process is a series of these reciprocating actions of the hind feet. As they continue, the nest grows to a depth that finally is equal to the reach of the hind leg. This depth usually is about 19 (18–22) inches. The nest is neatly urn-shaped, its diameter slightly smaller toward the top than near the bottom. The front-to-back diameter of the lower cavity tends to be a little greater than its side-to-side diameter.

OVIPOSITION. The nest-digging stage tapers off in a series of light, unproductive scrapes at the interior of the nest. Finally these stop, and both back fins come to rest, palm down, several inches on each side of the nest opening. The tail is then dropped low into the cavity, the cloacal opening is everted slightly, and extrusion of the eggs begins.

Throughout oviposition the hind legs keep their position at the right and left of the nest, and the fore fins rest half folded against the body and partly embedded in the sand. The first eggs may fall as far as 14 inches to the bottom of the nest. The whole clutch generally fills the cavity to within 5 to 8 inches of the level of the opening. Mucus is frequently secreted between the extrusions of eggs, but there is no wetting by other liquid from the cloaca.

As eggs emerge, the spread hind fins usually curl up sharply at the edges, and then relax as the eggs drop. In the hawksbill, as in all the other sea turtles, each extrusion of eggs is also accompanied by regular movements of the neck and head, evidently produced by contractions that help push the eggs down the oviduct and out the cloaca. After each extrusion the neck extends horizontally and the chin rests in a shallow recess in the sand, or in the wall of the body pit if one has been made. Just before the eggs are expelled, the neck is retracted and bent downward and the chin is pushed against the sand. It is at this moment that the eggs are pushed out, and, as they fall, the neck stretches horizontally forward again until the chin again rests in its mold in the sand.

The first extrusion is usually a single egg, while the main complement drops mostly in two's or three's, and the last eggs appear singly. The oviposition of the turtle tagged as number 3231 terminated with the extrusion of five single eggs; then the head movements associated with extrusion were executed, with no eggs appearing; then the covering of the nest began abruptly.

FILLING THE NEST. When the last egg has been laid, filling begins immediately. Sand is not scraped into the hole, as in *Chelonia*. Instead, the flippers, working alternately, reach far out beside the opening, pick up sand, and carry it in over the hole and drop it. As this process continues, two excavations grow beside the nest and a mound rises where the filled mouth was situated. The tail is repeatedly thrust into the sand of this pile, as if to determine its height. When the mound has reached a certain, somewhat variable, elevation, filling stops and the turtle begins to knead and press the sand of the fill with the leading edges of her back flippers. This process is long and fussy. The tail is constantly manipulated in its seemingly tactile role, and more sand is brought in from time to time as the fill is compacted. The stage ends when the filling action begins to lag and the front fins, until this time quietly bracing the body of the turtle, gradually make the jerky motions that are a prelude to the concealment tactics.

FILLING THE BODY PIT AND CONCEALING THE SITE. This stage begins when the front flippers start throwing sand backward, working at first alternately, then together, and when the pressing action of the hind feet is gradually converted into kicking strokes. This work of the four limbs not only obliterates all signs of the nest but pushes the turtle slowly forward away from its location. The slow advance may carry her 6 to 8 feet away from the place where her eggs are buried, leaving behind a broad zone of thrown and harrowed sand. The concealment operation ends when the work of the fore fins becomes desultory, and they begin to work separately instead of in unison, and with increasing intervals between periods of activity.

RETURN TO THE SEA. After the last sand-slinging stroke the turtle usually hesitates only a second or two before moving off in her return to the water. Unless lights are shone upon her, the very first shift in the axis of her body is nearly always a seaward correction of heading. While the return is rarely a straight perpendicular to the surf, it is always a clearly oriented course that is maintained even when elevations or brush completely hide the sea. The gait is mostly a lizard-like diagonal action of the four legs, with only occasional breast strokes like those of the green turtle. As in the coming in to nest, there is much more peering from side to side and more lowering of the muzzle against the sand than are characteristic of *Chelonia*. The return to the surf is nearly always far less protracted than the journey prospecting for the nest site. One Tortuguero hawksbill traveled half an hour before stopping to nest, while her return trip was made in four and a half minutes.

In general the hawksbill on shore gives the impression of being more typically reptilian in its behavior than the green turtle—more furtive, aware, and active. Much of the contrast is no doubt due to the more ponderous body of *Chelonia* and to the greater effort required to drag it forward. Moreover, the shorter, stiffer neck of the green turtle perhaps precludes the lizard-like peering about characteristic of the hawksbill on shore.

Throughout the entire interlude on shore, which may last as much as two hours, there is a constant slight secretion of tears from the eyes.

In four nests examined by Carr *et al.* (1966) the distances from the surface of the ground to the top of the egg clutch and to the bottom of the nest cavity respectively, were, 10.0 inches (9.0–12.0) and 17.1 inches (17.0–17.5). The egg chambers in the four nests averaged 9 by 11 inches, and none varied by more than 2 inches from this average in either dimension.

The white, calcareous eggs usually are spherical in shape, averaging about 38 mm (35–42) in diameter, but a few in each clutch may be slightly elongated. Eggs examined by Deraniyagala (1939) were thinly covered with a mucilaginous secretion, which appeared to absorb water and was found to remain moist for 48 hr. The average number of eggs in 57 nests examined by Carr *et al.* (1966) was 161.1 (53–206).

The average incubation period of 13 clutches moved to artificial nests by Carr *et al.* (1966) was 58.6 days (52–74). These clutches contained a total of 2,193 eggs that were artificially buried in nine nests, and 46.7% of these eggs hatched (range in the individual nests, 12–80%). Probably this mortality was influenced by the moving of the eggs.

Hatching usually occurs at night or in early morning. The eggs of any one clutch hatch almost simultaneously and the hatchlings follow one another to the surface in quick succession.

The hatchling carapace is heart-shaped and has a vertebral keel; the plastron has two longitudinal ridges. Hatchlings are black or very dark brown except for the keels, the shell edge, and areas on the neck and flippers, which are light brown. Sizes and weights are as follows: carapace length 39–50 mm, carapace width 27–35 mm, plastron length 30–37 mm, and weight 14–15 g.

Deraniyagala (1939) found that in a clutch laid by a senile female with completely closed fontanelles half of the 22 young examined showed deviations from the typical scute pattern.

GROWTH: According to Schmidt (1916) the hatchling increases its length to 70–80 mm during its 1st winter, to about 100 mm by the 1st spring, and to 200 mm by the next fall. Caldwell (1962b) maintained a hatchling from Tortuguero, Costa Rica, for nearly 3 years; it increased in length approximately 100 mm the 1st year, 60 mm the 2nd, and 100 mm the 3rd. The respective increases in weight were approximately 160 g, 900 g, and 2,330 g. Deraniyagala (1939) reported that in 16 months two captive juveniles grew 13 inches and put on 10 lb. Lewis (1940) reported a 280-lb hawksbill from the Cayman Islands—apparently the record weight for this species. Most adults weigh about 35 lb.

The horny scutes of the hawksbill's shell change in character as the length increases. In juveniles the scutes lie side by side until they reach a length of more than 100 mm. Then the scutes develop the shinglelike form they have in the adult. The scutes remain this way until the turtle reaches a length of 360-400 mm, when they return to a juxtaposed condition. This change usually begins first in the plastral scutes (Deraniyagala, 1939).

A captive in the Berlin Zoological Garden lived at least 16 years. Four females and a male were kept for more than 20 years at Marineland, in Florida.

FOOD AND FEEDING: *Eretmochelys* is omnivorous but seems to prefer invertebrates. It is known to have consumed sponges, coelenterates (Portuguese man-of-war, hydroids, coral), ectoprocts (*Amthia*, *Steganoporella*), sea urchins, gastropod and bivalve mollusks (*Pinna*, *Ostrea*), barnacles, crustaceans, ascidians, and fish. Plants consumed are algae, *Cymodocea*, *Conferva*, and *Sargassum*. Carr (1952) reported they ate the fruits, leaves, dead bark, and wood of the red mangrove. Captives eat fish, meat, bread, octopi, squid, crabs, mussels, and oysters. Hatchlings seem to be herbivorous, but they become more omnivorous as they age.

In seizing a crab, a hawksbill kept by Deraniyagala (1939) would swim up to it and examine it for a couple of seconds. If the prey was small it would be seized without further ado, but if it was large the turtle would maneuver for position and then wait until the crab moved, whereupon the turtle would seize the crab by one side and break its carapace by a sharp bite, preventing the use of the pincers. When eating a Portuguese man-of-war a hawksbill closes its eyes, presumably to avoid being stung (Carr, 1952).

PREDATORS: Hawksbill nests are robbed by man, dogs, raccoons, and other animals. On the shore, hatchlings are consumed by dogs, rats, sand crabs, and birds; once in the water they are eaten by many species of fishes. The adults are preyed on by sharks, but man is the dominant predator.

MOVEMENTS: Contrary to the beliefs of many of the earlier investigators, Carr *et al.* (1966) have gathered evidence that some kind and degree of migratory travel occurs in *Eretmochelys*. The young disappear from view when they enter the sea after hatching and are rarely seen again until they reach a carapace length of 125–150 mm. The hawksbills decrease in numbers at Tortuguero from November to April. Females tagged there have been recovered 285 miles away on the Miskito coast and 325 miles away in the Miskito Cays, Nicaragua. They occur as strays along the coast of the United States far north of the regular feeding and nesting ranges. Individuals, evidently from America, occasionally are taken in the British Isles and Europe; although it is unlikely that these are true migrants, they may be evidence of a tendency to travel in the open sea on the major currents. Such travel, however, could be little more than sporadic wandering.

The Nicaraguan record from the Miskito coast gives a little evidence on the speed of travel: that turtle had traveled 285 statute miles in not more than 60 days. Oliver (1955) reported the cruising speed of a medium-sized hawksbill as around 1 mph.

Carr *et al.* (1966) studied the sea-finding orientation in hatchling *Eretmochelys* at Tortuguero. The hatchlings were able to find the sea from a wide range of release situations, including all conditions of topography and seaward outlook that occur at Tortuguero between the surf and the coconut-grove or shore-forest vegetation. The most immediate orientation and most active locomotion occurred when the test nest was in sight of ocean surf and separated from it by beach that sloped toward the water. Orientation was successful, however, in rolling or cluttered ground, where the traveling turtle had to go over or around obstacles and climb long, blind, seaward slopes before the ocean came into view. Although most of the natural emergences are at night or at dawn, orientation in the trials was equally successful by day and by night. The greatest single natural hazard, other than exceptional concentrations of predators, appeared to be the heat of the midday sun, which immobilized or slowed the hatchlings within a few minutes—either killing them in the open or causing them to take refuge under debris, whence they rarely emerged. The sea-finding feat was clearly shown to be, in most cases at least, not a single-stimulus event but a composite event in which environmental information of diverse kinds is used. The dominant cue is some aspect of the sky over the ocean. What aspect of exposure or illumination is involved has not been shown.

The sea-finding ability and drive were found to be retained by hatchlings long after they had been placed in tanks of water. Tank-held turtles seemed less strongly motivated, however, and were easily confused by situations in which they had no direct visual contact with the sea. Pope (1939) reported that hatchlings were noticeably influenced by light

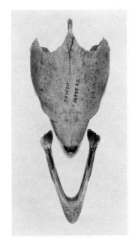

Skull of *Eretomochelys imbricata*

190. Swimming juvenile *Eretmochelys imbricata.*

229

when on the shore, but once placed in water they no longer were attracted by light.

When hatchlings were released on a spit between a river and the sea, the seaward tendency dominated across much of the width of the land. However, where the ocean was hidden and the river was visible from a few yards away, the turtles quickly entered the river.

During their first day in the water the hatchlings use their forelimbs chiefly as balancers while swimming largely by means of alternate strokes of the hind limbs. The presence of internal yolk material makes diving efforts ineffectual for several days. This inability affects the hatchlings' feeding habits, exposes them to predators, and allows them to be dispersed by wind and current.

The orientation processes that guide the nesting turtle inland are not understood, nor are those by which she returns to the sea. It is clear, however, that more than sand-smelling and direct appraisal of the landscape is involved. The orientation of the mature female in going from a nest back to the sea seems identical with that of the sea-finding feat in hatchlings; that is, it probably is a composite process dominated by a response to illumination, not a compass sense. Like hatchlings, the female has no trouble turning directly toward the ocean from any nest site, even when her view of the water is blocked. Whatever the nature of the process, the back-azimuth orientation that takes the turtle from the water to the upper beach must be the opposite of it (Carr and Ogren, 1960).

REMARKS: The hawksbill's chief claim to fame is the translucent scutes of the carapace—the tortoise-shell of commerce. The scutes are a clear amber, streaked with red, white, green, brown, and black. Usually the turtle is killed before the scutes are removed by the application of heat. There is evidence that if the scutes are removed carefully and the turtle is returned to the sea it can regenerate the lost scutes. This may be possible if the Malpighian cells of the epidermis are not damaged. A single turtle can yield 10–12 lb of tortoiseshell (called "carey" by the Caribbeans).

The flesh and eggs are eaten in many parts of the range. This requires caution, for *Eretmochelys* tends to store in its tissues the toxins of various poisonous organisms that it eats. Deraniyagala (1939) cites an instance in which 24 persons were poisoned by eating hawksbills that had fed on poisonous weeds. Seven died after 2 days; the others recovered.

The survival of the hawksbill is questionable. Throughout its range it is hunted mercilessly for the plates of its shell and for food. Existing conservation laws are ineffectively enforced and as long as there is a ready market for tortoiseshell the numbers of this turtle will continue to dwindle.

191. Young adult female *Caretta caretta*. This is the only reddish sea turtle.

CARETTA CARETTA (Linnaeus)

Loggerhead

RECOGNITION: A large (71–213 cm) sea turtle with five or more pairs of pleurals, with the first touching the cervical, and three poreless inframarginals on the bridge. The elongated carapace has a vertebral keel that becomes progressively smoother with age, is highest anterior to the bridge, and is serrated posteriorly. The marginal scutes average 12 or 13 on each side but vary from 11 to 15. The carapace is reddish-brown but may be tinged with olive, and the scutes often are bordered with yellow. The bridge and plastron are yellow to cream-colored. The plastron is hingeless and has two longitudinal ridges, which disappear with age. The large head is broad posteriorly and rounded in front; the snout is short and broad, and there are two pairs of prefrontals. The head varies from reddish or yellow-chestnut to olive-brown, with the scales often yellow-bordered. The jaws are yellowish-brown, and the bony surface of the lower jaw is smooth at the symphysis. The limbs and tail are dark centrally and yellowish toward the borders and below. Adults usually weigh about 300 lb, but truly massive size is sometimes attained. *Caretta* probably is the largest hard-shelled turtle living; it is exceeded in length and weight only by the leatherback (*Dermochelys coriacea*). Pritchard (1967a) reported that weights of up to 1,000 lb have been recorded and that there is a skull in the Bell collection at Cambridge University of such size (28.4 cm wide) as to indicate a weight of about 1,200 lb.

Males have narrow shells, which gradually taper posteriorly, and long, thick tails, which extend beyond the rear carapacial margin.

GEOGRAPHIC VARIATION: Two poorly marked subspecies are recognized. *C. c. caretta* (Linnaeus), the Atlantic loggerhead, ranges from Newfoundland and the British Isles south to Argentina and the Canary Islands and the western coast of tropical Africa; occasionally it enters the Mediterranean Sea. This race usually has seven or eight neural bones in the carapace and averages 12 marginal scutes on each side. *C. c. gigas* Deraniyagala, the Pacific loggerhead, occurs from southern California, Japan, India, and Kenya south through the Pacific and Indian oceans to Chile, Australia, and South Africa; there are also records from the eastern Atlantic. This subspecies has 7 to 12 neural bones in the carapace, the last 1 to 5 usually interrupted by costal bones, and 13 marginal scutes on each side.

CONFUSING SPECIES: The ridleys (*Lepidochelys*) have four inframarginals at the bridge; *L. kempii* is gray, and *L. olivacea* is olive-colored and usually has more than five pairs of pleurals on the carapace. *Chelonia mydas* and *Eretmochelys imbricata* have only four pairs of pleurals, with the first pair not touching the cervical. Also, *Chelonia* has but one pair of prefrontal scales. None of the other marine turtles is reddish.

DISTRIBUTION: *Caretta* occurs in the Pacific, Indian, and Atlantic Oceans from southern California, Japan, India, Kenya, the British Isles, and Newfoundland south to Chile, Australia, South Africa, tropical western Africa, and Argentina. It also occurs in the Caribbean and Mediterranean seas.

HABITAT: The loggerhead wanders widely throughout the marine waters of its range; it has been found as far as 500 miles out in the open sea. It enters bays, lagoons, salt marshes, creeks, and the mouths of large rivers. The loggerhead shares its nesting beaches with the other species of sea turtles.

BEHAVIOR: The daily activities of three captives, each about 38 cm long, appeared to be about equally divided between swimming and resting on the bottom of the tank. When resting they always selected a corner and would lie completely motionless with the head thrust into the corner, eyes open or half-shut, and flippers extended to about the normal midstroke swimming position. They were alert: the slightest movement above the water usually would bring them to the surface. Possibly they slept in this same position; on one occasion, when they were observed at night by dim light, the turtles were found in their corners with eyes tightly closed and were slower to rouse than during the daylight hours (Layne, 1952). Parrish (1958) reported that captives at Marineland, in Florida, did most of their sleeping before 1 AM, and they showed little activity in the predawn hours.

Carr (1952) pointed out that in the open sea loggerheads spent a great deal of time floating on the surface, presumably sleeping; but he never saw them do this in the sounds or estuaries, where they stay in the deeper parts of the channels and come up only to breathe or reconnoiter. They may be somewhat nocturnal in the small salt-marsh streams.

The respiration rate of the captives observed by Layne (1952) was variable. When actively swimming they surfaced for air an average of once every 2.1 min (0.25–24). When resting their average time between breaths was 12.7 min, and some remained on the bottom for as long as 25 min.

Walker (1959) noted that when moving underwater the turtles kept their nostrils open and moved the floor of the mouth slowly up and down. They also moved the lower jaw slightly. Presumably the loggerheads were passing water through the nostrils for olfaction. When they were sleeping or were resting on the bottom, there was no such movement and the nostrils were closed. Closure occurred partway within each nostril and was effected by the meeting of bulges from the laterodorsal and medioventral walls of the nasal passages. It took 23–45 sec for the nostrils to open completely.

Two of three individuals kept outdoors in shallow water at Beaufort, North Carolina, died when the air temperature dropped to 26 F; the third succumbed when it dropped to 13 F. They made no attempt to burrow into the mud bottom as the temperature fell (Pope, 1939).

Layne (1952) found evidence of possible territoriality in captive loggerheads. Usually each turtle occupied a particular corner of the tank while at rest, and once the regular occupant of a corner delivered a vicious snap at the head of another that attempted to occupy the same place.

Caretta is aggressive and belligerent. Pope (1939)

reported that Atlantic loggerheads kept at Beaufort, North Carolina, were gentle during the first 2 years of life but later became decidedly aggressive: they frequently fought each other and bit at any hand within reach. Caldwell (1963a) found a Pacific loggerhead extremely pugnacious: it killed two *Chelonia mydas* kept in a dry pen with it. After a stay out of water of some 10 days—in the pen and during airplane and automobile rides—the turtle still bit at a stick placed near its mouth. Some captives do not seem overly aggressive; for example, one large individual freely allowed its head to be scratched. However, such action is not recommended with wild loggerheads, if you value your fingers.

REPRODUCTION: Caldwell (1959) found that the size of mature females nesting at the Cape Romain Migratory Bird Refuge, in South Carolina, was 84.5–102.9 cm. Caldwell, Carr, and Ogren (1959) reported that at Jekyll Island, Georgia, nesting females were 79.4–114.9 cm long.

Mating has been observed at every hour from dawn to dark but doubtless also occurs at night. Paired loggerheads may copulate for extended periods—for more than 3 hr, according to Wood (1953) —and perhaps the females remate after each nesting. Mating occurs at the surface of the water off the nesting beaches. Although the female is completely submerged, the highest part of the male's carapace usually is out of the water. He grasps the anterolateral margins of her carapace with the claw of each foreflipper and the posterolateral margins with the claw of each hind flipper. He sometimes bites the nape of her neck. His head surfaces every few minutes for breathing; she struggles to the surface about every 5 min. His tail is bent down and under hers, so that the cloacal openings touch. The behavior of the female in mating ranges from passive acceptance to violent resistance.

C. c. caretta formerly nested on United States beaches, from Virginia to the Gulf coast, but today the breeding range probably is restricted to points south of Cape Lookout, North Carolina. This subspecies also nests in Costa Rica, Cuba, and the Cayman Islands. In the north the nesting season extends

192. Plastral view of *Caretta caretta.*

193. Face of *Caretta caretta.*

from April through August, with a peak in June; it occurs somewhat earlier in the southern part of the range. Little is known of the nesting habits of the Pacific race, *C. c. gigas*. It nests in Natal, Africa, in late November and December; on Heron Island, Queensland, Australia, it nests from November to March. Deraniyagala (1939) thought it probable that it nests in the Maldive Islands: in December 1932 he examined two nests, presumably of this subspecies, on Gulifalu Island. A study of the breeding habits of this turtle in the eastern Pacific is sorely needed.

Most nests are on open beaches or along narrow bays, if the soil is suitable. The nests are dug at night above the high-tide mark and usually seaward from the dune front. Although the females may come onto the beaches on any night during the season, most of them nest during periods of high tides. They nest two or three times a season on the same stretch of beach, at intervals of 12 to 15 days (Caldwell, 1962a). A female interrupted in nesting returns on the same night or on successive nights until she has nested successfully. Groups of females apparently nest together several times. From data on returns Caldwell (1962a) showed that both 2- and 3-year nesting cycles occur.

Caldwell, Carr, and Ogren (1959) presented a lucid account of the nesting of a female loggerhead, as follows:

On first leaving the water, and even until she has started to dig, the turtle is easily disturbed. She reacts strongly to a light thrown directly upon her. . . . after the site for the evening's activity is selected all turtles observed dug a preliminary excavation of varying extent. The female uses all four flippers in this process until she has lowered herself several inches below the surface of the sand. . . . Digging of the actual nest follows almost immediately, for which only the hind flippers working alternately are used. With its outer edge downward, one flipper is inserted into the sand or into the growing hole. . . . It is then cupped, and the outer edge is rotated inwardly. A small amount of sand is now scooped up . . . lifted to the top of the hole, and deftly laid to one side. Meanwhile the opposing flipper remains flat, "palm" down on the sand near the edge of the hole. . . .

The turtle now shifts her body so this other flipper comes into position over the hole. Just before she inserts it into the hole to dig, she flicks it out laterally and upward to brush the loose sand, deposited when this flipper last excavated, away from the edge of the hole. . . .

The digging process is then repeated as the turtle shifts to bring the first flipper into play again. Almost as soon as the nest is finished the flippers are laid straight back or pointed slightly outward, "palms" down . . . and the cloacal "ovipositer" is inserted. During the digging process the head has been held flat on the sand and the eyes kept open, although blinking occasionally. The eyes secrete copiously . . . during the digging and laying. Just before each group of eggs falls (in groups of one, two, or three) the neck is arched with the head still down . . . and the hind flippers are raised slightly. . . . As each group of eggs falls, the neck is lowered to the position held during digging and the flippers come down and lie flat again between extrusions. . . . During this interval, the head may be raised slightly . . . and the turtle may snort or sigh by expelling air from her nostrils or mouth. . . . When the nest is filled with eggs . . . covering begins almost immediately. Sand is drawn in by the hind flippers, usually working alternately, sometimes together. The outer edge of the flipper is used, the limb reaching well forward and out from the body to drag sand back to the hole. . . . As filling proceeds, the front flippers join in sweeping sand backward to replenish that pushed into the nest cavity by the hind legs and, like the hind flippers, the front ones are used either alternately or together. When the hole is full of loose sand, the hind flippers press it down firmly. . . . During the filling and packing process the head and fore part of the body are sometimes raised as if to shift weight to the hind flippers and help them exert more force. Perhaps this shifting and raising of the body to increase pressure at the hind flippers accounts for the impression that the site is "pounded." Although it was expressly watched for, no turtle was seen to pack or pound the nest with her plastron. . . . As the filling reaches completion, the front flippers aided somewhat by the hind ones begin to fling sand backward. This increased exertion pivots the turtle on the pedestal of sand her digging leaves under her plastron.

After completing the nest the turtle rests for a short period, and she also rests between the several subsequent outbursts of sand-flinging before moving away from the site. The flinging of sand—presumably aimed at concealing the site, and certainly effective—often enlarges the preliminary excavation. . . . Just as the turtle moves away from the site she raises her head high with the eyes still open, as they have been throughout the nesting process . . . and the hyoid aparatus becomes quite prominent as it moves in and out. When she leaves the nest, the site . . . is so camouflaged that the eggs are hard to find without the aid of a probing rod.

The return trip to the surf is usually made quickly and purposefully. Although the head is slightly raised while the turtle drags herself along . . . on reaching the water she drops her head into it. . . . After a moment she raises it again . . . before moving rapidly out of sight into the sea.

The egg chamber is 6–10 inches deep, 8–10 inches wide, and slightly wider at the bottom than at the top. The depth of the uppermost eggs in 317 nests was 5–22 inches, with two thirds of them between the 11- and 16-inch levels (Caldwell, 1959).

The spherical, white eggs have soft, leathery shells. Clutch size of 71 nests at Cape Romain, South Carolina, averaged 126 eggs (64–118). Three nests near Charleston contained 180, 219, and 341 eggs. Measurements of 827 eggs revealed that the greatest diameter of normal eggs averaged 41.5 mm (35–49) and that the average weight was 35 g. The variation of egg diameter within a clutch was 3–11 mm. Within a clutch the eggs laid last were smaller than those laid first. Larger females laid, on average, smaller eggs (Caldwell, 1959). Hughes, Bass, and Mentis (1967) and Hughes and Mentis (1967) reported that the clutch size of *C. c. gigas* in Natal, Africa, averaged 112 eggs (98 clutches) and 118 eggs (68 clutches) on 2 successive years. The diameters of 260 eggs in 26 clutches averaged 49.9 mm.

Cunningham and Hurwitz (1936) studied the water absorption of six loggerhead eggs, which were obtained about a week after they were laid. One was immediately desiccated to determine the dry content for comparison with that found in the other eggs, which were incubated for nearly 2 months. The average weight increase of the four eggs that developed was approximately 50%. Carr (1952) remarked that washing with the salt water of spring tides apparently does not kill the embryos, but Ragotzkie (1959) found that fresh water flooding does.

194. Nesting *Caretta caretta*.
(*Photo by John M. Mehrtens*)

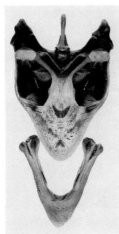

Skull of *Caretta caretta*

195. Young *Caretta caretta*.

The incubation period of the Atlantic loggerhead ranges up to 68 days. Caldwell (1959) reported that in 55 nests the incubation period averaged 55 days (49–62). Eggs of *C. c. gigas* in Natal, Africa, had incubation periods of 67–71 days (Hughes and Mentis, 1967).

Caldwell (1959) reported a hatching success of 16–98% for Atlantic loggerhead eggs. Hughes, Bass, and Mentis (1967) found that of 2,859 Pacific loggerhead eggs, 88.30% were fertile and 87.25% hatched. Hughes and Mentis (1967) found that of 10,238 eggs laid in the following year 85.70% were fertile and 83.39% hatched.

Caldwell (1959) discovered that 5.3% of the eggs laid among stands of the spike grass *Uniola paniculata* were destroyed by its roots. The root hairs formed thick mats around the individual eggs, eroded the shells, and desiccated them; often the sharp-pointed stolons pierced the eggs. A small number of the turtles that pipped their eggs were unable to completely escape the shell. Others escaped from the shell but were trapped in the nest, either because of their inability to climb through the tightly packed deposit of fractured eggshells and matted roots or because of their tendency to burrow horizontally into hard sand instead of perpendicularly to the surface.

Young loggerheads usually emerge from the nest at night. Caldwell (1959) found that heat probably is the factor controlling time of emergence: hatchlings 1–4 inches below the surface of the sand were inactive in the middle of the day but emerged in the cool of the following night.

The hatchling *C. c. caretta* has a heart-shaped, brown carapace with three dorsal keels. The whitish plastron has two longitudinal ridges. Caldwell (1959) measured 398 hatchlings from Cape Romain, South Carolina, and found that the carapace length averaged 45 mm (38–50) and the carapace width 35.5 mm (31–40). The average weight of 104 hatchlings was 21.2 g.

The hatchling *C. c. gigas* also has a heart-shaped carapace with three longitudinal keels, but it is yellowish-brown to grayish-black. The plastron has several longitudinal ridges and varies from cream-colored to a mottled grayish-black and white. Hughes and Mentis (1967) found that 499 Natal hatchlings averaged 45.0 mm in carapace length, 36.7 mm in carapace width, and 19.0 mm in body depth.

GROWTH: Parker (1929) kept a 48-mm, 20-g hatchling *C. c. caretta* for 4.5 years, during which it grew to 630 mm and 37 kg. Hildebrand and Hatsel (1927) reported that an Atlantic loggerhead, obtained as a yearling, grew in carapace length from 136 mm to 538 mm in 3.5 years. At age 4.5 years it weighed 45 lb; at 6 years, 61 lb. Smith (1968) reported that a young individual 64.3 mm in carapace length grew 42 mm in 3 months. Two captive hatchlings each grew 4.5 mm in 13 days. In a group of mixed juveniles one was 48 mm long about 2 weeks after hatching; others, 53–71 mm long, were approximately 11 weeks old; and one, 81 mm long, was about 13 weeks old (Caldwell *et al.*, 1955b). Five Atlantic loggerheads 46.7–52.0 mm in length when hatched had a mean length increase of 21.9 mm in 2 months (Caldwell, 1962b). Hughes, Bass, and Mentis (1967) reported that 2.5-year-old Pacific loggerheads were 20–25 cm in length.

Several specimens lived for 33 years (from 1898 to 1931) in the Vasco da Gama Aquarium, Lisbon, Portugal. One lived at least 23 years and possibly 25 years at the Berlin Zoological Gardens. Nine Atlantic loggerheads were kept in captivity for more than 20 years at Marineland, in Florida.

FOOD AND FEEDING: *Caretta* is omnivorous. It commonly noses about coral reefs, rocky places, and old boat wrecks for food. Animals consumed include sponges, jellyfish, mussels, clams, oysters, conchs, borers (*Natica*), squid, shrimp, amphipods, crabs, barnacles, sea urchins, tunicates, and various fish; whether the fish are caught fresh or consumed as carrion is not known. It also eats seaweed, turtle grass (*Zostera*, *Thalassia*), and *Sargassum*.

PREDATORS: The nests of the loggerhead are dug up and the eggs eaten by sand crabs, hogs, foxes, dogs, and raccoons. Routa (1967) reported that, contrary to the popular belief that most nests are destroyed by predators, the total predation may be low: only 7.8% of the 705 nests he counted on Hutchinson Island, Florida were destroyed. However, Holden (in Carr, 1967a) found that of 199 nests on a 5-mile stretch of the beaches of Cape Sable, Florida, 140 were destroyed by raccoons, which not only dug up fresh nests but also destroyed some that were several days old. Man is also a major nest-predator in parts of the world where the eggs are often the chief source of protein. On the beach the hatchlings are eaten by sand crabs, a racer (*Masticophis anthonyi*), raccoons, water mongooses (*Atilax paludinosus*), dogs, gulls, crows, and yellow kites (*Milvus aegyptius*); in the water they are the prey of numerous kinds of fish.

Bustard (1967a) reported that silver gulls (*Larus novae-hollandiae*) and ghost crabs (*Ocypode ceratophthalma*) are the two most important beach predators of hatchlings at the Heron Island rookery, in Australia. The gulls usually eat the few hatchlings that emerge during the day, and the ghost crabs are voracious nocturnal predators. In the water off Heron Island the hatchlings readily fall prey to carnivorous fish, including the black-tipped reef shark (*Carcharinus spallanzani*).

The adults apparently have few natural predators other than man. Sharks surely attack them in the sea, and dogs kill nesting females.

MOVEMENTS: The loggerhead is likely a confirmed wanderer; its wide range seems to substantiate this. Murphy (in Carr, 1952) saw large numbers of this species 400–500 miles off the coast of Uruguay.

Tagging studies have contributed some information on loggerhead movements. Caldwell *et al.* (1955b) reported that a female tagged at Fort Pierce, Florida, was recaptured 130 miles to the north, off Daytona Beach, Florida. A female tagged at Tongaland, Natal, Africa, was killed 1,500 miles to the north, near Mikindani, Tanzania, Africa, more than 1 year later (Hughes and Mentis, 1967). Bustard and Limpus (1970) reported that a female tagged at Mon Repos, Australia, was recovered after 63 days in the Trobriand Islands, at a straight-line distance of 1,100 miles; the probable course was 1,200 miles, but if the coastline was followed, the distance would have been about 2,000 miles. The journey was against the prevailing current.

Hughes, Bass, and Mentis (1967) reported the finding of a hatchling on a Durban, South Africa, beach some 300 miles from the Tongaland nesting locality; however, there were unconfirmed reports of turtles nesting at Tugeta Mouth, 65 miles north of Durban, and this individual may have come from there. Caldwell, Carr, and Ogren (1959) reported the capture of a young loggerhead 15 miles southwest of Key Largo, Florida. Carr (1967a) reported that two hatchlings were found in the stomach of a shark captured 135 miles east of Cumberland Island, Georgia, and that nine young were taken from a *Sargassum* raft in the Gulf Stream off Florida. Smith (1968) reported that a young loggerhead was captured at sea approximately 90 miles east of the mouth of the Savannah River, in Georgia. It was taken in a net along with *Sargassum* and juvenile fishes characteristic of a *Sargassum* community. It is probable that this turtle was associated with the weed, but this is uncertain because the net had been towed for about 2 miles; besides, Smith at other times saw young loggerheads on the surface that were not associated with *Sargassum*. Caldwell (1968) reported other instances of juveniles associated with this seaweed. One was 58.6 mm in carapace length —an indication that it had been at sea for 1–2 months. It is possible that after leaving the nesting beaches the hatchlings climb on *Sargassum* rafts and drift passively, feeding on the raft's associated animals.

Several studies give some idea of the mechanism of orientation by which *Caretta* hatchlings find the sea. Hooker (1908, 1911) demonstrated that hatchlings preferred blue over red, orange, or green. The hatchlings were attracted by large areas of light rather than intense point-sources and after entering the water were attracted by the darker blue of deep water. Parker (1922) reported that the hatchlings were positively geotropic and thus were guided by the downward slope of the beach to the sea. He also found that they were repelled by a broken horizon

and attracted by a low, unbroken one. Daniel and Smith (1947) observed that the young were guided by phototaxis and photokinesis, being attracted by bright surf and repelled by dark patterns; the orientation capacity was diminished on dark nights. McFarlane (1963) reported that loggerheads hatching at Fort Lauderdale, Florida, were disoriented by artificial lighting along an adjacent highway and crawled toward it, with the result that 90 of them were killed by the traffic. From these reports it can be concluded that hatchlings find their way to the sea by means of attraction to open areas of illumination, by visual cues, and, possibly, by positive geotaxis.

REMARKS: *Caretta* is most important economically for its food value. In many parts of the world the meat and eggs provide a much-needed source of protein.

The loggerhead has been so consistently persecuted at the nesting grounds and so many of them destroyed that the original nesting range cannot be discerned. The rapid development of beaches and coastal islands for home sites and recreational areas probably will destroy most of the North American nesting beaches and perhaps exterminate the Atlantic subspecies. The raccoon is a most efficient nest-predator, and the marked expansion of its coastal populations also threatens the future of *C. c. caretta*. The main hope for the survival of the Atlantic loggerhead lies in the development of state and national parks and reserves.

196. Female *Lepidochelys kempii* showing the heartshaped carapace.

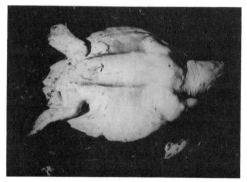

197. Plastral view of *Lepidochelys kempii*.

LEPIDOCHELYS KEMPII (Garman)

Atlantic Ridley

RECOGNITION: A small (50–70 cm) sea turtle with two pairs of prefrontals, four pairs of pore-bearing inframarginals on the bridge, and five pleurals on each side of the carapace. The heart-shaped, keeled, gray carapace often is wider than long in adults, is highest anterior to the bridge and serrated behind. The first pair of pleurals touch the cervical, and there are 12 to 14 marginals on each side. The bridge and the hingeless plastron are immaculate white, and the head and the paddlelike limbs are gray. The head is wide and somewhat pointed anteriorly, and the snout is short and broad. The bony alveolar surface of the upper jaw has a conspicuous ridge running parallel to the cutting edge.

Males have concave plastrons and long tails, which extend beyond the posterior carapacial margin.

GEOGRAPHIC VARIATION: No subspecies have been described.

CONFUSING SPECIES: *L. olivacea* is olive and usually has more than five pairs of pleurals on each side of the carapace. *Chelonia mydas* and *Eretmochelys imbricata* have only four pleurals on each side of the carapace, with the first not touching the cervical. *Caretta caretta* has only three inframarginals in the bridge and is red in color.

DISTRIBUTION: *L. kempii* ranges in the western Atlantic Ocean from Nova Scotia and, possibly, Newfoundland south to Bermuda and west through the Gulf of Mexico to Mexico. It also crosses the Gulf Stream to England, Ireland, the Scilly Isles, France, the Azores, and it occasionally enters the Mediterranean Sea.

HABITAT: The Atlantic ridley prefers shallow water. In the Florida Keys it is closely associated with the subtropical shoreline of red mangrove.

BEHAVIOR: Almost nothing is known of the habits

239

of this turtle. Several captives spent much of the time buried in the debris at the bottom of their tank, possibly foraging for food. *L. kempii* is generally bad-tempered, and freshly caught individuals exhibit hysterical violence and obstinacy. If kept out of water and placed on their backs they thrash about frantically with their flippers and often bite at nearby objects. Although captives become somewhat tame, they remain nervous. Parrish (1958) reported that captives slept with their eyes open and were never observed with their eyes more than half-closed.

Walker (1959) noted that *L. kempii* is capable of closing its nostrils underwater. Closure occurs part way within each nostril; it is effected by the meeting of bulges from the laterodorsal and medioventral walls of the nasal passages.

REPRODUCTION: *L. kempii* reaches sexual maturity at a carapace length of about 60 cm.

Courtship and mating occur shortly before nesting, at the surface of the water just off the beaches. The males become quite active at this time; Carr (1967a) reported that one even followed a nesting female onto the beach and attempted to mount her all the way. Chavez, *et al.* (1968b) observed a copulating pair at 11 AM off the Tamaulipas, Mexico, nesting beach.

Nesting occurs sporadically from April through mid-August on the beaches of the Gulf of Mexico between Corpus Christi, Texas, and southern Veracruz, Mexico, but most often occurs along a 90-mile stretch of the Tamaulipas coast north of Tampico. The most frequently selected locality is Rancho Nuevo, in the Municipio de Aldana; there, most activity is concentrated on some single mile of shore. Nesting usually is diurnal; Chavez *et al.* (1968b) reported that in Tamaulipas it takes place between 8:25 AM and 6:25 PM.

Although some females come up to nest individually, most do so in large groups—sometimes by the thousands. Carr (1963b) reported that during a 6-hr period there may be 10,000 females on the sand at one time. The turtle traffic is so dense at the place of maximum emergence that the eggs laid by one female are often dug up by a later-nesting female. Up to three clutches are laid each season, at intervals of 10 to 28 days; and a female may nest in successive years.

At the time of nesting the ridleys gather offshore from the nesting beaches in groups that may number 40,000—groups that Carr (1967a) has termed arribadas (Spanish, "arrivals"). These gatherings usually take place during a time of strong wind from the northeast and heavy surf, but they may also occur at full moon.

Chavez *et al.* (1968b) studied nesting in Tamaulipas and found that the nests were dug in fine sand, either on the beach or on the dunes, at distances of 13–45 m from the water. On the nesting beach at Tamaulipas the sea is to the east, so females leaving the water travel in a westerly direction; and even while they deposit their eggs they keep their heads pointed toward the west. When they have finished nesting they generally turn counterclockwise—that is, they start toward the left, or south—until they face the water; then they return to the sea.

Chavez *et al.* (1968b) observed a female leave the water at 12:34 PM (on 11 May 1966). She crawled in a more or less diagonal direction toward the dunes. On the way she stopped 11 times, apparently to rest. Sometimes while crawling she slightly buried the front of her jaw, apparently to test the texture of the sand. She reached the base of a dune at 12:42 PM; there she stopped, buried her jaw in the sand, and, while moving her head from side to side, began digging with her front flippers. She then began to dig the nest, using the posterior flippers alternately, the outer edges of which were curled so as to lift out the sand; the front flippers were at this time buried firmly in the ground for balance. When the nest was deep enough she lifted the forepart of her body, burying the flippers even deeper. At 12:57 PM, she finished the 41-cm excavation and, keeping the hind flippers on the sand, started to lay a clutch of 106 eggs. Most of the time two or three eggs fell together, but sometimes only one. At intervals a clear, viscous liquid was secreted over the eggs. While she was depositing the eggs the turtle lifted her head and expanded the hyoid apparatus; her mouth remained slightly open and at times a sound was produced by the exhaled air. From the beginning of nesting she kept her eyes almost completely closed; a lachrymal fluid was secreted from them. She finished laying at 1:09 PM and immediately began to cover the nest. When it was almost filled she began to press down by dipping the sides of her body alternately; this produced a sound. At intervals she threw more sand with her hind limbs. The nest was completely covered at 1:15 PM. Then she turned to the left (south), made a complete turn to face the sea, and departed. On the way she stopped five times finally arriving at the water at 1:22 PM. Her stay on the beach had lasted exactly 48 min.

The nest of *L. kempii* is flask-shaped; the surface diameter is 26–33 cm, and the cavity widens a few centimeters toward the bottom. The maximum depth is 37–49 cm, and the depth from the surface to the level of the eggs is 11–38 cm. The temperatures of eight nests, recorded after nesting, were 23–30 C (Chavez *et al.*, 1968b).

The spherical eggs have soft, white shells. Chavez *et al.* (1968b) reported that after being buried in the sand for two days the shell became even softer and dark spots appeared on the embryonic side. The diameter of 221 eggs averaged 38.9 mm (35.0–44.5). Among 271 females the number of eggs averaged 110 (54–185) per clutch; 62% of the females laid 100–129 eggs. A 61.8-cm female laid 118 eggs and when dissected was found to contain 258 large oviducal eggs (diameters 26.0–31.2 mm) and 11 smaller eggs (12.9–16.6 mm).

Chavez *et al.* (1968b) removed 29,937 eggs from 271 nests within 48 hr of their being laid and reburied them in a protected part of the beach. After an incubation period of 50–70 days 1,664 hatched. Most hatchings occurred after 53–56 days, and all hatchings took place between 5:17 AM and 8:50 AM; 87% of hatchings occurred before 7 AM. The hatchings took place in any kind of weather—even when it was raining or a strong wind was blowing. Two or 3 days before hatching the upper and central parts of the nests sank, producing a circular depression about 5 cm deep. From 27 to 31 hatchlings were seen emerging from a nest at intervals of 30–40

198. *Lepidochelys kempii.*

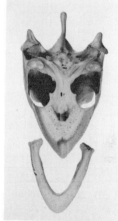

Skull of *Lepidochelys kempii*

min, and some left the same nest on different days.

Hatchlings have relatively elongated, oval carapaces with three tuberculate keels and a plastron with four longitudinal ridges. They are dark gray to black, with a white edge on both the flippers and the carapace. The measurements and weights of 124 examined by Chavez *et al.* (1968a) were as follows: carapace length 38–46 mm; carapace width 30–40 mm; plastron width 27–41 mm; head length 17–22 mm; and weight 13.5–21.0 g. In the hatchlings they examined, the carapace always was longer than wide —the opposite of the usual condition in adults. The mean length of the foreflippers was 38.9 mm (33–44) and that of the hind flippers was 26.0 mm (20–31).

GROWTH: At capture an Atlantic ridley was 260 mm long and weighed 3,178 g. After 316 days on a cutfish diet it had increased 45 mm in length and 1,589 g in weight and had changed from wider-than-long to longer-than-wide. Another measured 279 mm and weighed 2,838 g at capture. After 330 days on a cut-fish diet it had increased only 15 mm and 1,362 g. Almost exactly 1 year later this turtle had grown an additional 46 mm in length and 1,816 g in weight (Caldwell, 1962b). Four captive hatchlings averaging 44.5 mm in carapace length and 16.2 g in weight increased an average of 46.7 mm and 252.8 g in 188 days. Three females, tagged while nesting, increased 0.5–1.0 cm in carapace length in 349–373 days (Chavez, 1969).

Carr and Caldwell (1956) found that the length-weight relationship in *L. kempii* is best expressed by the following formula: log W = minus 1.69 + 2.49 log L, where L is the carapace length and W is the weight. They reported that at a carapace length of 42.5 cm an Atlantic ridley had a mean empirical weight of 20 lb and a calculated weight of 22.8 lb; specimens 50.8 cm long had a mean empirical weight of 35.3 lb (31–38) and a calculated weight of 35.4 lb; and those 64.8 cm long had a mean empirical weight of 58.5 lb (58–59) and a calculated weight of 64.9 lb. They calculated that the length of a 93-lb specimen would be 74.9 cm. The great variation in the length-width proportion

makes for correspondingly wide ranges in the length-weight ratios, because the *L. kempii* that are as wide as, or even wider than, long are heavier than those of more usual widths for the length class.

Four female *L. kempii* were kept in captivity for more than 20 years at Marineland, in Florida.

FOOD AND FEEDING: *L. kempii* is predominately carnivorous, feeding on crabs (*Callinectes*, *Ovalipes*, *Hepatus*), snails (*Nassarius*), clams (*Nuculana*, *Corbula*, *Mulinia*), and occasionally on various marine plants. It seems to be largely a bottom feeder. Captives readily eat fish.

PREDATORS: The nests are robbed by sand crabs and various mammals. On the beaches the hatchlings are eaten by sand crabs and various birds, and once they reach the sea many marine fishes prey on them. Chavez *et al.* (1968b) were told that a sea bass had 11 newly hatched ridleys in its stomach. The adults are occasionally attacked by sharks, but man is their most effective predator.

MOVEMENTS: Chavez (1969) and his co-workers tagged 285 nesting female *L. kempii* on the sands from Boca San Vicente to about 4 km to the south of Barra Coma, on the coast of Tamaulipas. Of these, 18 were recaptured. Nine were found in localities on the Gulf coast of the United States: seven from south of Brownsville, Texas, to the coast of Louisiana, and one from between the Marquesas Keys and the Dry Tortugas, off the southwestern coast of Florida (Sweat, 1968). This last individual had traveled at least 955 miles in 212 days. The other eight recaptures occurred in Mexican waters, from Veracruz to Campeche. The turtles were captured at distances of 200 m to 39 km off the coast; the majority were found at 4–12 km. The Florida specimen was exceptional in that it was captured about 165 km from land. The depths of the water at the capture sites were 1.8–4.3 m; most of the recaptures occurred in waters 3.5–9.0 m deep. Of 25 tagged near the Withlacoochee-Crystal River, Florida, by Carr and Caldwell (1956) only 2 were recovered: one at the site of original capture after an interval of 43 days, the other by a Cedar Key, Florida, fisherman. All these records tend to substantiate Carr's (1961a) assumption that this turtle migrates near the coast. They also indicate that the feeding grounds of this species extend along the Gulf coast from southern Florida to Yucatan.

Orientation in this species is known to be well developed, but the exact cues are not known. Nesting females must travel considerable distances from their feeding grounds to find a rather small nesting zone; for example the major nesting area in Tamaulipas is only 14 km in length.

POPULATIONS: Carr and Caldwell (1956) estimated on the basis of very scant data that the size of the *L. kempii* population on the Florida fishing grounds was 3,750 and that the total catch amounted to 300 turtles.

REMARKS: The ridleys (*Lepidochelys*) long were confused with the loggerheads (*Caretta*), and even today the Atlantic ridley is sometimes referred to as "Kemp's loggerhead." There are obvious differences between loggerheads and ridleys: see the account of *Caretta caretta*.

Grant (1946b) remarked that if the shell of a ridley is given a sharp rap with a hard object, the sound produced is hollow and dead, like that produced by tapping a piece of dead wood; but a loggerhead, similarly rapped, sounds like a "living thing."

The Atlantic ridley's chances of survival are more precarious than those of any other sea turtle. Its numbers have been decimated by fishing, nest-robbing, and the slaughter of nesting females. Fortunately, the Mexican government, in an effort to save this turtle, now protects the nesting females on the beaches of Tamaulipas. A group of concerned American conservationists is transplanting eggs and transporting hatchlings from Tamaulipas to Padre Island, Texas, a known natural nesting-site, in an attempt to reestablish a breeding colony there.

Both the eggs and adults of this species are eaten by man. Carr (1952) reported that he had eaten several of these turtles; he considered the young ridley to be as tasty as the young of any of the other sea turtles, but the adult seemed to him to be somewhat inferior to the green turtle, both for soup and for steaks. Nevertheless, *L. kempii* offers a ready source of protein in some places where this nutrient is scarce.

199. Swimming *Lepidochelys kempii* present an almost ghostly appearance.

200. Female *Lepidochelys olivacea.*
(*Photo by Charles M. Bogert*)

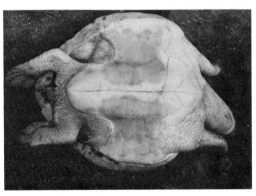

201. Plastron of *Lepidochelys olivacea.*
(*Photo by Peter C. H. Pritchard*)

LEPIDOCHELYS OLIVACEA (Eschscholtz)

Pacific Ridley   XXII

RECOGNITION: A small (60–71 mm) sea turtle with paddlelike flippers, two pairs of prefrontals, four pairs of pore-bearing inframarginals on the bridge, and usually six to eight (occasionally five to nine) pleurals on each side. The heart-shaped, olive carapace is flattened dorsally, is highest anterior to the bridge, and is serrated posteriorly. The first pair of pleurals touches the cervical, and there may be more pleurals on one side of the carapace than on the other; in specimens from the eastern Pacific, at least, the higher number usually is found on the left side. There are from 12 to 14 marginals on each side of the carapace. The bridge and the hingeless plastron are greenish-white or greenish-yellow. The skin is olive above and lighter below. The head is wide, with concave sides, especially on the upper part of the short, broad snout. The bony alveolar surface of the upper jaw may have a gentle elevation extending parallel to the cutting edge, but it lacks a conspicuous ridge.

Males have long thick tails, which extend well beyond the rear carapacial margin; females' tails usually do not reach the margin. Males have concave plastrons, a more gently sloping lateral profile, and a strongly developed, curved claw on each front flipper.

GEOGRAPHIC VARIATION: No subspecies are recognized; however, the possibility exists that the eastern Pacific and southern Atlantic populations are distinct.

CONFUSING SPECIES: *L. kempii* is gray and usually has only five pleurals on each side. *Chelonia mydas* and *Eretmochelys imbricata* have only four pleurals on each side, with the first not touching the cervical. *Caretta caretta* is reddish and has three inframarginals on the bridge.

DISTRIBUTION: *L. olivacea* occurs in the tropical waters of the Pacific and Indian oceans; in the Atlantic Ocean off the western coast of Africa and the coasts of Surinam and Guyana, in South America; and, occasionally, in the Carribean Sea as far north as Puerto Rico. There are California records from Monterey Bay and from a beach near Table Bluff, Humbolt County.

HABITAT: Most records are from protected, relatively shallow marine waters, but the Pacific ridley occasionally occurs in the open sea. Deraniyagala (1939) reported the habitat to be the shallow water between reefs and shore, the larger bays, and lagoons. *L. olivacea* nests on the same beaches as *Chelonia mydas*, *Eretmochelys imbricata*, *Caretta caretta*, and *Dermochelys coriacea*.

BEHAVIOR: Little is known of the behavior of this species. Pacific ridleys often travel in loosely aggregated groups; apparently they do not come ashore to bask. The temperatures of three *L. olivacea* were 28.0 C, 29.0 C, and 29.5 C when the sea temperature was approximately 28.0 C (Pritchard, 1969a).

REPRODUCTION: The majority of the nesting females in Surinam had a carapace length of 66–71 cm; the smallest of 241 mature females was 62 cm long (Pritchard, 1969a). Carr (1952) found that the carapace length of mature females from Honduras was 64.5–69.1 cm. Studies in Honduras by Pritchard (1969a) showed some females matured at 58.4 cm. The size at which the males mature is unknown.

The mating season probably coincides with the nesting period. Carr (1952) saw several adult males loafing in a narrow channel off a Honduras beach on which females were nesting at night, and boatmen told him that males were not found in the channel at other seasons. The courtship and mating acts have not been described.

L. olivacea may be found nesting in almost every month of the year in various parts of the range. The eggs are laid from mid-August through January in the eastern Pacific, from September to January in India and Ceylon, during March and April in Burma, during May on the coast of Eritrea, and from April through July in Surinam. Females start to emerge from the sea with a rising tide in late after-noon and are finished nesting by the advent of low tide at night. During the peaks of activity many nest on the same stretch of beach; Pritchard (1969a) saw 97 nesting simultaneously on a 230-yard stretch of beach in Surinam, and 115 were present on the entire beach. The complete nesting, from emergence to reentering the sea usually takes less than 1 hr to complete. Females may nest three times a season but usually do so only twice. Pritchard (1969a) found that in Surinam the usual intervals between successive nestings were about 17 days, 30 days, and, possibly, 44 days; one female was recovered after a 60-day interval. Nesting often occurs during periods of strong winds, and Pritchard felt that the interval between nestings was controlled more by environmental factors, such as the tide and weather, than by physiologic factors.

How do so many females manage to synchronize their nesting? Pritchard (1969a) thought it unlikely that eggs ripen within gravid females in such perfect synchrony that the urge to lay comes upon the whole population simultaneously. He thought it more likely that the eggs ripen in only approximate synchrony and that the female can hold the shelled eggs for a rather long period until the right combination of tide, moon, and wind brings about in all females a simultaneous urge to lay. This reasonable idea should be viewed in the light of the common observation that a turtle frightened back to the sea before it nests usually will try again, either later the same night or on the following night. It seems likely that once a turtle comes on the beach to nest, the eggs start moving towards the cloaca and produce a pressure that can be relieved only by laying them.

Pritchard (1969a) observed the nesting of a Pacific ridley; extracts from his account are as follows:

The turtle, found crawling up the beach with its carapace still wet, paused occasionally as she walked straight to the vegetation line, turned back a short way, and immediately began digging the body pit. Using rather disorganized strokes of all four flippers, the front ones usually working together . . . the rear ones alternately, she completed the pit in 4 minutes. She started digging the nest cavity at the rear of the body pit with great energy, but soon became rather sluggish. Her shell moved from side to side through a wide angle as she dipped her flippers alternately in the cavity. She jerked each flipper forward sharply before re-inserting it in the hole. As the cavity deepened her shell dipped lower to let the flipper scrape sand off the bottom. At first she moved the rear part of her carapace in a simple down–up movement, but towards the end of the excavation this movement became a little more complicated; she lowered the rear part of her shell to the full extent, the front of the shell raised high on the forelimbs and the neck lowered; then she raised the rear a little, lowered it the same amount, and finally raised it fully before switching to the other flipper. When the egg cavity reached its final flask shape, she continued to jerk the flipper sharply forward as if about to re-insert it in the cavity, but instead she merely curled the flipper and drew it under the overhanging rear margin of the carapace. There was no obvious reason for this movement, which she made about three times with each flipper.

Oviposition commenced with the foreflippers still braced in the sand and the hind flippers splayed outwards. . . . The sequence of movements preceding each deposition of one, two, three, or four eggs was as follows: 1) humeral region drawn slightly inwards and head simultaneously slightly extended, 2) above movements reversed, 3) rear part of shell moved up and down through a few millimeters with rear margins of hind flippers raised simultaneously . . . 4) eggs deposited. From time to time during oviposition she raised her head considerably and took a deep breath. About a minute after laying the last egg, she pulled sand into the egg cavity by alternate movement of the hind flippers. As soon as the hole was filled she pounded the loose sand down with alternate sides of the carapace. During this movement she braced her front flippers in the sand with her head pointed down and almost resting on the sand but providing no anchorage. She thumped down the side of her carapace and the hind flipper on the same side almost simultaneously. . . . After a few minutes she stopped pounding and with the hind flippers drew more sand into a small pile under the rear of her carapace. She then resumed thumping, always with a side-to-side rocking movement, never with the whole plastron. Then she began to throw sand backwards with one foreflipper and the opposite hind flipper. . . . This movement generated a slight turning effect and a slight motion away from the nest site. After four or five swipes she counteracted the turning movement with a single quick step and repeated the maneuver with the opposite flipper.

This continued for a long time, while she moved about 5 feet away, then turned round and returned toward the nest, possibly disoriented by the light. Into this movement she interposed a few simultaneous swipes of her foreflippers. Gradually the movement became the standard walking which carried her part way to the sea. Shortly before she reached the sea she turned a tight circle and thereafter seemed completely disoriented, again possibly by the flashlight. Eventually it was necessary to help her into the sea.

In Ceylon the nest site frequently is near some river mouth. This may be due either to a preference for the fine river-sand washed onto the beach or for the low salinity of the water; high salinity causes coagulation of the yolk. The nest usually is scooped out under the shelter of shrubs about 50 m from the sea and is at the apex of a V formed by the ingress and egress trails of the turtle (Deraniyagala, 1939).

The flask-shaped nests are 482–550 mm in overall depth, 178–205 mm in lateral diameter of the egg chamber, and 250–304 mm in front-to-back diameter (Carr, 1952).

Clutch size of 928 Surinam nests was 30–168 eggs (mean 116); only 4 nests contained fewer than 70 eggs and only 4 had more than 155. Of 45 Honduras females 20 that exceeded 66.7 cm in carapace length laid an average of 123.8 eggs each and the smaller ones averaged only 95.9 eggs each (Pritchard, 1969a).

The oval-to-spherical, white eggs have soft, leathery shells and are 37.5–45.4 mm in diameter. When newly laid they adhere to one another, owing to the strongly mucilaginous mucus that invests them; these agglutinated eggs present a morulalike appearance.

Pritchard (1969a) found strikingly high hatching percentages for Pacific ridley nests in Surinam. All the eggs in a clutch of 88 hatched normal offspring. In another clutch, of 126 eggs, 3 that he opened before hatching contained living embryos; of the remainder 118 hatched, 2 were infertile, and 3 were slow developers.

Under natural conditions eggs laid on Ceylon beaches hatch in 50 days, but if weather conditions are unfavorable the period may extend to 60 days

246

202. Nesting *Lepidochelys olivacea.*
(*Photo by Peter C. H. Pritchard*)

203. Nesting *Lepidochelys olivacea.*
(*Photo by Wayne Frair*)

(Deraniyagala, 1939). The time from laying of eggs to appearance of the hatchlings at the surface of 22 Surinam nests was 49–62 days (mean 55.7) (Pritchard, 1969a).

The relatively elongated, oval carapace of the hatchling usually has well-developed pale keels on the vertebrals and pleurals. There also are four longitudinal ridges on the plastron. Hatchlings are gray-black to olive-black, with a small white mark at each side at the supralabial scale, another on the hind part of the umbilical protuberance, and several where the ridges of the plastron cross the abdominal and femoral scutes. The skin and plastron may be dark grayish-brown. A fine white line borders the carapace and the trailing edge of the foreflippers and the hind flippers. Hatchlings are 40–50 mm in carapace length, 31–45 mm in carapace width, and 18–20 mm in head length, and they weigh 16–19 g.

GROWTH: Deraniyagala (1939) recorded the following growth data for individuals from the Indian Ocean: at age 30 days, carapace length 85 mm; 210 days, 170 mm; and 307 days, 185 mm. One grew from 43 mm to 74 mm from 1 February to 3 August 1929, and another grew from 45 mm to 490 mm from 18 January 1934 to 30 May 1936.

FOOD AND FEEDING: *L. olivacea* is highly carnivorous, feeding predominantly on fish, crabs, snails, oysters, sea urchins, and jellyfish. Sea weeds are occasionally eaten. Captives eat fish, meat, and bread, and at times they are cannibalistic.

PREDATORS: Many birds and mammals rob the nests, and the young are eaten by a host of crabs, birds, mammals, and oceanic fish. Adults often have their shells and limbs damaged, presumably by sharks. However, man is the leading predator on this turtle, gathering the eggs and slaughtering the females on the beaches. Some adults are taken at sea by turtle fishermen.

MOVEMENTS: A female tagged by Pritchard (1969a) in Surinam on 7 June 1966 was recovered on 17 September 1966, 300 miles upstream near Cape Cassipore, Brazil. Another, tagged the same day, was recovered 75 miles offshore from Paramaribo on 20 January 1967. Of three tagged in 1967 one was recovered from near the mouth of the Orinoco, one off the coast of Surinam, and one from Brazil between the mouths of the Oyapoque and Amazon rivers.

Oliver (1946) observed what may have been a migratory aggregation of Pacific ridleys in deep water off Guerrero, Mexico, in late November 1945.

POPULATIONS: The observation of Oliver (1946) of an unusually large number of *L. olivacea* in the Pacific Ocean, together with the observations of Carr (1952) and Pritchard (1969a) of numerous nesting females, suggest a rather large population of this turtle, at least locally.

Several Pacific ridleys have been collected at sea in the western Atlantic and the Carribean during September and October. This suggests either a resident population off northeastern South America and in the Antilles, a constant recruitment from Africa via the North or the South Equatorial Current, or a movement independent of the currents. A turtle merely riding the current after a late-summer nesting season would be swept far beyond Surinam and Puerto Rico by October.

REMARKS: Schmidt (1953) considered the differences between *L. olivacea* and *L. kempii* to be only subspecific and included three subspecies under *Lepidochelys olivacea: L. o. kempii*, the Atlantic race; *L. o. remivaga* (Hay, 1908a), the Pacific race; and *L. o. olivacea*, the race in the Indian Ocean.

The pleural scutes of *L. olivacea* are clearly divisible into whole and half scutes—the whole scutes being homologous with the five pleurals of *L. kempii*. Displacement of the homologues of the seams of *L. kempii* usually is slight, although in cases of extreme splitting (to eight or nine pleurals) the seams become displaced to lessen the size of the small 1st pleural and the large last vertebral. In almost every case division takes place in the posterior pleurals; for example, a 6–6 count is produced by division of the 5th pleurals on each side or an 8–8 count by division of the 3rd, 4th, and 5th pleurals.

Antiserum tests conducted by Frair (1969) did not discriminate between *L. olivacea* and *Caretta caretta*. This suggests that *Caretta* is closely related to *Lepidochelys*.

L. olivacea eggs and flesh are a source of protein in some impoverished regions where protein is scarce.

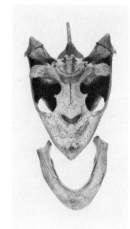

Skull of *Lepidochelys olivacea*

DERMOCHELYIDAE: *Leatherbacks*

This family is composed of a single living species, *Dermochelys coriacea*, the leatherback. It is the largest living turtle, and it ranges widely in tropical and subtropical seas.

The carapace lacks horny plates but is covered with a ridged, leathery skin. The paddlelike limbs are devoid of claws. The neck is short and incompletely retractile.

The shell bones, except the nuchal and the margin of the plastron, are lost; their place is taken by a mosaic of small platelets embedded in the leathery skin. The 4th vertebra is biconvex. The nuchal is attached to the neural arch of the last neck vertebra. The skull roof is complete. The vomer meets the premaxilla, thus separating both the nares and palatines. The basisphenoid does not touch the palatines, and the maxilla is separated from both the pterygoid and quadratojugal. A secondary palate and palatine fenestra are lacking. The quadrate is open posteriorly and does not inclose the stapes. The jaws are very short behind the coronoid process.

DERMOCHELYS CORIACEA (Linnaeus)

Leatherback   XXIII

RECOGNITION: A huge sea turtle with a shell covered with smooth skin instead of horny scutes. The brown-to-black, smooth carapace is elongated and triangular and has seven prominent longitudinal keels, which divide it into eight sections. The hingeless plastron is whitish and has five longitudinal ridges. The carapace and plastron consist of a layer of small, irregularly-shaped bones embedded in the leathery skin. A large number of small bones form a mosaic beneath this leathery layer. The head and neck are black or dark brown, with a few white or yellow blotches. There is a toothlike cusp on either side of the gray upper jaw. The paddlelike, clawless limbs are black and may have some white blotches.

This is the largest living turtle: adults are 118–244 cm in carapace length and weigh from 700–1,600 lb. There is some evidence that in the past individuals may have weighed a ton.

Males have concave plastrons and are rather de-

204. *Dermochelys coriacea.*
(*Photo by Peter C. H. Pritchard*)

pressed in profile. They are more tapering posteriorly and have tails that are longer than their hind limbs; the tails of females are barely half as long.

GEOGRAPHIC VARIATION: Two subspecies are recognized. *D. c. coriacea* (Linnaeus), the Atlantic leatherback, ranges through the Atlantic Ocean, the Gulf of Mexico, and the Caribbean Sea, from Newfoundland to the British Isles and south to Argentina and the Cape of Good Hope. Occasionally it enters the Mediterranean Sea. This race has longer forelimbs in comparison with total body length; has a shorter head; and is darker, with less light mottling on the back, lower jaw, and throat. *D. c. schlegelii* (Garman), the Pacific leatherback, ranges through the Pacific and Indian oceans, from British Columbia to Chile and west to Japan and eastern Africa. It has shorter forelimbs, a longer head, and is paler, with more light mottling on the back, lower jaw, and throat.

The subspecies seem to be poorly differentiated, and a detailed study will be necessary to determine the validity of the two races. Perhaps sexual dimorphism has been confused with subspeciation.

CONFUSING SPECIES: All other marine turtles have claws and a bony carapace covered with horny scutes.

DISTRIBUTION: *Dermochelys* ranges throughout the tropical waters of the Atlantic, Pacific, and Indian oceans, from Newfoundland, the British Isles, British Columbia, and Japan south to Argentina, Chile, Australia, and the Cape of Good Hope. It also enters the Mediterranean Sea.

HABITAT: The leatherback is pelagic, but occasionally it enters the shallow waters of bays and estuaries. It shares its major nesting beaches with most of the other species of marine turtles.

BEHAVIOR: Almost nothing is known of the behavior of free-living leatherbacks. Pope (1939) reported that they sometimes sleep while floating on the surface. Several writers have commented on the great strength of this turtle and have pointed out that it is a formidable adversary when captured: it flails its flippers violently and bites viciously. It is said to vocalize when in distress. Captive leatherbacks almost constantly thrash about and batter themselves against the sides of the tank; they usually succumb within a few weeks.

Dermochelys is subject to a wide variety of temperatures over its range. MacAskie and Forrester (1962) reported vigorous activity of a leatherback in water of 53 F (11.7 C) in the Queen Charlotte Islands of British Columbia; most reptiles are sluggish at that temperature. Bleakney (1965) reported that leatherbacks taken off the eastern coast of Canada had stomachs full of jellyfish, which meant that they had been feeding actively despite the low water-temperatures (55–65 F). Mrosovsky and Pritchard (in Pritchard, 1969a) took deep-body temperatures of four female leatherbacks and recorded readings of 30.00 C, 30.00 C, 30.50 C, and 31.25 C when the sea temperature was approximately 28 C.

REPRODUCTION: Bacon (1970) found that the mean carapace length of 20 nesting females in Trinidad was 158 cm (125–185). Pritchard (1969a) reported that nesting females from Bigi Santi and Eilanti, Surinam, were 148.6–169.2 cm in carapace length.

Courtship and mating have not been described, but they are believed to occur in the water off the nesting beaches at the period of laying.

Nesting of the Atlantic leatherback occurs from April through November. Nesting females have been reported from both coasts of Florida and from Jamaica (Pedro and Morant cays), St. Kitts, Nevis, Barbados, St. Croix, Tortola, Trinidad, Tobago, French Guiana, Surinam, Guyana, Costa Rica, Nicaragua, and Liberia. The Bahamas, the Cayman Islands, Brazil, and Honduras have also been listed, but these reports are questionable.

The Pacific race nests at various times throughout the year, depending on location. Nesting has been reported from Natal, Ceylon, India, Addu Island, Tenasserim, Thailand, Malaya, Australia, and Mexico.

Leatherbacks usually emerge at night to lay.

Bacon (1970) found that on Trinidad all observed females emerged from the sea between 9 PM and midnight and spent about 1.5 hr on the beach. They nest several times a season; evidence gathered by Pritchard (1969a) in Surinam indicated that they nest three times a season, at intervals of about 10 days. Hughes, Bass, and Mentis (1967) reported a similar period for leatherbacks in Natal.

Carr and Ogren (1959) observed a female come ashore and nest; their lucid description of the process is as follows:

STRANDING AND TRIP TO NEST SITE. No overt signs, such as the odd "smelling" of the sand that a green turtle sometimes engages in, of sensory appraisal of the stranding site were noted. During the process of coming ashore, and throughout the trip up the beach, the female trunkback [leatherback] seems far less skittish and easily frightened by lights and moving shapes than either the green turtle or the hawksbill . . . .

GAIT AND PACE. The gait is similar to that of the female green turtle—a labored hauling-forward of the body by simultaneous movements of all four legs. It also resembles locomotion in the sea-seeking young, except that the latter lifts itself off the sand at the beginning of each forward push, while the adult drags herself along.

SELECTION OF THE NEST SITE. Here again no specific orientation or assessment procedures are detectable. The female simply stops, after having moved for a certain distance over dry sand, and the stopping place becomes the nest site. . . . Each of the three . . . females stopped about midway up the beach, on level sand where no obstructions or changes in topography could be identified as stopping signs.

EXCAVATION OF THE BODY PIT. The concealing pit in which the turtle lies while digging the nest, laying, and covering the eggs is made by slow, bulldozer-like strokes of the fore limbs, working mostly together, while the hind legs scrape and push sand independently of the front fins and of each other. At the beginning of the operation, the most effective digging is that of the fore limbs, and, as this deepens the cavity more rapidly anteriorly, the body after a time comes to slope downward under the fore end of the turtle. Eventually, the work of the arms slows down and the kicking and scraping by the back flippers are accelerated, until eventually the latter are working alone.

205. Plastron of *Dermochelys coriacea*. (*Photo by Bob Ackman, courtesy of Wayne Frair*)

206. Head of *Dermochelys coriacea*. (*Photo by John Gilhen, courtesy of Wayne Frair*)

251

EXCAVATION OF THE EGG CAVITY. When the dwindling mound under the back end of the body has been reduced to the general level of the bottom of the body pit, the hind feet continue to work away at this point, and the cavity that grows there becomes the nest. . . . The hind feet work alternately in digging the nest, the body pivoting on its forward end to swing the working flipper directly over the hole. . . .

LAYING. When the nest is as deep as the fin will easily reach, the digging reflex wanes. The flippers are spread out flat behind the body, over and partly within the opening of the nest, into which the tail and cloaca are lowered. Almost immediately laying starts. Throughout the process part of one of the hind flippers remains in the nest, its distal sections pressed against the back edge of the nest. The eggs come out one, two, or three at a time. . . . Throughout the process the eyes are bathed by copious secretion. . . .

FILLING OF THE NEST. A few seconds after the last egg has dropped, and while the forelimbs are still anchored, motionless, the turtle starts filling the nest with her hind feet. Again they work alternately, each pulling and pushing in sand from the accumulation on its side of the opening. When the fill, rising in the nest, is high enough to be felt by the working flippers, the edges of these tilt downward anteriorly in such a way as to press the fore margin into the sand over the nest. This is the beginning of a packing operation which increases as the filling nears completion. For several minutes the flippers keep up the packing work, sometimes pressing downward so hard that the plastron is raised from the sand.

COVERING AND CONCEALING THE PIT. When packing has gone on for a while, the forelegs join in the work of filling. They work mostly together, making swiping, lateral strokes that begin far forward and throw sand back over the sides of the body and into the pit. This operation . . . is accompanied by a steady slow dragging in of sand by the hind feet, which results in the building of a growing mound under the back end of the body. The strong strokes of the forelimbs drag the body a few inches forward each time, and as the original site is slowly left behind, the trail is marked by an irregular ridge, representing the mounding work of the hind feet, and two deep crescentic cavities show where the fore flippers did their last scooping. After the turtle has moved off thus for some feet, the concealment effort suddenly stops. Without discernible cues, the sand-throwing strokes of the fore flippers are supplanted by crawling strokes, and the turtle drags herself out of the

207. Nesting of *Dermochelys coriacea*.
The longitudinal keels are obvious.
(*Photo by Wayne Frair*)

208. Hatchling *Dermochelys coriacea*.
(*Photo by Peter C. H. Pritchard*)

cavity from which she was last throwing sand and without hesitation turns and moves in the general direction of the surf....

The nest may be flask-shaped or not, depending on whether the turtle digs down to damp sand. Deraniyagala (1939) reported a nest 100 cm deep, including the body pit.

Hendrickson and Balasingam (1966) found that the nesting beaches in Malaya had a predominance of coarse sand, which would not pass a 30-mesh sieve. Bacon (1970) found the same situation in Trinidad. The Malaya beaches were steeply sloping, and characteristically there was deep water close inshore.

The usual clutch size is 50–170 eggs. A rather large percentage of the eggs are yolkless, and apparently some of these occur in every clutch. Carr and Ogren (1959) found four clutches with ratios of normal eggs to yolkless eggs as follows: 73:34, 80:41, 66:38, and 45:7. Hughes, Bass, and Mentis (1967) found that Natal nests averaged 106 normal and 30 abnormal eggs. Pritchard (1969a) recorded 71–166 eggs in each of eight nests in Surinam; the normal eggs numbered 58–126 per clutch, the yolkless ones 1–40.

Normal eggs are spherical; have soft, white shells; are 49–65 mm in diameter; and weigh 70–80 g. The abnormal eggs may be ellipsoidal, small and spherical, or somewhat dumbbell-shaped, and they are 15–45 mm in greatest diameter.

Hendrickson (1962) found that of 95 clutches transplanted in Malaya, 11 (876 eggs) were sterile. From the remaining 84 clutches (7,490 eggs) 3,699 hatchlings emerged (mean 49%+; range 14–84%). This emergence percentage was the percentage of the normal eggs that hatched and the young that successfully made their way to the surface through at least 2 ft of sand. No attempt was made to determine the number of hatchlings that failed to reach the surface.

Incubation periods of leatherback eggs are 53–74 days. Deraniyagala (1939) stated that the incubation period in Ceylon is 58–65 days and varies with the intensity of the sun. Carr and Ogren (1959) reported that the incubation periods of three nests observed in Costa Rica were 74 days, 66 days, and 51–58 days. Hendrickson (1962) reported that transplanted eggs hatched after 53 days in Malaya. McAllister *et al.* (1965) reported that the incubation period for a Natal clutch was 72 days. Pritchard (1969a) recorded incubation periods of 60–68 days for seven naturally incubated clutches in Surinam.

Hatchlings are dark brown or black, with white or yellow carapacial keels and flipper margins. The skin is covered with small scales and the tail is keeled dorsally; the scales and the keel soon disappear. Carr and Ogren (1959) gave the following mean measurements for 30 hatchling Atlantic leatherbacks from Costa Rica: carapace length 62.8 mm, carapace width 41.8 mm, plastron length 53.6 mm, depth 26.3 mm, and head width 18.04 mm. Hughes and Mentis (1967) reported that the average measurements of 18 hatchling Pacific leatherbacks from Natal were as follows: carapace length 60.78 mm, carapace width 39.90 mm, and depth 18.00 mm. Deraniyagala (1939) reported that hatchlings of the Pacific subspecies in Ceylon were about 85 mm long and weighed 32.62–33.57 g.

GROWTH: Little is known of the growth rates of the leatherback turtle. Carr and Ogren (1959) reported that 44 9-day-old leatherbacks from Costa Rica had a mean carapace length of 67.2 mm and a mean carapace width of 47.9 mm. Deraniyagala (1939) kept a specimen until it died, at 169 days of age; at that time it was 160 mm in carapace length, 133 mm in plastron length, and 40 mm in head length, and the extended forelimbs, tip-to-tip, were 280 mm. Another specimen reached the following carapace lengths at the ages indicated: 195 days, 225 mm; 218 days, 302 mm (weight 3,005.1 g); 308 days, 350 mm (4,536 g); 624 days, 433 mm (6,804 g); and 662 days, 545 mm.

FOOD AND FEEDING: The little information available on the food habits of *Dermochelys* indicates that it probably is omnivorous but has a predilection for jellyfish. Stomachs of wild specimens examined have contained jellyfish (including *Physalia*), sea

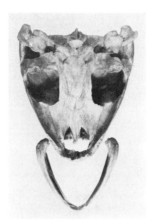

Skull of *Dermochelys coriacea*

urchins, squid, crustaceans, tunicates, fish, blue-green algae, and floating seaweeds. Captives are known to eat fish, raw meat, octopi, chicken liver, jellyfish, crustaceans, bread, and green algae.

PREDATORS: Man, monitor lizards, and dogs are known to dig up nests and eat the eggs. The hatchlings have many predators: on their trip across the beach to the sea they are preyed on by mongooses, dogs, cats, pigs, monitor lizards, gulls, crows, and vultures, and once they reach the water a host of fish predators, as well as cuttlefish and octopi, devour them. The adults have few predators other than man. Sharks and other large predacious fish probably attack them occasionally, and the killer whale (*Orcinus orca*) eats them (Caldwell and Caldwell, 1969).

MOVEMENTS: *Dermochelys* is the most powerful swimmer of all turtles and has been found far out in the open sea. Leatherbacks travel great distances; but whether these trips are random wanderings or regular migrations is unknown. The only recapture is that reported by Moulton (1963). A large individual was struck on the head with the butt of a harpoon as it lay at the surface about 1,700 yards northeast of the Portland, Maine, lightship in late August 1962. The blow left a light-colored scar of unique, easily recognizable shape on the top of the head slightly behind the eyes. The turtle was caught 1 week later 5.25 nautical miles north-northeast of the point where it had been struck. This time it was towed alive to Bailey Island and released. Photographs taken there clearly showed the fresh scar atop the head.

Dermochelys sometimes travel in groups. Leary (1957) observed a concentration of about 100 leatherbacks along a 30-mile line off the Texas coast on 17 December 1956. The turtles seemed to be most numerous in a dense school of the jellyfish *Stomolophus meleagris*.

Carr and Ogren (1959) studied the sea-finding orientation of hatchling leatherbacks at Tortuguero, Costa Rica, and found that they had a positive reaction to open areas and to large areas of illumination. They also discovered that the basic kinesis was clearly supplemented by the capacity to use information of various sorts for repeated topical reorientation in a complex landscape: on their way across the beach the hatchlings regularly executed circles, presumably for orientation by visual cues.

POPULATIONS: Hughes, Bass, and Mentis (1967) estimated that there were 27–50 nesting female leatherbacks on the Natal coast during the 1965–66 season. Fitter (1961) estimated the world leatherback population to be possibly as low as 1,000 mature females, of which 850 nested in the state of Trengganu, Malaya. This estimate seems low in view of the numerous nesting grounds; nevertheless the total leatherback population probably is somewhat smaller than that of the green turtle, the loggerhead, or the hawksbill.

REMARKS: *Dermochelys* is of all turtles the most highly adapted to an aquatic life, but its origins and relationships are not clear. Studies on the components of its blood (Cohen and Strickler, 1958; Frair, 1964, 1969) have shown that it is most closely related to the other sea turtles (family Cheloniidae), and studies on the penial morphology by Zug (1966) have confirmed this.

Some of the nesting beaches are still being raided for eggs; but Carr (1967a) felt that *Dermochelys* may have the least dreary survival possibility of any sea turtle: it has the great advantage of being almost everywhere considered inedible, it has no shell, and yields no calipee (gelatinous fat). But its oils may be its downfall: some cosmetics have the oils of this turtle as their base. If they are hunted for their oils, leatherbacks may well be exterminated just to make milady more beautiful.

TRIONYCHIDAE:
Soft-shelled Turtles

The 22 living species of softshells, in seven genera, are found in Africa, Asia, and North America. Four species of the genus *Trionyx* occur in the United States. These rounded, flattened freshwater turtles lack horny scutes and are covered by a leathery skin. The neck is long and retractile, and the limbs are paddlelike, with three claws on each.

The bony elements of the shell are secondarily reduced; peripherals and pygals are absent, and the distal ends of the ribs project freely. There are 7 to 8 neurals and 7 to 10 costals, with the last pairs at times meeting centrally. The plastron is reduced and has central lacunae and lateral fontanelles. There is no entoplastron. The neck vertebrae are slender, and none is biconvex. The 4th digit has four to six phalanges; the 5th has two to four. The temporal region of the skull is widely open. The premaxillae are fused, and neither the parietal nor the postorbital touches the squamosal. The vomer is reduced, does not separate the palatines, and is separated from the premaxillae but touches the maxillae and separates the internal nares. The nasopalatine foramen is large; the palatine fenestra is small. The maxilla contacts the pterygoid but not the quadratojugal. The basisphenoid is separate from the pterygoid but contacts the palatines. The quadrate incloses the stapes, and an epipterygoid is present. The jaw is very deep at the level of the coronoid process, and the dentary reaches laterally nearly to the posterior end of the jaw.

Morphologically the softshells are thought to resemble most closely the cryptodiran turtle *Carettochelys insculpta*, of New Guinea. However, Frair (1964) reported that all serologic tests indicate that the softshells are distinct not only from pleurodires but also from cryptodires, among which they are presently classified. Possibly they should be placed in a separate suborder.

209. Young adult female *Trionyx muticus muticus*. The limbs are uniformly colored.

TRIONYX MUTICUS Le Sueur
Smooth Softshell   XXIII

RECOGNITION: A medium-sized to large (11.0–34.5 cm), flat, soft-shelled turtle without spines or raised knobs on the leathery shell, usually without a pattern on its limbs, and with no septal ridges in the nostrils. The round, smooth, keelless carapace is olive to orange-brown, with a pattern of darker dots, dashes, or blotches; often there is a lighter marginal band bordered on the inside by a darker area. The hingeless plastron is immaculate white or gray, and the underlying bones usually can be seen through it. The head, neck, and limbs are olive to orange above and gray to white below; there may be a few scattered dark dots on the limbs. A black-bordered light line extends through the eye and onto the neck. The tubular snout usually terminates somewhat obliquely, and the round nostrils are slightly inferior; the mandibles are very sharp. The anterior surface of each forelimb has four cornified antebrachial scales. The feet are webbed, and the webbing extends up the shank of the hindlimbs.

Males have long thick tails, with the anal opening near the tail-tip. Females have longer hind claws while males have longer foreclaws. Large females may have a mottled or blotched carapacial pattern. Adult males are 11.0–17.5 cm in carapace length, adult females 17.0–34.5 cm.

GEOGRAPHIC VARIATION: Two subspecies are recognized. *T. m. muticus* Le Sueur, the midland smooth softshell, ranges in the central United States from extreme western Pennsylvania to southern Minnesota and South Dakota, south to Tennessee, Louisiana, and Oklahoma, and west into Texas and New Mexico. This subspecies is distinguished by a juvenile pattern of dusky dots and short lines, ill-defined pale stripes on the snout, and pale postocular stripes with black borders less than half their width, except in some individuals in the Colorado River drainage of Texas. *T. m. calvatus* Webb, the Gulf coast smooth softshell, occurs along the Gulf coast from the Escambia River system of Alabama and the Florida panhandle west to Louisiana and Mississippi, including the Pearl River drainage. It has a juvenile pattern of large circular (often ocellate) carapacial spots, no stripes on the dorsal surface of the snout, a pattern of fine markings on the dorsal surface of the limbs, and pale postocular

210. Plastron of *Trionyx muticus*. In this as in other *Trionyx* the underlying bones of the plastron are often visible externally.

Skull of *Trionyx muticus*

257

stripes having thick black borders approximately half their width on adult males.

CONFUSING SPECIES: All other American softshells have ridges on the internasal septum and spines or knobs on the anterior border of the carapace.

DISTRIBUTION: *T. muticus* ranges from western Pennsylvania, Minnesota, and South Dakota south to the Florida panhandle, southern Texas, and New Mexico.

HABITAT: The smooth softshell occurs in large rivers and streams having moderate to fast currents. *T. m. calvatus* has been taken only from such habitats, but *T. m. muticus* is also known from lakes, impoundments, and shallow bogs. Waterways with sandy bottoms and few rocks or aquatic plants are preferred. The species occurs with most of the other fresh-water turtles within its range.

BEHAVIOR: *T. muticus* probably is more aquatic than the other American softshells. It rarely moves overland. If trapped in a drying pool of water, it simply buries itself in the mud. It is an agile and powerful swimmer, able to capture fish with ease; the highly extensible neck gives it a great advantage. Cahn (1937) saw one capture a small brook trout, one of the fastest of our fish. The turtle rapidly overtook the darting fish and when within reach shot out its head and grabbed it. The smooth softshell is also fast on land: it can often outdistance a man on a level, unobstructed surface.

It is a shy turtle, but it has been reported to be quite a fighter when handled; however, some individuals never attempt to bite.

T. muticus seldom leaves the water to bask. When it does, it chooses a sandy beach or a mud flat within 10 ft of the water. In basking the legs are drawn up under the carapace and the neck usually is stretched to its full extent and laid on the ground, usually facing the water. Even when relaxed this turtle is alert: it scampers into the water at the slightest disturbance.

When not browsing or basking it spends long

211. Face of *Trionyx muticus*. This species lacks tubercles on the anterior edge of the carapace.

Distribution of *Trionyx muticus*.

periods under water, buried in the bottom at a depth that just allows the snout to reach the surface. Smooth softshells bury themselves by a shuffling motion that stirs up the bottom; when it settles down the carapace is concealed and only the head is visible. In addition to breathing air, they probably can obtain oxygen from water by pharyngeal and cloacal absorption: Cahn (1937) demonstrated pharyngeal currents by inserting grains of carmine in the water close to the nostrils and observing them disappear into the nostrils as the hyoid apparatus drops, and he also demonstrated currents in and out of the anus.

REPRODUCTION: Females are sexually mature when the carapace is 17–22 cm long. Some may mature in their sixth year, but most of them probably mature in their 7th year. Males are sexually mature at a carapace length of 11.0–12.6 cm.

Nothing is know about courtship and mating in this species.

The nesting period lasts from late May through July. Nests are dug on sandbars, banks, and islands in full sunlight, usually within 60 ft of the water. Females seem never to dig nests in hard-packed soil. Goldsmith (1945) reported that when the water level is high and sand plots are covered *T. muticus* will make nests at any place it can find sand—even among weeds or bushes. The nest is dug entirely with the hind feet and is 6–9 inches deep. As the eggs are laid they are arranged in the nest cavity by the hind feet, and after laying the female uses her hind feet to fill the cavity and rake soil over the nest. In sandy soil the completed nests appear as small craters, and in pebbly places they are marked by circular patches of clear sand.

Muller (1921) reported that, if disturbed while laying, females would desert the nest and return to the water. However, Goldsmith (1945) found that an observer could approach and touch a laying female without disturbing the process—but when finished she would scurry to the water without covering the eggs and would not return. Those frightened in the process of digging would not return to complete the nest.

Clutches consist of 4–33 eggs; 18–22 are usual. The number laid is proportional to the size of the female; that is, small individuals lay fewer eggs than do large ones. There is some evidence that up to three clutches may be laid annually. The eggs are spherical and have thick, brittle, white shells. They are 20–23 mm in diameter and weigh about 7 g.

The incubation period is 65–77 days. Instead of using the caruncle, the hatchling escapes from the egg by means of its forelimbs. It then tunnels almost straight upward through the sand, leaving the egg shell below the surface and a hole in the sand about 1 inch in diameter.

The dull-olive carapace of the hatchling is marked with numerous short, black lines and bordered with a pale margin, which broadens posteriorly. Like adults, the young are nearly circular in outline. Hatchlings average 41.3 mm (34–45) in carapace length, 38.6 mm (31–40) in carapace width, and 30.1 mm (21–32) in plastron length, and they weigh about 5 g. The umbilical scar is approximately 2 mm in diameter. The caruncle drops off in about 1 week.

GROWTH: Males lose the juvenile carapacial pattern with age, but in the females it is replaced by a mottled and blotched pattern of variable contrast. The juvenile pattern on the dorsal surface of the soft parts is correspondingly modified in females larger than 8 cm.

FOOD AND FEEDING: Smooth softshells are decidedly carnivorous; however, some plant material is eaten —perhaps accidentally. They (and the other softshells) obtain food by prowling about, on the bottom or on submerged debris, actively pursuing and capturing prey or ambushing it by lying concealed on the bottom. *T. muticus* feeds on fish, frogs, tadpoles, mudpuppies (*Necturus*), crayfish, aquatic insects, snails, bivalves, and worms. Plant material reportedly taken includes algae, fruits, and "hard nuts" (Anderson, 1965; Carr, 1952). Captives feed readily on canned or fresh fish and various meats.

PREDATORS: Skunks, raccoons, and crows feed on

the eggs, and Muller (1921) thought moles may destroy some nests. Juveniles are eaten by large fish, turtles, snakes, wading birds, and various mammals. Adults have few enemies other than man, but alligators take some.

MOVEMENTS: Anderson (1958) reported that hatchling *T. muticus* leave their nests within 3 hr after sunset and make their way to the water by a direct route. To study their means of orientation he released three at night on a sand beach 20 ft from a forest and 100 yards from the water. After raising their heads and looking about briefly, the hatchlings moved in the direction of the water, although it was not visible to them. He laid a flashlight on the sand with its beam shining at right angles across their path. One hatchling showed positive phototaxis in repeated trials—stopping, turning, and following the beam until halted by the flashlight lens. The second showed a similar reaction in stopping in the light beam, but it continued towards the water. The third seemed uninfluenced by the light.

Similar variation was observed by Anderson when a kerosene lamp was placed between hatchlings and the water. The flame was approximately 10 inches above the ground. When several turtles were simultaneously released 15 ft from the lamp on the landward side all proceeded toward the water. Some went past the lamp without deviation. Others approached the base of the lamp, passed it, and then began to circle it; of these individuals some continued toward the water after one circle, but others circled the light at a distance of 6–10 ft until retrieved. Further tests were made in a Y maze, using a flashlight or the light of the moon as a stimulus; a positive response to light was generally obtained.

Contrasting behavior was exhibited during the day. Anderson's hatchlings retained in large, sand-filled cans were active on the surface at night but burrowed beneath the sand during the daytime. If released in bright sunlight, even within 2 ft of the water, they would burrow.

Anderson examined trails left in the sand by undisturbed hatchlings as they moved from nests to water. At the nest a conical depression, 2–3 inches wide and 1 inch deep, marked their point of emergence. Inasmuch as all emerged within 2 hr, the light conditions, temperature, and landmarks varied only slightly; and although the trails typically radiated somewhat from the nest, they followed the same broad pattern.

An oil lamp was placed on the sandbar and left burning during the night. Hatchlings emerged from a nest on the landward side of the lamp and proceeded past it toward the water. As indicated by their trails, their reaction to the light gave no evidence of phototropism. However, the trails indicated some confusion: although the light failed to attract them it did mask some important cue or cues normally used. The pattern of trails suggested that hatchlings may react in some way to the mass of forest shadow or to the forest skyline. Postulation of orientation through negative response to dark masses was compatible with all observed trail patterns. Such an initial orientation—possibly later reinforced by a tendency to telotaxis or some direct visual response to the water—satisfactorily explains the movements of *T. muticus* hatchlings from nest to water.

REMARKS: The flesh of *T. muticus* is delicious but is seldom marketed.

This turtle may feed on some game fish, but it is doubtful if it is a sufficiently abundant or successful predator to ever cause a serious decimation of the fish population.

TRIONYX SPINIFERUS (Le Sueur)
Spiny Softshell   XXIII

RECOGNITION: A medium-sized to large (12.7–45.7 cm), flat, soft-shelled turtle with a round, keelless, leathery carapace having a sandpaperlike surface. Conical projections or spines are present along the anterior edge of the shell. The carapace is olive to tan, with a pattern of black ocelli or dark blotches and a marginal dark line. The hingeless plastron is immaculate white or yellow, and the underlying bones can often be seen through the leathery covering. The head and limbs are olive to gray, with a pattern of dark spots and streaks. Two separate, dark-bordered, light stripes are found on each side of the head: one extending backward from the eye, the other backward from the angle of the jaw. The tubular snout is truncated, with large nostrils, each of which contains a septal ridge; the lips are yellowish with dark spotting, and the jaws are sharp. The anterior surface of each forelimb has four cornified antebrachial scales. All four feet are webbed, and the webbing extends up the shank of the hind limbs.

Adult males have long thick tails with the anal opening near the tip; and they retain the juvenile pattern of ocelli, spots, and lines. Adult females develop a mottled or blotched pattern. Males are 12.7–21.6 cm in carapace length, females 16.5–45.7 cm.

GEOGRAPHIC VARIATION: Six subspecies are recognized. *T. s. spiniferus* Le Sueur, the eastern spiny softshell, ranges east of the Mississippi River, from Vermont and extreme southeastern Canada west to Wisconsin and south to North Carolina, western Virginia, and Tennessee. It can be distinguished from the other subspecies by the presence of large black ocelli in combination with only one dark marginal line. *T. s. hartwegi* (Conant and Goin), the western spiny softshell, ranges west of the Mississippi River, from Minnesota to Montana and south to northern Louisiana, Oklahoma and northeastern New Mexico. It has uniform small dots and ocelli on the carapace and only one dark marginal line.

212. Male *Trionyx spiniferus spiniferus*. Adult males of this species retain the juvenile pattern of ocelli.

213. Female *Trionyx spiniferus spiniferus*. With increasing age the females of this species lose the ocelli and develop blotches.

261

T. s. asper (Agassiz), the Gulf coast spiny softshell, occurs from southern North Carolina to southeastern Louisiana; its range includes the Florida panhandle but not peninsular Florida. This race has more than one black line paralleling the rear margin of the carapace, and there is often a fusion of the postlabial and postocular stripes on each side of the head. *T. s. pallidus* Webb, the pallid spiny softshell, occurs west of the Mississippi in the upper Red River drainage and in rivers that drain into the Gulf of Mexico east of the Brazos River in Texas. It is pale and has white tubercles on the posterior half of the carapace; the tubercles gradually decrease in size anteriorly and are indistinct or absent on the anterior third of the carapace, and they are not surrounded by black ocelli. *T. s. guadalupensis* Webb, the Guadalupe spiny softshell, occurs in the Nueces and Guadalupe–San Antonio drainage systems of south-central Texas. It is dark and has white tubercles surrounded by narrow black ocelli on the anterior third of the carapace; some tubercles are as large as 3 mm in diameter. Small black dots are sometimes interspersed among the white tubercles. *T. s. emoryi* (Agassiz), the Texas spiny softshell, occurs in the Rio Grande drainage in Texas and New Mexico and the Colorado River drainages in Arizona, New Mexico, and southern Nevada; it also occurs in northeastern Mexico. There is some evidence that this subspecies was introduced into the Gila–Colorado drainage system (Miller, 1946). It has a pale rim on the carapace that is four or five times wider posteriorly than laterally. There is a dark, slightly curved line connecting the anterior margins of the orbits, and the postocular stripes usually are interrupted, leaving a pale blotch behind each eye.

CONFUSING SPECIES: *T. muticus* usually lacks a pattern on the limbs, spiny tubercles on the carapace, and a septal ridge in the nostril. *T. ferox* has a marginal ridge on the carapace.

DISTRIBUTION: This species ranges from northwestern Vermont, southern Ontario, and Quebec to North Dakota and Montana and south to the Gulf coastal states and New Mexico. It also occurs in the Colorado River system of California, Nevada, Arizona, and New Mexico and in the northern parts of Tamaulipas, Nuevo León, Coahuila, and eastern Chihuahua, Mexico. Individuals have also been taken from the Red River of the North along the Minnesota–North Dakota line, and introduced *T. spiniferus* have become established in Salem County, New Jersey.

HABITAT: *T. spiniferus* inhabits a great variety of aquatic habitats, including marshy creeks, large swift-flowing rivers, bayous, oxbows, lakes, and impoundments. A soft bottom with some aquatic vegetation is essential, and sandbars and mud flats are preferred. Fallen trees with spreading underwater limbs are frequented. *T. spiniferus* has been taken with almost every other aquatic turtle inhabiting its range.

BEHAVIOR: The spiny softshell is highly aquatic. It spends most of its time in the water, either foraging, floating at the surface, or buried in the soft bottom with only the head and neck protruding. It buries itself by flipping silt over its back until it is entirely concealed. Often it lies buried under water shallow enough to allow the nostrils to reach the surface when the neck is extended; but it also burrows under deep water.

Gage and Gage (1886) demonstrated that *T. spiniferus* and *T. muticus* pump water in and out of the mouth and pharynx at an average rate of 16 times/min by alternately raising and lowering the hyoid apparatus, and that the vascular lining of the pharynx serves in gaseous exchange. Dunson (1960) confirmed these findings. He also reported that either dermal or cloacal respiration is sufficient to sustain life during forced submersion of 5 hrs in a closed system at room temperature.

Spiny softshells spend much time basking on rocks, logs, mud or sand banks, or floating debris. When basking on steep banks they often face the water, ready to make a rapid escape. Usually they bask alone, but occasionally they bask in groups. Basking seldom begins before 10 AM.

Hutchison *et al.* (1966) reported that 10 *T. spiniferus* had a mean critical thermal maximum of 41.05 C (39.9–42.3).

Bentley and Schmidt-Nielsen (1970) found that the skin of this turtle is three or four times more permeable to water than that of *Chrysemys scripta*, whether in air or in hypotonic or hypertonic solutions. This may indicate a more restricted permeability of the typical turtle shell than of the softer cutaneous covering of *Trionyx*.

The spiny softshell sleeps buried in the mud or among the branches of submerged trees. There is some evidence that it is somewhat nocturnal.

In the northern parts of the range it is active from late March to early October, but it has also been observed in December. Hibernation occurs under water, beneath 2–4 inches of mud. In the deep South it is probably active throughout the year.

The disposition of spiny softshells is generally bad: they bite and scratch savagely when handled. Because of their speed and agility they are difficult to catch by hand, either on land or in water.

REPRODUCTION: Webb (1956, 1962) found that male *T. s. emoryi* become sexually mature at plastron lengths of 8–9 cm and males of the other subspecies at 9–10 cm. Females of all subspecies except some *T. s. emoryi* may be sexually mature when the plastron is 18.0–20.0 cm in length. Probably all physiologically normal females are adult at 22 cm.

Courtship and mating have not been adequately described. Mating takes place in April or May. On two occasions Conant (1951a) saw pairs of spiny softshells in positions that indicated mating, but neither time were they actually copulating. The male had placed his forefeet on the back of the female in such a way that his hind feet were beyond the posterior border of her shell and his tail could be turned so that its ventral surface met hers.

Legler (1955) observed a captive male *T. spiniferus* swim behind or above a female *T. muticus* and nip at the anterior part of her carapace. During these movements the posterior edge of her carapace was turned up slightly, whereas his was turned down. They frequently surfaced to breathe, and she

214. Female *Trionyx spiniferus emoryi*. The carapacial spines of this species may be seen on this specimen. (*Photo by Robert G. Webb*)

215. Male *Trionyx spiniferus asper*. This subspecies has more than one black line paralleling the rear carapacial margin.

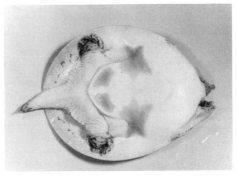

216. Plastron of *Trionyx spiniferus*. The large, elongated tail is characteristic of male *Trionyx*.

217. *Trionyx spiniferus spiniferus*. This species has patterned limbs and tubercles along the anterior edge of the carapace.

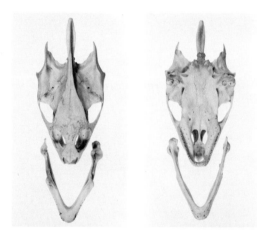

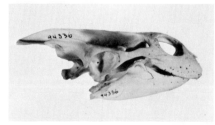

Skull of *Trionyx spiniferus*

occasionally followed him. When they settled to the bottom he crawled onto her carapace from the rear but did not clasp it with his feet. Legler observed five coital unions in 30 min, each preceded by the same courtship.

June and July are the usual months of nesting, but the nesting season may begin in May and extend into August. Places in full sunlight on sand or gravel banks or old roadbeds close to the water are selected as nest sites. The nests are dug entirely with the hind feet, and the bladder contents may be voided into the cavity to facilitate digging. The nests are flask-shaped and extend to a depth of 4–10 inches; the neck has a diameter of 1–3 inches and the egg cavity is 3–5 inches across. Spiny softshells usually will cease nesting activities and retreat to the water if surprised before egg deposition begins. Breckenridge (1960) reported that a Minnesota female dug a cavity in 15 min, deposited a clutch of 17 eggs in 6 min, and covered the eggs in another 5 min.

The white, brittle eggs are spherical or nearly so and average about 28 mm (24–32) in diameter. Clutch size is 4–32 eggs, and probably more than one clutch is laid each year.

Hatching occurs from late August to October, but the incubation period is unknown. Overwintering in the nest by hatchlings probably occurs in the northern parts of the range.

The young resemble adults in shape and color. The pale, olive-to-tan, rounded carapace has a well-marked pattern of small, dark ocelli or spots and a yellowish border set off by a black line. The granulation of its surface is pronounced, but the spines along the anterior edge are small and poorly developed. Hatchlings are 30–40 mm in carapace length.

GROWTH: The smallest Minnesota individual from which Breckenridge (1955) obtained growth-rate data was 2.25 inches long and about 1 year old. He estimated that the growth rate for a hatchling 1.5 inches long is 1.88 inches/year, but when it has grown to 2 inches its rate of growth decreases to 1.66 inches/year. Breckenridge estimated that a 10-year-old female is about 9.8 inches in carapace length; a 15-year-old, 11.7 inches; a 20-year-old, 13.1 inches; and a 30-year-old, 15.0 inches. He thought that a 17-inch female would be approximately 53 years old. He calculated that a 10-year-old male would be approximately 6.25 inches in carapace length and a 15-year-old would be only 6.75 inches long.

FOOD AND FEEDING: *T. spiniferus* is predominantly carnivorous; however, it consumes some plant material—possibly by accident. It eats crayfish, aquatic insects, mollusks, earthworms, fishes, tadpoles, and frogs. Lagler (1943) examined the stomach contents of 11 spiny softshells from Michigan and found crayfish in 47% and insects in 52%. Breckenridge (1944) reported that 18 *T. spiniferus* in Minnesota contained 44% crayfish, 29% aquatic insects, and 8% fish. Anderson (1965) examined the stomachs of 11 from Missouri and found 61.2% crayfish, 34.8% insects, and 2.0% fish. Penn (1950) found crayfish constituted 46% (58% frequency) of the food. Lagler (1943) reported finding cryptogams in *T. spiniferus*, and Surface (1908) found one stomach full of corn. Captives eat fresh and canned fish, chicken, beef, and pork.

While feeding, spiny softshells crawl or swim along the bottom in a somewhat random fashion, thrusting their snouts under stones and into masses of aquatic vegetation. They sometimes actively pursue and capture small animals, and may take prey from ambush on the bottom. They may use the forefeet to hold the food while tearing it into smaller pieces with the jaws, but sometimes they swallow it whole, using the forefeet to assist in forcing it down.

PREDATORS: Skunks and raccoons destroy many nests. The young are eaten by fishes, other turtles, snakes, wading birds, and mammals. Alligators and man prey on the adults.

POPULATIONS: Spiny softshells made up less than 1% of more than 1,000 turtles collected from a drainage ditch near Jacob, Illinois; however, they made up 16% of 214 turtles at Elkville, Illinois. Of the 43 softshells collected at these two localities 2 were juveniles, 24 males, and 17 females—a 1.4:1 ratio of males to females (Cagle, 1942).

Cagle and Chaney (1950) found that Louisiana *T. spiniferus* were most abundant in streams with some current (Caddo Dam Spillway, 52.9% of the turtles caught; Lacassine Refuge, 25.3%; Sabine River, 66.6%) but that they also occurred in quiet waters (Caddo Lake, 31.2%; False River, 8.6%; Lake Providence, 12.8%).

The relative abundance of *T. spiniferus* in swift water probably is the result of the inability of other species to compete as successfully as *Trionyx* in currents.

REMARKS: Four of the subspecies—*T. s. spiniferus*, *T. s. hartwegi*, *T. s. pallidus*, and *T. s. asper*—intergrade in the Mississippi River drainage of Louisiana; *T. s. asper* is the subspecies least represented there.

Ernst and Hamilton (1969) reported that in a four-choice situation of red, yellow, green, and blue compartments a *T. spiniferus* entered the yellow compartment in 10 of 12 trials.

The flesh of *T. spiniferus* is excellent and is eaten locally throughout its range, but it is not offered frequently in the markets.

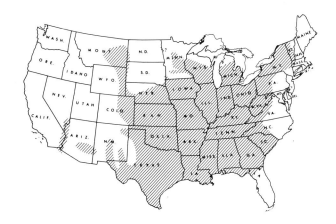

Distribution of *Trionyx spiniferus* in the United States.

218. Male *Trionyx ferox*.

TRIONYX FEROX (Schneider)

Florida Softshell　　　　　XXIV

RECOGNITION: A medium-sized to large (15–46 cm), flat, soft-shelled turtle with a marginal ridge on the leathery carapace. The oval, keelless carapace has blunt, knobby tubercles clustered along its anterior edge and on the marginal ridge. Often there are longitudinal rows of indentations and raised areas on the dorsal surface. The carapace is gray to brown and may have darker blotches. The hingeless plastron is gray to white, and the underlying bones can often be seen through the leathery covering. The head and limbs are gray to brown and sometimes bear light mottlings or reticulations. Often a red or yellow band extends from the posterior corner of the eye to the base of the lower jaw. The lips are fleshy and the jaws are sharp. The tubular snout is terminally truncated, and each nostril contains a lateral ridge that projects from the nasal septum. The anterior surface of each forelimb has four cornified antebrachial scales. All four feet are webbed, and the webbing extends up the shank of the hind limbs.

Adult females are 20–46 cm in carapace length, males 15–29 cm. Males have long, thick tails, with the anal opening near the tip. Older males may develop an expanded crushing surface in the upper jaw.

GEOGRAPHIC VARIATION: No subspecies have been described.

CONFUSING SPECIES: All other softshells within the range of *T. ferox* lack a marginal ridge on the carapace.

DISTRIBUTION: *Trionyx ferox* ranges from South Carolina and southern Georgia through Florida, except for the Keys and most of the panhandle.

HABITAT: This softshell occurs in all freshwater habitats, but in the northern parts of the range it seems to be more at home in still waters than in the southern part of the range. It prefers deep water with sand or mud bottoms, or bubbling mud-sand springs where there is foliage overhead. It sometimes occurs in brackish water near the mouths of streams; there the tides occasionally carry it out to sea. It can be found with most of the other freshwater turtles within its range.

BEHAVIOR: The Florida softshell spends much time buried in the soft bottom in either shallow or deep water, with only its head protruding. Marchand (1942) stated that when buried in the mud it appears to consider itself perfectly concealed and protected: at such times the carapace may be handled or even pulled about, and the snout may be rubbed without the turtle's showing any concern. It can burrow into and tunnel through mud with amazing speed.

According to Marchand (1942) some areas on the bottom of Crystal Springs, in Florida, have been so thoroughly disturbed by the burrowing of softshells that these places are bare and soft. An area treated thus by *T. ferox* assumes a characteristic appearance and can be easily recognized. Rainbow Run, in Marion County, Florida, has bottom areas of bare white sand, and softshells are fond of burrowing there. Whenever they do so a school of fish invariably is attracted to the spot—a clue to the location of the softshells (Marchand, 1942).

T. ferox spends much time floating on the surface or lying along the banks. It seems quite fond of basking.

Hutchison *et al.* (1966) reported that two *T. ferox* lost the righting response at 36.9 C and 37.4 C and had critical thermal maxima of 38.9 C and 39.1 C; but Brattstrom (1965) reported that the critical maximum temperature appeared to be about 42.3 C.

T. ferox practices pharyngeal and cloacal respiration. Marchand (1942) reported that he dropped a small amount of silt directly in front of the nostrils of a submerged *T. ferox* and could easily detect the water currents set up by the intake and expulsion of water, presumably for pharyngeal respiration. He often saw *T. ferox* gulping water.

Meehean (in Carr, 1952) used large amounts of derris (a toxic plant) in Florida lakes to collect fish

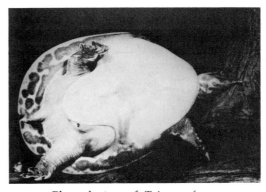

219. Plastral view of *Trionyx ferox.*

220. Anterior view of *Trionyx ferox.* The spines on the leading edge of the carapace seem to become gradually transformed into the marginal ridge.

for population analyses. He found that in nearly all the lakes poisoned *T. ferox* were killed in numbers while no other turtles were affected. Rotenone, the active ingredient of derris, works through the respiratory system to kill fish; therefore one assumes that in killing *T. ferox* it affected the pharyngeal and cloacal respiration. Even so, it is not clear why rotenone, which causes suffocation, should affect *T. ferox*, a turtle in which the surfaces for aquatic respiration are of limited function and only supplement the lungs.

The Florida softshell occasionally migrates overland; it is commonly seen on the highways in Florida.

REPRODUCTION: Some males mature at 12 cm in plastron length (Webb, 1962). The smallest recorded mature female had a carapace length of approximately 22 cm (Hamilton, 1947).

Nesting occurs from mid-March to July in southern Florida and from June through July in the northern portions of the range. Sandy soil in full sunlight usually is chosen as the nest site, and the nest is dug in the morning. A typical nest has an entrance about 2 inches in diameter and an egg chamber 4 inches in diameter; the total depth is about 5 inches. The nest is dug by alternate scraping of the hind feet, and the bladder contents may be used to soften the earth and moisten the cavity. The eggs are covered by scraping dirt into the burrow with the hind feet.

Harper (in Hamilton, 1947) reported that after she has completed nesting the female moves a few yards away and there vigorously scratches up the ground, scattering the earth about and leaving a conspicuous trace of its presence. He suggested that this may serve to draw the attention of predators away from the actual nest.

The spherical, white eggs have thin, brittle shells; they are 24–32 mm in diameter and weigh about 12 g. Oviducal eggs are slightly smaller: about 25–27 mm in diameter. Clutches consist of 4–22 eggs—most commonly 17–22.

Goff and Goff (1935) incubated eggs at temperatures of 82.3–89.2 F and found the incubation pe-

riod to be 64 days. They examined some of these eggs and found the following embryonic growth-rates: 10 days, 6 mm; 26 days, 10 mm; 40 days, 20 mm; 55 days, 35 mm; and 64 days, 50 mm.

Hatchlings are less round than are those of other North American *Trionyx*. The carapace is yellowish-olive with dusky spots and a narrow yellow or orange border. The spots are large, and the narrow light lines separating them give a reticulated appearance. The plastron is dark gray. The olive skin is mottled with lighter color. A Y-shaped figure extends from the anterior edge of each orbit to the middle of the snout. Carr (1952) gave the following measurements of a very young *T. ferox*: carapace length 38 mm, carapace width 33.5 mm, and depth 12.5 mm. Newly hatched *T. ferox* weighed by Goff and Goff (1935) averaged 8.82 g (8.50–9.25).

FOOD AND FEEDING: *T. ferox* is thought to be omnivorous but not overly fond of plant material. The bulk of the diet apparently consists of invertebrates, and the turtle is known to do some scavenging. Its natural foods include crayfish, snails, mussels, frogs, fish, and waterfowl. Captives readily feed on canned and fresh fish, canned dog food, raw beef, and chicken. The expanded crushing surface of the jaws in some large individuals may be an adaptation for crushing the shells of mollusks.

PREDATORS: Skunks, raccoons, foxes, bears, and crows rob the nests. Fish, turtles, snakes, wading birds, and mammals take their toll of the young. Alligators feed on adults, but man is probably the greatest predator.

REMARKS: Herald (1949) reported that a field observer found a *T. ferox* eating a DDT-killed bluegill on the morning after spraying. An attempt was made to capture the turtle but it escaped. Ten days later an individual of approximately the same size was found dead, and it was suspected that this was the same turtle. It is likely that turtles that feed often on carrion, including the bodies of animals killed by pesticides, ingest enough poison to be harmed by it.

T. ferox shares the marginal ridge and the longitudinal ridges of small knobs on the carapace with the Asiatic species of *Trionyx*. These characters are lacking in other North American softshells. Therefore *T. ferox* may be more closely related to the Old World softshells than to either *T. muticus* or *T. spiniferus*.

The flesh of this turtle is excellent, and it is sold in the southern markets. Oliver (1955) mentioned the sale in Florida of about 146,000 lb in a recent year.

T. ferox sometimes causes damage in duck ponds, and on occasion it probably takes small wading birds.

A captive lived 25 years (Pope, 1939).

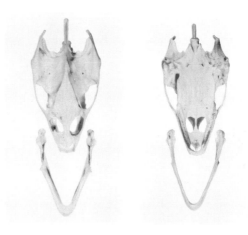

Skull of *Trionyx ferox*

Distribution of *Trionyx ferox*.

221. Juvenile *Trionyx sinensis*. The marginal ridge and the fine longitudinal ridges on the carapace are evident.

222. *Trionyx sinensis*, introduced into Hawaii from the Orient, is the only softshell in the United States with a patterned plastron.

TRIONYX SINENSIS Weigmann

Chinese Softshell   XXIV

RECOGNITION: A medium-sized to large (18–25 cm), soft-shelled turtle with a marginal ridge on the leathery, oval, keelless carapace. The flat carapace is slightly longer than wide, and in juveniles it exhibits rows of blunt tubercles, which soon disappear. The carapace is olive to gray and in juveniles is patterned with round, light-bordered, black spots. The hingeless, white-to-yellow plastron is immaculate in adults but has large black blotches in juveniles. The head and limbs are olive to yellowish-white, and the head and neck may have fine black lines. The throat is either light with vermiculations or dark with yellow spots. There often are fine black lines radiating from the eyes. The tubular snout has a lateral ridge projecting from each side of the nasal septum; the lips are fleshy and the jaws are sharp. The anterior surface of each forelimb bears cornified antebrachial scales. All four feet are webbed, and the webbing extends up the shank of the hind limbs.

Males differ from females in being shallower and having long, thick tails, with the anal opening near the tip.

GEOGRAPHIC VARIATION: Two subspecies are recognized, but only one occurs in the United States: *T. s. sinensis* Weigmann, the Chinese softshell, which has been introduced into the Hawaiian Islands.

CONFUSING SPECIES: *T. sinensis* can be distinguished from all other American softshells by the presence of a juvenile plastral pattern and the dark lines radiating from the eye and by the absence of a dark-bordered, pale stripe passing through the eye.

DISTRIBUTION: This species inhabits central and southern China, Vietnam, and the islands of Hainan and Formosa. It has been introduced into the Hawaiian Islands, one of the Bonin Islands, Timor, and Japan.

HABITAT: In China *T. sinensis* is found in rivers,

lakes, ponds, canals, and creeks with slow currents. In Hawaii it seems to be established only on Kauai. According to Paul Kawamoto, aquatic biologist for the Hawaiian Division of Fish and Game, extensive stream-surveys conducted by the division have shown that *T. sinensis* inhabits the marshlands and many small streams and drainage ditches feeding the Kapaa Canal.

BEHAVIOR: Almost nothing is known of this turtle's behavior. The basking habit is not well developed, but *T. sinensis* occasionally will sun itself on the bank. Captives in Japan hibernated buried in the mud bottom of ponds from October to April or May (Mitsukuri, 1905).

REPRODUCTION: Mitsukuri (1905) reported that captive females of the Japan population reach maturity and may begin to deposit eggs in their 6th year. He also found that copulation takes place in spring at the water surface.

In Japan nesting begins in late May and continues to mid-August (Mitsukuri, 1905). Licent (in Pope, 1935) discovered quantities of eggs on 14 June, in southeastern Kansu, China.

The digging of the nest is done entirely by alternating actions of the hind legs. Each leg, with claws extended, is moved firmly from side to side, and the body is also swayed, in rhythm with the motion of the legs. The force put in the lateral sweeps of the feet is so great that dirt is sometimes thrown 10 ft or more, although most of it is piled up around the hole.

The nest is a squarish hole with the corners rounded off; it generally is about 3–4 inches across at the entrance and 4 inches or more in depth and width. When the cavity is finished the eggs are deposited in the hole in a disordered pile; the entire clutch is deposited in about 20 min. The hind legs are then used to scrape dirt to fill the nest.

The whitish, spherical eggs average about 20 mm in diameter but may be as large as 24 mm. Clutch size is 17–28+, and two to four clutches are laid each year.

The incubation period is about 60 days (40–80)

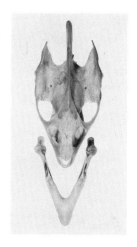

Skull of *Trionyx sinensis*

223. Front view of *Trionyx sinensis*. This species has unpatterned limbs like *Trionyx muticus*, spines on the front of the carapace like *Trionyx spiniferus*, and a marginal ridge on the carapace like *Trionyx ferox*.

By the time the last clutches are laid, in August, those deposited in May or June are ready to hatch.

Hatchlings average 27 mm in carapace length and are about 25 mm wide. The carapace is olive, and it may have a pattern of small, dark-bordered ocelli. The marginal fold is prominent, as are the longitudinal rows of spiny tubercles. The plastron is white to yellow, with large dark blotches. The limbs and head are olive above and lighter below. The head has dark flecks, and dark lines radiate from the eyes. The throat is mottled, and the lips may have small, dark bars. There is a pair of dark blotches in front of the tail and a black band on the posterior side of each thigh.

GROWTH: Juvenile *T. sinensis* average 45 mm in carapace length and 23 g in weight at the end of their 1st year, 105 mm and 169 g after the 2nd year, 125 mm and 300 g after the 3rd year, 160 mm and 563 g after the 4th year, and 175 mm and 750 g after the 5th year (Mitsukuri, 1905).

FOOD AND FEEDING: *T. sinensis* is predominantly carnivorous. Heude (in Pope, 1935) found the remains of fish, crustaceans, mollusks, insects, and seeds of marsh plants in the stomachs he examined. Mitsukuri (1905) reported that juveniles feed on fish and that adults feed on fish and bivalves. Captives eat canned and fresh fish, canned dog food, raw beef, and chicken.

PREDATORS: The young are sometimes eaten by the adults, but little else is known of predation. Surely many other vertebrates prey on the eggs and young.

POPULATIONS: The population inhabiting Kauai is quite limited.

REMARKS: The Chinese and the Japanese make wide use of *T. sinensis* as food and have propagated it in turtle ponds. The turtles were exported to the Hawaiian Islands for food, and it is believed that the Kauai turtles arrived in this way before World War II, when importation was interrupted. Mitsukuri (1905) reported that *T. sinensis* sold in Osaka,

Tokyo, Nagoya, and a few other Japanese cities in a single year weighed about 16,500 lb and were worth about $3.25 to $3.75 each. Brock (1947) reported that the price in Hawaii during World War II reached $6.00/lb and in 1947 they were selling for about $1.00/lb. Paul Kawamoto told us that during the 1950s Hawaiian *T. sinensis* averaging 1–3 lb sold for $15 to $20 each.

Distribution of *Trionyx sinensis* in the United States.

Origin & Evolution
of North American Turtles

The origin of the turtle remains one of the mysteries of paleontology. The first fossils that are clearly turtles are from the early Triassic, more than 185 million years ago. Remote ancestors are to be found among the cotylosaurs ("stem reptiles"—the basic reptilian stock) from the Carboniferous nearly 275 million years ago. They have the anapsid (solid-roofed) skull lacking temporal openings that is characteristic of present-day turtles. However, no transitional fossils with turtle characters have been found to date.

Holman (1969) has listed the following criteria for the ancestral Permian turtle: (1) the skull would be solidly roofed and lack temporal openings; (2) teeth might be dropping out around the margins of the jaws; (3) the palatal bones might be in some stage of the development of a partial secondary palate; (4) a large otic notch should be forming in the rear of the skull, and this notch should be high and short rather than long and narrow; (5) the jaws should be relatively short and braced to the skull by vertical bones; (6) the limb bones should be primitive and the posture sprawling; (7) the body form would be short, with a reduced number of vertebrae and with a short tail but with a rather long neck; and (8) there should be some indication of the developing shell: expanded ribs might be in some stage of fusing with bony elements of the carapace, or expanded gastralia might be in some stage of fusion with elements of the shoulder girdle, and furthermore the ribs might be in some stage of overgrowth of the girdles and the vertebral column might be starting to fuse with the bony plates along the back.

Several fossil forms have been suggested by paleontologists as a possible ancestor of the turtle. Watson (1914) asserted that *Eunotosaurus africanus* possibly represented a missing link in the evolution of the turtle. This small fossil, from the Middle Permian of South Africa, is known only from a small series of poorly preserved specimens. *Eunotosaurus* is only about 4 inches high, and it has only a few vertebrae, as in turtles. Following a reduced 1st rib there are eight expanded ribs, which almost touch each other. There is no evidence of separate bony plates that might fuse with the expanded ribs in turtles. Also, there is no trace of the development of a plastron. The limbs are poorly known, but the girdles appear to have been of primitive structure and the pectoral girdle is overlapped by the ribs. The pelvic girdle apparently lies outside the ribs. Teeth are present. Unfortunately, the roof of the skull is missing, so nothing is known of temporal openings or an otic notch. Romer (1956, 1966) pointed out that although *Eunotosaurus* is not a true turtle it is far from being a typical cotylosaur. Romer suggested that perhaps it may be provisionally included in the Testudines in a broad sense but placed in a separate suborder, Eunotosauria. Parsons and Williams (1961) felt that *Eunotosaurus* does show a number of resemblances to turtles but that these resemblances are often to advanced types instead of to the early, primitive turtles. The apparent prototype of a carapace found in *Eunotosaurus* is in fact basically different in plan and is primarily interesting as another method by which a similar result may be achieved. Parsons and Williams stated that the relation of limb girdles to ribs in *Eunotosaurus* is merely primitive and helps no more than do similar conditions in other groups in visualizing the way in which the strange girdles-to-ribs relationship characteristic of turtles may have come about.

A small cotylosaur, *Nyctiphruretus*, from the Permian of Russia shows skull features that are somewhat intermediate between those of the stem reptiles and the turtles (Romer, 1966; Holman, 1969). The skull is solidly roofed, but the back of the skull has a structure that appears to be the beginning of a turtlelike otic notch. The jaws are shortened and vertically braced by bones from the roof of the skull, but the body skeleton is that of a primitive reptile. This reptile occurs so late in time as to be excluded from the direct turtle ancestry.

Gregory (1946) and Olson (1947, 1950) considered an assemblage of Carboniferous, Permian, and Triassic genera, collectively termed diadectomorphs, to be possible turtle ancestors. These include the diadectids, pareiasaurids, and procolophonids (including *Nyctiphruretus*). Diadectomorphs are primitive, have skulls with solid-roofed temporal regions, and usually have a well-developed otic notch formed by posterior emargination of the quadrate. The most advanced members have a crushing dentition, with the palate solidly attached to the cranium. The jaw is short, and its point of articulation has moved forward. Gregory (1946) pointed out the many points of resemblance between turtles and pareiasaurs, such as the presence of occipital openings for the temporal musculature and the general structure of the limbs and girdles. Olson (1947) compared primitive turtles and diadectids and particularly stressed the structure of the otic region; he suggested that turtles, diadectomorphs, and seymouriamorphs should be classified together as the subclass Parareptilia, separate from other reptilian groups. Such a relationship would imply that turtles evolved from a group of amphibians different from those that gave rise to other living reptiles. Olson's further studies (1965, 1966) on diadectids and seymouriamorphs led him to believe that the resemblances between diadectids and turtles are not indicative of close relationship; rather, he suggested that turtles may have evolved from other diadectomorphs, such as the procolophonids or pareiasaurs, and that these in turn may possibly have evolved from seymouriamorphs. Romer (1964) in recent studies of diadectomorphs concluded they are not a natural group. He suggested that *Diadectes* is an amphibian, possibly related to the seymouriamorphs. Romer (1964, 1968) further suggested that turtles may share a common ancestry with the reptilian pareiasaurs and procolophonids.

Hay (1898) asserted that the extra row of scutes —the supramarginals—on the carapace of *Macroclemys temminckii* was all that was needed to establish the homology of the shell scutes of all turtles, including the longitudinal keels of the leatherbacks (*Dermochelys*). He thus concluded that *Macroclemys* is the most primitive living turtle and most like the ancestral form. However, the oldest fossils of *Macroclemys* are from rather late geologic deposits (Miocene), and therefore it seems questionable that this genus is ancestral.

Deraniyagala (1930), while studying the structure and relationships of the turtles of Ceylon, developed an alternate theory of the evolution of turtles and their later differentiation. He saw the primitive turtle as a marsh-dweller that was covered with scales. It was lizardlike, and the lateral dermal folds formed the margins of the future carapace. The pectoral girdle was shifted anteriorly over the ribs to avoid constriction between them and the dermal corselet, and this girdle sent out bony processes to stabilize its position. At this point the scapula was still external to the ribs, and its distal end was in contact with the nuchal fold of the carapace. One branch of these reptiles remained aquatic, but the rest came ashore, where they remained for varying periods before returning to an aquatic existence. The original skull had the temporal region roofed over, but this roof was lost when the turtle came ashore. Deraniyagala felt that the period spent on land could be determined by the comparative amount of change undergone by the temporal roof. During the terrestrial period the turtles first protected themselves by rolling up like armadillos, and this habit broke up the corselet skin into scutes. Later the corselet ossified, and complete withdrawal into the shell was substituted for coiling up. Deraniyagala divided the turtles into two divisions: the Atheca and the Thecophora. The Atheca is restricted to the leatherback turtle, *Dermochelys*, which Deraniyagala considered to have remained in water and retained many primitive characters. The Thecophora comprises all other known turtles, which lost the primitive characters while on shore. Deraniyagala proposed that there are two sets of dermal platelets in turtles: an upper, athecan one of ossified scales and a lower, thecophoran layer. The first has disappeared entirely from modern turtles, which still retain a few remnants of the second layer. Deraniyagala's hypothesis, however interesting, is not accepted today. Modern studies have shown that *Dermochelys* has actually evolved from the bony-shelled sea turtles of the family Cheloniidae and secondarily lost the solidity of the shell, as have freshwater soft-shelled turtles of the family Trionychidae.

The oldest fossil turtles have been found in the Triassic deposits of Germany. These fossils have been assigned to the genus *Proganochelys* (=*Triassochelys*), which, along with the fossil genera *Proterochersis*, *Saurischiocomes*, and *Chelytherium*, are assigned to the suborder Proganochelydia. The skeletal features of none of these are known completely. The skull is solidly roofed, with the external parts sculptured. The postfrontal, lacrimal, and supratemporal appear to have been present, and the external nares are separated by a bony bar. The quadrate lacks the strong curvature around the stapes that is characteristic of most turtles. There are small teeth on bones of the palate and rudimentary teeth on the jaw margins. Proganochelydians possess seven cervicals—the 8th vertebra is a dorsal rather than a cervical, its arch fused to the nuchal—and the cervicals are amphicoelous, with two-headed ribs. The bones of the pectoral girdle, although partially fused with the plastron, can still be identified individually as clavicle, interclavicle, and cleithrum. The pelvis probably was more or less firmly attached, even sometimes fused, to the plastron. The peripherals of the carapace apparently were very numerous; the neurals are long and narrow; and there are nine costals. The plastron contains several extra bones, in the form of two pairs of mesoplastrals, which are absent in most modern turtles. The buttress elements of the plastron do not reach the carapacial costals. There are dermal tubercles on the neck and tail, and presumably the head and limbs could not be pulled into the shell. Likely these primitive turtles were amphibious.

Dominant during the Jurassic and lasting until the Pleistocene was a somewhat more advanced group of turtles, which is assigned to the suborder Amphichelydia. They include, among others, the genera *Craspedochelys*, *Glyptops*, *Helochelys*, *Kallokibotion*, *Parachelys*, *Platychelys*, *Plesiochelys*, *Pleurosternum*, and *Stegochelys*, of the Jurassic and Cretaceous of Europe; *Naomichelys*, of the upper Jurassic of North America; *Baena*, of the upper Cretaceous and Eocene of North America; *Chisternon*, of the Eocene of North America; *Niolamia*, of the upper Cretaceous of South America; *Crossochelys*, of the Eocene of South America; and *Meiolania*, of the Pleistocene of Australia. The Amphichelydia have toothless, elongated skulls with sculptured or tuberculate exposed parts, and the roof of the skull is somewhat emarginate. The parietal–squamosal contact has been lost, or rarely the temporal roofing is absent. The postfrontal, lacrimal, and supratemporal are absent. The bony external nares generally are confluent and the quadrate is typically developed. The vertebrae are amphicoelous, and there are eight cervicals present, with no free ribs and with the last cervical free of the nuchal. The shoulder girdle lacks a coracoid foramen and a cleithrum. The pubis apparently was united with the plastron in some cases. There is only one pair of mesoplastra in the plastron. The plastral buttresses are narrow, and they reach the carapacial costals; the neurals usually are long and narrow. The epiplastra and entoplastron are small. None could pull the head or limbs into the shell. They were mainly amphibious, but some species were terrestrial or marine. The amphichelydians gave rise to the two modern suborders of turtles: the Cryptodira, during the Jurassic, and the Pleurodira, during the Cretaceous. The Crypotodira continued as the main evolutionary line of turtles, with the Pleurodira appearing as an aberrant but structurally conservative side-branch.

The earliest cryptodirans are from the close of the Jurassic. By the Upper Cretaceous they had become the dominant turtles of northern regions, and some species had invaded the oceans; all of the modern turtles inhabiting the United States are cryptodirans. The temporal region of the cryptodiran skull frequently is emarginate posteriorly, and the parietal and squamosal usually do not touch. Nasal bones rarely are present, and lacrimals are absent. The prefrontals have processes that descend to the vomer. The quadrate is often closed behind the stapes and does not extend inward to the basiphenoid. The articular surface of the mandible is concave. The cervical vertebrae have the central articulations well developed, broad, and usually double on the posterior cervicals. The postzygapo-

physes are widely separated. The posterior cervical spines are low, and the transverse processes are barely present. The head can be withdrawn in a vertical flexure, because the cervical vertebrae can be bent into a sigmoid curve. Mesoplastra are present only as anomalies (see Pritchard, 1966b). The pelvic girdle is not attached to the shell. The Cryptodira are considered to be the most advanced group of turtles.

The Pleurodira are considered by most herpetologists to be more primitive than the Cryptodira. Surprisingly, these turtles appear in the fossil record an entire period later than the cryptodirans: the oldest pleurodirans are from the upper Cretaceous. The pleurodiran skull is depressed, and the temporal roof may be emarginated posteriorly and variable ventrally. The frontals enter the orbit, and nasals may be present or absent; lacrimals are always absent. There are no descending processes on the prefrontals. The quadrate usually is closed behind the stapes and extends inward to the basisphenoid. The articular surface of the mandible is convex. The cervical vertebrae have high spines posteriorly, well-developed transverse processes, and well-developed, single central articulations. The pleurodirans withdraw their necks laterally; that is, they wrap the head around the side of the shell. This has given rise to their common name: side-necked turtles. The pelvis is fused to the shell. Mesoplastral bones are present in some genera.

The turtle fauna of North America during the Cretaceous was not as diversified as today's, and it included several primitive groups. The amphichelydid turtles were represented by the genera *Baena, Boremys, Eubaena, Glyptops, Naomichelys, Neurankylus, Probaena,* and *Thescelus;* of these only *Baena* survived into the Eocene. The primitive cryptodiran family Dermatemydidae was represented by *Adocus, Agomphus, Basilemys, Compsemys,* and *Hoplochelys;* of these *Adocus* and *Compsemys* lasted until the Paleocene and *Basilemys* and *Hoplochelys* until the Eocene. The sea turtles (Cheloniidae) were much more numerous in the upper Cretaceous than they are today; there were about 15 genera, including *Chelonia, Caretta,* and the giant *Archelon,* which was about 12 ft in length. The softshell turtles (Trionychidae) were represented by *Trionyx.* Only three genera of Pleurodira —*Amblypeza, Bothremys,* and *Podocnemis*—occurred in North America during the upper Cretaceous; species of *Podocnemis* exist today in South America.

Between the end of the Cretaceous and the beginning of the Paleocene a wave of extinction passed over the Reptilia. Among the turtles most of the amphichelydids became extinct, as did many of the marine turtles.

The Paleocene found a rather poor and somewhat different turtle fauna in North America. Of the amphichelydids only *Baena* has been recorded later than the Cretaceous, and of the pleurodirans only *Bothremys* persisted. The family Dermatemydidae was dominant in North America, with four genera: *Adocus, Basilemys, Compsemys,* and *Hoplochelys.* Of the marine turtles (Cheloniidae) only *Chelonia* and *Caretta* have been recorded. The softshells were still represented, by *Trionyx.* The first genus of the modern freshwater turtles (Emydidae) appeared: *Clemmys.*

During the next epoch, the Eocene, only two genera of amphichelydids and one genus of pleurodiran were present in North America. However, during this epoch turtles of the families Emydidae and Testudinidae became the dominant turtle groups. The tortoises, of the family Testudinidae, were represented by *Cymatholcus, Geochelone,* and possibly others. Among the Emydidae were *Clemmys, Rhinoclemys,* and *Echmatemys* (possibly the ancestor of the modern *Chrysemys* complex). Five genera of the Dermatemydidae—*Adocus, Baptemys, Basilemys, Compsemys,* and *Hoplochelys*—were present. The leatherback sea turtles (Dermochelyidae) made their first appearance, in the form of the extinct genus *Psephophorus.* There was also a transitory appearance of two extinct genera —*Anosteria* and *Pseudanosteria*—of the family Carettochelyidae.

Between the Eocene and Oligocene all of the archaic turtle groups—the amphichelyids, dermatemydids, carettochelyids, and pleurodirans—became

TABLE 6

THE FOSSIL RECORD OF SOME SPECIES
OF NORTH AMERICAN TURTLES

Chelydra serpentina	Pliocene (Hemphillian)
C. osceola	Pre-Columbian deposits
Macroclemys temminckii	Pliocene (Clarendonian)
Sternotherus odoratus	Pleistocene (Sangamon)
S. minor	Pleistocene (Wisconsin)
Kinosternon subrubrum	Pleistocene (Wisconsin)
K. baurii	Pleistocene (Wisconsin)
K. flavescens	Pliocene (Blancan)
Clemmys guttata	Archeological records
C. insculpta	Pleistocene (Yarmouth)
C. marmorata	Pliocene (Blancan)
Terrapene carolina	Pliocene (Hemphillian)
T. ornata	Pliocene (Clarendonian)
Graptemys geographica	Pleistocene (Sangamon)
G. pseudogeographica	Pleistocene
Chrysemys picta	Miocene–Pliocene
C. scripta	Pleistocene (Kansan)
C. concinna	Pleistocene (Wisconsin)
C. floridana	Pleistocene (Illinoian)
C. nelsoni	Pre-Columbian deposits
Deirochelys reticularia	Pleistocene (Illinoian)
Emydoidea blandingii	Pliocene
Gopherus agassizii	Pleistocene (Wisconsin)
G. polyphemus	Pleistocene (Illinoian)
Chelonia mydas	Pleistocene (Wisconsin)
Caretta caretta	Pleistocene (Wisconsin)
Trionyx muticus	Archeological records
T. spiniferus	Pleistocene (Kansan)
T. ferox	Pleistocene (Illinoian)

extinct. Those turtles that remained formed the core of our modern North American fauna.

During the Oligocene the first Kinosternidae made their appearance, in the form of the genus *Xenochelys*. The tortoises (Testudinidae) were represented by the living genera *Gopherus* and *Geochelone* and the extinct *Stylemys*. Emydid genera included *Clemmys*, *Chrysemys*, and possibly *Graptemys*. The Trionychidae and Dermochelyidae also were present.

The Miocene of North America saw the development of the last modern family, the Chelydridae, with the appearance of *Macroclemys*, *Chelydrops*, and *Archerontemys*. The Testudinidae of this epoch included *Gopherus*, *Geochelone*, and *Stylemys*. The family Emydidae was represented by *Clemmys*, *Chrysemys*, *Terrapene*, and possibly *Graptemys*. *Trionyx* was present, as also were *Chelonia*, *Caretta*, *Peritresius*, and *Syllomus* (Cheloniidae) and *Psephophorus* (Dermochelyidae).

The Pliocene witnessed an increase in types and a modernization of the North American turtle fauna. The family Chelydridae was now represented by its two modern genera, *Macroclemys* and *Chelydra*. The genera *Kinosternon* and *Sternotherus* of the Kinosternidae came into existence. The family Testudinidae was represented by *Gopherus*, *Geochelone*, *Floridemys*, and *Stylemys*, and the Emydidae included *Clemmys*, *Chrysemys*, and *Terrapene*. The freshwater-softshell and marine-turtle fauna was much like it is today. Most Pliocene species, however, are now extinct.

By the beginning of the Quarternary the North American turtle fauna was composed mainly of modern genera. Those found only in more recent deposits include *Deirochelys* (Pleistocene), *Emydoidea* (Pliocene), and *Malaclemys* (Recent). Table 6 presents the fossil history of some living species of North American turtles.

Care of Turtles in Captivity

The use of turtles in research and their acquisition as pets has increased in recent years, and many people are now obligated to care for these creatures in captivity. Most of our North American species make good captives; but it is not advisable to keep marine turtles, which need constantly circulating seawater and much room for swimming. If turtles are to be kept as pets it is best to keep local species: if they do poorly they can be released in suitable habitats and thus need not die in captivity.

To keep a turtle successfully a well-rounded knowledge of its biology is necessary. With this knowledge and a little common sense one can keep most specimens healthy. The needs for proper care can be divided into three categories: living quarters, temperature and light, and diet.

LIVING QUARTERS: Aquatic species can be kept nicely in aquaria. Tap water may be used: a moderate amount of chlorination does not bother them. An area of about 1 sq ft per specimen is ideal, but they can stand considerable crowding. Two small turtles can be kept in a 5-gal aquarium, three in a 10-gal, and two medium-sized turtles usually are enough for a 15-gal aquarium. If large specimens or a great number are to be kept for experimental purposes, cattle watering tanks (with drain plugs) or children's plastic wading pools may be used with success: they can easily be hosed down.

The use of gravel or sand and aquatic plants, although nice to look at, is undesirable because the turtles often uproot the plants and stir the gravel and sand, making it harder to keep the tank clean. Some sort of filter should be used to cleanse the water; however, the larger turtles sometimes break filters installed inside the aquarium. The water should be changed frequently to avoid fouling.

Table salt, added in a proportion of 3 oz per 5 gal of water, helps supplement the diet and control fungus and algae. If brackish-water species such as *Malaclemys terrapin* are to be kept, one cup of salt per 10 gal of water provides a suitable medium. It is also advisable to add some copper—an essential element; for this a few copper coins placed on the bottom of the tank will suffice.

Basking platforms must be provided. These allow the turtles to emerge from the water to rest. They are particularly necessary for *Chrysemys*, *Graptemys*, and *Deirochelys*, which must dry their shells if the proper shedding of the horny scutes is to occur. Care must be taken that these platforms are not abrasive: the turtle may bruise its plastron while climbing onto them. Underwater hiding places should be available to bottom dwellers like *Chelydra*, *Kinosternon*, *Sternotherus*, and *Trionyx*.

Terrestrial turtles such as *Terrapene* and *Gopherus* can be kept indoors in a terrarium. The spacing ratio for aquatic turtles, less one (see above), should be used in determining the area needed. Some soil and a water dish large enough for them to enter should be present. The water must be changed each day. A few copper coins and a small amount of table salt added to the water will be beneficial.

During the summer terrestrial turtles are best kept outdoors if a suitable place is available. Such a place should be enclosed to prevent their escape and should include a water source and some shrubs for shade. The burrowing *Gopherus* may cause some problems, but if a shelter (a hut or a doghouse) is provided they will probably use it instead of digging. Care must be taken that the turtles are not put out so early in the spring or left out so late in the fall that a surprise frost may kill them. Within their normal range *Terrapene* can be left out all year; all that is needed for winter is a large pile of vegetation (rotting leaves or grass) that they can burrow under. *Gopherus*, on the other hand, is best kept indoors during the colder months.

Cleanliness of the living quarters is most important. No matter what turtle you have, its surroundings must be kept free of leftover food and fecal matter, which serve as growth media for microbes and worms and, besides, cause a foul odor.

TEMPERATURE AND LIGHT: Aquatic specimens are best maintained at 75–85 F. In the summer the water in the aquarium normally will stay within this range, but in winter a source of heat must be provided. Both aquarium heaters and lighted aquarium hoods work well, and for larger tanks infrared heat lamps may be used. In air-conditioned rooms some artificial heat is necessary. A hand towel placed over the top of a small aquarium containing hatchlings and juveniles will help to retain heat at night.

Turtles need sunlight for proper health. Solar ultraviolet light allows the turtle to synthesize vitamin D from skin sterols. Vitamin D is essential for the calcium and phosphate uptake that is so important for the maintenance of a good healthy shell. Sunlight also kills fungus, algae, and skin ectoparasites. The increased body temperature caused by basking speeds up the rate of metabolism and aids in digestion.

During the warm weather aquaria should be placed near open windows so the turtles can get the benefit of sunlight unfiltered by glass. A sun lamp is an alternate source of ultraviolet rays, but care must be taken not to use it too long: the excess heat may kill the turtles.

DIET: Food preferences vary among species; that is, food acceptable to one turtle may be rejected by another. One should attempt to provide a nearly natural diet for the captive. The diet should contain the A, C, D, and B-complex vitamins, protein, and a calcium–phosphorus source.

If a natural diet cannot be provided an artificial diet can easily be prepared. This consists of canned fish (usually salmon and mackerel), liquid multiple vitamins, and powdered bone meal. The vitamins are added—mixing thoroughly—at the rate of 15 cc per 2 lb of fish and the bone meal at the rate of 3 tablespoons per 2 lb of fish. The 2-lb lots can be frozen for later use. This combination has been fed successfully to turtles of all the freshwater genera. However, most freshwater species are omnivorous, so some plant material (lettuce, for example) should be made available. This is especially true of adult *Chrysemys* and *Deirochelys*, which are more herbivorous than are the juveniles. *Malaclemys* and *Graptemys* are mollusk-eaters, so some snails and small bivalves should be provided.

The box turtles (*Terrapene*) and the wood turtle,

Clemmys insculpta, need a variety of animal and plant foods. They do well on a diet of canned dog food, tomatoes, apples, bananas, watermelon, cantaloupe, lettuce, and hard-boiled eggs. Vitamins and bone meal should be added to this diet. A raw egg mixed with the dog food is beneficial.

The tortoises (*Gopherus*) are chiefly herbivorous. They should be given a variety of plants, such as lettuce, cabbage, spinach, tomatoes, bananas, grapes, watermelon, cantaloupe, and apples. They also eat bread, hard-boiled eggs, eggshells, and canned dog food; and they relish yellow flowers, such as dandelions. Vitamins and bone meal should be added.

If marine turtles are to be kept they should be fed a variety of marine annelids, crustaceans, mollusks, and plants.

Aquatic turtles should be fed in a container large enough to allow them to eat underwater. Small species and juveniles are best fed in bowls separate from their aquaria; this keeps the aquaria free of oils and putrefying leftover food.

Adult turtles should be fed once or twice a week, juveniles two or three times a week. It is better to underfeed captives somewhat, for they are limited in the amount of their activity. Newly acquired turtles may not feed readily on artificial diets, but placing them with regular feeders of similar size usually induces them to eat. However, this may have to be repeated several times.

If captives are given proper care and diet few problems should arise. Occasionally, though, health problems do occur. Wild specimens usually harbor parasites, so they should be quarantined for a time and checked for unwanted guests before they are placed with other captives.

Terrestrial turtles often have ticks or mites attached to their skin. Ticks should be carefully removed and any resulting wound treated with an antiseptic, such as mercurochrome. Mites are harder to eradicate: they burrow beneath the scales. A generous application of olive oil to an infested spot will clog the breathing pores of the mites and kill them. Some terrestrial turtles may have lumps on their limbs, neck, or head; these usually are

the sacs of flesh-fly maggots. They can easily be removed by a veterinarian. Aquatic turtles often have leeches attached to their skin and shells. These should be removed and the resulting wound treated with mercurochrome; allow the solution to dry before placing the turtle back in the water.

Turtles are internally parasitized by a variety of bacteria, protozoa, and worms. Newly caught turtles often will pass worms in their fecal matter if kept without food for several days. Piperazine compounds added to the water or food once a week are excellent in controlling worms. These compounds, which are used on dogs and cats, are obtainable from a veterinarian. Bacterial and protozoan infections are harder to control; a veterinarian should be consulted. Turtles usually respond to treatment with antibiotics, but the dosage is best set by a veterinarian. Any turtle showing signs of a bacterial, protozoan, or worm infection should be immediately isolated from other turtles, in order to prevent an epidemic.

Fungi sometimes attack the shell and limbs of aquatic turtles. A fungus infection takes the form of white growths on swollen, puffy skin, but it may resemble eczema or it may cause pitted, eroded areas on the shell. The infection can be treated by direct applications of a strong table-salt solution or of a solution of iodine (5%), gentian violet, merthiolate, or malachite green. The solution should be allowed to dry before the turtle is returned to the water. Ultraviolet light is also effective in controlling fungi.

Algal colonies often occur on the shells of wild turtles, and if introduced into an aquarium they can become a problem. The shell of a newly acquired turtle should be swabbed with a 70% alcohol solution, which will kill any attached colonies or spores of algae that might be present.

Occasionally accidents occur that crack the shell of a captive. Cracks may be repaired with Canadian balsam, once bleeding has stopped. (The use of Peruvian balsam is not recommended.) Turtle shells should never be painted: because they are composed of living tissue, painting can cause distorted shell growth, especially in hatchlings and juveniles.

281

Parasites, Commensals, & Symbionts

A number of organisms live within or attached to the body of the turtle, and they form several kinds of associations with their host. Some, such as certain protozoa and bryozoa attached to the shell, live in a commensal relationship with the turtle: they derive the advantages of protection and mobility while neither benefiting nor harming the host. The relationship between alga and turtle seems to be symbiotic: the algae gain protection from small algae-eating animals and, possibly, a means of dissemination as the turtle moves about; in return the turtle gains camouflage. In view of the fact that few animals feed on adult turtles, this would seem to be of little value; however, camouflage can also conceal a predator from its prey. A little algae along the carapacial seams breaks up the turtle's outlines and causes it to resemble an inanimate object rather than a living creature. (A disadvantage of algal growth is the possibility that it might penetrate beneath the epidermal scutes and cause necrosis.) Some bacteria, protozoa, worms (trematodes, cestodes, nematodes, acanthocephalans, leeches), barnacles, insects, mites, and ticks parasitize turtles. They benefit from the relationship while harming the turtle by consuming nutrients, damaging tissues and organs, destroying red blood cells, forming tumors and nodules, and causing dermatitis. It is often difficult to determine whether certain bacteria, protozoa, and barnacles are commensals or parasites.

An annotated list of the parasites, algae, and commensals of the turtles covered in this volume follows.

CHELYDRA SERPENTINA

PARASITES.

1. Protozoa: *Eimeria chelydrae, Entamoeba* sp., *Haemogregarina stepanowi, Haemoproteus metchnikovi, Hexamita* sp., *Myxidium chelonarum, Trepomonas* sp., *Trichomonas* sp., and *Trypanosoma chrysemydis.*

2. Trematodes: *Allosostomoides parvum, Auridistomum chelydrae, A. georgiense, Cephalogonimus compactus, Cercaria ramonae, Cotylaspis stunkardi, Didtyangium chelydrae, Eustomus chelydrae, Hapalorhyn-*

chus gracilis, *Herpetodiplostomum dellei*, *Heronimus chelydrae*, *Microphallus opacus*, *Neopolystoma domitilae*, *N. orbiculare*, *Polystoma hassalli*, *Polystomoides coronatum*, *Polystomoidella oblongum*, *Spirorchis elegans*, *S. haematobium*, *S. magnitestis*, *S. minutum*, *Telorchis attenuatus*, *T. corti*, and *T. singularis*.

3. Nematodes: *Aplectana* sp., *Camallanus microcephalus*, *C. trispinosus*, *Capillaria serpentina*, *Dracunculus globocephalus*, *Eustrongylides* sp., *Folleyella* sp., *Spironoura chelydrae*, *S. wardi*, and *Spiroxys contortus*.

4. Acanthocephalans: *Neoechinorhynchus chrysemydis* and *N. emydis*.

5. Leeches: *Actinobdella annectens*, *Placobdella multilineata*, *P. parasitica*, and *P. rugosa*.

6. Insect: *Aedes canadensis*.

7. Mite: *Cloacarus faini*.

Hunt (1957) reported the death of two snapping turtles from tuberculosis. Nolan *et al.* (1965) isolated the virus of eastern equine encephalitis from the brain of a snapping turtle.

ALGAE. *C. serpentina* is known to harbor *Basicladia chelonum*, *B. crassa*, *Dermatophyton radians*, *Entophysalis rivularis*, and *Plectonema tenue*. Proctor (1958) found *Basicladia* on 75% or more of the snapping turtles he examined, and Edgren *et al.* (1953) found algae attached to the carapace of 40% of those they examined.

CHELYDRA OSCEOLA

PARASITES. One we examined had several leeches of the species *Placobdella parasitica*. Frank J. Ligas told us he had found several nematodes in the gut of a specimen.

ALGAE. Adults often harbor colonies of *Basicladia* on their shells. Carr (1940) found two individuals with the head, legs, and carapace entirely covered with algae, the filaments of which were 2–3 inches long.

MACROCLEMYS TEMMINCKII

PARASITES. The trematodes *Lophotaspis interiora* and *Distomum* sp. occur in the alligator snapper. Cahn (1937) reported that the nematode *Zanolophorus* sp. is usually abundant in the large intestine; more than 250 were taken from one specimen. He also found an undetermined linguatulid (a parasitic arthropod) in the large intestine. The leech *Placobdella parasitica* is commonly found on this turtle.

ALGAE. The carapace usually is heavily overgrown with algae. *Basicladia chelonum*, *B. crassa*, *Cladophora* sp., *Rhizoclonium* sp., *Lyngbya* sp., *Oscillatoria* sp., and *Trichodesmium* sp. have been found on *Macroclemys*. Proctor (1958) found *Basicladia* attached to 75% or more of the *Macroclemys* he examined. The roughened carapacial surfaces of *Macroclemys* and *Chelydra* provide a good place of attachment for the algae. The algae sometimes grow over almost all of the body.

STERNOTHERUS ODORATUS

PARASITES.

1. Protozoan: *Myxidium chelonarum*.

2. Trematodes: *Hapalorhynchus reelfooti*, *Heronimus chelydrae*, *Pleorchis mollis*, *Polystomoidella oblongum*, *Telorchis medius*, and *T. robustus*.

3. Nematode: *Spiroxys contortus*.

4. Leech: *Placobdella parasitica*.

ALGAE. The epizoophytic algae *Basicladia chelonum*, *B. crassa*, *Dermatophyton radians*, *Entophysalis rivularis*, *Lyngbya* sp., *Oscillatoria splendida*, and *Rhizoclonium hieroglyphicum* have been found on the stinkpot. Dixon (1960) found the small epiphytic alga *Derepyxis dispar* on a few filaments of *Basicladia chelonum* growing on the carapace of a stinkpot.

Edgren *et al.* (1953) found that 36 of 66 (54.6%) of the *S. odoratus* examined had algae attached; of these 43% had *Basicladia chelonum* and 12% had *B. crassa*. Proctor (1958) found *Basicladia* colonies attached to more than 75% of the *S. odoratus* he examined.

Algae grow not only on the carapace but also on the upper surface of the limbs. In these areas the skin decays and falls away, exposing the underlying muscle; death soon results. Possibly the decay is produced by a fungus or other organism secondarily invading tissues weakened by heavy algal growth (Neill and Allen, 1954).

Moski (1957a) thought that *S. odoratus* might be responsible for spreading spores of *Basicladia chelonum*, which form colonies on other turtles.

COMMENSALS. Evermann and Clark (1916) found a dense growth of a stalked, branched protozoan, *Opercularia*, on the plastrons of stinkpots in Indiana. Dixon (1960) found a bryozoan, *Plumatella*, attached to the plastron of Texas stinkpots.

STERNOTHERUS CARINATUS

PARASITES. The blood protozoan *Haemogregarina*, the trematodes *Cercorchis bairdi*, *Hapalorhynchus stunkardi*, *Polystomoidella oblongum*, and *Telorchis medius*, and the nematode *Spiroxys contortus* occur in this turtle.

ALGAE. Dixon (1960) recorded *Basicladia chelonum* and *B. crassa* on 69% of the *S. carinatus* he examined. Proctor (1958) found *Basicladia* colonies on 75% of another group.

STERNOTHERUS MINOR

PARASITES. Edney (1949) found the blood protozoan *Haemogregarina stepanowi* in a Tennessee specimen. Byrd (1939) described the blood fluke *Hapalorhynchus stunkardi* from a Georgia specimen. Gibbons and Esch (1970) found the nematode *Spiroxys contortus*, the trematodes *Eustomus chelydrae*, *Polystomoidella* sp., *Telorchis* sp., and an unidentifiable trematode of the subclass Aspidocotylea in the intestines of Florida loggerhead musk turtles.

ALGAE. *S. minor* is often covered with algae.

KINOSTERNON SUBRUBRUM

PARASITES.
1. Protozoa: *Entamoeba* sp., *Haemogregarina stepanowi*, *Hexamita*, sp., *Trepomonas* sp., and *Trichomonas* sp.
2. Trematodes: *Heronimus chelydrae*, *Neopolystoma orbiculare*, *Polystomoidella oblongum*, *P. whartoni*, *Telorchis diminutus*, and *T. medius*.
3. Nematodes: *Camallanus trispinosus*, *Oxyuroidea* sp. and *Spiroxys contortus*.
4. Acanthocephalan: *Neoechinorhynchus* sp.
5. Insect: *Aedes canadensis*.
6. Leech: *Placobdella parasitica*.

ALGAE. The epizoophytic algae *Basicladia chelonum* and *B. crassa* have been found attached to mud turtles. Proctor (1958) found that more than 75% of the *K. s. hippocrepis* he examined supported colonies of *Basicladia*.

KINOSTERNON BAURII

PARASITE. *Kinosternon baurii* is a host of the trematode *Polystomoidella whartoni*.

ALGAE. This species often supports a growth of algae. Loennberg (1894) reported a shell of *K. baurii* eroded by algae.

KINOSTERNON FLAVESCENS

ALGAE. *Basicladia chelonum* and *B. crassa* occurred on 65% of the *K. flavescens* examined by Dixon (1960). Proctor (1958) found *Basicladia* on 75% of another group.

KINOSTERNON SONORIENSE

PARASITE. The protozoan *Myxidium chelonarum* occurs in the bile ducts and gall bladder of this turtle.

ALGAE. *Basicladia chelonum* and *B. crassa* often are attached to the shell.

KINOSTERNON HIRTIPES

PARASITES. The trematodes *Heronimus chelydrae*, *Polystomoidella oblongum*, and *P. whartoni* parasitize this turtle.

CLEMMYS GUTTATA

PARASITES.
1. Trematodes: *Telorchis corti* and *T. robustus*.
2. Nematode: *Spironoura affine*.
3. Acanthocephalan: *Neoechinorhynchus emydis*.
4. Leech: *Placobdella* sp.
5. Mosquitoes: *Aedes canadensis* and *A. atlanticus*.

ALGAE. *Cladophora kuetzingiana* and *Dermatophyton radians* occur on the shell, but algae of the genus *Basicladia* apparently do not grow on spotted turtles.

CLEMMYS MUHLENBERGII

PARASITES. Barton and Price (1955) found an adult harboring three oxyurid nematodes apparently related to the genus *Aplectana*.

CLEMMYS INSCULPTA

PARASITES. The wood turtle is a host of the trematodes *Spirorchis innominata* and *Telorchis corti*, the acanthocephalan *Neoechinorhynchus emydis*, the leech *Placobdella parasitica*, and the flesh fly *Sarcophaga cistudinis*.

CLEMMYS MARMORATA

PARASITES. The trematodes *Neopolystoma orbiculare*, *Ophioxenos dienteros*, *Polystomoides coronatum*, *Spirorchis artericola* and *Telorchis corti*, and the nematodes *Spironoura affine* and *Spiroxys contortus* parasitize this turtle.

ALGAE. Despite this turtle's strong aquatic tendencies algae have not been recorded from it.

TERRAPENE CAROLINA

PARASITES.
   1. Protozoa: *Trepomonas* sp., *Trichomonas* sp., *Hexamita* sp., and *Entamoeba* sp.
   2. Trematodes: *Brachycoelium salamandrae*, *Neopolystoma terrapenis*, *Polystomoidella oblongum*, *P. whartoni*, *Telorchis medius*, and *T. robustus*.
   3. Tapeworms: *Oochoristica whitentoni* and *Proteocephalus* sp.
   4. Nematodes: *Aplectana* sp., *Atractis carolinae*, *Cardianema cistudinis*, *Cosmocercoides dukae*, *Cruzia testudines*, *Oswaldocruzia leidyi* (?), *O. pipiens*, and *Spironoura affine*.
   5. Mite: *Trombicula irritans*.
   6. Tick: *Ambylomma tuberculatum*.
   7. Insects: mosquitoes—*Aedes atlanticus*, *A. canadensis*, *A. cantator*, *A. sollicitans*, *A. triseriatus*, and *Culex salinarius*; flesh fly—*Sarcophaga cistudinis*.

ALGAE. The terrestrial habits of *T. carolina* usually prevent the growth of algae on its carapace; however, Belusz and Reed (1969) found *Rhizoclonium hookeri* and *Dermatophyton radians* on a Michigan specimen.

TERRAPENE ORNATA

PARASITES. The nematodes *Cosmocercoides dukae* and *Oswaldocruzia pipiens* parasitize this turtle. Larvae of the chigger mite, *Trombicula alfreddugesi*, occur abundantly on summer specimens, and larvae of the bot fly, *Sarcophaga cistudinis*, can be found on *T. ornata* throughout the year. Infestations by bot fly larvae can be fatal.

MALACLEMYS TERRAPIN

PARASITES. The fleshy parts of a *Malaclemys* kept in a tank of freshwater were attacked by a fungus, which soon killed the turtle (Babcock, 1919). Barney (1922) reported that the cause of increased mortality in winter-fed individuals was a disease, cancerous in nature, that attacked the head, the limbs, and especially, the tail. It soon spread to the body proper, causing paralysis and death.

The trematodes *Neopolystoma orbiculare* and *Telorchis corti* occur in the diamondback terrapin.

ALGAE. *Basicladia chelonum* and *B. crassa* sometimes grow on the carapace.

GRAPTEMYS GEOGRAPHICA

PARASITES.
   1. Protozoa: *Haemoproteus metchnikovi* and *Trypanosoma chrysemydis*.
   2. Trematodes: *Cotylaspis cokeri*, *Dictyongium chelydrae*, *Heronimus chelydrae*, *Macrovestibulum eversum*, *Microphallus opacus*, *Polystomoides coronatum*, *Spirorchis artericola*, *S. innominata*, and *Telorchis corti*.
   3. Nematodes: *Camallanus microcephalus*, *Spiroxys constricta*, *S. contortus*, *Spironoura affine*, *S. concinnae*, and *S. wardi*.
   4. Acanthocephalan: *Neoechinorhynchus emydis*.
   5. Leech: *Placobdella* sp.

ALGAE. *Basicladia chelonum*, *B. crassa*, *Dermatophyton radians*, and *Gongrosira debaryona* occur on this turtle. Edgren *et al.* (1953) reported that of 44 map turtles (*Graptemys* sp.), only 4 (4.5%) supported algae. The basking habits and the annual shedding of the carapacial scutes inhibit algal attachment.

GRAPTEMYS PULCHRA

PARASITE. The protozoan *Myxidium chelonarum* occurs in the bile ducts and gall bladder.

GRAPTEMYS KOHNII

PARASITES. The trematode *Polystomoides coronatum* occurs in the mouth and the acanthocephalan *Neoechinorhynchus stunkardi* in the intestines of this species of turtle.

285

GRAPTEMYS PSEUDOGEOGRAPHICA

PARASITES.

1. Protozoan: *Myxidium chelonarum*.

2. Trematodes: *Cotylaspis* sp., *Spirorchis artericola*, *S. scripta*, and *Unicaecum ruszkowskii*.

3. Acanthocephalans: *Neoechinorhynchus emydis* and *N. stunkardi*.

4. Leech: *Placobdella* sp.

Webb (1961) found numerous nematodes, four small trematodes, and a tapeworm in the intestines of this turtle.

ALGAE. *Basicladia chelonum, B. crassa, Dermatophyton radians, Lyngbya* sp., and *Rhizoclonium hieroglyphicum* have been reported from the false map turtle. Both Proctor (1958) and Dixon (1960) reported that 50% of the individuals they examined supported colonies of *Basicladia*. The basking habits and annual shedding of the scutes probably keep this turtle relatively free of algae.

COMMENSALS. Dixon (1960) found a bryozoan, *Plumatella*, attached to one.

CHRYSEMYS PICTA

PARASITES.

1. Protozoa: digestive tract—*Eimeria chrysemydis, E. delagei, E. mitrarium, Endolimax clevelandi, Endamoeba testudinis,* and *Myxidium chelonarum*; blood—*Haemogregarina stepanowi, Haemoproteus metchnikovi,* and *Trypanosoma chrysemydis*.

2. Trematodes: intestinal—*Allassostomoides parvum, Eustomas chelydrae, Microphallus opacus, Protenes angustus, Telorchis attentuatus, T. corti, T. dimenutis,* and *T. nematoides*; blood and heart—*Spirorchis artericola, S. elegans, S. elephantis, S. haemotobium, S. innominata, S. parvus, S. pseudemyae,* and *S. scripta*; oral and pharyngeal—*Polystomoides coronatum* and *P. oris*; lung—*Heronimus chelydrae*; bladder—*Neopolystoma orbiculare* and *Polystomoidella oblongum*.

3. Nematodes: intestinal—*Aplectana* sp., *Camallanus microcephalus, C. trispinosus, Physaloptera* sp., *Spironoura* sp., *Spiroxys constricta, S. contortus,* and *S. sulcata*.

4. Acanthocephalans: *Neoechinorhynchus chrysemydis, N. emydis,* and *N. pseudemydis*.

5. Leeches: *Placobdella parasitica* and *P. rugosa*.

6. Insects: biting flies and mosquitoes—*Aedes cana-densis, A. fitchii, A. triseriatus, Culex salinrius, Culicoides* sp., *Chrysops* sp., and *Mansonia perturbans*; flesh flies—Sarcophagidae.

7. Mite: *Cloacarus beeri*.

Rausch (1947) reported an unidentifiable immature cestode from an Ohio painted turtle and thought it possibly an accidental infection. Experimental infections have been produced with the intestinal trematode *Telorchis medius* by McMullen (1934) and the fish eye trematode *Diplostomum flexicaudum* by Ferguson (1943); whether these are natural parasites of the painted turtle is not known.

ALGAE. *Basicladia chelonum, B. crassa, Cladophora kuetzingiana, Dermatophyton radians, Gongrosira deboryona,* and *Rhizoclonium hieroglyphicum* have been found on the painted turtle. Edgren *et al.* (1953) reported algal growth on 9.5% of 549 painted turtles they examined; we found 69% of 929 Pennsylvania *C. picta* supporting algae; and Proctor (1958) found 50% infestation on *C. p. bellii*.

The basking habits of *C. picta* and the periodic shedding of the scutes surely reduce the amount of algae.

COMMENSALS. Goodrich and Jahn (1943) listed the epizoic suctorian protozoa *Acineta limnetis, Anarma brevis, A. multiruga, Multifasciculatum elegans, Podophrya okobojiensis, Squalorophyra macrostyla,* and *Tokophyra quadripartita* from the western painted turtle.

CHRYSEMYS SCRIPTA

PARASITES. The relative ease with which *C. scripta* can be obtained has made this turtle a favorite subject for parasitologic research; consequently a wide variety of parasites have been found associated with it.

1. Protozoa: *Eimeria scriptae, Entamoeba terrapinae, Haemogregarina stepanowi, Haemoproteus metchnikovi,* and *Myxidium chelonarum*.

2. Trematodes: *Allossostoma magnum, Heronimus chelydrae, Macravestibulum obtusicaudum, Neopolystoma domitilae, N. orbiculare, Polystomoides coronatum, P. microcotyle, P. oblonga, Protenes angustus, P. chapmani, Schizamphistomoides tabascensis, Spirorchis artericola, S. blandingioides, S. elegans, S. pseudemyae, S. scripta, Telorchis corti, T. dissimilis, T. medius, T. nematoides, T. robustus, T. singularis, T. texanus, Unicaecum dissimilis,* and *U. ruszkowskii*.

3. Cestode: *Opithiotaenia testudo*.

286

4. Nematodes: *Camallanus microcephalus, C. trispinosus, Falcaustra chelydrae, F. procera, Oxyuroidea* sp., *Spironoura concinnae,* and *Spiroxys contortus.*

5. Acanthocephalans: *Leptorhynchus* sp., *Neoechinorhynchus chelonos, N. chrysemydis, N. constrictus, N. emydis, N. emyditoides, N. magnapipillatus,* and *N. pseudemydis.*

6. Leech: *Placobdella parasitica.*

ALGAE. *Basicladia chelonum, B. crassa, Cladophora glomerata, Dermatophyton radians, Lyngbya* sp., *Oscillatoria splendida,* and *Trichodesmium* sp. have been reported from *Chrysemys scripta.* Edgren *et al.* (1953) found algae on 11% of the *C. scripta* they examined, Proctor (1958) reported *Basicladia* on 50–75%, and Dixon (1960) found colonies on 77%. Most pond sliders are not so heavily colonized as snapping, musk, or mud turtles; this probably is due to their basking habit and the annual shedding of the scutes.

COMMENSALS. Dixon (1960) found a bryozoan, *Plumatella,* attached to *C. s. elegans.*

CHRYSEMYS CONCINNA

PARASITES.

1. Protozoa: *Endolimax clevelandi, Haemogregarina stepanowi,* and *Myxidium chelonarum.*

2. Trematodes: *Neopolystoma orbiculare, Polystomoides coronatum, P. stunkardi,* and *Spirorchis innominata.*

3. Nematodes: *Camallanus trispinosus, Falcaustra procera, Spironoura concinnae,* and *Spiroxys contortus.*

4. Acanthocephalan: *Neoechinorhynchus emydis.*

5. Leech: *Placobdella* sp.

ALGAE. *Basicladia chelonum* and *B. crassa* often attach to *Chrysemys concinna.* Pritchard and Greenhood (1968) reported that Florida individuals with extensive algal growth basked longer than those with less algae.

Since the river cooter annually sheds the epidermal scutes, it periodically divests itself of any algae established on the shell.

CHRYSEMYS FLORIDANA

PARASITES.

1. Protozoan: *Myxidium chelonarum.*

2. Trematodes: *Allosotomoides parvum, Cephalo-*

gonimus compactus, Macravestibulum sp., *Polystomoides coronatum, P. multifalx, Spirorchis artericola, S. blandingioides, S. innominata, S. scripta,* and *Telorchis* sp.

3. Acanthocephalans: *Neoechinorhynchus chrysemydis* and *N. emyditoides.*

4. Leech: *Placobdella* sp.

ALGAE. *Basicladia chelonum* and *B. crassa* often grow on *C. floridana.* Proctor (1958) found colonies of *Basicladia* on 50–75% of the *Chrysemys f. hoyi* he examined.

CHRYSEMYS RUBRIVENTRIS

PARASITES. Hughes *et al.* (1941a) reported the trematode *Neopolystoma orbiculare* from *Chrysemys rubriventris.* Harwood (1932) listed this turtle as a host of the nematode *Falcaustra procera.* Graham (1969) reported the passage of several medium-sized nematodes by a captive adult. Crans and Rockel (1968) collected the mosquito *Aedes canadensis* while it fed on a *C. rubriventris* in New Jersey.

CHRYSEMYS NELSONI

PARASITES. The protozoan *Myxidium chelonarum* lives in the bile duct and gall bladder, and a large female that we examined was infested with 82 *Placobdella parasitica.*

CHRYSEMYS ALABAMENSIS

PARASITE. *Neopolystoma orbiculare* occurs in the urinary bladder.

DEIROCHELYS RETICULARIA

PARASITES. The protozoan *Myxidium chelonarum,* the trematodes *Neopolystoma orbiculare* and *Telorchis corti,* the nematodes *Camallanus trispinosus* and *Spiroxys contortus,* and leeches of the genus *Placobdella* parasitize this turtle.

ALGAE. Dixon (1960) found *Basicladia chelonum* and *B. crassa* on 33% of the *Deirochelys* he examined. Proctor (1958) found *Basicladia* colonies on 50–75% of those he examined.

EMYDOIDEA BLANDINGII

PARASITES.

1. Protozoan: *Haemogregarina stepanowi*.
2. Trematodes: *Heronimus chelydrae, Microphallus opacus, Polystomoides* sp., *Spirorchis blandingi, S. innominata, S. pseudemyae, Telorchis compactus,* and *T. medius*.
3. Nematodes: *Aplectana* sp., *Camallanus microcephalus, Spironoura affine,* and *Spiroxys contortus*.
4. Acanthocephalans: *Neoechinorhynchus emydis, N. emyditoides,* and *N. pseudemydis*.
5. Leech: *Placobdella* sp.
6. Mosquito: *Aedes canadensis*.

ALGAE. *Basicladia crassa* and *Cladophora glomerata* were found on 40% of the *Emydoidea* examined by Edgren et al. (1953). Proctor (1958) found *Basicladia* on 50–75% of the *Emydoidea* he examined. Belusz and Reed (1969) described the alga *Cladophora kosterae* from Blanding's turtle.

GOPHERUS AGASSIZII

PARASITES. The adobe tick, *Ornithodorus turicata*, has been recorded from desert tortoises by Harbison (1937) and Woodbury and Hardy (1948). The latter also found maggots in a wound on one tortoise and mold growing on two other tortoises.

GOPHERUS BERLANDIERI

PARASITES. Strecker (1927a) attributed the death of a captive to internal parasites with which it became infested while in a terrarium. He suggested that in nature tortoises usually can survive parasitic infestations but when weakened by captivity often succumb to their ravages.

GOPHERUS POLYPHEMUS

PARASITES. Young and Goff (1939) found the tick *Amblyomma tuberculatum* on gopher tortoises. It is also possible that the tick *Ornithodoros turicata*, which inhabits the burrows, occasionally parasitizes them. Pope (1939) reported that a large blood-sucking mite lives in the burrow and attacks *G. polyphemus* as bedbugs do humans.

288

CHELONIA MYDAS

PARASITES. Because *Chelonia mydas* is an economically important animal it has been extensively studied, and many parasites have been found associated with it.

1. Blood protozoan: *Trypanosoma testundinis*.
2. Trematodes: *Amphiorchis amphiorchis, Angiodyctium parallelum, Calycodes anthos, Charaxicephalus robustus, Cricocephalus albus, C. megastomus, C. resectus, C. ruber, Cymatocarpus solearis, Desmogonius desmogonius, Deuterobaris proteus, D. viridis, Diaschistorchis lateralis, D. pandus, Distoma testudinis mydae, Distomum constrictum, Enodiotrema megachondrus, Glyphicephalus lobatus, G. solidus, Haemoxenicon chelonenecon, H. stunkardi, Learedius europaeus, L. learedi, L. orientalis, L. similis, Medioporus cheloniae, Metacetabulum invaginatum, Microscaphidium aberrans, M. reticulare, Monostoma pseudamphistomum, Monticellius indicum, Neoctangium travassosi, Neospirorchis schistosomatoides, Octangium hasta, O. sagitta, O. takonoi, Orchidasma amphiorchis, Pachypsolus irroratus, Phyllodistomum cymbiforme, Pleurogonius bilobus, P. chelonii, P. linearis, P. longiusculus, P. minutissimus, Polyangium linguatula, P. miyajimai, Polystoma mydae, Pronocephalus obliguus, Pyelosomum cochlear, Rhytidodes gelatinosus, Rhytidodoides intestinalis, R. similis, Schizamphistomoides chelonei, S. spinulosum, Schizamphistomum scleroporum, Spirorchis parvum,* and *Squaroacetabulum solus*.
3. Cestodes: *Ancistrocephalus imbricatus* and *Tentacularia coryphaenae*.
4. Leech: *Ozobranchus branchiatus*.
5. Barnacles: *Chelonibia testudinaria, Platylepas hexastylos, Stephanolepas muricata,* and *Stomatolepas elegans*.
6. Isopod: *Eurydice* sp.

The burrowing barnacle *Stephanolepas muricata* can do considerable damage to the shell and skin of the green turtle, but it is not known if the other species of barnacles associated with this turtle are parasitic or only epizoic. This is also true of the isopods of the genus *Eurydice*, which are found clinging to the margins of the eyelids.

ALGAE. Deraniyagala (1939) reported that lagoon-dwelling *Chelonia* in Ceylon usually are distinguished by a growth of algae on their shells.

ERETMOCHELYS IMBRICATA

PARASITES. The following trematodes have been reported from the hawksbill: *Amphiorchis lateralis, Amphistoma cheloniae-imbricatae, Cricocephalis albus, Diaschistorchis pandus, Medioporus microphallus, Pachypsolus brachus, Pleurogonius ozakii, P. trigonocephalus, Pyelosomum posterorchis, Rhytidodes gelatinosus,* and *R. indicus.*

The barnacle *Chelonibia testudinaria* may encrust the shell and flippers of the hawksbill, and another barnacle, *Stephanolepas muricata,* infests this turtle by boring deep into its flippers and shell.

ALGAE. Cribb (1969) reported that an *Eretmochelys* collected at North West Island, Australia, carried crusts of calcareous algae on its plastron and an intermittent, fine fur of filamentous algae over both the carapace and plastron. Later examination of material scraped from the turtle revealed a surprising total of 38 algal species, as follows:

1. Cyanophyta: *Anacystis dimidiata, Calothrix crustacea, Entophysalis conferta, E. deusta, Microcoleus lyngbyaceus, Oscillatoria lutea, Schizothrix calcicola, S. tenerrima,* and *Spirulina subsala.*

2. Chlorophyta: *Bryopsis pennata, Cladophora crystallina, Enteromorpha clathrata, Ochlochaete ferox, Phaeophila dentroides, Pilinia* sp., *Pseudopringsheimia* sp., *Rhizoclonium implexum,* and an undetermined filamentous species.

3. Phaeophyta: *Ectocarpus irregularis, E. mitchellae, E. rhodochortonoides, Sphacelaria furcigera, S. novae-hollandiae,* and *S. tribuloides.*

4. Rhodophyta: *Acrochaetium catenulatum, A. daviesii, A. robustum, Ceramium gracillimum* var. *byssoideum, C. serpens, Erythrotrichia carnea, Fosliella* sp., *Gelidiella* sp., *Goniotrichum elegans, Herposiphonia tenella, Lophosiphonia scopulorum,* and *Melobesia* sp.

CARETTA CARETTA

PARASITES. The following trematodes have been reported from the loggerhead: *Adenogaster serialis, Carettacola bipora, Cricocephalus albus, C. delitescens, Cymatocarpus undulatus, Diaschistorchis ellipticus, D. pandus, Distoma pachyderma, D. testudinus, Enodiotrema acariaeum, E. instar, E. megachondrus, E. reductum, Epibathra crassa, Hapalotrema loossi, H. mistroides, H. synorchis, Learedius europaeus, Lophotaspis vallei, Neo-*

spirorchis pricei, Orchidasma amphiorchis, Pachypsolus irroratus, P. ovalis, P. tertius, Phyllodistomum cymbiforme, Pleurogonius trigonocephalus, Polystoma mydae, Polystomoides ocellatus, Pyelosomum longicaecum, Rhytidodes gelatinosus, R. secundus, Schizamphistomum scleroporum, and *Styphlotrema solitaria.* The tapeworms *Ancistrocephalus imbricatus* and *Tentacularia coryphaenae* also parasitize *Caretta.*

Considerable numbers of the leech *Ozobranchus maggoi* often can be found adhering to the cloacal regions of Pacific loggerheads.

Hughes, Bass, and Mentis (1967) found a number of pits in the carapaces and, in one case, on the head. The shape of the pits indicated that they might have been caused by barnacles. Some of the pits were as much as 12.7 mm deep. These authors thought it possible that the barnacles may have had an adverse effect on the turtles, because several barnacles were found occupying sites that showed incipient pitting. They even fix themselves in the turtle's mouth. It is not known if the barnacles are parasitic or only epizoic. *Chelonibia caretta, C. testudinaria, Coronula regina, Lepas ansifera, Platylepas hexastylos,* and *Stomatolepas elegans* occur on loggerheads.

COMMENSALS. Caldwell (1968) found that several juveniles associated with the seaweed *Sargassum* had light encrustations of the bryozoa and tube worms typical of *Sargassum* communities; these probably were epizoic.

LEPIDOCHELYS KEMPII

PARASITES. Chavez (1969) reported that small captive *L. kempii* that were fed a diet based exclusively on fish were attacked by fungi, which apparently killed two.

LEPIDOCHELYS OLIVACEA

PARASITES. Hughes *et al.* (1941a) listed the Pacific ridley as the host of the trematode *Orchidasma amphiorchis.* Pritchard (1969a) reported that mosquitoes descend in clouds on nesting females. Hiro (1936) found the barnacle *Stomatolepas elegans* on a Japanese *L. olivacea.*

DERMOCHELYS CORIACEA

PARASITES. The only identified endoparasite is the trematode *Astrorchis renicapite.* The barnacles *Chelonibia tes-*

tudinaria, *Platylepas* sp., and *Stomatolepas elegans* have been reported from the leatherback and may be ecto-parasitic. The oily body-covering of this turtle probably restricts the attachment of most ectoparasites.

COMMENSALS. Certain fish, such as the remora, often attach themselves and ride on leatherbacks.

TRIONYX MUTICUS

PARASITES. The blood protozoan *Haemogregarina* and the trematodes *Cephalogonimus* sp., *Crepidostomum cooperi*, *Opisthorchis ovalis*, and *Telorchis corti* parasitize this softshell. Muller (1921) found that eggs occasionally were inhabited by maggots, but these eggs may have been spoiled prior to invasion.

TRIONYX SPINIFERUS

PARASITES.

1. Protozoa: *Eimeria amydae*, *E. dericksoni*, *Haemoproteus metchnikovi*, *Haemogregarina stepanowi*, and *Myxidium americanum*.

2. Trematodes: *Hapalorhynchus evaginatus*, *Opisthorchis ovalis*, *Polystomoides coronatus*, *Teloporia aspidenectes*, *Vasotrema amydae*, *V. attenuatum*, *V. longitestis*, and *V. robustum*.

3. Cestode: *Proteocephalus testudo*.

4. Nematodes: *Camallanus trispinosus*, *Falcaustra chelydrae*, *Spiroxys amydae*, and *S. contortus*.

5. Acanthocephalans: *Neoechinorhynchus emyditoides* and *N. chrysemydis*.

ALGAE. *Dermatophyton radians* and *Stigeoclonium* have been found on the spiny softshell.

TRIONYX FEROX

PARASITES. The trematodes *Neopolystoma orbiculare*, *N. rugosa*, *Polystomoides coronatum*, *P. opacum*, *Teloporia aspidonectes*, *Vasotrema amydae*, *V. attentuatum*, and *V. robustum* and the cestode *Proteocephalus trionychinus* parasitize the Florida softshell.

TRIONYX SINENSIS

PARASITES. The trematodes *Aspidogaster conchicola*, *Astiotrema amydae*, *A. fukuii*, *A. orientale*, *Cephalogonimus japonicus*, *Cotylaspis sinensis*, *Kaurma orientalis*,

Lophotaspis orientalis, and *Neopolystoma palpebrae* parasitize this turtle.

REFERENCES

Acholonu (1968, 1969a, b), Babcock (1919), Bacon (1970), Barker and Covey (1911), Barker and Parsons (1914), Barney (1922), Barton and Price (1955), Belusz and Reed (1969), Bogitsh (1959), Bychowsky (1961), Byrd (1939), Cable and Fisher (1961), Cable and Hopp (1954), Cable and Sanborn (1970), Cahn (1937), Camin et al. (1967), Caldwell (1963a, 1968), Carr (1940), Chavez (1969), Chidester (1916), Collins (1907), Crandall (1960), Crans (1968), Crans and Rockel (1968), Cribb (1969), Crites (1963), DasGupta (1935), Deeds and Jahn (1939), DeFoliart (1967), DeGuisti (1970), DeGuisti and Batten (1951), Deraniyagala (1939), Dixon (1960), Driml (1961), Edgren (1968), Edgren et al. (1953), Edney (1949), Ernst (1969, 1970c, 1971a), Ernst et al. (1969), Esch and Gibbons (1967), Everhart (1958), Evermann and Clark (1916), Ewing (1926), Ferguson (1943), Fisher (1960), Fried and Fee (1968), Gibbons (1968a), Gibbons and Esch (1970), Goodchild and Dennis (1967), Goodchild and Kirk (1960), Goodrich and Jahn (1943), Graham (1969), Gupta (1961), Gutierrez-Ballesteros and Wenrich (1950), Harbison (1937), Harrah (1922), Harwood (1932a, b), Hayes (1965), Hedrick (1932, 1935), Hendrickson (1958), Herban and Yaeger (1969), Herrmann (1970), Hiro (1936), Holliman and Fisher (1968), Hopp (1945, 1954), Hughes (1970b), Hughes, Bass, and Mentis (1967), Hughes et al. (1941a, b), Hunt (1957, 1958a), Jackson et al. (1969), Johnson (1967, 1969a, b). Kepner (1912), Knipling (1937), Legler (1960a), Little and Hopkins (1968), Lönnberg (1894), Loftin (1960), Luhman (1935), Mackin (1927, 1936), Manter (1932), Manter and Larson (1950), Martin and Bamberger (1952), Mathers (1948), McAllister, Bass, and Van Schoor (1965), McMullen (1934, 1935), Meyer (1968), Moski (1955, 1957a, b), Muller (1921), Neill and Allen (1954), Nigrelli (1940, 1941, 1942), Nolan et al. (1965), Parker (1941), Peters (1948), Pope (1939), Price (1934, 1939), Pritchard (1969a), Pritchard and Greenhood (1968), Proctor (1958), Rainey (1953), Rausch (1946, 1947a, b), Reiber (1941), Richards (1930), Rokosky (1948), Roudabush and Coutney (1937), Sampson and Ernst (1969), Sanders and Cleveland (1930), Schmidt et al. (1970), Schroeder and Ulmer (1959), Simha and Chattopadhyaya (1969, 1970), Smith et al.

(1941), Strecker (1927a), Stunkard (1923, 1924, 1927, 1943), Thatcher (1954, 1963), Ulmer (1957, 1959), Vinyard (1953), Walker *et al.* (1953), Wall (1941, 1951), Wang and Hopkins (1965), Ward (1921), Webb (1961, 1962), Wieczorowski (1939), Williams (1953), Wilson and Friddle (1950), Woo (1969), Woodbury and Hardy (1948), Young and Goff (1939), and Zullo and Bleakney (1966).

Glossary
of Scientific
Names

agassizii	(ăg-a-sē′-zĭ-ī′), a proper name —L. Agassiz
alabamensis	(ăl′-a-băm-en′-sis), belonging to Alabama
asper	(ăs′-per), rough
bangsi	(bangs′-ī′), a proper name— O. Bangs
barbouri	(bär′-ber-ī), a proper name— T. Barbour
bauri	(baur′-i′), a proper name—G. Baur
baurii	(baur′-ĭ-ī′), a proper name— G. Baur
bellii	(bĕll′-ĭ-ī′), a proper name— T. Bell
berlandieri	(ber-lan′-di-ere′-ī), a proper name—L. Berlandier
bissa	(bĭs′-a), biting
blandingii	(blăn-ding′-ĭ-ī′), a proper name—W. Blanding
calvatus	(căl-vāt′-us), smooth, bald
Caretta	(că-rĕt′-tă), a tortoise shell
carinatus	(kăr′-ĭ-nāt′-us), keeled
carolina	(kăr′-ō-lī′-na), a proper name —Carolina
centrata	(sĕn-trä′-ta), centered
Chelonia	(che-lō′-nĭ-ă), tortoise
Chelydra	(chĕ-lee′-dră), water turtle
chrysea	(cry′-see-a), golden one
Chrysemys	(cry′-sĕ-mēz), golden turtle
Clemmys	(clem′-eez), tortoise
concinna	(kŏn-sĭn′-a), elegant, neatly arranged
coriacea	(kō′-rĭ-ā′-ce-a), leathery
Deirochelys	(dīre-ä′-kĕ-leez), hill, or hump, turtle
delticola	(dĕl-tĭ′-co-lă), delta-inhabiting
Dermochelys	(dĕr-mä′-kĕ-leez), leather tortoise
dorsalis	(dor-săl′-us), dorsal
elegans	(ĕl′-e-găns′), elegant

emoryi	(ĕm'-o-rĭ-ī'), a proper name—W. H. Emory
Emydoidea	(em'-ĭ-doi'-dē-ă), *Emys*-like one
Eretmochelys	(ĕ-rĕt'-mock'-kĕ-leez), oar turtle
ferox	(fĕr'-ox'), wild, savage
flavescens	(fla-vĕs'-ens), yellowish
flavimaculata	(fla'-vi-mac-u-lā'-tă), yellow-spotted
floridana	(flor-i-dā'-na), a proper name—Florida
gaigeae	(gā'-jē), a proper name—H. T. Gaige
geographica	(jē-ō-grā'-fi-ca), geographic, maplike
gigas	(jī'-găs), giant
Gopherus	(gō'-fer-us), burrower
Graptemys	(grap'-te-mēz), inscribed turtle
guadalupensis	(gwä'-dä-loop-en'-sis), belonging to Guadalupe (river in Texas)
guttata	(gŭ-tāt'-a), spotted
hartwegi	(härt'-weg-ī'), a proper name—N. E. Hartweg
hieroglyphica	(hī'-rō-glĭf'-ĭ-kă), mysterious markings
hippocrepis	(hip-oh-crē'-pis), horseshoe
hirtipes	(her'-ti-peez), rough foot
hoyi	(hoy'-ī'), a proper name—P. R. Hoy
imbricata	(ĭm-brĭ-kāt'-a), overlapping
insculpta	(ĭn-skŭlp'-ta), engraved
kempii	(kemp'-ĭ-ī'), a proper name R. M. Kemp
Kinosternon	(kī-no-stĕr'-non), movable breast
kohnii	(kohn'-ĭ-ī') a proper name—G. Kohn
Lepidochelys	(lep'-id-ō-kē'-leez), scaly turtle
littoralis	(lĭt-ō-răl'-is), of the seashore
luteola	(lū-tē-ō'-la), yellowish
Macroclemys	(mack'-rō-clem'-mēz), large tortoise
macrospilota	(mack'-rō-spill-ō'-ta), large-spotted
major	(mā'-jer), larger, major
Malaclemys	(măl'-ă-clem'-mēz), gentle tortoise
marginata	(mär-jĭ-nāt'a), margined
marmorata	(mär'-mō-rā'-ta), marbled
miaria	(mē-air'-ia), stained (referring to plastral pattern)
minor	(mī'-ner), smaller, minor
mobilensis	(mō-beel'-ĕn'-sis), belonging to Mobile (Alabama)
muhlenbergii	(mū-len-berg'-ĭ-ī'), a proper name—G. H. E. Muhlenberg
murrayi	(mûr'-ray-ī'), a proper name—L. T. Murray
muticus	(mū'-tĭ-cus), curtailed, unarmed, cut off
mydas	(my'-das), wet
nelsoni	(nĕl'-sŏn-ī'), a proper name—E. W. Nelson
nigrinoda	(nī'-grĭ-nō'-da), black-knobbed
oculifera	(ŏc-ū-lĭ'-fur-ă), eye-bearing
odoratus	(ō-dōr-ā'-tus), smelly
olivacea	(ŏl'-ĭ-vā'-cea), olive-colored
ornata	(ôr-nāt'-a), ornate
osceola	(ŏss-ē-ō'-lä), a proper name—Osceola (Florida)
ouachitensis	(wash-ĭ-ten'-sis), belonging to Ouachíta (river in Louisiana)
pallida	(păl'-ĭd-a), pale
pallidus	(păl'-ĭd-us), pale
palmarum	(palm-air'-um), of the palms
peltifer	(pĕlt'-ĭ-fer), shield-bearer
peninsularis	(pĕn-ĭn'-su-lăr'-is), pertaining to a peninsula
picta	(pick'-ta), painted

293

pileata	(pĭ'-lē-āt'-a), capped, covered with a cap
polyphemus	(pŏl'-ĭ-fē'-mus), many-voiced
pseudogeographica	(sū'-dō-jē-ō-grã'-fi-ca), false-ly maplike
pulchra	(pŭl'-kra), beautiful
reticularia	(re-tick'-ū-lăr'-ia), netlike
rhizophorarum	(rī'-zō-fō-rare'-um), bearing roots (refers to habitat)
rubriventris	(roo'-brĭ-věn'-trĭs), red-bellied
sabinensis	(sā'-ben-ĕn'-sis), belonging to Sabine (river in Louisiana)
schlegelii	(shlā'-gĕl-ĭ-ī'), a proper name —H. Schlegel
scripta	(skrĭpt'-a) written
serpentina	(sur'-pĕn-tēn'-a), snakelike
sinensis	(sĭ-něn'-sis), belonging to China
sonoriense	(sō-no'-ri-en'-sē), belonging to Sonora (Mexico)
spiniferus	(spī-nĭ'-fer-us), bearing spines
spooneri	(spoon'-er-ī'), a proper name —C. S. Spooner
steindachneri	(stein-doc'-ner-ī'), a proper name—H. Steindachner
stejnegeri	(stĕn'-ĕ-gẽr-ī'), a proper name —L. Stejneger
Sternotherus	(stir-nŏ'-thĕr-us), hinged chest
subrubrum	(sŭb-rūb'-rūm), red under-side
suwanniensis	(sū-wän'-ĭ-en'-sis), belonging to Suwannee (river in Florida)
temminckii	(tĕ-mink'-ĭ-ī'), a proper name —C. J. Temminck
tequesta	(tē-quest'-a), a proper name —Tequesta (Indian tribe)
Terrapene	(tĕr'-ă-pē'-nē), turtle
terrapin	(tĕr'-a-pin), turtle
texana	(tex-ān'-a), a proper name—Texas
Trionyx	(trī-ŏ'-nĭks), three-clawed one
triunguis	(trī-un'-gū-iss), three-clawed
troostii	(troost'-ĭ-ī'), a proper name —G. Troost
versa	(vur'-sa), turn, change

Bibliography

We have attempted to include all the papers on the ecology, ethology, and systematics of North American turtles published between 1 January 1950 and 31 December 1970. Only the more pertinent papers on physiology and morphology have been included, and then only if they are related to the above fields of study. Some important studies published before 1950 are listed, but the reader is referred to Carr (1952) for other pre-1950 papers. Publications marked with an asterisk (*) are those that contain the original description of a species or subspecies of North American turtle.

Those who are seriously interested in turtle research should regularly consult the following journals: *Copeia*, published by the American Society of Ichthyologists and Herpetologists; *Herpetologica*, published by the Herpetologists' League; and the *Journal of Herpetology*, published by the Society for the Study of Amphibians and Reptiles. Furthermore, anyone with a serious and lasting interest in turtles should join one or more of these societies.

The turtle hobbyist may want to consult the *International Turtle & Tortoise Society Journal*. This society is dedicated to the conservation of turtles throughout the world and to the proper care of captives. The journal, published bimonthly, contains much useful information of a general nature on the biology and care of turtles.

Acholonu, A. D.
  1968   Studies on the digenetic trematodes of Louisiana turtles. Trans. Amer. Microsc. Soc. 87: 124–125
  1969a   Some monogenetic trematodes from Louisiana turtles. Proc. Louisiana Acad. Sci. 32: 20–25.
  1969b   Acanthocephala of Louisiana turtles with a redescription of *Neoechinorhynchus stunkardi* Cable and Fisher, 1961. Proc. Helminthol. Soc. Washington 36:177–183.

Ackman, R. G., and R. D. Burgher
  1965   Cod liver oil fatty acids as secondary reference standards in the GLC of polyunsaturated fatty acids of animal origin: analysis of a dermal oil of the Atlantic leatherback turtle. J. Amer. Oil Chem. Soc. 42:38–42.

Adams, D. E.
1966   More about the ridley. Operation: Padre Island. Egg transplanting. Int. Turtle & Tortoise Soc. J. 1(1):18–20, 40–43, 45.

Adler, K. K.
1960   Notes on lateral expansion of the periphery in juveniles of *Sternothaerus odoratus*. Copeia 1960:156.
1961   Egg-laying in the spotted turtle, *Clemmys guttata* (Schneider). Ohio J. Sci. 61:180–182.
1968   *Pseudemys scripta* in West Virginia: archeological and modern records. J. Herpetol, 2: 117–120.
1970   The influence of prehistoric man on the distribution of the box turtle. Ann. Carnegie Mus. 41:263–280.

Agassiz, L.
*1857 Contributions to the natural history of the United States of America. Little, Brown and Co., Boston, Vol. 1–2; 452 pp.

Akers, T. K., and M. G. Damm
1963   The effect of temperature on the electrocardiograms of two species of turtles. Copeia 1963:629–634.

Albrecht, P. W.
1967   The cranial arteries and cranial arterial foramina of the turtle genera *Chrysemys*, *Sternotherus*, and *Trionyx*: a comparative study with analysis of possible evolutionary implications. Tulane Stud. Zool. 14:81–99.

Alexander, J. D.
1961   Notes on the Gulf Coast softshell in the vicinity of Albany. Philadelphia Herpetol. Soc. Bull. 9(5):11–14.

Alexander, M. M.
1943   Food habits of the snapping turtle in Connecticut. J. Wildlife Mgt. 7:278–282.

Allard, H. A.
1935   The natural history of the box turtle. Sci. Monthly 41:325–338.
1939   Mating of the box turtle ending in death to the male. Copeia 1939:109.
1948   The eastern box-turtle and its behavior. J. Tennessee Acad. Sci. 23:307–321.

Allen, E. R.
1938   Notes on the feeding and egg-laying habits of the *Pseudemys*. Proc. Florida Acad. Sci. 3:105–108.
1950   Sounds produced by the Suwannee terrapin. Copeia 1950:62.

Allen, E. R., and W. T. Neill
1950   The alligator snapping turtle, *Macrochelys temminckii*, in Florida. Spl. Publ. Ross Allen's Rept. Inst. 4:1–15.
1952   Know your reptiles: the diamondback terrapin. Florida Wildlife, Nov.:8.
1953   Juveniles of the tortoise *Gopherus polyphemus*. Copeia 1953:128.
1957   Another record of the Atlantic leatherback, *Dermochelys c. coriacea*, nesting on the Florida coast. Copeia 1957:143–144.

Allen, J. F., and R. A. Littleford
1955   Observations on the feeding habits and growth of immature diamondback terrapins. Herpetologica 11:77–80.

Allen, W. B.
1955   Some notes on reptiles. Herpetologica 11:228.

Anderson, P. K.
1958   The photic responses and water-approach behavior of hatchling turtles. Copeia 1958:211–215.
1965   The reptiles of Missouri. Univ. Missouri Press, Columbia. 330 pp.

Anonymous
1967   Once upon a time. Int. Turtle & Tortoise Soc. J. 1(4):24–29.

Arata, A. A.
1958   Notes on the eggs and young of *Gopherus polyphemus* (Daudin). Quart. J. Florida Acad. Sci. 21:274–280.

Armington, J. C.
1954   Spectral sensitivity of the turtle *Pseudemys*. J. Comp. Psychol. 47:1–6.

Ash, R. P.
1951   A preliminary report on the size, egg number, incubation period, and hatching in the common snapping turtle, *Chelydra serpentina*. Virginia Acad. Sci. 2:312.

Ashe, V. M.
1970   The righting reflex in turtles: a description and comparison. Psychon. Sci. 20:150–152.

Ashley, L. M.
1955   Laboratory anatomy of the turtle. Wm. C. Brown Co., Dubuque, Iowa. 48 pp.

Atland, P. D.
1951   Observations on the structure of the reproductive organs of the box turtle. J. Morphol. 89:599–621.

Atland, P. D., and K. C. Brace
1962   Red cell life span in the turtle and toad. Amer. J. Physiol. 203:1188–1190.

Atland, P. D., B. Higman, and B. Wood
1951   Some effects of X-irradiation on turtles. J. Exp. Zool. 118:1–17.

Atland, P. D., and M. Parker
1955   Effects of hypoxia upon the box turtle. Amer. J. Physiol. 180:421–427.

Atland, P. D., and E. C. Thompson
1958   Some factors affecting blood formation in turtles. Proc. Soc. Exp. Biol. Med. 99:456–459.

Auffenberg, W.
1958   Fossil turtles of the genus *Terrapene* in Florida. Bull. Florida St. Mus. 3:53–92.
1963   Fossil testudinine turtles of Florida genera *Geochelone* and *Floridemys*. Bull. Florida St. Mus. 7:53–97.
1964   A redefinition of the fossil tortoise genus *Stylemys* Leidy. J. Paleontol. 38:316–324.
1966a   The carpus of land tortoises (Testudininae). Bull. Florida St. Mus. 10:159–192.
1966b   On the courtship of *Gopherus polyphemus*. Herpetologica 22:113–117.
1969   Tortoise behavior and survival. Rand McNally & Co., Chicago. 38 pp.

Auffenberg, W., and W. G. Weaver
1969   *Gopherus berlandieri* in southeastern Texas. Bull. Florida St. Mus. 13:141–203.

Babbitt, L. H.
1932   Some remarks on Connecticut herpetology. Bull. Boston Soc. Nat. Hist. 63:23–28.

Babcock, H. L.
1916   An addition to the chelonian fauna of Massachusetts. Copeia 1916(38):95–98.
1919   The turtles of New England. Mem. Boston Soc. Nat. Hist. 8:323–431.
*1937   A new subspecies of the red-bellied terrapin *Pseudemys rubriventris* (LeConte). Occ. Pap. Boston Soc. Nat. Hist. 8:293.
1938   Field guide to New England turtles. New England Mus. Nat. Hist., Nat. Hist. Guide 2:1–56.
1939   Growth of an individual box turtle. Copeia 1939:175.

Bacon, P. R.
1967   Leatherback turtles. J. Trinidad Field Nat. Club 1967:2–3.
1969   The leatherback turtle project, progress report 1967–1968, and recommendations. J. Trinidad Field Nat. Club 1969:8–9.
1970   Studies on the leatherback turtle *Dermochelys coriacea* (L.), in Trinidad, West Indies. Biol. Conserv. 2:213–217.

Baird, S. F., and C. Girard
*1852   Descriptions of new species of reptiles collected by the U.S. exploring expedition under the command of Capt. Charles Wilkes, U.S.N. Proc. Acad. Nat. Sci. Philadelphia 1852:174–177.

Balasingam, E.
1965a   The giant leathery turtle conservation programme—1964. Malayan Nat. J. 19:145–146.
1965b   Conservation of green turtles (*Chelonia mydas*) in Malaya. Malayan Nat. J. 19:235–236.
1967a   Turtle conservation: results of the 1965 hatchery programme. Malayan Nat. J. 20:139–141.
1967b   The ecology and conservation of the leathery turtle (*Dermochelys coriacea*) in Malaya. Micronesia 3:37–43.
1969   Marine turtles in West Malaysia. IUCN Publ. (n.s.) 20:67–70.

Baldwin, H. A., D. L. Brumbaugh, and A. Carr
1969   Initial experiments with migrating *Chelonia mydas* using telemetry. Prelim. Tech. Rep. Sensory Syst. Lab. Mimeo; 33 pp.

Banks, E.
1937 The breeding of the edible turtle (*Chelone mydas*). Sarawak Mus. J. 4:523–532.

Banta, B. H.
1963 On the occurrence of *Clemmys marmorata* (Reptilia: Testudinata) in western Nevada. Wasmann J. Biol. 21:75–77.

Barbour, R. W.
1950 The reptiles of Big Black Mountain, Harlan County, Kentucky. Copeia 1950:100–107.
1971 Amphibians and reptiles of Kentucky. Univ. Press Kentucky, Lexington. 334 pp.

Barden, A. A.
1952 A Maine record for Blanding's turtle. Copeia 1952:279–280.

Barkalow, F. S.
1948 Notes on the breeding habits of the turtle *Kinosternon s. subrubrum*. Copeia 1948:130.

Barker, F. D., and G. W. Covey
1911 A new species of trematode from the painted terrapin, *Chrysemys marginata*. Univ. Nebraska Stud. 11:193–216.

Barker, F. D., and M. Parsons
1914 A new aspidobothrid trematode from Lesseur's terrapin. Trans. Amer. Microsc. Soc. 33:261–262.

Barney, R. L.
1922 Further notes on the natural history and artificial propagation of the diamond-back terrapin. Bull. U. S. Bur. Fish. 38:91–111.

Barton, A. J., and J. W. Price
1955 Our knowledge of the bogturtle, *Clemmys muhlenbergi*, surveyed and augmented. Copeia 1955:159–165.

Baur, G.
*1888 Notes on the American Trionychidae. Amer. Nat. 22:1121–1122.
*1890 Two new species of tortoises from the South. Science 16:262–263.
*1893a Notes on the classification and taxonomy of the Testudinata. Proc. Amer. Phil. Soc. 31:210–225.
*1893b Two new species of North American Testudinata. Amer. Nat. 27:675–676.

Baze, W. B., and F. R. Horne
1970 Ureogenesis in Chelonia. Comp. Biochem. Physiol. 34:91–100.

Behler, J. L.
1970 The bog turtle (*Clemmys muhlenbergi*) in Monroe County, Pennsylvania. Bull. Maryland Herpetol. Soc. 6:52–53.

Belkin, D. A.
1962 Anaerobiosis in diving turtles. Physiologist, Washington 5:105.
1963 Anoxia: tolerance in reptiles. Science 139:492–493.
1964 Variations in heart rate during voluntary diving in the turtle *Pseudemys concinna*. Copeia 1964:321–330.
1965a Reduction of metabolic rate in response to starvation in the turtle *Sternotherus minor*. Copeia 1965:367–368.
1965b Critical oxygen tensions in turtles. Physiologist, Washington 8:109.
1968a Aquatic respiration and underwater survival of two freshwater turtle species. Resp. Physiol. 4:1–14.
1968b Anaerobic brain function: effects of stagnant and anoxic anoxia on persistence of breathing in reptiles. Science 162:1017–1018.

Belkin, D. A., and C. Gans
1968 An unusual chelonian feeding niche. Ecology 49:768–769.

Bellairs, A. d'A.
1957 Reptiles. Hutchinson Univ. Libr., London. 200 pp.

Bellairs, A. d'A., and R. Carrington
1966 The world of reptiles. Amer. Elsevier Publ. Co., New York. 154 pp.

Bellamy, D., and J. A. Petersen
1968 Anaerobiosis and the toxicity of cyanide in turtles. Comp. Biochem. Physiol. 24:543–548.

Beltz, R. E.
1954a Miscellaneous observations on captive Testudininae. Herpetologica 10:45–47.
1954b Notes on the winter behavior of captive nonindigenous Chelonia in southern California. Herpetologica 10:124.

Belusz, L. C., and R. J. Reed
1969   Some epizoophytes on six turtle species collected in Massachusetts and Michigan. Amer. Midl. Nat. 81:598–601.

Bennett, D. H., J. W. Gibbons, and J. C. Franson
1970   Terrestrial activity in aquatic turtles. Ecology 51:738–740.

Bentley, P. J., W. L. Bretz, and K. Schmidt-Nielsen
1967   Osmoregulation in the diamondback terrapin, *Malaclemys terrapin centrata*. J. Exp. Biol. 46:161–167.

Bentley, P. J., and K. Schmidt-Nielsen
1966   Cutaneous water loss in reptiles. Science 151:1547–1549.
1970   Comparison of water exchange in two aquatic turtles, *Trionyx spinifer* and *Pseudemys scripta*. Comp. Biochem. Physiol. 32:363–365.

Berkson, H.
1966   Physiological adjustments to prolonged diving in the Pacific green turtle (*Chelonia mydas agassizii*). Comp. Biochem. Physiol. 18:101–119.
1967   Physiological adjustments to deep diving in the Pacific green turtle (*Chelonia mydas agassizii*). Comp. Biochem. Physiol. 21:507–524.

Bierly, E. J.
1954   Turtles in Maryland and Virginia. Atlantic Nat. 9:244–249.

Bishop, S. C., and F. J. W. Schmidt
1931   The painted turtles of the genus *Chrysemys*. Field Mus. Nat. Hist. Zool. Ser. 18:123–139.

Bissett, D.
1968   Box turtle nesting. Int. Turtle & Tortoise Soc. J. 2(6):12–16, 36.

Blake, S. F.
1922   Sexual differences in coloration in the spotted turtle, *Clemmys guttata*. Proc. U. S. Natl. Mus. 59:463–469.

Blanchard, F. N.
1928   Amphibians and reptiles of the Douglas Lake region in northern Michigan. Copeia 1928 (167):42–51.

Blaney, R. M.
1968   Hybridization of the box turtles *Terrapene carolina* and *T. ornata* in western Louisiana. Proc. Louisiana Acad. Sci. 31:54–57.

Bleakney, J. S.
1955   Four records of the Atlantic ridley turtle, *Lepidochelys kempi*, from Nova Scotia waters. Copeia 1955:137.
1957   A snapping turtle, *Chelydra serpentina serpentina*, containing eighty-three eggs. Copeia 1957:143.
1958   Postglacial dispersal of the turtle *Chrysemys picta*. Herpetologica 14:101–104.
1963   Notes on the distribution and life histories of turtles in Nova Scotia. Canadian Field-Nat. 77:67–76.
1965   Reports of marine turtles from New England and Eastern Canada. Canadian Field-Nat. 79:120–128.
1967   Food items in two loggerhead sea turtles, *Caretta caretta caretta* (L.) from Nova Scotia. Canadian Field-Nat. 81:269–272.

Bocourt, M. F.
*1868   Description de quleques cheloniens nouveaux appartenant a la faune mexicaine. Ann. Sci. Nat. (5), 10:121–122.

Bogert, C. M.
1937   Note on the growth rate of the desert tortoise, *Gopherus agassizi*. Copeia 1937:191–192.
1957   The snorkel turtle. Nat. Hist. 66:240–241.

Bogert, C. M., and R. B. Cowles
1947   Moisture loss in relation to habitat selection in some Floridian reptiles. Amer. Mus. Novitates 1358:1–34.

Bogert, C. M., and J. A. Oliver
1945   A preliminary analysis of the herpetofauna of Sonora. Bull. Amer. Mus. Nat. Hist. 83:301–425.

Bogitsh, B. J.
1959   A new species of *Auridistomum* (Trematoda: Auridistomidae) from snapping turtles of Georgia. J. Parasitol. 45:631–633.

Boice, R.
1970   Competitive feeding behaviours in captive

Terrapene c. carolina. Anim. Behav. 18:703–710.

Bond, G. C.
1940   Serological studies of the Reptilia. III. Hemagglutinins and hemagglutinogens of turtle-blood. J. Immunol. 39:125–131.

Booth, K.
1958   Development of eggs and young of desert tortoise. Herpetologica 13:261–263.

Boycott, B. B., and R. W. Guillery
1962   Olfactory and visual learning in the red-eared terrapin, *Pseudemys scripta elegans* (Wied). J. Exp. Biol. 39:567–577.

Boycott, B. B., and M. W. Robins
1961   The care of young red-eared terrapins (*Pseudemys scripta elegans*) in the laboratory. British J. Herpetol. 2:206–210.

Boyer, D. R.
1963   Hypoxia: effects on heart rate and respiration in the snapping turtle. Science 140:813–814.
1965   Ecology of the basking habit in turtles. Ecology 46:99–118.

Brace, K. C., and P. D. Atland
1955   Red cell survival in the turtle. Amer. J. Physiol. 183:91–94.

Bragg, A. H., and W. N. Bragg
1957   The southern painted turtle in Oklahoma. Copeia 1957:307–308.

Brambel, C. E.
1941   Prothrombin activity of turtle blood and the effect of a synthetic vitamin K derivative. J. Cell. Comp. Physiol. 18:221–232.

Brattstrom, B. H.
1955   Notes on the herpetology of the Revillagigedo Islands, Mexico. Amer. Midl. Nat. 54:219–229.
1961   Some new fossil tortoises from western North America with remarks on the zoogeography and paleontology of tortoises. J. Paleontol. 35:543–560.
1965   Body temperatures of reptiles. Amer. Midl. Nat. 73:376–422.

Brattstrom, B. H., and A. Sturn
1959   A new species of fossil turtle from the Pliocene of Oregon, with notes on other fossil *Clemmys* from western North America. Bull. So. California Acad. Sci. 58:65–71.

Breckenridge, W. J.
1944   Reptiles and amphibians of Minnesota. Univ. Minnesota Press, Minneapolis. 202 pp.
1955   Observations on the life history of the soft-shelled turtle *Trionyx ferox*, with especial reference to growth. Copeia 1955:5–9.
1957   A large spiny soft-shelled turtle. Copeia 1957:232.
1960   A spiny soft-shelled turtle nest study. Herpetologica 16:284–285.

Breder, R. B.
1927   Turtle trailing: a new technique for studying the life habits of certain Testudinata. Zoologica 9:231–243.

Brenner, F. J.
1970   The influence of light and temperature on fat utilization in female *Clemmys insculpta*. Ohio J. Sci. 70:233–237.

Brock, V. E.
1947   The establishment of *Trionyx sinensis* in Hawaii. Copeia 1947:142.

Brode, W. E.
1958   Prehensility of the tails of two turtles (family Chelydridae). Copeia 1958:48.
1959   Notes on behavior of *Gopherus polyphemus*. Herpetologica 15:101–102.

Brongersma, L. D.
1961   Notes upon some sea turtles. Zool. Verh. Mus. Leiden 51:1–46.
1968a   Notes upon some sea turtles from Surinam. Proc. Koninkl. Nederlandse Acad., Ser. C 71:114–127.
1968b   Notes upon some turtles from the Canary Islands and Madeira. Proc. Koninkl. Nederlandse Acad., Ser. C 71:128–136.

Brown, B. C.
1950   An annotated check list of the reptiles and amphibians of Texas. Baylor Univ. Press, Waco, Texas. 257 pp.
1967   *Trionyx muticus muticus* in the Texas panhandle. S. W. Nat. 12:487.

Brown, B. C., and J. Haver
1952   An unusually large congregation of turtles. Herpetologica 8:2.

Brown, D. A.
1964   Nesting of a captive *Gopherus berlandieri* (Agassiz). Herpetologica 20:209–210.

Brown, J. R.
1927   A Blanding's turtle lays its eggs. Canadian Field-Nat. 41:185.

Brown, K. T.
1969   A linear area centralis extending across the turtle retina and stabilized to the horizon by non-visual cues. Vision Res. 9:1053–1062.

Brown, W. S.
1968   A northern range extension for *Trionyx spiniferus emoryi* in New Mexico. S. W. Nat. 13:106–107.

Brumwell, M. J.
1940   Notes on the courtship of the turtle, *Terrapene ornata*. Trans. Kansas Acad. Sci. 43:391.

Bundy, R. E.
1951   New locality records of reptiles in New Mexico. Copeia 1951:314.

Burda, D. J.
1965   Development of intracranial arterial patterns in turtles. J. Morphol. 116:171–188.

Burger, J. W.
1937   Experimental sexual photoperiodicity in the male turtle, *Pseudemys elegans* (Wied). Amer. Nat. 71:481–487.

Burger, W. L.
1952   A neglected subspecies of the turtle *Pseudemys scripta*. J. Tennessee Acad. Sci. 27:75–79.

Burghardt, G. M., and E. H. Hess
1966   Food imprinting in the snapping turtle, *Chelydra serpentina*. Science 151:108–109.

Burkett, R. D.
1967   An extension of known range in Texas for the stinkpot turtle, *Sternothaerus odoratus*. Trans. Kansas Acad. Sci. 69:361.

Burne, R. H.
1905   Anatomy of the leatherback turtles, *Dermochelys coriacea*. Proc. Sci. Meet. Zool. Soc. London 1:291–324.

Burnley, J. M.
1969   Diamondback terrapin. Int. Turtle & Tortoise Soc. J. 3(5):32–34.

Bury, R. B.
1963   Occurrence of *Clemmys m. marmorata* in north coastal California. Herpetologica, 18:283.
1970   *Clemmys marmorata*. Cat. Amer. Amphib. Rept. 100:1–3.

Bush, F. M.
1959   Foods of some Kentucky herptiles. Herpetologica 15:73–77.

Bustard, H. R.
1967a   Turtle biology at Heron Island. Int. Turtle & Tortoise Soc. J. 1(6):6–8, 37.
1967b   Mechanism of nocturnal emergence from the nest in green turtle hatchlings. Nature 214:317.
1969   Marine turtles in Queensland, Australia. IUCN Publ. (n.s.) 20:80–87.
1970   The adaptive significance of coloration in hatchling green sea turtles. Herpetologica 26:224–227.

Bustard, H. R., and P. Greenham
1968   Physical and chemical factors affecting hatching in the green sea turtle, *Chelonia mydas* (L.). Ecology 49:269–276.
1969   Nesting behavior of the green sea turtle on a Great Barrier Reef island. Herpetologica 25:93–102.

Bustard, H. R., and C. Limpus
1969   Observations on the flatback turtle *Chelonia depressa* Garman. Herpetologica 25:29–34.
1970   First international recapture of an Australian tagged loggerhead turtle. Herpetologica 26:358–359.

Bustard, H. R., K. Simkiss, and N. K. Jenkins
1969   Some analyses of artificially incubated eggs and hatchlings of green and loggerhead sea turtles. J. Zool. Soc. London 158:311–315.

Bustard, H. R., and K. P. Tognetti
1969   Green sea turtles: a discrete simulation of

density-dependent population regulation. Science 163:939–941.

Bychowsky, B. E.
1961 Monogenetic trematodes. Their systematics and physiology. AIBS, Washington. 627 pp.

Byrd, E. E.
1939 Studies on the blood flukes of the family Spirorchidae. Part II. Revision of the family and description of new species. J. Tennessee Acad. Sci. 14:116–161.

Cable, R. M., and F. M. Fisher
1961 A fifth species of *Neoechinorhynchus* (Acanthocephala) in turtles. J. Parasitol. 47:666–668.

Cable, R. M., and W. B. Hopp
1954 Acanthocephalan parasites of the genus *Neoechinorhynchus* in North American turtles with the descriptions of two new species. J. Parasitol. 40:674–680.

Cable, R. M., and C. R. Sanborn
1970 Two oviduct flukes from reptiles in Indiana: *Telorchis compactus* sp. n. and a previously described species. Proc. Helminthol. Soc. Washington 37:211–215.

Cagle, F. R.
1937 Egg laying habits of the slider turtle (*Pseudemys troostii*), the painted turtle (*Chrysemys picta*), and the musk turtle (*Sternotherus odoratus*). J. Tennessee Acad. Sci. 12:87–95.
1939 A system of marking turtles for future identification. Copeia 1939:170–172.
1942 Turtle populations in southern Illinois. Copeia 1942:155–162.
1944a Activity and winter changes of hatchling *Pseudemys*. Copeia 1944:105–109.
1944b Home range, homing behavior and migration in turtles. Misc. Publ. Mus. Zool. Univ. Michigan 61:1–34.
1944c Sexual maturity of the female of the turtle *Pseudemys scripta elegans*. Copeia 1944:149–152.
1945 Recovery from serious injury in the painted turtle. Copeia 1945:45.
1946 The growth of the slider turtle *Pseudemys scripta elegans*. Amer. Midl. Nat. 36:685–729.
1947 Color abnormalities in *Pseudemys scripta troostii* (Holbrook). Nat. Hist. Misc. 6:1–3.
1948a Sexual maturity in the male turtle, *Pseudemys scripta troostii*. Copeia 1948:108–111.
1948b The growth of turtles in Lake Glendale, Illinois. Copeia 1948:197–203.
1950 The life history of the slider turtle, *Pseudemys scripta troostii* (Holbrook). Ecol. Monogr. 20:31–54.
1952a A key to the amphibians and reptiles of Louisiana. Tulane Univ., New Orleans, 42 pp.
1952b The status of the turtles *Graptemys pulchra* Baur and *Graptemys barbouri* Carr and Marchand, with notes on their natural history. Copeia 1952:223–234.
1952c A Louisiana terrapin population (*Malaclemys*). Copeia 1952:74–76.
*1953a Two new subspecies of *Graptemys pseudogeographica*. Occ. Pap. Mus. Zool. Univ. Michigan 546:1–17.
1953b The status of the turtle *Graptemys oculifera* (Baur). Zoologica 38:137–144.
*1954a Two new species of the genus *Graptemys*. Tulane Stud. Zool. 1:167–186.
1954b Observations on the life cycles of painted turtles (genus *Chrysemys*). Amer. Midl. Nat. 52:225–235.
1955 Courtship behavior in juvenile turtles. Copeia 1955:307.

Cagle, F. R., and A. H. Chaney
1950 Turtle populations in Louisiana. Amer. Midl. Nat. 43:383–388.

Cagle, F. R., and J. Tihen
1948 Retention of eggs by the turtle *Deirochelys reticularia*. Copeia 1948:66.

Cahn, A. R.
1937 The turtles of Illinois. Illinois Biol. Monogr. 35:1–218.

Caldwell, D. K.
1958 On the status of the Atlantic leatherback turtle, *Dermochelys coriacea coriacea*, as a visitant to Florida nesting beaches, with natural history notes. Quart. J. Florida Acad. Sci. 21:285–291.

1959 The loggerhead turtles of Cape Romain, South Carolina. Bull. Florida St. Mus. 4:319–348.

1960 Sea turtles of the United States. Bur. Comm. Fish. Leaflet 492:1–20.

1962a Comments on the nesting behavior of Atlantic loggerhead sea turtles, based primarily on tagging returns. Quart. J. Florida Acad. Sci. 25:287–302.

1962b Growth measurements of young captive Atlantic sea turtles in temperate waters. Los Angeles Co. Mus. Cont. Sci. 50:1–8.

1962c Sea turtles in Baja Californian waters (with special reference to those of the Gulf of California), and the description of a new subspecies of north-eastern Pacific green turtle. Los Angeles Co. Mus. Cont. Sci. 61:1–31.

1962d Carapace length-body weight relationship and size and sex ratio of the northeastern Pacific green sea turtle, *Chelonia mydas carrinegra*. Los Angeles Co. Mus. Cont. Sci. 62:1–10.

1963a Second record of the loggerhead sea turtle, *Caretta caretta gigas*, from the Gulf of California. Copeia 1963:568–569.

1963b The sea turtle fishery of Baja California, Mexico. California Fish and Game 49:140–151.

1966 A nesting report on the American ridley. Int. Turtle & Tortoise Soc. J. 1(1):10–13, 30, 48.

1968 Baby loggerhead turtles associated with sargassum weed. Quart. J. Florida Acad. Sci. 31:271–272.

1969 Hatchling green sea turtles, *Chelonia mydas*, at sea in the northeastern Pacific Ocean. Bull. So. California Acad. Sci. 68:113–114.

Caldwell, D. K., F. H. Berry, A. F. Carr, and R. A. Ragotzkie
1959 Multiple and group nesting by the Atlantic loggerhead turtle. Bull. Florida St. Mus. 4:309–318.

Caldwell, D. K., and M. C. Caldwell
1962 The black "steer" of the Gulf of California. Los Angeles Co. Mus., Quart. Sci. Hist. 1:14–17.

1969 Addition of the leatherback sea turtle to the known prey of the killer whale, *Orcinus orca*. J. Mammal. 50:636.

Caldwell, D. K., and A. F. Carr
1957 Status of the sea turtle fishery in Florida. Trans. Twenty-second North Amer. Wildlife Conf. 457–463.

Caldwell, D. K., A. F. Carr, and T. R. Hellier
1955a A nest of the Atlantic leatherback turtle, *Dermochelys coriacea coriacea* (Linnaeus), on the Atlantic Coast of Florida, with a summary of American nesting records. Quart. J. Florida Acad. Sci. 18:279–284.

1955b Natural history notes on the Atlantic loggerhead turtle, *Caretta caretta caretta*. Quart. J. Florida Acad. Sci. 18:292–302.

Caldwell, D. K., A. F. Carr, and L. H. Ogren
1959 Nesting and migration of the Atlantic loggerhead turtle. Bull. Florida St. Mus. 4:295–308.

Caldwell, D. K., and R. S. Casebeer
1964 A note on the nesting of the eastern Pacific ridley sea turtle, *Lepidochelys olivacea*. Herpetologica 20:213.

Caldwell, D. K., and D. S. Erdman
1969 Pacific ridley sea turtle, *Lepidochelys olivacea*, in Puerto Rico. Bull. So. California Acad. Sci. 68:112.

Caldwell, D. K., and W. F. Rathjen
1969 Unrecorded West Indian nesting sites for the leatherback and hawksbill sea turtles, *Dermochelys coriacea* and *Eretmochelys i. imbricata*. Copeia 1969:622–623.

Caldwell, D. K., W. F. Rathjen, and B. C. C. Hsu
1969 Surinam ridleys at sea. Int. Turtle & Tortoise Soc. J. 3(1):4–5, 23.

Caldwell, M. C., and D. K. Caldwell
1962 Factors in the ability of the northeastern Pacific green turtle to orient toward the sea from the land, a possible coordinate in long-range navigation. Los Angeles Co. Mus. Cont. Sci. 60:1–27.

Camin, J. H., W. W. Moss, J. H. Oliver, Jr., and G. Singer
1967 Cloacariidae, a new family of cheyletoid mites from the cloaca of aquatic turtles (Acari: Acariformes: Eleutherengona). J. Med. Entomol. 4:261–272.

Camp, C. L.
1916   Notes on the local distribution and habits of the amphibians and reptiles of southeastern California in the vicinity of the Turtle Mountains. Univ. California Publ. Zool. 12:503–544.

Campbell, H. W.
1960   The bog turtle in Maryland. Maryland Nat. 30:15–16.
1969   The unsung chicken turtle. Int. Turtle & Tortoise Soc. J. 3(5):22–24, 36.

Campbell, H. W., and W. E. Evans
1967   Sound production in two species of tortoises. Herpetologica 23:204–209.

Carl, G. C.
1944   The reptiles of British Columbia. British Columbia Prov. Mus., Handbook 3:5–60.

Carpenter, C. C.
1955   Sounding turtles: a field locating technique. Herpetologica 11:120.
1956   Carapace pits in the three-toed box turtle, *Terrapene carolina triunguis* (Chelonia—Emydidae). S. W. Nat. 1:83–86.
1957   Hibernation, hibernacula and associated behavior of the three-toed box turtle (*Terrapene carolina triunguis*). Copeia 1957:278–282.

Carr, A. F.
1935   The identity and status of two turtles of the genus *Pseudemys*. Copeia 1935:147–148.
*1937a A new turtle from Florida, with notes on *Pseudemys floridana mobilensis* (Holbrook). Occ. Pap. Mus. Zool. Univ. Michigan 348:1–7.
1937b The status of *Pseudemys scripta* (Schoepff) and *Pseudemys troostii* (Holbrook). Herpetologica 1:75–77.
*1938a *Pseudemys nelsoni*, a new turtle from Florida. Occ. Pap. Boston Soc. Nat. Hist. 8:305–310.
*1938b A new subspecies of *Pseudemys floridana*, with notes on the *floridana* complex. Copeia 1938:105–109.
1938c Notes on the *Pseudemys scripta* complex. Herpetologica 1:131–135.
1940   A contribution to the herpetology of Florida. Univ. Florida Biol. Sci. Ser. 3:1–118.
1942a Notes on sea turtles. Proc. New England Zool. Club 21:1–16.
1942b The status of *Pseudemys floridana texana* with notes on parallelism in *Pseudemys*. Proc. New England Zool. Club 21:69–76.
1946   Status of the mangrove terrapin. Copeia 1946:170–172.
1948   Sea turtles on a tropical island. Fauna 10:50–55.
1949   The identity of *Malacoclemmys kohnii* Baur. Herpetologica 5:9–10.
1952   Handbook of turtles. Comstock Publ. Assoc., Ithaca, N.Y. 542 pp.
1954a The passing of the fleet. AIBS Bull. October:17–19.
1954b The zoogeography and migrations of sea turtles. Yrbk. Amer. Philos. Soc. 1954:138–140.
1955   The windward road. Alfred A. Knopf, Inc., New York. 258 pp.
1957   Notes on the zoogeography of the Atlantic sea turtles of the genus *Lepidochelys*. Rev. Biol. Trop. 5:45–61.
1961a The ridley mystery today. Anim. Kingdom 58:7–12.
1961b Pacific turtle problem. Nat. Hist. 70:64–71.
1962   Orientation problems in the high seas travel and terrestrial movements of marine turtles. Amer. Sci. 50:359–374.
1963a The reptiles. Life Nature Library. Time, Inc., New York. 192 pp.
1963b Panspecific reproductive convergence in *Lepidochelys kempi*. Ergebnisse der Biologie 26:298–303.
1964   Transoceanic migrations of the green turtle. BioScience 14:49–52.
1965   The navigation of the green turtle. Sci. Amer. 212:78–86.
1967a So excellent a fishe. Natural History Press, Garden City, N.Y. 248 pp.
1967b Adaptive aspects of the scheduled travel of *Chelonia*. In Storm, R. M. (ed.): Animal orientation and navigation. Oregon St. Univ. Press, Corvallis. Pp. 35–55.
1967c 100 turtle eggs. Nat. Hist. 76:46–51.
1967d No one knows where the turtles go. Nat. Hist. 76:40–43, 52–59.
1968a Sea turtles: a vanishing asset. IUCN Publ. (n.s.) 13:162–168.
1968b Turtles endangered. Florida Nat. 41:83–84.
1969   Survival outlook of the West Caribbean green turtle colony. IUCN Publ. (n.s.) 20:13–16.

Carr, A. F., and D. K. Caldwell
1956   The ecology and migrations of sea turtles, 1. Results of field work in Florida, 1955. Amer. Mus. Novitates 1793:1–23.
1958   The problem of the Atlantic ridley turtle. Rev. Biol. Trop. 6:245–262.

Carr, A. F., and M. H. Carr
1970   Modulated reproductive periodicity in *Chelonia.* Ecology 51:335–337.

Carr, A. F., and J. W. Crenshaw, Jr.
1957   A taxonomic reappraisal of the turtle *Pseudemys alabamensis* Baur. Bull. Florida St. Mus. 2:25–42.

Carr, A. F., and L. Giovannoli
1957   The ecology and migrations of sea turtles, 2. Results of field work in Costa Rica, 1955. Amer. Mus. Novitates 1835:1–32.

Carr, A. F., and C. J. Goin
1955   Guide to the reptiles, amphibians and freshwater fishes of Florida. Univ. Florida Press, Gainesville. 341 pp.

Carr, A. F., and D. Goodman
1970   Ecologic implications of size and growth in *Chelonia.* Copeia 1970:783–786.

Carr, A. F., and H. Hirth
1961   Social facilitation in green turtle siblings. Anim. Behav. 9:68–70.
1962   The ecology and migrations of sea turtles, 5. Comparative features of isolated green turtle colonies. Amer. Mus. Novitates 2091:1–42.

Carr, A. F., H. Hirth, and L. Ogren
1966   The ecology and migrations of sea turtles, 6. The hawksbill turtle in the Caribbean Sea. Amer. Mus. Novitates 2248:1–29.

Carr, A. F., and R. M. Ingle
1959   The green turtle (*Chelonia mydas mydas*) in Florida. Bull. Mar. Sci. Gulf & Caribbean 9:315–320.

Carr, A. F., and L. T. Marchand
*1942   A new turtle from the Chipola River, Florida. Proc. New England Zool. Club 20:95–100.

Carr, A. F., and L. Ogren
1959   The ecology and migrations of sea turtles,

3. *Dermochelys* in Costa Rica. Amer. Mus. Novitates 1958:1–29.
1960   The ecology and migrations of sea turtles, 4. The green turtle in the Caribbean Sea. Bull. Amer. Mus. Nat. Hist. 121:1–48.

Carr, A. F., and R. E. Schroeder
1967   Caribbean green turtle, imperiled gift of the sea. Natl. Geog. 131:876–890.

Carr, A. F., and D. Sweat
1969   Long-range recovery of a tagged yearling *Chelonia* on the east coast of North America. Biol. Conserv. 1:341–342.

Chaikoff, I. L., and C. Entenman
1946   The lipides of blood, liver, and egg yolk of the turtle. J. Biol. Chem. 166:683–689.

Chaney, A., and C. L. Smith
1950   Methods for collecting mapturtles. Copeia 1950:323–324.

Chavez, H.
1966   Propositos y finalidades. Bol. Progr. Nac. Marc. Tortugas Mar., Mexico. 1(1):1–16.
1967   Nota preliminar sobre la recaptura de ejemplares marcados de tortuga lora, *Lepidochelys olivacea kempii.* Bol. Progr. Nac. Marc. Tortugas Mar., Mexico. 1(6):1–5.
1969   Tagging and recapture of the lora turtle (*Lepidochelys kempi*). Int. Turtle & Tortoise Soc. J. 3(4):14–19, 32–36.

Chavez, H., M. Contreras G., and T. P. E. Hernandez D.
1968a   On the coast of Tamaulipas. I. Int. Turtle & Tortoise Soc. J. 2(4):20–29, 37.
1968b   On the coast of Tamaulipas. II. Int. Turtle & Tortoise Soc. J. 2(5):16–19, 27–34.

Chermock, R. L.
1952   A key to the amphibians and reptiles of Alabama. Alabama Mus. Nat. Hist. Pap. 33:1–88.

Chidester, F. E.
1916   Sarcophagid larvae from the painted turtle. J. Parasitol. 2:48–49.

Clark, D. B., and J. W. Gibbons
1969   Dietary shift in the turtle *Pseudemys scripta* (Schoepff) from youth to maturity. Copeia 1969:704–706.

Clark, H. W.
1935   On the occurrence of a probable hybrid between the eastern and western box turtles, *Terrapene carolina* and *T. ornata*, near Lake Maxinkuckee, Indiana. Copeia 1935:148–150.

Clark, H. W., and J. B. Southall
1920   Fresh water turtles: a source of meat supply. U. S. Bur. Fish. Doc. 889:3–20.

Clark, N. B.
1965   Experimental and histological studies of the parathyroid glands of freshwater turtles. Gen. Comp. Endocrinol. 5:297–312.
1967   Influence of estrogens upon serum calcium phosphate and protein concentrations of fresh-water turtles. Comp. Biochem. Physiol. 20:823–834.
1968   Calcitonin studies in turtles. Endocrinology 83:1145–1148.

Clarke, R. F.
1950   Notes on the ornate box turtle. Herpetologica 6:54.
1953   Additional turtle records for Kansas. Trans. Kansas Acad. Sci. 56:438–439.
1956   A case of possible overwintering of *Terrapene o. ornata* in a well. Herpetologica 12:131.
1958   An ecological study of reptiles and amphibians in Osage County, Kansas. Emporia St. Res. Stud. 7(1):1–52.

Cloudsley-Thompson, J. L.
1968   Hot blood or cold? Thermoregulation in terrestrial poikilotherms. Science Prog. 56:499–509.

Cochran, D. M.
1952   Nature's tank, the turtle. Natl. Geog. 101:665–684.

Cochran, D. M., and C. J. Goin
1970   The new field book of reptiles and amphibians. G. P. Putnam's Sons, New York. 359 pp.

Cohen, E.
1954   A comparison of the total protein and albumin content of the blood sera of some reptiles. Science 119:98–99.

Cohen, E., and G. B. Strickler
1958   Absence of albuminlike serum proteins in turtles. Science 127:1392.

Coker, R. E.
1906   The cultivation of the diamond-back terrapin. North Carolina Geol. Survey Bull. 14:1–69.
1920   The diamond-back terrapin: past, present and future. Sci. Monthly 11:171–186.

Collins, F. S.
1907   Some new green algae. Rhodora 9:197–202.

Conant, R.
1938   On the seasonal occurrence of reptiles in Lucas County, Ohio. Herpetologica 1:137–144.
1945   An annotated list of the amphibians and reptiles of the Del-Mar-Va Peninsula. Publ. Soc. Nat. Hist. Delaware, 8 pp.
1951a   The reptiles of Ohio. Univ. Notre Dame Press, Notre Dame, Indiana. 284 pp.
1951b   The red-bellied terrapin, *Pseudemys rubriventris* (LeConte), in Pennsylvania. Ann. Carnegie Mus. 32:281–290.
1958   A field guide to reptiles and amphibians. Houghton Mifflin Co., Boston. 366 pp.
1961   The softshell turtle, *Trionyx spinifer*, introduced and established in New Jersey. Copeia 1961:355–356.
1962   Notes on the distribution of reptiles and amphibians in the Pine Barrens of southern New Jersey. New Jersey Nat. News 17:16–21.

Conant, R., and R. M. Bailey
1936   Some herpetological records from Monmouth and Ocean counties, New Jersey. Occ. Pap. Mus. Zool. Univ. Michigan 328:1–10.

Conant, R., and A. Downs
1940   Miscellaneous notes on the eggs and young of reptiles. Zoologica 25:33–48.

Conant, R., and C. J. Goin
*1948   A new subspecies of soft-shelled turtle from the central United States, with comments on the application of the name *Amyda*. Occ. Pap. Mus. Zool. Univ. Michigan 510:1–19.

Conant, R., and R. G. Hudson
1949   Longevity records for reptiles and amphibians in the Philadelphia Zoological Garden. Herpetologica 5:1–8.

Conant, R., M. B. Trautman, and E. B. McLean
1964   The false map turtle, *Graptemys pseudo-*

geographica (Gray), in Ohio. Copeia 1964: 212–213.

Cooper, J. E.
1956   A Maryland hibernation site for herptiles. Herpetologica 12:238.

1958   Some albino reptiles and polydactylous frogs. Herpetologica 14:54–56.

1959   The turtle *Pseudemys scripta* feral in Maryland. Herpetologica 15:44.

1961   Further notes on non-indigenous turtles in Maryland. Herpetologica 17:209–210.

Cooper, J. G.
*1863   Description of *Xerobates agassizii*. Proc. California Acad. Sci. 2:118–123.

Cooper, T. E.
1968   Courtship patterns of *Terrapene carolina*. Int. Turtle & Tortoise Soc. J. 2(3):38.

Cosgrove, G. E.
1965   The radiosensitivity of snakes and box turtles. Rad. Res. 25:706–712.

Coulter, M. W.
1957   Predation by snapping turtles upon aquatic birds in Maine marshes. J. Wildlife Mgt. 21:17–21.

1958   Distribution, food, and weight of the snapping turtle in Maine. Maine Field Nat. 14:53–62.

Cowan, F. B. M.
1967   Comparative studies on the cranial glands of turtles with special reference to salt secretion. Amer. Zool. 7:810.

1969   Gross and microscopic anatomy of the orbital glands of *Malaclemys* and other emydine turtles. Canadian J. Zool. 47:723–729.

Cozzolino, A.
1938   Osservazioni etologiche sulla *Chelonia mydas* delle coste Somalia Italiana. Riv. Biol. Colon. 1:241–248.

Crandall, R. B.
1960   The life history and affinities of the turtle lung fluke, *Heronimus chelydrae* MacCallum, 1902. J. Parasitol. 46:289–307.

Crans, W. J.
1968   *Aedes atlanticus* Dyar and Knab, feeding on turtles. Mosquito News 28:239.

Crans, W. J., and E. G. Rockel
1968   The mosquitoes attracted to turtles. Mosquito News 28:332–337.

Crenshaw, J. W.
1962   Variation in the serum albumins and other blood proteins of turtles of the Kinosternidae. Physiol. Zool. 35:157–165.

1965   Serum protein variation in an interspecies hybrid swarm of turtles of the genus *Pseudemys*. Evolution 19:1–15.

Crenshaw, J. W., and M. N. Hopkins
1955   The relationships of the soft-shelled turtles *Trionyx ferox ferox* and *Trionyx ferox aspera*. Copeia 1955:13–23.

Cribb, A. V.
1969   Algae on a hawk's bill turtle. Queensland Nat. 19:108–109.

Crites, J. L.
1963   Dracontiasis in Ohio carnivores and reptiles with a discussion of the dracunculid taxonomic problem. (Nematoda: Dracunculidae). Ohio J. Sci. 63:1–6.

Crooks, F. D., and P. W. Smith
1958   An instance of twinning in the box turtle. Herpetologica 14:170–171.

Culbertson, G.
1907   Some notes on the habits of the common box turtle (*Cistudo carolina*). Proc. Indiana Acad. Sci. 1907:78–79.

Cunningham, B.
1923   Some phases in the development of *Chrysemys cinerea*. J. Elisha Mitch. Soc. 38:51–73.

1939   Effect of temperature upon the developmental rate of the embryo of the diamond-back terrapin (*Malaclemys centrata* Lat.). Amer. Nat. 73:381–384.

Cunningham, B., and E. Huene
1938   Further studies on water absorption by reptile eggs. Amer. Nat. 72:380–385.

Cunningham, B., and A. Hurwitz
1936   Water absorption by reptile eggs during incubation. Amer. Nat. 70:590–595.

Cunningham, J. G.
1960   Observations on *Sternothaerus odoratus* in Marshall County, Indiana. Copeia 1960:53.

Daniel, R. S., and K. V. Smith
1947   Migration of newly hatched loggerhead turtles toward the sea. Science 106:398–399.

Dantzler, W. H., and B. Schmidt-Nielsen
1966   Excretion in fresh-water turtle (*Pseudemys scripta*) and desert tortoise (*Gopherus agassizii*). Amer. J. Physiol. 210:198–210.

DasGupta, B. M.
1935   The occurrence of a *Trepomonas* sp. in the caecum of turtles. J. Parasitol. 21:125–126.

Daudin, F. M.
*1802   Histoire naturelle des reptiles. Paris. 2:1–326.

Davis, J. D., and C. G. Jackson
1970   Copulatory behavior in the red-eared turtle, *Pseudemys scripta elegans* (Wied). Herpetologica 26:238–240.

Daw, J. C., D. P. Wenger, and R. M. Berne
1967   Relationship between cardiac glycogen and tolerance to anoxia in the western painted turtle, *Chrysemys picta bellii*. Comp. Biochem. Physiol. 22:69–73.

Decker, J. D.
1967   Motility of the turtle embryo, *Chelydra serpentina* (Linné). Science 157:952–954.

Deeds, O. J., and T. L. Jahn
1939   Coccidian infections of western painted turtles. Trans. Amer. Micros. Soc. 58:249–253.

DeFoliart, G. R.
1967   *Aedes canadensis* (Theobald) feeding on Blanding's turtle. J. Med. Entomol. 4:31.

DeGiusti, D. L.
1970   Additional studies on the life cycle of *Haemoproteus metchnikovi* from the turtle, *Chrysemys picta marginata*. J. Parasitol. 56(4) sect. 2:70–71.

DeGiusti, D. L., and P. J. Batten
1951   Notes on *Haemoproteus metchnikovi* in turtles from Wisconsin, Michigan, and Louisiana. J. Parasitol. 37 (suppl.):12.

Deraniyagala, P. E. P.
1930   Testudinate evolution. Proc. Zool. Soc. London 48:1057–1070.

*1933   The loggerhead turtles (Carettidae) of Ceylon. Ceylon J. Sci. (B), 18:61–72.

1939   The tetrapod reptiles of Ceylon. Vol. I. Colombo Mus. Nat. Hist. Ser. 412 pp.

1952   The loggerhead turtles (Carettinae) of Europe. Herpetologica 8:57–58.

1957   The breeding grounds of the luth and the ridley. Herpetologica 13:110.

1964   A comparison of the cephalic scalation of *Dermochelys coriacea* with that of the Cheloniidae (Reptilia, Testudinata). Senck. biol. 45:349–352.

DeSilva, G. S.
1969a   Turtle conservation in Sabah. Sabah Soc. J. 5:6–26.

1969b   Statement on marine turtles in the State of Sabah. IUCN Publ. (n.s.) 20:75–79.

DeSola, C. R., and F. Abrams
1933   Testudinata from southeastern Georgia, including the Okefinokee Swamp. Copeia 1933:10–12.

Dickinson, W. E.
1965   Handbook of amphibians and turtles of Wisconsin. Milwaukee Pub. Mus. Pop. Handbk. Ser. 10:1–45.

Dimond, M. T.
1954   The reactions of developing snapping turtles, *Chelydra serpentina serpentina* (Linné), to thiourea. J. Exp. Zool. 127:93–115.

1970   Iodine uptake and thyroid activity in developing turtles. Amer. Zool. 10:492.

Dinkins, A.
1954   A brief observation on male combat in *Clemmys insculpta*. Herpetologica 10:20.

Ditmars, R. L.
1934   A review of the box turtles. Zoologica (N.Y.) 17:1–44.

Dixon, J. R.
1960   Epizoophytic algae on some turtles of Texas and Mexico. Texas J. Sci. 12:36–38.

Dobie, J. L.
1968   Shelled eggs in the urinary bladder of an alligator snapping turtle, *Macroclemys temmincki*. Herpetologica 24:328–330.

Dobie, J. L., L. H. Ogren, and J. F. Fitzpatrick
1961   Food notes and records of the Atlantic ridley turtle (*Lepidochelys kempi*) from Louisiana. Copeia 1961:109–110.

Dodge, C. H.
1956a The musk turtle in Iowa. Herpetologica 12: 176.
1956b An unusually large Blanding's turtle from Iowa. Herpetologica 12:328.

Dodge, C. H., and G. E. Folk
1963   Notes on comparative tolerance of some Iowa turtles to oxygen deficiency (hypoxia). Proc. Iowa Acad. Sci. 70:438–441.

Dodge, C. H., and L. S. Mitler
1955   The yellow mud turtle, *Kinosternon flavescens spooneri* Smith, in Iowa. Nat. Hist. Misc. 144:1–3.

Dodge, C. H., and C. C. Wunder
1962   Growth of turtles during continual centrifugation. Proc. Iowa Acad. Sci. 69:594–599.

Dolbeer, R. A.
1969   Population density and home range size of the eastern box turtle (*Terrapene c. carolina*) in eastern Tennessee. A.S.B. Bull. 16:49.

Donoso-Barros, R.
1964   Nota sobre *Lepidochelys kempi* en las costas de Cumaná. Lagena 2:20–21.

Dowling, H. G.
1956   Geographic relations of Ozarkian amphibians and reptiles. S. W. Nat. 1:174–189.
1957   A review of the amphibians and reptiles of Arkansas. Univ. Arkansas Mus. Occ. Pap. 3:1–51.

Doyle, R. E., and A. F. Moreland
1968   Diseases of turtles. Lab. Anim. Dig. 4:3–6.

Dozy, A. M., C. A. Reynolds, J. M. Still, and T. H. J. Huisman
1964   Studies on animal hemoglobins. I. Hemoglobins in turtles. J. Exp. Zool. 155:343–347.

Driml, M.
1961   Electron and light microscope studies of *Endamoeba terrapinae*. Proc. Iowa Acad. Sci. 68:581–585.

Duellman, W. E.
1965   A biogeographic account of the herpetofauna of Michoacán, Mexico. Univ. Kansas Publ. Mus. Nat. Hist. 15:627–709.

Duellman, W. E., and A. Schwartz
1958   Amphibians and reptiles of southern Florida. Bull. Florida St. Mus. 3:81–324.

Dundee, H. A.
1950   *Kinosternon subrubrum hippocrepis* (Gray) in Oklahoma. Herpetologica 6:138–139.

Dunlap, C. E.
1955   Notes on the visceral anatomy of the giant leatherback turtle (*Dermochelys coriacea* Linnaeus). Bull. Tulane Med. Fac. 14:55–69.

Dunlap, D. G.
1967   Selected records of amphibians and reptiles from South Dakota. Proc. South Dakota Acad. Sci. 46:100–106.

Dunn, R. S., and A. M. Perks
1970   A new plasma kinin in the turtle, *Pseudemys scripta elegans*. Experientia (Basel) 26:1220–1221.

Dunson, W. A.
1960   Aquatic respiration in *Trionyx spinifer asper*. Herpetologica 16:277–283.
1967a Relationship between length and weight in the spiny softshell turtle. Copeia 1967:483–485.
1967b Sodium fluxes in fresh-water turtles. J. Exp. Zool. 165:171–182.
1970   Some aspects of electrolyte and water balance in three estuarine reptiles, the diamondback terrapin, American and "salt water" crocodiles. Comp. Biochem. Physiol. 32:161–174.

Dunson, W. A., and R. D. Weymouth
1965   Active uptake of sodium by softshell turtles (*Trionyx spinifer*). Science 149:67–69.

Edgren, R. A.
1942   A nesting rendezvous of the musk turtle. Chicago Nat. 5:63.
1949   Variation in the size of eggs of the turtles *Chelydra s. serpentina* (Linné) and *Sternotherus odoratus* (Latreille). Nat. Hist. Misc. 53:1.

1956   Egg size in the musk turtle, *Sternotherus odoratus* Latreille. Nat. Hist. Misc. 152:1–3.

1960a   Ovulation time in the musk turtle, *Sternothaerus odoratus*. Copeia 1960:60–61.

1960b   A seasonal change in bone density in female musk turtles, *Sternothaerus odoratus* (Latreille). Comp. Biochem. Physiol. 1:213–217.

1968   Mossbacks. Turtle-algae relationships. Int. Turtle & Tortoise Soc. J. 2(6):30–31.

Edgren, R. A., and M. K. Edgren
1955   Thermo-regulation in the musk turtle, *Sternotherus odoratus* Latreille. Herpetologica 11:213–217.

Edgren, R. A., M. K. Edgren, and L. H. Tiffany
1953   Some North American turtles and their epizoophytic algae. Ecology 34:733–740.

Ediminster, F. C.
1953   Snapping turtle catches pheasant. J. Wildlife Mgt. 17:383.

Edney, J. M.
1949   *Haemogregarina stepanowi* Danilewsky (1885) in middle Tennessee turtles. J. Tennessee Acad. Sci. 24:220–222.

Edney, J. M., and W. R. Allen
1951   Age of the box turtle, *Terrapene carolina carolina* (Linnaeus). Copeia 1951:312.

Eglis, A.
1962   Tortoise behavior: a taxonomic adjunct. Herpetologica 18:1–8.

1967   *Clemmys muhlenbergi*, rarest of North American turtles. Anim. Kingdom 70:58–61.

Ehrenfeld, D. W.
1967   North, south, east, or west. Int. Turtle & Tortoise Soc. J. 1(5):24–29.

1968   The role of vision in the sea-finding orientation of the green turtle (*Chelonia mydas*). 2. Orientation mechanisms and range of spectral sensitivity. Anim. Behav. 16:281–287.

Ehrenfeld, D. W., and A. F. Carr
1967   The role of vision in the sea-finding orientation of the green turtle (*Chelonia mydas*). Anim. Behav. 15:25–36.

Ehrenfeld, D. W., and A. L. Koch
1967   Visual accommodation in the green turtle. Science 155:827–828.

Einem, G. E.
1956   Certain aspects of the natural history of the mud turtle, *Kinosternon bauri*. Copeia 1956:186–188.

Emerson, D. N.
1967   Preliminary study on seasonal liver lipids and glycogen and blood sugar levels in the turtle *Graptemys pseudogeographica* (Gray) from South Dakota. Herpetologica 23:68–70.

Emlen, S. T.
1969   Homing ability and orientation in the painted turtle *Chrysemys picta marginata*. Behaviour 33:58–76.

Englebert, V. E., and A. D. Young
1970   Erythropoiesis in peripheral blood of tuatara (*Sphenodon punctatus*) and turtle (*Malaclemys terrapin*). Canadian J. Zool. 48:209–212.

Ernst, C. H.
1964a   Further suggestions for the care of juvenile aquatic turtles. Philadelphia Herpetol. Soc. Bull. 12(1–4):18.

1964b   Social dominance and aggressiveness in a juvenile *Chrysemys picta picta*. Philadelphia Herpetol. Soc. Bull. 12(1–4):18–19.

1965   Bait preferences of some freshwater turtles. J. Ohio Herpetol. Soc. 5:53.

1966   Overwintering of hatchling *Chelydra serpentina* in southeastern Pennsylvania. Philadelphia Herpetol. Soc. Bull. 14(2):8–9.

1967a   Intergradation between the painted turtles *Chrysemys picta picta* and *Chrysemys picta dorsalis*. Copeia 1967:131–136.

1967b   Serum protein analysis: a taxonomic tool. Int. Turtle & Tortoise Soc. J. 1(3):34–36.

1967c   A mating aggregation of the turtle *Clemmys guttata*. Copeia 1967:473–474.

1967d   Notes on the herpetofauna of the White Oak Bird Sanctuary. Philadelphia Herpetol. Soc. Bull. 15:32–36.

1968a   Homing ability in the spotted turtle, *Clemmys guttata* (Schneider). Herpetologica 24:77–78.

1968b   Evaporative water-loss relationships of turtles. J. Herpetol. 2:159–161.

1968c   A turtle's territory. Int. Turtle & Tortoise Soc. J. 2(6):9, 34.

1969   Natural history and ecology of the painted

turtle, *Chrysemys picta* (Schneider). Ph.D. dissertation, University of Kentucky. 202 pp.

1970a   Home range of the spotted turtle, *Clemmys guttata* (Schneider). Copeia 1970:391–393.

1970b   Reproduction in *Clemmys guttata*. Herpetologica 26:228–232.

1970c   *Chrysemys picta* and its parasites. Int. Turtle & Tortoise Soc. J. 4(3):28–30.

1970d   The status of the painted turtle *Chrysemys picta* in Tennessee and Kentucky. J. Herpetol. 4:39–45.

1970e   Homing ability in the painted turtle, *Chrysemys picta* (Schneider). Herpetologica 26:399–403.

1971a   Seasonal incidence of leech infestation in the painted turtle, *Chrysemys picta*. J. Parasitol. 57:32.

1971b   Sexual cycles and maturity of the turtle *Chrysemys picta*. Biol. Bull. 140:191–200.

1971c   Growth in the painted turtle, *Chrysemys picta*, in southeastern Pennsylvania. Herpetologica. 27:135–141.

1971d   *Chrysemys picta*. Cat. Amer. Amphib. Rept. 106:1–4.

1971e   *Clemmys guttata*. Cat. Amer. Amphib. Rept. 124:1–2.

1971f   *Clemmys insculpta*. Cat. Amer. Amphib. Rept. 125:1–2.

1971g   Population dynamics and activity cycles of *Chrysemys picta* in southeastern Pennsylvania. J. Herpetol. 5:151–160.

1971h   Observations on the painted turtle, *Chrysemys picta*. J. Herpetol. 5:216–220.

1971i   Observations on the egg and hatchling of the American turtle, *Chrysemys picta*. British J. Herpetol. In press.

1971j   Temperature–activity relationships in the painted turtle, *Chrysemys picta*. Copeia. In press.

Ernst, C. H., and E. M. Ernst
1969   Turtles of Kentucky. Int. Turtle & Tortoise Soc. J. 3(5):13–15.

1971   The taxonomic status and zoogeography of the painted turtle, *Chrysemys picta*, in Pennsylvania. Herpetologica 27:390–396.

Ernst, C. H., and H. F. Hamilton
1969   Color preferences of some North American turtles. J. Herpetol. 3:176–180.

Ernst, C. H., and B. G. Jett
1969   An intergrade population of *Pseudemys scripta elegans* × *Pseudemys scripta troosti* in Kentucky. J. Herpetol. 3:103.

Ernst, C. H., S. Soenarjo, and H. F. Hamilton
1970   The retinal histology of the stinkpot, *Sternotherus odoratus*. Herpetologica 26:222–223.

Ernst, J. V., T. B. Stewart, J. R. Sampson, and G. T. Fincher
1969   *Eimeria chelydrae* n. sp. (Protozoa: Eimeriidae) from the snapping turtle, *Chelydra serpentina*. Bull. Wildlife Dis. Assoc. 5:410–411.

Esch, G. W., and J. W. Gibbons
1967   Seasonal incidence of parasitism in the painted turtle, *Chrysemys picta marginata* Agassiz. J. Parasitol. 53:818–821.

1970   Stress and parasitism. J. Parasitol. 56(4) sect. 2:420.

Eschscholtz, J. F.
*1829   Zoologischer Atlas, enthaltened Abbildungen und Beschreibungen neuer Thierarten während des Flottcapitains v. Kotzebue zweiter Reise um die Welt, auf den russisch-kairerlichen Kriegsschlupp Predpriaetie in dem Jahren 1823–1826. G. Reimer, Berlin. 1:1–28.

Evans, L. T.
1952   Endocrine relationships in turtles. III. Some effects of male hormone in turtles. Herpetologica 8:11–14.

1953   The courtship pattern of the box turtle, *Terrapene c. carolina*. Herpetologica 9:189–192.

1967   How are age and size related to mating in the wood turtle, *Clemmys insculpta*? Amer. Zool. 7:799.

1968   The evolution of courtship in the turtle species, *Terrapene carolina*. Amer. Zool. 8:695–696.

Evenden, F. G.
1948   Distribution of the turtles of western Oregon. Herpetologica 4:201–204.

Everhart, B. A.
1958   Notes on the helminths of *Pseudemys scripta elegans* (Wied, 1838) in areas of Texas and Oklahoma. Proc. Oklahoma Acad. Sci. 38:38–43.

Evermann, B. W., and H. W. Clark
1916 The turtles and bactrachians of the Lake Maxinkuckee region. Proc. Indiana Acad. Sci. 1916:472–518.

Ewing, H. E.
1926 The common box-turtle, a natural host for chiggers. Proc. Biol. Soc. Washington 39:19–20.
1933 Reproduction in the eastern box turtle, *Terrapene carolina carolina*. Copeia 1933:95–96.
1943 Continued fertility in female box turtles following mating. Copeia 1943:112–114.

Fahy, W. E.
1954 Loggerhead turtles, *Caretta caretta caretta*, from North Carolina. Copeia 1954:157–158.

Ferguson, D. E.
1962 Fish feeding on imported fire ants. J. Wildlife Mgt. 26:206–207.
1963 Notes concerning the effects of heptachlor on certain poikilotherms. Copeia 1963:441–443.

Ferguson, M. S.
1943 Development of eye flukes of fishes in the lenses of frogs, turtles, birds, and mammals. J. Parasitol. 29:136–142.

Feuer, R. C.
1970 Key to the skulls of recent adult North and Central American turtles. J. Herpetol. 4:69–75.

Fichter, L. S.
1969 Geographical distribution and osteological variation in fossil and recent specimens of two species of *Kinosternon* (Testudines). J. Herpetol. 3:113–119.

Finneran, L. C.
1948 Reptiles at Branford, Connecticut. Herpetologica 4:123–126.

Fishbeck, D. W., and J. C. Underhill
1959 A check list of the amphibians and reptiles of South Dakota. Proc. South Dakota Acad. Sci. 38:107–113.

Fisher, C.
1945 Early spring mating of the wood turtle. Copeia 1945:175–176.

Fisher, F. M.
1960 On acanthocephala of turtles, with the description of *Neoechinorhynchus emyditoides* n. sp. J. Parasitol. 46:257–266.

Fitch, H. S.
1956 Temperature responses in free-living amphibians and reptiles of northeastern Kansas. Univ. Kansas Publ. Mus. Nat. Hist. 8:417–476.
1958 Home ranges, territories, and seasonal movements of vertebrates of the University of Kansas Natural History Reservation. Univ. Kansas Publ. Mus. Nat. Hist. 11:63–326.

Fitter, R. S. R.
1961 The leathery turtle or luth. Oryx 6:116–125.

Folkerts, G. W.
1967 Notes on a hybrid musk turtle. Copeia 1967:479–480.
1968 Food habits of the striped-necked musk turtle, *Sternotherus minor peltifer* Smith and Glass. J. Herpetol. 2:171–173.

Folkerts, G. W., and R. H. Mount
*1969 A new subspecies of the turtle *Graptemys nigrinoda* Cagle. Copeia 1969:677–682.

Folkerts, G. W., and A. C. Skorepa
1967 A spotted turtle, *Clemmys guttata* (Schneider), from southeastern Georgia. Herpetologica 23:63.

Forbes, A., H. W. Deane, M. Neyland, and M. S. Gongaware
1958 Electroretinogram of fresh-water turtle: quantitative response to color shift. J. Neurophysiol. 21:247–262.

Forbes, R. B., and D. McKey-Fender
1968 A green turtle from the Oregon coast. Canadian J. Zool. 46:1079.

Fowler, H. W.
*1906 Some cold blooded vertebrates from the Florida Keys. Proc. Acad. Nat. Sci. Philadelphia. 59:77–113.

Fox, A. M.
1961 Active transport of sugar by turtle small intestine. Amer. Zool. 1:15.

Fox, A. M., and X. J. Musacchia
1959 Notes on the pH of the digestive tract of *Chrysemys picta*. Copeia 1959:337–339.

Frair, W.

1962a   Comparative serology of turtles with systematic implications. Diss. Abstr. 23:2262.

1962b   Current studies on chelonian serology. Serol. Mus. Bull. 27:7–8.

1963   Blood group studies with turtles. Science 140:1412–1414.

1964   Turtle family relationships as determined by serological tests. In Leone, C. A. (ed.): Taxonomic biochemistry and serology. Ronald Press, New York. Pp. 535–544.

1969   Aging of serum proteins and serology of marine turtles. Serol. Mus. Bull. 42:1–3.

1970   The world's largest living turtle. Salt Water Aquar. 6:235–241.

Frair, W., and B. Prol

1970   "Aitkanti" blood sampling. Int. Turtle & Tortoise Soc. J. 4(3):12–15, 33–34.

Frankel, H. M., A. Spitzer, J. Blaine, and E. P. Schoener

1969   Respiratory response of turtles (*Pseudemys scripta*) to changes in arterial blood gas composition. Comp. Biochem. Physiol. 31:535–546.

Frankel, H. M., G. Steinberg, and J. Gordon

1966   Effects of temperature on blood gases, lactate and pyruvate in turtle, *Pseudemys scripta elegans*, in vivo. Comp. Biochem. Physiol. 19:279–283.

Freeman, H. L.

1970   A comment on: a new subspecies of the turtle *Graptemys nigrinoda* Cagle. Herpetol. Rev. 2(1):3.

Fried, B., and W. Fee

1968   A method of obtaining turtle blood fluke eggs and miracidia. Turtox News 46:186–187.

Fuentes, C. D.

1967   Perspectivas del cultivo de tortugas marinas en el Caribe mexicano. Biol. Progr. Noc. Marc. Tortugas Mar., Mexico 1(10):1–9.

Fugler, C. M., and R. G. Webb

1957   Some noteworthy reptiles and amphibians from the states of Oaxaca and Veracruz. Herpetologica 13:103–108.

Gaffney, E. S.

1968   A revision of the chelonian genus *Bothremys*

(Pleurodira: Pelomedusidae). Fieldiana: Geol. 16:193–239.

Gage, S. H., and S. P. Gage

1886   Aquatic respiration in soft-shelled turtles: a contribution to the physiology of respiration in vertebrates. Amer. Nat. 20:233–236.

Galbreath, E. C.

1961   Two alligator snappers, *Macroclemys temmincki*, from southern Illinois. Trans. Illinois St. Acad. Sci. 54:134–135.

Gans, C., and A. S. Gaunt

1969   Shell and physiology of turtles. African Wildlife 23:197–207.

Gans, C., and T. S. Parsons (eds.)

1969–70   The biology of the Reptilia. I (1969), II (1970), III (1970). Academic Press, New York.

Garman, S.

*1880   On certain species of Chelonioidae. Bull. Mus. Comp. Zool. 6:123–126.

*1884   The reptiles of Bermuda. U. S. Natl. Mus. Bull. 25:285–303.

*1891   On a tortoise found in Florida and Cuba, *Cinosternum Baurii*. Bull. Essex Inst. 23:141–144.

Gaumer, A. E. H., and C. J. Goodnight

1957   Some aspects of the hematology of turtles as related to their activity. Amer. Midl. Nat. 58:332–340.

Gaunt, A. S., and C. Gans

1969   Mechanics of respiration in the snapping turtle, *Chelydra serpentina* (Linné). J. Morphol. 128:195–228.

Gehlbach, F. R.

1956   Annotated records of southwestern amphibians and reptiles. Trans. Kansas Acad. Sci. 59:364–372.

1965   Amphibians and reptiles from the Pliocene and Pleistocene of North America: a chronological summary and selected bibliography. Texas J. Sci. 17:56–70.

Gehlbach, F. R., and B. B. Collette

1959   Distributional and biological notes on the Nebraska herpetofauna. Herpetologica 15:141–143.

Gemmell, D. J.
 1969 Additional distribution records of the false
        map turtle and the short-horned lizard in
        North Dakota. Prairie Nat. 1:30.
 1970 Some observations on the nesting of the west-
        ern painted turtle, *Chrysemys picta belli*, in
        northern Minnesota. Canadian Field-Nat.
        84:308–309.

Gentry, G.
 1956 An annotated check list of the amphibians
        and reptiles of Tennessee. J. Tennessee Acad.
        Sci. 31:242–251.

Gibbons, J. W.
 1967a Variation in growth rates in three populations
        of the painted turtle *Chrysemys picta*. Her-
        petologica 23:296–303.
 1967b Possible underwater thermoregulation by tur-
        tles. Canadian J. Zool. 45:585.
 1968a Carapacial algae in a population of the
        painted turtle, *Chrysemys picta*. Amer. Midl.
        Nat. 79:517–519.
 1968b Population structure and survivorship in the
        painted turtle, *Chrysemys picta*. Copeia 1968:
        260–268.
 1968c Reproductive potential, activity, and cycles in
        the painted turtle, *Chrysemys picta*. Ecology
        49:399–409.
 1968d Observations on the ecology and population
        dynamics of the Blanding's turtle, *Emydoidea
        blandingi*. Canadian J. Zool. 46:288–290.
 1968e Growth rates of the common snapping turtle,
        Chelydra serpentina, in a polluted river. Her-
        petologica 24:266–267.
 1969a Structure and dynamics of the yellow-bellied
        turtle, *Pseudemys scripta* (Reptilia: Chelonia:
        Emydidae) in an artificially heated reservoir.
        A.S.B. Bull. 16:52.
 1969b Ecology and population dynamics of the
        chicken turtle, *Deirochelys reticularia*. Copeia
        1969:669–676.
 1970a Terrestrial activity and the population dy-
        namics of aquatic turtles. Amer. Midl. Nat.
        83:404–414.
 1970b Reproductive characteristics of a Florida
        population of musk turtles (*Sternothaerus
        odoratus*). Herpetologica 26:268–270.
 1970c Reproductive dynamics of a turtle (*Pseu-
        demys scripta*) population in a reservoir re-

ceiving heated effluent from a nuclear reactor.
Canadian J. Zool. 48:881–885.
 1970d Sex ratios in turtles. Res. Popul. Ecol. 12:
        252–254.

Gibbons, J. W., and G. W. Esch
 1970 Some intestinal parasites of the loggerhead
        musk turtle (*Sternothaerus m. minor*). J. Her-
        petol. 4:79–80.

Gibbons, J. W., and M. H. Smith
 1968 Evidence of orientation by turtles. Herpe-
        tologica 24:331–334.

Gibbons, J. W., and D. W. Tinkle
 1969 Reproductive variation between turtle popu-
        lations in a single geographic area. Ecology
        50:340–341.

Gilles-Baillien, M.
 1970 Urea and osmoregulation in the diamondback
        terrapin *Malaclemys centrata centrata* (La-
        treille). J. Exp. Biol. 52:691–697.

Gillette, D. D.
 1970 Breathing adaptations in *Trionyx*. Int. Turtle
        & Tortoise Soc. J. 4(3):18–19.

Glass, B. P.
 1949 Records of *Macrochelys temminckii* in Okla-
        homa. Copeia 1949:138–141.

Glass, B. P., and N. Hartweg
 *1951 *Kinosternon murrayi*, a new muskturtle of
        the *hirtipes* group from Texas. Copeia 1951:
        50–52.

Goff, C. C., and D. S. Goff
 1932 Egg laying and incubation of *Pseudemys flori-
        dana*. Copeia 1932:92–94.

Goff, D. S., and C. C. Goff
 1935 On the incubation of a clutch of eggs of
        Amyda ferox (Schneider). Copeia 1935:156.

Goin, C. J., and C. C. Goff
 1941 Notes on the growth rate of the gopher tur-
        tle, *Gopherus polyphemus*. Herpetologica
        2:66–68.

Goin, C. J., and O. B. Goin
 1962 Introduction to herpetology. W. H. Freeman
        and Co., San Francisco. 341 pp.

Goin, C. J., and C. G. Jackson
1965   Hemoglobin values of some amphibians and reptiles from Florida. Herpetologica 21:145–146.

Goldsmith, W. M.
1945   Notes on the egg laying habits of the softshell turtles. Proc. Iowa Acad. Sci. 51:447–449.

Goodchild, C. G., and E. S. Dennis
1967   Comparative egg counts and histopathology in turtles infected with *Spirorchis* (Trematoda: Spirorchiidae). J. Parasitol. 53:38–45.

Goodchild, C. G., and D. E. Kirk
1960   The life history of *Spirorchis elegans* Stunkard, 1923 (Trematoda: Spirorchiidae) from the painted turtle. J. Parasitol. 46:219–229.

Goodchild, C. G., and V. L. Martin
1969   A study of the validity of certain *Spirorchis* species (Trematoda: Digenea). A.S.B. Bull. 16:52.

Goodrich, J. P., and T. L. Jahn
1943   Epizoic Suctoria from turtles. Trans. Amer. Microsc. Soc. 62:245–253.

Gordon, H., and J. A. Fowler
1961   A new locality record for *Pseudemys scripta elegans* in Michigan. Copeia 1961:350.

Gordon, J., and H. M. Frankel
1963   Turtle blood gas composition at different body temperatures. Bull. New Jersey Acad. Sci. 8:23.

Gossette, R. L., and H. Hombach
1968   Body temperature change in the snapping turtle (*Chelydra serpentina*). Psychon. Sci. 13:177–178.

Gould, E.
1957   Orientation in box turtles, *Terrapene c. carolina* (Linnaeus). Biol. Bull. 112:336–348.
1959   Studies on the orientation of turtles. Copeia 1959:174–176.

Gourley, E. V.
1969   Orientation of the gopher tortoise, *Gopherus polyphemus* (Daudin). Diss. Abstr. Int. B. 31:446.

Graf, V.
1967   A spectral sensitivity curve and wavelength discrimination for the turtle *Chrysemys picta picta*. Vision Res. 7:915–928.

Graham, T. E.
1969   Pursuit of the Plymouth turtle. Int. Turtle & Tortoise Soc. J. 3(1):10–13.
1970   Growth rate of the spotted turtle, *Clemmys guttata*, in southern Rhode Island. J. Herpetol. 4:87–88.

Graham, T. E., and V. H. Hutchison
1969   Centenarian box turtles. Int. Turtles & Tortoise Soc. J. 3(3):25–29.

Granda, A. M.
1962   Electrical responses of the light-and-dark-adapted turtle eye. Vision Res. 2:343–356.
1965   Differential spectral sensitivity in the optic tectum and eye of the turtle. J. Gen. Physiol. 48:901–917.

Granda, A. M., and C. E. Stirling
1966   The spectral sensitivity of the turtle's eye to very dim lights. Vision Res. 6:143–152.

Grant, C.
1935   Notes on the spotted turtle in northern Indiana. Proc. Indiana Acad. Sci. 44:244–247.
1936a Herpetological notes from northern Indiana. Proc. Indiana Acad. Sci. 45:323–333.
1936b The southwestern desert tortoise, *Gopherus agassizii*. Zoologica 21:225–229.
1946a Data and field notes on the desert tortoise (*Gopherus agassizii*). Trans. San Diego Soc. Nat. Hist. 10:399–402.
1946b Identification of *Lepidochelys kempii* (Garman). Herpetologica 3:39.
1956   Aberrant lamination in two hawksbill turtles. Herpetologica 12:302.
1960a Differentiation of the southwestern tortoises (genus *Gopherus*) with notes on their habits. Trans. San Diego Soc. Nat. Hist. 12:441–448.
1960b *Gopherus*. Herpetologica 16:29–31.

Gray, J. E.
*1831 Synopsis reptilium. Part I. Cataphracta. Tortoises, crocodiles, and enaliosaurians. Treuttel, Wurtz, and Co., London. 78 pp.
*1856 On some new species of freshwater tortoises from North America, Ceylon and Australia, in the collection of the British Museum. Proc. Zool. Soc. London 1855:197–202.

Green, N. B.
1969   The occurrence and distribution of turtles in West Virginia. Proc. West Virginia Acad. Sci. 41:1-14.

Gregory, W. K.
1946   Pareiasaurs versus placodonts as near ancestors to the turtles. Bull. Amer. Mus. Nat. Hist. 86:279–326.

Grundhauser, J. W.
1960   Water balance in the turtle in response to season and hypothermia. Diss. Abstr. 20: 3803–3804.

Guidry, E. V.
1953   Herpetological notes from southeastern Texas. Herpetologica 9:49–56.

Gupta, S. P.
1961   On some trematodes from the intestine of the marine turtle, *Chelonia mydas*, from the Caribbean Sea. Canadian J. Zool. 39:293–298.

Gutierrez-Ballesteros, E., and D. H. Wenrich
1950   *Endolimax clevelandi*, n. sp., from turtles. J. Parasitol. 36:489–493.

Hadžiselimović, H., and M. Andelić
1967   Contribution to the knowledge of the ear in the sea turtle. Acta Anat. 66:460–477.

Hallinan, T.
1923   Observations made in Duval County, northern Florida, on the gopher tortoise (*Gopherus polyphemus*). Copeia 1923(115):11–20.

Hamilton, R. D.
1944   Notes on mating and migration in Berlandier's turtle. Copeia 1944:62.

Hamilton, W. J., Jr.
1940a   The summer foods of minks and raccoons on the Montezuma Marsh, New York. J. Wildlife Mgt. 4:80–84.
1940b   Observations on the reproductive behavior of the snapping turtle. Copeia 1940:124–126.
1947   Egg laying of *Trionyx ferox*. Copeia 1947:209.

Hammer, D. A.
1969   Parameters of a marsh snapping turtle population Lacreek Refuge, South Dakota. J. Wildlife Mgt. 33:995–1005.

Hansen, K. L.
1963   The burrow of the gopher tortoise. Quart. J. Florida Acad. Sci. 26:353–360.

Harbison, C. F.
1937   The adobe tick on *Gopherus agassizii*. Herpetologica 1:80.

Hardy, J. D.
1962   Comments on the Atlantic ridley turtle, *Lepidochelys olivacea kempi*, in the Chesapeake Bay. Chesapeake Sci. 3:217–220.
1969   Records of the leatherback turtle, *Dermochelys coriacea coriacea* (Linnaeus), from the Chesapeake Bay. Bull. Maryland Herpetol. Soc. 5:92–96.

Harlan, R.
*1835   Genera of North American Reptilia and a synopsis of the species. Medical and Physical Researches. Lydia R. Bailey, Philadelphia. Pp. 84–160.

Harless, M.
1970   Social behavior in wood turtles. Amer. Zool. 10:289.

Harrah, E. C.
1922   North American monostomes primarily from fresh water hosts. Illinois Biol. Monogr. 7:1–107.

Harrisson, T.
1950   The Sarawak Turtle Islands "semah." J. Malay British Asiatic Soc. 23:105–126.
1951   The edible turtle (*Chelonia mydas*) in Borneo. 1. Breeding season. Sarawak Mus. J. 3:592–596.
1952   Breeding of the edible turtle. Nature 169:198.
1954   The edible turtle (*Chelonia mydas*) in Borneo. 2. Copulation. Sarawak Mus. J. 6:126–128.
1955   Notes on edible turtles. 3. Young turtles (in captivity). Sarawak Mus. J. 6:633–641.
1956a   Tagging green turtles, 1951–56. Nature 178:1479.
1956b   The edible turtle (*Chelonia mydas*) in Borneo. 4. Growing turtles and growing problems. Sarawak Mus. J. 7:233–239.
1956c   The edible turtle in Borneo. 5. Tagging turtles and why. Sarawak Mus. J. 7:504–516.
1958   Notes on the edible green turtle (*Chelonia mydas*). 7. Long term tagging returns, 1952–58. Sarawak Mus. J. 8:772–774.

1969   The marine turtle situation in Sarawak. IUCN Publ. (n.s.) 20:71–74.

1970   The turtle tragedy. Int. Turtle & Tortoise Soc. J. 4(2): 26–28.

Hartman, W. L.
1958   Integradation between two subspecies of painted turtle, genus *Chrysemys*. Copeia 1958:261–265.

Hartweg, N.
*1938   *Kinosternon flavescens stejnegeri*, a new turtle from northern Mexico. Occ. Pap. Mus. Zool. Univ. Michigan 371:1–5.

*1939   A new American *Pseudemys*. Occ. Pap. Mus. Zool. Univ. Michigan 397:1–4.

1946   Confirmation of overwintering in painted turtle hatchlings. Copeia 1946:255.

Harwood, P. D.
1932a   Some parasites of Oklahoma turtles. J. Parasitol. 18:98–101.

1932b   The helminths parasitics in the Amphibia and Reptilia of Houston, Texas, and vicinity. Proc. U. S. Natl. Mus. 81:1–71.

Hay, O. P.
1898   On *Protostega*, the systematic position of *Dermochelys*, and the morphogeny of the chelonian carapace and plastron. Amer. Nat. 32:929–948.

1908a   On three existing species of sea-turtles, one of them (*Caretta remivaga*) new. Proc. U. S. Natl. Mus. 34:183–198.

1908b   The fossil turtles of North America. Carnegie Inst. Washington Publ. 75:1–568.

Hay, W. P.
*1904   A revision of *Malaclemmys*, a genus of turtles. Bull. U. S. Bur. Fish. 24:1–20.

Hayes, J.
1965   New host record for *Aedes canadensis*. Mosquito News 25:344.

Hayes, W. N., and E. I. Saiff
1967   Visual alarm reactions in turtles. Anim. Behav. 15:102–106.

Hedrick, L.
1932   Life history of *Spiroxys* sp. from American turtles. J. Parasitol. 18:120.

1935   The life history and morphology of *Spiroxys contortus* (Rudolphi); Nematoda: Spiruridae. Trans. Amer. Microsc. Soc. 54:307–335.

Hedrick, R. M., and J. C. Holmes
1956   Additional Minnesota herpetological notes. Flicker 28:123–126.

Heidt, G. A., and R. G. Burbidge
1966   Some aspects of color preference, substrate preference, and learning in hatchling *Chrysemys*. Herpetologica 22:288–292.

Helms, D. R., and H. J. Stains
1966   Kill of mammals and birds and entrapment of turtles on railroad tracks. Trans. Illinois St. Acad. Sci. 59:297.

Hendrickson, J. R.
1958   The green sea turtle, *Chelonia mydas* (Linn.) in Malaya and Sarawak. Proc. Zool. Soc. London 130:455–535.

1962   The programme for conservation of the giant leathery turtle, 1961. Malayan Nat. J. 16: 64–69.

1969   Report on Hawaiian marine turtle populations. IUCN Publ. (n.s.) 20:89–95.

Hendrickson, J. R., and E. R. Allard
1961   Nesting populations of sea-turtles on the east coast of Malaya. Bull. Raffles Mus. 26:190–196.

Hendrickson, J. R., and E. Balasingam
1966   Nesting beach preferences of Malayan sea turtles. Bull. Nat. Mus. Singapore 33:69–76.

Hendrickson, J. R., and J. S. Winterflood
1961   Hatching leathery turtle eggs. Bull. Raffles Mus. 26:187–189.

Herald, E. S.
1949   Effects of DDT-oil solutions upon amphibians and reptiles. Herpetologica 5:117–120.

Herban, N. L., and R. G. Yaeger
1969   Blood parasites of certain Louisiana reptiles and amphibians. Amer. Midl. Nat. 82:600–601.

Herrmann, S. J.
1970   Systematics, distribution, and ecology of Colorado Hirudinea. Amer. Midl. Nat. 83: 1–37.

Hildebrand, H. H.
1963　Hallazgo del área de anidación de la tortuga marina "lora," *Lepidochelys kempi* (Garman), en la costa occidental del Golfo de México (Rept., Chel.). Ciencia 22:105–112.

Hildebrand, S. F.
1929　Review of experiments on artificial culture of diamond-back terrapin. Bull. U. S. Bur. Fish. 45:25–70.

1932　Growth of diamond-back terrapins, size attained, sex ratio, and longevity. Zoologica (N.Y.) 9:551–563.

1933　Hybridizing diamond-back terrapins. J. Heredity 24:231–238.

Hildebrand, S. F., and C. Hatsel
1926　Diamond-back terrapin culture at Beaufort, N.C. U. S. Bur. Fish., Econ. Cir. 60:1–20.

1927　On the growth, care and age of loggerhead turtles in captivity. Proc. Natl. Acad. Sci. 13:374–377.

Hildebrand, S. F., and H. F. Prytherch
1947　Diamond-back terrapin culture. Fish and Wildlife Serv. Fish. Leaflet 216:1–5.

Hinds, V. T.
1965　The green turtle in South Arabia. Port of Aden Ann. 1964–65:54–57.

Hiro, F.
1936　Occurrence of the cirriped, *Stomatolepas elegans*, on a loggerhead turtle found at Seto. Ann. Zool. Japan 15:312–320.

Hirschfeld, W. J., and A. S. Gordon
1961　Studies on erythropoiesis in turtles. Anat. Rec. 139:306.

1964　Erythropoietic response of the turtle (*Pseudemys scripta elegans*) to bleeding. Amer. Zool. 4:305.

1965　The effect of bleeding and starvation on blood volumes and peripheral hemogram of the turtle, *Pseudemys scripta elegans*. Anat. Rec. 153:317–324.

Hirth, H. F.
1962　Cloacal temperatures of the green and hawksbill sea turtles. Copeia 1962:647–648.

1968　The green turtle resource of South Arabia and the status of the green turtle in the Seychelles Islands. F.A.O. (Rome) TA2467.

1969　Marine turtles in the Seychelles and Aldabra. IUCN Publ. (n.s.) 20:54–55.

Hirth, H. F., and A. Carr
1970　The green turtle in the Gulf of Aden and the Seychelles Islands. Ver. Kon. Nederlandse Akad. Wetenschap. Nat. 58:1–44.

Holbrook, J. E.
*1836　North American herpetology I. Philadelphia. 55 pp.

*1838　North American herpetology II. Philadelphia. 55 pp.

Holliman, R. B., and J. E. Fisher
1968　Life cycle and pathology of *Spirorchis scripta* Stunkard, 1923 (Digenea: Spirorchiidae) in *Chrysemys picta picta*. J. Parasitol. 54:310–318.

Holman, J. A.
1967　The age of the turtle. Int. Turtle & Tortoise Soc. J. 1(4):15–21, 45.

1969　The ancestral turtle. Int. Turtle & Tortoise Soc. J. 3(2):16–19.

Holmes, P. A., and M. E. Bitterman
1966　Spatial and visual habitat reversal in the turtle. J. Comp. Physiol. Psychol. 62:328–331.

Holmes, W. N., and R. L. McBean
1964　Some aspects of electrolyte excretion in the green turtle, *Chelonia mydas mydas*. J. Exp. Biol. 41:81–90.

Honegger, R. E.
1967　The green turtle (*Chelonia mydas japonica*) Thunberg in the Seychelles Islands. British J. Herpetol. 4:8–11.

Hooker, D.
1908　Preliminary observations on the behavior of some newly hatched loggerhead turtles (*Thalassochelys caretta*). Carnegie Inst. Washington Yrbk. 6:111–112.

1911　Certain reactions to color in young loggerhead turtles. Carnegie Inst. Washington Publ. 132:71–76.

Hopp, W. B.
1945　Notes on the life history of *Neoechinorynchus emydis* (Leidy), an acanthocephalan parasite of turtles. Proc. Indiana Acad. Sci. 55:183.

1954 Studies on the morphology and life cycle of *Neoechinorhynchus emydis* (Leidy), an acanthocephalan parasite of the map turtle, *Graptemys geographica* (LeSueur). J. Parasitol. 40: 284–299.

Hornell, J.
1927 The turtle fisheries of the Seychelles Islands. H. M. Stationery Office, London, 55 pp.

Houck, W. J., and J. G. Joseph
1958 A northern record for the Pacific ridley, *Lepidochelys olivacea*. Copeia 1958:219–220.

Housholder, V. H.
1950 Courtship and coition of the desert tortoise. Herpetologica 6:11.

Hoyt, J. S. Y.
1941 The incubation period of the snapping turtle. Copeia 1941:180.

Hughes, G. R.
1969a Report to the Survival Service Commission on marine turtles in southern Africa. IUCN Publ. (n.s.) 20:56–66.
1969b Marine turtle hatchlings of Tongaland. African Wildlife 23:5–19.
1970a Marine turtles: an introduction to the sea turtles of South East Africa. S. Africa J. Sci. 66:239–246.
1970b Further studies on marine turtles in Tongaland. III. Lammergeyer 12:7–25.
1970c Further studies on marine turtles in Tongaland. IV. Lammergeyer 12:26–36.
1970d Sea turtle research. Bull. South African Assoc. Mar. Biol. Res. 8:21–25.

Hughes, G. R., A. J. Bass, and M. T. Mentis
1967 Further studies on marine turtles in Tongaland. I. Lammergeyer 3:5–54.

Hughes, G. R., and M. T. Mentis
1967 Further studies on marine turtles in Tongaland. II. Lammergeyer 3:55–72.

Hughes, R. C., J. W. Higginbotham, and J. W. Clary
1941a The trematodes of reptiles. Part II. Host catalogue. Proc. Oklahoma Acad. Sci. 21:35–43.

Hughes, R. C., J. R. Baker, and C. B. Dawson
1941b The tapeworms of reptiles. Part II. Host catalogue. Wasmann Coll. 4:97–104.

Hunsaker, D.
1966 Parasitism in turtles. Int. Turtle & Tortoise Soc. J. 1(1):6–7, 23, 37, 46.

Hunt, T. J.
1957 Notes on diseases and mortality in Testudines. Herpetologica 13:19–23.
1958a Influence of environment on necrosis of turtle shells. Herpetologica 14:45–46.
1958b The ordinal name for tortoises, terrapins and turtles. Herpetologica 14:148–150.

Huse, W. H.
1901 The Testudinata of New Hampshire. Proc. Manchester Inst. Arts Sci. 2:47–51.

Hutchison, V. H.
1963 Record of the bog turtle, *Clemmys muhlenbergi*, in southwestern Virginia. Copeia 1963: 156–157.

Hutchison, V. H., and R. J. Kosh
1965 The effect of photoperiod on the critical thermal maxima of painted turtles (*Chrysemys picta*). Herpetologica 20:233–238.

Hutchison, V. H., and A. Vinegar
1963 The feeding of the box turtle, *Terrapene carolina*, on a live snake. Herpetologica 4:284.

Hutchison, V. H., A. Vinegar, and R. J. Kosh
1966 Critical thermal maxima in turtles. Herpetologica 22:32–41.

Hutt, A.
1967 The gopher tortoise, a versatile vegetarian. Florida Wildlife 21:20–24.

Hutton, K. E.
1960 Seasonal physiological changes in the red-eared turtle, *Pseudemys scripta elegans*. Copeia 1960:360–362.
1961 Blood volume, corpuscular constants and shell weight in turtles. Amer. J. Physiol. 200:1004–1006.
1964 Effects of hypothermia on turtle blood glucose. Herpetologica 20:129–132.

Hutton, K. E., D. R. Boyer, J. C. Williams, and P. M. Campbell
1960 Effects of temperature and body size upon heart rate and oxygen consumption in turtles. J. Cell. Comp. Physiol. 55:87–94.

Hutton, K. E., and C. J. Goodnight
1957   Variations in the blood chemistry of turtles under active and hibernating conditions. Physiol. Zool. 30:198–207.

Ingle, R. M., and F. G. W. Smith
1949   Sea turtles and the turtle industry. Spec. Publ. Univ. Miami. 107 pp.

Jackson, C. G.
1965   Carapace erosion in the loggerhead musk turtle *Sternothaerus minor minor* Agassiz. Herpetologica 20:279–281.
1966   A biometrical study of form and growth in *Pseudemys concinna suwanniensis* Carr (Order: Testudinata). Diss. Abstr. 26:4126–4127.
1967   Blood serum cholesterol levels in turtles. Comp. Biochem. Physiol. 20:311–312.
1968   A study of allometric growth in *Pseudemys concinna suwanniensis* Carr (Order Testudinata). A.S.B. Bull. 15:41.
1969   Agonistic behavior in *Sternotherus minor minor* Agassiz. Herpetologica 25:53–54.
1970   A biometrical study of growth in *Pseudemys concinna suwanniensis*. I. Copeia 1970:528–534.

Jackson, C. G., and C. E. Cantrell
1964   Total body water in neonatal Suwannee terrapins, *Pseudemys concinna suwanniensis* Carr. Comp. Biochem. Physiol. 12:527–528.

Jackson, C. G., and A. D. Conger
1969   Radiographic techniques for turtle osteology. J. Herpetol. 3:97–99.

Jackson, C. G., and M. Fulton
1970   A turtle colony epizootic apparently of microbial origin. J. Wildlife Dis. 6:466–468.

Jackson, C. G., C. M. Holcomb, and M. M. Jackson
1970   The relationship between age, blood serum cholesterol level and aortic calcification in the turtle. Comp. Biochem. Physiol. 35:491–493.

Jackson, C. G., and M. M. Jackson
1968   The egg and hatchling of the Suwannee terrapin. Quart. J. Florida Acad. Sci. 31:199–204.

Jackson, C. G., M. M. Jackson, and J. D. Davis
1969   Cutaneous myiasis in the three-toed box turtle, *Terrapene carolina triunguis*. Bull. Wildlife Dis. Assoc. 5:114.

Jackson, D. C.
1968   Metabolic depression and oxygen depletion in the diving turtle. J. Appl. Physiol. 24:503–509.
1969   Buoyancy control in the freshwater turtle, *Pseudemys scripta elegans*. Science 166:1649–1651.

Jackson, D. C., and K. Schmidt-Nielsen
1966   Heat production during diving in the fresh water turtle, *Pseudemys scripta*. J. Cell. Physiol. 67:225–231.

Jackson, M. M., C. G. Jackson, and M. Fulton
1969   Investigation of the enteric bacteria of the Testudinata—I: occurrence of the genera *Arizona*, *Citrobacter*, *Edwardsiella* and *Salmonella*. Proc. Ann. Conf. Bull. Wildlife Dis. Assoc. 5:328–329.

Jacques, F. A.
1961   Variations in concentrations of a metachromatic staining anticoagulant in plasma of the turtle, *Pseudemys scripta elegans*. Copeia 1961:222–223.
1963   Blood coagulation and anticoagulant mechanisms in the turtle *Pseudemys elegans*. Comp. Biochem. Physiol. 9:241–251.

Jacques, F. F., X. J. Musacchia, and D. H. Bowden
1960   Effect of induced cold torpor on blood coagulation of *Pseudemys elegans*. Physiologist 2:64–65.

James, D.
1961   The measurements of an aged box turtle. Proc. Arkansas Acad. Sci. 15:26–28.

Johlin, J. M., and F. B. Moreland
1933   Studies on the blood picture of the turtle after complete anoxia. J. Biol. Chem. 103:107–114.

Johnson, C. A.
1967   Helminth parasites in turtles collected from farm ponds in Lee County, Alabama. J. Alabama Acad. Sci. 38:325.
1969a   *Neoechinorhynchus magnapapillatus* sp. n. (Acanthocephala) from *Pseudemys scripta scripta* (Chelonia). Proc. Helminthol. Soc. Washington 36:277–281.
1969b   A redescription of *Myxidium chelonarum*

Johnson, 1969 (Cnidospora: Myxidiidae) from various North American turtles. J. Protozool. 16:700–702.

Johnson, R. M.
1954 The painted turtle, *Chrysemys picta picta*, in eastern Tennessee. Copeia 1954:298–299.
1964 The herpetofauna of the Oak Ridge area. Publ. Oak Ridge Natl. Lab. 3653:1–28.

Johnson, W. R.
1952a *Lepidochelys kempii* and *Caretta c. caretta* from a south Florida Indian mound. Herpetologica 8:36.
1952b Range of *Malaclemmys terrapin rhizophorarum* on the west coast of Florida. Herpetologica 8:100.

Jolicoeur, P., and J. E. Mosimann
1960 Size and shape variation in the painted turtle. A principal component analysis. Growth 24:339–354.

Judd, W. W.
1951 The snapping turtle (*Chelydra serpentina* L.) in the Dundas Marsh, Hamilton, Ontario. Canadian Field-Nat. 65:37–39.
1965 Studies of the Byron Bog in southwestern Ontario. XXII. Observations on toads, frogs, and turtles. Canadian Field-Nat. 79:142–144.

Kaplan, H. M.
1956 Anticoagulants isotonic with turtle blood. Herpetologica 12:269–272.
1958 Marking and banding frogs and turtles. Herpetologica 14:131–132.
1960a Variation with age of the electrophoretic protein pattern in turtle blood. Herpetologica 16:202–206.
1960b Electrophoretic analysis of protein changes during growth of *Pseudemys* turtles. Anat. Rec. 138:359.

Kaplan, H. M., and W. Rueff
1960 Seasonal blood changes in turtles. Proc. Anim. Care Panel June:63–68.

Kenefick, J. H.
1954 Observations on egg laying of the tortoise *Gopherus polyphemus*. Copeia 1954:228–229.

Kennedy, M. E.
1969 *Salmonella* serotypes isolated from turtle en-

vironment. Canadian J. Microbiol. 15:130–132.

Kepner, W. A.
1912 The larva of *Sarcophaga*, a parasite of *Cistudo carolina* and the histology of its respiratory apparatus. Biol. Bull. 22:163–172.

Kirk, K. L., and M. E. Bitterman
1965 Probability-learning by the turtle. Science 148:1484–1485.

Klimstra, W. D.
1951 Notes on late summer snapping turtle movements. Herpetologica 7:140.
1959a Foods of the racer, *Coluber constrictor*, in southern Illinois. Copeia 1959:210–214.
1959b Food habits of the cottonmouth in southern Illinois. Nat. Hist. Misc. 168:1–8.

Klimstra, W. D., and F. Newsome
1960 Some observations on the food coactions of the common box turtle, *Terrapene c. carolina*. Ecology 41:639–647.

Knapp, H., and D. S. Kang
1968 The visual pathways of the snapping turtle (*Chelydra serpentina*). Brain Behav. Evol. 1:19–42.

Knepton, J. C.
1956 County records of Testudinata collected in Georgia. J. Tennessee Acad. Sci. 31:322–324.

Knight, A. W., and J. W. Gibbons
1968 Food of the painted turtle, *Chrysemys picta*, in a polluted river. Amer. Midl. Nat. 80:559–562.

Knipling, E. F.
1937 The biology of *Sarcophaga cistudinis* Aldrich (Diptera), a species of Sarcophagidae parasitic on turtles and tortoises. Proc. Ent. Soc. Washington 39:91–101.

Koch, A. L., A. Carr, and D. W. Ehrenfeld
1969 The problem of open-sea navigation: the migration of the green turtle to Ascension Island. J. Theoret. Biol. 22:163–179.

Korschgen, L. J., and T. S. Baskett
1963 Foods of impoundment- and stream-dwelling bullfrogs in Missouri. Herpetologica 19:89–99.

Kosh, R. J., and V. H. Hutchison
1968   Daily rhythmicity of temperature tolerance in eastern painted turtles, *Chrysemys picta.* Copeia 1968:244–246.

Krefft, G.
1951   *Deirochelys reticularia* (Latreille), eine wenig bekannte Schmuckschildkröte der USA. Aqua. Terrar. Z. 4:157–160.

Lacépède, B. G. E.
*1788   Histoire naturelle des quadrupèdes ovipares et des serpens. Paris. 1:18–651.

Lagler, K. F.
1941   Fall mating and courtship of the musk turtle. Copeia 1941:268.

1943   Food habits and economic relations of the turtles of Michigan with special reference to fish management. Amer. Midl. Nat. 29:257–312.

Lagler, K. F., and V. C. Applegate
1943   Relationship between the length and the weight in the snapping turtle *Chelydra serpentina* Linnaeus. Amer. Nat. 77:476–478.

Landreth, H. F.
1968   *Deirochelys reticularia* in Mississippi. J. Mississippi Acad. Sci. 14:130.

Lardie, R. L.
1963   A length record for *Trionyx spinifer emoryi* (Agassiz). Herpetologica 19:150.

1965   Pugnacious behavior in the softshell *Trionyx spinifer pallidus.* Herpetologica 20:281–284.

Latham, R.
1916   Notes on *Cistudo carolina* from Orient, Long Island. Copeia 1916(34):64–67.

Latham, R., and F. C. Schlauch
1969   Inscribed eastern box turtles. Int. Turtle & Tortoise Soc. J. 3(4):13.

Layne, J. N.
1952   Behavior of captive loggerhead turtles, *Caretta c. caretta* (Linnaeus). Copeia 1952:115.

Leary, T. R.
1957   A schooling of leatherback turtles, *Dermochelys coriacea coriacea,* on the Texas coast. Copeia 1957:232.

LeBuff, C. R., Jr.
1969   The marine turtles of Sanibel and Captive islands, Florida. Spec. Publ. Sanibel–Captive Conserv. Found. 1:1–13.

1970   Turner Beach Sanctuary. Int. Turtle & Tortoise Soc. J. 4(2):14–16.

Le Conte, J.
*1836   Description of the species of North American tortoises. Ann. Lyceum Nat. Hist., New York 3:91–131.

*1853   Description of four new species of *Kinosternum.* Proc. Acad. Nat. Sci. Philadelphia 7: 180–190.

Lee, D. S.
1968   Herpetofauna associated with central Florida mammals. Herpetologica 24:83–84.

1969   Save Barbour's map turtle. Florida Nat. 42(1): 38.

Lee, H. H.
1963   Egg-laying in captivity by *Gopherus agassizi* Cooper. Herpetologica 19:62–65.

Legler, J. M.
1954   Nesting habits of the western painted turtle, *Chrysemys picta belli* (Gray). Herpetologica 10:137–144.

1955   Observations on the sexual behavior of captive turtles. Lloydia 18:95–99.

1956a   A social relationship between snapping and painted turtles. Trans. Kansas Acad. Sci. 59: 461–462.

1956b   A simple and practical method of artificially incubating reptile eggs. Herpetologica 12:290.

1958a   Extra-uterine migration of ova in turtles. Herpetologica 14:49–52.

1958b   The Texas slider (*Pseudemys floridana texana*) in New Mexico. S. W. Nat. 3:230–231.

1960a   Natural history of the ornate box turtle, *Terrapene ornata ornata* Agassiz. Univ. Kansas Publ. Mus. Nat. Hist. 11:527–669.

1960b   Remarks on the natural history of the Big Bend slider, *Pseudemys scripta gaigeae* Hartweg. Herpetologica 16:139–140.

1960c   A simple and inexpensive device for trapping aquatic turtles. Proc. Utah Acad. Sci., Arts, Lett. 37:63–66.

1962   The *os transiliens* in two species of tortoises, genus *Gopherus.* Herpetologica 18:68–69.

Lemkau, P. J.
1970   Movements of the box turtle, *Terrapene c. carolina* (Linnaeus), in unfamiliar territory. Copeia 1970:781–783.

Leone, C. A., and F. E. Wilson
1961   Studies of turtle sera I. The nature of the fastest-moving electrophoretic component in the sera of nine species. Physiol. Zool. 34:297–305.

Le Sueur, C. A.
*1817   An account of the American species of tortoise, not noticed in the systems. J. Acad. Nat. Sci. Philadelphia 1:86–88.
*1827   Note sur deux espèces de tortues du genre *Trionyx* Gffr. St. H. Mem. Mus. Hist. Nat. Paris. 15:257–268.

Lewin, V.
1963   First record of the western painted turtle in Alberta. Copeia 1963:446–447.

Lewis, G. B.
1940   The Cayman Islands and marine turtle. Bull. Inst. Jamaica 2.(appendix):56–65.

Lin, N.
1958   Coital movement patterns in pairings of a male *Terrapene c. bauri* with a female *T. c. triunguis*. British J. Herpetol. 2:96–97.

Liner, E. A.
1954   The herpetofauna of Lafayette, Terrebonne, and Vermilion parishes, Louisiana. Proc. Louisiana Acad. Sci. 17:65–85.

Linnaeus, C.
*1758   Systema Naturae, 10th ed. Holmiae. 1:1–824.
*1766   Systema Naturae, 12th ed. Halae Magdeburgicae. 1:1–532.

Liepitz, L. E., and R. M. Hill
1970   Discrimination characteristics of the turtle's retinal ganglion cells. Experientia (Basel) 26:373–374.

List, J. C.
1951   The ornate box turtle, *Terrapene ornata* (Agassiz), in Indiana. Amer. Midl. Nat. 45:508.

Little, J. W., and S. H. Hopkins
1968   *Neoechinorhynchus constrictus* sp. n., an acanthocephalan from Texas turtles. Proc. Helminthol. Soc. Washington 35:46–49.

Lönnberg, E.
1894   Notes on reptiles and batrachians collected in Florida in 1892 and 1893. Proc. U. S. Natl. Mus. 17:317–339.

Loftin, H.
1960   An annotated check-list of trematodes and cestodes and their vertebrate hosts from northwest Florida. Quart. J. Florida Acad. Sci. 23:302–314.

Logier, E. B. S.
1925   Notes on the herpetology of Point Pelee, Ontario. Canadian Field-Nat. 39:91–95.

Logier, E. B. S., and G. C. Toner
1955   Check-list of the amphibians and reptiles of Canada and Alaska. Contr. Royal Ontario Mus. Zool. Palaeont. 41:1–88.

Loomis, R. B., and J. C. Geest
1964   The desert tortoise *Gopherus agassizi* in Sinaloa, Mexico. Herpetologica 20:203.

Loveridge, A.
1955   The generic name of the alligator snapper turtle. Herpetologica 11:16.

Loveridge, A., and E. E. Williams
1957   Revision of the African tortoises and turtles of the suborder Cryptodira. Bull. Mus. Comp. Zool. 115:163–557.

Lowe, C. H., and K. S. Norris
1955   Measurements and weight of a Pacific leatherback turtle, *Dermochelys coriacea schlegeli*, captured off San Diego, California. Copeia 1955:256.

Luhman, M.
1935   Two new trematodes from the loggerhead turtle (*Caretta caretta*). J. Parasitol. 21:274–276.

Lynn, W. G., and M. C. Ullrich
1950   Experimental production of shell abnormalities in turtles. Copeia 1950:253–262.

Lynn, W. G., and T. Von Brand
1945   Studies on the oxygen consumption and water metabolism of turtle embryos. Biol. Bull. 88:112–125.

MacAskie, I. B., and C. R. Forrester
  1962 Pacific leatherback turtles (*Dermochelys*) off the coast of British Columbia. Copeia 1962: 646.

Mackin, J. G.
  1927 *Dracunculus globocephalus* n. sp. from *Chelydra serpentina*. J. Parasitol. 14:91–94.
  1936 Studies on the morphology and life history of nematodes in the genus *Spironoura*. Illinois Biol. Monogr. 14:7–64.

MacMahon, J. A.
  1961 A technique for the preparation of turtle shells. Herpetologica 17:138–139.

Mahmoud, I. Y.
  1967 Courtship behavior and sexual maturity in four species of kinosternid turtles. Copeia 1967:314–319.
  1968a Nesting behavior in the western painted turtle, *Chrysemys picta belli*. Herpetologica 24: 158–162.
  1968b Feeding behavior in kinosternid turtles. Herpetologica 24:300–305.
  1969 Comparative ecology of the kinosternid turtles of Oklahoma. S. W. Nat. 14:31–66.

Mahmoud, I. Y., and N. Lavenda
  1969 Establishment and eradication of food preferences in red-eared turtles. Copeia 1969:298–300.

Malkin, P.
  1969 At loggerheads . . . man vs. *Caretta*. Mus. News (Miami) 1:190–193.

Manter, H. W.
  1932 Continued studies on trematodes of Tortugas. Carnegie Inst. Washington Yrbk. 31:287–288.

Manter, H. W., and M. I. Larson
  1950 Two new blood flukes from a marine turtle, *Caretta caretta*. J. Parasitol. 36:595–599.

Mansuetti, R., and D. H. Wallace
  1960 Notes on the soft-shell turtle (*Trionyx*) in Maryland waters. Chesapeake Sci. 1:71–72.

Manwell, C., and C. V. Schlesinger
  1966 Polymorphism of turtle hemoglobin and geographical differences in the frequency of varients of *Chrysemys picta* "slow" hemoglobin —an example of "temperature anti-adaptation?" Comp. Biochem. Physiol. 18:627–637.

Marchand, L. J.
  1942 A contribution to a knowledge of the natural history of certain freshwater turtles. Master's thesis, Univ. Florida. 83 pp.
  1944 Notes on the courtship of a Florida terrapin. Copeia 1944:191–192.
  1945 The individual range of some Florida turtles. Copeia 1945:75–77.

Marquez, R.
  1969 Additional records of the Pacific loggerhead turtle, *Caretta caretta gigas*, from the north Mexican Pacific coast. J. Herpetol. 3:108–110.

Marquez, R., and M. Contreras
  1967 Marcado de tortuga lora (*Lepidochelys kempi*) en la costa de Tamaulipas, 1967. Bol. Progr. Noc. Marc. Tortugas Mar., Mexico. 2(1):1–8.

Martin, W. E., and J. W. Bamberger
  1952 New blood flukes (Trematoda: Spirorchiidae) from the marine turtle, *Chelonia mydas* (L.). J. Parasitol. 38:105–110.

Martof, B. S.
  1956 Amphibians and reptiles of Georgia, a guide. Univ. Georgia Press, Athens. 94 pp.

Masat, R. J., and H. C. Dessauer
  1968 Plasma albumins of reptiles. Comp. Biochem. Physiol. 25:119–128.

Masat, R. J., and X. J. Musacchia
  1963 A study of serum proteins in *Chrysemys picta*. Amer. Zool. 3:216.
  1965 Serum protein concentration changes in the turtle, *Chrysemys picta*. Comp. Biochem. Physiol. 16:215–225.

Maslin, T. P.
  1959 An annotated check list of the amphibians and reptiles of Colorado. Univ. Colorado Stud., Ser. Biol. 6:1–98.

Masters, C. O.
  1970 Sea turtles. Ward's Bull. 10(70):1, 5.

Mathers, C. K.
  1948 The leeches of the Okoboji region. Proc. Iowa Acad. Sci. 55:397–425.

McAllister, H. J., A. J. Bass, and H. J. van Schoor
1965   The marine turtles of Tongaland. Lammergeyer 3:10–40.

McCauley, R. H.
1945   The reptiles of Maryland and the District of Columbia. Privately printed, Hagerstown, Maryland. 194 pp.

McCoy, C. J.
1968   The development of melanism in an Oklahoma population of Chrysemys scripta elegans (Reptilia—Testudinidae). Proc. Oklahoma Acad. Sci. 47:84–87.

McDowell, S. B.
1961   On the major arterial canals in the ear-region of the testudinoid turtles and the classification of the Testudinoidea. Bull. Mus. Comp. Zool. 125:23–39.
1963   Muscles in the region of the eustachian tube of turtles: two corrections. Copeia 1963:153–154.
1964   Partition of the genus Clemmys and related problems in the taxonomy of the aquatic Testudinidae. Proc. Zool. Soc. London 143:239–279.

McFarlane, R. W.
1963   Disorientation of loggerhead hatchlings by artificial road lighting. Copeia 1963:153.

McGinnis, S. M.
1968   Respiration rate and body temperature of the Pacific green turtle Chelonia mydas agassizii. Amer. Zool. 8:766.

McMullen, D. J.
1934   The life history of the turtle trematode, Cercorchis medius. J. Parasitol. 20:248–250.
1935   The life cycle and a discussion of the systematics of the turtle trematode, Eustomos chelydrae. J. Parasitol. 21:52–53.

Medem, F. J.
1962   Estudio sobre tortugas marinas: informe sobre la commission realizada en la costa Atlantica. Corp. Autonoma Reg. de los Valles del Magdalena y del Sinu. Pp. 1–11.

Mehrtens, J. M., and C. F. Herrmann
1951   Saurophagous box turtle. Herpetologica 7:101.

Mertens, R.
1961   How do turtles orientate themselves? Philadelphia Herpetol. Soc. Bull. 9(5):16–17.

Mertens, R., and H. Wermuth
1955   Die rezenten Schildkröten, Krokodile und Brückeneschsen. Zool. Jahrb. 83:323–440.

Meseth, E. H., and O. J. Sexton
1963   Response of painted turtles, Chrysemys picta, to removal of surface vegetation. Herpetologica 19:52–56.

Metcalf, E., and A. L. Metcalf
1970   Observations on ornate box turtles (Terrapene ornata ornata Agassiz). Trans. Kansas Acad. Sci. 73:96–117.

Meyer, M. C.
1968   Moore on the Hirudinea with emphasis on his type-specimens. Proc. U. S. Natl. Mus. 125:1–32.

Millen, J. E., H. V. Murdaugh, C. B. Bauer, and E. D. Robin
1964   Circulatory adaptation to diving in the freshwater turtle. Science 145:591–593.

Miller, L.
1932   Notes on the desert tortoise (Testudo agassizii). Trans. San Diego Soc. Nat. Hist. 7:187–208.
1955   Further observations on the desert tortoise, Gopherus agassizi, of California. Copeia 1955:113–118.

Miller, M. D.
1968   An additional observation of the leatherback turtle off Newfoundland. Canadian Field-Nat. 82:226.

Miller, R. R.
1946   The probable origin of the soft-shelled turtle in the Colorado River basin. Copeia 1946:46.

Milstead, W. W.
1969   Studies on the evolution of box turtles (genus Terrapene). Bull. Florida St. Mus. 14:1–113.

Milstead, W. W., and D. W. Tinkle
1967   Terrapene of western Mexico, with comments on the species groups in the genus. Copeia 1967:180–187.

Minton, S. A.
1944   Introduction to the study of the reptiles of In-
        diana. Amer. Midl. Nat. 32:438–477.
1959   Observations on amphibians and reptiles of
        the Big Bend region of Texas. S. W. Nat. 3:
        28–54.

Miranti, J. P., H. M. Kaplan, and T. Hirano
1964   The spermatozoan of the turtle, *Pseudemys
        scripta elegans*. Copeia 1964:209–211.

Mitsukuri, K.
1905   The cultivation of marine and fresh-water
        animals in Japan. The snapping turtle, or
        soft-shell tortoise, "suppon." Bull. U. S. Bur.
        Fish. 24:260–266.

Mittleman, M. B.
1947   Notes on *Gopherus berlandieri* (Agassiz).
        Copeia 1947:211.

Moll, E. O., and J. M. Legler
1971   The life history of a neotropical slider turtle,
        Pseudemys scripta (Schoepff), in Panama.
        Bull. Los Angeles Co. Mus. Nat. Hist. In
        press.

Moll, E. O., and K. L. Williams
1963   The musk turtle *Sternothaerus odoratus* from
        Mexico. Copeia 1963:157.

Montoya, A. E.
1966   Programa nacional de marcado de tortugas
        marinas. Inst. Nat. Invest. Biol.-Pesq., Mexi-
        co. 14:1–39.
1969   Programas de investigación y conservación
        de los tortugas marinas. IUCN Publ. (n.s.)
        20:34–53.

Moore, J. C.
1953   Shrew on box turtle menu. Everglades Nat.
        Hist. 1:129.

Moorhouse, F. W.
1933   Notes on the green turtle (*Chelonia mydas*).
        Rept. Great Barrier Reef Comm. 4:1–22.

Morejohn, G. V.
1969   Occurrence of a Pacific ridley and a young
        northern fur seal in Monterey Bay. California
        Fish Game 55:239–242.

Mosimann, J. E.
1958   An analysis of allometry in the chelonian
        shell. Rev. Canadienne Biol. 17:137–228.

Mosimann, J. E., and J. R. Bider
1960   Variation, sexual dimorphism, and maturity
        in a Quebec population of the common snap-
        ping turtle, *Chelydra serpentina*. Canadian J.
        Zool. 38:19–38.

Moski, H. C.
1955   Algal growth on the turtle *Chrysemys picta
        picta*. Copeia 1955:61.
1957a   Further notes concerning algal growth on
        painted turtles. Herpetologica 13:46.
1957b   Algal occurrence on the turtle *Clemmys gut-
        tata*. Copeia 1957:50–51.

Moss, D.
1955   The effect of the slider turtle "*Pseudemys
        scripta scripta*" (Schoepff) on the production
        of fish in farm ponds. Proc. Southeastern
        Assoc. Game Fish Comm. Meet. 1955:97–
        100.

Moulton, J. M.
1953   The collection of a map-turtle in eastern Mas-
        sachusetts. Copeia 1953:181.
1963   The recapture of a marked leatherback turtle
        in Casco Bay, Maine. Copeia 1963:434–435.

Mount, R. H.
1969   Distributional notes on two southern turtles.
        J. Herpetol. 3:191.

Mowbray, L. S., and D. K. Caldwell
1958   First record of the ridley turtle from Bermuda,
        with notes on other sea turtles and the turtle
        fishery in the islands. Copeia 1958: 147–148.

Moyle, V.
1949   Nitrogenous excretion in chelonian reptiles.
        Biochem. J. 44:581–584.

Mrosovsky, N.
1967   How turtles find the sea. Sci. J. 3:53–57.
1968   Nocturnal emergence of hatchling sea turtles:
        control by thermal inhibition of activity. Na-
        ture 220:1338–1339.
1970   The influence of the sun's position and ele-
        vated cues on the orientation of hatchling sea
        turtles. Anim. Behav. 18:648–651.

Mrosovsky, N., and B. B. Boycott
1966   Intra- and interspecific differences in photo-
        tactic behaviour of freshwater turtles. Be-
        haviour 26:215–227.

Mrosovsky, N., and A. Carr
1967 Preference for light of short wavelengths in hatchling green sea turtles, *Chelonia mydas*, tested on their natural nesting beaches. Behaviour 28:217–231.

Mrosovsky, N., and S. J. Shettleworth
1968 Wavelength preferences and brightness cues in the water finding behaviour of sea turtles. Behaviour 32:211–257.

Muller, J. F.
1921 Notes on the habits of the soft-shell turtle *Amyda mutica*. Amer. Midl. Nat. 7:180–184.

Muntz, W. R. A., and D. P. M. Northmore
1968 Background light, temperature and visual noise in the turtle. Vision Res. 8:787–800.

Murphy, T. D.
1964 Box turtle, *Terrapene carolina*, in stomach of copperhead, *Agkistrodon contortrix*. Copeia 1964:221.

Musacchia, X. J.
1959 The viability of *Chrysemys picta* submerged at various temperatures. Physiol. Zool. 32:47–50.

Musacchia, X. J., and M. J. Chladek
1961 Investigation of the cloacal bladder in turtles. Amer. Zool. 1:376.

Musacchia, X. J., and W. Grundhauser
1958 Water content in turtle tissues. Fed. Proc. 17:115.
1962 Seasonal and induced alternations of water content in organs of the turtle *Chrysemys picta*. Copeia 1962:570–575.

Musacchia, X. J., and M. L. Sievers
1956 Effects of induced cold torpor on blood of *Chrysemys picta*. Amer. J. Physiol. 187:99–102.
1962 Effects of cold torpor and fasting on the erythrocytes of the turtle, *Pseudemys elegans*. Trans. Amer. Microsc. Soc. 81:198–201.

Myers, C. W.
1952 *Terrapene carolina triunguis* winters in the egg. Herpetologica 8:80.
1956 An unusual feeding habit in the box turtle. Herpetologica 12:155.

Myszka, J.
1960 Notes on reproductive behavior in the eastern box turtle. Philadelphia Herpetol. Soc. Bull. 8(1):17–18.

Nakagawa, K., S. Klahr, and N. S. Bricker
1967 Sodium transport by isolated epithelium of the urinary bladder of the freshwater turtle. Amer. J. Physiol. 213:1565–1569.

Neill, W. T.
1948a Hibernation of amphibians and reptiles in Richmond County, Georgia. Herpetologica 4:107–114.
1948b Use of scent glands by prenatal *Sternotherus minor*. Herpetologica 4:148.
1948c Odor of young box turtles. Copeia 1948:130.
1948d The musk turtles of Georgia. Herpetologica 4:181–183.
1951a The taxonomy of North American soft-shelled turtles, genus *Amyda*. Publ. Res. Div. Ross Allen's Rept. Inst. 1:7–24.
1951b Notes on the role of crawfishes in the ecology of reptiles, amphibians, and fishes. Ecology 32:764–766.
1958 The occurrence of amphibians and reptiles in saltwater areas, and a bibliography. Bull. Mar. Sci. Gulf Caribbean 8:1–97.

Neill, W. T., and E. R. Allen
1954 Algae on turtles: some additional considerations. Ecology 35:581–584.
1957 The laminal spurs of the juvenile gopher tortoise, *Gopherus polyphemus* (Daudin). Copeia 1957:307.

Nemuras, K.
1966 Genus *Clemmys*. Int. Turtle & Tortoise Soc. J. 1(1):26–27, 39, 44.
1967a Genus *Clemmys*. Int. Turtle & Tortoise Soc. J. 1(2):38–40.
1967b Notes on the natural history of *Clemmys muhlenbergi*. Bull. Maryland Herpetol. Soc. 3:80–96.
1968 Again, the spotted turtle. Int. Turtle & Tortoise Soc. J. 2(3):32–35.
1969 Survival of the Muhlenberg. Int. Turtle & Tortoise Soc. J. 3(5):18–21.

Netting, M. G.
1936 Hibernation and migration of the spotted turtle, *Clemmys guttata*. Copeia 1936:112.

1944   The spineless soft-shelled turtle, *Amyda mutica* (Le Sueur), in Pennsylvania. Ann. Carnegie Mus. 30:85–88.

Newman, H. H.
1906   The habits of certain tortoises. J. Comp. Neurol. Psychol. 16:126–152.

Nichols, J. T.
1933   Further notes on painted turtles. Copeia 1933: 41–42.
1939a   Data on size, growth and age in the box turtle, *Terrapene carolina*. Copeia 1939:14–20.
1939b   Range and homing of individual box turtles. Copeia 1939:125–127.
1947   Notes on the mud turtle. Herpetologica 3: 147–148.

Nichols, U. G.
1953   Habits of the desert tortoise, *Gopherus agassizii*. Herpetologica 9:65–69.
1957   The desert tortoise in captivity. Herpetologica 13:141–144.

Nigrelli, R. F.
1940   Observations on trematodes of the marine turtle, *Chelonia mydas*. Anat. Rec. 78 (suppl.):178.
1941   Parasites of the green turtle, *Chelonia mydas* (L.), with special reference to the rediscovery of trematodes described by Looss from his host species. J. Parasitol. 27 (suppl.):15–16.
1942   Leeches (*Ozobranchus branchiatus*) on fibro-epithelial tumors of marine turtles (*Chelonia mydas*). Anat. Rec. 84:539–540.

Niles, D. M.
1962   Records for the Sonora mud turtle, *Kinosternon sonoriense*, in New Mexico. Herpetologica 18:205–206.

Nishimura, S.
1964   Records of occurrence of the leatherback turtle in adjacent waters to Japan. Physiol. Ecol. 12:286–290.
1967   The loggerhead turtle in Japan and neighboring waters (Testudinate: Chelonidae). Publ. Seto. Mar. Biol. Lab. 15:1–4, 19–35.

Noble, G. K., and A. M. Breslau
1938   The senses involved in the migration of young fresh-water turtles after hatching. J. Comp. Psychol. 25:175–193.

Nolan, M. P., M. A. Moussa, and D. E. Hayes
1965   *Aedes* mosquitoes feeding on turtles in nature. Mosquito News 25:218–219.

Norris, K. S., and R. G. Zweifel
1950   Observations on the habits of the ornate box turtle, *Terrapene ornata* (Agassiz). Nat. Hist. Misc. 58:1–4.

Norris-Elye, L. T. S.
1949   The common snapping turtle (*Chelydra serpentina*) in Manitoba. Canadian Field-Nat. 63:145–147.

Northcutt, R. G.
1970   The telencephalon of the western painted turtle (*Chrysemys picta belli*). Illinois Biol. Monogr. 43:1–113.

Olexa, A.
1969   Breeding of common musk turtles *Sternotherus odoratus* at Prague Zoo. Int. Zoo Yrbk. 9:28–29.

Oliver, J. A.
1946   An aggregation of Pacific sea turtles. Copeia 1946:103.
1954   "Old 1844," the Hope Valley turtle. Nature Mag. 47:71–74, 108–109.
1955   The natural history of North American amphibians and reptiles. D. van Nostrand Co., Princeton, N.J. 359 pp.

Oliver, J. A., and C. E. Shaw
1953   The amphibians and reptiles of the Hawaiian Islands. Zoologica (N.Y.) 38:65–95.

Olson, E. C.
1947   The family Diadectidae. Fieldiana: Geol. 11: 3–53.
1950   The temporal region of the Permian reptile *Diadectes*. Fieldiana: Geol. 10:63–77.
1965   Relationships of *Seymouria*, *Diadectes*, and Chelonia. Amer. Zool. 5:295–307.
1966   Relationships of *Diadectes*. Fieldiana: Geol. 14:199–227.

Olson, R. E.
1956   The amphibians and reptiles of Winnebago County, Illinois. Copeia 1956:188–191.

1959   Notes on some Texas herptiles. Herpetologica 15:48.

Ortleb, E. P., and O. J. Sexton
1964   Orientation of the painted turtle, *Chrysemys picta*. Amer. Midl. Nat. 71:320–334.

Overmann, S. R.
1970   Social facilitation of feeding in box turtles and American toads. Bull. Ecol. Soc. Amer. 54(4):23.

Pallas, D. C.
1960   Observations on a nesting of the wood turtle, *Clemmys insculpta*. Copeia 1960:155–156.

Parker, M. V.
1939   The amphibians and reptiles of Reelfoot Lake and vicinity, with a key for the separation of species and subspecies. J. Tennessee Acad. Sci. 14:72–101.
1941   The trematode parasites from a collection of amphibians and reptiles. J. Tennessee Acad. Sci. 16:27–45.

Parker, G. H.
1922   The crawling of young loggerhead turtles toward the sea. J. Exp. Zool. 6:323–331.
1929   The growth of the loggerhead turtle. Amer. Nat. 63:367–373.

Parrish, F. K.
1958   Miscellaneous observations on the behavior of captive sea turtles. Bull. Mar. Sci. Gulf Caribbean 8:348–355.

Parsons, J. J.
1962   The green turtle and man. Univ. Florida Press, Gainesville. 126 pp.

Parsons, T. S.
1958a   The choanal papillae of the Cheloniidae. Breviora 85:1–5.
1958b   The Jacobson's organ of turtles. Anat. Rec. 132:486.
1959   Studies on the comparative embryology of the reptilian nose. Bull. Mus. Comp. Zool. 120:101–277.
1960   The structure of the choanae of the Emydinae (Testudines: Testudinidae). Bull. Mus. Comp. Zool. 123:111–127.
1962   Variation in the structure of the choanae of turtles. Amer. Zool. 2:90.

1968   Variations in the choanal structure of Recent turtles. Canadian J. Zool. 46:1235–1263.

Parsons, T. S., and S. M. Stephens
1968   The nasal anatomy of *Kinosternon* and *Sternotherus* (Testudines: Kinosternidae). Canadian J. Zool. 46:399–404.

Parsons, T. S., and E. E. Williams
1961   Two Jurassic turtle skulls: a morphological study. Bull. Mus. Comp. Zool. 125:43–107.

Paxson, D. W.
1962   An observation of eggs in a tortoise shell. Herpetologica 17:278–279.

Payne, H. J., and J. D. Burke
1964   Blood oxygen capacity in turtles. Amer. Midl. Nat. 71:460–465.

Pearse, A. S.
1923   The growth of the painted turtle. Biol. Bull. 45:145–148.

Pearse, A. S., S. Lepkovsky, and L. Hintze
1925   The growth and chemical composition of three species of turtles fed on rations of pure foods. J. Morphol. Physiol. 41:191–216.

Penn, G. H.
1950   Utilization of crawfishes by cold-blooded vertebrates in the eastern United States. Amer. Midl. Nat. 44:643–658.

Penn, G. H., and K. E. Pottharst
1940   The reproduction and dormancy of *Terrapene major* in New Orleans. Herpetologica 2:25–29.

Perry, S. F., J. T. Albright, and D. I. Patt
1970   On the anatomy and histology of the lungs of the red-eared turtle *Pseudemys scripta elegans*. Anat. Rec. 166:361.

Pert, A., and M. E. Bitterman
1969   A technique for the study of consummatory behavior and instrumental learning in the turtle. Amer. Psychol. 24:258–261.

Peters, J. A.
1948   The box turtle as a host for dipterous parasites. Amer. Midl. Nat. 40:472–474.
1957   The eggs (turtle) and I. Biologist 39:21–24
1964   Dictionary of herpetology. Hafner Publ. Co., New York. 392 pp.

Peters, K.
1959 A physiological study of the effect of hibernation on the ornate box turtle. Trans. Kansas Acad. Sci. 62:15–20.

Peterson, A.
1965 On the ecology of turtles in northern Indiana. Philadelphia Herpetol. Soc. Bull. 13: 6–11.

Pilsbry, H. A.
1910 *Stomatolepas,* a barnacle commensal in the throat of the loggerhead turtle. Amer. Nat. 44:304–306.

Pope, C. H.
1935 The reptiles of China. Natural History of Central Asia. Vol. X. Amer. Mus. Nat. Hist., New York. 604 pp.
1939 Turtles of the United States and Canada. Alfred A. Knopf, Inc., New York. 343 pp.
1955 The reptile world. Alfred A. Knopf, Inc., New York. 325 pp.

Pough, F. H.
1966 Turtle trailing. Int. Turtle & Tortoise Soc. J. 1(1):9, 29, 40, 48.
1970 A quick method for permanently marking snakes and turtles. Herpetologica 26:328–330.

Pough, F. H., and M. B. Pough
1968 The systematic status of painted turtles (*Chrysemys*) in the northeastern United States. Copeia 1968:612–618.

Powell, C.
1967 Female sexual cycles of *Chrysemys picta* and *Clemmys insculpta* in Nova Scotia. Canadian Field-Nat. 81:134–140.

Price, E. W.
1934 New genera and species of blood flukes from a marine turtle, with a key to the genera of the family Spirorchidae. J. Washington Acad. Sci. 24:132–141.
1939 North American monogenetic trematodes. IV. The family Polystomatidae (Polystomatoidea). Proc. Helminthol. Soc. Washington 6:80–92.

Price, J. W.
1951 A half-century-old box turtle, *Terrapene caro-*
lina carolina (Linnaeus) from northern Ohio. Copeia. 1951:312.

Pritchard, P. C. H.
1963 Turtles of Georgia. British J. Herpetol. 3: 128–130.
1964 Turtles of British Guiana. Proc. British Guiana Mus. and Zoo 39:19–45.
1966a Sea turtles on Shell Beach, British Guiana. Copeia 1966:123–125.
1966b Occurrence of mesoplastra in a cryptodiran turtle, *Lepidochelys olivacea.* Nature 210: 652.
1967a Living turtles of the world, T.F.H. Publ., Inc., Jersey City, N.J. 288 pp.
1967b To find the ridley. Int. Turtle & Tortoise Soc. J. 1(4):30–35, 48.
1969a Sea turtles of the Guianas. Bull. Florida St. Mus. 13:85–140.
1969b Summary of world sea turtle survival situation. IUCN Bull. 2:90–91.
1969c Report on sea turtle survival situation in the Guianas. IUCN Publ. (n.s.) 20:17–18.

Pritchard, P. C. H., and W. F. Greenhood
1968 The sun and the turtle. Int. Turtle & Tortoise Soc. J. 2(1):20–25, 34.

Proctor, V. W.
1958 The growth of *Basicladia* on turtles. Ecology 39:634–645.

Rageot, R. H. de
1968 The occurrence of the eastern chicken turtle in southeastern Virginia. Virginia Herpetol. Soc. Bull. 57:2.

Ragotzkie, R. A.
1959 Mortality of loggerhead turtle eggs from excessive rainfall. Ecology 40:303–305.

Rainey, D. G.
1953 Death of an ornate box turtle parasitized by dipterous larvae. Herpetologica 9:109–110.

Ramey, K.
1970 Turtle lore: fact and fiction. Bull. Field Mus. Nat. Hist. 41(11):8–10.

Ramirez, J. R., and H. C. Dessauer
1957 Isolation and characterization of two hemoglobins found in the turtle, *Pseudemys scripta*

elegans. Proc. Soc. Exp. Biol. Med. 96:690–694.

Raney, E. C., and R. A. Josephson
1954   Record of combat in the snapping turtle, *Chelydra serpentina.* Copeia 1954:228.

Raney, E. C., and E. A. Lachner
1942   Summer food of *Chrysemys picta marginata* in Chautauqua Lake, New York. Copeia 1942:83–85.

Rapatz, G. L., and X. J. Musacchia
1957   Metabolism of *Chrysemys picta* during fasting and during cold torpor. Amer. J. Physiol. 188:456–460.

Raun, G. G.
1965   Western limits of distribution of the stinkpot, *Sternothaerus odoratus,* in Texas. Herpetologica 21:69–71.

Rausch, R.
1946   New host records for *Microphallus ovatus* Osborn, 1919. J. Parasitol. 32:93–94.
1947a   Some observations on the host relationships of *Microphallus opacus* (Ward, 1894) (Trematoda: Microphallidae). Trans. Amer. Microsc. Soc. 66:59–63.
1947b   Observations on some helminths parasitic in Ohio turtles. Amer. Midl. Nat. 38:434–442.

Ray, C., and C. W. Coates
1958   Record and measurement of a leatherback turtle from the Gulf of Maine. Copeia 1958:220–221.

Ream, C., and R. Ream
1966   The influence of sampling methods on the estimation of population structure in painted turtles. Amer. Midl. Nat. 75:325–338.

Reed, C. F.
1956   Distribution of the wood turtle, *Clemmys insculpta,* in Maryland. Herpetologica 12:80.

Reiber, R. J.
1941   Nematodes of Amphibia and Reptilia. I. Reelfoot Lake, Tennessee. Rept. Reelfoot Lake Biol. Sta. 5:92–99.

Reid, G. K.
1955   Reproduction and development in the north-

ern diamondback terrapin, *Malaclemys terrapin terrapin.* Copeia 1955:310–311.

Reilly, E. M.
1958   Turtles of New York. New York St. Conserv. June-July:1–6.

Richard, O. J.
1970   Bog turtle. Maine Field Nat. 26(4):34–37.

Richards, H. G.
1930   Notes on barnacles from Cape May County, New Jersey. Proc. Acad. Nat. Sci. Philadelphia 82:143–144.

Richmond, G.
1970   The marsh awakens. Int. Turtle & Tortoise Soc. J. 4(1):28–29.

Richmond, N. D.
1945   Nesting habits of the mud turtle. Copeia 1945:217–219.
1958   The status of the Florida snapping turtle *Chelydra osceola* Stejneger. Copeia 1958:41–43.
1964   The mechanical functions of the testudinate plastron. Amer. Midl. Nat. 72:50–56.

Richmond, N. D., and C. J. Goin
1938   Notes on a collection of amphibians and reptiles from New Kent County, Virginia. Ann. Carnegie Mus. 27:301–310.

Ridgway, S. H., E. G. Wever, J. G. McCormick, J. Palin, and J. H. Anderson
1969   Hearing in the giant sea turtle, *Chelonia mydas.* Proc. Natl. Acad. Sci. 64:884–890.

Risley, P. L.
1930   Anatomical differences in the sexes of the musk turtle, *Sternotherus odoratus* (Latreille). Pap. Michigan Acad. Sci. Arts Lett. 11:445–464.
1933   Observations on the natural history of the common musk turtle, *Sternotherus odoratus* (Latreille). Pap. Michigan Acad. Sci. Arts Lett. 17:685–711.
1934   The activity of the coelomic (germinal) epithelium of the male musk turtle, *Sternotherus odoratus* (Latreille). J. Morphol. 56:59–99.
1937   A preliminary study of sex development in

turtle embryos following administration of testosterone. Anat. Rec. 70:103.

1938 Seasonal changes in the testes of the musk turtle *Sternotherus odoratus* L. J. Morphol. 63:301–317.

1941 Some observations on hermaphroditism in turtles. J. Morphol. 68:101–117.

Robin, E. D., J. W. Vester, H. V. Murdough, and J. E. Millen

1964 Prolonged anaerobiosis in a vertebrate: anaerobic metabolism in the freshwater turtle. J. Cell. Comp. Physiol. 63:287–297.

Robinson, D. C.

1956 *Clemmys muhlenbergi* in western Connecticut. Copeia 1956:257.

Robotham, G. R.

1963 The bog turtle, a gift of responsibility. Philadelphia Herpetol. Soc. Bull. 11:68–70.

Rodbard, S., F. Samson, and D. Ferguson

1950 Thermosensitivity of the turtle brain as manifested by blood pressure changes. Amer. J. Physiol. 100:402–408.

Rokosky, E. J.

1948 A bot-fly parasitic in box turtles. Nat. Hist. Misc. 32:1–2.

Romer, A. S.

1956 Osteology of the reptiles. Univ. Chicago Press, Chicago. 772 pp.

1964 *Diadectes* an amphibian? Copeia 1964:718–719.

1966 Vertebrate paleontology. Univ. Chicago Press, Chicago. 468 pp.

1968 Notes and comments on vertebrate paleontology. Univ. Chicago Press, Chicago. 304 pp.

Romeyer, T., and G. T. Haneveld

1956 Turtle meat (*Eretmochelys imbricata*) poisoning in Netherlands New Guinea. Doc. Med. Geog. Tropica 8:380–382.

Root, R. W.

1949 Aquatic respiration in the musk turtle. Physiol. Zool. 22:172–178.

Rose, F. L.

1969 Desiccation rates and temperature relationships of *Terrapene ornata* following scute removal. S. W. Nat. 14:67–72.

1970 Tortoise chin gland fatty acid composition: behavioral significance. Comp. Biochem. Physiol. 32:577–580.

Rose, F. L., R. B. Drotman, and W. G. Weaver

1969 Electrophoresis of chin gland extracts of *Gopherus* (tortoises). Comp. Biochem. Physiol. 29:847–851.

Rose, F. L., and W. G. Weaver

1966 Two new species of *Chrysemys* (=*Pseudemys*) from the Florida Pliocene. Tulane Stud. Zool. 5:41–48.

Rosenbaum, C. P.

1968 Can box turtles be trained? Int. Turtle & Tortoise Soc. J. 2(5):38.

Ross, A., and W. A. Newman

1967 Eocene Balanidae of Florida, including a new genus and species with a unique plan of "turtle-barnacle" organization. Amer. Mus. Novitates 2288:1–21.

Roudabush, R. L., and G. R. Coatney

1937 On some blood protozoa of reptiles and amphibians. Trans. Amer. Microsc. Soc. 56:291–297.

Routa, R. A.

1967 Sea turtle nest survey on Hutchinson Island, Florida. Quart. J. Florida Acad. Sci. 30:287–294.

Routtenberg, A., and S. Glickman

1964 Visual cliff behavior in undomesticated rodents, land and aquatic turtles, and cats (*Panthera*). J. Comp. Physiol. Psychol. 58:143–146.

Rüppell, E.

*1835 Neue Wirbelthiere zu der Fauna von Abyssinian gehörig. III. Amphibien. Frankfurt am. M. 18 pp.

Russo, P. M.

1969 The annual behavioral thermoregulation cycle in *Terrapene c. carolina*. Ecol. Soc. Amer. Bull. 50:76–77.

Sabath, M.

1960 Eggs and young of several Texas reptiles. Herpetologica 16:72.

Salazar, B. M.
1967   The disappearing Muhlenberg. Int. Turtle &
       Tortoise Soc. J. 1(5):37, 39.

Sampson, J. R., and J. V. Ernst
1969   *Eimeria scriptae* n. sp. (Sporozoa: Eimeriidae)
       from the red-eared turtle *Pseudemys scripta
       elegans*. J. Protozool. 16:444–445.

Sanders, E. P., and L. R. Cleveland
1930   The morphology and life-cycle of *Entamoeba
       terrapinae* spec. nov., from the terrapin,
       Chrysemys elegans. Arch. Protista 70:267–
       272.

Sanderson, R. A.
1970   Notes on a communal nesting site of *Sterno-
       therus odoratus*. Bull. Maryland Herpetol.
       Soc. 6:81–82.

Scattergood, L. W., and C. Packard
1960   Records of marine turtles in Maine. Maine
       Field Nat. 16:46–50.

Schaefer, G. C., and A. W. Romano
1968   *Ambystoma opacum* and *Graptemys geo-
       graphica* in northeastern Pennsylvania. J.
       Herpetol. 1:103–104.

Schilb, T. P., and W. A. Brodsky
1970   Transient acceleration of transmural water
       flow by inhibition of sodium transport in
       turtle bladders. Amer. J. Physiol. 219:590–
       596.

Schlauch, F. C.
1969   Eggs of a stinkpot. Int. Turtle & Tortoise Soc.
       J. 3(5):25.

Schmidt, C.
1962   Conservation of sea turtles. Inter. Zoo Yrbk.
       4:70–71.

Schmidt, G. D., G. W. Esch, and J. W. Gibbons
1970   *Neoechinorhynchus chelonos*, a new species
       of acanthocephalan parasite of turtles. Proc.
       Helminthol. Soc. Washington 37:172–174.

Schmidt, J.
1916   Marking experiments with turtles in the Dan-
       ish West Indies. Meddelelser Kommissionen
       Havundersogelser, Ser. Fiskeri 5:1–26.

Schmidt, K. P.
1953   A check list of North American amphibians

and reptiles. 6th ed. Amer. Soc. Ichth. Herp.,
Univ. Chicago Press, Chicago. 280 pp.

Schmidt, K. P., and R. F. Inger
1957   Living reptiles of the world. Hanover House,
       Garden City, N.Y. 287 pp.

Schmidt-Nielsen, K., and P. J. Bentley
1966   Desert tortoise *Gopherus agassizii*: cutaneous
       water loss. Science 154:911.

Schmidt-Nielsen, K., and R. Fange
1958   Salt glands in marine reptiles. Nature 182:
       783–785.

Schneider, J. G.
*1783 Allgemeine naturgeschichte der schildkröten,
       nebst einem system. Verzeichnisse der ein-
       zeinen Arten. Leipzig. 364 pp.
*1792 Beschreibung und Abbildung einer neun Art
       von Wasserschildkröte. Schr. Ges. Naturf.
       Fruende Berlin 10:259–283.

Schoepff, J. D.
*1792 Historia testudinum. Io. Iac., Palmii. 136 pp.
*1801 Historia testudinum iconibus [illustrated]. 6.
       Io. Iac., Palmii. 136 pp.

Schoffeniels, E., and R. R. Tercafs
1965   Adaptation d'un reptile marin, *Caretta ca-
       retta* L. à l'eau douce et d'un reptile d'eau
       douce, *Clemmys leprosa* L. à l'eau de mer.
       Annals Soc. r. Zool. Belgium 96:1–8.

Schroeder, P. J., and M. J. Ulmer
1959   Host-parasite relationships of *Spirorchis ele-
       gans* Stunkard (Trematoda: Spirorchiidae).
       Trans. Iowa Acad. Sci. 66:443–454.

Schroder, R. C.
1957   Range extension of *Macrochelys temmincki*.
       Copeia 1957:234.

Schulz, J. P.
1964   Zeeschildpadden, deel II: Zeeschildpadden in
       Suriname. Dienst Landsbosbeheer Suriname.
       Paramaribo. Pp. 1–44.
1967   Zeeschildpadden, deel I (2nd ed.): ein litera-
       tuurstudie. Dienst Landsbosbeheer Suriname.
       Paramaribo. Pp. 1–79.
1969   National situation report re marine turtles in
       Surinam. IUCN Publ. (n.s.) 20:19–33.

Schwartz, A.
1954   A record of the Atlantic leatherback turtle

(*Dermochelys coriacea coriacea*) in South Carolina. Herpetologica 10:7.

*1955   The diamondback terrapins (*Malaclemys terrapin*) of peninsular Florida. Proc. Biol. Soc. Washington 68:157–164.

*1956a   Geographic variation in the chicken turtle. Fieldiana: Zool. 34:461–503.

1956b   The relationships and nomenclature of the soft-shelled turtles (genus *Trionyx*) of the southeastern United States. Charleston Mus. Leaflet 26:1–21.

Schwartz, F. J.
1961   Maryland turtles. Ed. Ser. Maryland Dept. Res. Ed. 50:1–44.

Schwartz, F. J., and B. L. Dutcher
1961   A record of the Mississippi map turtle, *Graptemys kohni*, in Maryland. Chesapeake Sci. 2:100–101.

Sealander, J. A., and B. J. Forsyth
1966   Amphibian and reptile records for southern Nevada. S. W. Nat. 11:132–134.

Seeliger, L. M.
*1945   Variation in the Pacific mud turtle. Copeia 1945:150–159.

Sergeev, A.
1937   Some materials to the problem of the reptilian post-embryonic growth. Zool. J. Moscow 16:723–735.

Sexton, O. J.
1957   Notes concerning turtle hatchlings. Copeia 1957:229–230.

1959a   Spatial and temporal movements of a population of the painted turtle, *Chrysemys picta marginata* (Agassiz). Ecol. Monogr. 29:113–140.

1959b   A method of estimating the age of painted turtles for use in demographic studies. Ecology 40:716–718.

1965   The annual cycle of growth and shedding in the midland painted turtle, *Chrysemys picta marginata*. Copeia 1965:314–318.

Shah, R. V.
1960   The mechanisms of carapacial and plastral hinges in chelonians. Breviora 130:1–15.

1962   A comparative study of the respiratory muscles in Chelonia. Breviora 161:1–16.

1963   The neck musculature of a cryptodire (*Deirochelys*) and a pleurodire (*Chelodina*) compared. Bull. Mus. Comp. Zool. 129:343–368.

Shannon, F. A., and H. M. Smith
1949   Herpetological results of the University of Illinois Field Expedition, Spring 1949. I. Introduction, Testudines, Serpentes. Trans. Kansas Acad. Sci. 52:494–509.

Shaw, C. E.
1959   Record size desert tortoises. Herpetologica 15:69.

Shields, L. M., and R. G. Lindeborg
1956   Records of the spineless soft-shelled turtle and the snapping turtle from New Mexico. Copeia 1956:120–121.

Shoop, C. R.
1967   *Graptemys nigrinoda* in Mississippi. Herpetologica 23:56.

Siebenrock, K. F.
*1906   Eine neue *Cinosternum*-Art aus Florida. Zool. Anz. 30:727–728.

Simha, S. S., and D. R. Chattopadhyaya
1969   Studies on the family Rhytidodidae Odhner, 1926, with a description of a new species *Rhytidodes indicus*, from the intestine of *Eretmochelys squamosa* from Rameswaram, India. Riv. Parasit. 30:95–100.

1970   A new genus and species of a blood fluke, *Squaroacetabulum solus*, from the ventricle of the heart of a marine turtle, *Chelone mydas*. Zool. Anz. 184:290–294.

Simkiss, K.
1962   The source of calcium for the ossification of the embryos of the giant leathery turtle. Comp. Biochem. Physiol. 7:71–79.

Skorepa, A. C.
1966   The deliberate consumption of stones by the ornate box turtle. J. Ohio Herpetol. Soc. 5:108.

Skorepa, A. C., and J. E. Ozment
1968   Habitat, habits, and variation of *Kinosternon subrubrum* in southern Illinois. Trans. Illinois St. Acad. Sci. 61:247–251.

Slater, J. R.
1962   Variations and new range of *Clemmys marmorata marmorata*. Occ. Pap. Dept. Biol. Univ. Puget Sound 20:204–205.

1963a   A key to the adult reptiles of Washington state. Occ. Pap. Dept. Biol. Univ. Puget Sound 23:209–211.

1963b   Distribution of Washington reptiles. Occ. Pap. Dept. Biol. Univ. Puget Sound 24:212–232.

Smith, C. G.
1968   Variations in the blood proteins of the musk turtle, *Sternotherus odoratus* (Latreille). Diss. Abstr. 28:3931–3932.

Smith, G. M., C. W. Coates, and R. F. Nigrelli
1941   A papillomatous disease of the gallbladder associated with infection by flukes, occurring in the marine turtle, *Chelonia mydas* (Linnaeus). Zoologica 26:13–16.

Smith, H(obart) M.
1947   Kyphosis and other variations in soft-shelled turtles. Univ. Kansas Publ. Mus. Nat. Hist. 1:117–124.

1955   The generic name of the alligator snapper turtle. Herpetologica 11:16.

1956   Handbook of amphibians and reptiles of Kansas. Univ. Kansas Mus. Nat. Hist. Misc. Publ. 9:1–356.

1958   Total regeneration of the carapace in a box turtle. Turtox News 36:234–235.

1961   Function of the choanal rakers of the green sea turtle. Herpetologica 17:214.

Smith, H(obart) M., and B. P. Glass
*1947   A new musk turtle from southeastern United States. J. Washington Acad. Sci. 37:22–24.

Smith, H(obart) M., and L. F. James
1958   The taxonomic significance of cloacal bursae in turtles. Trans. Kansas Acad. Sci. 61:86–96.

Smith, H(obart) M., D. C. Kritsky, and R. L. Holland
1969   Reticulate melanism in the painted turtle. J. Herpetol. 3:173–176.

Smith, H(obart) M., T. P. Maslin, and R. L. Brown
1965   Summary of the distribution of the herpetofauna of Colorado. Univ. Colorado Stud. 15:1–52.

Smith, H(obart) M., and D. C. Nickon
1961   Preliminary experiments on the role of the cloacal bursae in hibernating turtles. Nat. Hist. Misc. 178:1–8.

Smith, H(obart) M., and L. W. Ramsey
*1952   A new turtle from Texas. Wasmann J. Biol. 10:45–54.

Smith, H(obart) M., and O. Sanders
1952   *Terrapene carolina major* in Arkansas. Herpetologica 8:93.

Smith, H(obart) M., and E. H. Taylor
1950   An annotated checklist and key to the reptiles of Mexico exclusive of the snakes. Bull. U. S. Natl. Mus. 199:1–253.

Smith, H(obart) M., K. L. Williams, and E. O. Moll
1963   Herpetological explorations on the Rio Conchos, Chihuahua, Mexico. Herpetologica 19:205–215.

Smith, H(ugh) M.
1904   Notes on the breeding of the yellow-bellied terrapin. Smithsonian Misc. Coll. 45:252–253.

Smith, H. W.
1929   The inorganic composition of the body fluids of the Chelonia. J. Biol. Chem. 82:651–661.

Smith, M. A.
1931   The fauna of British India, including Ceylon and Burma. Reptilia and Amphibia. Vol. I. Loricata, Testudines. Taylor and Francis, London. 185 pp.

Smith, P. W.
*1951   A new frog and a new turtle from the western Illinois sand prairies. Bull. Chicago Acad. Sci. 9:189–199.

1955   Presumed hybridization of two species of box turtles. Nat. Hist. Misc. 146:1–3.

1957   An analysis of post-Wisconsin biogeography of the Prairie Peninsula region based on distributional phenomena among terrestrial vertebrate populations. Ecology 38:205–218.

1961   The amphibians and reptiles of Illinois. Illinois Nat. Hist. Surv. Bull. 28:1–298.

Smith, P. W., and M. M. Hensley
1957   The mud turtle, *Kinosternon flavescens stejnegeri* Hartweg, in the United States. Proc. Biol. Soc. Washington 70:201–204.

Smith, P. W., and J. C. List
1955   Notes on Mississippi amphibians and reptiles. Amer. Midl. Nat. 53:115–125.

Smith, P. W., and S. A. Minton
1957   A distributional summary of the herpetofauna of Indiana and Illinois. Amer. Midl. Nat. 58:341–351.

Smith, W. G.
1968   A neonate Atlantic loggerhead turtle, *Caretta caretta caretta*, captured at sea. Copeia 1968:880–881.

Snyder, L. L.
1921   Some observations on Blanding's turtle. Canadian Field-Nat. 35:17–18.

Sonnini, C. S., and P. A. Latreille
*1801   Histoire naturelee des reptiles avec figures dessinèes d'apres nature. I. Deterville, Paris. 280 pp.

Spearman, R. I. C.
1969   The epidermis of the gopher tortoise *Testudo polyphemus* (Daudin). Acta Zool. (Stockholm) 50:1–9.

Spigel, I. M.
1963   Running speed and intermediate brightness discrimination in the fresh water turtle (*Chrysemys*). J. Comp. Physiol. Psychol. 56:924–928.

Spigel, I. M., and K. R. Ellis
1965   Climbing suppression: passive avoidance in the turtle. Psychon. Sci. 3:215–216.
1966   Cerebral lesions and climbing suppression in the turtle. Psychon. Sci. 5:211–212.
1967   Excretory electrolytes and habituation in the turtle. Psychon. Sci. 8:381–382.
1968   Electrolyte balance and deficit drinking in a reptile. J. Comp. Physiol. Psychol. 65:384–387.

Spigel, I. M., K. R. Ellis, and Y. E. Kaiser.
1967   Electrolyte balance and drinking in the fresh water turtle. J. Comp. Physiol. Psychol. 64:313–317.

Spigel, I. M., and A. Ramsay
1969a   Stress and water consumption in a reptile. Psychon. Sci. 15:29–30.

1969b   Excretory electrolytes and response to stress in a reptile. J. Comp. Physiol. Psychol. 68:18–21.
1970a   Cerebral lesions and the excretory alkali metal response (EAMR) in reptile. Psychon. Sci. 18:59–60.
1970b   Extinction of the excretory alkali metal response (EAMR) to stress in a reptile. Psychon. Sci. 19:261–263.

Spoczynska, J. O. I.
1970   Rearing hatchlings of *Dermochelys coriacea*. British J. Herpetol. 4:189–192.

Squires, H. J.
1954   Records of marine turtles in the Newfoundland area. Copeia 1954:68.

St. John, R., and R. M. Nardone
1957   Eosinophil levels of the turtle after exposure to cold and epinephrine. Amer. J. Physiol. 188:420–422.

Stebbins, R. C.
1954   Amphibians and reptiles of western North America. McGraw-Hill Book Co., New York. 536 pp.
1966   A field guide to western reptiles and amphibians. Houghton Mifflin Co., Boston. 279 pp.

Stegeman, L. C.
1955   An abnormal carapace in the snapping turtle, *Chelydra serpentina*. Copeia 1955:255.

Steggerda, F. R., and H. E. Essex
1957   Circulation and blood pressure in the great vessels and heart of the turtle (*Chelydra serpentina*). Amer. J. Physiol. 190:320–326.

Stein, H. A.
1954   Additional records of amphibians and reptiles in southern Illinois. Amer. Midl. Nat. 51:311–312.

Stejneger, L.
*1918   Description of a new snapping turtle and a new lizard from Florida. Proc. Biol. Soc. Washington 31:89–92.
*1925   New species and subspecies of American turtles. J. Washington Acad. Sci. 15:462–463.
1944   Notes on the American soft-shell turtles with

special reference to *Amyda agassizii*. Bull. Mus. Comp. Zool. 94:1–75.

Stenroos, O. C., and W. M. Bowman
1968   Turtle blood—I. Concentrations of various constituents. Comp. Biochem. Physiol. 15: 219–222.

Stephen, A. C.
1953   Scottish turtle records previous to 1953. Scottish Nat. 65:108–114.

Stickel, L. F.
1950   Population and home range relationships of the box turtle, *Terrapene c. carolina* (Linnaeus). Ecol. Monogr. 20:351–378.
1951   Wood mouse and box turtle populations in an area treated annually with DDT for five years. J. Wildlife Mgt. 15:161–164.

Stitt, J. T., R. E. Sample, and D. W. Sigsworth
1970   Effect of changes in body temperature on circulating plasma volume of turtles. Amer. J. Physiol. 219:683–686.

Storer, T. I.
1930   Notes on the range and life-history of the Pacific fresh-water turtle, *Clemmys marmorata*. Univ. California Publ. Zool. 32:429–441.

Strecker, J. K.
1926   Chapters from the life histories of Texas reptiles and amphibians. Contr. Baylor Univ. Mus. 8:1–12.
1927a Notes on a specimen of *Gopherus berlandieri* (Agassiz). Copeia 1927(161):189–190.
1927b Observations on the food habits of Texas amphibians and reptiles. Copeia 1927(162):6–9.
1929   The eggs of *Gopherus berlandieri* Agassiz. Contr. Baylor Univ. Mus. 18:6.

Stuart, G. R.
1954   Observations on reproduction in the tortoise *Gopherus agassizi* in captivity. Copeia 1954: 61–62.

Stunkard, H. W.
1923   Studies on North American blood flukes. Bull. Amer. Mus. Nat. Hist. 48:165–221.
1924   On some trematodes from Florida turtles. Trans. Amer. Microsc. Soc. 43:97–113.

1927   A new trematode, *Vasotrema amydae*, n. g., n. sp., from the vascular system of the soft-shelled turtle *Amyda*. J. Parasitol. 13:218.
1943   A new trematode, *Dictyangium chelydrae* (Microscaphidiidae = Angiodictyidae), from the snapping turtle, *Chelydra serpentina*. J. Parasitol. 29:143–150.

Sturn, A., and B. H. Brattstrom
1958   A serial abnormality in the painted turtle. Herpetologica 13:277–278.

Sullivan, B., and A. Riggs
1967a Structure, function and evolution of turtle hemoglobins. I. Distribution of heavy hemoglobins. Comp. Biochem. Physiol. 23:437–447.
1967b Structure, function and evolution of turtle hemoglobins. II. Electrophoretic studies. Comp. Biochem. Physiol. 23:449–458.
1967c Structure, function and evolution of turtle hemoglobins. III. Oxygenation properties. Comp. Biochem. Physiol. 23:459–474.
1967d The subunit dissociation properties of turtle hemoglobins. Biochim. Biophys. Acta 140: 274–283.

Surface, H. A.
1908   First report on the economic features of the turtles of Pennsylvania. Zool. Bull. Div. Zool. Pennsylvania Dept. Agric. 6:105–196.

Suzuki, H. K.
1963   Studies on the osseous system of the slider turtle. Ann. New York Acad. Sci. 109:351–410.

Swanson, P. L.
1952   The reptiles of Venango County, Pennsylvania. Amer. Midl. Nat. 47:161–182.

Sweat, D. E.
1968   Capture of a tagged ridley turtle. Quart. J. Florida Acad. Sci. 31:47–48.

Tanzer, E. C., E. O. Morrison, and C. Hoffpauir
1966   New locality records for amphibians and reptiles in Texas. S. W. Nat. 11:131–132.

Taylor, E. H.
1933   Observations on the courtship of turtles. Univ. Kansas Sci. Bull. 21:269–271.
1935   Arkansas amphibians and reptiles in the Kan-

sas University Museum. Univ. Kansas Sci. Bull. 22:207–218.

1970   The turtles and crocodiles of Thailand and adjacent waters. Univ. Kansas Sci. Bull. 49:87–179.

Taylor, W. E.

*1895   The box turtles of North America. Proc. U. S. Natl. Mus. 17:573–588.

Telford, S. R.

1952   A herpetological survey in the vicinity of Lake Shipp, Polk County, Florida. Quart. J. Florida Acad. Sci. 15:175–185.

Tercafs, R. R., E. Schoffeniels, and G. Goussef

1963   Blood composition of a sea-turtle *Caretta caretta* L., reared in fresh water. Arch. Int. Physiol. Biochim. 71:614–615.

Thatcher, V. E.

1954   Some helminths parasitic in *Clemmys marmorata*. J. Parasitol. 40:481–482.

1963   Trematodes of turtles from Tabasco, Mexico, with a description of a new species of *Dodaytrema* (Trematoda: Paramphistomidae). Amer. Midl. Nat. 70:347–355.

Thomas, E. S., and M. B. Trautman

1937   Segregated hibernation of *Sternotherus odoratus* (Latreille). Copeia 1937:231.

Thompson, F. G.

1953   Further evidence of the occurrence of the wood turtle, *Clemmys insculpta* (LeConte), in northeastern Ohio. Herpetologica 9:74.

Thorson, T. B.

1968   Body fluid partitioning in Reptilia. Copeia 1968:592–601.

Timken, R. L.

1968   *Graptemys pseudogeographica* in the Upper Missouri River of the northcentral United States. J. Herpetol. 1:76–82.

1969   Ornate box turtle distribution in South Dakota. Herpetologica 25:70.

Tinkle, D. W.

1958a   The systematics and ecology of the *Sternothaerus carinatus* complex (Testudinata, Chelydridae). Tulane Stud. Zool. 6:3–56.

1958b   Experiments with censusing of southern tur-

tle populations. Herpetologica 14:172–175.

1959a   The relation of the fall line to the distribution and abundance of turtles. Copeia 1959:167–170.

1959b   Observations of reptiles and amphibians in a Louisiana swamp. Amer. Midl. Nat. 62:189–205.

1959c   Additional remarks on extra-uterine migration of ova in turtles. Herpetologica 15:161–162.

1961   Geographic variation in reproduction, size, sex ratio and maturity of *Sternothaerus odoratus* (Testudinata: Chelydridae). Ecology 42:68–76.

1962   Variation in shell morphology of North American turtles. I. The carapacial seam arrangements. Tulane Stud. Zool. 9:331–349.

Tinkle, D. W., and R. G. Webb

1955   A new species of *Sternotherus* with a discussion of the *Sternotherus carinatus* complex (Chelonia, Kinosternidae). Tulane Stud. Zool. 3:52–67.

Tinklepaugh, O. L.

1932   Maze learning of a turtle. J. Comp. Psychol. 13:201–206.

Toner, G. C.

1933   Over winter eggs of the snapping turtle. Copeia 1933:221–222.

1940   Delayed hatching in the snapping turtle. Copeia 1940:265.

Ulmer, M. J.

1957   Notes on *Spirorchis haematobium* (Stunkard, 1922) (Trematoda: Spirorchiidae) in the definitive host. J. Parasitol. 43 (suppl.):32.

1959   Studies on *Spirorchis haematobium* (Stunkard, 1922) Price, 1934 (Trematoda: Spirorchiidae) in the definitive host. Trans. Amer. Microsc. Soc. 78:81–89.

Urban, E. K.

1970   Nesting of the green turtle (*Chelonia mydas*) in the Dahlak Archipelago, Ethiopia. Copeia 1970:393–394.

Uzzell, T. M., and A. Schwartz

1955   The status of the turtle *Kinosternon bauri palmarum* Stejneger with notes on variation in the species. J. Elisha Mitch. Soc. 71:28–35.

Van Denburgh, J.
1922   The reptiles of western North America. Vol. II. Snakes and turtles. Occ. Pap. California Acad. Sci. 10:623–1028.

Villiers, A.
1958   Tortues et crocodiles de l'Afrique Noire Francaise. Inst. Francais d'Afrique Noire, Init. Africaines 15:1–354.

Vinyard, W. C.
1953   Epizoophytic algae from mollusks, turtles, and fish in Oklahoma. Proc. Oklahoma Acad. Sci. 34:63–65.

Viosca, P.
1933   The *Pseudemys troostii-elegans* complex, a case of sexual dimorphism. Copeia 1933: 208–210.

Virginia Herpetological Survey
1968a   Description of the turtles of Virginia. Virginia Herpetol. Soc. Bull. 57:1, 3–9, 13–15.
1968b   Distribution of the turtles of Virginia (1968). Virginia Herpetol. Soc. Bull. 58:1–7.

Vose, R. N.
1964   Nesting habits of the soft-shelled turtles (*Trionyx* sp.). J. Minnesota Acad. Sci. 31: 122–124.

Wade, S. E., and C. E. Gifford
1965   A preliminary study of the turtle population of a northern Indiana lake. Proc. Indiana Acad. Sci. 74:371–374.

Wagler, J.
*1830   Natürliches System der Amphibien. München, Stuttgart and Tübigen. 354 pp.

Wahlquist, H.
1970   Sawbacks of the Gulf Coast. Int. Turtle & Tortoise Soc. J. 4(4):10–13, 28.

Walker, W. F.
1959   Closure of the nostrils in the Atlantic loggerhead and other sea turtles. Copeia 1959: 257–259.

Walker, W. F., D. M. Green, and G. T. Jones
1953   Growth of algae on the turtle *Emys blandingi.* Copeia 1953:61.

Wall, L. D.
1941   Life history of *Spirorchis elephantis* (Cort, 1917) a new blood fluke from *Chrysemys picta.* Amer. Midl. Nat. 25:402–411.
1951   The life history of *Vasotrema robustum* (Stunkard, 1928), Trematoda: Spirorchidae. Trans. Amer. Microsc. Soc. 70:173–184.

Wang, C. C., and S. H. Hopkins
1965   *Haemogregarina* and *Haemoproteus* (Protozoa, Sporozoa) in blood of Texas freshwater turtles. J. Parasitol. 51:682–683.

Wangersky, E. D., and C. E. Land
1960   Interaction between the plasma of the loggerhead turtle and toxin of the Portugese man-of-war. Nature 185:330–331.

Ward, H. B.
1921   A new blood fluke from turtles. J. Parasitol. 7:114–128.

Waters, J. H.
1962   Former distribution of the red-bellied turtle in the northeast. Copeia 1962:649–651.
1964   Subspecific intergradation in the Nantucket Island, Massachusetts, population of the turtle *Chrysemys picta.* Copeia 1964:550–553.
1966   Second find of red-bellied turtle on Martha's Vineyard Island, Massachusetts. Copeia 1966:592.
1969   Additional observations of southeastern Massachusetts insular and mainland populations of painted turtles, *Chrysemys picta.* Copeia 1969:179–182.

Watson, D. M. S.
1914   *Eunotosaurus africanus* Seeley, and the ancestry of the Chelonia. Proc. Zool. Soc. London 1914:1011–1020.

Weaver, W. G.
1970   Courtship and combat behavior in *Gopherus berlandieri.* Bull. Florida St. Mus. 15:1–43.

Weaver, W. G., and J. S. Robertson
1967   A re-evaluation of fossil turtles of the *Chrysemys scripta* group. Tulane Stud. Geol. 5:53–66.

Weaver, W. G., and F. L. Rose
1967   Systematics, fossil history, and evolution of the genus *Chrysemys.* Tulane Stud. Zool. 14:63–73.

Webb, R. G.

1950   Range extension of the chicken turtle in Oklahoma. Herpetologica 6:137–138.

1956   Size at sexual maturity in the male softshell, *Trionyx ferox emoryi*. Copeia 1956:121–122.

1959   Description of a new softshell turtle from the Southeastern United States. Univ. Kansas Publ. Mus. Nat. Hist. 11:517–525.

1960   Type and type locality of the Gulf coast spiny softshell turtle, *Trionyx spinifer asper* (Agassiz). Breviora 129:1–8.

1961   Observations on the life histories of turtles (genus *Pseudemys* and *Graptemys*) in Lake Texoma, Oklahoma. Amer. Midl. Nat. 65:193–214.

1962   North American soft-shelled turtles (family Trionychidae). Univ. Kansas Publ. Mus. Nat. Hist. 13:429–611.

1970   Reptiles of Oklahoma. Univ. Oklahoma Press, Norman, 370 pp.

Wermuth, H., and R. Mertens

1961   Schildkröten, Krocodile, Brückenechsen. G. Fischer, Jena. 422 pp.

Werner, W. E.

1959   Amphibians and reptiles of the Thousand Islands region, New York. Copeia 1959:170–172.

Wetmore, A.

1920   Observations on the hibernation of the box turtle. Copeia 1920(77):3–5.

Wever, E. G., and J. A. Vernon

1956a   The sensitivity of the turtle's ear as shown by its electrical potentials. Proc. Natl. Acad. Sci. 42:213–220.

1956b   Sound transmission in the turtle's ear. Proc. Natl. Acad. Sci. 42:292–299.

1956c   Auditory responses in the common box turtle. Proc. Natl. Acad. Sci. 42:962–965.

White, F. N.

1968   Functional anatomy of the heart of reptiles. Amer. Zool. 8:211–219.

White, F. N., and G. Ross

1966   Circulatory changes during experimental diving in the turtle. Amer. J. Physiol. 211:15–18.

Wickham, M. M.

1922   Notes on the migration of *Macrochelys lacertina*. Proc. Oklahoma Acad. Sci. 2:20–22.

Wieczorowski, E.

1939   Parasitic lesions in turtles. J. Parasitol. 25:395–399.

Wied, M. zu.

*1838   Reise in des innare Nord-America in den Jahren 1832 bis 1834. J. Hoelscher, Coblenz. 213 pp.

*1865   Verzeichnis der Reptilien welche auf einer Reise im nördlichen America beobachtet wurden. Nova Acta Leopold. Carol. Nat. Curios 32:1–143.

Wiegmann, A. F. A.

*1835   Beiträge zur Zoologie, gesammelt auf einer Reise um die Erde, von Dr. F. J. F. Meyen. Amphibien. Nova Acta Acad. Leopold Carol. 17:183–268.

Wilber, C. G.

1962   Some circulatory problems in reptiles and amphibians. Ohio J. Sci. 62:132–138.

Wilcox, L.

1933   Incubation of painted turtle's eggs. Copeia 1933:41.

Willgohs, J. F.

1957   Occurrence of the leathery turtle in the northern North Sea and off western Norway. Nature 179:163–164.

Williams, E. C.

1961   A study of the box turtle, *Terrapene carolina carolina* (L.), population in Allee Memorial Woods. Proc. Indiana Acad. Sci. 71:399–406.

Williams, E. E.

1950a   Variation and selection in the cervical central articulations of living turtles. Bull. Amer. Mus. Nat. Hist. 94:510–561.

1950b   *Testudo cubensis* and the evolution of Western Hemisphere tortoises. Bull. Amer. Mus. Nat. Hist. 95:1–36.

1952   A new fossil tortoise from Mona Island, West Indies, and a tentative arrangement of the tortoises of the world. Bull. Amer. Mus. Nat. Hist 99:541–560.

1954   Fossils and the distribution of chelyid turtles. 2. Additional reputed chelyid turtles on northern continents: *Palaeapsis conybearii* (Owen)—a pelomedusid. Breviora 32:1–6.

1956   *Pseudemys scripta callirostris* from Venezuela with a general survey of the *scripta* series. Bull. Mus. Comp. Zool. 115:145–160.

1959   Cervical ribs in turtles. Breviora 101:1–12.

Williams, E. E., and S. B. McDowell
1952   The plastron of soft-shelled turtles (Testudinata, Trionychidae): a new interpretation. J. Morphol. 90:263–280.

Williams, J. E.
1952   Homing behavior of the painted turtle and musk turtle in a lake. Copeia 1952:76–82.

Williams, K. L.
1957a Yolk retraction as a possible cause of kyphosis in turtles. Herpetologica 13:236.

1957b Possible overwintering of a turtle egg in east-central Illinois. Herpetologica 13:248.

1961   Aberrant mudturtles, *Kinosternon flavescens*, from Coahuila, Mexico. Herpetologica 17:72.

Williams, K. L., and P. Han
1964   A comparison of the density of *Terrapene coahuila* and *T. carolina*. J. Ohio Herpetol. Soc. 4:105.

Williams, K. L., H. M. Smith, and P. S. Chrapliwy
1960   Turtles and lizards from northern Mexico. Trans. Illinois St. Acad. Sci. 53:36–45.

Williams, R. W.
1953   Helminths of the snapping turtle, *Chelydra serpentina*, from Oklahoma, including the first report and description of the male of *Capillaria serpentina* Harwood, 1932. Trans. Amer. Microsc. Soc. 72:175–178.

Williams, W.
1950   Snappers—underwater fishermen. Nat. Hist. 59:178–179.

Wilson, L. W., and S. B. Friddle
1950   The herpetology of Hardy County, West Virginia. Amer. Midl. Nat. 43:165–172.

Witham, R.
1970   Breeding of a pair of pen-reared green turtles. Quart. J. Florida Acad. Sci. 33:288–290.

Witham, R., and A. F. Carr
1968   Returns of tagged pen-reared green turtles. Quart. J. Florida Acad. Sci. 31:49–50.

Woo, P. T. K.
1969   Trypanosomes in amphibians and reptiles in southern Ontario. Canadian J. Zool. 47:981–988.

Wood, F. G.
1953   Mating behavior of captive loggerhead turtles, *Caretta caretta caretta*. Copeia 1953:184–186.

Wood, J. T.
1953   Protective behavior and photic orientation in hatchling snapping turtles, *Chelydra serpentina serpentina* (Linné), in an aquatic environment. J. Elisha Mitchell Soc. 69:54–59.

Wood, J. T., and O. K. Goodwin
1954   Observations on the summer behavior and mortality of box turtles in eastern Virginia. Virginia J. Sci. 5:60–63.

Woodbury, A. M.
1952   Hybrids of *Gopherus berlandieri* and *G. agassizii*. Herpetologica 8:33–36.

Woodbury, A. M. and R. Hardy
1940   The dens and behavior of the desert tortoise. Science 92:529.

1948   Studies of the desert tortoise, *Gopherus agassizii*. Ecol. Monogr. 18:145–200.

Woods, G. T.
1945   Rate of travel of the wood turtle. Copeia 1945:49.

Woolverton, E.
1961   Winter survival of hatchling painted turtles in northern Minnesota. Copeia 1961:109.

1963   Winter survival of hatchling painted turtles in northern Minnesota. Copeia 1963:569–570.

Wright, A. H.
1918   Notes on *Clemmys*. Proc. Biol. Soc. Washington 31:51–58.

Wurth, M. A., and X. J. Musacchia
1964   Renewal of intestinal epithelium in the fresh-

water turtle, *Chrysemys picta*. Anat. Rec. 148: 427–439.

Wyatt-Smith, J.
1960   The conservation of the leathery turtle. Malayan Nat. J. 1960:194–199.

Yañez, P. A.
1951   Vertebrados marinos chilenos, III. Reptiles. Rev. Biol. Marina 3(1–2):119.

Yerger, R. W.
1965   The leatherback turtle on the Gulf coast of Florida. Copeia 1965:365–366.

Yerkes, R. M.
1905   The color pattern of *Nanemys guttata* Schneider. Science 21:386.

Yntema, C. L.
1970a   Twinning in the common snapping turtle, *Chelydra serpentina*. Anat. Rec. 166:491–498.
1970b   Extirpation experiments on embryonic rudiments of the carapace of *Chelydra serpentina*. J. Morphol. 132:235–243.
1970c   Survival of xenogenic grafts of embryonic pigment and carapace rudiments in embryos of *Chelydra serpentina*. J. Morphol. 132:353–359.
1970d   Observations on females and eggs of the common snapping turtle, *Chelydra serpentina*. Amer. Midl. Nat. 84:69–76.

Young, F. N., and C. C. Goff
1939   An annotated list of the arthropods found in the burrows of the Florida gopher tortoise, *Gopherus polyphemus* (Daudin). Florida Entomol. 12:53–62.

Young, J. D.
1950   The structure and some physical properties of the testudinian eggshell. Proc. Zool. Soc. London 120:455–469.

Zangerl, R.
1948–60 The vertebrate fauna of the Selma Formation of Alabama. I (1948). Introduction. II (1948). The Pleurodiran turtles. III (1953). The turtles of the family Protostegidae. IV (1953). The turtles of the family Toxochelyidae. V (1960). An advanced cheloniid sea turtle. Fieldiana: Geol. Mem. 3:1–312.

1969   The turtle shell. In Gans, C., and T. S. Parsons (eds.): Biology of the Reptilia, I. Academic Press, New York. Pp. 311–339.

Zangerl, R., and R. G. Johnson
1957   The nature of shield abnormalities in the turtle shell. Fieldiana: Geol. 10:345–382.

Zug, G. R.
1966   The penial morphology and the relationships of cryptodiran turtles. Occ. Pap. Mus. Zool. Univ. Michigan 647:1–24.
1969   Locomotion and the morphology of the pelvic girdle and hindlimbs of cryptodiran turtles. Diss. Abstr. Int. B. 30:2474–2475.

Zullo, V. A., and J. S. Bleakney
1966   The cirriped *Stomatolepas elegans* (Costa) on leatherback turtles from Nova Scotian waters. Canadian Field-Nat. 80:162–165.

Zweig, G., and J. W. Crenshaw
1957   Differentiation of species by paper electrophoresis of serum proteins of *Pseudemys* turtles. Science 126:1065–1067.